The Sotheby's Directory of Silver

The Sotheby's Directory of SILVER

1600–1940

Vanessa Brett

SOTHEBY'S PUBLICATIONS

© 1986 Text: Philip Wilson Publishers
Illustrations: Sotheby's

First published 1986 for Sotheby's Publications by
Philip Wilson Publishers Ltd
Russell Chambers, Covent Garden, London WC2E 8AA

Distributed in the USA by
Harper & Row, Publishers, Inc
10 East 53rd Street, New York, NY 10022

All rights reserved. No part of this publication may be reproduced, stored in a
retrieval system or transmitted in any form or by any means without the prior
permission of the Publisher.

ISBN 0 85667 193 2
Library of Congress Catalog Card Number 85–050360

Edited by Michael Graham-Dixon
Designed by Alan Bartram
Phototypeset by Tradespools Ltd, Frome
Printed and bound in Singapore by Khai Wah Litho Pte Limited

Contents

Acknowledgements 6

Introduction
The Silver Trade 7
Styles 14
Collecting silver 46
The arrangement of the Directory 47
Notes on the Introduction 49

The Directory
Germany, Austria and Switzerland 51
The Low Countries 101
Great Britain and Ireland 122
North America 325
France 348
Italy 387
Russia 395
Scandinavia 406

Appendix 1
Family trees of Augsburg goldsmiths 416

Appendix 2
Currency conversion and bullion price tables 422

Bibliography 423

Index of objects 425

Index of goldsmiths, including assay masters, designers, retailers and engravers 428

Index of heraldry and inscriptions 431

Acknowledgements

I have spent so many days in Sotheby's over the past nine months that at times it seemed as though I was once more on the staff. I received help and guidance, for which I am enormously grateful, from Eleanor Thompson, John Culme, Peter Waldron, Eileen Goodway, Annabel Panchaud, Harry Charteris, Peter Lowe, Lydia Cresswell-Jones, Jane Alexander, Derek Shrub, Adriana Turpin, Julia Clarke, Heinrich Graf von Spreti, Maril Murchie and Nicola Redway; in New York from Kevin Tierney, Ian Irving and Pam Pinto, and also from the photography departments in London and New York. Michael Graham-Dixon, the editor, and Alan Bartram, the designer, have been immensely helpful and patient in guiding me in the task of compiling this book – for which I am very grateful.

VANESSA BRETT
May 1984

Introduction

The catalogues of the leading auctioneers and dealers provide a wealth of material for anyone interested in the arts. This book explores the catalogues of silver sales held by Sotheby's from the 1920s until the spring of 1984.

The names of a dozen or so of the 'great' goldsmiths are perhaps generally known but, on the whole, buyers have been content with knowing that a piece of silver comes from, say, the English Georgian and Victorian or the French Empire or Régence periods. However, in recent years increasing interest has been shown by collectors in the men and women whose marks appear on silver. Thus, when considering how to present a selection of the many thousands of objects sold by Sotheby's, I thought the emphasis should be placed on the goldsmiths and silversmiths (terms which are synonymous).

The Silver Trade

The objects chosen for illustration have been grouped according to the maker's mark. This focus on goldsmiths leads one to consider in particular four aspects of their work. Firstly, the meaning of the maker's mark; secondly, the associations between goldsmiths, also their connections with the retailers who sold their work and the men who designed for them; thirdly, the extent to which some goldsmiths specialized in the type of object they made; and lastly, the styles in which they fashioned their silver.

The maker's mark

This can be (a) the mark of an individual silversmith; (b) the mark of a silversmith who employed assistants and who, like (a), perhaps had his work decorated by self-employed chasers or engravers; (c) the initials of the head of a large firm, registered on its behalf, for example, F. Elkington for Elkington and Company; (d) the mark of a retailer, the object actually having been made by a firm of manufacturing silversmiths such as Liberty and Company, most of whose silver was made by W.H. Haseler.

Firstly, it must be understood that when a description states that an object is 'by' someone, it means it is *marked by* the person who sponsors the piece when it is sent for assay, rather than *made by* him. An object may have been both made and marked by the same person, but not necessarily.

The sponsor may be the head of a workshop or a retailer. The number of people involved in the creation of a piece of silver varies enormously. Occasionally an object may be the work of one man; more usually the process involves some or all of the following: the designer, manufacturer or head of workshop; his workmen and apprentices; the chaser, gilder, engraver or enameller; and the retailer. Some or all of these people might be involved in the marking of a piece and, depending on the period, the quantity of information given on an object varies.

Today, the sharing of work between craftsmen is sometimes acknowledged, as can be seen in the following catalogue entry: 'Parcel-gilt beaker (1981) made by Alan Evans, maker's mark of Gerald Benney designer and enameller, engraved by Malcolm Long. The names of the craftsmen are engraved on the base'.[1]

It must not be forgotten, however, that many goldsmiths created and decorated their pieces themselves, without any outside assistance.

K. Citroen quotes from the text of the oath of a goldsmith on being admitted to the freedom of the Corporation, 'the master to be pledged not only himself but his journeymen and apprentices as well'.[2] Here there is an acknowledgement of the master's responsibility for the quality of his assistants' work. The master, whose mark was struck on an object, was often the head of a large workshop. Frequently, as a goldsmith became successful he turned from actually making silver to design and management, dealing with clients and supervising his journeymen and apprentices. Large workshops or manufacturers sometimes required their workmen to mark their pieces in addition to the 'maker's mark'; this is most noticeable on cutlery and the workman's mark usually takes the form of incuse designs. The size of workshops varied greatly, increasing substantially in the nineteenth century, with the emergence of large manufacturers during the Industrial Revolution. Elkington and Company employed over a thousand people in 1865; Christofle had fifteen hundred employees in 1907.

Associations between craftsmen, retailers and designers

Whereas in the seventeenth century the connection between the client or patron and craftsman is of considerable importance, by the nineteenth century emphasis had shifted to the relationship between retailer and manufacturer. Our knowledge of this influence in the Regency period in England has been enlarged by Shirley Bury[3] and John Culme.[4] Some of the most successful retail businesses had close, and in some cases exclusive, ties with independent craftsmen – for example, the relationship between Storr, Scott and Smith and Rundells, or that between the workshops of Rappoport or Perchin with Fabergé. The methods of marking silver differ from firm to firm. Sometimes the retailer or head of the business marked objects with a punch or his own 'maker's mark'; and sometimes he inscribed them.[5]

When a piece of silver was made by one goldsmith on behalf of another, or when one man's work was sponsored by another when sent for assay, we sometimes find the former's mark overstruck by that of the latter.[6] This is also found, principally in the seventeenth and eighteenth centuries, in pairs of items of which a piece by one maker is matched some

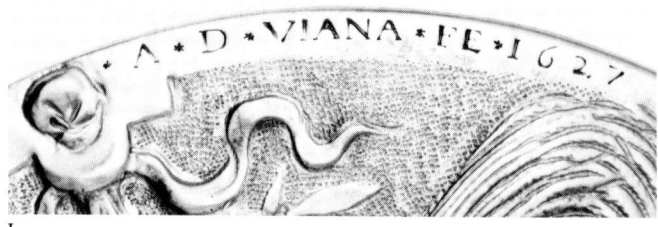

I

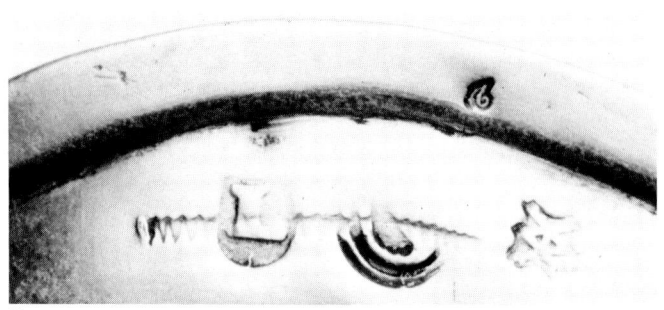

II

V

III IV

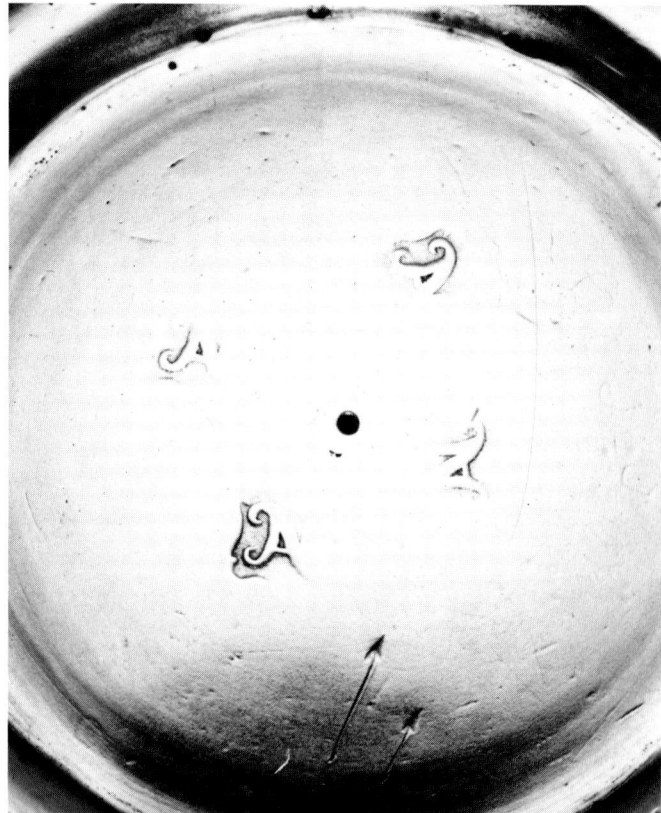

VI

VII

I Engraved signature of Adam van Vianen; from tazza, no.297.

II Seventeenth-century Low Countries marks. *Left to right*: date (1628); town (Utrecht); maker (Adam van Vianen). *Top*: later Dutch control mark; from tazza, no.297.

III Seventeenth-century German marks. *Left*: town (Nuremberg); *right*: maker (Hans Petzoldt). From cup and cover, no.13.

IV Seventeenth-century French provincial marks, from a fork. *Top to bottom*: charge; town (Toulouse); discharge; maker (François Becané); *maison commune*

V Maker's mark only: Henricus Boelen. American, seventeenth-century. With engraved owners' initials in a triad G^{T}A; from bowl, no.1556. Objects bearing only the maker's mark are found universally; see VI

VI Maker's mark only struck four times: Anthony Nelme. English, late seventeenth-century. See V

VII Seventeenth-century English marks (Britannia Standard), with maker overstruck. *Left to right*: 'maker' (Thomas Jenkins overstriking mark of Philip Rollos I); standard (Britannia); town (London); date (1698). From covered jug, no.473

VIII Seventeenth-century English marks (Sterling Standard). *Left to right*: 'maker' (Thomas Jenkins); town (London); standard (Sterling); date (1685). From covered jug, no.473

IX Late eighteenth-century English marks. *Left to right*: maker (James Young); date (1785); standard (Sterling); town (London); duty; drawback

THE SILVER TRADE 9

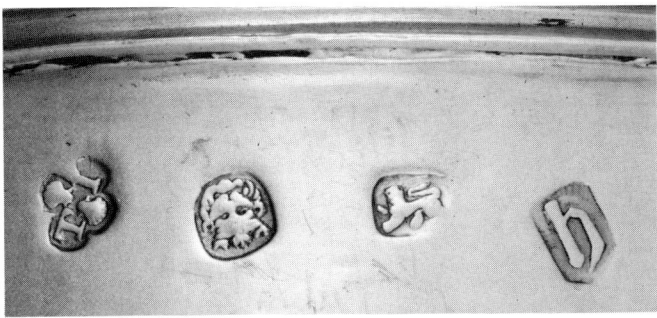
VIII

IX

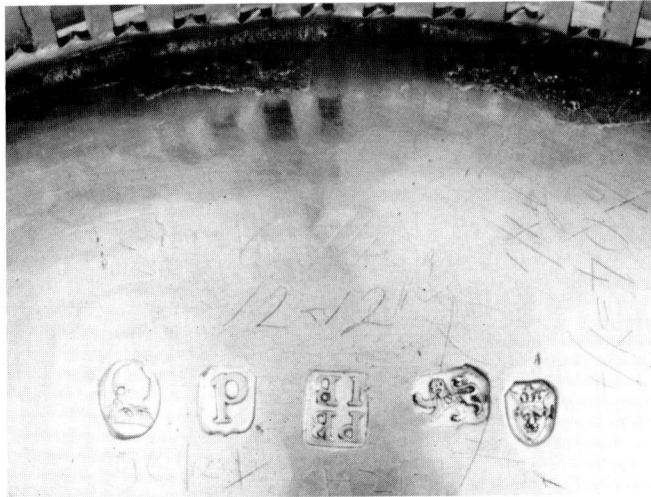
X

XI

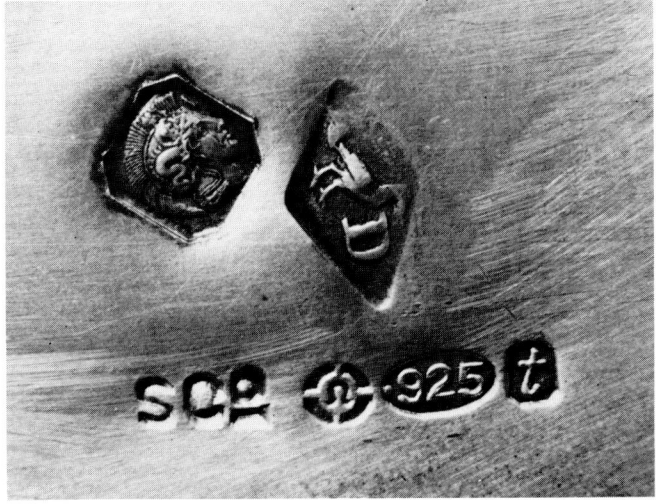
XII

XIII

XIV

X Late eighteenth-century English marks. *Left to right*: duty; date (1790); maker (Peter and Jonathan Bateman); standard (Sterling); town (London). Note in particular the numerous scratched letters and numbers surrounding the marks. These are references of the retailers and dealers who have owned the piece

XI Nineteenth-century English marks. *Top*: stamp of retailer; *bottom*: maker/sponsor

XII Nineteenth-century French marks. *Top left*: standard; *top right*: maker. With twentieth-century United Kingdom import marks. *Left to right*: sponsor, town, standard, date

XIII Nineteenth-century French marks. *Top*: maker's stamp (Froment-Meurice); *centre*: standard (950); *bottom*: maker's mark

XIV Nineteenth-century English P.O.D.R. (Patent Office Design Registry) mark

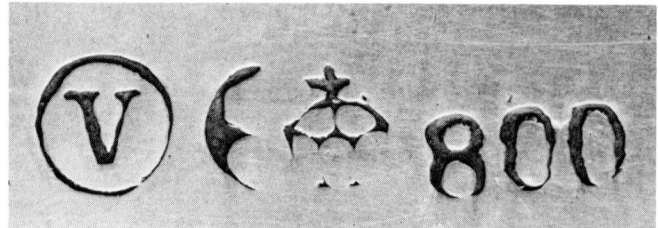
XV

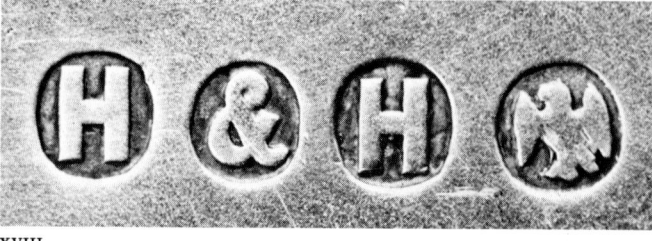
XVIII

XVI

XVII

XIX

XX

XXI

years later by another. This practice of overstamping is seen on no.473, where Thomas Jenkins overstruck the mark of Phillip Rollos. Sometimes the overstamping has obliterated the first mark so thoroughly that the identity of the maker of the piece remains a mystery. A successful goldsmith was often a shopkeeper also, selling jewellery and objects of vertu as well as silver plate, and sometimes acting as pawnbroker and banker.[7] He might buy items for stock from other specialist goldsmiths. Many Sheffield-made candlesticks are found with marks overstruck by the London maker who bought them for re-sale. The casters illustrated as no.725 have Paul de Lamerie's mark overstruck by that of Phillips Garden. Garden is known to have purchased some of Lamerie's tools after his death and presumably he obtained some of Lamerie's stock also.

If a large order was received it was sometimes sub-contracted, and on these occasions it was unusual to tamper with the marks of the individual makers. In the pieces made for these orders we can see an excellent example of the exchange of patterns (see pp. 23, 24), which is an important aspect of the trade. We become aware of the relationships between goldsmiths also: these connections usually occur either through families and their inter-marriage, or through the master/apprentice association. Catherine the Great's order for a service in 1734 included pieces (probably provided from stock, as they vary in style) by Paul Crespin, Anne Tanqueray and Simon Pantin, all of Huguenot origin.[8] In 1770 the Empress commissioned another service (this time from Paris) to present to Prince Gregory Orloff. Jacques Roettiers and his son Jacques-Nicolas were helped by

THE SILVER TRADE 11

XXII

XXIII

XXIV

XXV

XXVI

XXVII

XV German marks for 800 standard silver; used from 1 January 1888. Such pieces are described in English sale catalogues as 'silver coloured metal'

XVI Nineteenth-century English marks. *Top*: workman; *bottom*: maker/sponsor (Jonathan Hayne)

XVII Nineteenth-century English workman's mark

XVIII Manufacturer's mark (H & H) on English electroplate: Hukin and Heath. Late nineteenth century. See no.1486 ff.

XIX Twentieth-century English marks. *Top*: trade mark (Roberts and Belk, the manufacturer). *Centre, left to right*: maker/sponsor, in this case the retailer (Richard Burbidge, managing director, for Harrods Stores); town (Sheffield); standard (Sterling); date (1915). *Bottom*: manufacturer's stamped reference number

XX Nineteenth-century Russian marks: Peter Carl Fabergé; see no.1930 ff.

XXI Nineteenth-century American marks. *Left*: manufacturer's stamp (Sy and Wagner); *right*: design/stock number

XXII Nineteenth-century American marks: Tiffany and Company; see no.1633 ff.

XXIII Nineteenth-century English marks. *Top, left to right*: maker (Charles Dumesnil); standard (Sterling); town (London); date (1898). *Bottom*: retailer (Tiffany and Company, London)

XXIV Engraved signature of Latino Movio; see nos 1524, 1525

XXV Twentieth-century English marks. *Top*; house mark or trademark (unofficial). *Bottom*: maker/sponsor (H.G. Murphy; see no.1546)

XXVI English electroplate marks: Roberts and Belk

XXVII English electroplate marks

Edmé-Pierre Balzac and Louis-Joseph Lenhendrick, among others, in completing the commission (see no. **1747***).

In Germany, too, and particularly in Augsburg, we repeatedly find evidence of these connections. The service made for the Prince Bishop of Hildesheim (nos 181–3, 192, etc) undoubtedly offers a marvellous demonstration of a close-knit community working together to fulfil an important order. The travelling services which must have helped so much to ease the discomforts of long journeys are also good examples. No.206 includes work by J.C. Engelbrecht, Gottlieb Christian Drentwett, John Jacob Adam and Johan Christian Girschner, whilst another set[9] includes pieces by Johann Pepfenhauser II, Abraham Drentwett IV, Johan Gelb and Abraham Warnberger IV. The family trees in Appendix I illustrate their connections.

Whereas some goldsmiths employed chasers and engravers in their workshops, there were large numbers of freelance workers to whom a maker could send an object for decoration. They seldom signed their work and the credit for their skill tends to be given to the person whose mark is on the piece. The earliest example illustrated here is no.**29**, the shield from Munster. The work was most probably shared between Herman Potthof, whose mark it bears, and a follower of the chaser Anton Eisenhoit. The piece itself gives no specific clue to the chaser's identity (such as a mark or signature), and this can only be deduced by the skill with which such a successful design has been implemented.

Nos 949–951 are the work of the chaser G.M. Moser, described in 1763 as 'chaser and painter in enamel colours' and a specialist in the chasing of small gold items such as watch cases. Likewise, William Pitts in the early nineteenth century is one of the few chasers whose skills are recorded and whose standing is equal to that of the silversmiths whose work he decorated. The Shield of Achilles (no.1161) is undoubtedly the most prestigious piece he is thought to have worked on. In the group of seventeenth-century silver pieces flat-chased in chinoiserie style (nos 477, 482, 488, 491, 493, 502, 507, etc) we see a variety of items bearing the marks of several makers, which are thought to have been decorated perhaps by only one or two chasers, who specialized in this type of decoration, making use of contemporary engravings for source material.[10]

The use of pattern books as sources of design is more usual in engraved than in embossed silver and is discussed later. The close connection is clear. Theodor de Bry and his son Jan Theodor, Simon Gribelin and William Hogarth are but a handful of the printmakers who are known to have engraved silver. The de Passe family, too, were engravers rather than silversmiths (see p.17). Close ties obviously developed between a silversmith and a favoured engraver: for example, William Lukin and Joseph Sympson, Isaac Liger and Simon Gribelin.[11] The engraving on three tankards (56, 57, 58) helps us to link an unmarked piece with two marked pieces from Hamburg. Engraved armorials, too, became increasingly popular as a means of decoration, and, together with the elaborate cartouches which frame them, sometimes form the only decoration. Nineteenth-century directories contain the listing of 'heraldic engraver'.

A large number of designs by known artists for objects to be made in silver and other metals survive from the sixteenth

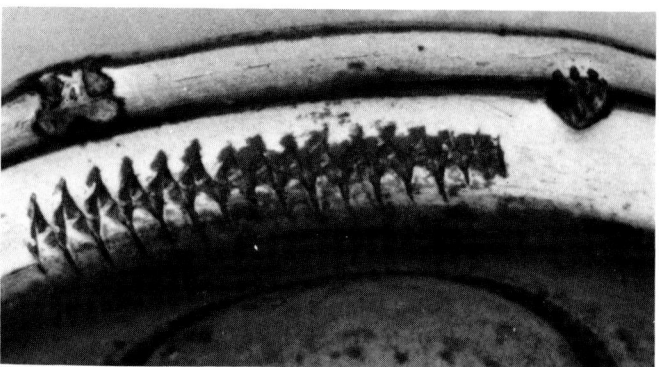

XXVIII

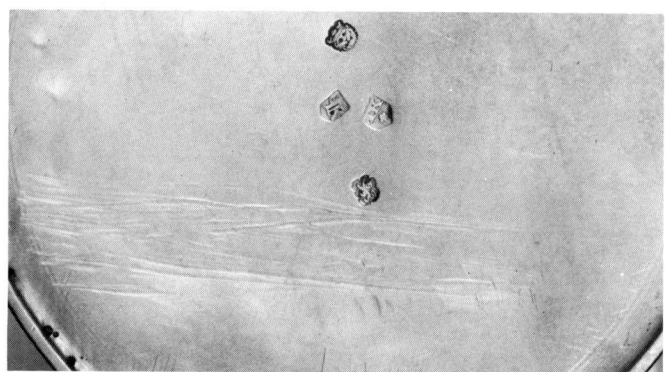

XXIX

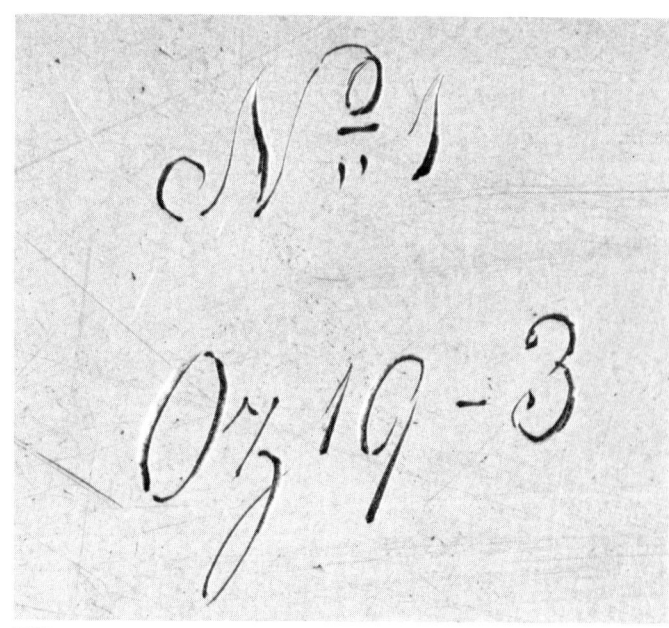

XXX

* References to catalogue numbers which are printed in bold indicate items which are illustrated in the Introduction

XXVIII Seventeenth-century German assay scrape. *Top*: maker; town (Augsburg). *Bottom*: zigzag assay scrape, typical of Continental assay scrapes

XXIX Seventeenth-century English assay scrape from the base of a tankard; London, 1687

XXX *Above*: Numbering (No.1); sets of items (such as dinner plates or candlesticks) were often numbered. *Below*: scratchweight (Oz.19-3), showing the original weight of the piece. English, eighteenth century

THE SILVER TRADE 13

XXXI

XXXIV

XXXII

XXXV

XXXIII

XXXVI

XXXI Embossing and chasing; detail of no. 1843

XXXII Embossing and chasing; no. 422

XXXIII Casting; detail of no. 1264

XXXIV Pricked or pounced initials and date. This style of lettering is commonly found on German and Scandinavian silver

XXXV Engraving; detail of no. 1043

XXXVI Etching; detail of no. 18

and seventeenth centuries.[12] From the eighteenth century, in the work of Meissonier, William Kent and Robert Adam, to the twentieth century, and the designs of Josef Hoffman and C.R. Mackintosh, we can see how the work of some designers unites the fields of architecture, furniture, sculpture, porcelain and silver in the discipline of a particular style. However, before the late eighteenth century the majority of silversmiths were most probably their own designers, making liberal use of pattern books and engravings. As far as we know, Rundells were probably the first firm to employ designers on a regular basis. The association between artists and silversmiths is discussed more fully below.

Specialization

One interesting aspect of the subject which emerges from the way in which the items have been grouped in this directory is the specialization of some makers. Spoon-makers are perhaps the earliest and most specialist of all. We find also makers who are specialist 'smallworkers' – that is, makers of small objects such as boxes and vinaigrettes. In England in the late eighteenth century and in the nineteenth they were known as 'toymakers' and worked chiefly in Birmingham. Larger articles were sometimes divided between makers of hollow-ware (coffee pots, mugs and so on) and makers of flat-ware (such as dishes and salvers).

It may be helpful to select a few examples: John and William Cafe and James Gould appear to have made a high proportion of the candlesticks produced in London in the mid-eighteenth century. J.G. Kloss and J.W. Kolb of Augsburg made coffee pots and teapots that varied little in style over a number of years. In the seventeenth century Nathaniel Pressding's mark appears on Danzig tankards chased with biblical and mythological scenes; Reinhold Riel of Nuremberg and Heinrich Mannlich of Augsburg made objects usually embossed in the bold manner of the baroque, and at the same period Balthasar Haydt, also from Augsburg, appears to have specialized in embossed sweetmeat dishes. Examples of more renowned goldsmiths are Paul van Vianen from Utrecht, the creator of outstanding plaques, and Hans Petzoldt of Nuremberg, who is particularly famed for his standing cups.

Styles

Mannerism and Baroque, 1600–1690

The style of the late Renaissance known as mannerism was popular with goldsmiths well into the seventeenth century, spreading north from Italy to France and thence to the Netherlands, Germany and the rest of Europe. It is an architectural style full of richness and detail, well suited to the goldsmith's craft.

The basin and salt illustrated as nos 1673–4, although made by unknown craftsmen, have decoration which derives from the engravings of Etienne Delaune. 'Delaune's drawings have an elegance and refinement that show him to have been one of the chief exponents of the Mannerist style ... [His] engravings were widely distributed and were exploited by goldsmiths and by masters of engraved ornament working in other countries.'[13] Like many of his contemporaries, Delaune travelled widely, leaving his native France to work in

Mannerism (France): detail of basin, after Etienne Delaune, last quarter of the sixteenth century (no.1673)

Strasbourg and Augsburg before returning to Paris. He died in 1583.

This mobility amongst leading craftsmen, particularly in the sixteenth century, was one way in which knowledge of a style was spread. A second was through the circulation of pattern books and engravings; a third was through gifts. Large quantities of plate changed hands through presentations between rulers, councils and guilds.

The salt (no.1674) is decorated with engraving; the basin (no.1673) is embossed and chased. These are the two forms of surface decoration most frequently seen on silver. Engraving is executed with a burin, the engraver cutting into metal and removing some of it in a linear design. Embossing and chasing is carried out with hammer and punches, pushing the metal into the desired shape without any of it being removed. Etching was also used as surface decoration, most commonly in Germany (no.18). In the late sixteenth and early seventeenth centuries many pieces were also decorated with intricate cast work, which required the making of many different moulds, and with scrolling sheet silver (nos 17, 31, 34). The popularity of the different methods of making and decorating silver changed frequently at all periods, as silversmiths used whichever technique was best suited to the current fashion.

STYLES: MANNERISM AND BAROQUE, 1600–1690 15

Mannerism (Italy): detail of dish, maker's mark S.B., Genoa, 1621 (no.1843)

Mannerism (Germany): shield, Herman Potthof, Munster, 1613 (no.29)

Mannerism (Low Countries): plaquette, circle of Paul van Vianen, early seventeenth century (no.299)

Perhaps the most easily recognizable characteristics of mannerist decoration on silver are the use of figures in typically graceful, even languorous poses, within scroll and strapwork cartouches (nos **29**, 293, **1843**), of grotesque and demi-figures amidst stylized scrolling leafage (nos 8, 10), of the arabesque, and of caryatid handles and brackets (nos 9, 11, 27). Silver was used to portray biblical, mythological and allegorical scenes, which were all popular at this time. The shield from Munster of 1613 (no.**29**), mentioned above, shows a highly developed use of the mannerist style in its treatment of the figures and the quantity of detail it incorporates. It is centred by three standing cups in a popular contemporary form.

Drinking vessels are perhaps the objects from this period most commonly seen at auction today, particularly those from Germany and the Low Countries. The standing cup and cover was a symbol of wealth and position, used for display on a buffet or sideboard and for ceremonial purposes. They were also a popular choice when a presentation was called for. In the late sixteenth and early seventeenth centuries many cups were made in a 'neo-gothic' style and are commonly known as 'bunch of grapes' or 'pineapple cups' (nos 18, 21, 31–5). One of the most outstanding makers of such standing cups was Hans Petzolt. He was one of the leading goldsmiths in Nuremberg, and much of his work was done for the City Council, although the example shown (no. 13) was a private commission for a gift to a member of the Imhof family, whose arms are incorporated in the design. Many charming examples of cups take naturalistic forms (nos 4–6) or make use of precious objects such as shells, ivory, jewels, crystal and coconuts, which are mounted by the goldsmiths. There was also a fashion for animal and bird cups – bears, owls, horses, unicorns (nos 28, 45)[14] – and for others in the form of figures (nos 2, 113). Many of these cups were made for guilds and symbolize their trade. They were intended for ceremonial use – some part, usually the head, is normally detachable – and also for display as a decorative and sculptural object. Some were kept in the treasuries or 'cabinets' of their usually royal or aristocratic owners.

Many of the squat beakers illustrated (nos 14, 23, 26) were originally part of a set, stacking one on top of the other. Their borders are usually decorated, in a variety of techniques, with domestic or allegorical scenes; if from a set of twelve, they frequently depict the months of the year. German tankards of the late sixteenth and early seventeenth centuries usually have a tapering cylindrical body, richly decorated with strapwork and fruit (nos 9, 11) with thin caryatid handles. Similar decoration is found on standing cups (nos 1, 3, 282) and on tazze (no.37). These shallow drinking vessels were often displayed on the table, for close inspection of their craftsmanship.[15] The shallow bowl or tazza created an ideal space for the skilled engraver or chaser (nos 293, 305). Theodor de Bry and his son Johan Theodor (of Liège, although active chiefly in Frankfurt) were amongst the finest exponents of engraving on silver, particularly on tazze. Like those of Etienne Delaune, their designs were widely circulated and were very influential (nos 280–81).

The most renowned goldsmiths from the Low Countries in the early seventeenth century were Paul and Adam van Vianen. Paul van Vianen travelled extensively, finally settling in Prague, where he was 'the most outstanding goldsmith' at the court of Rudolph II. His plaques became widely known, not least through castings in different metals (no.295), and his development of the auricular or lobate style, continued by his brother Adam in Utrecht, was to be

Auricular (Low Countries): tazza, Christian van Vianen, Utrecht, 1628 (no.300)

enormously influential. The auricular style forms the transition between mannerism and the baroque; mannerist and auricular motifs can be found side by side until the middle of the seventeenth century (nos 57, 307). In the work of Adam van Vianen this combination of styles can be seen in the pair of tazze (299) and in the sconces (296), where 'the pierced borders are of exceptional extravagance with human figures and animals developing into auricular scrolls while the classical scenes they enclose show the delicate manner associated with the earlier style of the van Vianens'.[16] Contemporaries of the van Vianens include Arent van Bolten (nos 291–2), Thomas Boogaert (nos 304–6) and Adam's son Christian (nos 300–2), who published his father's designs in 1650. The esteem in which these craftsmen were held placed them on an equal footing with painters and sculptors, some of whom owned their silver and who portrayed their work in still-life paintings and in portraits, such as Rembrandt's etching of the important Amsterdam goldsmith Jan Lutma. 'Sandrart (in 1675) says that Adam enjoyed great fame, making bowls, tazze, salts, book covers and so on for collectors in Amsterdam and all over Holland.'[17]

The auricular style was not universally popular, principally because there were few craftsmen sufficiently skilled to form pieces of such complexity. It is seldom seen, for example, in France or Scandinavia. In Germany, where it was adopted quite widely, it was rarely used to create the overall form of a piece. Rather we see it in borders and forming cartouches enclosing engraved or embossed scenes (no. 57), and it is often evident in the handles of tankards (for example, nos 447–9). The group of tankards from Hamburg (nos 57–9) are decorated with engravings after Abraham Bosse within cartouches in the lobate style. Another example with embossed cartouches is illustrated by Carl Hernmark.[18] In England the style was also used with restraint, but there are exceptions – no. **445** for example. However this piece may be the work of an immigrant goldsmith, possibly directly influenced by Christian van Vianen, who worked for Charles I.

The series of portrait medallions by Simon de Passe (nos 284–90) illustrate the period of English history immediately preceding the last melting of silver on a large scale for political reasons. De Passe came from a family of Dutch engravers and worked in England between 1615 and 1622. Although the technique he used when creating his medallions is not known exactly, it is now thought that many were originally die-stamped. Much of the silver made in England in the first forty years of the seventeenth century, together with many earlier items, was probably melted during the Civil War. Pieces that survive from the 1630s and 1640s are often of light gauge and rather naively embossed (nos 417–19). 'Many a customer when ordering plate in the reign of Charles I must have reflected that, if his purchase

Auricular (England): cup and cover, unmarked, c.1665 (no.455)

was likely to be melted down within a short space of time, it would be extravagant to stipulate for an elaborate finish. If it was melted, the value of the silver and even of the gilding could be recovered, but what had been paid for workmanship would be irretrievably lost.'[19]

However, certain English goldsmiths do stand out for the quality of their work, which no doubt reflects the prosperity of their patrons – notably the one whose mark is a hound sejant (nos 409–11).

The finest silver that appears regularly at auction from the late sixteenth and early seventeenth centuries comes from Germany and the Low Countries. Comparatively little silver is seen from southern Europe and Iberian silver has not been included in this book. The famous dish by Gaspare Mola (no.1844) must represent the work of Italian goldsmiths during the transition between mannerism and baroque.

As with many artistic periods that of the baroque appears to present conflicting faces. In silver the baroque style is most frequently associated with the robust floral or naturalistic style that developed in Germany and the Low Countries (nos **68–9**, 85, 323) and which at its demise mingled with the more formal acanthus decoration of the 1670s and 1680s (nos 324, **474**). The foliate baroque style coincided with the period in Dutch history that has become known as Holland's 'Golden Age'. Following the dissemination of the lobate style, Dutch silversmiths indulged the native passion for flowers in their adoption of botanical decoration, both engraved and chased. Alongside this flamboyance, we find undecorated pieces, notably in France, England and Holland (nos 322, 494), and the adoption of classical forms which, by the end of the seventeenth century, crystallized into the style favoured by the Huguenots.

Stylistic similarities in silver often mirror geographical areas. Shifting frontiers resulting from marriages between royalty, wars and subsequent treaties, religious conflicts or the economic climate must always be borne in mind. The de Bry family, Etienne Delaune and François Briot were all victims of religious persecution. So were, most probably, a group of Groningen craftsmen who crossed the border into Germany, where, in Emden, they produced beakers of a type

Baroque (Germany): beaker, Reinhold Riel, Nuremberg, c.1670 (no.69)

Baroque (Germany): tankard, Reinhold Riel, Nuremberg, c.1660 (no.68)

usually associated with their native town (nos 317–20). The changing prosperity of Flemish and Dutch cities, for example, is reflected in the silver produced there, and towns along the Baltic coast of Germany have also been subject to changing influences. Thus much of the silver from north Germany is close in feeling to that of Scandinavia. It is noticeable, for example, in beakers and tankards where the use of three feet, either ball, pomegranate or lion, is widespread (nos 86, 96, 1948, 1954–8). Scandinavian silver has an affinity with some Russian work; indeed, many Scandinavian silversmiths went to work in Russia. The military triumphs of one of Sweden's most famous monarchs, Gustavus Adolphus, were often celebrated by goldsmiths, on both sides of the Baltic.

The middle years of the seventeenth century saw a variety of decorative techniques. The supreme skill of the van Vianens could not be emulated by many craftsmen, but the quality of most embossing in the mid-seventeenth century was good. The chasers worked the silver in high relief, making the foliate forms appear more realistic than was possible in engraving: '... there developed in the Netherlands two other styles that are perhaps even more exclusive to this country. In the first place there was a sudden rise of engraving on silver ... the smooth surface of the silver was decorated with engraved ornament of a quality found nowhere else in the world.... In the second place the completely new discovery ... that silver can perfectly well be left completely or virtually completely undecorated....'[20] A cheaper and easier method of decorating silver than chasing or engraving was matting – used in every period as a background to chasing. 'Its use as a primary form of decoration became widespread in Germany during the Thirty Years War even in areas not deeply involved in the struggle. [In England it] proved so acceptable that it competed successfully with the more expensive forms of ornament which returned at the Restoration'.[21] (nos 81, 95, 479)

The foliate baroque style, inspired by the silver of the Low Countries, suited the mood of the supporters of Charles II returning to England in 1660; the country's carefree and lavish mode of living, overthrowing the years of austerity, is

Baroque (England): wall sconce, Thomas Jenkins, London, 1687 (no.474)

Baroque (England): detail of porringer and cover, Francis Garthorne, London, 1682 (no.509)

reflected in much Restoration silver; however, a softening of form had already been evident in the silver made in the last years of the Commonwealth (nos 421–2). Money was spent more freely and surplus cash was once again invested in plate. One of the most interesting craftsmen working in London in the years following the Restoration used the mark IB, with a crescent below, attributed to a goldsmith of German origin, Jacob Bodendick. In the series of tankards illustrated (nos 447–9) the cast handles, still showing the influence of auricular forms, are unlike any by other London craftsmen. The embossed scenes on no. 450, too, are untypical of English tankards. Bodendick's other work, however, has close parallels in the work of English silversmiths and also reflects the fashion popular in France and Holland (nos 453, 551, 1676). The work of English craftsmen appeared to blossom under the influence of the times. The work of Arthur Manwaring is perhaps the most illustrative of the change in the fortunes of the trade (nos 424–33).

The use of heraldry as a means of decoration became more important at this time. Hitherto, armorials had been used as a means of identifying the owner of a piece and were often very attractively executed (particularly when enamel was used), but, although important, the coat-of-arms had not usually been dominant. In England we now see armorials becoming a major vehicle for displaying an engraver's art: indeed, to the eyes of many modern collectors a piece often appears barren without a coat-of-arms.

In the 1670s and 1680s parallel with the foliate style, in England especially, there was a fashion for chinoiserie (see p. 12), which sometimes influenced the shape of objects (nos 91, 551) as well as their surface decoration (no. 507). In these decades, too, the introduction of stiff palm and acanthus decoration became evident, and gradually superseded the earlier naturalism (nos 470, 492).

The Dutch ewer (no. 324), made in the third quarter of the seventeenth century, is in marked contrast to the free naturalism seen so far, but is contemporary with it. This ewer would have been part of a large toilet set similar to that known as the Lennoxlove toilet set (no. 1676), made in France by an unidentified master in 1674. Another set, bearing the mark of Pierre Prevost, Paris, 1670, is in the collection of the Duke of Devonshire. The influence of French silver on English is apparent from a comparison of the two illustrated pairs of candlesticks (nos **444, 1675**). All these pieces are decorated with stiff acanthus leafage, so characteristic of the late phases of foliate baroque, but their form is classical.

Baroque Classicism: the Huguenot and Régence Style, 1670–1730

In the last quarter of the seventeenth century there was a marked change in the use of silver and therefore in the type of object made. As manners became more sophisticated and houses more comfortable, the range of articles needed increased: toilet sets, table ware, furniture, utensils for the new drinks of chocolate, tea and coffee. The ewer and basin,

Baroque (France): candlestick, Pierre Massé, Paris, 1664 (no. 1675)

Baroque (England): candlestick, Robert Smythier, London, 1670 (no. 444)

no longer necessary for washing hands at meals, became the principal item of display on the buffet. These stupendous shows of wealth can best be seen in contemporary paintings and prints.[22] When an Englishman was appointed ambassador, he was given a quantity of plate, calculated by weight, which he was allowed to retain after his term of office ended. This practice accounts for the existence of much of the finest plate, most of which bears the Royal Arms or monogram. The influence of Louis XIV and his court at Versailles penetrated all the courts and aristocratic houses of Europe. Architects and designers such as Jean Berain and Daniel Marot spread the language of the baroque interpretation of classicism through published designs. However, goldsmiths were still working for a very small minority of the population – those who possessed both power and wealth – and, of course, for the Church.

Comparatively little French silver survives from the turn of the seventeenth and eighteenth centuries. In order to finance his wars, Louis XIV required thousands of ounces of plate to be melted and the silver lost in this way included not only domestic items but the silver furnishings of the palace of Versailles. However, sufficient silver survives to show the high quality of most pieces made at this period throughout France, and we know of it also through designs and contemporary engravings. Paintings such as the still life by Alexandre François Desportes in the Metropolitan Museum, New York,[23] show the massive character of some French silver of this period. A comparable piece is perhaps the Italian ewer (no.1847) or John le Sage's ewer of 1725 (no.763). More typical of extant domestic pieces are the group of candlesticks (nos 1681, 1682, 1686) and the casket and ewer (nos **1683**, 1687). The decorative motifs of entwined strapwork, classical busts, lambrequins and guilloche that were introduced late in Louis XIV's reign, and were to continue to develop through the period of the French Regency, derive principally from the designs of architects and designers such as Berain and Marot. These pieces show how skilled the French craftsmen were at casting silver and the very high standard to which they finished their work. The use of applied strapwork on the body of hollow ware (nos 1698, 652) was one of the features that became most popular with English goldsmiths, who developed through casting the technique known as cut-card work (for which sheet silver was normally used) that had been seen in the Carolean period (nos 476, 567), and which had also come from France.

The persecution of French Huguenots, culminating in the revocation of the Edict of Nantes in 1685, helped further to spread the French taste. The Huguenot craftsmen, starting life afresh in England and other Protestant nations, brought with them not only new designs but a higher level of craftsmanship than had been generally current hitherto in the countries of their adoption. It was not the court style, however; most of the exiled Huguenots came from the provinces rather than from Paris.

Despite attempts to prevent the Huguenots from working in London and having their silver marked, London goldsmiths were forced, in the end, to accept them and to learn from them. 'It is not, in fact, surprising that the less successful London goldsmiths should have been so sensitive to the effect upon their livelihood of the foreign competitors.

The main advantage enjoyed by the latter was that they could offer fashions that were as yet unknown or only beginning to become known in England, and they tended, therefore, to obtain important commissions from those rich patrons who attached great significance to keeping up with the latest fashions.'[24] Not all Londoners were so antagonistic, however, and the initial reluctance of the Goldsmiths Company to admit Huguenots led to the practice of a friendly freeman occasionally including the work of Huguenot colleagues with his own when having silver assayed. Amongst surviving pieces from this period there might be many whose marks deceive us in this way.

The first Huguenot to be admitted to the Goldsmiths Company in London was Pierre Harache in 1682, three years before Louis XIV revoked the Edict of Nantes; examples of his work are illustrated (nos 614–21). There follows a group of some of the finest Huguenot craftsmen, including David Willaume, Louis Mettayer, Philip Rollos, Pierre Platel and his pupil Paul de Lamerie, who has become the goldsmith perhaps best known to present-day collectors.

The work of Englishmen such as Anthony Nelme and Benjamin Pyne illustrates the changing taste during the years 1680–1720. Both were signatories of petitions attempting to limit the work of Huguenots. The ginger jar of 1693 (no.551) shows Nelme working in the foliate style influenced by Holland, using formal acanthus leafage but also classical motifs. The tankard made the previous year (no.544) is a development of the style of tankards made during the

Baroque classicism/Régence (France): ewer, Louis Cordier, Paris, 1729 (no.1683)

preceding two decades (which was to remain popular amongst English craftsmen into the eighteenth century) but chased with lobing and fluting. Nelme, however, instead of continuing to work in this style, adopted the Huguenot techniques, developing his work in the utterly simple form that was to typify silver made in the reigns of Queen Anne and George I. Benjamin Pyne, too, though apparently a less efficient businessman, kept abreast of the new fashion and techniques and therefore remained prominent in the trade, as evidenced by the toilet set (no.541) and the salts with guilloche borders (no.538), so typical of much French work.

'After 1700 the French taste was generally dominant and the most important pieces of plate were either made by Huguenots or executed in a style that was derived from them. Alongside this rich Huguenot style, however, another fashion for plate of extreme sobriety arose, a reduction of the Huguenot designs to their fundamental form, free of all ornamentation.'[25] The absolute simplicity of this latter style, with the emphasis on octagonal forms, is peculiar to England (nos **599**, 602, 609, 610). The facets thus created displayed to particular advantage the colour of the higher standard of silver (known as Britannia Standard) used at this time. The style was also well suited to the range of new articles needed for the drinking of tea, coffee and chocolate. It was only at this period that the domesticity which was beginning to influence the general way of life created the desire for lighter, functional utensils to be made in silver.

By contrast, it would be hard to find more richness of detail than is seen in the set of three casters (no.668). More usually it is items made for display that show the Huguenot style to best advantage – for example, cups and covers, and ewers and dishes. Smaller, equally grand, ewers and basins were made

Baroque classicism/Huguenot (England): cup and cover, David Willaume I, London, 1712 (no.641)

for toilet purposes. In either case, large areas of silver were frequently left vacant for armorials to be displayed prominently. The engravers took every advantage of this, creating elaborate architectural cartouches incorporating scrollwork and sometimes figures. The accompanying ewers are frequently the objects which show the skilled use of casting to greatest effect. The helmet shape, that most commonly used, shows obvious classical inspiration (nos 592, **632**, 672).

The family ties of goldsmiths must have been as important as the continuing connection between master and apprentice. This has already been touched upon (p.12) and is particularly noticeable amongst the Huguenot community in London and in Augsburg. The similarities in the design of some pieces cannot be solely attributable to the fact that two associated goldsmiths were working in the current mode.

Moulds or patterns for casting silver were expensive to make and therefore frequently re-used. On the death or retirement of a goldsmith the moulds were often bequeathed or sold to other members of the trade. This had always been so. In Germany in the seventeenth century, for example, the use of the same castings can be confirmed from standing cups bearing the marks of different makers. This may be the result of the loan of moulds; alternatively one man may have made, say, a batch of finials and another a batch of bracket supports, some of which they then exchanged. In England in the eighteenth century 'certain widely-used designs for handles, feet or finials owe their common features to suppliers of cast components to the trade, although again their identities are not yet known.'[26] See, for example, the chocolate pot bearing William Lukin's mark (no.662) and that of Thomas Corbet,[27] or nineteenth-century examples illustrated by John Culme

Baroque classicism/Huguenot (England): ewer, David Willaume I, London, 1702 (no.632)

Baroque classicism/Huguenot (England): candlestick, Matthew Cooper I, London, 1715 (no.599)

Baroque classicism/Régence (Germany): casket, Michael Heckel II, Augsburg, c.1725 (no.151)

from the workshops of Storr and Garrard.[28] Nor is it surprising to find the mark of Phillips Garden on cake baskets (no.908) of a type made earlier by Lamerie.[29] The candlesticks illustrated here bearing the marks of Charles Hatfield and C.F. Kandler (nos 830, 835) are further examples. (The similarity of their marks should also be borne in mind.) Similar relationships, both as regards style and the way in which the trade worked, can be seen everywhere. The family trees in Appendix 1 may help to show how many of the leading Augsburg families were connected – notably the Biller and Drentwett families.

Augsburg had taken the place of Nuremberg as the centre for goldsmiths. The first thirty years of the eighteenth century was the period when Augsburg goldsmiths produced their finest work. The form of much Augsburg silver at this time is softened by vertical fluting, the principal form of decoration being entwined strapwork, frequently heightened by a textural background and interspersed with plaques bearing classical busts and mythological scenes (nos 110, 151, 152, 155, 158). 'Amongst the earliest examples of angular fluting are the works of the Augsburg master Johann Erhard Heuglin II, known for his toilet and breakfast services. In the 1720s he also engraved patterns for such services, clearly stressing the flutings.... Both Heuglin's pattern sheets and the services he actually made show decoration with Berain-inspired strapwork, and this combination of un-French angular fluting with French-influenced strapwork ornamentation thereafter became commonplace in Augsburg and in other places where Augsburg exerted a strong influence'[30] (see nos 152–158).

The subtle change in the use of fluting is one of the clearest indications of the change of mood between baroque classicism and its successor, rococo. In England, we can see this change in the work produced in the largest and most successful workshop of the mid-eighteenth century, that of Paul de Lamerie (nos 699–735).

Rococo, 1730–70

The inspiration for rococo came from France. Juste Aurèle Meissonier was the man primarily responsible for its influence on silver design. Rococo is a light-hearted style, a reaction against the formality of classicism. 'It is sometimes considered that the essence of rococo design is its asymmetry, but in fact there are many pieces of silver in the style which are, in form at least, perfectly symmetrical . . . the essential characteristic of the style is movement as being the inherent nature of the design which prevents the eye from resting on a static form . . . and compels one's

Baroque classicism Régence (Germany): toilet vase, Albrecht Biller, Augsburg, c.1705 (no.110)

observation to move from part to part through the interplay of flowing outline and decoration....'[31]

The change in the style of living which first became noticeable in the baroque period continued to gather momentum and to influence goldsmiths, particularly in the type of object they produced. Several objects appear for the first time, particularly for use in the dining room: for example, the soup tureen and epergne. The sauceboat, introduced in England in the reign of George I, and the wine cooler, first seen at the turn of the century (although earlier in France), are found in increasing quantities. Teapots, coffee pots and all the appurtenances of these drinks became ever more popular, but sets (including teapot, coffee pot, sugar basin and milk jug) are rarely seen until the neo-classical period. The high price of tea is reflected in lockable tea caddies. Cake or bread baskets, too, proved well suited to the rococo style, although baskets were no new invention. Those illustrated (no.708) are in the style of the late sixteenth century.[32] By contrast, silver beakers and wine cups are less commonly found, glass and porcelain having proved more popular media. Apart from travelling services, it is rare to find sets of table silver (cutlery or flatware) dating from the seventeenth century;[33] by the eighteenth century, however, changing table manners demanded greater numbers of eating implements. It is possible for the present-day collector to buy sets of spoons and forks from the first decades of the century (no.587), but examples from the rococo period are the earliest which are available in large quantities.

The growing popularity of porcelain meant that goldsmiths faced new competition. Many of the large dinner services now being ordered were of porcelain, and only a few of the wealthiest patrons also wanted to acquire plate on a large scale. There was compensation, however, in the increasing wealth of the gentry and middle classes, many of whom, like the aristocracy, no doubt wished to own a silver teapot or coffee pot to use with porcelain cups. The use of pieces such as those illustrated (nos 186–9) can be seen in a portrait of the Remy family by Januarius Zich now in Nuremberg.[34] The period of the rococo seems to see the gap widen between objects such as centrepieces and epergnes, soup tureens, ewers and cups and covers, into which the goldsmith poured all his creative skill in terms of design and craftsmanship, and the more utilitarian objects, only a small proportion of which merited the same care as the larger pieces. The elaborate detail of most rococo silver was expensive to produce and perhaps too flamboyant for everyday use in the eyes of many clients. Thus much domestic silver throughout the period 1730–65 remains very simple, with only hints of rococo forms (nos 171, 858, 1720).

Although the first signs of rococo can be seen in silver in the late 1720s, it is not until the mid-1730s that its influence really shows. In France Meissonier's contemporaries, Jacques Roettiers and Thomas Germain, created some of the finest silver to have survived; some is now housed in the Museu Nacional in Lisbon. The service from Berkeley Castle (no.**1707**) shows all the elements of the style that were to remain popular for the next thirty years: the extensive use of rocaille ornament, foliage and crustacea; the highly skilled use of casting and embossing; above all, the sense of movement and love of display. The group of candlesticks which follow (nos 1711–13, 1719) show a wide range of the motifs used for decoration in the middle years of the century. Some are surprisingly plain, and all inherit the basic form developed in the late seventeenth century. The dishes of 1744 (1709) show the crispness and quality of finish that characterize so much French silver from this period. The swirled fluting seen on nos 1725–6 is rarely seen on English silver but in varying forms was almost universally popular on the Continent for the decoration of domestic items. It is a simple development of the vertical fluting popular in Germany earlier in the century and is perhaps even more commonly seen there than in France (**173**, 184, **189**). Rococo lingered on in Germany some time after the French and English had turned, perhaps with some relief, to neo-classicism.

Scandinavia, having been relatively slow to adopt the rococo style, still made use of its forms well into the 1770s. Designs were commissioned from France and executed by local goldsmiths. Influenced by France and Germany, many of the earlier pieces are fluted (nos 1967, 1969), but later coffee pots and jugs display floral and rocaille motifs (nos 1976, 1977). 'Really sumptuous pieces are few but the quality is ... often very high.'[35] The typical Swedish beaker, of flared form, continued to be made in large quantities (nos 1978–83),

Rococo (France): detail of service, Jacques Roettiers, Paris, 1735–8 (no.1707)

Rococo (Germany): toilet box, Gottlieb Satzger, Augsburg, 1759–61 (no.195)

Rococo (Germany): chocolate pot, Johann Christoph Engelbrecht, Augsburg, 1755-7 (no.189)

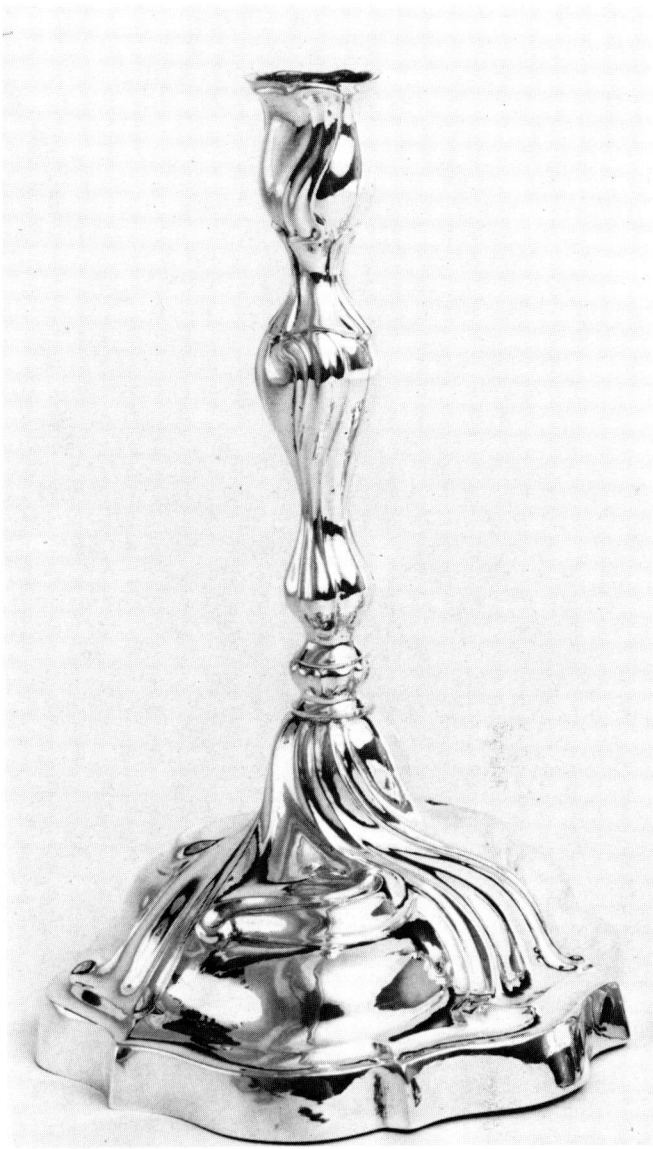

Rococo (Germany): candlestick, Hans Jakob Baur IV, Augsburg, 1769-71 (no.173)

some examples incorporating a token of rococo ornament.

By the mid-eighteenth century the Low Countries had lost their position in the forefront of artistic and political life in Europe: '... those working in the applied arts were subject to influences from abroad, but they managed to assimilate them into something that was entirely their own.... Amsterdam, a town which traditionally had a strong Classicist bias, did not take so much interest in the light-hearted Louis XV style, this in contrast to The Hague, ... there leafy twigs, which do not appear in France itself, were much used round the rims of tureens and baskets [nos 361, 386]. Amsterdam felt more at home with stricter, more stylized forms.'[36]

French designs and ideas were brought rapidly to England, where Paul de Lamerie became the principal exponent of rococo. The size of his workshop and the wealth of many of his clients enabled him to produce large quantities of plate in varying degrees of lavishness. At the start of his career, Lamerie worked in the classical style of his fellow Huguenots, engraving and flat-chasing his work with strapwork and leafage (nos 702, 703). His workshop continued to produce relatively simple pieces throughout his career, no doubt varying the work according to the taste and affluence of the client (nos 715, 728, **731**). The English goldsmiths developed the rococo style in their own manner, with restraint, and it is interesting that many of the more exuberant pieces bear the marks of masters who were probably of German, Scandinavian or French origin: for example, Nicolas Sprimont, C.F. Kandler, James Shruder, Christian Hillan and Emick Romer.

Many of the more fanciful pieces made in the 1750s and 1760s show the renewed interest in chinoiserie, so popular also in furniture and porcelain. Epergnes were well suited to this taste, and so were tea caddies (no.735). Towards the end of the rococo period there was also a fleeting interest in gothic once more, although the revival at this time was not so widespread as was to be that which occurred in the early nineteenth century (no.834).

The mid-eighteenth century is the period when we can begin seriously to look at American silver. Very few examples dating from earlier years appear at auction, but it is noticeable that the silver from the late seventeenth and early eighteenth century illustrated here follows English styles

Rococo (England): cup and cover, Paul de Lamerie, London, 1739 (no.731)

quite closely (nos 1547, 1554). Other pieces were influenced by Dutch and German silver, depending on the origins of the immigrant craftsmen. There is, however, usually a delay of up to twenty years or so in the use of patterns. Thus, flat-lidded tankards of a type common in England in the 1680s were still being made in North America in the 1720s. Bleeding bowls, or porringers, also follow this pattern; American examples dating well into the eighteenth century are commonly found, but English specimens are rare after 1700 (no.1549). This object is one of the best examples of changes in terminology. 'In England a porringer implies a two handled bowl, while in America a shallow, single flat-handled bowl. Today, in England, it is this latter which is known as a bleeding bowl. However, opinion is divided as to their use, and the fact that they are, and always have been, known as "porringers" in America supports the view that their use as a bleeding bowl was exceptional and it is likely that the American usage is more correct.'[37] Another example is the pitcher, for which the terms 'ewer' or 'jug' are now more commonly used in England.

Rococo (England): beer jug, Phillip(s) Garden, London, 1754 (no.907)

Amongst the illustrated items of American silver of the period 1730–70 are a number that closely parallel English pieces, notably the teapots (nos 1575, 1586) and the milk jugs or creamers (nos 1571–2). The form of teapot seen in nos 1567, 1570 is not found in silver in England, however, but in pewter – especially pewter made for export to New England. 'The rococo style of decoration, except in rare instances, never caught the imagination of the 18th century American.'[38] The objects illustrated here bear this out, all of them being in simple taste.

Neo-Classicism, 1760–1820

The years during which neo-classicism was in vogue were years of revolution – not only political and social revolution but industrial revolution also. The revolution in France affected the fortunes of many goldsmiths, those who survived financially being those who found new patrons in the age of Bonaparte. Napoleon spent large sums of money on plate, but as a result of his rule countries such as Austria witnessed a number of years during which silver had to be melted down to replenish the country's finances and relatively little new silver was made. By contrast, the trade in England flourished, having in the Prince of Wales (later George IV) a patron prepared to spend extravagantly (mainly through Rundell, Bridge and Rundell) and, as a result of the increasing wealth of the population, a ready market for the cheaper range of articles fashioned with the aid of new machinery (discussed below).

Stylistically, the period can be divided: the first phase was closely associated with the work of the British architect Robert Adam and was greatly influenced by French goldsmiths; the second phase derived its inspiration not only from Greek but also from Egyptian sources and is generally known as the Regency style (in England) or the Empire style (in France). After the delightful interlude of rococo, design returned to a classical fold.

The impetus for the design of most early neo-classical works came from the discoveries made at Herculaneum and Pompeii which were published in the 1750s and 1760s, and from books containing engravings of Greek pottery, notably examples from Sir William Hamilton's collection. In the work of François-Thomas Germain we can see the use of classical ideas at a time when other goldsmiths were still deeply involved with the rococo style. By 1770–71 neo-classicism was sufficiently established for Roettiers to produce the candlesticks illustrated here (no.**1747**) and Thomas Heming the punch bowl (no.**990**), the latter being strongly influenced by the designs of Robert Adam.

Very few designs for silver can be ascribed with certainty to Adam himself (1006). 'Some of the best Adamite silver was made without the direct agency of Robert at all, by inventing in the manner of the Ancients, using often the same sources as he did, and indeed seeing through similarly conditioned eyes.'[39] The French style, by contrast, 'was heavier and its ornamentation cast in rather strong relief.... At first it was the French style which swept triumphantly over Europe but in the 1780s the English style began to exert a greater influence.'[40]

The components of the style that came to be used almost universally in the first phase of neo-classicism are a general outline of vase or urn form, laurel swags, paterae, stiff palm leaves and rams' masks. Medallions of classically inspired figures were sometimes incorporated (nos 994, **1015**). Beaded borders and piercing, both made considerably easier to achieve by the new machinery, also became part of the repertoire of popular motifs (nos 1073, 1074). 'It was unfortunate, if to be expected, that it was generally the clichés of the style which made up that Adam manner to be seen in European silver from Scandinavia to Southern Italy in the later 1770s'[41] (see nos 380, 1985). American goldsmiths were quick to follow the English patterns, too, sometimes

Neo-classicism (England): detail of punch bowl, Thomas Heming, London, 1771 (no.990)

copying quite closely the English manner (no.1592), but also developing their own (no.1595). The use of bright-cut engraving, which produced a faceted design, was tremendously popular in England for the last twenty years of the eighteenth century (nos **1082**, 1086, 1093) and was also common in America, but was seldom adopted on the Continent (no.1603).

The 1780s saw England leading Europe in the techniques used for the manufacture of silver, techniques which in turn influenced its design.

At the turn of the eighteenth century the hand, horse and water power previously employed was, in some factories, already being superseded by steam power. The flatting or rolling mills ... became necessary for the preparation of the manufacturers' raw material ... the use of easily available sheet metal had already had a profound effect ... on the styles in plate currently available. Work from the Bateman manufactory, headed by the legendary Hester Bateman, shows how domestic items could, almost unthinkingly, be fashioned in great quantity from the sheet. The banality of their designs, however, cannot overshadow their importance as early examples of London-made 'factory' work[42] [see nos 1063–81].

The name of Hester Bateman, like one or two others, such as that of Paul Storr, has in past years had an almost magical effect on the market, resulting in high prices for objects bearing her mark. But, as the passage just quoted suggests, her importance lies less in the aesthetic merit of her silver than in the way in which, under her direction, her workshops seized the available opportunities for expansion and produced designs the market wanted at relatively modest

Neo-classicism (France): candlesticks, Jacques-Nicolas Roettiers, Paris, 1771 (no.1747)

Neo-classicism (England): detail of toilet box, Daniel Smith and Robert Sharp, London, 1783 (no.1015)

prices. She was not alone in this – as the quantity of silver from this period available today testifies.

Goldsmiths now faced new competition from within their own ranks – from Sheffield plate. Although, with a few exceptions, plated items have not been included in this book, the subject of plated wares must be briefly mentioned here. Discovered by accident in 1742, the technique of fusing silver onto a copper base was developed over the succeeding years. Plated wares were being produced in considerable quantities in Sheffield by the 1760s, and later in Birmingham, where Matthew Boulton had his Soho factory. The influence of the new industry was far-reaching, not least because, for the first time, the London trade faced competition from the provinces. Boulton epitomized the age in which he lived, being an astute and cultured industrialist. He developed the steam engine in partnership with James Watt and produced ormolu and silver as well as Sheffield plate. His friendship with Josiah Wedgwood involved mutual enthusiasms and friendly rivalry, such as the desire to produce copies of the Portland Vase (no.1158).

Wedgwood's patronage of the sculptor John Flaxman was the result of a need for sophisticated design. 'The impact of the work of Robert Adam saw the beginning in England of what we would now call interior design, in which all elements of a room create an artistic unity. It was to this new taste that Wedgwood addressed himself.'[43] The designs Flaxman produced for Wedgwood and his partner Thomas Bentley were sometimes used by goldsmiths (for example, in

Neo-classicism (England): detail of hot water jug, Peter and Ann Bateman, London, 1796 (no.1082)

the bowl illustrated as no.1031). Flaxman went on to design for silver and later worked for Rundell, Bridge and Rundell, the firm that was to dominate the English trade in the early nineteenth century. Much of Rundell's work was in the Greek and Egyptian style that is associated with the second phase of neo-classicism.

The tureen by Henry Auguste dated 1787 heralds the new taste (no.1759). During the first twenty years of the nineteenth century, despite the divisions of war, goldsmiths on both sides of the Channel worked along parallel lines, creating pieces often criticized for the severity of their design but which nonetheless displayed the wealth and confidence of their patrons. In France 'Napoleon set aside 100,000 francs a year for silver, most of which was purchased from Biennais and his only serious rival in Imperial favour, Jean-Baptiste-Claude Odiot. But this was seldom enough for his needs.'44 Henry Auguste, also patronized by Napoleon, left France in 1809 after suffering financial problems.

Inspired perhaps by Napoleon's Egyptian campaign, goldsmiths added sphinxes and snakes to their repertoire, alongside Grecian motifs. Borders were formed from tight palm leaves. The rest of Europe followed France's lead, but with subdued enthusiasm. In Italy the work of Giuseppe Valadier was of the highest quality (nos 1864–6). German goldsmiths produced silver which incorporated classical and Egyptian motifs (nos 231, 234), jugs and teapots frequently having animal spouts (nos 228, 236), in the manner also seen in France and Italy. The leading Parisian exponents of the Empire style were Percier and Fontaine; acting as architects and interior designers, they also produced designs for the Imperial goldsmiths.

The practice of a firm of retail or manufacturing goldsmiths of employing designers trained in other disciplines was established at this time. As far as is known, Rundell's were the first to do this in England, employing John Flaxman (no.1129), William Theed (no.1145), Thomas Stothard (no.1146), E.H. Baily (no.1153), and the Frenchman Jean Jacques Boileau. Rundell's' artists were kept busy adapting designs—often in the interests of economy.45

Neo-classicism (France): coffee pot, Martin-Guillaume Biennais, Paris, 1798–1809 (no.1767)

Neo-classicism (England): centrepiece, Rundell, Bridge and Rundell, London, 1809 (no.1138)

Neo-classicism (England): tea urn, Rundell, Bridge and Rundell, London, 1805 (no.1118)

More and more we see the practices of exchanging models, and of elaborating or simplifying designs, with the object of creating pieces which would appeal to clients of varying affluence and of ensuring that not too many identical articles were made. The juggling of component parts can be seen, for example, in the group of ewers by Thomas Holland (nos 1107–10) and in the group of sugar vases (nos 1121, 1122, 1150).

Although there was no need to melt old plate for political reasons, it would be fascinating to know how much of it was converted into the enormous quantity of new wares which were made for virtually every large household in the Regency

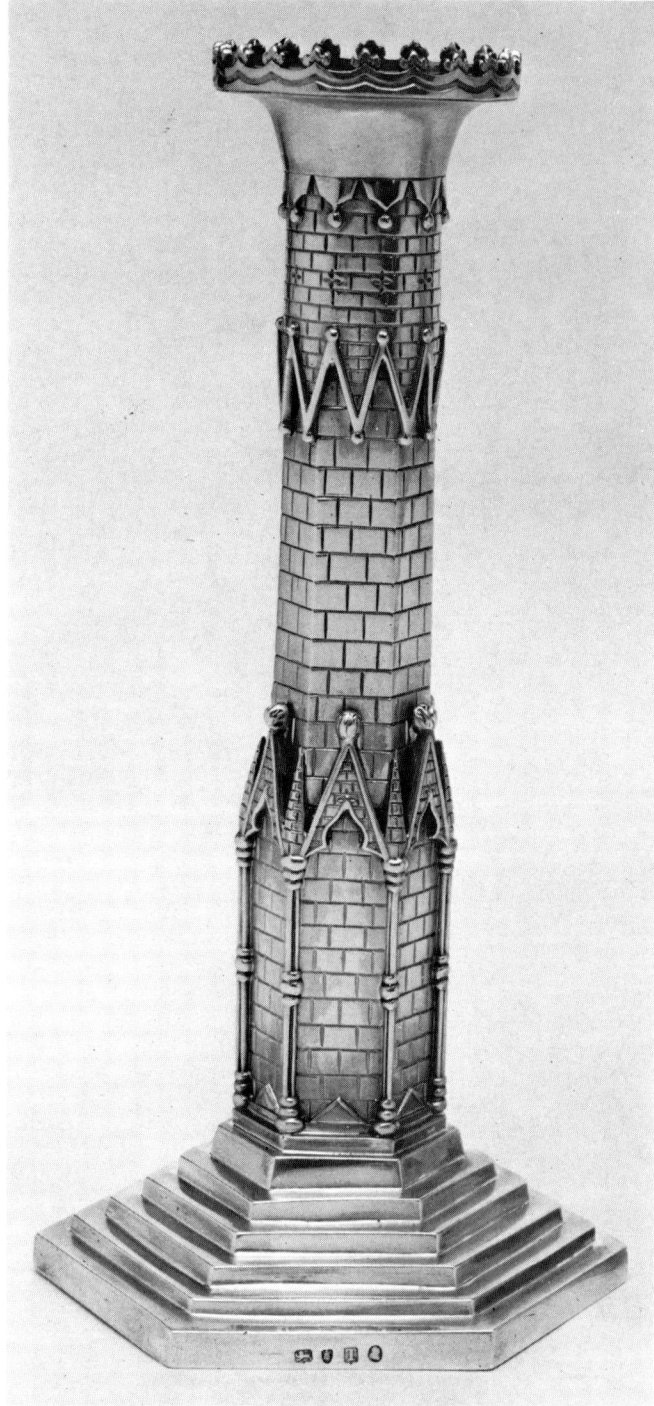

Gothic revival (England): candlestick, William Elliott, London, 1814 (no.1248)

Gothic revival (England): chalice and paten, John Hardman and Company, Birmingham, 1869/77 (no.1365)

period in England. Rundell's are known to have acquired pieces from the Royal Collection, which, however, they did not melt as they were expected to do. Much of this silver was to provide the inspiration for Rundells' designers to revive the past styles which are discussed below.[46]

Naturalism and the revivals of Rococo and Gothic, 1815–40

The work produced in Rundell's workshops is extraordinarily eclectic and influenced the entire trade. In the period between 1815 and 1830, and even as early as 1810, there was a renewed interest in Chinoiserie (no.1139), and in the revival of gothic and rococo (the latter blending with a vogue for naturalism), as well as occasional hints of early neo-classicism (no.1162) and baroque (no.1241). The work of goldsmiths must be seen against a background of architectural fantasies such as George IV's Brighton Pavilion and William Beckford's Fonthill Abbey (nos 1049, 1111), of the novels of Walter Scott and of the romantic paintings of Constable, de Loutherbourg, Cotman and Turner. Many of the more esoteric pieces, however, appealed to only a small intellectual elite. The bulk of the trade's output was for the general market.

This mixture of styles was also evident on the Continent, where it was exacerbated by the uncertain political situation after the fall of Napoleon. In Austria the period between 1815 and 1848 has come to be known as Biedermeier, during which pieces such as nos 235 and **241** were produced. Here, as in Holland, there also developed a style of domestic silver which, in its extreme simplicity, foreshadowed the work of twentieth-century designers. In Paris the firm of Odiot, continued by Jean-Baptiste Claude's son, Charles Nicholas (who worked for a time in England), continued to produce a large output. Services such as the illustrated example (no.1802) closely mirror English work of the time.

Interest in the gothic style was more widespread in

Rococo revival (Austria): ewer and basin, Stephan Mayerhofer and Joseph Klinkosch, Vienna, 1836; the ewer unmarked (no.241)

Naturalism (France): tea set, Charles-Nicholas Odiot, Paris, c.1825 (no.1803)

England during the nineteenth century than it was during the revivals of the seventeenth and eighteenth centuries. The style remained popular amongst architects, cabinet-makers and goldsmiths throughout the century. One of its earliest exponents, A.W.N. Pugin, designed silver for Rundell's and later for J. Hardman and Company. The choice of gothic was perhaps more widespread for church furnishings (no.**1365**) than for domestic articles, but a wide variety of objects is found which display arches and trellis-work in the gothic manner (nos **1248**, 1351, 1357). Mannerist motifs also reappear (nos **1404**, 1413).

As connoisseurs began to show an interest in early plate there developed a vogue for 'historical' pieces. This trend had started in about the 1750s and 1760s amongst a small band of the cognoscenti. The mounting of gemstones and enamelling achieved limited popularity. Goldsmiths such as Edward Farrell incorporated pieces of early silver into their own work (no.1240). The name of the sixteenth-century Italian goldsmith Benvenuto Cellini inspired such adulation that pieces were named after him: Cellini-pattern ewers and goblets (no.1342) were made by a number of manufacturers over a long period. Objects such as the illustrated cup and cover (no.1289) were made in imitation of earlier examples.

Direct copies were made of old silver, sometimes to make a pair for better display (no.1333). Later, as the possibility of deceiving collectors entered the minds of goldsmiths and retailers, pieces were probably made with that object in view (no.**248**). The influences behind the use of gothic and historical forms coincided with an interest in mediaevalism. This was due, in no small measure, to literature. The Duke of Cambridge was presented with a dish depicting the Battle of Agincourt (no.1184); the Doncaster Cup of 1857 (no.1420) was one of many presentation pieces which romanticized the age of chivalry (no.1323).

However, in terms of silver design rococo appeared to have longer lasting appeal than gothic. In a tray such as that bearing the mark of Paul Storr (no.1274) or in the ewer of 1835 (no.1315), the pervasive motifs of rocaille and shells are evident once more, as is the use of assymetrical scrolls and leafage in the mustard pot of 1854 (no.1325) and, spectacularly, in the epergne by Edward Barnard and Sons (no.1383). Naturalism is often confused with the revival of rococo and the two can be seen together frequently. But when naturalism is used to create the overall form of an object, rather than as surface decoration, it can result in objects of immense charm, such as the taper stick now in the Victoria

Naturalism (England): cruet bottles, William Bateman II, London, 1836 (no.1183)

and Albert Museum (no.1384), the ladle (no.1319) or the inkstand (no.1335). 'The revived rococo style, and its offspring the "Louis Quatorze", accounted for much that was bad or careless in the design of mid-century plate. Even by 1835... voices were raised against the trend. The witnesses [at a Parliamentary Select Committee] without exception condemned the current rococo revival.'[47] Nevertheless, rococo continued to be used, with varying degrees of enthusiasm, throughout Europe for the rest of the century (nos 247, 250, 1815, 1986).

Products of the revival of rococo in the nineteenth century are sometimes hard to distinguish from examples of eighteenth-century rococo; however, as a general rule (to which there are always exceptions), nineteenth-century rococo lacks the lightness of touch of the earlier period. For example, the chasing is executed in a denser, more contrived manner and usually covers a greater surface area of the object. It was at this time, too (the early 1820s), that the practice began of chasing earlier pieces of silver to suit the current taste. Thus tankards, mugs, coffee pots and milk jugs (such as nos 753 and 813), that would originally have been plain, can be found elaborately embossed with foliate, scroll and rocaille decoration added later.

Naturalism (England): taperstick, Edward Barnard and Sons, London, 1840 (no.1384)

This was not the first time that goldsmiths had looked at the work of their predecessors and recreated their designs in a modern idiom, but it was perhaps the first period during which silver created in revived historical tastes was dominant. This trend was to continue for the next half-century, but, for the most part, without the inventiveness and good craftsmanship that characterize so much silver made in England in the years leading up to Victoria's reign.

The middle and later nineteenth century, 1840–1900

Until recently the years 1830–1900 were dismissed as of little interest to collectors and students of silver. This sweeping condemnation was probably based on the undeniable fact that the majority of silver made during this period was mass-produced by manufacturing goldsmiths using techniques different from those generally associated with the production of good-quality silver. However, even when the trade was generally regarded as being at a low ebb, some goldsmiths were making pieces of consistently high quality. 'Familiarity breeds contempt', and it may be that the sheer quantity of nineteenth-century silver in existence has been prejudicial to its reputation. It may also be that the nineteenth century has only lately receded sufficiently from us for a proper evaluation to be made, and, as a result, modern commentators see the silver of this period in a new and more favourable light. 'Such an extraordinary multiplicity of designs, such ingenious new methods of manufacture, such creative inventiveness on a scale unrivalled in any other century is displayed by the silver of the Victorian period that it would be absurd for us to treat its aspirations and achievements with scorn or indifference.'[48]

The Great Exhibition held in London in 1851 was not the first exhibition ever held, but it was the first international exhibition and as such the most ambitious and the most successful. It was the precursor of many more throughout Europe and North America. These included another in London in 1862, and those in Paris (1855, 1867 and 1889), Vienna (1873) and Philadelphia (1876), to name only a few. These exhibitions became the showcase of the industry, displaying its strengths and weaknesses in a way not always foreseen by the exhibitors. The earlier exhibitions were exciting for the variety of their displays. Objects shown at the 1851 exhibition included, for example, the tea set (no.1362) and the Macready testimonial (no.1266). The work of J-V. Morel aroused particular admiration: several English firms employed designers from the Continent (nos 1402, 1406, 1409–11). The exhibitions held in the 1870s and 1880s, however, showed that the English trade, although still producing a large quantity of goods, was no longer in the forefront in terms of design and workmanship. From the 1860s onwards English manufacturers turned increasingly to the manufacture of trinkets, toys and jewellery; the industry went into a steady decline. The vogue for 'novelty silver' was widespread and led to the specialization of certain 'smallworkers'. French, German and Austrian manufacturers dominated exhibitions held in the latter years of the century, with increasingly important contributions from America. This trend has not been easy to demonstrate in this book, however, since comparatively little nineteenth-century Continental silver has been illustrated in auction catalogues.

Renaissance revival (France): cup, attributed to J.V. Morel, c.1850 (no.1811)

Mannerist revival (England): card case, Elkington and Company, Birmingham, 1864 (no.1404)

The middle decades of the century were the period when manufacturing silversmiths, many of whom ran very large workshops, prevailed in the trade. It was also the time when the process of electroplating came to dominate the cheaper end of the market. Electroplating was patented by G.R. Elkington in 1840. 'In industrial technology, the Elkingtons had a far-reaching effect, for they changed the face of the silver and plating trades all over the world.'[49] Elkingtons spent much time and effort in producing pieces by their leading designers in electroplate – for example, the series of shields and dishes by Morel-Ladeuil (nos 1406, 1409–11). Some of these objects were made from a mould, and are known as electrotypes, 'an electrical equivalent of casting'.[50] The process was used to reproduce earlier masterpieces and to electrotype from nature,[51] as well as to create new designs. In order to safeguard their work, English manufacturers registered a new design at the Patent Office, marking their wares with the Patent Office Design Registry (PODR) mark, which shows the date on which the design was registered.[52]

The chief energies of the designers working for many of the leading English firms, such as Garrards, Hancocks, Edward Barnard and Sons and Hunt and Roskell, went into producing show pieces such as testimonials and racing trophies (1419, 1425). For the most part, everyday articles, such as tea sets, flatware and candlesticks, were mass-produced as an alternative to and in competition with electroplate, the purchaser choosing between the two according to the amount of money he or she wished to spend. Although there was considerable rivalry between the major firms, they also worked occasionally in close association. For example, Hennells, who were manufacturers to the trade, made a great deal of silver for C.F. Hancock, who were retail jewellers and silversmiths as well as having their own factory (nos 1420–26). C.F. Hancock had originally been connected with Hunt and Roskell, whose work is notable for its high standard.

At no time in the nineteenth century can it be said clearly that the use of one style stopped and the use of another started. Once a style had been reintroduced into the silversmiths' vocabulary it continued to appear, in combination with others, some forms being more popular with one manufacturer than another. The reappearance of rococo and gothic and the interest in naturalism, already discussed, were followed by a revival of mannerism (nos 1406, 1413, 1423) and an enthusiasm for pieces of eastern inspiration, including examples with arabesque decoration (nos 1360, 1644, 1812). The Renaissance revival was particularly evident in France (no.**1811**), Austria and Germany (no.254). The objects made included the mounting of hardstones and an extensive use of enamelling. Hermann Böhm (nos 257–9) and Hermann Ratzersdorfer (nos 254–6), both of Vienna, were leading manufacturers of such work. There was also a continuing interest in classical forms. After a period when cast and chased ornament was especially popular, engraving was used again on a variety of objects (nos 1348, 1392). In the last thirty years of the century there was a revival of neo-classicism: the vase shape became popular once more and pieces were sometimes decorated with bright-cut engraving (nos 1444, 1477). The greatest exponent of neo-classicism at the turn of the century was Carl Fabergé (nos 1933, **1935**, 1938).

STYLES: THE MIDDLE AND LATER NINETEENTH CENTURY, 1840–1900

Renaissance revival (mid-European): cup and cover, unmarked, c.1870 (no.248)

Rococo revival (Germany): wine cooler, Hermann Julius Wilm, Berlin, c.1855 (no.247)

Rococo revival (France): vegetable dish, André Aucoc, c.1900 (no.1815)

The London exhibition of 1862, whilst not especially auspicious for English manufacturers, displayed a variety of wares from Japan which were to be the inspiration for the Aesthetic Movement. The silver trade in England followed the lead of ceramics manufacturers in the production of wares in the Japanese taste. Between 1870 and 1890 a number of articles, such as tea sets, trays, cigar cases and card cases, were decorated with birds, butterflies and blossom in an oriental manner. Many have a frosted or pearl finish; some are also parcel-gilt (nos 1393, 1398–9, **1417**). The Japanese taste was also popular in America, although in a distinctive manner quite different from the English style (nos **1630**, 1649, 1656, 1664).

Throughout the nineteenth century the American silver trade had been gathering momentum, increasingly so after the Civil War. Several manufacturers of silver, plate and Britannia Metal rivalled the major European firms in their output, notably Tiffany, Gorham, Reed and Barton and the Whiting Manufacturing Company. Stylistic influences were similar to those prevalent in Europe, although for the most

Neo-classical revival (Russia): candelabrum, Peter Carl Fabergé, c.1900 (no.1935)

part American silversmiths were much more independent of European taste than formerly. During the last twenty years of the century American export of silver increased considerably.[53]

Japan was also an important influence on two of the most interesting personalities in the trade during the last quarter of the nineteenth century: Christopher Dresser and Arthur Lasenby Liberty – whose work will be considered below.

Aesthetic movement (England): salver, Elkington and Company, Birmingham, 1879 (no.1417)

Aesthetic movement (America): pitcher, Theodore B. Starr, New York, c.1885 (no.1630)

Art Nouveau, Art Deco and Modernism, 1890–1940

The rift between what a small group of intellectuals considered to be good design and what most people wanted was as apparent in late nineteenth and early twentieth century silver as it is in architecture today. This division of taste had been growing since the eighteenth century; by the second half of the nineteenth, when vastly greater numbers of people could afford a piece of silver, the gap was very wide indeed. The bulk of the silver produced by members of the Arts and Crafts movement, and in the Art Nouveau style, had limited appeal, but it reflected the tastes of people who were influential in artistic and intellectual (often socialist) circles and who wrote and talked about the need for a new approach to design (see nos 1493–4, **1499**, 1822). What was considered smart, however, amongst both the aristocracy and middle classes, was the eighteenth century. The continuing popularity of eighteenth-century silver permitted the majority of manufacturers to make only token gestures to new trends in design. The production of 'Queen Anne' and 'Georgian', or 'Louis Quatorze' and 'Louis Seize', silver – which, whilst often of good quality, required little imagination to create – continued to be a mainstay of the silver trade in England (nos **1528**, 1530) and on the Continent (nos **1824**, 1828).

The decline of the silver trade in England during the second half of the nineteenth century resulted in the emergence of different schools of thought. Firstly, there were the manufacturers who continued to produce objects in earlier tastes and who, as a small part of their business, made some wares in the contemporary manner. Secondly, there were Dr Christopher Dresser and his adherents, who believed that good design should take into account the requirements of industrial production. Thirdly, there were the protagonists of the Arts and Crafts movement, who rejected machinery and returned to craftsmanship. (This conflict of ideals was not unique to England, but was also apparent, for example, in Austria.) Dresser wrote, 'Modes of economizing material, when we are forming vessels of costly substances, are of the utmost importance, and should be carefully thought out. If the designer forms works which are expensive, he places them beyond the reach of those who might otherwise enjoy them.'[54] Pieces designed by Dresser, or after his designs, were made in silver and electroplate by Hukin and Heath, James Dixon and Sons and Elkingtons from the mid-1870s (nos 1486–94). They were way ahead of the general taste of the time.

The Arts and Crafts movement resulted in the founding of numerous craft groups. C.R. Ashbee started the Guild of Handicraft in 1888. His silver was notable, but reached only a small buying public (nos 1497–1504). Using modern methods and employing designers such as Archibald Knox and Rex Silver, Liberty sold pieces in the manners of both the Arts and Crafts movement and of the Art Nouveau style, under the Cymric label from 1899.

Arts and Crafts and Art Nouveau enjoyed their greatest popularity at the same time, the period 1890–1910. Art Nouveau was a completely new style, sometimes incorporating themes from earlier periods, adopted by goldsmiths in many countries. Its flowing curvilinear forms, sometimes known as 'whiplash curves', incorporated flowers and maidens with flowing hair and trailing gowns. In France

'Régence style' (France): tea and coffee set, Cardeilhac, Paris, c.1905 (no.1824)

one of the most famous designers, although he worked principally as a jeweller, was Lalique (nos 1820–22), with large firms such as Cardeilhac also producing work of fine quality (nos 1823–5). German manufacturers, such as W.M.F. (Württembergische Metallwarenfabrik), also produced plated wares and pewter. In America, the major output came from the established firms, such as Tiffany and Gorham, whose Art Nouveau silver was sold under the Martele label.

The modern movement was established some years before Art Nouveau went completely out of fashion, and while the conflict over the design of mass-produced objects still continued. One of its leaders was Josef Hoffman, who was amongst the founders of the Wiener Werkstätte in Vienna in 1903. He continued to design silver of enormous variety over the following decades (nos 264–275). 'Hoffman did not share the Arts and Crafts anxiety about designing for an elite. From the outset the workshops served a rich, sophisticated and cosmopolitan clientele, producing furniture, fabrics, metalware and ceramics in forms and patterns that anticipate the stylistic preoccupation of the 1920s and 1930s.'[55]

The style that developed in the 1920s in France, and which dominated the 1925 Paris Exposition des Arts Décoratifs et Industriels, has come to be known as Art Deco. In silver and jewellery Art Deco can best be seen in the work of firms such as Cartier, Christofle and Puiforcat (nos 1831, 1841). English and American manufacturers followed the French lead. Tea sets, vases and boxes have clean outlines, with a minimum of decorative detail (no.1543).

Scandinavia, and in particular Sweden and Denmark, emerged in the 1920s and 1930s as a major force in modern design. From the point of view of silver, Scandinavian design is to many people synonymous with the name of Georg Jensen. Jensen worked in close collaboration with Johan Rohde; their designs progress from the influence of Art Nouveau to the precise forms of the modern movement in

'Queen Anne style' (England): coffee pot, William Comyns and Sons, London, 1910 (no.1528)

Arts and Crafts movement (England): decanter, Guild of Handicraft Ltd, London, 1901 (no. 1499)

Art Nouveau (Germany): centrepiece, Louis Sy and Albert Wagner, Berlin, *c.*1900 (no.263)

Art Nouveau (France): sugar basin, Cardeilhac, Paris, *c.*1895 (no.1823)

STYLES: ART NOUVEAU, ART DECO AND MODERNISM, 1890–1940   45

Art Deco (France): bowl, Jean Goulden, 1929 (no.1839)

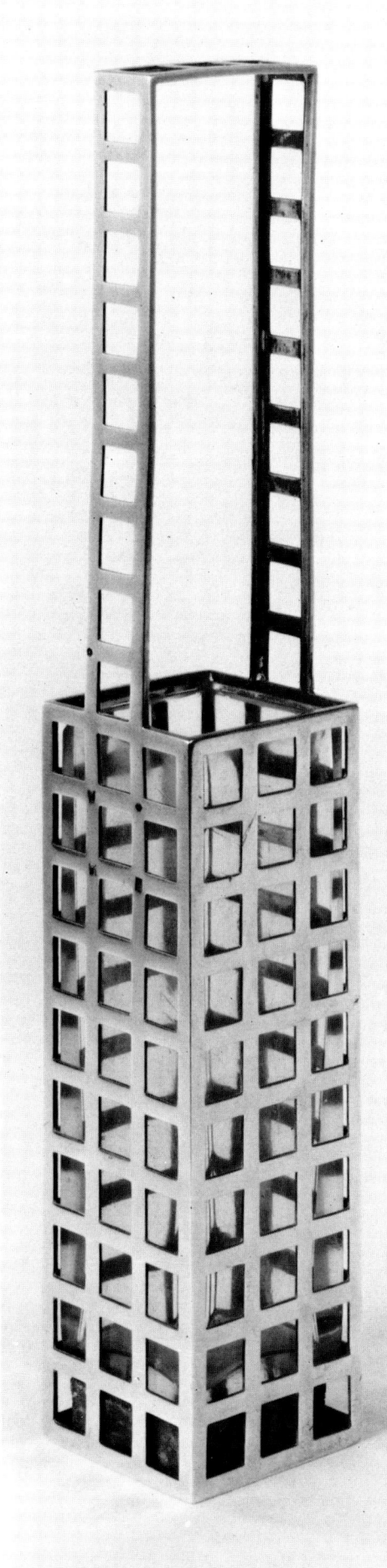

Modernism (Austria): vase, Wiener Werkstätte, Vienna, c.1920 (no.275)

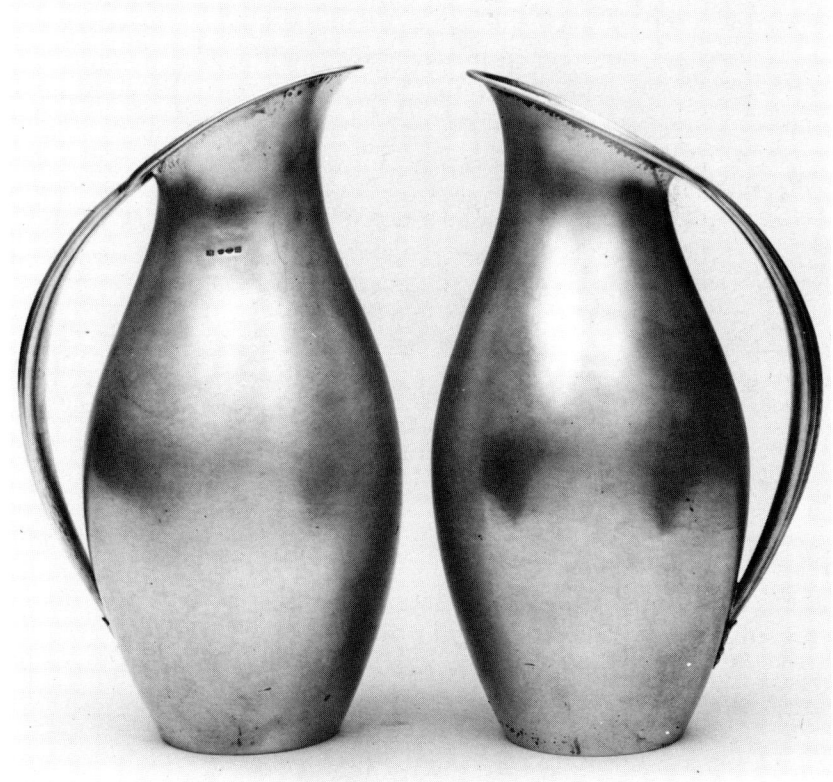

Modernism (Denmark): jug, Georg Jensen, Copenhagen, c. 1927 (no.1999)

the inter-war years. Some of their designs from this period are still being produced today.

The debate over 'modernism' continues. In the 1980s a considerable quantity of silver in earlier styles is still being produced by manufacturing silversmiths alongside contemporary pieces by leading designers. The ideals of the Arts and Crafts movement also survive in the ever-increasing numbers of men and women who run their own workshops and whose clients or patrons include both companies and private individuals.

Collecting silver

In looking through past auction catalogues one is constantly reminded how current fashion is reflected in the taste of collectors and therefore the market.

Until the 1960s relatively few items were photographed for catalogues and these were usually either early in date or by a maker respected at the time – a piece by Paul de Lamerie, for example, has nearly always been accorded an illustration. The first sales of nineteenth-century silver in 1969, the success and daring of which came as something of a surprise to a market used to regarding Victorian silver as worth little more than its melt value, revealed a different aspect of silver. Then, with developments in printing techniques in the 1970s and 1980s, it has been feasible to illustrate a wider range of objects, including the smaller and cheaper items, and with the emphasis on the unusual. This possibly reflects the taste and interests of those working at Sotheby's – who hope both to follow and to influence the current trends in collecting – as much as the taste of the buyers.

There is one paramount criterion for a collector: buy only what you like. Having decided this, the hopeful buyer should turn to practical questions.

The collector must first make sure that the piece he wishes to buy is what it purports to be. When attempting to identify a piece of silver one should first try to establish its area and date of manufacture by judging its style. It might then be possible to identify the maker from distinctive characteristics in his work. In order to confirm this one can turn to the marks. These must be genuine and correctly placed: placing will vary according to the date and provenance of the pieces and the type of object. Provided that the marks have not been faked or transposed, they should give a quantity of information, varying in detail according to the time and place of marking. Town mark, date letter and quality marks are relatively uncomplicated and can be checked in the relevant reference books – as can the maker's mark, which has already been discussed at length early in this Introduction.

When assessing the style of the piece, one should take into consideration the chasing or engraving with which it is decorated. Is it contemporary or has it been added later? It was a common practice in the nineteenth century to chase a plain object and so bring it in line with current fashion. Engraving can wear with use and cleaning. If a coat-of-arms appears suspiciously crisp it may have been re-engraved. Armorials and inscriptions are often added some time after the piece was made – they should be in the same style as the object they adorn. Whereas a good contemporary coat-of-arms can add to the value of an object, later engraving makes a piece less desirable.

The weight is helpful when one is judging the quality of an object: a pair of eighteenth-century cast candlesticks weighing 40 oz will normally be of better quality than a pair weighing 20 oz. It reflects the affluence of the original owner, as silver was sold by its weight, with additional charges for decoration and gilding. The weight can also offer a clue to possible alterations. If a mug, for example, is unusually heavy, or if its present weight is greater than the scratch weight (if this is shown), this would usually indicate an addition, or perhaps plating of the inside to strengthen any weakness.

Condition makes an enormous difference to value. A piece of domestic silver that has had heavy wear may be split at the borders or near the handle, be damaged at the feet, had holes repaired, and so on. In standing up to such wear, light products of the late eighteenth century have suffered worse than the hand-raised pieces of the classical and rococo periods. Over-zealous cleaning can also cause damage, especially affecting the value of a piece today if the marks have been badly rubbed. Cleaning can also alter the colour of silver. A good patination and colour are amongst the most desirable attributes sought by a collector. Old silver develops a marvellously deep tone over the years, but this can be destroyed by a misguided restorer or owner. It is difficult to understand what is meant by colour and patination in silver without holding a seventeenth or early eighteenth century piece in one hand and a modern piece in the other.

Once these and perhaps other considerations have been taken into account, the prospective buyer can then decide how much to pay for the piece. This is where expert advice can be helpful, because no amount of reading – whether of books relating to history and style or of price guides – is a substitute for the experience which comes from having handled many objects over a long period. And without this experience it is often difficult to assess quality.

The elusive noun 'quality' can cause puzzlement. Why is it that one soup tureen (no.1794) is worth £172,388 ($275,820) and another only a tenth of that price? Quality, in the context of silver, is a distillation and combination of a number of the attributes discussed so far. The very finest silver, made for the wealthiest patrons, combines good design with excellence of craftsmanship. Also, to meet the requirements of the most discerning collector today, an item of silver should be in good condition, not worn, and have a good colour. If such a piece also has an interesting provenance, its value will be enhanced further.

It is pieces such as these that will weather the fluctuations of the market best. Silver has its ups and downs like nearly every sector of the art market. There was a boom in English silver in 1968–9, when prices for Georgian silver rose rapidly. Then they fell in a matter of weeks in 1969, and prices for certain items took over ten years to recover. Candlesticks and coffee pots of average quality, for example, were amongst the slowest to regain the prices reached at the peak of the boom. Since that time, we have seen an enormous increase in interest in nineteenth-century silver. Silver made between 1890 and 1939, and in the Art Nouveau and Art Deco styles, is generally sold in sales specializing in that period, rather than in general silver sales, and tends to appeal to a different group of buyers. It is in this field that a significant modern trend – the view that value is not necessarily related to the age of a piece – is most apparent.

For the present generation of collectors appears to esteem quality and current fashion more than age. The prices realized by two tazze (no.1333) provide an example of this. Today, too, when the occupations of interior decorator and antique dealer are often combined by one person, the decorative aspect of a piece of silver is becoming more important. Hence the popularity of items such as the knights in armour (nos 261–62) and the nef (no.260). The flamboyance of much early nineteenth-century silver – see, for example, the wine wagons (no.1373) or candelabra (no.1317) – is also greatly sought after. However, this aspect of the market can change very quickly as the demand for certain items rises or falls. In contrast, the finest silver from the reigns of Queen Anne and George I, which is of the utmost simplicity, seems to maintain its popularity and its strong market value.

The style of living of most collectors today must also be taken into account. People who live in small houses inevitably collect small objects. Another factor which has increased buyer's interest in small items is the enormous cost of insurance today. To avoid this, some people, particularly those who buy for investment rather than for the pleasure of using and owning fine silver, keep their silver in bank vaults. Since storage problems anywhere lead to the buying of small objects, we find items such as spoons, boxes or wine labels – categories which offer an almost infinite variety of pieces to collect – fetching relatively high prices in comparison with many larger and more utilitarian objects. Spoon collecting is a highly specialized field which has barely been touched upon in this book.

Silver has always had one check on its value: the bullion price. The market value today of most of the silver illustrated in this book does not compare in any way with its melt value. Some items sold at auction are priced according to their bullion value, but this is usually at the lower end of the market, applying to modern silver of inferior quality or pieces that are very worn. Only rarely does it appear profitable to melt old silver, the most recent occasion being late in 1979 and early in 1980, when the bullion price rose suddenly to over £20 an ounce, after which it fell as rapidly. For those who might like to check bullion prices over a number of years, table 3 in Appendix 2 may be of interest.

Some readers may wish to use this directory as a price guide. Every time the hammer falls on a lot a new indication of market value is given. Every lot is different and, just because one item realizes a good price, it does not mean that another apparently similar piece is worth the same amount. Nor is the trend always upwards, as some would like to think. Last year's prices are no sure guide to today's, but an examination of pieces sold, say, over the previous six years should give the reader some guidance. Many of the prices given here will therefore be of value only for the record. An example is the coffee pot by Paul de Lamerie first sold at Sotheby's in 1929 for £580 ($2,813), together with a milk jug, as quoted here (no.721). The coffee pot subsequently appeared at auction in 1971 and most recently in 1982, when it fetched $275,000 (£184,563). One problem is that, in any book planned on the lines of this one, it is impracticable to give details of condition – an important factor, as has been explained.

There are two other factors which may affect the market value of an item in a totally unpredictable – and, sometimes, quite irrational – way. One is the sudden whim of a buyer, who feels that he or she must own a piece, almost regardless of price. If two people have the same feeling at the same time the result can be extraordinary. The other is the fun offered by a piece with a good story behind it, although sometimes this only comes to light after the sale. I will give three examples. The sconces by Lamerie (no.701) were 'at the outbreak of war in Lady Trent's home in Jersey. There was no time to remove them in 1940 (when the Germans invaded) and her chef, who was forced to act as stoker, was able to conceal silver and other valuables under the ashes, which he wheeled to a tip at the bottom of the garden where he hid these sconces . . . in a well in the greenhouses. Still in charge at the end of the war, he retrieved them and had them in place for the owner's return.' The charming ashtray (no.1437) was found by new owners of a house in the remains of a bonfire in the garden. The story of the bowl (no.1677) is perhaps what many people dream of: it was bought in a jumble sale along with football boots (the reason for the purchase) and other items for less than £1.

In conclusion, I repeat the advice that a collector should buy what he or she likes, buy the best he can afford, and take advice if he does not have complete confidence in his ability to judge a piece of silver.

The arrangement of the Directory

In most books of this type the entries in the directory are classified by the different categories of object: coffee pots, salvers, epergnes and so on. A different arrangement has been adopted here. The emphasis is on the goldsmith. In addition to this, the book aims to show how goldsmiths worked in the prevailing fashion and in the native interpretation of that style.

Selections have been made from catalogues from the 1920s until the spring of 1984. Because of the history of Sotheby's, it is perhaps inevitable that a high proportion of illustrations are of English silver. Parke-Bernet, in New York, became part of Sotheby's in 1964 and sales on the Continent have been held regularly since 1977. Since then the proportion of Continental and North American silver sold has risen dramatically and this may be expected to continue.

The book covers the silver of Europe (excluding Iberia) and North America only. The amount of English silver sold also reflects the enormous quantity of English eighteenth- and nineteenth-century domestic silver that is still in existence. The ravages of history must be borne in mind. There have been no large-scale meltings of silver in England since the Civil War in the mid-seventeenth century. By contrast, most Continental countries, France in particular, have suffered greatly from the compulsory melting of silver in times of war or financial distress. No attempt has been made to correct this imbalance. Priority has been given to named goldsmiths and, wherever possible, to those whose work is most commonly seen at auction. These restrictions have not mitigated the problems of attempting a fair representation of each country.

Another factor in the choice of illustrations must be taken into consideration. The most famous goldsmiths – those whose work is important because of their skill and the quality of their designs – are not necessarily those whose work appears frequently at auction. Thus many great names – Jamnitzer, Meissonier, Dinglinger, Sprimont, Thomas Germain, for example – do not appear in the following pages and it may seem that others, of less repute, have a disproportionate representation. This merely points the contrast between what appears at auction and what is usually written about.

It is hoped that the large number of items included from each of the chosen countries will show a cross-section of the silver they produced. The tremendous cultural influence of the Continent on England must always be remembered. The inspiration for goldsmiths' designs, and the skills with which they were executed, spread from Italy, France and Germany to the rest of Europe.

The various styles in which artists and craftsmen work have been defined by art historians in an attempt to help us understand works of art and relate the fine to the decorative arts. These styles have been discussed above in their relation to silver. We can see the elements of neo-classicism, for example, appear in the porcelain and furniture people used in the late eighteenth and early nineteenth centuries, in the paintings that adorned their walls and portrayed their way of life, and in the architecture of their houses and public monuments. Silver cannot always be labelled easily in this way, but in most cases the form or decoration of a piece will offer some clue. The study of these terms and stylistic influences brings rewards in the greater appreciation and understanding of all works of art.

In the selection of items to illustrate the principle has been always to choose pieces which typify the work of a particular goldsmith. Pieces of relatively low value have usually had priority over very expensive examples, many of which have already been illustrated in other books and articles. As many pieces as possible have been included which display characteristics unusual for their period, or which are simply amusing or pretty.

The book deals principally with domestic silver, and only a handful of ecclesiastical objects have been selected for inclusion. Judaica and the many religious objects generally included in sales of works of art have not been touched upon. A few excursions have been made into the associated fields of vertu and jewellery. Enamelling and the mounting of gemstones require specialist skills. Such pieces are not generally sold in silver auctions, but a handful of items have been included to remind the reader how closely associated are the jeweller and goldsmith. Also, no.1236 is a reminder that many goldsmiths, particularly in the sixteenth and seventeenth centuries, were medallists. With a few exceptions, examples of Sheffield plate and electroplate are not included.

A small number of unmarked objects have been selected; these have been listed in their stylistic, national and chronological context. Examples of unmarked silver survive from all periods and are of widely differing quality. As has already been mentioned, it is sometimes possible to attribute a master's name to a piece through its similarity to authenticated pieces of his work. The major difference for the collector is the substantially lower price that an unmarked piece will command (see, for example, nos 1272, 1273). This applies also to objects bearing only a maker's mark. Indeed, any incomplete set of marks can affect the market value of an object.

Some readers will undoubtedly wish to trace the designs of specific objects – to see how the form of teapots developed, for example. It is possible to do this by using the 'Index of Objects', where most objects have been subdivided by country and period.

Entries and their illustrations are grouped under the mark of the 'maker' according to his or her nationality. The work of each goldsmith is grouped in roughly chronological order according to the year in which he or she registered their mark or were made 'free' of their guild or livery company (in other words, made Master). In cases where this date is not known, the goldsmith has been placed according to the date of the pieces shown and sometimes according to the stylistic influences on his work. Thus Arent van Bolten, for example, has been placed next to Paul van Vianen, both being makers of plaques. There are other deviations from a strict chronological order, most notably amongst English eighteenth-century goldsmiths. In certain cases family connections or business partnerships have taken precedence over date. Thus William and James Gould are placed together, as are the various partnerships of Nicholas Dumee, Francis Butty and Lewis Herne. Where such partnerships span a great number of years and different stylistic influences, they have been split: for example David Willaume I and II, or the business of George Wickes, which continues from the eighteenth to the twentieth century. The work of such partnerships, in terms both of style and of the type of object produced, has been a deciding factor in their order of placement, although every attempt has been made to maintain a chronological sequence. Two other exceptions should be explained. Because of their immense influence on the English trade, some of the major Huguenot masters working at the turn of the seventeenth and eighteenth centuries have been grouped together. And in the early nineteenth century information regarding Rundell, Bridge and Rundell (see p.248) is followed by the men most closely connected with the firm (no.1115ff.).

Sotheby's cataloguing has been followed in the listing of objects. Sometimes, particularly in the early sales, the details are tantalizingly brief. Recent sale catalogues usually give far more information and are more profusely illustrated than those from the first half of this century – and the selection has been made only from objects illustrated in the catalogues. Most of the information in commentaries on individual items has been taken from catalogue footnotes. Occasionally it has been possible to up-date the description of a piece in the light of recent research; this usually amounts to the attribution of a mark not known at the time of sale, or a slight alteration in the dating of a piece where detailed information on a goldsmith's life has since become available.

However, because none of the silver has perforce been re-examined, the description given reproduces the original catalogue description, including the occasional mis-readings of marks and catalogue misprints.

Several of the items in the following pages have appeared at auction at Sotheby's on more than one occasion. No single principle has been followed in the choice of date made for the purpose of the directory. Sometimes the choice has been made for the historical interest of the price (discussed above on p.47), sometimes because of the availability of the photograph. It would have been fascinating to follow the life of each object through sales at Sotheby's and other auction houses throughout the world, but to do this accurately would have been an almost impossible task. It would often, too, have made sad reading, as we see toilet sets and sets of candlesticks and plates divided by a succession of buyers and sellers. By contrast, it is gratifying occasionally to find evidence of a collector piecing together a group of silver divided at auction many years before.

The precise date of sale has been given in the hope that the reader may be sufficiently interested to consult the sale catalogue, which, in the case of the more important pieces, will often contain information which space does not permit inclusion of here. Certain refinements of cataloguing terminology have also been excluded: for example, the distinction in the quality of metal (which in English catalogues is described as silver or silver-coloured metal) and whether the weight is 'all in' – that is, whether it includes part of the piece which is not silver (for example, a wooden handle or finial).

Where relevant, prices have been altered to include the 10 per cent. buyers's premium which for some years was not shown in the published price lists. However, prices do not include local sales taxes, which vary in each selling venue and which are explained in each catalogue. Exchange rates given for the period 1971–84 are the average rates given in Sotheby's yearbook, *Art at Auction*, for each season (September–July); those for the preceding years have been taken from R.L. Bidwell's *Currency Conversion Tables* (1970), unless shown in Sotheby's printed price lists. See the tables in Appendix 2.

Measurements have been translated to show metric and imperial to the nearest quarter-inch, and weights to give troy ounces and grammes (one troy ounce = 31.1 grammes). In each case there will no doubt be some loss of accuracy.

It may help the reader to have the following terms explained:

Silver-gilt (later)
The gilding is not contemporary with the manufacture of the object

(Augsburg), 1600
When the town is in brackets, this indicates where the object was made, although it does not bear a town mark

1721/2
Objects bear different date letters

Scratch weight
The original weight engraved on the piece when it was made (see p.12)

Notes
Authorities listed in the Bibliography are cited by author and title, or title of exhibition, only.

1. Exhibition, 'The Goldsmith and the Grape', no.199.
2. *Amsterdam Silversmiths and their Marks*, p.ix.
3. Bury, 'The Lengthening Shadow of Rundells'.
4. Culme, 'Kensington Lewis, a Nineteenth Century Businessman'.
5. See the entries for Kensington Lewis, Green Ward and Green, Ball Black and Company and others listed in the 'Index of Goldsmiths, Designers and Retailers'.
6. See Oman, *Caroline Silver*, p.7.
7. Elaine Barr's study of the ledgers of George Wickes (*George Wickes, Royal Goldsmith*) gives us a clear picture of the way in which a firm was run during the eighteenth century.
8. Hayward, *Huguenot Silver in England*, p.11.
9. Sold Christie's, Geneva, 12 May 1983, lot 137.
10. Oman, *Caroline Silver*, p.16; Dauterman, 'Dream-pictures of Cathay, Chinoiserie on Restoration Silver'.
11. Oman, *English Engraved Silver*, ch. IV.
12. See Hayward, *Virtuoso Goldsmiths*.
13. Ibid., pp.180–81.
14. See also the catalogue for Sotheby's, London, 8 December 1983, lot 94.
15. Gruber, in *Silverware*, illustrates two paintings which include tazze: pl.60 shows a still-life painting by Clara Peeters; pl.63 a painting by Dirk Hals of a man drinking from a tazza.
16. Hayward, *Virtuoso Goldsmiths*, p.292.
17. Exhibition, 'Art in 17th Century Holland', London, National Gallery, 1976, catalogue, p.106.
18. Hernmarck, *The Art of the European Silversmith*, pl.216.
19. Oman, *Caroline Silver*, p.3.
20. Exhibition, 'Dutch Silver 1580–1830', catalogue, p.xxvi.
21. Oman, *Caroline Silver*, p.15.
22. See, for example, those reproduced in Thornton, *17th Century Interior Decoration*, and Gruber, *Silverware*.
23. See Gruber, *Silverware*, pl.9.
24. Hayward, *Huguenot Silver in England*, p.15.
25. Ibid., p.3.
26. Exhibition, 'Rococo', catalogue, p.104.
27. Hayward, *Huguenot Silver in England*, pl.50B.
28. *Nineteenth Century Silver*, pp.138, 146.
29. Grimwade, *Rococo Silver*, pl.42B.
30. Hernmarck, *The Art of the European Silversmith*, p.63.
31. Grimwade, *Rococo Silver*, p.1.
32. See Clayton, ed., *Collector's Dictionary of Silver and Gold*, ill. no.8, which shows a basket made in London in 1597.
33. One of the few examples to appear in a saleroom in recent years was a set of twelve trefid spoons sold at Sotheby's, London, on 12 December 1974, lot 196.
34. Gruber, pl.132.
35. Hernmarck, *The Art of the European Silversmith*, p.37.
36. Exhibition, 'Dutch Silver 1580–1830', p.xxviii.
37. Clayton, ed., *Collector's Dictionary of ... Silver and Gold*, p.28.
38. Ibid., p.13.
39. Rowe, *Adam Silver*, p.39.
40. Hernmarck, *The Art of the European Silversmith*, pp.71–2.
41. Rowe, *Adam Silver*, p.70.
42. Culme, *Nineteenth Century Silver*, p.8.
43. Exhibition, 'John Flaxman, R.A.', catalogue, p.47.
44. Honour, *Goldsmiths and Silversmiths*, p.236.
45. See Oman, 'A Problem of Artistic Responsibility'.
46. Bury, Wedgwood and Snodin, 'The Antiquarian Plate of George IV'
47. Culme, *Nineteenth Century Silver*, p.80.
48. Inglis, *Silver*, p.105.
49. Bury, *Victorian Electroplate*, p.3.
50. John Fleming and Hugh Honour, *The Penguin Dictionary of Decorative Arts* (Harmondsworth, 1977), p.265.
51. Bury, *Victorian Electroplate*, p.26.
52. Ibid., pp.62–3.
53. Culme, *Nineteenth Century Silver*, p.208.
54. Quoted in ibid., p.207.
55. Gillian Naylor, 'Modernism', *Phaidon Encyclopaedia of Decorative Arts*, p.30.

The Directory

Note
All the pieces described in the Directory are silver unless it is stated otherwise.

Germany
Austria
Switzerland

Christof Ritter I
Nuremberg; master 1547
Mark Rosenberg, 3880

1 Cup and cover
silver-gilt
Nuremberg, c. 1590
12 in (31 cm) high
13 oz 2 dwt (410 gr)
Geneva, 12 XI 1980, 186
SFr.18,700 (£4,358 $9,021)

2 Cup
silver-gilt
Nuremberg, c. 1590
5¼ in (13.7 cm) high
3 oz 4 dwt (100 gr)
Zurich, 7 V 1980, 209
SFr.19,440 (£4,984 $11,712)

Hans Straub
Nuremberg; master 1568, died 1610
Son-in-law of Wenzel Jamnitzer.
Mark Rosenberg, 3969

3 Cup and cover
silver-gilt
Nuremberg, c. 1580
19½ in (49.3 cm) high
37 oz 4 dwt (1,160 gr)
Geneva, 15 XI 1983, 73
SFr.52,800 (£16,869 $23,447)

Melchior Bair
Augsburg; born Nuremberg
c. 1550, master 1576, died 1634
Mark Seling, 895

4 Standing cup
parcel-gilt
Augsburg, c. 1615
5¼ in (13.4 cm) high
4 oz (125 gr)
Geneva, 10 XI 1981, 183
SFr.11,000 (£3,072 $5,498)

5 Standing cup
parcel-gilt
Augsburg, c. 1610
6 in (15.5 cm) high
3 oz 16 dwt (120 gr)
Geneva, 12 XI 1980, 275
SFr.27,500 (£6,410 $13,268)

6 Standing cup
parcel-gilt
Augsburg, c. 1610
7¼ in (18.3 cm) high
4 oz 6 dwt (135 gr)
Geneva, 12 XI 1980, 276
SFr.30,800 (£7,180 $14,862)

1 C. RITTER I

2 C. RITTER I

3 HANS STRAUB

4 M. BAIR

5 M. BAIR

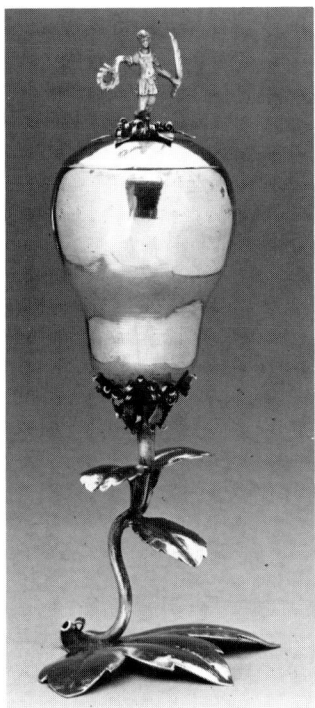
6 M. BAIR

GERMANY AUSTRIA SWITZERLAND

7 M. BAIR

8 M. BAIR

9 C. RITTER II

10 UNMARKED

11 UNMARKED

12 UNMARKED

7 Wager cup
parcel-gilt
Augsburg, c. 1580
10 in (25.2 cm) high
11 oz 10 dwt (360 gr)
Zurich, 18 XI 1977, 185
SFr.30,240 (£8,150 $15,077)

8 Trencher salts, pair
silver-gilt
Augsburg, 1620–25
2½ in (6.5 cm) square
9 oz 4 dwt (287 gr)
Geneva, 10 XI 1981, 184
SFr.17,600 (£4,916 $8,800)

Christof Ritter II
Nuremberg; master 1577, died 1616
Mark Rosenberg, 3881

9 Tankard
silver-gilt
Nuremberg, c. 1600
5½ in (13.8 cm) high
9 oz 6 dwt (290 gr)
Geneva, 12 XI 1980, 314
SFr.15,400 (£3,590 $7,431)

Unmarked

10 Spice stand
German, c. 1630
5 in (13 cm) wide
4 oz 16 dwt (150 gr)
Geneva, 12 XI 1980, 317
SFr.11,000 (£2,564 $5,307)

11 Tankard
silver-gilt
German, c. 1600
5¼ in (13.4 cm) high
14 oz 14 dwt (457 gr)
London, 26 VI 1975, 140
£1,150 ($2,645)

12 Beaker
silver-gilt
Transylvanian, c. 1600
8¾ in (22cm) high
14 oz 8 dwt (450 gr)
Monaco, 30 XI 1975, 80
FFr.13,200 (£1,466 $2,932)

Hans Petzolt
Nuremberg; born 1551, master 1578, died 1633. Worked for Emperor Rudolph II in Prague and for Nuremberg City Council, for whom he made standing cups. A large quantity of his work survives. See Hayward, *Virtuoso Goldsmiths*, pp.218–20; Honour, *Goldsmiths and Silversmiths*, pp.87–90
Mark Rosenberg, 4002, 4003

13 Cup and cover
silver-gilt
Nuremberg, c. 1625
18½ in (47 cm) high
42 oz (1,306 gr)
Arms: Imhoff
An inscription records the posthumous presentation of the cup in 1626 by Veit Georg Holtzschuher (who died 1606) to Andreas Imhof.
The scenes round the body depict the mining of silver.
London, 25 X 1973, 127
£40,000 ($96,000)

13 (DETAIL)

13 (DETAIL)

15 KELLER (KELLNER)

13 (PETZOLT)

14 HOHMAN

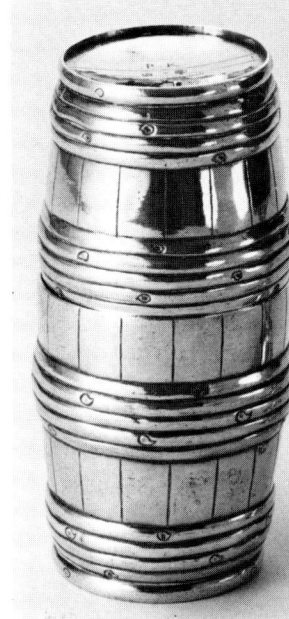
16 EMMERLING

Eustachius Hohman
Nuremberg; master 1582, died 1612
Mark Rosenberg, 4033

14 Beaker (*Setzbecher*)
silver-gilt
Nuremberg, c. 1600
3¼ in (8.2 cm) high
5 oz 4 dwt (164 gr)
Geneva, 15 XI 1983, 81
SFr.30,800 (£9,840 $13,677)

Hans Keller (Kellner)
Nuremberg; master 1582, died 1609. See Hayward, *Virtuoso Goldsmiths* p.220
Mark Rosenberg, 4031, 4032

15 Beaker
silver-gilt
Nuremberg, c. 1600
3½ in (8.9 cm) high
3 oz 8 dwt (108 gr)
Geneva, 15 XI 1983, 234
SFr.13,750 (£4,392 $6,104)

Nicolaus Emmerling
Nuremberg; master 1582, died 1606
Mark Rosenberg, 4029

16 Double beaker
silver-gilt
Nuremberg, c. 1600
5 in (13 cm) high
6 oz 18 dwt (215 gr)
Geneva, 12 V 1983, 84
SFr.13,200 (£3,940 $6,304)

17 WINTERSTEIN

18 STOER THE ELDER

19 MAIR

20 H.J. BAIR I

22 UNMARKED

Heinrich Winterstein
Augsburg; born Salzungen
c. 1552, master 1586, died 1634
Mark Seling, 1018

17 Nef
parcel-gilt
Augsburg, c. 1600
11½ in (29.3 cm) high
8 oz 10 dwt (265 gr)
Geneva, 12 XI 1980, 279
SFr.33,000 (£7,692 $15,922)

Thomas Stoer the elder
Nuremberg; master 1597, died 1611
Mark Rosenberg, 4081

18 Double cup
silver-gilt
Nuremberg, c. 1600
17 in (43.2 cm) high
37 oz 19 dwt (1,180 gr)
London, 11 VI 1970, 222
£4,600 ($11,040)

Melchior Mair
Augsburg; born c. 1565, master c. 1598, died 1613
Mark Seling, 1131

19 Tankard
ivory, silver-gilt mounts
Augsburg, c. 1610
10¾ in (27.2 cm) high
Geneva, 15 XI 1983, 237
SFr. 28,600 (£9,137 $12,700)

Hans Jakob Bair (Bayr) I
Augsburg; born c. 1564, master c. 1603, died 1628
Mark Seling, 1168

20 Tazza
parcel-gilt
Augsburg, c. 1620–30
9 in (23 cm) diameter
32 oz 8 dwt (1,010 gr)
Geneva, 12 V 1983, 178
SFr.99,000 (£26,865 $42,984)

21 WIBER

25 LAMBRECHT

26 STRAUB

24 J. RITTER

27 STRAUB FAMILY

23 J. RITTER

Peter Wiber
Nuremberg; master 1603, died 1641. See Hayward, *Virtuoso Goldsmiths*, p.220
Mark Rosenberg, 4119

21 Cup and cover
silver-gilt
Nuremberg, c. 1620
16½ in (41.8 cm) high
24 oz 2 dwt (750 gr)
Geneva, 12 XI 1980, 48
SFr.12,100 (£2,820 $5,837)

Unmarked

22 Plaque
silver-gilt
German, c. 1600
5½ in (14.5 cm) diameter
Mentmore, 19 V 1977, 685
£2,640 ($4,488)

Jeremias Ritter
Nuremberg; master 1605, died 1646
Mark Rosenberg, 3882

23 Beaker (*Setzbecher*)
silver-gilt
Nuremberg, c. 1610
3½ in (8.9 cm) high
8 oz 9 dwt (262 gr)
London, 28 IV 1937, 216
£90 ($442)

24 Model of a warrior on horseback
Nuremberg, c. 1640
11 in (27.8 cm) high
53 oz 7 dwt (1,659 gr)
London, 30 XI 1972, 70
£1,150 ($2,875)

Hinrich Lambrecht
Hamburg; died 1628
Mark Scheffler, *Niedersachsens*, p.413, no.12

25 Sweetmeat dish
silver-gilt
Hamburg, c. 1610
6 in (15.5 cm) high
42 oz 18 dwt (1,335 gr)
Arms: Royal, of Denmark
Provenance: King Christian IV of Denmark; the Czar of Russia, Archangel, 1628.
This dish formed part of a group of silver pawned by King Christian IV in 1628 to pay for military equipment; the king was unable to redeem the pieces, and they were bought by the Czar.
Geneva, 12 XI 1980, 52
SFr.275,000 (£64,102 $132,691)

Heinrich Straub
Nuremberg; master 1608, died 1636.
No. 27 attributed to a member of the Straub family
Mark Rosenberg, 4130

26 Beaker (*Monatsbecher*)
silver-gilt
Nuremberg, c. 1610
3½ in (9 cm) high
7 oz 14 dwt (240 gr)
Geneva, 15 V 1984, 106
SFr.46,200

27 Bowl and cover
silver-gilt
Nuremberg, c. 1630
5¼ in (13.5 cm) overall
5 oz 18 dwt (185 gr)
Geneva, 12 XI 1980, 296
SFr.17,600 (£4,102 $8,491)

28 SCHALLER

29 POTTHOF

30 ECKLOFF

31 MULLER

32 BAIR

Matthäus Schaller
Augsburg; born c. 1580, master c. 1607, died 1652
Mark Seling, 1212

28 Squirrel model/cup
silver-gilt
Augsburg, c. 1630
10¾ in (27.3 cm) high
25 oz 10 dwt (793 gr)
Inscription dated 1682
London, 21 XI 1957, 109
£850 ($2,371)

Herman Potthof
Munster; apprenticed to Bartel Jamnitzer, master 1607, died 1635
Mark Scheffler (Westfalens), p. 786, no. 47

29 Shield of the Munster Goldschmiedezunft
parcel-gilt
Munster, 1613
Signed: Herman Pothof 1613
6½ in (16.5 cm) high
3 oz 14 dwt (117 gr)
Arms: of the guild, surrounded by shields bearing the arms or devices of Munster goldsmiths. The shield was probably fixed to the cloth covering the coffin of a deceased master of the guild. See p. 12
Geneva, 6 V 1982, 166
SFr.286,000 (£79,888 $143,000)

Paul Eckloff
Königsberg; master 1612
Mark Scheffler, Ostpreussens, p.73, no.73

30 Beaker and cover
silver-gilt
(Königsberg), c. 1620
Maker's mark only
8¼ in (20.8 cm) high
19 oz 2 dwt (595 gr)
See Brunner, Old Table Silver, pl.89
Geneva, 12 V 1983, 86
SFr.99,000 (£29,552 $47,283)

Michael Muller
Nuremberg; master 1612, died 1650
Mark Rosenberg, 4151

31 Cup and cover
silver-gilt
Nuremberg, c. 1635
15¾ in (40 cm) high
16 oz 11 dwt (514 gr)
London, 12 XII 1974, 187
£1,500 ($3,450)

Paulus Bair
Nuremberg; master 1613
Mark Rosenberg, 4159

32 Cup and cover
parcel-gilt
Nuremberg, c. 1620
10¾ in (27.2 cm) high
7 oz 4 dwt (225 gr)
Zurich, 16 V 1979, 56
SFr.4,536 (£1,277 $2,617)

33 Cup and cover
silver-gilt
Nuremberg, c. 1620
12¼ in (31.5 cm) high
10 oz 18 dwt (340 gr)
Zurich, 18 XI 1977, 182
SFr.3,888 (£1,047 $1,936)

34 Cup and cover
parcel-gilt
Nuremberg, c. 1620
11¾ in (29.5 cm) high
8 oz 12 dwt (270 gr)
Geneva, 10 XI 1981, 43
SFr.7,150 (£1,997 $3,574)

35 Cup and cover
silver-gilt
Nuremberg, c. 1625
12½ in (31.6 cm) high
10 oz 4 dwt (317 gr)
London, 19 VII 1973, 95
£800 ($2,000)

Nicolaus Weiss
Nuremberg; born 1544, master 1613, died 1631
Mark Rosenberg, 4160

36 Tankard
silver-gilt
Nuremberg, c. 1630
5¾ in (14.3 cm) high
11 oz 8 dwt (354 gr)
New York, 17 VI 1981, 5
$6,875 (£3,321)

Tobias Kramer
Augsburg; born c. 1582, master c. 1613, died 1634
Mark Seling, 1277

37 Tazza
silver-gilt
Augsburg, c. 1615
7½ in (19.4 cm) diameter
11 oz 2 dwt (345 gr)
London, 22 V 1969, 217
£1,800 ($4,320)

38 Tankard
silver-gilt
Augsburg, c. 1620
9¾ in (25 cm) high
44 oz 6 dwt (1,380 gr)
Zurich, 7 V 1980, 213
SFr.38,880 (£9,970 $23,429)

33 BAIR

34 BAIR

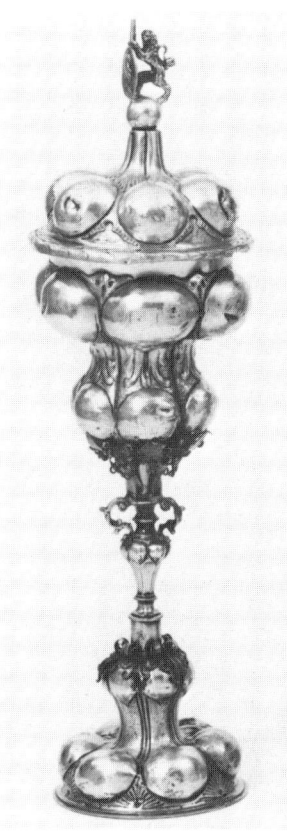

35 BAIR

36 WEISS

38 KRAMER

37 KRAMER

39 BLANK

40 W. C. RITTER

41 M. GELB I

42 N.R.

43 KRAER

Matthäus Blank (Plank)
Augsburg; born c. 1584, master c. 1615, died 1657
Mark Seling, 1298

39 Standing cup
silver-gilt
Augsburg, c. 1625
7¼ in (18.3 cm) high
6 oz 14 dwt (210 gr)
Geneva, 10 XI 1981, 61
SFr.6,600 (£1,843 $3,298)

Wolff Christof Ritter
Nuremberg; master 1617, died c. 1660
Mark Rosenberg, 3884

40 Tankard
silver-gilt
Nuremberg, c. 1620
9¾ in (25 cm) high
13 oz 18 dwt (435 gr)
Zurich, 22 XI 1978, 176
SFr.10,260 (£2,890 $5,924)

Melchior Gelb I
Augsburg; born Ulm c. 1581, master c. 1616, died 1654.
Married 1616 the widow of Hans Pfleger IV.
Mark Seling, 1305

41 Tankard
parcel-gilt
Augsburg, c. 1620
9½ in (24.3 cm) high
36 oz 16 dwt (1,144 gr)
London, 9 V 1974, 184
£10,000 ($24,000)

N.R.
42 Figures of grape pickers, two carved wood with silver-gilt mounts
Probably Bavarian, c. 1628
Town mark: double-headed eagle
10 in (26 cm) high
Mentmore, 19 V 1977, 656
£24,200 ($41,140)

Jacob Kraer
Nuremberg; master 1625, died 1669
Mark Rosenberg, 4196

43 Beaker (*Roemer*)
Nuremberg, c. 1635
3½ in (8.8 cm) high
3 oz 4 dwt (99 gr)
New York, 17 VI 1981, 12
$4,400 (£2,125)

Thomas Stoer the younger
Nuremberg; master 1629, died before 1660
Mark Rosenberg, 4207

44 Tazza
silver-gilt
Nuremberg, c. 1630
7 in (17.6 cm) diameter
15 oz 2 dwt (470 gr)
Geneva, 5 V 1981, 47
SFr.26,400 (£6,153 $12,736)

45 Model of a rampant horse
silver-gilt
Nuremberg, c. 1635
11 in (28 cm) high
25 oz 14 dwt (800 gr)
Zurich, 18 XI 1977, 102
SFr.77,760 (£20,960 $38,776)

46 Cup and cover
silver-gilt
Nuremberg, c. 1635
21 in (53.6 cm) high
20 oz 8 dwt (635 gr)
Zurich, 13 XI 1979, 53
SFr.11,340 (£4,825 $11,338)

47 Standing cup
silver-gilt
Nuremberg, c. 1635
7 in (18 cm) high
3 oz 14 dwt (115 gr)
London, 4 V 1978, 140
£550 ($1,017)

Esaias Busch I
Augsburg; master c. 1632, died 1679. See Appendix 1.
Mark Seling, 1457

48 Double beaker
Augsburg, 1650
5.5 in (14 cm) high
8 oz 4 dwt (258 gr)
London, 4 VII 1983, 359
£3,300 ($5,280)

44 T. STOER THE YOUNGER

45 T. STOER THE YOUNGER

46 T. STOER THE YOUNGER

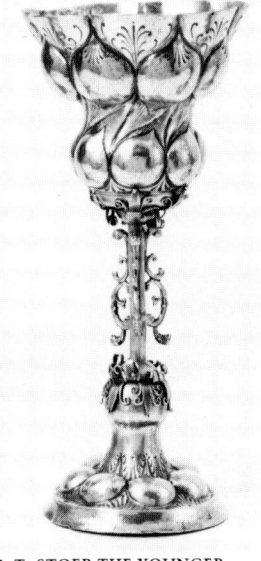

47 T. STOER THE YOUNGER

48 E. BUSCH I

49 KOLB(E)

Hans (Johann) Kolb(e)
Augsburg; born Neisse, died 1640
Mark Seling, 1374; Rosenberg, 517

49 Canister
parcel-gilt
Augsburg, c. 1640
7½ in (19 cm) high
35 oz 15 dwt (1,111 gr)
London, 4 IV 1957, 66
£190 ($530)

50 FESENMAYR

51 UNICORN & STAR

52 MACKENSEN

55 UNMARKED

Georg Wilhelm Fesenmayr
Augsburg; born Neresheim, master 1639, died 1672
Mark Seling, 1496

50 Trencher salt
parcel-gilt
Augsburg, c. 1650
2¾ in (6.9 cm) high
5 oz 6 dwt (166 gr)
London, 4 VII 1983, 350
£5,060 ($8,096)

Unicorn and Star
Nuremberg
Mark Rosenberg, 4220

51 Beaker
silver-gilt
Nuremberg, c. 1650
3¾ in (9.5 cm) high
6 oz (186 gr)
New York, 27 IV 1976, 164
$3,200 (£1,777)

Andrew (Andrzej) Mackensen
Cracow and Danzig; born c. 1600 of Scottish parentage, appointed Royal Goldsmith in Cracow 1628, moved to Danzig 1643, died 1670. See the catalogue of the exhibition 'Objects for a *Wunderkammer*', Colnaghi, London, 1981, no.30

52 Candlesticks, pair
Danzig, c. 1660
8½ in (21.6 cm) high
63 oz (1,960 gr)
Initialled for Venceslaus de Leszno Leszczynski (1605–66), private secretary to Sigismund III of Poland 1629, Bishop of Warmia 1644–58, Archbishop of Gniezno and Primate of the Realm 1658
Exhibited in London, Colnaghi, 1981 (see above).
Zurich, 16 V 1979, 46
SFr.45,000 (£12,676 $25,985)

53 MAIR

Abraham Mair
Augsburg; died 1670
Mark Seling, 1548

53 Canister
silver-gilt
Augsburg, 1653–5
4 in (10.2 cm) high
8 oz 12 dwt (270 gr)
The foliate decoration is etched.
Geneva, 15 V 1984, 129
SFr.11,000 (£3,514 $4,884)

54 UNMARKED

Unmarked

54 Beaker
parcel-gilt
Hungarian, c. 1666
8¼ in (21.2 cm) high
20 oz 4 dwt (630 gr)
Geneva, 15 XI 1983, 60
SFr.22,000 (£7,028 $9,768)

55 Tankard
silver-gilt
Possibly North German
c. 1660–80
8 in (20.3 cm) high
25 oz (777 gr)
Arms: Kniphof, Hamburg
Inscribed: Gottes Reiche Segen
Hand Bindet Treuer Freunde Bad
['God's generous blessing will
unite true friendship ties']
New York, 10–12 VI 1980, 75
$9,350 (£3,978)

56 Tankard
parcel-gilt
German, c. 1650
7 in (18 cm) high
25 oz 8 dwt (790 gr)
Similar tankards were made by
members of the Lambrecht
family c. 1650 (see no.58). The
engravings relate closely to a
series by Abraham Bosse:
*Le Jardin de la Noblesse
Française*.
Geneva, 12 V 1983, 157
SFr.12,100 (£3,612 $5,779)

Claus Sulsen Hamburgensis
Hamburg; master 1613, died
1662
Mark Scheffler, *Niedersachsens*,
p.426, no.38

57 Tankard
Hamburg, c. 1645
8 in (20.2 cm) high
29 oz 11 dwt (919 gr)
London, 7 XII 1981, 141
£4,620 ($8,270)

Lambrecht Family

58 Tankard
parcel-gilt
Hamburg, c. 1650
9 in (22.8 cm) high
46 oz 15 dwt (1,454 gr)
The maker's mark on this
tankard, HL conjoined, could be
that of Hans Lambrecht II (died
1633) or that of Henrich
Lambrecht II. The engraved
figures are derived from
engravings by Abraham Bosse
See no.56
New York, 22 V 1973, 78A
$15,000 (£6,000)

59 Ewer
parcel-gilt
Hamburg, c. 1640
19½ in (49.5 cm) high
66 oz 8 dwt (2,065 gr)
London, 4 VII 1968, 126
£1,100 ($2,640)

56 UNMARKED

57 HAMBURGENSIS

58 LAMBRECHT FAMILY

59 LAMBRECHT FAMILY

Peter or Salomon von der Rennen
Danzig
Mark Rosenberg, 1550–1551

60 Ewer and sideboard dish
silver-gilt
Danzig, c. 1650
Ewer: 13 in (33 cm) high
Dish (illustrated): 25¼ in
(64 cm) wide
173 oz 10 dwt (5,395 gr)
New York, 26–27 X 1976, 159
$32,000 (£18,823)

60 VON DER RENNEN

Ritter Family

61 Four plaques
Nuremberg, 1656
10¼ in (26.2 cm) diameter
Probably from the guild chapel of the Rotschmiede and Bronzegiesser in Nuremberg. Each plaque is embossed with the name of a guild member and the objects he manufactured. See 'Ein rheinischer Silberschatz', Cologne, Kunstgewerbemuseum, 1980, no.291.
London, 13 II 1969, 144
£2,200 ($5,280)

Johann Baptist Biller

Augsburg; master 1637, died 1683
Mark Seling, 1478

62 Sweetmeat dish
silver-gilt
Augsburg, c. 1670
5¼ in (13.7 cm) wide
4 oz 10 dwt (140 gr)
London, 16 III 1978, 113
£770 ($1,424)

63 Sweetmeat dish
parcel-gilt
Augsburg, c. 1670
5¾ in (14.5 cm) wide
3 oz 10 dwt (110 gr)
Geneva, 6 V 1982, 170
SFr.4,400 (£1,229 $2,200)

61 RITTER FAMILY

62 J.B. BILLER

63 J.B. BILLER

64 HAYDT

65 HAYDT

68 RIEL

69 RIEL

67 HAYDT

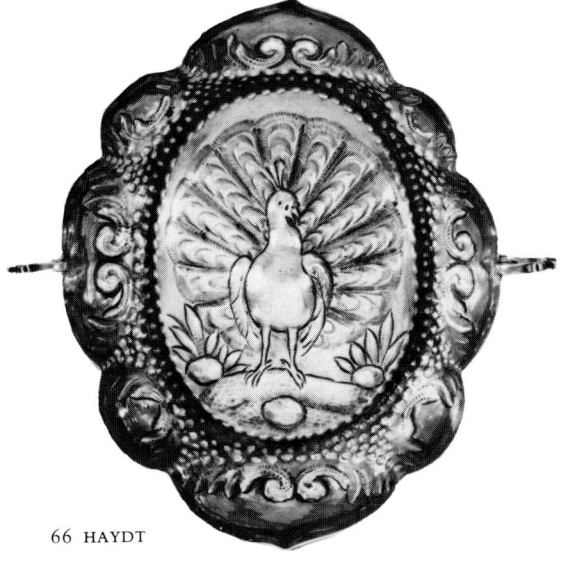
66 HAYDT

70 RIEL

71 RIEL

Balthasar Haydt
Augsburg; born Seefeld, master
c. 1645, died 1680
Mark Seling, 1534

64 Sweetmeat dish
parcel-gilt
Augsburg, c. 1675
4½ in (11.6 cm) wide
2 oz 4 dwt (70 gr)
Geneva, 5 V 1981, 71
SFr.3,080 (£718 $1,486)

65 Sweetmeat dish
parcel-gilt
Augsburg, c. 1675
7 in (17.6 cm) wide
4 oz 16 dwt (150 gr)
London, 7 III 1983, 284
£990 ($1,584)

66 Sweetmeat dish
parcel-gilt
Augsburg, c. 1680
6¼ in (15.8 cm) wide
3 oz 16 dwt (118 gr)
London, 26 VI 1975, 99
£420 ($966)

67 Sweetmeat dish
parcel-gilt
Augsburg, c. 1680
4½ in (11.2 cm) wide
1 oz 19 dwt (60 gr)
London, 12 II 1981, 69
£605 ($1,252)

Reinhold Riel
Nuremberg; master 1652, died
c. 1686
Mark Rosenberg, 4232

68 Tankard
parcel-gilt
Nuremberg, c. 1660
9½ in (24 cm) high
20 oz 14 dwt (643 gr)
London, 3 VII 1980, 90
£6,600 ($15,510)

69 Beaker (*Roemer*)
silver-gilt
Nuremberg, c. 1670
4½ in (11.5 cm) high
3 oz 16 dwt (120 gr)
Zurich, 13 XI 1979, 170
SFr.6,480 (£1,661 $3,903)

70 Beaker and cover
parcel-gilt
Nuremberg, c. 1675
7½ in (19.3 cm) high
8 oz (248 gr)
Geneva, 15 XI 1983, 95
SFr.4,400 (£1,405 $1,952)

71 Beakers, three
silver-gilt
Nuremberg, c. 1680
3¼ in (8.2 cm) high
8 oz 14 dwt (270 gr)
London, 2 VI 1977, 135
£2,640 ($4,488)

Peter Rohde II
Danzig; master 1654, died c. 1677
Mark Rosenberg, 1560

72 Tankard
parcel-gilt
Danzig, c. 1660
8 in (20.3 cm) high
35 oz 8 dwt (1,100 gr)
London, 2 VI 1977, 125
£2,420 ($4,114)

73 Tankard
silver-gilt
Danzig, c. 1670
8¾ in (22.4 cm) high
53 oz 3 dwt (1,652 gr)
London, 13 VII 1967, 143
£300 ($840)

74 Tankard
parcel-gilt
Danzig, c. 1675
9¼ in (23.5 cm) high
38 oz (1,181 gr)
New York, 16 VI 1982, 10
$13,200 (£7,374)

Unmarked

75 Dishes, six
parcel-gilt
Hungarian, c. 1696
9¾ in (24.5 cm) wide
52 oz 8 dwt (1,630 gr)
Geneva, 15 XI 1983, 53
SFr.99,000 (£31,629 $43,964)

Nathaniel Pressding I
Danzig; master 1658, died 1670
Mark Rosenberg, 1561

76 Tankard
parcel-gilt
Danzig, c. 1660
8 in (20.4 cm) high
26 oz (808 gr)
New York, 10–11 II 1976, 148
$4,000 (£2,222)

77 Bowl and cover
Danzig, c. 1665
8½ in (21.7 cm) diameter
28 oz 6 dwt (880 gr)
London, 4 V 1978, 150
£1,980 ($3,663)

Heinrich Mannlich
Augsburg; born Troppau, married Sophia Drentwett 1659, died 1698. See Appendix 1.
Mark Seling, 1613

78 Dish
silver-gilt
Augsburg, c. 1660
25½ in (64.8 cm) wide
62 oz 14 dwt (1,950 gr)
Zurich, 7 V 1980, 212
SFr.12,960 (£3,323 $7,809)

79 Dish
silver-gilt
Augsburg, c. 1670
27½ in (70 cm) wide
74 oz 10 dwt (2,230 gr)
London, 7 III 1983, 303
£5,500 ($8,800)

72 P. ROHDE II

73 P. ROHDE II

74 P. ROHDE II

76 N. PRESSDING I

75 UNMARKED

80 Ewer
parcel-gilt
Augsburg, c. 1675
18¼ in (46.3 cm) high
41 oz 16 dwt (1,300 gr)
London, 7 III 1983, 322
£4,950 ($7,920)

Martin Heuglin II
Augsburg; born 1619, died 1675
Mark Seling, 1508

81 Tankard
silver-gilt
Augsburg, c. 1670
5½ in (13.9 cm) high
11 oz 14 dwt (365 gr)
Geneva, 5 V 1981, 31
SFr.9,350 (£2,179 $4,510)

Jürgen Richels
Hamburg; master 1664, died 1710
Mark Scheffler, *Niedersachsens*, p.486, no.188

82 Canisters, pair
silver-gilt
Hamburg, c. 1670
8 in (20.2 cm) high
48 oz 10 dwt (1,508 gr)
New York, 16–17 XII 1980, 19
$26,400 (£12,753)

77 N. PRESSDING I

80 MANNLICH

78 MANNLICH

81 M. HEUGLIN II

79 MANNLICH

82 RICHELS

83 S.B.F.

84 S.B.F.

85 S.B.F.

86 SCHMIDT

87 A. DRENTWETT II

S.B.F.
Nuremberg; attributed to a member of the Ferrn family, second half of the 17th century
Mark Rosenberg, 4227

83 Beaker
silver-gilt
Nuremberg, *c.* 1680
4 in (10.4 cm) high
2 oz 8 dwt (75 gr)
London, 7 III 1983, 328
£1,320 ($2,112)

84 Bowl and cover
silver-gilt
Nuremberg, *c.* 1680
9½ in (24 cm) diameter
43 oz 5 dwt (1,345 gr)
London, 20 X 1966, 105
£1,800 ($5,022)

85 Beaker
Nuremberg, *c.* 1685
3½ in (8.9 cm) high
3 oz 19 dwt (122 gr)
London, 11 VI 1970, 211
£300 ($720)

Niklaus Schmidt
Lübeck; died *c.* 1694
Mark Rosenberg, 3209

86 Bowl and cover
parcel-gilt
Lübeck, *c.* 1680
8¾ in (21.6 cm) diameter
53 oz 16 dwt (1,673 gr)
Arms (detachable): Williams Wynn
London, 2 VI 1977, 162
£11,000 ($18,700)

Abraham Drentwett II
Augsburg; born 1647, master *c.* 1675, died 1729. See Appendix I
Mark Seling, 1728

87 Figures, pair
parcel-gilt
Augsburg, *c.* 1700
7 in (18 cm) high
57 oz 6 dwt (1,782 gr)
London, 9 XII 1976, 80
£4,620 ($7,854)

Johann Christoph Treffler I
Augsburg; born *c.* 1652, master *c.* 1680, died 1722. See Appendix I
Mark Seling, 1773

88 Pilgrim bottle
silver-gilt
Augsburg, *c.* 1690
7¾ in (19.6 cm) high
19 oz 13 dwt (611 gr)
Engraved in the manner of Adrian van Ostade.
London, 16 X 1975, 134
£8,800 ($17,600)

89 Dish
silver-gilt
Augsburg, *c.* 1700
7 in (18 cm) diameter
7 oz 19 dwt (247 gr)
London, 21 VI 1973, 96
£780 ($1,950)

88 J.C. TREFFLER I

89 J.C. TREFFLER I

91 M. BAUR II

90 M. BAUR II

Matthäus Baur II
Augsburg; born c. 1653, master c. 1681, died 1728. See Appendix 1
Mark Seling, 1776

90 Beaker
parcel-gilt
Augsburg, c. 1690
6¾ in (17.1 cm) high
11 oz 6 dwt (351 gr)
London, 17 VI 1971, 113
£950 ($2,280)

91 Teapot
silver-gilt
Augsburg, c. 1690
7 in (17.5 cm) high
22 oz 16 dwt (710 gr)
See Hernmark, *The Art of the European Silversmith*, p.116, no.311. The portraits of the Ottoman emperors are after engravings by Theodor de Bry. This teapot was probably made to commemorate the victory of the Imperial army over the Turks after the siege of Vienna in 1683.
Geneva, 12 V 1983, 154
SFr.198,000 (£59,104 $94,566)

92 POPPE

94 T.H., I.B.

T.H., I.B.
Hamburg

94 Double beaker
parcel-gilt
Hamburg, c. 1690
5¾ in (14.6 cm) high
11 oz 9 dwt (356 gr)
London, 4 V 1961, 29
£380 ($1,067)

Hans Jakob Baur III
Augsburg; born c. 1655, master
c. 1682, died 1703. See
Appendix 1
Mark Seling, 1786

95 Beaker
silver-gilt
Augsburg, c. 1685
3¾ in (9.3 cm) high
4 oz 10 dwt (140 gr)
London, 7 III 1983, 271
£748 ($1,196)

92 (DETAIL)

Cornelius Poppe
Augsburg; born Hamburg
c. 1650, died 1723
Mark Seling, 1815

92 Beaker
parcel-gilt
Augsburg, c. 1695
6½ in (16.2 cm) high
11 oz 15 dwt (365 gr)
New York, 26–27 X 1976, 158
$7,500 (£4,411)

93 Beaker
Augsburg, c. 1705
3½ in (9.2 cm) high
4 oz 8 dwt (136 gr)
London, 9 X 1969, 219
£290 ($696)

93 POPPE

95 H. J. BAUR III

Johann Drentwett I
Augsburg; baptized 1654, master
c. 1685, died 1703. See
Appendix 1
Mark Seling, 1812

96 Beaker and cover
parcel-gilt
Augsburg, 1689
5¾ in (14.5 cm) high
7 oz 16 dwt (244 gr)
London, 5 VII 1982, 74
£1,100 ($1,969)

Paul Solanier
Augsburg; born Nuremberg
1635, died 1724
Mark Seling, 1669

97 Beaker
silver-gilt
Augsburg, c. 1680
3½ in (8.8 cm) high
4 oz 19 dwt (154 gr)
London, 27 XI 1975, 95
£440 ($880)

98 Tankard
parcel-gilt
Augsburg, c. 1673
5½ in (14 cm) high
14 oz 12 dwt (454 gr)
New York, 16 VI 1982, 11
$7,425 (£4,148)

99 Dish
silver-gilt
Augsburg, c. 1720
14¾ in (37.5 cm) wide
15 oz 10 dwt (485 gr)
London, 12 III 1984, 389
£1,100 ($1,529)

96 J. DRENTWETT I

97 SOLANIER

Nathaniel Pressding II

Danzig; master 1686, died 1732
Mark Rosenberg, 1576–7

100 Tankard
parcel-gilt
Danzig, c. 1690
8 in (20 cm) high
29 oz (905 gr)
Zurich, 7 V 1980, 195
SFr.14,040 (£3,600 $8,460)

Peter Rohde III

Danzig; master 1688, died 1717
Mark Rosenberg, 1580

101 Tankard
parcel-gilt
Danzig, c. 1700
9 in (23.2 cm) high
31 oz 16 dwt (988 gr)
London, 12 II 1981, 65
£3,080 ($6,375)

Nathaniel Schlaubitz

Danzig; master 1690, died 1726
Mark Rosenberg, 1584

102 Tankard
parcel-gilt
Danzig, c. 1700
7¾ in (19.7 cm) high
41 oz 16 dwt (1,300 gr)
Geneva, 10 XI 1981, 198
SFr.11,550 (£3,226 $5,774)

103 Tankard
parcel-gilt
Danzig, c. 1700
8½ in (21.5 cm) high
29 oz 15 dwt (925 gr)
New York, 19 I 1973, 21
$3,100 (£1,240)

98 SOLANIER

99 SOLANIER

100 N. PRESSDING II

101 P. ROHDE III

102 SCHLAUBITZ

103 SCHLAUBITZ

104 SCHLAUBITZ

105 SCHLAUBITZ

106 HAAS

107 WAGNER

108 WAGNER

109 N.R.

Johann Wilhelm Haas

Nuremberg; born 1649, died 1723. Founder of a family of trumpet-makers that continued until 1817. See no. 106, catalogue of the sale, lot 183, footnote.
Mark Rosenberg, 4012

106 Waldhorn
parcel-gilt
Nuremberg, 1681
Signed: Johann Wilhelm Hass Nurnb. 1681
4¼ in (11 cm) overall
7 oz, 14 dwt (240 gr)
Geneva, 5 V 1981, 183
SFr.46,200 (£10,769 $22,291)

Johann Wagner

Augsburg; born 1646, died 1724
Mark Seling, 1750

107 Beakers, three
parcel-gilt
Augsburg, 1695–1700
5 in (12.7 cm) high
15 oz 2 dwt (470 gr)
Geneva, 10 XI 1981, 226
SFr.66,000 (£18,435 $32,998)

108 Beaker and cover
parcel-gilt
Augsburg, c. 1700
7¼ in (18.5 cm) high
18 oz 4 dwt (566 gr)
London, 2 V 1968, 112
£720 ($1,728)

104 Tankard
parcel-gilt
Danzig, c. 1685
6½ in (16.4 cm) high
21 oz (655 gr)
Geneva, 15 V 1984, 77
SFr.7,150 (£2,284 $3,174)

105 Tankard
parcel-gilt
Danzig, c. 1695
8 in (20.4 cm) high
31 oz 8 dwt (976 gr)
London, 17 V 1973, 71
£1,500 ($3,750)

N.R. in script

109 Blackamoor
parcel-gilt and painted
Bamberg, c. 1690
14¾ in (37.7 cm) high
53 oz 14 dwt (1,670 gr)
Mentmore, 19 V 1977, 692
£18,700 ($31,790)

Johann Andreas Thelott

Augsburg; born 1655, master 1689, died 1734. Specialized in chased relief work, including many plaques. His work is frequently signed. See H. Prael-Himmer, *Johann Andreas Thelott*, Munich, 1978.
Mark Seling, 1846

117 Cup and cover
parcel-gilt
Signed: JA Thelot; dated 1688
15½ in (39.4 cm) high
67 oz 7 dwt (2,094 gr)
The cup commemorates the Austro-German victories over the Turks
London, 14 V 1959, 64
£640 ($1,798)

119 THELOTT

120 THELOTT

121 THELOTT

122 UNMARKED, MANNER OF THÉLOTT

118 Sweetmeat dish
silver-gilt
Augsburg, c. 1680
4¼ in (10.8 cm) wide
1 oz 18 dwt (59 gr)
London, 26 VI 1975, 100
£270 ($621)

119 Tankard
ivory, silver-gilt mounts
Augsburg, c. 1690
9 in (22.9 cm)
London, 15 XI 1962, 83
£680 ($1,910)

120 Tankard
parcel-gilt
Augsburg, c. 1700
6 in (15 cm) high
19 oz 4 dwt (598 gr)
Geneva, 15 XI 1983, 71
SFr.9,350 (£2,987 $4,151)

121 Plaque
Signed: J.A. Thelot
10½ in (26.8 cm) overall
The scene depicts the pleasures of summer.
London, 12 XII 1974, 176
£1,050 ($2,415)

122 Plaque
Unmarked in the manner of J.A. Thelott
7 in (17.8 cm) wide
The scene shows Dido greeting Aeneas at Carthage
London, 25 X 1973, 119
£850 ($2,040)

123 Plaquette
(Augsburg), c. 1700
Signed: J.A. Thelot
8¾ in (22.5 cm) overall
The scene depicts King Cyrus of Persia and Panthea.
London, 13 VII 1967, 149
£190 ($532)

123 THELOTT

124 J. BARTERMANN I

125 J. BARTERMANN I

126 STENGLIN

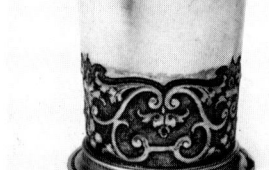

127 STENGLIN

Johann Bartermann I
Augsburg; born Danzig 1661, master c. 1693, died 1732. See Appendix 1
Mark Seling, 1874

124 Wine fountains, pair
Augsburg, c. 1695
24½ in (62 cm) high
630 oz (19,593 gr)
See G. Biermann, *Deutsches Barock und Rokoko*, Leipzig 1914.
London, 23 VII 1931, 55
£320 ($1,558)

125 Vase
Augsburg, c. 1700
18½ in (47 cm) high
130 oz 4 dwt (4,050 gr)
Provenance: Baron von Weyhe
Zurich, 13 XI 1979, 72
SFr.19,800 (£5,077 $11,930)

128 STENGLIN

129 WINTER

130 WINTER

131 WINTER

132 REHM

133 J. PEPFENHAUSER II   134 J. PEPFENHAUSER II

130 Dishes and covers, pair
silver-gilt
Augsburg, c. 1730
18¾ in (47.5 cm) diameter
3,858 oz (120,000 gr)
Arms: Augustus I ('the Strong'), Elector of Saxony and King of Poland (1670–1733)
For a smaller pair see catalogue, Sotheby's, Zurich, 18 XI 1977, 86, SFr.130,000 (£35,040 $64,824).
Monaco, 27 XI 1979, 855
FFr.387,500 (£143,040 $336,144)

131 Dinner plates, twelve
silver-gilt
Augsburg, c. 1730
9¾ in (24.6 cm) diameter
260 oz (8,115 gr)
Arms: Augustus I ('the Strong') Elector of Saxony and King of Poland (1670–1733)
From the same service as no.130
Zurich, 7 V 1980, 171
SFr.259,200 (£66,461 $156,183)

Johann Matthäus Rehm
Augsburg; master c. 1696, died c. 1714
Mark Seling, 1910

132 Tankard
parcel-gilt
Augsburg, c. 1700
7¾ in (19.8 cm) high
26 oz 19 dwt (838 gr)
London, 20 IV 1972, 53
£1,100 ($2,750)

Johann Pepfenhauser II
Augsburg; born 1666, master 1697, died 1754. See Appendix 1
Mark Seling, 1919

133 Candlesticks, pair
parcel-gilt
Augsburg, c. 1700
5¼ in (13.5 cm) high
13 oz 10 dwt (419 gr)
London, 12 II 1981, 95
£3,740 ($7,741)

134 Candlesticks, pair
Augsburg, c. 1720
7½ in (19.3 cm) high
23 oz 2 dwt (720 gr)
Geneva, 6 V 1982, 172
SFr.16,500 (£4,608 $8,248)

Philipp Stenglin
Augsburg; born 1667, master 1693, died 1744
Mark Seling, 1880

126 Beaker
parcel-gilt
Augsburg, c. 1715
5½ in (14 cm) high
7 oz 4 dwt (223 gr)
London, 18 XI 1976, 145
£1,650 ($2,805)

127 Beaker
parcel-gilt
Augsburg, c. 1725
5¼ in (13.3 cm) high
7 oz 14 dwt (550 gr)
London, 15 VI 1978, 102
£1,760 ($3,256)

128 Tankard
parcel-gilt
Augsburg, 1732–3
6 in (15.5 cm) high
16 oz 16 dwt (525 gr)
Arms: Weibel of Basel
Geneva, 5 V 1981, 201
SFr.24,200 (£5,641 $11,676)

Christian Winter
Augsburg; born Berlin 1661, master 1694, died 1737. See Appendix 1
Mark Seling, 1894

129 Beaker
parcel-gilt
Augsburg, c. 1723
5¾ in (14.6 cm) high
9 oz (280 gr)
New York, 28 X 1980, 56
$12,100 (£5,845)

GERMANY AUSTRIA SWITZERLAND

135 J. PEPFENHAUSER II

136 I.S. OR S.I.

135 Candlesticks, pair
Augsburg, c. 1725
7½ in (18.9 cm) high
18 oz 12 dwt (580 gr)
Zurich, 13 XI 1979, 145
SFr.11,880 (£3,046 $7,158)

I.S or S.I

136 Candlesticks, four
silver-gilt
Cologne, early 18th century
9 in (23 cm) high
72 oz 18 dwt (2,267 gr)
London, 1 XI 1956, 76
£800 ($2,240)

Johann Conrad Weiss
Nuremberg; master 1699
Mark Rosenberg, 4279

137 Tankard
ivory, silver-gilt mounted
Nuremberg, c. 1725
9¾ in (24.5 cm) high
Zurich, 7 V 1980, 226
SFr.21,060 (£5,400 $12,690)

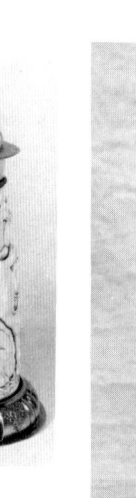

137 WEISS

138 I.C

139 KLINGE

I.C

138 Guild Cup of the Silversmiths' Guild of Ratibor in Silesia
c. 1725
22½ in (57.2 cm) high
44 oz 10 dwt (1,383 gr)
London, 23 VII 1931, 43
£85 ($413)

J. Klinge
Breslau; master 1704, died 1737

139 Beaker
parcel-gilt
Breslau, c. 1730
8¾ in (22.3 cm) high
16 oz 6 dwt (510 gr)
Geneva, 12 V 1983, 158
SFr.82,500 (£24,626 $39,400)

140 DEDEKE

141 A. HORNUNG

Lewin Dedeke
Celle; born c. 1660
Mark Scheffler, Niedersachsens, p.249, no.3

140 Ecuelle and cover
Celle, c. 1730
7 in (17.8 cm) diameter
20 oz 5 dwt (629 gr)
London, 9 V 1974, 90
£2,800 ($6,720)

Andreas Hornung
Hanover; born 1661, master 1689
Mark Scheffler, *Niedersachsens*, p.756, no.106a

141 Bowl and cover, possibly by Hornung
Hanover, c. 1730
10 in (25.4 cm) overall
21 oz 6 dwt (665 gr)
Geneva, 12 V 1983, 167
SFr.22,000 (£6,567 $10,507)

Philip Christian Hornung
Göttingen
Mark Scheffler, *Niedersachsens*, p.373, no.11

142 Coffee pot
Göttingen, c. 1730
7 in (17.4 cm) high
12 oz (375 gr)
Geneva, 12 V 1983, 168
SFr.15,400 (£4,597 $7,355)

Tilman Wendel(s)
Cologne; born 1684
Mark Scheffler, *Rheinland-Westfalens*, p.598, no.1706

143 Candlesticks, pair
silver-gilt
Cologne, c. 1720
7¾ in (20 cm) high
19 oz 2 dwt (595 gr)
Zurich, 7 V 1980, 172
SFr.23,760 (£6,092 $14,316)

Esaias Busch III
Augsburg; born 1676, master 1704, died 1759. See Appendix 1
Mark Seling, 1973

144 Travelling service
silver-gilt and Böttger Meissen porcelain, in fitted leather case
Augsburg, c. 1720
42 oz 9 dwt (1,320 gr) of silver
London, 7 III 1957, 58
£1,100 ($3,069)

145 Toilet box
silver-gilt
Augsburg, c. 1725
4¼ in (10.6 cm) wide
5 oz 12 dwt (175 gr)
Geneva, 12 XI 1980, 69
SFr.13,200 (£3,077 $6,370)

146 Teapot
silver-gilt
Augsburg, 1732–3
5¾ in (14.6 cm) high
15 oz 4 dwt (475 gr)
Geneva, 12 V 1983, 166
SFr.20,900 (£6,238 $9,980)

142 P.C. HORNUNG

143 WENDEL(S)

144 E. BUSCH III

145 E. BUSCH III

146 E. BUSCH III

GERMANY AUSTRIA SWITZERLAND

147 SCHAFFLER

148 G.D. WEISS

149 ADAM

150 M. HECKEL II

151 M. HECKEL II

(Johann) Daniel Schaffler I
Augsburg; born Dresden 1659, master 1701, died 1727. See Appendix 1
Mark Seling, 1951

147 Ecuelle and cover
silver-gilt
Augsburg, 1716
9 in (23.2 cm) wide
18 oz 8 dwt (575 gr)
Geneva, 5 V 1981, 48
SFr.30,800 (£7,179 $14,860)

Georg Daniel Weiss
Nuremberg; master 1706
Mark Rosenberg, 4284

148 Coffee urn
silver-gilt
Nuremberg, c. 1715
11¼ in (28.7 cm) high
26 oz 9 dwt (822 gr)
London, 26 II 1976, 98
£1,375 ($2,475)

152 J.E. HEUGLIN II

153 J.E. HEUGLIN II

154 J.E. HEUGLIN II

155 J.E. HEUGLIN II

156 J.E. HEUGLIN II

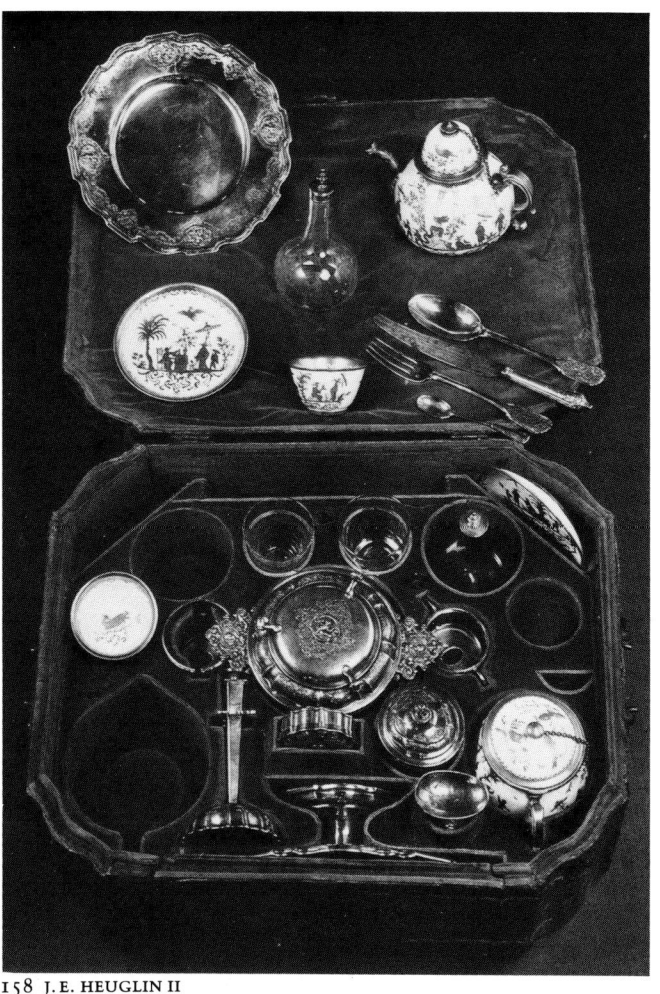

158 J.E. HEUGLIN II

157 J.E. HEUGLIN II

Elias Adam
Augsburg; born Zullichau
c. 1669, master 1703, died 1745.
See Appendix 1
Mark Seling, 1964

149 Coconut cup and cover, of a weaver's guild
silver-gilt mounts
Augsburg, 1735–6
13 in (33 cm) high
Geneva, 15 XI 1983, 100
SFr.19,800 (£6,325 $8,791)

Michael Heckel II
Augsburg; baptized 1686, master
c. 1717, died 1726. See
Appendix 1
Mark Seling, 2095

150 Beaker
silver-gilt
Augsburg, c. 1720
4¾ in (12.1 cm) high
8 oz 16 dwt (275 gr)
Geneva, 5 V 1981, 204
SFr.44,000 (£10,256 $21,230)

151 Casket
silver-gilt
Augsburg, c. 1725
6 in (15.2 cm) wide
35 oz 17 dwt (1,115 gr)
London, 18 VII 1974, 177
£1,700 ($4,080)

Johann Erhard Heuglin II
Augsburg; baptized 1687, master
1717, died 1757. See p.24
Mark Seling, 2096

152 Salver
silver-gilt
Augsburg, c. 1720
10 in (25.5 cm) wide
16 oz (500 gr)
Geneva, 12 XI 1980, 73
SFr.12,100 (£2,820 $5,837)

153 Salver-on-foot
silver-gilt
Augsburg, c. 1730
9¾ in (25.2 cm) wide
17 oz 15 dwt (552 gr)
New York, 4–5 X 1979, 113
$7,700 (£3,276)

154 Ecuelle and stand
silver-gilt
Augsburg, c. 1725
5¼ in (13.5 cm) diameter
24 oz 5 dwt (754 gr)
London, 5 XI 1964, 24
£1,350 ($3,780)

155 Dish
silver-gilt
Augsburg, c. 1730
24 in (61 cm) diameter
101 oz (3,141 gr)
London, 9 VII 1959, 64
£380 ($1,067)

156 Ecuelle and cover
silver-gilt
Augsburg, 1731–3
8 in (20 cm) overall
11 oz 8 dwt (355 gr)
Geneva, 15 XI 1983, 279
SFr.22,000 (£7,028 $9,768)

157 Candlesticks, pair
silver-gilt
Augsburg, c. 1720
7¼ in (18.5 cm) high
20 oz (622 gr)
Zurich, 7 V 1980, 173
SFr.28,080 (£7,200 $16,920)

158 Travelling service
silver-gilt and Böttger Meissen
porcelain
Augsburg, c. 1730
Case: 19½ in (49.5 cm) wide
60 oz 2 dwt (2,150 gr) of
weighable silver
Zurich, 18 XI 1977, 101
SFr.75,600 (£20,377 $37,697)

Ludwig Schneider
Augsburg; born Bachern, died 1729
Mark Seling, 1806

159 Ewer
silver-gilt
Augsburg, c. 1725
9 in (22.8 cm) high
19 oz 11 dwt (608 gr)
The preceding lots comprised a casket and clothes brush from the same set.
London, 1 II 1968, 125
£1,150 ($2,760)

Unmarked

160 Travelling set (*nécessaire*)
gold
Augsburg, c. 1735
28 oz 12 dwt (890 gr)
Monaco, 27 XI 1979, 852
FFr.283,080 (£29,183 $68,580)

159 SCHNEIDER

160 UNMARKED

Johann Nikolaus Spickermann
Augsburg; born Schifelbein c. 1700, died 1747. See Appendix 1
Mark Seling, 2337

161 Ecuelle and stand
silver-gilt
Augsburg, 1743–5
9 in (22.8 cm) diameter
38 oz 8 dwt (1,194 gr)
London, 1 II 1968, 126
£1,200 ($2,880)

162 Tea kettle
(Augsburg), mid-18th century
Maker's mark only
12 in (30.8 cm) high
56 oz 2 dwt (1,745 gr)
Zurich, 13 XI 1979, 152
SFr.8,100 (£2,076 $4,878)

Biller Family

163 Tumbler cup
Augsburg, 1735–6
Maker's mark: IIB
2 in (5 cm) high
Zurich, 22 XI 1978, 154
SFr.3,240 (£912 $1,869)

161 SPICKERMANN

Johannes Treffler I
Augsburg; born 1693, master 1720, died 1751. See Appendix 1
Mark Seling, 2130

164 Beaker and cover
parcel-gilt
Augsburg, c. 1725
6¾ in (17.2 cm) high
10 oz 18 dwt (340 gr)
Geneva, 15 XI 1983, 241
SFr.8,800 (£2,811 $3,907)

C.O.D.

165 Two coffee pots
c. 1740
Maker's mark only
12½ in (31.8 cm) and 9¾ in (24.8 cm) high
107 oz 9 dwt (3,341 gr)
London, 22 X 1970, 87, 88
£2,100 ($5,040)

Johannes Biller
Augsburg; born c. 1696, master 1724, died 1745. See Appendix 1
Mark Seling, 2161

166 Cup and cover
silver-gilt
Augsburg, 1735
12 in (30.5 cm) high
33 oz 7 dwt (1,037 gr)
London, 17 XI 1960, 81
£280 ($786)

Etienne Terroux
Geneva; born 1694, master 1719, died 1774
Mark Catalogue of exhibition, 'Schweizer Tafelsilber 1650–1850', no.195

162 SPICKERMANN

167 Coffee pot
Geneva, c. 1725
6¾ in (17.3 cm) high
13 oz 6 dwt (415 gr)
Geneva, 12 XI 1980, 115
SFr.15,950 (£3,718 $7,696)

168 Feeding vessel
Geneva, c. 1730
Assay Master: Jacob or Jean Chevrier
7¾ in (19.5 cm) overall
7 oz 6 dwt (230 gr)
Geneva, 6 V 1982, 133
SFr.18,700 (£5,223 $9,349)

163 BILLER FAMILY

164 J. TREFFLER I

165 C.O.D.

166 J. BILLER

167 TERROUX

169 TERROUX

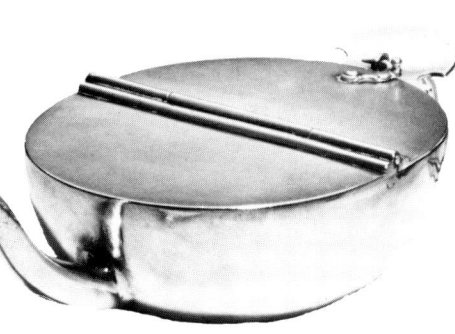

168 TERROUX

169 Coffee pot
Geneva, 1774
Assay Master: Pierre Lossier
6 in (15 cm) high
7 oz 6 dwt (230 gr)
Pierre Lossier was in office 1774–6.
Geneva, 6 V 1982, 128
SFr.6,050 (£1,690 $3,025)

170 TERROUX

171 TERROUX

174 DREYER

172 BARDE

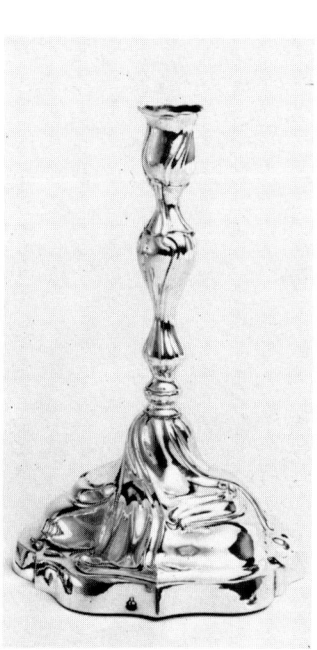

173 H.J. BAUR IV

175 INGERMANN

170 Salver
Geneva, c. 1770
10½ in (27 cm) diameter
16 oz 19 dwt (527 gr)
London, 10 III 1977, 150
£1,078 ($1,832)

171 Candlesticks, pair
Geneva, c. 1760
Assay Master: Jacques Girod
9½ in (24 cm) high
34 oz (1,060 gr)
Geneva, 6 V 1982, 140
SFr.16,500 (£4,609 $8,250)

Jean-Daniel Barde
Geneva; born 1705, master 1731, died 1780
Mark Gruber, no. 178

172 Hot milk jug
Geneva, c. 1740
7¼ in (18.5 cm) high
19 oz (590 gr)
London, 25 X 1973, 89
£2,400 ($5,760)

Hans Jakob Baur IV
Augsburg; born c. 1683, master 1712, died 1774. See Appendix 1
Mark Seling, 2046

173 Candlesticks, pair
Augsburg, 1769–71
8¾ in (22.2 cm) high
18 oz 19 dwt (590 gr)
Zurich, 16 V 1979, 49
SFr.8,640 (£2,433 $4,987)

Salomon Dreyer
Augsburg; born Elbing c. 1699, master 1735, died 1762. See Appendix 1
Mark Seling, 2263

174 Candlesticks, four
Augsburg, 1753–5
9¼ in (23.3 cm) high
56 oz 18 dwt (1,770 gr)
Geneva, 12 XI 1980, 255
SFr.63,800 (£14,870 $30,780)

Christian Heinrich Ingermann
Dresden; master 1732
Mark Rosenberg, 1798

175 Candlesticks, six
silver-gilt
Dresden, c. 1750
9¾ in (24.5 cm) high
162 oz 16 dwt (5,065 gr)
Cypher of Augustus III, Duke of Saxony and King of Poland (reigned 1733–63)
See J.L. Sponsel, *Das Grüne Gewölbe zu Dresden*, 1928, vol.II, p.127. These candlesticks are probably part of a set of thirty-six (see Rosenberg, vol.II, no.1661).
Geneva, 12 V 1983, 80
SFr.385,000 (£114,925 $183,880)

Johann Mittnacht III
Augsburg; born 1706, master 1735, died 1758. See Appendix 1
Mark Seling, 2271

176 Tankard
parcel-gilt
Augsburg, 1741–3
6 in (15.3 cm) high
14 oz 6 dwt (445 gr)
Geneva, 10 XI 1981, 223
SFr.14,300 (£3,995 $7,151)

177 Beaker
silver-gilt
Augsburg, 1751–3
3¼ in (8.3 cm) high
3 oz 3 dwt (98 gr)
Geneva, 12 V 1983, 188
SFr.13,200 (£3,940 $6,304)

Gottfried Bartermann
Augsburg; born c. 1705, master 1733, died 1769. See Appendix 1
Mark Seling, 2248

178 Meat dishes, pair
Augsburg, 1763–5
21 in (53.5 cm) wide
70 oz 11 dwt (2,194 gr)
London, 4 III 1965, 58
£1,000 ($2,800)

Emanuel Drentwett
Augsburg; baptized 1681, master 1713, died 1753. See Appendix 1
Mark Seling, 2056

179 Ewer and basin
Augsburg, 1749–51
20 in (51 cm) diameter
62 oz 14 dwt (1,950 gr)
Geneva, 12 XI 1980, 229
SFr.24,200 (£5,640 $11,675)

176 J. MITTNACHT III

177 J. MITTNACHT III

178 BARTERMANN

179 E. DRENTWETT

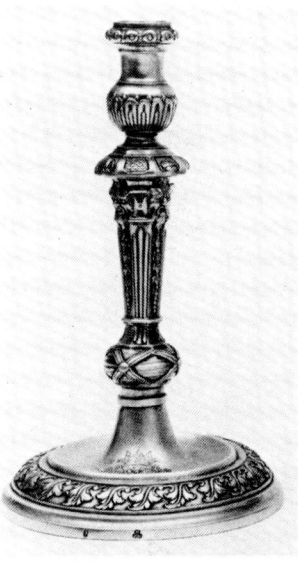
180 WEY(H)E

Bernhard Heinrich Wey(h)e
Augsburg; born Osnabruck c. 1701, master 1735, died 1782. See the introduction to entry on the service made for the Prince-Bishop of Hildesheim, where he is described as 'one of the major goldsmiths of his time' (catalogue, Sotheby's, Geneva, 12 XI 1980, p.80); see also Appendix 1
Mark Seling, 2275

180 Candlesticks, two
Augsburg, 1743–5; 1747–9
10 in (25.5 cm) high
61 oz (1,897 gr)
Arms: Counts of Leiningen impaling Solus-Baruth
New York, 16–17 XII 1976, 150
$4,000 (£2,352)

181 WEY(H)E

182 WEY(H)E

181 Soup tureens and stands, pair
Augsburg, 1759–61
23¼ in (59 cm) wide
466 oz 4 dwt (14,500 gr)
Geneva, 12 XI 1980, 216
SFr.550,000 (£128,205 $265,384)

182 Centrepiece
Augsburg, 1761–3
28½ in (72.5 cm) wide
Geneva, 12 XI 1980, 207
SFr.616,000 (£143,590 $297,231)

183 Caster and mustard pot, with spoon
Augsburg, 1761–3
7¾ in (19.7 cm) high
29 oz (905 gr)
Geneva, 12 XI 1980, 209
SFr.57,200 (£13,333 $27,599)

Johann Christian Girschner

Augsburg; master 1738, died 1772
Mark Seling, 2298

184 Teapot
Augsburg, 1747–9
5 in (12.7 cm) high
8 oz 2 dwt (251 gr)
New York, 19–20 I 1973, 42
$1,300 (£520)

185 Teapot
Augsburg, 1763–5
4¾ in (12 cm) high
9 oz 12 dwt (300 gr)
Geneva, 15 V 1984, 121
SFr.8,250 (£2,635 $3,662)

Johann Georg Kloss(e)

Augsburg; born Winzig, master 1738, died 1766. See Appendix 1 and nos 211, 212
Mark Seling, 2300

186 Chocolate pot
Augsburg, 1753–5
12 in (30.2 cm) high
26 oz (810 gr)
Geneva, 30 XI 1982, 226
SFr.7,700 (£2,298 $3,676)

187 Coffee pot
Augsburg, 1757–9
5 in (12.6 cm) high
4 oz 12 dwt (145 gr)
Geneva, 15 XI 1983, 277
SFr.5,940 (£1,897 $2,636)

188 Teapot
Augsburg, 1761–3
3½ in (8.4 cm) high
7 oz (220 gr)
Geneva, 15 XI 1983, 278
SFr.6,050 (£1,932 $2,685)

183 WEY(H)E

184 GIRSCHNER

186 KLOSS(E)

185 GIRSCHNER

187 188 KLOSS(E)

189 ENGELBRECHT

190 ECKART

191 A. DRENTWETT IV

Johann Christoph Engelbrecht

Augsburg; born c. 1707, master 1739, died 1758. See the nécessaire, no.206. See Appendix 1
Mark Seling, 2307

189 Chocolate pot
Augsburg, 1755–7
9¼ in (23.1 cm) high
14 oz 12 dwt (455 gr)
Geneva, 12 XI 1980, 183
SFr.7,150 (£1,666 $3,448)

Johann Christoph Eckart

Augsburg; born c. 1708, master 1741, died 1766
Mark Seling, 2330

190 Chocolate pots, two
Augsburg, 1761–3
8¾ in and 12¼ in (22.3 cm and 31.5 cm) high
38 oz 2 dwt (1,185 gr)
Geneva, 12 XI 1980, 261
SFr.35,200 (£8,205 $16,985)

Abraham Drentwett IV

Augsburg; baptized 1711, master 1741, died 1785. See Appendix 1
Mark Seling, 2329

191 Meat dishes, pair
Augsburg, 1761–3
19 in (48 cm) wide
130 oz (4,020 gr)
Arms: Ernst August, King of Hanover (1837–51)
Geneva, 12 XI 1980, 237
SFr.55,000 (£12,820 $26,537)

192 Salvers-on-foot, pair
silver-gilt
Augsburg, 1761–3
12½ in (32 cm) diameter
106 oz 14 dwt (3,320 gr)
Geneva, 12 XI 1980, 219
SFr.33,000 (£7,692 $15,792)

Gottlieb Satzger
Augsburg; born *c.* 1709, master 1746, died 1783. See Appendix 1
Mark Seling, 2373

193 Toilet box
silver-gilt
Augsburg, 1749–51
8¼ in (21 cm) wide
28 oz 13 dwt (894 gr)
London, 5 II 1970, 158
£1,600 ($3,840)

194 Toilet boxes, pair
silver-gilt
Augsburg, 1753–5
10 in (25.3 cm) wide
72 oz (2,240 gr)
Zurich, 22 XI 1978, 170
SFr.97,200 (£27,380 $56,129)

195 Toilet box
silver-gilt
Augsburg, 1759–61
6¼ in (16.1 cm) wide
16 oz (500 gr)
Geneva, 5 V 1981, 25
SFr.18,700 (£4,358 $9,021)

Johann Gottlieb Ackermann
Celle; born 1716, master 1743, died 1792
Mark Scheffler, *Niedersachsens*, p.262, no.36

196 Sauceboat
Celle, *c.* 1765
8 in (20.3 cm) overall
12 oz 10 dwt (390 gr)
Arms: Dincklage of Prussia
Geneva, 5 V 1981, 61
SFr.13,200 (£3,077 $6,369)

192 A. DRENTWETT IV

196 ACKERMANN

193 SATZGER

197 J.P. HECKENAUR

194 SATZGER

195 SATZGER

198 J.P. HECKENAUR

199 J.P. HECKENAUER

200 J.J. BILLER II

201 J.J. BILLER II

Johann Philipp Heckenauer

Augsburg; born 1705, master 1741, died 1793. See Appendix 1
Mark Seling, 2332

197 Candelabra, pair
Augsburg, 1761–3
12½ in (31.4 cm) high
92 oz 12 dwt (2,880 gr)
Geneva, 12 XI 1980, 253
SFr.82,500 (£19,230 $39,806)

198 Candelabra, pair
Augsburg, 1761–3
18¾ in (47.6 cm) high
118 oz 8 dwt (3,685 gr)
Monogram: Ernst August, King of Hanover (1837–51)
Geneva, 12 XI 1980, 235
SFr.49,500 (£11,538 $23,883)

199 Candlesticks, pair
Augsburg, 1755–7
10¼ in (25.8 cm) high
35 oz 6 dwt (1,100 gr)
Geneva, 10 XI 1981, 205
SFr.14,300 (£3,995 $7,151)

Johann Jakob Biller II

Augsburg; born 1715, master 1746, died 1777. See Appendix 1
Mark Seling, 2366

200 Beaker
silver-gilt
Augsburg, 1743–5
3¾ in (9.7 cm) high
5 oz 8 dwt (168 gr)
Geneva, 12 XI 1980, 46
SFr.4,180 (£974 $2,016)

201 Dishes, pair
Augsburg, 1757–9
17 in (42.5 cm) overall
60 oz (1,866 gr)
New York, 25–26 IV 1979, 77
$7,975 (£3,890)

202 J.J. BILLER II

203 J.J. BILLER II

202 Candlesticks, pair
Augsburg, 1759–61
7¼ in (18.5 cm) high
15 oz 15 dwt (490 gr)
Geneva, 5 V 1981, 181
SFr.14,300 (£3,333 $6,700)

203 Candlesticks, pair
Augsburg, 1767–9
8¼ in (21.1 cm) high
20 oz (622 gr)
New York, 16–17 XII 1980, 10
$5,170 (£2,500)

Johann Wilhelm Dammann

Augsburg; born 1716, master 1748, died 1784. See Appendix 1
Mark Seling, 2387

204 Soup tureens and stands, pair
Augsburg, 1761–3
21¾ in (55.3 cm) wide
255 oz 6 dwt (7,940 gr)
Geneva, 12 XI 1980, 243
SFr.66,000 (£15,385 $31,846)

204 DAMMANN

205 G.C. DRENTWETT

Gottlieb Christian Drentwett

Augsburg; baptized 1723, master c. 1749, died 1754. See Appendix 1
Mark Seling, 2394

205 Toilet box
silver-gilt
Augsburg, 1753–5
3½ in (9 cm) wide
4 oz 16 dwt (150 gr)
Geneva, 12 V 1983, 189
SFr.11,000 (£3,283 $5,252)

206 Nécessaire
silver-gilt
Augsburg, c. 1750
Includes pieces by Johann Christian Girschner, Joh.Jacob Adam, J.C. Engelbrecht, Johann Abraham Winkler and others.
Monaco, 24 VI 1976, 210
FFr.555,500 (£66,130 $119,035)

Emanuel Abraham Drentwett

Augsburg; born 1723, master 1750, died 1770. See Appendix 1
Mark Seling, 2407

207 Sauceboats, two
Augsburg, 1755/9
8 in (21 cm) overall
29 oz (902 gr)
London, 13 VII 1967, 142
£270 ($756)

Emanuel Gottlieb Oernster

Augsburg; born Danzig 1718, master 1755, died 1767. See Appendix 1.
Mark Seling, 2435

208 Teapot
Augsburg, 1757–9
4½ in (11.8 cm) high
15 oz 10 dwt (482 gr)
London, 12 II 1981, 61
£3,520 ($7,286)

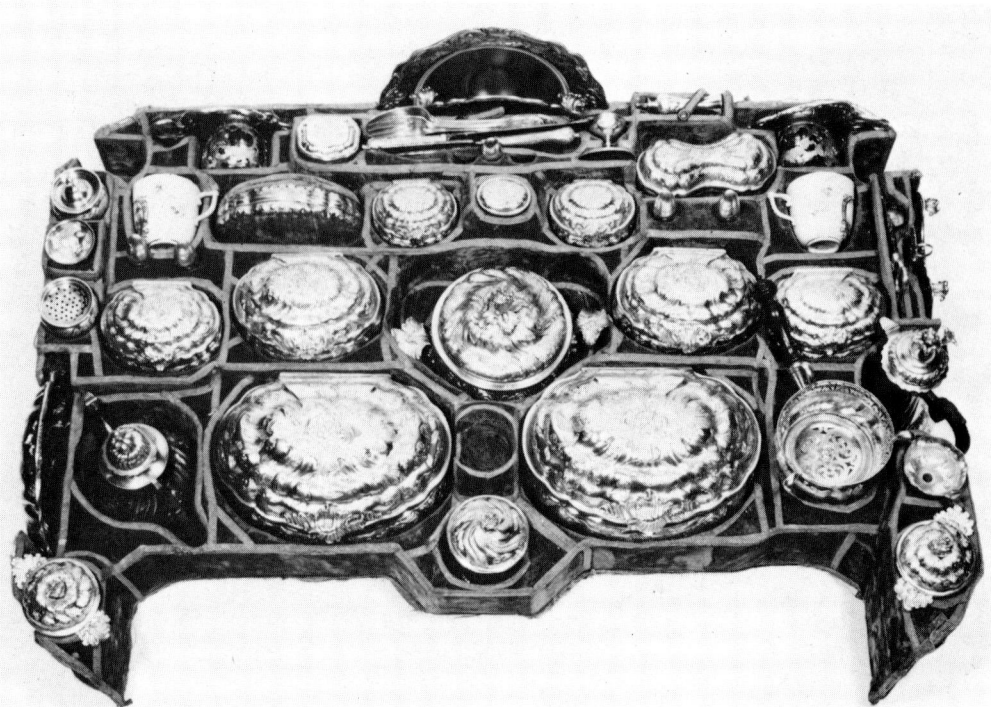

206 G.C. DRENTWETT

Christian Drentwett II

Augsburg; born 1729, master 1754, died 1801. See Appendix 1
Mark Seling, 2427

209 Ewer and basin
Augsburg, 1761–3
19¼ in (49 cm) diameter
67 oz 10 dwt (2,100 gr)
Geneva, 12 XI 1980, 233
SFr.26,400 (£6,154 $12,738)

210 Bowl and stand
The stand, Carl Samuel Bettkober (1773–5)
Augsburg, 1775–7
8¾ in (22.5 cm) overall
20 oz 8 dwt (635 gr)
London, 12 III 1984, 350
£2,200 ($3,058)

207 E.A. DRENTWETT

208 OERNSTER

211 KOLB

Jakob (Johann) Wilhelm Kolb
Augsburg; born Stuttgart c. 1743, master 1768, died 1782. Married in 1768 the widow of J.G. Kloss, who had run the workshop after the latter's death in 1766. See Appendix 1
Mark Seling, 2522

211 Chocolate pot
Augsburg, 1779–81
10½ in (27 cm) high
21 oz 16 dwt (680 gr)
London, 7 III 1983, 294
£2,090 ($3,344)

212 Chocolate pot
Augsburg, 1769–71
11¼ in (28.4 cm) high
23 oz 16 dwt (740 gr)
London, 30 XI 1972, 54
£1,050 ($2,625)

209 C. DRENTWETT II

212 KOLB

Jean Frédéric Pastre
Berlin; born c. 1722 in Kassel, died 1789
Mark Scheffler, *Berlin*, 901

213 Candlesticks, pair
silver-gilt
Berlin, c. 1776
9¼ in (13.5 cm) high
31 oz 16 dwt (973 gr)
London, 1 VII 1971, 110
£950 ($2,280)

210 C. DRENTWETT II

Johannes Adam Kördell
Kassel; master 1767
Mark Scheffler *Hesse* p.596, no.146

214 Coffee pot
Kassel, 1766
11 in (27.9 cm) high
29 oz (901 gr)
New York, 18 II 1982, 218
$10,725 (£5,990)

214 KÖRDELL

213 PASTRE

215 DULLIKER

216 DULLIKER   217 PAPUS & DAUTUN

Johann Jakob Dulliker
Berne; born 1731, master 1759, died 1810
Mark Gruber, 200

215 Tea caddy
Berne, *c.* 1770
4¼ in (10.5 cm) high
5 oz 2 dwt (160 gr)
Geneva, 6 V 1982, 132
SFr.6,600 (£1,843 $3,299)

216 Bowl
Berne, *c.* 1775
7¼ in (18.5 cm) diameter
13 oz 6 dwt (415 gr)
Geneva, 30 XI 1982, 143
SFr.7,150 (£2,135 $3,416)

218 PAPUS & DAUTUN

219 PAPUS & DAUTUN

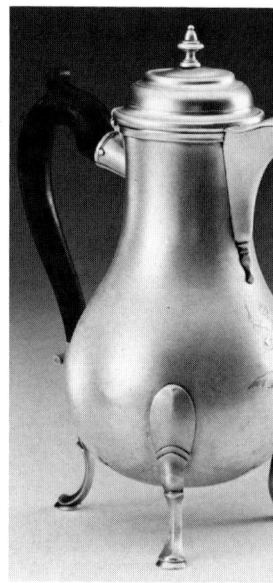

220 PAPUS & DAUTUN

Elie Papus and Pierre Henry Dautun
Lausanne; in partnership 1760–93. Papus: born 1703, died 1793; Dautun born 1729, died 1803
Mark Gruber, 86, 274–7

217 Teapot
Lausanne, *c.* 1760
4¾ in (11.4 cm) high
11 oz 7 dwt (353 gr)
London 17 V 1973, 76
£950 ($2,375)

218 Candlesticks, pair
Lausanne, *c.* 1770
9 in (22.8 cm) high
24 oz (745 gr)
Zurich, 7 V 1980, 164
SFr.11,340 (£2,907 $6,831)

219 Cream jug
Lausanne, *c.* 1770
6 in (15 cm) high
8 oz 12 dwt (270 gr)
Geneva, 30 XI 1982, 158
SFr.4,620 (£1,380 $2,208)

220 Coffee pot
Lausanne, *c.* 1775
8¼ in (21.1 cm) high
10 oz 12 dwt (330 gr)
Zurich, 16 V 1979, 61
SFr.6,480 (£1,825 $3,741)

221 BUNSEN

222 BUNSEN

223 SCHULTZ

Frantz Peter Bunsen
Hanover; born 1725
Mark Scheffler, *Niedersachsens*,
p.765, no.126a

221 Candlesticks, six
Hanover, c. 1794
11¾ in (30 cm) high
357 oz 10 dwt (11,120 gr)
Monogram: George III, King of
England and Elector of Hanover.
See no.222
Monaco, 27 XI 1979, 825
FFr.710,400 (£73,237 $172,106)

222 Cruet
Hanover, c. 1794
12¾ in (32.5 cm) wide
68 oz 2 dwt (2,120 gr)
Monogram: see no.221
Monaco, 27 XI 1979, 823
FFr.88,800 (£9,154 $21,512)

224 J.C. NEUSS

225 J.C. NEUSS

226 UNMARKED

227 J.G. FOURNIER II

Christian Friedrich Schultz
Celle; master 1764
Mark Scheffler, *Niedersachsens*,
p.266, no.47

223 Sugar box and cover
Celle, c. 1780
5 in (12.5 cm) high
7 oz 10 dwt (235 gr)
London, 7 III 1983, 268
£1,100 ($1,760)

Johann Christian Neuss
Augsburg; born 1740, master
1766, died 1803. See Appendix 1
Mark Seling, 2511

224 Coffee pot
Augsburg, 1799
11¼ in (28.5 cm) high
23 oz 6 dwt (724 gr)
London, 15 VII 1976, 54
£990 ($1,782)

225 Wine cooler
Augsburg, 1783–5
9¼ in (23.5 cm) high
63 oz (1,959 gr)
New York, 14–16 VI 1976, 326
$7,300 (£4,055)

Unmarked

226 Coffee pot
silver-gilt
German, c. 1800
9¼ in (23.4 cm) high
34 oz (1,058 gr)
Zurich, 18 XI 1977, 35
SFr.3,024 (£815 $1,507)

Johann Georg Fournier II
Berlin
Mark Scheffler, *Berlin*, 1281a

227 Coffee pot and milk jug
parcel-gilt
Berlin, c. 1800
8¾ in (22 cm) and 4¾ in
(12.2 cm) high
29 oz 10 dwt (917 gr)
London, 15 VII 1976, 78
£1,430 ($2,574)

228 H. & K. ROSSBACH

229 J.G.C. NEUSS

230 J.G.C. NEUSS

231 J.G.C. NEUSS

232 NEUSS FAMILY

Hertler and Kranert Rossbach
Dresden
Mark Rosenberg, 1824

228 Tea and coffee set
silver-gilt
Dresden, 1813
104 oz 12 dwt (3,253 gr)
New York, 13–15 X 1981, 13
$7,700 (£4,301)

Johann Georg Christoph Neuss
Augsburg; born 1774, master 1803, died 1857. See Appendix 1
Mark Seling, 2665

229 Coffee pots, two
Augsburg, 1805
11½ in (29.3 cm) and 9¾ in (24.5 cm) high
46 oz 18 dwt (1,460 gr)
Zurich, 22 XI 1978, 147
SFr.4,536 (£1,277 $2,617)

233 NEUSS FAMILY

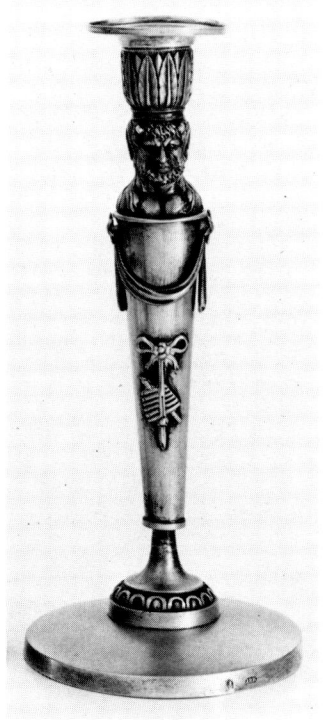

234 J.B. HECKENAUER

230 Coffee pots, two
Augsburg, 1814
10¾ in (27.3 cm) and 9¼ in (23.7 cm) high
46 oz (1,430 gr)
London, 22 V 1969, 176
£550 ($1,320)

231 Candelabra
Augsburg, 1817
23½ in (59.7 cm) high
132 oz 16 dwt (4,130 gr)
New York, 13–15 X 1981, 12
$3,850 (£2,150)

Neuss Family

232 Candelabra, pair
silver (loaded)
Augsburg, 1819
22 in (56 cm) high
New York, 27 IV 1976, 154
$1,500 (£833)

233 Soup tureen and stand
Augsburg, 1811
17¼ in (44 cm) wide
203 oz 17 dwt (6,340 gr)
Arms (later): Duke of Brunswick-Luneburg and King of Hanover, for Ernest Augustus, Duke of Cumberland, 5th son of King George III of England, who succeeded to the crown of Hanover on the death of William IV in 1837
London, 18 V 1967, 108
£950 ($2,660)

Jakob Balthasar Heckenauer

Augsburg; born 1784, master 1811, died after 1825. See Appendix 1
Mark Seling, 2693

234 Candlesticks, pair
Augsburg, c. 1810
8¼ in (21 cm) high
18 oz 18 dwt (587 gr)
London, 12 II 1981, 97
£715 ($1,480)

Maler

235 Tea and coffee set, with tray
Warsaw, c. 1840–50
Tray: 34 in (86.2 cm) wide
518 oz (16,109 gr)
New York, 10–12 VI 1980, 56
$13,200 (£5,617)

236 REHFUS

238 REHFUS

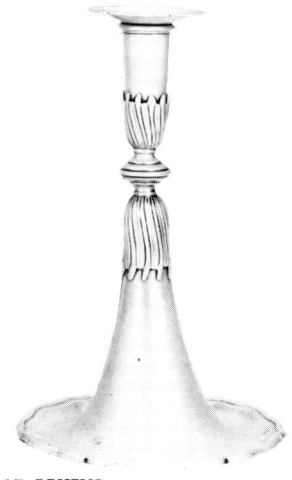

237 REHFUS

Georg Adam Rehfus

Berne; born 1784, active from 1807, died 1858
Mark Gruber, 301

236 Teapot and stand
Berne, c. 1815
6 in (15.4 cm) high
27 oz 12 dwt (860 gr)
Zurich, 13 XI 1979, 136
SFr.4,860 (£1,246 $2,928)

237 Candlesticks, pair
Berne, c. 1820
9½ in (23.9 cm) high
23 oz 2 dwt (719 gr)
Geneva, 6 V 1982, 162
SFr.4,400 (£1,229 $2,199)

238 Tea set
Berne, c. 1825
44 oz 6 dwt (1,380 gr)
Geneva, 10 XI 1981, 75
SFr.3,850 (£1,075 $1,924)

235 MALER

GERMANY AUSTRIA SWITZERLAND

239 MAYERHOFER & KLINKOSCH

240 MAYERHOFER & KLINKOSCH

241 MAYERHOFER & KLINKOSCH

242 KLINKOSCH

243 KLINKOSCH

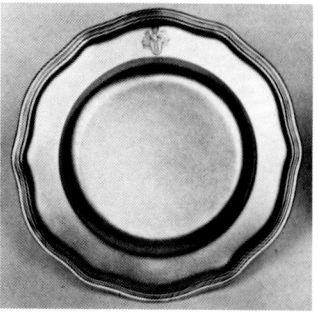

244 KLINKOSCH

Stephan Mayerhofer and Josef Klinkosch

Vienna; in partnership from ?1838; subsequently the firm was taken over by J.C. Klinkosch (see below). See catalogue of exhibition, 'The Adjectives of History', London, Colnaghi, 1983, no.39.
Mark Neuwirth, vol. I, p.296, and vol. II, p.58

239 Cup and cover
parcel-gilt
Vienna, 1844
28¾ in (73 cm) high
376 oz 4 dwt (11,700 gr)
Geneva, 15 XI 1983, 208
SFr.22,000 (£7,028 $9,768)

240 Ink stand
silver and mother-of-pearl
Vienna, 1821
11¾ in (29.7 cm) wide
18 oz 6 dwt (569 gr)
London, 6 VII 1981, 156
£770 ($1,593)

241 Ewer and basin
silver-gilt
Vienna, 1836
The ewer unmarked
12 in (30.5 cm) high
112 oz (3,483 gr)
New York, 18 II 1982, 172
$6,600 (£3,687)

J.C. Klinkosch

Vienna; founded 1797 by Isidor von Klinkosch. See Stephan Mayerhofer and Josef Klinkosch, above
Mark Neuwirth, vol. I, p.296, and vol. II, p.58

242 Centrepiece
Vienna, c. 1910
14½ in (36.5 cm) overall
57 oz (1,772 gr)
New York, 4–5 II 1981, 210
$1,320 (£637)

243 Bowl and a pair of Tazze
Vienna, c. 1925
12 in (30.5 cm) and 8 in (20 cm) overall
New York, 10–11 IV 1981, 242, 243
$1,210 (£584) each lot

244 Dessert plates, twelve
silver-gilt
Vienna, c. 1880
133 oz 2 dwt (4,140 gr)
Monaco, 6 XII 1983, 1161
FFr.42,180 (£3,629 $5,044)

245 Pill box
Vienna, late 19th century
1¾ in (4.2 cm) overall
London (Belgravia), 17 XII 1981, 244
£242 ($433)

246 Fruit basket
Vienna, c. 1900
10 in (25.6 cm) overall
31 oz 16 dwt (992 gr)
London (Belgravia), 18 X 1979, 270
£308 ($723)

Hermann Julius Wilm

Berlin; born 1812 in Hamburg, died 1907
Mark Scheffler, *Berlin*, 2008

247 Wine cooler
Berlin, c. 1855
15½ in (39.7 cm) high
316 oz 14 dwt (9,850 gr)
Geneva, 15 XI 1983, 266
SFr.19,800 (£6,325 $8,791)

245 KLINKOSCH

246 KLINKOSCH

247 WILM

248 UNMARKED

249 UNMARKED

250 BOSSARD

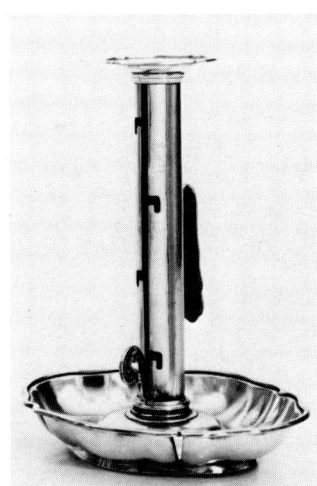

251 BOSSARD

Unmarked

248 Cup and cover
silver-gilt
Mid-European, c. 1870
30½ in (77.5 cm) high
153 oz 17 dwt (4,784 gr)
London (Belgravia), 30 V 1974, 148
£2,200 ($5,280)

249 Cup
silver-gilt, enamel and agate
Probably Continental, c. 1865
11¾ in (29.7 cm) high
London (Belgravia), 25 VII 1974, 90
£1,200 ($2,880)

Johann Karl Bossard
Lucerne
Mark Gruber, nos 32–35

250 Candelabra, pair
Lucerne, late 19th century
24½ in (63.2 cm) high
325 oz (10,107 gr)
London, 18 XI 1976, 73
£4,400 ($7,480)

251 Chamber candlesticks, pair
(Lucerne), c. 1880
8½ in (21.5 cm) high
26 oz 7 dwt (819 cm)
London, 10 II 1977, 59
£935 ($1,590)

96 GERMANY AUSTRIA SWITZERLAND

252 POSEN

253 UNMARKED

254 RATZERSDORFER

255 RATZERSDORFER

256 RATZERSDORFER

257 BÖHM

Lazarus Posen
Frankfurt; exhibited at Munich Exhibition (1888)

252 Tankard
Frankfurt, c. 1900
18¾ in (47.5 cm) high
119 oz 2 dwt (3,705 gr)
London (Belgravia), 25 VI 1981, 272
£2,090 ($4,326)

258 BÖHM

Unmarked

253 Jug
silver-mounted hardstone
Austro-Hungarian, c. 1910
9¼ in (23.7 cm) high
London (Belgravia), 1 V 1980, 651
£2,640 ($6,204)

Hermann Ratzersdorfer

Vienna; firm founded 1845, holder of the Royal Warrant; exhibited at the Great Exhibition in London (1851) and Paris Exhibition (1855).
Mark Neuwirth, p.129

254 Cup
silver-mounted hardstone
Vienna, c. 1885
3½ in (9 cm) high
London (Belgravia), 19 II 1976, 65
£286 ($514)

255 Vase
silver-gilt and enamel
Vienna, late 19th century
4¾ in (12 cm) high
London (Belgravia), 19 VI 1975, 84
£580 ($1,392)

256 Cup
rock crystal, enamel and silver-gilt
Vienna, late 19th century
9 in (23 cm) high
London (Belgravia), 19 VI 1975, 85
£2,900 ($6,670)

Hermann Böhm

Vienna
Mark Neuwirth, p.116

257 Musical box
silver and enamel
Vienna, late 19th century
5¼ in (13.4 cm) wide
London, 16 XII 1982, 384
£2,310 ($3,696)

258 Standing cup
silver-mounted enamel
Vienna, late 19th century
15 in (38.3 cm) high
London (Belgravia), 17 XII 1981, 216
£4,400 ($7,876)

259 Vases, pair
silver-mounted enamel
Vienna, third quarter of the 19th century
The vases depict scenes from the lives of Perseus and Andromeda.
London (Belgravia), 25 VII 1974, 56
£820 ($1,968)

259 BÖHM

Neresheimer

Hanau; established 1893

260 Nef
Hanau, imported London 1927
32 in (81.5 cm) high
200 oz (6,222 gr)
London (Belgravia), 17 XII 1981, 252
£5,170 ($9,254)

261 Figures of knights, three
Hanau, imported London and Chester, 1904/08/13
Importer's mark: B.H. Muller for B. Muller and Son
9¼ in (23.5 cm) to 11 in (28 cm) high
50 oz 2 dwt (1,561 gr)
London (Belgravia), 11 XII 1980, 86
£1,375 ($2,846)

262 Figures of equestrian knights, pair
Hanau, imported London 1911
Importer's mark: B.H. Muller for B. Muller and Son
12 in (30.4 cm) and 13½ in (34.5 cm) high
89 oz 16 dwt (2,795 gr)
London (Belgravia), 22 XI 1979, 264
£3,080 ($7,238)

260 NERESHEIMER

261 NERESHEIMER

262 NERESHEIMER

98 GERMANY AUSTRIA SWITZERLAND

Louis Sy and Albert Wagner
Berlin; exhibited at London Exhibition (1862)

263 Centrepiece
Berlin, c. 1900
25 in (63.5 cm) overall
104 oz 10 dwt (3,250 gr)
New York, 5–6 X 1977, 332
$1,100 (£594)

Wiener Werkstätte
Vienna: The Wiener Werkstätte-Produktiv-Gemeinschaft von Kunsthandwerkern in Wien were founded 1903. Designers and craftsmen included Josef Hoffmann (1870–1956), founder member of the Vienna Secession; Koloman Moser (1868–1918), Otto Prutscher (1880–1949), Dagobert Peche (1887–1923). See Werner J. Schweiger, *Wiener Werkstätte 1903–1932*, Vienna, 1982
Mark See Schweiger

264 Table silver, six pieces
c. 1904
Designer: Josef Hoffmann
Monaco, 11 III 1984, 250
FFr.177,600 (£15,283 $21,243)

265 Butter knife
c. 1903
Designer: Josef Hoffmann
6½ in (16.5 cm) overall
Monaco, 18 XI 1978, 155
FFr.2,220 (£244 $500)

266 Napkin ring
c. 1905
Designer: Koloman Moser
1¼ in (3 cm) diameter
Monaco, 18 XI 1978, 158
FFr.3,330 (£366 $750)

267 Bottle top
c. 1905
Designer: Josef Hoffmann
1¾ in (4.5 cm) high
Monaco, 18 XI 1978, 160
FFr.1,998 (£219 $448)

268 Spoon
c. 1905
Maker: Anton Pribil
Designer: Josef Hoffmann
6¾ in (17 cm) overall
London, 28 IV 1983, 99
£17,600 ($28,160)

263 SY & WAGNER

264 WIENER WERKSTÄTTE

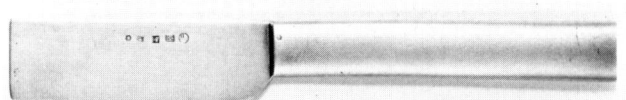

265 WIENER WERKSTÄTTE

266 267 WIENER WERKSTÄTTE

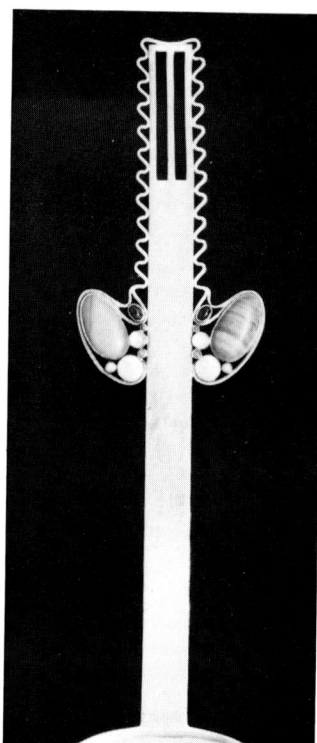

268 WIENER WERKSTÄTTE

269 WIENER WERKSTÄTTE

270 WIENER WERKSTÄTTE

269 Bottle top
electroplate
c. 1910
Designer: Josef Hoffmann
2¼ in (5.5 cm) high
Monaco, 11 III 1984, 259
FFr.3,885 (£334 $464)

270 Bowl
c. 1920
Designer: Josef Hoffmann
7 in (17.8 cm) high
19 oz 12 dwt (609 gr)
New York, 4–5 II 1981, 209
$12,523 (£6,050)

271 Desk set
electroplate
c. 1910–20
Stamped: 'Made in Austria'
13¾ in (35 cm) overall
London (Belgravia), 12 VII 1978, 197
£1,210 ($2,238)

272 Coffee set
electroplate
1911
Designer: Josef Hoffmann
Maker's mark: Otto Prutscher
London (Belgravia), 25 IX 1981, 249
£1,870 ($3,347)

273 Tea set
c. 1920
Designers: Josef Hoffmann and Dagobert Peche
Tray: 17 in (43 cm) wide
96 oz 6 dwt (2,995 gr)
Monaco, 9 X 1983, 290
FFr.105,450 (£9,074 $12,612)

274 Vase
c. 1920–30
Designer: Josef Hoffmann
Stamped: Wiener Werkstätte
10¾ in (27.2 cm) high
London (Belgravia), 28 II 1979, 171
£990 ($2,029)

275 Vase
c. 1920
Designer: Josef Hoffmann
9½ in (24.2 cm) high
London (Belgravia), 22 VI 1972, 73
£220 ($550)

276 Tea set
Stamped: made in Austria 1928
Designer: Josef Hoffmann
London (Belgravia), 20 VII 1977, 75
£5,280 ($8,976)

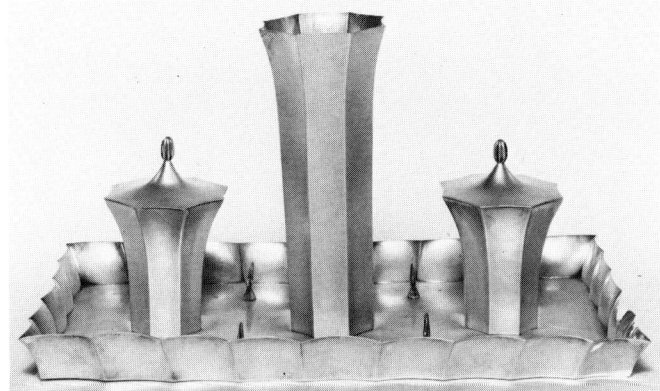

271 WIENER WERKSTÄTTE

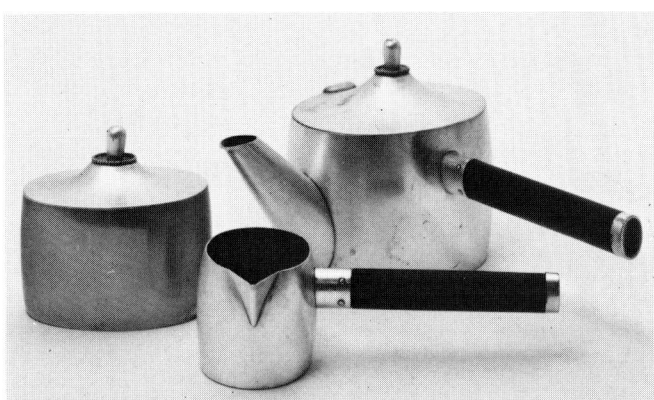

272 WIENER WERKSTÄTTE

274 WIENER WERKSTÄTTE

273 WIENER WERKSTÄTTE

275 WIENER WERKSTÄTTE

276 WIENER WERKSTÄTTE

277 H. SUDFELD & CO

278 FRIEDMAN

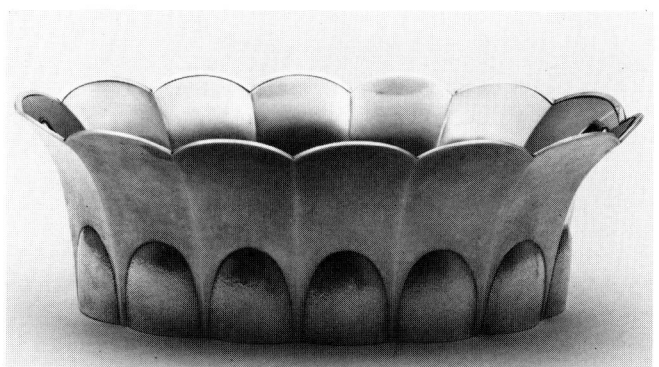

279 FRIEDMAN

H. Sudfeld and Company

Vienna; founded in Prague by A.B. Bacher 1835; continued from 1867 by his sons in Vienna; taken over by Hermann Sudfeld in 1881; owned by Heinrich Tandler 1914–22
Mark Neuwirth, p.240

277 Tea set
Vienna, 1915
74 oz 10 dwt (2,317 gr)
New York, 26–27 III 1980, 268
$1,540 (£655)

E. Friedman

Vienna

278 Tea set
Austrian, c. 1920
Tray: 32½ in (82.5 cm) overall
326 oz (10,138 gr)
New York, 31 X 1979, 37
$10,175 (£4,329)

279 Basket
Vienna, c. 1920
15 in (38.1 cm) overall
38 oz (1,181 gr)
New York, 10–11 IV 1981, 241
$1,320 (£637)

The Low Countries

Theodor de Bry
Engraver; born 1528 in Liège, in 1570 went with his son Johan Theodor to live in Frankfurt, died 1598. See Hayward, *Virtuoso Goldsmiths*, pp.294-7.

280 Travelling knife and fork, in German boxwood case
Unmarked
Dutch, first half of 17th century
The handles are engraved with Old and New Testament scenes relating to marriage and with figures symbolizing Faith, Hope and Charity, after Theodor de Bry.
Geneva, 30 XI 1982, 17
SFr.6,050 (£3,781 $6,049)

Unmarked

281 Knife and fork
Dutch, early 17th century
Engraved with scenes from the New Testament.
London 21 X 1971, 154
£280 ($700)

Franssoys Eelioet
Utrecht; born *c.* 1585 in Antwerp, master 1608, died 1642
Mark  Stag's antlers; see catalogue of exhibition, 'Dutch Silver 1580-1830'

282 Standing cup
Utrecht, 1618
9¼ in (23.5 cm) high
10 oz 10 dwt (326 gr)
London, 20 IV 1972, 58
£1,700 ($4,250)

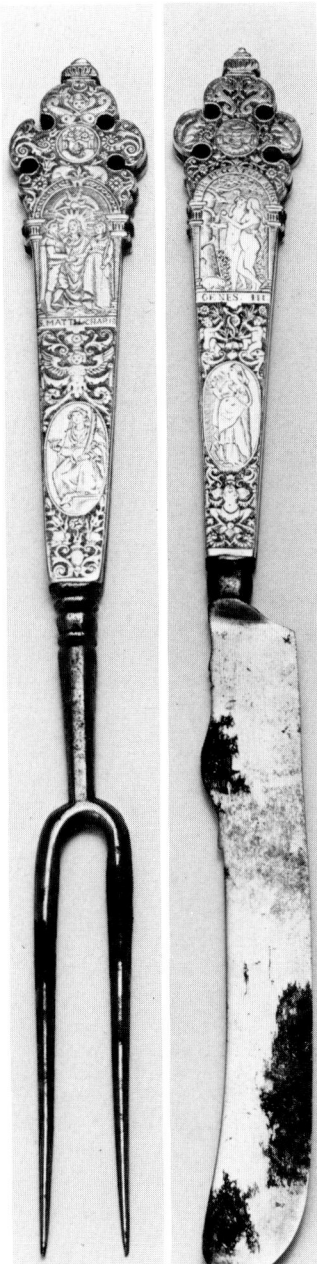

280 DE BRY

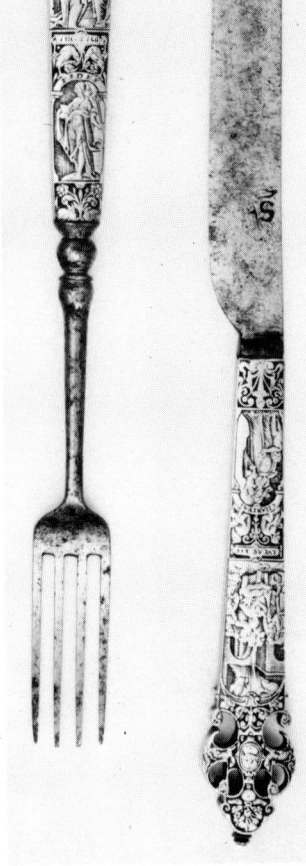

281 UNMARKED

282 EELIOET

283 UNMARKED

Unmarked

283 Beaker
silver-gilt
Probably Dutch, *c.* 1610
3¾ in (9.7 cm) high
The body is applied with embossed plaques depicting the parable of the Prodigal Son, after engravings by Hans Sebald Beham.
London, 20 IV 1972, 126
£1,650 ($4,125)

284 DE PASSE
285 DE PASSE 
286 DE PASSE 
287 DE PASSE 
288 DE PASSE 
289 DE PASSE 

Simon de Passe

Engraver, born c. 1595 in Cologne, worked in Utrecht 1612–15, London 1615–22, Copenhagen 1624 until his death in 1647.

284 Medallion
c. 1615–22
2½ in (6.3 cm) overall
Portraits of James I of England, Queen Anne and Prince Charles
London, 22 VI 1972, 129
£680 ($1,700)

285 Medallion
Dated: 1616
Signed: Si.Pa. fecit
2 in (5.5 cm) overall
Portrait of Charles, Prince of Wales
London, 9 IV 1981, 193D
£440 ($910)

286 Medallion
c. 1616
2 in (5.5 cm) overall
Portrait of James I
London 9 IV 1981, 193B
£770 ($1,593)

290 DE PASSE

291 VAN BOLTEN

292 VAN BOLTEN

293 BIRD'S CLAW

287 Medallion
c. 1616
Signed: Simon Passevs Sculp
2¼ in (6 cm) overall
Portrait of James I
London, 9 IV 1981, 193C
£1,595 ($3,301)

288 Medallion
c. 1616–20
Signed: Sim.Passe Sculpsit
2¼ in (6 cm) overall
Portrait of Emperor Matthias
London, 9 IV 1981, 193F
£2,420 ($5,009)

289 Medallion
c. 1620
2½ in (6.3 cm) overall
Portraits of the Emperor
Frederick V, Princess Elizabeth
and Prince Frederick
London, 18 VII 1974, 161
£540 ($1,296)

290 Medallion
gold
c. 1615
3 in (7.7 cm) overall
Portrait of Queen Elizabeth I
London, 25 V 1977, 210
£22,000 ($37,400)

Arent van Bolten

Zwolle; born 1573, died 1624–6; signed his work AVB in monogram. See catalogue of exhibition, 'Dutch Silver 1580–1830'

291 Plaque 'The Entombment'
Zwolle, early 17th century
Signed in monogram: AVB
7 in (17.6 cm) high
London, 11·II 1971, 95
£2,000 ($4,800)

292 Plaquette, 'The Resurrection'
Zwolle, early 17th century
attributed to van Bolten
8½ in (21.7 cm) wide
London, 17 V 1973, 87
£700 ($1,750)

Bird's Claw

293 Tazze, pair
silver-gilt
Delft, 1604/6
7½ in (19 cm) diameter
42 oz 18 dwt (1,336 gr)
Embossed with scenes emblematic of the seasons and the elements after prints by Jan Sadeler.
Geneva, 15 V 1984, 30
SFr.935,000 (£298,722 $415,223)

294 P. VAN VIANEN

295 P. VAN VIANEN

298 A. VAN VIANEN

Paul van Vianen

Born c. 1568–70; in 1601 was court goldsmith to the Archbishop of Salzburg, in 1603 *Kammergoldschmied* to Rudolph II in Prague, where he remained until his death in 1613. See pp.16–17; Honour, *Goldsmiths and Silversmiths*, pp.96–103; catalogue, 'De Utrechtse Edelsmeden van Vianen', Centraal Museum, Utrecht, 1984–5

294 Plaque, 'The Resurrection'
Signed: PV 1605
12¼ × 8¾ in (31.1 × 22.2 cm)
17 oz 18 dwt (556 gr)
London, 13 XI 1958, 73
£2,000 ($5,620)

295 Plaquette
gilded lead
c. 1612
6¼ in (16 cm) diameter
Compare with Frederiks, vol. I, no.93, 'Susanna and the Elders'.
Amsterdam, 20–23 I 1975, 872
DFl.4,510 (£812 $1,867)

Circle of Paul van Vianen

296 Plaquette
From a tazza
silver-gilt
Early 17th century
6¼ in (16 cm) diameter
Depicts Bacchus and Ceres walking
London, 3 VII 1980, 188
£4,180 ($9,823)

297 Plaquette
First quarter of 17th century
4½ in (11.4 cm) diameter
London, 17 V 1973, 86
£620 ($1,550)

Adam van Vianen

Utrecht; born c. 1565–9, master c. 1593, died 1627. Brother of Paul. Whereas Paul travelled widely, Adam van Vianen remained in Utrecht and developed the auricular or lobate style of which the brothers were the finest exponents. See catalogue, 'De Utrechtse Edelsmeden van Vianen', Centraal Museum, Utrecht, 1984–5
Mark Rosenberg, 7711

298 Wall sconces, pair
Utrecht, dated 1622
23½ in (59.8 cm) high
119 oz 2 dwt (3,704 gr)
The scenes from mythology on these sconces are recorded on vessels by Paul van Vianen and on a ewer and basin (see no.303).
London, 17 VI 1971, 126
£62,000 ($148,800)

299 Tazze, pair
silver-gilt (later)
Utrecht, 1627
Signed: A.D. Viana Fe 1627
6¾ in (17.3 cm) high
41 oz 17 dwt (1,301 gr)
Emblematic of Summer and Winter.
London, 25 X 1973, 124
£30,000 ($72,000)

Christian van Vianen

Born 1598–1600, apprenticed to his father Adam, master 1628, lived in London 1635–47 and 1660–67; died there. In 1650 he published his father's designs for silver, engraved by Th. van Kessel, *Modelles artificiels de divers vaisseaux d'argent* (1650). See Lightbown, 'Christian van Vianen at the Court of Charles I'; catalogue, 'De Utrechtse Edelsmeden van Vianen', Centraal Museum, Utrecht, 1984–5
Mark Rosenberg, 7721

300 Tazza
silver-gilt (later)
Utrecht, 1628
4¼ in (10.6 cm) high
9 oz 5 dwt (287 gr)
London, 25 X 1973, 125
£24,000 ($57,600)

296 CIRCLE OF P. VAN VIANEN

297 CIRCLE OF P. VAN VIANEN

299 A. VAN VIANEN

300 C. VAN VIANEN

301 C. VAN VIANEN

301 (DETAIL)

302 C. VAN VIANEN

304 BOOGAERT

301 Ewer and basin
Utrecht, 1632
Ewer: 9½ in (24.3 cm) high
Basin: 20½ in (52 cm) wide
Arms: probably a member of the van Tongeren family; added later: Duke of Sussex (1773–1843)
Previously sold at Christie's, 22 VI 1843 (collection of Duke of Sussex), lot 78, for £85. See Lightbown, cited above.
London, 2 VI 1977, 186
£137,500 ($233,750)

302 Dish
c. 1640
Unmarked, in the manner of Christian van Vianen
12¼ in (31.2 cm) wide
19 oz 1 dwt (592 gr)
See Fredericks, vol.I, no.57
London, 20 IV 1972, 62
£600 ($1,500)

303 (DETAIL)

303 (DETAIL)

GB in monogram

303 Ewer and basin
silver-gilt
Utrecht, early 17th century
Bears the monogram MAF, possibly the signature of the chaser
Ewer: 12¾ in (32.7 cm) high
Basin: 17¾ in (45.5 cm) diameter
76 oz 17 dwt (2,390 gr)
Now in the Rijksmuseum, Amsterdam
See Hayward, *Virtuoso Goldsmiths*, no.635: '... suggesting that these vessels were embossed by a master working either in Prague or Utrecht who had access to Paul van Vianen's drawings or plaquettes'.
London, 26 VI 1969, 172
£16,000 ($38,400)

Thomas Boogaert

Born 1597/8 Utrecht, master 1625 after which date he left Utrecht, died 1653. His work is strongly influenced by that of Adam van Vianen.
Mark Citroen (Amsterdam), 848

304 Standing salts
silver-gilt (later)
Utrecht, 1624
7¼ in (18.5 cm) high
26 oz 5 dwt (816 gr)
Provenance: The Duke of Hamilton and Brandon
London, 2 VI 1977, 127
£24,200 ($41,140)

303 GB

305 BOOGAERT

306 LUTMA

307 UNMARKED

305 Tazza
Amsterdam, probably 1633
6½ in (16.8 cm) diameter
11 oz 10 dwt (357 gr)
London, 11 II 1971, 191
£650 ($1,560)

Johannes Lutma I
Amsterdam, born 1587, died 1669
Mark Citroen (Amsterdam), 954

306 Toilet box
Amsterdam, 1654
4¾ in (12.2 cm) wide
6 oz 4 dwt (195 gr)
See catalogue of exhibition 'De Utrechtse edelsmeden Van Vianen', Centraal Museum, Utrecht, 1984, no.107
Zurich, 16 V 1979, 122
SFr.7,500 (£2,112 $4,329)

308 UNMARKED

309 UNMARKED

Unmarked

307 Wedding heart
Dutch, c. 1640
3 in (7.6 cm) high
London, 12 III 1984, 336
£2,420 ($3,363)

308 Marriage casket
Friesian, c. 1625
3 in (7.5 cm) wide
London, 20 II 1975, 130
£1,100 ($2,530)

309 Book cover
Dutch, second quarter of 17th century
3½ in (9 cm) overall
London, 17 II 1971, 92
£650 ($1,560)

310 UNMARKED

311 UNKNOWN MAKER

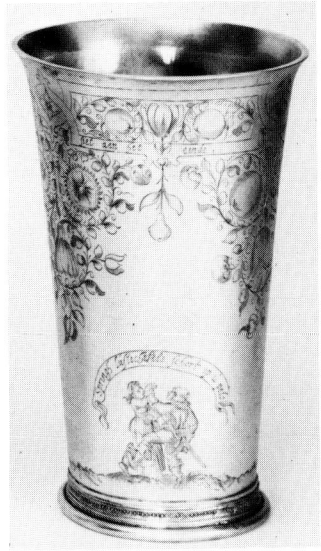

312 UNKNOWN MAKER

310 Marriage casket
silver-gilt (later)
Dutch, c. 1630
3 in (7.5 cm) wide
3 oz 17 dwt (119 gr)
London, 16 II 1978, 114
£2,090 ($3,866)

Unknown maker

311 Windmill cup
silver-gilt
No maker's mark
Amsterdam, 1635
8½ in (21.8 cm) high
6 oz 7 dwt (197 gr)
London, 13 II 1969, 154
£1,800 ($4,320)

312 Beaker
Dutch, c. 1630
7¼ in (18.7 cm) high
13 oz 5 dwt (412 gr)
London, 11 II 1971, 87
£850 ($2,040)

313 BAS

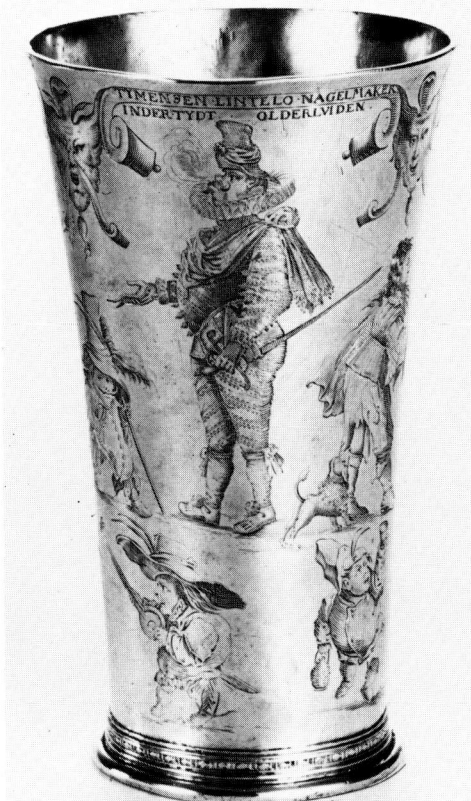

315 MAGNUS

Willem Tobias
Amsterdam; born 1604 in
Workum, active 1624–41
Mark Citroen (Amsterdam), 997

314 Dish
silver-gilt
(Amsterdam), c. 1640
10½ in (26.7 cm) wide
16 oz 4 dwt (503 gr)
London, 22 V 1958, 71
£1,150 ($3,321)

Antoni Magnus
Deventer; described as a
journeyman in 1630, died after
1677. See catalogue of
exhibition, 'Dutch Silver 1580–
1830'.

315 Beaker
Deventer, 1664
7¼ in (18.4 cm) high
11 oz 12 dwt (362 gr)
Arms: Lintelo family
The engravings are after
Abraham Bosse and Jacques
Callot.
Geneva, 15 V 1984, 25
SFr.132,000 (£42,172 $58,619)

Hans Bas
Hans Bas was probably a
member of the Antwerp family
of engravers.

313 Beaker
parcel-gilt
Signed: Hans Bas 1632;
monogrammed: HB
8 in (20 cm) high
18 oz 12 dwt (578 gr)
The engraving shows 'The
Labours of the Months',
'Caprices' and 'Seven Deadly
Sins', after Jacques Callot.
£3,000 ($8,400)

314 TOBIAS

110 THE LOW COUNTRIES

316 W.F. CONJOINED   317 MUNTINCK   318 MUNTINCK

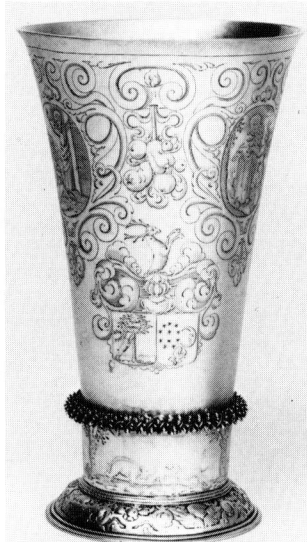

319 EVERTS   320 EVERTS   321 UNMARKED

322 METTING

323 VAN DER LELY

W.F. conjoined

316 Beaker
Possibly Friesian, c. 1628
5 in (12.9 cm)
London, 28 XI 1968, 137
£500 ($1,200)

Hindrick Muntinck

Groningen; active c. 1644–62.
See catalogue of exhibition,
'Dutch Silver 1580–1830'

317 Beaker
Groningen, 1648
4¾ in (12 cm) high
4 oz 8 dwt (136 gr)
London, 2 VI 1977, 98
£2,640 ($4,488)

318 Beaker
Groningen, 1657
Maker's mark I.M., probably a member of the Muntinck family
7½ in (19.4 cm) high
11 oz 10 dwt (357 gr)
London, 11 II 1971, 189
£700 ($1,680)

Warner Everts

Groningen. See catalogue of exhibition, 'Groninger Zilver'

319 Beaker
Groningen, 1663
7½ in (19.2 cm) high
9 oz (279 gr)
London, 11 II 1971, 75
£700 ($1,680)

320 Beaker
Groningen, 1670
4¼ in (10.9 cm) high
3 oz 14 dwt (115 gr)
London, 6 VII 1981, 255
£1,540 ($3,187)

Unmarked

321 Beaker
Probably Dutch, inscribed 1683
8¼ in (21 cm) high
12 oz 2 dwt (438 gr)
London, 10 IV 1930, 57
£130 ($633)

Jan Metting
Groningen; active 1655–73. See catalogue of exhibition, 'Dutch Silver 1580–1830'.

322 Brandy bowl
Groningen, 1656–7
7½ in (19 cm) overall
6 oz 12 dwt (207 gr)
Amsterdam, 9 XI 1978, 525
DFl.9,000 (£2,093 $4,290)

Tjeerd Jarigs van der Lely
Leeuwarden; born 1631, master 1662, died 1705
Mark Voet (Friesland), 420

323 Mustard pot
Leeuwarden, 1687
4¼ in (11 cm) high
7 oz (220 gr)
Amsterdam, 16 III 1983, 4017
DFl.9,280 (£2,048 $3,276)

Unmarked

324 Ewer
silver-gilt (later)
Dutch, c. 1650–75
7¼ in (18.4 cm) high
25 oz 10 dwt (793 gr)
Monogram: probably that of Princess Anna, granddaughter of William the Silent. The same monogram is on a toilet set (1665–78) now in the Museum of the Hague.
New York, 14–16 IX 1972, 480
$3,500 (£1,400)

325 Tobacco box
Dutch
4½ in (11.6 cm) wide
7 oz 12 dwt (236 gr)
The engraving on the cover is after a print by Jan Sadeler after a composition by Dirck Barendsz; that on the base is after Matthys Pool after a painting by Barent Graat.
London, 21 VI 1973, 97
£5,800 ($14,500)

326 Box
silver-gilt
Dutch, 17th century
2¼ in (5.6 cm) diameter
London, 18 V 1978, 128
£396 ($732)

327 Scissors case, with scissors
Dutch, late 17th century
3¼ in (8.2 cm) overall
London, 21 X 1971, 155
£210 ($525)

328 Tobacco rasp
Dutch, 17th century
3½ in (9.1 cm) high
London, 25 X 1973, 114
£1,450 ($3,480)

324 UNMARKED

326 UNMARKED

327 UNMARKED

325 UNMARKED

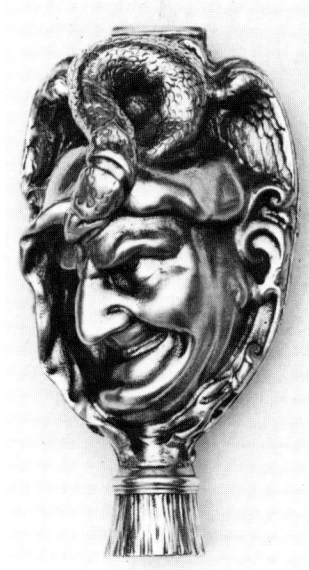

328 UNMARKED

Unidentified Maker

329 Wine cistern
Probably Brussels, c. 1690
44½ in (113 cm) wide
Arms: Middleton, Barons
Engraved scratch weight: 1,353 oz (42,078 gr)
The cistern bears Brussels marks of c. 1690, but these may have been added when the piece entered the country, for it is akin to English work of the period.
London, 20 V 1965, 98
£15,000 ($42,000)

Daniel Bouman

Amsterdam; born 1644, died 1692.
Mark Citroen (Amsterdam), 1068

330 Teapot
Amsterdam, 1696
4 in (10.2 cm) high
9 oz 13 dwt (300 gr)
London, 25 X 1973, 96
£1,400 ($3,360)

Jan du Vignon

The Hague; born 1660, master 1683, died 1746
Mark Voet (The Hague), 59

331 Candlesticks, pair
The Hague, 1703
6¾ in (17.4 cm) high
22 oz 2 dwt (688 gr)
Monaco, 30 XI 1975, 82
FFr.26,400 (£2,933 $5,866)

Bernt Wolff

Nijmegen; see catalogue of exhibition, Nijmeegs Zilver 1400–1900, 1983, p.55

332 Candlesticks, four
Nijmegen, apparently 1710
8¼ in (21 cm) high
69 oz (2,146 gr)
London, 3 VII 1980, 162
£17,050 ($40,067)

Pieter de Keen

Amsterdam; born 1659, master 1682, died 1742
Mark Citroen (Amsterdam), 962, 963

333 Candlesticks, pair
Amsterdam, 1733
8¼ in (20.8 cm) high
33 oz 14 dwt (1,050 gr)
Geneva, 15 XI 1983, 25
SFr.16,500 (£5,111 $7,104)

329 UNIDENTIFIED

330 BOUMAN

331 DU VIGNON

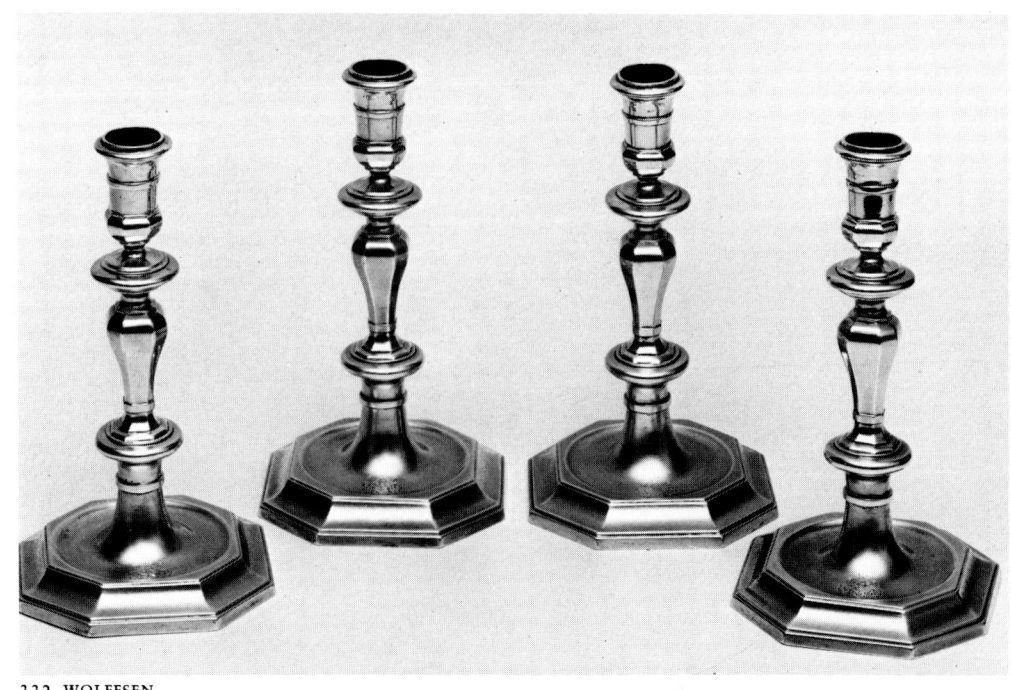
332 WOLFFSEN

Johannes Logerat
The Hague; born c. 1698, master 1726, died 1754
Mark Voet (The Hague), 93

334 Candlesticks, pair
The Hague, 1730
8 in (20.3 cm) high
30 oz 10 dwt (950 gr)
Geneva, 15 XI 1983, 44
SFr.18,150 (£5,798 $8,059)

Jacques Tuillier
The Hague; master 1701
Mark Voet (The Hague), 56

335 Dressing table mirror
silver-gilt
The Hague, 1702
16 in (41 cm) high
London, 18 V 1967, 120
£800 ($2,240)

336 Salver
The Hague, 1721
9½ in (24.2 cm) diameter
14 oz 13 dwt (455 gr)
Arms: Ahlefeldt and Blome, Denmark
London, 8 XII 1977, 372
£1,760 ($3,256)

Jan de Vries
Amsterdam; born 1686, master 1710, died 1753
Mark Citroen (Amsterdam), 966–7

337 Teapot
Amsterdam, c. 1735
6 in (15.4 cm) high
9 oz 5 dwt (287 gr)
London, 16 XI 1978, 181
£572 ($1,172)

François van Stapele
The Hague; born 1697/8 in s'Hertogenbosch, master 1723, died 1773
Mark Voet (The Hague), 97

338 Hot milk jug
The Hague, 1759
6¼ in (16.2 cm) high
10 oz 13 dwt (331 gr)
London, 26 II 1976, 101
£1,045 ($1,881)

339 Teapot
The Hague, 1739
4½ in (11.7 cm) high
12 oz (373 gr)
London, 12 II 1981, 255
£825 ($1,707)

333 DE KEEN

334 LOGERAT

335 TUILLIER

336 TUILLIER

337 DE VRIES

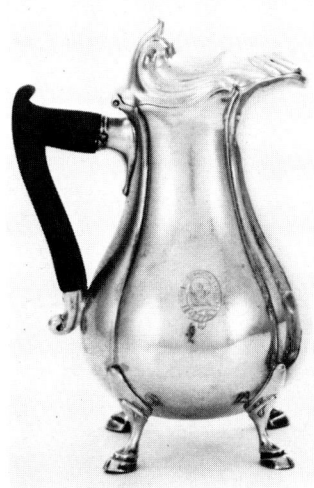

338 F. VAN STAPELE

339 F. VAN STAPELE

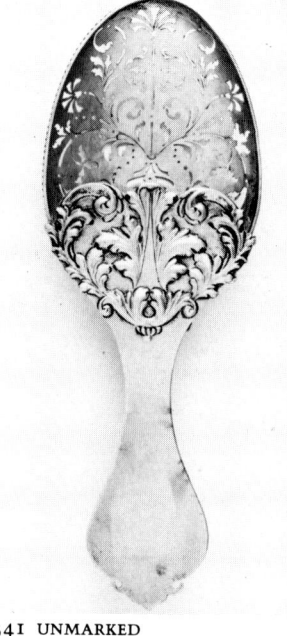

340 BLENCKE   341 UNMARKED

   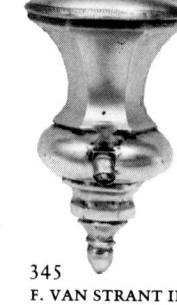

342 W. VAN STRANT   343 W. VAN STRANT   344 W. VAN STRANT   345 F. VAN STRANT II

346 F. VAN STRANT II   347 F. VAN STRANT II   348 A. VAN GEFFEN   349 A. VAN GEFFEN

  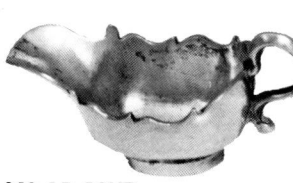

350 J.A. VAN GEFFEN   351 DULLER   352 J.D. PONT

Bernardus Blencke
Groningen
Mark B.B.; see catalogue of exhibition, 'Groninger Zilver'

340 Snuffers and stand
Groningen, 1742
10 oz 2 dwt (315 gr)
Amsterdam, 20–23 I 1975, 1200
DFl.7,200 (£1,297 $2,983)

Unmarked

341 Sugar sifter
Probably Friesland, 18th century
8 in (20.3 cm) overall
3 oz (93 gr)
New York, 28 X 1980, 142
$550 (£265)

Willem van Strant
Amsterdam; uncle of Frederick van Strant II (see below), born 1682, master 1727, died 1742
Mark Citroen (Amsterdam), 899

342 Miniature tea kettle
Amsterdam, 1734
2 in (5.5 cm) high
London, 20 X 1977, 92
£99 ($183)

343 Miniature: child
Amsterdam, 1737
1 in (3 cm) high
London, 4 V 1978, 44
£132 ($244)

344 Miniature coffee grinder
Amsterdam, 1738
1½ in (3.8 cm) high
London, 22 X 1970, 59
£80 ($192)

Frederik van Strant II
Amsterdam; born 1709, master 1727, died c. 1749
Mark Citroen (Amsterdam), 235

345 Miniature water cistern
Amsterdam, 1738
3¾ in (7.3 cm) high
London, 22 X 1970, 66
£80 ($192)

346 Miniature tea kettle
Amsterdam, 1738
2¼ in (5.5 cm) high
New York, 18 VI 1974, 51
$300 (£125)

347 Miniature coffee urn
Amsterdam, 1738
2¾ in (7.2 cm) high
New York, 18 VI 1974, 48
$475 (£197)

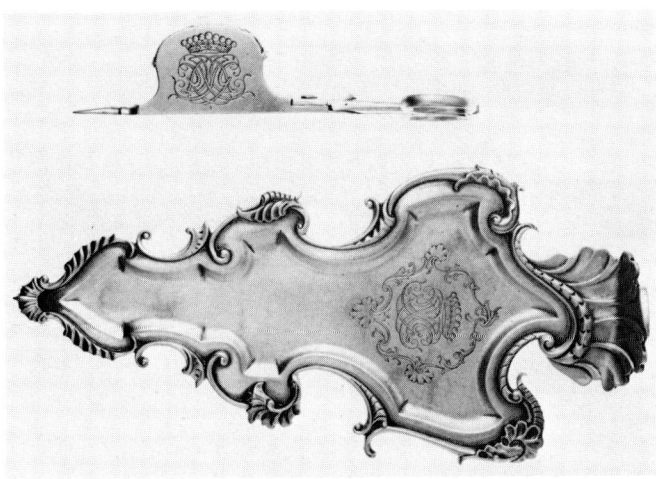

353 J.D. PONT

Arnoldus van Geffen
Amsterdam; born 1700, master 1728, died 1769
Mark Citroen (Amsterdam), 1199

348 Miniature bird cage
Amsterdam, 1745
3 in (7.8 cm) high
London, 22 X 1970, 68
£160 ($384)

349 Miniature brazier
Amsterdam, 1768
1½ in (4.2 cm) diameter
London, 20 X 1977, 103
£165 ($305)

354 J.D. PONT

Johannes Adrianus van Geffen
Amsterdam; born 1734, master 1766, died 1795
Mark Citroen (Amsterdam), 1218

350 Miniature: milkmaid
Amsterdam, 1772
1½ in (3.7 cm) high
London, 4 V 1978, 46
£176 ($325)

Hendrik Duller
Amsterdam; born 1749, master 1776, active until c. 1811, died 1820
Mark Citroen (Amsterdam), 308

351 Miniature tobacco box
Amsterdam, 1787
1¼ in (3.2 cm) diameter
London, 20 X 1977, 102
£121 ($223)

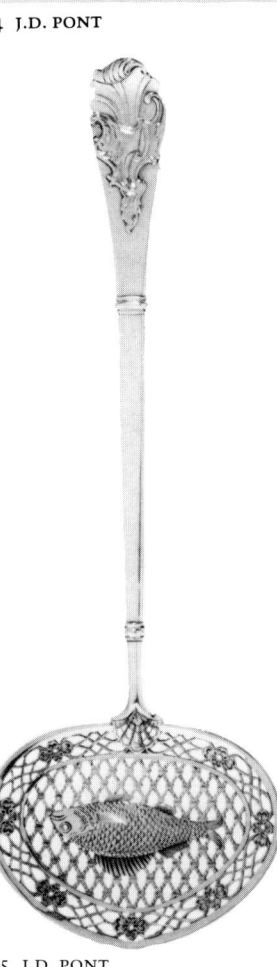

355 J.D. PONT

356 M. DE HAAN

357 M. DE HAAN

Jan Diederik Pont
Amsterdam; born 1702, master 1729, died 1767
Mark Citroen (Amsterdam), 716

352 Miniature sauceboats, pair
Amsterdam, 1749
2 in (5 cm) overall
London, 20 X 1977, 105
£528 ($976)

353 Snuffers stand and pair of snuffers
Amsterdam, 1756
9 oz 18 dwt (307 gr)
London, 26 II 1976, 102
£2,530 ($4,554)

354 Tobacco box
Amsterdam, c. 1755
6 in (15.5 cm) high
20 oz 18 dwt (650 gr)
Geneva, 12 V 1983, 7
SFr.9,350 (£2,791 $4,465)

358 R. DE HAAN

355 Fish slice
Amsterdam, 1760
15 in (38 cm) overall
6 oz 15 dwt (210 gr)
London, 21 II 1980, 143
£1,265 ($2,972)

Marcelus de Haan
The Hague; born 1707, master 1731, died 1790
Mark Voet (The Hague), 125

356 Caster
The Hague, c. 1730
4 in (10 cm) high
3 oz 2 dwt (96 gr)
London, 11 II 1971, 91
£230 ($552)

357 Tea caddies, pair
The Hague, 1739
5¼ in (13.3 cm) high
13 oz (404 gr)
London, 14 XI 1968, 171
£850 ($2,040)

Reynier de Haan
The Hague; born 1712, master 1731, died 1783, brother-in-law of Gregorius van der Toorn (see below, no.359).
Mark Voet (The Hague), 106

358 Casters, pair
The Hague, 1781
9½ in (24.2 cm) high
28 oz 10 dwt (888 gr)
Geneva, 15 V 1984, 26
SFr.11,000 (£3,514 $4,884)

359 G. VAN DER TOORN

360 BRANDT

361 BRANDT

362 BRANDT

363 BRANDT

364 BRANDT

Gregorius van der Toorn
The Hague; born 1715, master 1738, died 1768
Mark Voet (The Hague), 103

359 Punch bowl
The Hague, 1768
24¾ in (63 cm) overall
195 oz 11 dwt (6,081 gr)
Arms: probably Hillebrandes

London, 25 X 1973, 88
£12,000 ($28,800)

Reynier Brandt
Amsterdam; born 1702, master 1734, died 1788
Mark Citroen (Amsterdam), 783

360 Salvers, pair
Amsterdam, 1763
11½ in (29.2 cm) wide
55 oz 5 dwt (1,718 gr)
New York, 1–2 III 1978, 445
$5,250 (£2,837)

361 Cake basket
Amsterdam, 1769
15¾ in (40 cm) wide
32 oz 12 dwt (1,016 gr)
Amsterdam, 16 III 1983, 4053
DFl.27,840 (£6,145 $9,832)

362 Cake basket
Amsterdam, 1776
9½ in (24 cm) wide
21 oz 4 dwt (660 gr)
Geneva, 15 XI 1983, 42
SFr.7,700 (£2,460 $3,419)

363 Salver
Amsterdam, 1782
9¾ in (24.8 cm) square
19 oz (591 gr)
New York, 18–19 II 1981, 419
$1,562 (£754)

364 Coffee urn on lamp stand
Amsterdam, *c.* 1760
14¾ in (37.5 cm) high
72 oz (2,239 gr)
New York, 16–17 IV 1980, 440
$11,000 (£4,680)

Rudolph Sondagh
Rotterdam; born 1726, master 1746, died 1812. Sondagh was the most important silversmith in Rotterdam.
Mark a sun; see catalogue of exhibition, 'Dutch Silver 1580–1830'

365 Tobacco box
Rotterdam, 1764
6¾ in (17 cm) high
18 oz 4 dwt (567 gr)
Amsterdam, 16 III 1983, 4050
DFl.8,584 (£1,894 $3,030)

366 Salt cellars, pair
Rotterdam, 1780
5 in (12.5 cm) overall
4 oz 17 dwt (150 gr)
London, 15 II 1979, 130
£286 ($586)

367 Candlesticks, pair
Rotterdam, 1796
12½ in (32 cm) high
37 oz 10 dwt (1,169 gr)
Amsterdam, 16 III 1983, 4062
DFl.8,584 (£1,895 $3,032)

365 SONDAGH

366 SONDAGH

Willem Pont
Amsterdam; born 1733, master 1755, died 1797
Mark Citroen (Amsterdam), 718

368 Fish slice
Amsterdam, 1772
15¼ in (39 cm) overall
6 oz 14 dwt (208 gr)
London, 9 XII 1976, 77
£616 ($1,047)

Cornelis de Haan
The Hague; born 1735 son of Marcelus; master 1755, died 1788
Mark Voet (The Hague), 128

369 Table bell
silver-gilt
The Hague, 1775
5½ in (14 cm) high
10 oz 10 dwt (326 gr)
Lennoxlove, 24 VI 1980, 302
£2,640 ($6,204)

370 Cake basket
The Hague, 1777
17 in (45.5 cm) wide
49 oz 10 dwt (1,540 gr)
London, 20 X 1966, 80
£1,350 ($3,780)

371 Candlesticks, pair
The Hague, 1770
9 in (23 cm) high
34 oz 19 dwt (1,087 gr)
London, 11 II 1971, 181
£800 ($1,920)

372 Candlesticks, pair
The Hague, 1778
9½ in (24 cm) high
34 oz 13 dwt (1,080 gr)
London, 19 XII 1963, 77
£550 ($1,540)

367 SONDAGH

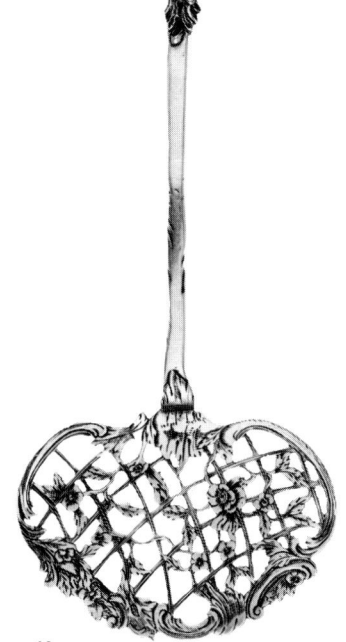

368 W. PONT

369 C. DE HAAN

370 C. DE HAAN

371 C. DE HAAN   372 C. DE HAAN

373 M. VAN STAPELE

374 M. VAN STAPELE

375 M. VAN STAPELE

376 M. VAN STAPELE

Martinus van Stapele

The Hague; born 1731, son of François van Stapele (see above, no.338f.); master 1757, died 1806
Mark Voet (The Hague), 130

373 Candlesticks, four
The Hague, 1782
9½ in (24 cm) high
62 oz (1,928 gr)
New York, 3–4 X 1974, 152
$3,600 (£1,500)

374 Candlesticks, six
The Hague, 1792
11¾ in (29.9 cm) high
109 oz 6 dwt (3,400 gr)
Geneva, 15 XI 1983, 35
SFr.24,200 (£7,731 $10,746)

375 Tea caddies, three, in a filigree box
The Hague, 1786
87 oz (2,710 gr)
Amsterdam, 20–23 I 1975, 344
DFl.3,400 (£612 $1,407)

376 Sauceboats, pair
The Hague, 1785
8 in (20.3 cm) overall
26 oz 19 dwt (838 gr)
London, 9 XII 1976, 129
£3,190 ($5,423)

377 L'HERMINOTTE

Joannes Andreas Gerardus l'Herminotte

Maastricht
Mark I.L. Szenassy, *Maastrichts Zilver*, Maastricht, 1978, p.190

377 Candlesticks, pair
Maastricht, 1758–60
8½ in (21.6 cm) high
25 oz 4 dwt (785 gr)
Geneva, 5 V 1981, 177
SFr.15,400 (£3,590 $7,431)

378 Caster and mustard pot
Maastricht, 1770–72
7½ in (19 cm) and 6¾ in (17 cm) high
14 oz 10 dwt (454 gr)
Amsterdam, 16 III 1983, 4031
DFl.13,920 (£3,072 $4,915)

378 L'HERMINOTTE

379 L'HERMINOTTE

379 Sauceboats, pair
Maastricht, 1768–70
6½ in (16.5 cm) overall
24 oz (745 gr)
Geneva, 15 V 1984, 31
SFr.13,200 (£4,217 $5,861)

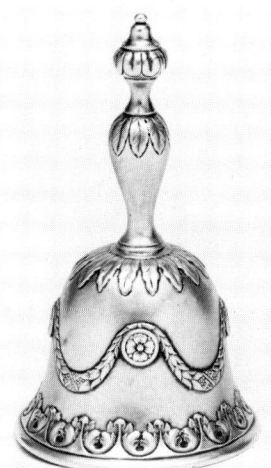

380 SCHIOTLING

Johannes Schiotling

Amsterdam; born 1730 in Gothenburg, master 1762, died 1799. See catalogue of exhibition, 'Johannes Schiotling'.
Mark Citroen (Amsterdam), 573–575

380 Bell
Amsterdam, 1776
5¾ in (14.5 cm) high
8 oz 11 dwt (265 gr)
London, 3 XII 1964, 72
£215 ($602)

381 Cruet
Amsterdam, 1777
11¼ in (28.5 cm) wide
41 oz 10 dwt (1,290 gr)
New York, 26–27 X 1976, 110
$5,250 (£3,088)

382 Tray
Amsterdam, 1785
20 in (51 cm) overall
83 oz 10 dwt (2,596 gr)
New York, 4–5 XII 1974, 227
$3,700 (£1,608)

383 Tobacco box
Amsterdam, 1782
23 oz 18 dwt (743 gr)
Amsterdam, 20–23 I 1975, 480
DFl.3,400 (£612 $1,407)

384 Tobacco box
Amsterdam, 1789
6¾ in (17.4 cm) high
19 oz 2 dwt (594 gr)
London, 3 VII 1980, 179
£3,520 ($8,272)

385 Teapot and hot water jug
Amsterdam, 1786/90
4 in (10 cm) and 4¾ in (12 cm) high
19 oz 4 dwt (600 gr)
Amsterdam, 9 XI 1978, 495
DFl.6,600 (£1,534 $3,144)

381 SCHIOTLING

382 SCHIOTLING

383 SCHIOTLING

384 SCHIOTLING

385 SCHIOTLING

386 NIEWENHUYS

387 NIEWENHUYS

388 NIEWENHUYS

389 SMIT

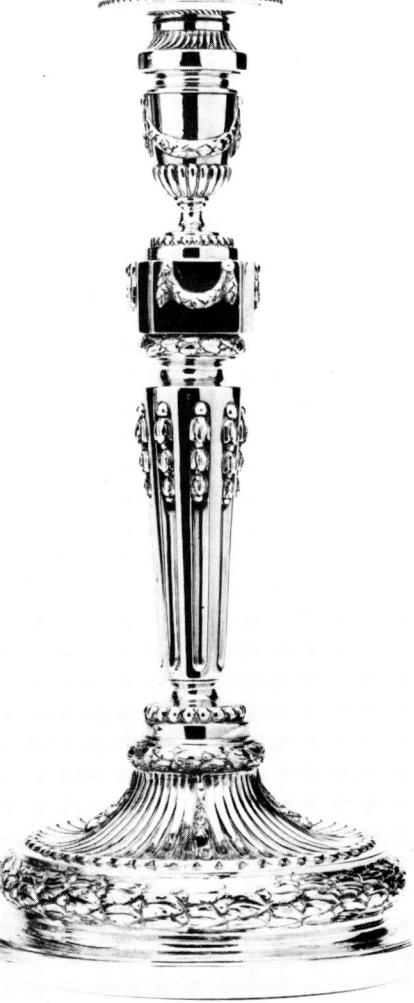

390 SMIT

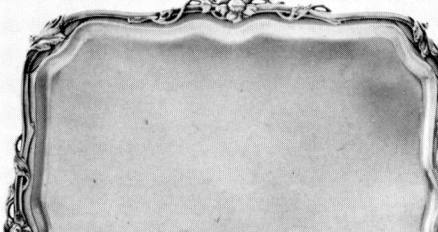

391 J. VAN DER TOORN

Hendrik Niewenhuys

Amsterdam; born 1742, master 1763, died 1803
Mark Citroen (Amsterdam), 346, 347

386 Sauce tureen and cover
Amsterdam, 1765
8 in (20 cm) wide
14 oz 4 dwt (443 gr)
Amsterdam, 16 III 1983, 4049
DFl.19,720 (£4,353 $6,964)

387 Teapot
Amsterdam, 1766
5 in (13 cm) high
14 oz 6 dwt (445 gr)
Amsterdam, 22 V 1981, 835
DFl.6,960 (£1,298 $2,686)

388 Tobacco box
Amsterdam, 1779
5¾ in (14.6 cm) wide
15 oz 12 dwt (485 gr)
London, 20 VII 1978, 94
£2,090 ($3,866)

Jan Smit
Amsterdam; born 1741 in Nijmegen, master 1769, died 1796
Mark Citroen (Amsterdam), 1220

389 Candlesticks, four
Amsterdam, 1784
10¾ in (27.5 cm) high
86 oz 12 dwt (2,693 gr)
London, 2 VI 1977, 107
£6,600 ($11,220)

390 Candlesticks, pair
Amsterdam, 1778
11¾ in (30 cm) high
Amsterdam, 9 XI 1978, 573
DFl.15,500 (£3,604 $7,388)

Johannes van der Toorn
The Hague; born 1747, master 1771, died 1832.
Mark Voet (The Hague), 145–6

391 Salver
The Hague, 1777
11 in (28.3 cm) square
23 oz 11 dwt (732 gr)
London, 14 XII 1972, 138
£520 ($1,300)

392 Tea caddies, three, in satinwood case
The Hague, 1783
4¼ in (10.8 cm) high
16 oz 5 dwt (505 gr)
London, 11 II 1971, 84
£450 ($1,080)

Gerardus Hendrikus Nieuwenhuzen
Leiden; born c. 1768, master 1792
Mark Catalogue of exhibition, 'Leids Zilver', p.161

394 Tea caddy
Leiden, 1804
4½ in (11.7 cm) high
10 oz 12 dwt (329 gr)
London, 16 XI 1978, 178
£638 ($1,307)

Anton Hendrik Paap
Amsterdam; born 1746, master 1775, died 1816
Mark Citroen (Amsterdam), 36–37

393 Candlesticks, eight
Amsterdam, 1789
11 in (28 cm) high
123 oz 14 dwt (3,847 gr)
London, 17 VI 1971, 125
£2,400 ($5,760)

392 J. VAN DER TOORN

394 NIEWENHUZEN

393 PAAP

396 J. DUFOUR ET FRÈRES

397 J. DUFOUR ET FRÈRES

Jean Dufour et Frères
Brussels; goldsmiths to the King of the Belgians from 1857

396 Ewer
Brussels, c. 1868
10¼ in (26 cm) high
31 oz 14 dwt (985 gr)
London (Belgravia), 24 II 1972, 38
£230 ($575)

397 Tea kettle on lamp stand
Brussels, c. 1868
20½ in (52 cm) high
94 oz 1 dwt (2,925 gr)
London (Belgravia), 20 VII 1972, 76
£390 ($975)

J.A. Bonnebakker
Amsterdam; active 1822–53, the firm continued as Bonnebakker and Zn (1854–1944)
Mark Meestertekens, 5127

395 Candlesticks, four
silver (loaded)
Amsterdam, c. 1840
11 in (28 cm) high
New York, 28 X 1980, 134
$1,870 (£903)

395 BONNEBAKKER

Great Britain
Ireland

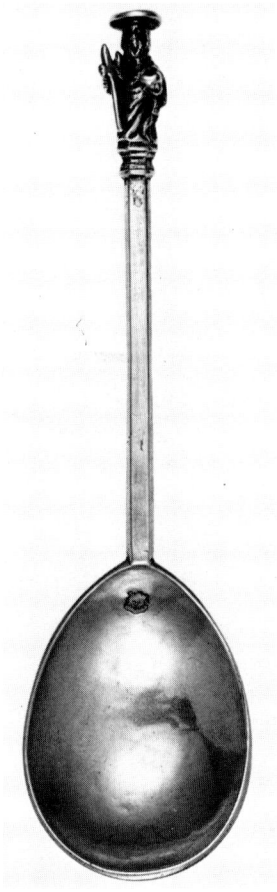

398 D ENCLOSING C

Daniel Cary
London; free 1604, died 1641/2
Mark Kent p.19, Jackson p.119
(D enclosing C)

398 Apostle spoon, St Matthias
London, 1622
London, 15 VI 1978, 59
£990 ($1,831)

399 Apostle spoon, St Bartholomew
London, 1622
London, 9 V 1974, 38
£550 ($1,320)

399 D ENCLOSING C

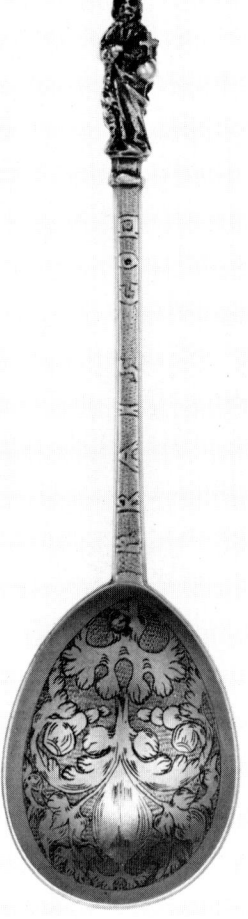

400 QUYCKE FAMILY

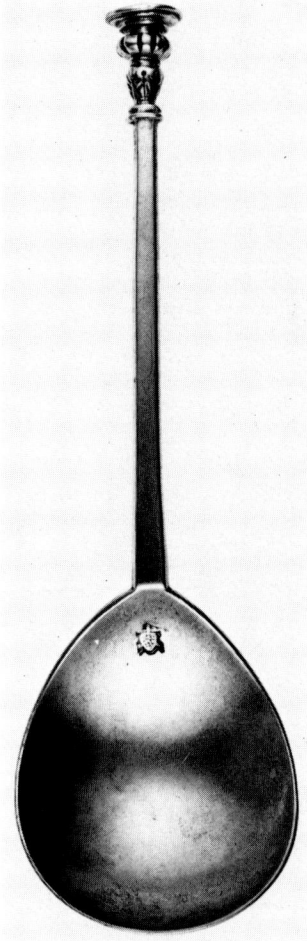

401 QUYCKE FAMILY

Quycke family
Barnstaple; Peter Quycke I and his son Peter (born 1575) recorded in late 16th/early 17th century. John (active c. 1590–1630) may have been another son of Peter Quycke I.
Mark See How, vol.II, pp.202–6

400 Spoon, the Master
Attributed to John Quycke
silver-gilt
Barnstaple, c. 1600
See How, op. cit., ch.II sect. VII, pls 14, 15.
London, 18 XI 1976, 112
£1,870 ($3,179)

401 Spoon, seal top
Barnstaple, c. 1610
London, 9 V 1974, 43
£500 ($1,200)

402 Spoon, Buddha knop
parcel-gilt
Barnstaple, c. 1620
London, 15 VI 1978, 63
£935 ($1,729)

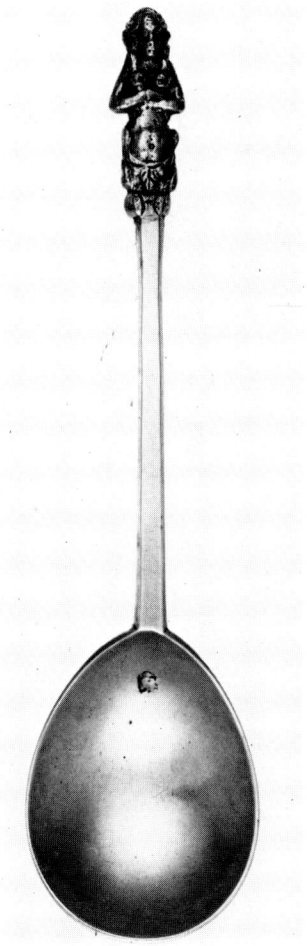

402 QUYCKE FAMILY

403 A B CONJOINED

404 A B CONJOINED

405 A B CONJOINED

406 A B CONJOINED

407 CB IN MONOGRAM

408 CB IN MONOGRAM

AB conjoined
London
Mark Jackson, p.109

403 Wine cup
London, 1597
4 in (10.2 cm) high
4 oz 19 dwt (150 gr)
London, 1 II 1968, 162
£800 ($1,920)

404 Wine cup
London, 1605
7 in (17.8 cm) high
6 oz 5 dwt (194 gr)
London, 1 II 1973, 140
£2,600 ($6,500)

405 Wine cup
silver-gilt
London, 1606
8 in (20.3 cm) high
9 oz 14 dwt (301 gr)
London, 8 VI 1972, 92
£4,200 ($10,500)

406 Wine cup
silver-gilt
London, 1607
5½ in (14 cm) high
4 oz 5 dwt (132 gr)
London, 19 X 1961, 152
£1,100 ($3,080)

CB in monogram
London
Mark Jackson, p.119

407 Dessert stand
London, 1619
9 in (22.9 cm) diameter
11 oz 12 dwt (360 gr)
London, 16 III 1961, 133
£1,250 ($3,512)

408 Dish
London, 1631
11¾ in (29.8 cm) diameter
19 oz 10 dwt (606 gr)
London, 31 I 1963, 152
£1,300 ($3,640)

409 HOUND SEJANT

410 HOUND SEJANT

411 HOUND SEJANT

Hound Sejant

London; active mid-17th century; worked chiefly for Royalist clients. See Oman, *Caroline Silver*, p.27: 'the most important goldsmith active in the middle years of the century'.
Mark Jackson, p.123

409 Porringer (bleeding bowl)
London, 1649
5¼ in (13.3 cm) diameter
8 oz (248 gr)
Arms: Weld impaling Pindar
New York, 1–2 III 1978, 731
$6,000 (£3,243)

410 Sweetmeat box
London 1650
7¾ in (19.7 cm) wide
17 oz 16 dwt (553 gr)
Arms: Weld impaling Pindar for George Weld of Willey Park, co.Salop, and his wife, Mary.
London, 12 XII 1974, 203
£9,000 ($20,700)

411 Porringer and cover
(London), c. 1650
Maker's mark only
9 in (22.8 cm) high
48 oz (1,492 gr)
Arms: Berkeley
London, 16 III 1961, 147
£6,500 ($18,265)

Patrick Borthwick

Edinburgh; admitted to Incorporation 1642
Mark Jackson, p.499

412 Communion cups, pair
(Edinburgh), c. 1645
Deacon: Adam Lamb
9 in (23.2 cm) high
62 oz 5 dwt (1,935 gr)
Inscribed: For the Kirke of Hadingtoune 1645
London, 30 XI 1972, 113
£20,000 ($50,000)

Unmarked

413 Gaming counters, thirty-six in a box
English, c. 1631
1 in (2.6 cm) diameter
Each counter bears a portrait of one of the twenty-seven crowned kings and queens of England from Edward the Confessor to Charles I; Mary, Queen of Scots and Henry, Earl of Darnley (parents of James I); Anne of Denmark (James I's wife); Frederick and Elizabeth of Bohemia and their son (James's and Anne's daughter and son-in-law); Henrietta Maria, Henry, Prince of Wales and Prince Charles (later Charles II) as a child.
London, 18 IX 1975, 93
£385 ($770)

412 BORTHWICK

413 UNMARKED

417 T. MAUNDY

419 W. MAUNDY

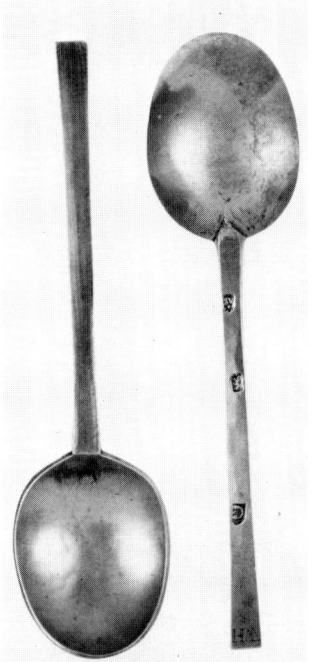
414 415 VENABLES

418 T. MAUNDY

420 IN

416 UNMARKED

Stephen Venables
London; baptized 1613/14, apprenticed to Daniel Cary, free 1640, died 1683
Mark Kent, p.20

414 Puritan spoon
London, 1655
1 oz 14 dwt (52 gr)
London, 18 VI 1981, 63
£1,155 ($2,390)

415 Puritan spoons, pair
London, 1671
4 oz 4 dwt (130 gr)
London, 18 VI 1981, 60
£2,860 ($5,920)

Unmarked

416 Recusant chalice and paten
Sold with a pyx
English, c. 1650
5¾ in (14.6 cm) high
9 oz 5 dwt (287 gr)
London, 18 XI 1976, 109
£572 ($972)

Thomas Maundy
London; active c. 1640–65
Mark Jackson, p.122

417 Sweetmeat dish
London, 1641
6¼ in (15.9 cm) wide
2 oz 18 dwt (90 gr)
London, 12 XII 1974, 96
£600 ($1,380)

418 Bowl
London, 1640
10¾ in (27.3 cm) diameter
15 oz 3 dwt (471 gr)
London, 24 IV 1969, 265
£5,500 ($13,200)

William Maundy
London; active c. 1630–34
Mark Jackson, p.119

419 Sweetmeat dish
London, 1633
8¼ in (21 cm) diameter
8 oz 1 dwt (250 gr)
London, 12 XII 1974, 100
£1,550 ($3,565)

IN with bird below
London
Mark Jackson, p.128

420 Porringer
silver-gilt
London, 1661
9 in (22.8 cm) high
33 oz 15 dwt (1,049 gr)
Arms: Sir Edward Walker, Garter King of Arms (died 1676)
London, 8 VI 1972, 85
£26,000 ($65,000)

421 SHEPHERD

422 SHEPHERD

423 SHEPHERD

424 MANWARING

425 MANWARING

426 MANWARING

Gilbert Shepherd

London; free 1631, died by 1668.
See Oman, *Caroline Silver*, p.40
Mark Jackson, p.127

421 Porringer
London, 1659
3½ in (8.9 cm) high
8 oz 16 dwt (273 gr)
London, 20 VII 1978, 196
£1,540 ($2,849)

422 Caudle cup and cover
London, 1660
6¼ in (15.9 cm) high
12 oz 2 dwt (376 gr)
London, 17 VI 1971, 170
£1,050 ($2,520)

423 Dram cup
London, 1660
2¾ in (7 cm) high
1 oz 13 dwt (51 gr)
London, 19 VII 1982, 76
£1,540 ($2,756)

Arthur Manwaring

London; active *c.* 1643–96. See
Oman *Caroline Silver*, pp.30–31
Mark Jackson, p.124 (attributed
to A. Moore)

424 Porringer and salver-on-foot
silver-gilt (later)
London, 1655
Salver: 11¼ in (28.6 cm)
diameter
Porringer: 4¾ in (12.1 cm) high
43 oz 17 dwt (1,363 gr)
London, 24 III 1960, 42
£1,200 ($3,372)

427 MANWARING

428 MANWARING

429 MANWARING

430 MANWARING

431 MANWARING

425 Porringer and salver-on-foot
London, 1657
Salver: 13¼ in (33.6 cm) diameter
Porringer: 5½ in (14 cm) high
44 oz 4 dwt (1,374 gr)
London, 2 VI 1977, 247
£8,800 ($14,960)

426 Basin
London, 1650
13¼ in (33.7 cm) diameter
39 oz 12 dwt (1,231 gr)
London, 25 X 1973, 148
£3,200 ($7,680)

427 Porringer and cover
London, 1657
6 in (15 cm) diameter
22 oz 10 dwt (699 gr)
New York, 20–23 IV 1983, 325
$20,900 (£13,062)

428 Caudle cup and cover
London, 1659
7 in (17.8 cm) high
34 oz (1,057 gr)
London, 10 II 1949, 145
£850 ($3,425)

429 Salver-on-foot
London, 1657
15¼ in (39 cm) diameter
46 oz 17 dwt (1,457 gr)
Arms: Chester of Amesbury, co.Wilts
Illus. Oman, *Caroline Silver*, pl.19A
London, 18 I 1962, 161
£3,200 ($8,992)

430 Beakers, pair
(London), c. 1660
Maker's mark only
12 in (30.5 cm) high
55 oz 15 dwt (1,733 gr)
London, 22 XI 1951, 123
£230 ($644)

431 Toilet set
Rectangular casket, octagonal boxes and powder vases Manwaring, 1673 and c. 1673; the remainder unmarked or by others, c. 1675.
London, 5 II 1970, 211
£4,000 ($9,600)

432 Tankard
London, 1677
8 in (20.3 cm) high
41 oz 17 dwt (1,301 gr)
Arms: 9th Earl of Rutland, who married 1673/4 Katherine, daughter of 3rd Viscount Campden.
London, 20 VI 1974, 87
£6,500 ($15,600)

433 Salver-on-foot
silver-gilt
London, 1677
8½ in (21.6 cm) diameter
11 oz 14 dwt (363 gr)
Lot 156 in this sale was a chalice and paten, Manwaring, 1677, bearing the same armorials
London, 8 IV 1948, 155
£320 ($1,289)

432 MANWARING

433 MANWARING

John Plummer

York; free 1648, active until c. 1688. See Oman *Caroline Silver*, p.20: 'The most important provincial goldsmith of this period'; Oman, *English Engraved Silver*, pp.66–9
Mark Jackson, p.290

434 Tankard
York, 1649
6 in (15.2 cm) high
16 oz 17 dwt (524 gr)
The barrel is engraved with the cardinal virtues and the temptation of Eve; the cover is inscribed: 'When this you se remember me' 'whome God Joynes together let no man separate'.
London, 30 XI 1978, 95
£11,000 ($22,550)

435 Tankard
York, 1663
7¾ in (19.7 cm) high
29 oz 12 dwt (920 gr)
London, 24 VII 1975, 183
£3,100 ($7,130)

436 Porringer and cover
York, 1657
6½ in (16.5 cm) high
22 oz 18 dwt (712 gr)
Exhibition: Park Lane, no.97
London, 16 III 1961, 144
£1,800 ($5,058)

437 Tankard
York, 1673
8 in (20.3 cm) high
32 oz 18 dwt (1,023 gr)
London, 27 VI 1963, 11
£980 ($2,744)

438 Bowl
York, 1659
2 in (4.9 cm) high
3 oz 12 dwt (115 gr)
Monaco, 1 XII 1975, 324
FFr.6,820 (£757 $1,514)

434 PLUMMER

435 PLUMMER

436 PLUMMER

437 PLUMMER

438 PLUMMER

439 ORB & CROSS

440 ORB & CROSS

441 F.W.

442 F.W.

443 RF

Orb and Cross
London
Mark Jackson, p.127

439 Salver-on-foot
London, 1659
15½ in (39.4 cm) diameter
30 oz 15 dwt (1,205 gr)
London, 16 VII 1970, 31
£1,350 ($3,240)

440 Salver-on-foot
London, 1660
15¾ in (40 cm) diameter
44 oz 10 dwt (1,383 gr)
London, 5 VII 1956, 51
£600 ($1,680)

F.W.
London
Mark Jackson, p.131

441 Flagon
silver-gilt
London, 1663
12 in (30.5 cm) high
51 oz 5 dwt (1,593 gr)
See no.433.
London, 8 IV 1948, 154
£850 ($3,425)

442 Tankard
London, 1664
6¼ in (15.9 cm) high
21 oz 3 dwt (657 gr)
London, 6 XII 1979, 73
£5,500 ($12,925)

RF, mullet below
London
Mark Jackson, p.124

443 Tankard
London, 1654
8 in (20.3 cm) high
36 oz 4 dwt (1,125 gr)
New York, 17 VI 1981, 49
$30,800 (£14,880)

444 SMYTHIER

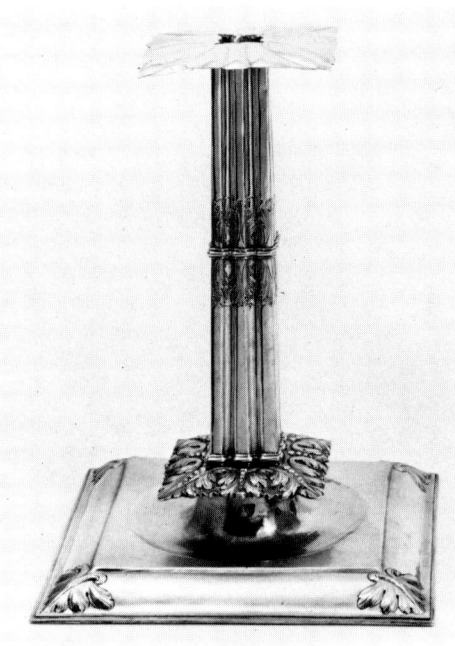

446 BODENDICK

445 UNMARKED

447 BODENDICK

448 BODENDICK

449 BODENDICK

Robert Smythier

London; free 1660, died before 1689. See Oman, *Caroline Silver*, p.31: 'Probably more plate has survived bearing the mark S crowned than any other ... in the reign of Charles II'.
Mark Jackson, p.137

444 Candlesticks, two
silver-gilt
London, 1670/76
One maker's mark: IH
6¾ in (17.1 cm) high
36 oz 19 dwt (1,149 gr)
London, 13 VI 1983, 16
£20,900 ($33,440)

Unmarked

445 Cup and cover
gold
English, c. 1665
3½ in (9 cm) high
8 oz 14 dwt (270 gr)
London, 24 III 1960, 41
£1,000 ($2,810)

Jacob Bodendick

London; 'native of the city of Limburg, Germany', granted denization 1661; active not later than 1688. Several of his pieces are in the German style. See Oman, *Caroline Silver*, pp.34–5; catalogue of exhibition, 'Touching Gold and Silver', no.65
Mark Jackson, p.130 (IB crescent below)

446 Candlesticks, pair
London, 1669
12¼ in (31.1 cm) high
84 oz 12 dwt (2,631 gr)
For a similar pair of candlesticks by Bodendick (1667), see catalogue of sale, London 2 VI 1977, 232.
London, 12 XII 1974, 202
£38,000 ($87,400)

447 Tankard
parcel-gilt
(London), c. 1670
Maker's mark only
6¾ in (17.2 cm) high
48 oz 13 dwt (1,516 gr)
London, 19 V 1955, 82
£250 ($697)

450 BODENDICK

451 BODENDICK

452 BODENDICK

448 Tankard
silver-gilt and carved walnut root
London, 1664
8¼ in (21 cm) high
London, 12 XII 1974, 151
£3,000 ($6,900)

449 Tankard
parcel-gilt
London, 1674
7¾ in (19.7 cm) high
41 oz 3 dwt (1,279 gr)
Arms: Hunhulton
The scene round the barrel represents Mercury, Venus, Cupid and Diana with Mars and Minerva in a wooded landscape.
London, 19 XI 1970, 229
£1,850 ($4,440)

450 Tankard
(London), c. 1670
Maker's mark only
9¼ in (23.5 cm) high
72 oz 8 dwt (2,251 gr)
London, 14 VII 1960, 118
£500 ($1,405)

451 Vases, pair
London, 1674
13½ in (34.3 cm) high
71 oz (2,208 gr)
New York, 11–12 XI 1975, 259
$13,000 (£6,500)

452 Sweetmeat dish
London, 1671
8½ in (21.6 cm) overall
6 oz 8 dwt (199 gr)
London, 8 VII 1936, 124
£121.12.0d ($596)

453 Ginger jar
London, 1674
20 in (50.8 cm) high
108 oz 14 dwt (3,380 gr)
London, 17 XI 1960, 174
£1,250 ($3,512)

453 BODENDICK

454 BODENDICK

455 BODENDICK

454 Porringer and cover
London, 1668
6 in (15.2 cm) high
22 oz 19 dwt (713 gr)
London, 16 III 1961, 122
£1,150 ($3,231)

455 Porringer and cover
silver-gilt
(London), c. 1670
Maker's mark only
8 in (20.3 cm) high
45 oz 16 dwt (1,424 gr)
London, 15 XII 1966, 180
£520 ($1,456)

456 BODENDICK

456 Candlesticks, pair
silver-gilt
(London), c. 1675
Maker's mark only
9¾ in (24.8 cm) high
61 oz 11 dwt (1,914 gr)
London, 9 VII 1964, 106
£2,100 ($5,880)

457 Toilet water bottles, pair
(London), c. 1680
Maker's mark only
6 in (15.2 cm) high
23 oz (715 gr)
Probably the bottles from the set, no.458
London, 15 VI 1978, 127
£1,012 ($1,872)

458 Toilet set
(London), c. 1680
Mirror: 21½ in (54.6 cm) high
Boxes: 3½ in (8.9 cm) diameter
London, 22 XI 1951, 124, 125
124 (mirror): £210 ($588); 125 (pair scent bottles and pair boxes): £200 ($560)

459 Toilet boxes, pair
London, 1680
3½ in (8.9 cm) diameter
14 oz 11 dwt (452 gr)
London, 15 VI 1978, 128
£2,860 ($5,291)

457 BODENDICK

Unmarked

460 Tray
English, c. 1670
26½ in (67.3 cm) overall
97 oz (3,016 gr)
New York, 6–7 II 1980, 767
$10,560 (£4,493)

461 Andirons, pair
English, c. 1670
18½ in (47 cm) high
168 oz 10 dwt (5,240 gr)
Cypher: crowned, of Charles II
Compare Christie's, 29 May 1963, lot 23: a pair of andirons, maker's mark GC in monogram
London, 8 VII 1936, 147
£360 ($1,774)

458 BODENDICK

459 BODENDICK

460 UNMARKED

461 UNMARKED

463 UNMARKED

464 UNMARKED

462 UNMARKED

462 Cup and cover
parcel-gilt
English, c. 1675
8 in (20.5 cm) high
44 oz 2 dwt (1,371 gr)
London, 4 III 1965, 168
£360 ($1,008)

465 UNMARKED

463 Ginger jars, three
silver-gilt
English, c. 1675
7½ in (19 cm) high
29 oz 16 dwt (926 gr)
London, 12 XII 1974, 192
£1,900 ($4,370)

464 Toilet set
English, c. 1680
158 oz (4,913 gr)
London, 20 VII 1978, 182
£22,000 ($40,700)

465 Incense burner
English, c. 1675
14¾ in (37.5 cm) high
78 oz 19 dwt (2,455 gr)
See Sir C.J. Jackson, *History of English Plate*, London, 1911, 2 vols, vol.I, fig.255 for another example
London, 1 II 1968, 100
£1,200 ($2,880)

466 UNMARKED

467 PR

468 JENKINS

469 JENKINS

466 Bowls and covers, pair
silver-gilt
English, c. 1680
Scratch weight: 15.16 and 15.11.
5¼ in (13.5 cm) diameter
31 oz 16 dwt (985 gr)
Provenance: Chatsworth collection
London, 19 VII 1982, 71
£5,280 ($9,451)

PR in cypher
London
Mark Jackson, p.140

467 Wax Jack
London, c. 1680
9¼ in (23.5 cm) high
26 oz 4 dwt (814 gr)
London, 16 III 1961, 140
£3,600 ($10,116)

Thomas Jenkins
London; active c. 1668–1705.
See A. Grimwade and J. Banister, 'Thomas Jenkins Unveiled', *Connoisseur*, July 1977.
Mark Jackson, pp.130, 142; Grimwade, 1422, 1430

468 Garniture; two ginger jars and two vases (illustrated)
London, 1675
Vases: 12 in (30.5 cm) high
118 oz (3,670 gr)
London, 2 XI 1950, 149
£1,600 ($4,480)

469 Wine cistern
London, 1677
18½ in (47 cm) wide
232 oz 18 dwt (7,243 gr)
Now in the Victoria and Albert Museum, London.
London, 9 V 1957, 147
£1,500 ($4,185)

470 Tankard
London, 1677
7¼ in (18.4 cm) high
32 oz 1 dwt (996 gr)
London, 20 II 1975, 141
£2,500 ($5,750)

471 Ewer and dish
London, 1686
Ewer: 9¼ in (23.5 cm) high
Dish: 21½ in (54.6 cm) diameter
157 oz 14 dwt (4,904 gr)
Inscribed: The Gift of Sr Tho Wagstaffe & Frances his wife to Edw: Bagot Esq. and Frances his wife ye 15 Apr: 1697.
See no.476
London, 18 V 1967, 167
£9,800 ($27,342)

470 JENKINS

473 JENKINS

471 JENKINS

474 JENKINS

472 JENKINS

475 JENKINS

472 Tankard
London, 1688
8½ in (21.6 cm) high
47 oz 13 dwt (1,481 gr)
London, 23 VII 1970, 162
£2,900 ($6,960)

473 Covered jugs, two
London, 1685/98
14 in (36 cm) high
186 oz (5,784 gr)
One jug bears the mark of Philip Rollos I overstruck by Thomas Jenkins (1698). See p.11
Exhibitions: Park Lane, 1929, no.139; Seaford House, 1929, no.401.
London, 20 II 1975, 178
£18,000 ($41,400)

474 Wall sconces, six
London, 1687
12½ in (31.7 cm) high
220 oz 10 dwt (6,857 gr)
Arms: Joliffe
London, 20 IV 1972, 100
£26,000 ($65,000)

475 Caudle cup and cover
London, 1698
9¼ in (23.5 cm) high
61 oz 10 dwt (1,912 gr)
New York, 2 XII 1975, 271
$4,750 (£2,375)

TK rosette below

London
Mark Jackson, p.132

476 Ewer
London, 1674
Scratchweight 33 oz 17 dwt
8½ in (21.6 cm) high
33 oz 9 dwt (1,040 gr)
Arms: Charles Salusbury of Bachymbydd, co. Denbigh, and his wife Elizabeth, whose daughter married Sir Walter Bagot, 3rd Bt. The recipient (their son) was born 1674.
Inscribed: The gifte of Mrs Elizabeth Salesbury to her Grande-childe Edward Bagot as an heire loome neauer to be changed
See no.471
London, 18 V 1967, 166
£4,000 ($11,200)

477 Salver
London, 1679
13¼ in (33.6 cm) diameter
32 oz 16 dwt (1,020 gr)
Arms: Ashburnham
London, 20 IV 1972, 102
£3,400 ($8,500)

478 Tankard
London, 1668
7 in (17.8 cm) high
30 oz 18 dwt (960 gr)
London, 27 VI 1963, 91
£860 ($2,408)

Francis Leake

London
Mark Jackson, p.126

479 Tankard
silver-gilt
London, 1675
8¼ in (21 cm) high
61 oz (1,897 gr)
Arms: General George Monck (1608–69), created Duke of Albermarle 1660.
London, 13 VI 1983, 25
£85,800 ($137,280)

John Sutton

London; free 1668
Mark Jackson, p.134; Grimwade, 2649

480 Tankard
London, 1674
6¾ in (17.2 cm) high
28 oz 14 dwt (892 gr)
London, 12 XII 1974, 70
£2,700 ($6,210)

476 TK

477 TK

478 TK

479 LEAKE

480 SUTTON

481 SUTTON

482 SUTTON

485 FELLING

Gabriel Felling

Bruton, Somerset; first recorded London 1676, then Bruton 1678; died 1714. See Kent, 'Gabriel Felling, Goldsmith of Bruton'.
Mark See Kent, cited above; GF and GF above a swan.

483 Tankard
(Bruton), c. 1683
Maker's mark only struck four times
7 in (18 cm) high
24 oz (764 gr)
London, 24 IV 1969, 258
£2,000 ($4,800)

484 Porringer
(Bruton), c. 1690
4¾ in (12.1 cm) high
13 oz 6 dwt (413 gr)
London, 18 VI 1981, 183
£2,640 ($5,464)

485 Porringer
(Bruton), c. 1687
4 in (10.2 cm) high
7 oz 5 dwt (225 gr)
London, 4 XII 1969, 140
£500 ($1,200)

486 Tankard
(Bruton), c. 1685
Maker's mark only struck four times
7 in (18 cm) high
23 oz 3 dwt (719 gr)
London, 29 IV 1976, 169
£2,310 ($4,158)

483 FELLING

486 FELLING

WF knot above

London
Mark Jackson, p.140

487 Toilet box
London, 1683
3½ in (8.9 cm) diameter
7 oz 6 dwt (227 gr)
London, 16 II 1978, 212
£1,210 ($2,238)

488 Casket
London, 1683
9¼ in (23.5 cm) wide
43 oz 11 dwt (1,354 gr)
Compare with a toilet set by this maker in the Victoria and Albert Museum, London.
London, 17 XI 1960, 99
£1,500 ($4,215)

484 FELLING

487 WF

481 Tankard
London, 1688
6¼ in (15.9 cm) high
22 oz 5 dwt (691 gr)
London, 18 VII 1974, 47
£1,200 ($2,880)

482 Porringer
London, 1692
2½ in (6.4 cm) high
3 oz 16 dwt (118 gr)
London, 28 XI 1968, 45
£1,800 ($4,320)

488 WF

Goose in a dotted circle
London; late 17th century
Mark Jackson, p.138

489 Porringer
London, 1680
3 in (7.6 cm) high
4 oz 10 dwt (140 gr)
London, 17 XI 1966, 139
£340 ($952)

490 Tankard
London, 1680
5¾ in (19.3 cm) high
37 oz (1,150 gr)
New York, 5–9 VI 1979, 599
$9,350 (£4,560)

491 Porringer and cover
London, 1686
7½ in (19 cm) high
32 oz 2 dwt (998 gr)
London, 24 VII 1980, 247
£23,100 ($54,285)

492 Tankards, two
London, 1681
6½ in (16.5 cm) and 8 in (20.3 cm) high
53 oz 17 dwt (1,674 gr)
London, 17 XI 1966, 131
£3,000 ($8,400)

493 Tankard
London, 1683
7 in (17.8 cm) high
37 oz 8 dwt (1,163 gr)
London, 19 VI 1958, 150
£580 ($1,629)

494 Flagons, two
London, 1687/90
9 in (22.9 cm) high
56 oz 7 dwt (1,752 gr)
Arms: Cooks Company; initialled M.G. for Matthew Gunnell, a liveryman of the company.
Provenance: Church of St Michael, Easthampstead, Berkshire
London, 14 X 1976, 137
£6,050 ($10,285)

495 Porringer
London, 1690
3½ in (8.9 cm) high
10 oz 10 dwt (326 gr)
London, 9 X 1969, 236
£2,000 ($4,800)

489 GOOSE

490 GOOSE

491 GOOSE

492 GOOSE

493 GOOSE

494 GOOSE

James Cockburne
Edinburgh; admitted to
Incorporation 1669
Mark Jackson, p.500

496 Tankards, pair
Edinburgh, 1685
Assay Master: John Borthwick
7 in (17.8 cm) high
65 oz 10 dwt (2,037 gr)
See Ian Finlay, *Scottish Gold
and Silverwork*, London, 1956,
p.116.
London, 24 III 1960, 37
£4,600 ($12,926)

497 Mugs, pair
Edinburgh, 1693
Assay Master: James Borthwick
3¼ in (8 cm) high
13 oz 4 dwt (410 gr)
London, 24 IV 1969, 264
£5,200 ($12,480)

498 Mug
Edinburgh, 1694
Assay Master: James Borthwick
3 in (7.6 cm) high
5 oz 12 dwt (174 gr)
Gleneagles, 27–28 VIII 1979,
248
£1,430 ($2,931)

499 Salvers-on-foot, pair
Edinburgh, 1692
Assay Master: John Borthwick
9¼ in (23.5 cm) diameter
24 oz 1 dwt (747 gr)
Gleneagles, 28 VIII 1969, 176
£1,600 ($3,840)

EG between mullets
London
Mark Jackson, p.144

500 Porringer (bleeding bowl)
London, 1683
5½ in (14 cm) diameter
6 oz 12 dwt (205 gr)
London, 11 IV 1968, 83
£1,400 ($3,360)

501 Tankard
London, 1684
7¾ in (19.7 cm) high
36 oz 11 dwt (1,136 gr)
London, 17 X 1968, 158
£1,750 ($4,200)

495 GOOSE

496 COCKBURNE

497 COCKBURNE

498 COCKBURNE

499 COCKBURNE

500 EG

501 EG

140 GREAT BRITAIN IRELAND

502 EG

506 BB

502 Mug
London, 1688
4 in (10.2 cm) high
6 oz 6 dwt (195 gr)
London, 29 IV 1971, 135
£950 ($2,280)

503 Bowl
London, 1688
5 in (12.7 cm) diameter
8 oz 8 dwt (261 gr)
London, 30 V 1963, 49
£750 ($2,100)

503 EG

506 BB

BB crescent below
London
Mark Jackson, p.143

504 Sweetmeat box
London, 1676
7¼ in (18.4 cm) wide
21 oz 12 dwt (671 gr)
London, 28 II 1974, 134
£18,000 ($43,200)

505 Teapot
London, 1689
5 in (12.7 cm) high
11 oz 3 dwt (346 gr)
London, 8 VI 1972, 79
£3,700 ($9,250)

506 Toilet boxes, pair
London, 1685
4¾ in (12 cm) wide
33 oz (1,026 gr)
New York, 28–29 X 1977, 606
$6,750 (£3,648)

504 BB

509 F. GARTHORNE

505 BB

510 F. GARTHORNE

507 D IN SCRIPT

512 F. GARTHORNE

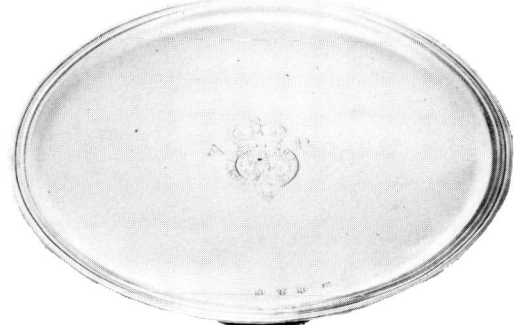

513 F. GARTHORNE

508 D IN SCRIPT

511 F. GARTHORNE

D in script
London
Mark Jackson, pp.142, 147

507 Ginger jars and stands, pair
London, 1682
Salvers: 8 in (20.3 cm) square
Jars: 7½ in (19 cm) high
72 oz 18 dwt (2,267 gr)
London, 21 VI 1962, 15
£18,000 ($50,400)

508 Wine cup, paten and salver-on-foot
silver-gilt
London, 1691
Numbered 17 and 18
9½ in (24.2 cm) high
55 oz 12 dwt (1,729 gr)
London, 17 V 1973, 118
£2,100 ($5,250)

Francis Garthorne
London; active c. 1677?–1726
Mark Grimwade, 736, 3570;
Jackson, p.138

509 Porringer and cover
London, 1682
6½ in (16.5 cm) high
22 oz 6 dwt (693 gr)
Arms: Streatfeild; probably for
Henry Streatfeild 1639–1719, of
Chiddingstone, co. Kent
London, 13 VII 1961, 152
£860 ($2,416)

510 Porringer and cover
silver-gilt
London, 1690
6½ in (16.5 cm) high
19 oz 11 dwt (608 gr)
London, 31 X 1974, 144
£750 ($1,725)

511 Dinner plates, pair
silver-gilt
London, 1690
9½ in (24.2 cm) diameter
41 oz (1,275 gr)
Cypher: Royal
London, 9 VII 1964, 96
£3,400 ($9,520)

512 Chamber candlestick
London, 1708
5 in (12.7 cm) diameter
18 oz (560 gr)
Arms: Royal, of Queen Anne
London, 15 X 1970, 14
£1,000 ($2,400)

513 Salver-on-foot
silver-gilt
London, 1701
9 in (23.2 cm) diameter
16 oz 15 dwt (520 gr)
Arms: Queen Anne
New York, 28–29 X 1977, 614
$3,250 (£1,756)

142 GREAT BRITAIN IRELAND

514 Salvers-on-foot, pair
silver-gilt
London, 1718
7 in (18 cm) diameter
27 oz (839 gr)
Arms: George I
Initials: E.D.C., for Ernest, Duke of Cumberland; and EAFs for Ernest Augustus Fidiekommis (the entailed estate of Ernest Augustus, Duke of Cumberland)
New York, 28–29 X 1977, 613
$5,500 (£2,972)

514 F. GARTHORNE

516 G. GARTHORNE

George Garthorne

London; apprenticed to Francis Garthorne, free 1680, died 1730
Mark Grimwade, 739; Jackson, p.148

515 Mug
London, 1693
4¼ in (10.8 cm) high
8 oz 16 dwt (273 gr)
London, 17 X 1974, 160
£800 ($1,840)

515 G. GARTHORNE

517 G. GARTHORNE

518 TT

519 TT

516 Mugs, pair
London, 1688
4 in (10 cm) high
19 oz 2 dwt (594 gr)
London, 3 V 1984, 47
£2,420 ($3,363)

517 Tobacco box
London, 1690
3½ in (8.9 cm) wide
5 oz 13 dwt (175 gr)
London, 4 XII 1969, 228
£820 ($1,968)

TT crowned

London; attributed to T. Townley or Tucker.
See Y. Hackenbroch, 'Gribelin's designs engraved on English Silver', Connoisseur, June 1968
Mark Jackson, p.146.

518 Beaker and spice box
silver-gilt
(London), c. 1680
Beaker: 3¼ in (8 cm) high, unmarked
Box: 2¾ in (7 cm) wide
5 oz 7 dwt (166 gr)
Arms: Banks impaling Dethick
London, 27 XI 1975, 190
£2,585 ($5,170)

519 Travelling set
(London), c. 1690
Beaker: 3¼ in (8.2 cm) high
7 oz 8 dwt (230 gr)
Inscribed: The Guift of the Honoble Lady Tipping, April y[e] 15 1708
London, 3 XII 1970, 248
£620 ($1,488)

520 FS/s

521 FS/s   523 FS/s

522 FS/s   524 UNMARKED

FS crown above small s below

London. See Y. Hackenbroch, 'Gribelin's designs engraved on English Silver', *Connoisseur*, June 1968
Mark Y. Hackenbroch, *English and other Silver in the Collection of Irwin Untermeyer*, New York 1974, p.56

520 Beaker and spice box
silver-gilt
Beaker unmarked; spice box, maker's mark only
(London), c. 1690
Box: 2½ in (6.7 cm) wide
Beaker: 3½ in (9 cm) high
4 oz 9 dwt (138 gr)
Engraved with figures of Diana and Endymion, the box depicting Love and Fortitude and inscribed with French proverbs. See also catalogue, Sotheby's, 15 June 1978, lot 126, and Clayton, ed., *Collector's Dictionary of ... Silver and Gold*, p.17, for two travelling sets engraved as Bartholomew Fairings.
London, 13 VI 1983, 9
£2,860 ($4,576)

521 Cordial pot
Maker's mark only
(London), c. 1685
4½ in (11.5 cm) high
Compare with a similar example in the Museum of Fine Arts, Boston.
London, 18 V 1967, 163
£450 ($1,260)

522 Travelling set
silver-gilt
Maker's mark only
(London), c. 1690
Beaker: 3¼ in (8.2 cm) high
9 oz 17 dwt (306 gr)
London, 14 XII 1972, 233
£900 ($2,250)

523 Spice box
silver-gilt
(London), c. 1690
Maker's mark only
2½ in (6.3 cm) wide
See also catalogue, Sotheby's, London, 20 November 1980, lot 257.
London, 11 XI 1971, 125
£440 ($1,100)

Unmarked

524 Spice box
silver-gilt
English, c. 1690
2½ in (6.3 cm) wide
See no.523
London, 11 XI 1971, 126
£420 ($1,050)

144 GREAT BRITAIN IRELAND

525 UNMARKED

527 LEEKE

526 LEEKE

528 PYNE

531 PYNE

529 PYNE

530 PYNE

532 PYNE

525 Beaker and cover
silver-gilt
English, c. 1690
3¼ in (8.3 cm) high
4 oz 16 dwt (149 gr)
Arms: Henry Mordaunt, 2nd Earl of Peterborough
London, 4 VII 1968, 93
£1,200 ($2,880)

Ralph Leeke
London; mark entered 1699, free 1671
Mark Grimwade, 1914, 3717

526 Cup
silver-gilt
London, apparently 1683
2 in (5 cm) high
1 oz 15 dwt (54 gr)
London, 2 XII 1965, 175
£480 ($1,344)

527 Wine cisterns, pair
London, 1698
22¼ in (56.5 cm) wide
746 oz 10 dwt (23,216 gr)
Arms: Sir Nathaniel Curzon of Kedlestone, 5th Bt, created Baron Scarsdale in 1761
Exhibition: Seaford House, 1929 no. 395.
London, 9 VII 1964, 104
£5,800 ($16,240)

Benjamin Pyne

London; free 1676, financially distressed by 1727, died 1732
Mark Jackson, p.149; Grimwade, 2244–5, 3748

528 Punch bowl (monteith)
London, 1685
11 ½ in (29.2 cm) diameter
37 oz 5 dwt (1,158 gr)
London, 21 XI 1957, 176
£800 ($2,232)

529 Cups and covers, pair (known as the Croft Cups)
London, 1685
One maker's mark: S.H.
14½ in (36.9 cm) high
196 oz 4 dwt (6,101 gr)
Now in the British Museum. See Tait, 'The Advent of the Two-handled Cup'.
London, 17 XI 1937, 81
£2,650 ($13,011)

530 Mug
London, 1688
4¾ in (12 cm) high
13 oz 18 dwt (432 gr)
London, 19 III 1964, 120
£1,500 ($4,200)

531 Candlesticks, pair
London, 1701
6¼ in (15.8 cm) high
21 oz 9 dwt (667 gr)
London, 4 III 1971, 175
£1,200 ($2,880)

532 Casters, three
London, 1702
8 in and 5¾ in (20.2 cm and 14.6 cm) high
22 oz 19 dwt (713 gr)
London, 16 III 1961, 73
£720 ($2,023)

533 Dishes, four
silver-gilt
London, 1698
9½ in (24 cm) wide
94 oz 19 dwt (2,953 gr)
Arms: Sir William Courtnay
Now in the Victoria and Albert Museum, London. The engraving of the armorials is possibly by Simon Gribelin; the chased border is after an etching by Stefano della Bella. See catalogue of exhibition, 'Pattern and Design', 2.l.b.
London, 30 X 1947, 111
£1,100 ($4,433)

534 Punch bowl
London, 1697
11 in (28 cm) diameter
40 oz 13 dwt (1,264 gr)
London, 11 XI 1971, 187
£740 ($1,850)

533 PYNE

534 PYNE

535 PYNE

536 PYNE

535 Teapot
London, 1705
5 in (12.7 cm) high
9 oz 15 dwt (303 gr)
London, 6 XI 1969, 159
£700 ($1,680)

536 Mug
London, 1699
4¼ in (10.8 cm) high
9 oz 16 dwt (304 gr)
Inscribed: The Gift of Tho. Mansell to his Godson and Nephew Tho. Mansell born 3 Jan 1699 1700
London, 8 VI 1972, 75
£1,000 ($2,500)

537 PYNE

538 PYNE

539 PYNE

540 PYNE

537 Livery badge
London, 1708
4½ in (11.4 cm) overall
1 oz 19 dwt (60 gr)
Emery Hill, brewer (1610–77), endowed almshouses in Rochester Row and Petty France, London. He is buried in the Church of St Margaret, Westminster, where he was churchwarden.
London, 11 X 1979, 77a
£495 ($1,014)

538 Salt cellars, six
London, 1719
4¼ in (10.8 cm) wide
67 oz 17 dwt (2,110 gr)
London, 22 X 1970, 206
£3,600 ($8,640)

539 Hot milk jug
London, 1709
5¾ in (14.6 cm) high
9 oz (279 gr)
London, 29 IV 1971, 134
£650 ($1,560)

540 Tea kettle on lamp stand
London, 1709
14½ in (36.9 cm) high
99 oz (3,078 gr)
London, 13 X 1955, 123
£1,150 ($3,208)

541 Toilet set, twelve pieces
silver-gilt
London, 1711
285 oz (8,863 gr)
Initials: EAFs, for Ernest Augustus Fideikommis (the entailed estate of Ernest Augustus, Duke of Cumberland)
New York, 28–29 X 1977, 617
$32,000 (£17,297)

541 PYNE

542 PYNE

543 PYNE

544 A. NELME

545 A. NELME

547 A. NELME

545 (DETAIL)

546 A. NELME

Anthony Nelme

London; free 1679/80, died 1723.
See Honour, *Goldsmiths and Silversmiths*, pp.122–127; see also no.812
Mark Jackson, p.146; Grimwade, 68–9, 3741

544 Tankard
London, 1692
6¾ in (17.2 cm) high
24 oz 4 dwt (752 gr)
London, 9 V 1974, 229
£2,500 ($6,000)

545 Toilet set
London, 1691
354 oz (11,009 gr) approx.
London, 30 V 1935, 166
£1,700 ($8,381)

546 Chamber candlestick
London, 1691
4¼ in (10.8 cm) diameter
8 oz 13 dwt (269 gr)
London, 3 XI 1966, 77
£600 ($1,680)

547 Toilet boxes, pair
London, 1686
5¼ in (13.4 cm) wide
23 oz 3 dwt (720 gr)
London, 21 II 1952, 134
£38 ($106)

542 Soup plates, twelve
silver-gilt
London, 1720
9¾ in (24.9 cm) diameter
241 oz 6 dwt (7,504 gr)
Arms: Methuen, for Sir Paul Methuen (1672–1757); also bearing later crests.
London, 13 VI 1983, 41
£41,800 ($66,880)

543 Inkstand
London, 1725
9¼ in (23.5 cm) wide
36 oz 6 dwt (1,128 gr)
London, 20 II 1964, 81
£2,500 ($7,000)

548 A. NELME

549 A. NELME

550 A. NELME

551 A. NELME

552 A. NELME

548 Cadinet
Converted into an inkstand
London, 1696
9¼ in (23.5 cm) wide
28 oz 10 dwt (886 gr)
New York, 28–29 X 1977, 610
$3,250 (£1,756)

549 Inkstand
London, 1703
11½ in (29.2 cm) wide
48 oz 6 dwt ($1,502)
London, 21 III 1963, 132
£1,850 ($5,180)

550 Bowl and cover
London, 1704
4¾ in (12 cm) diameter
16 oz 4 dwt (503 gr)
London, 16 VII 1970, 45
£500 ($1,200)

551 Ginger jar
London, 1693
Scratch weight: 170 oz 4 dwt; no.1
22 in (58 cm) high
167 oz (5,200 gr)
London, 13 VI 1983, 17
£36,300 ($58,080)

553 A. NELME

554 A. NELME

555 A. NELME

556 A. NELME

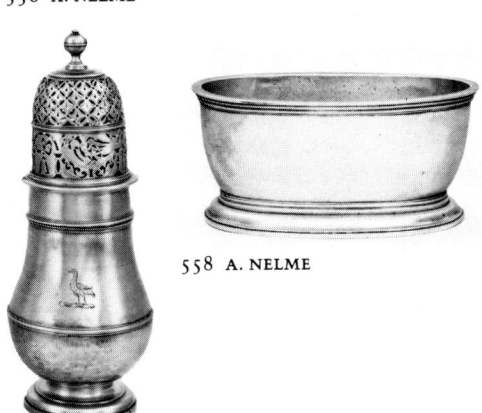

557 A. NELME

558 A. NELME

552 Candlesticks, pair
(London), c. 1695
Maker's mark only
9¼ in (23.5 cm) high
43 oz 6 dwt (1,346 gr)
See Clayton, ed., *Collector's Dictionary of ... Silver and Gold*, ill.no.82, for a similar pair, Nelme, 1697.
London, 11 IV 1968, 87
£1,050 ($2,520)

553 Teapot
London, 1705
5¾ in (14.6 cm) high
12 oz 17 dwt (399 gr)
London, 20 IV 1972, 157
£1,050 ($2,625)

554 Tankard
London, 1705
7 in (17.8 cm) high
27 oz 11 dwt (856 gr)
London, 4 IX 1975, 104
£902 ($1,804)

555 Set of communion plate
silver-gilt
London, 1717
Dish: 12 in (30.5 cm) diameter
Arms: Sir William Courtenay of Powderham, co. Devon, 2nd Bt, and his wife Anne, daughter of the 1st Earl of Abingdon
Inscribed: This Chalice [Plate/Salver] for the Communion Service in the Chapel at Powderham Castle.
London, 4 III 1965, 183
£2,900 ($8,120)

556 Cups and covers, pair
London, 1714
11 in (28 cm) high
118 oz 16 dwt (3,694 gr)
Arms: 4th Earl of Coventry (1668–1719), who married in 1715 Anne, daughter of Sir Streynsham Master.
London, 22 X 1970, 205
£2,500 ($6,000)

557 Caster
London, 1706
9 in (23 cm) high
14 oz 13 dwt (455 gr)
London, 20 III 1980, 201
£1,045 ($2,455)

558 Wine bottle stand
London, 1715
Scratch weight: Pr 37; 7:0
7 in (17.5 cm) wide
18 oz (559 gr)
London, 23 VII 1981, 220
£4,840 ($10,018)

559 A. NELME

560 A. NELME

564 TIMBRELL

565 TIMBRELL

561 SYNG

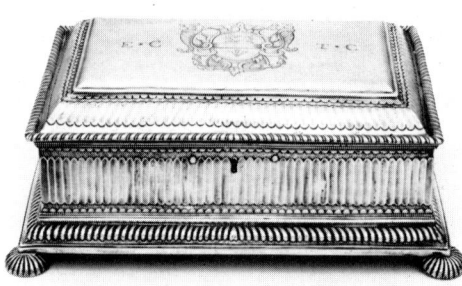
562 SYNG

563 SYNG

566 BODINGTON

559 Censer
London, 1722
8¾ in (22.2 cm) high
27 oz 1 dwt (841 gr)
London, 19 X 1978, 131
£1,320 ($2,706)

560 Tea kettle on lamp stand
London, 1718/19
16 in (40.6 cm) high
106 oz 15 dwt (3,319 gr)
Arms: Bulkeley impaling Bertie, for Richard, 4th Viscount Bulkeley (died 1724), and his wife Bridget, daughter of the 1st Earl of Abingdon.
London, 28 I 1965, 160
£2,200 ($6,160)

Richard Syng
London; free 1687
Mark Grimwade, 2673

561 Candlesticks, pair
London, 1703
9¼ in (23.5 cm) high
23 oz 10 dwt (730 gr)
London, 10 X 1983, 491
£2,200 ($3,058)

562 Casket
London, 1702
10¼ in (26 cm) wide
47 oz 10 dwt (1,477 gr)
London, 23 VII 1981, 224
£2,530 ($5,237)

563 Chocolate pot
London, 1706
8½ in (21.6 cm) high
21 oz 3 dwt (657 gr)
London, 17 VII 1969, 260
£1,800 ($4,320)

Robert Timbrell
London; free 1685. See Robert Timbrell and Joseph Bell (in partnership 1707) below, nos 609, 610
Mark Grimwade, 2810

564 Punch bowl (monteith)
London, 1698
10¾ in (27.3 cm) diameter
48 oz 10 dwt (1,508 gr)
London, 3 III 1983, 72
£6,050 ($9,680)

565 Porringer
London, 1705
4¾ in (12 cm) high
12 oz 10 dwt (388 gr)
London, 10 II 1977, 179
£825 ($1,402)

John Bodington
London; free 1688, died 1727, active until c. 1714.
Mark Grimwade, 201

566 Wine bottles, pair
silver-gilt
London, 1699
16¾ in (42.5 cm) high
208 oz 7 dwt (6,479 gr)
Arms: John Holles, created Duke of Newcastle-upon-Tyne 1694, died 1711
London, 26 VI 1975, 64
£62,000 ($142,600)

567 BODINGTON

568 BODINGTON

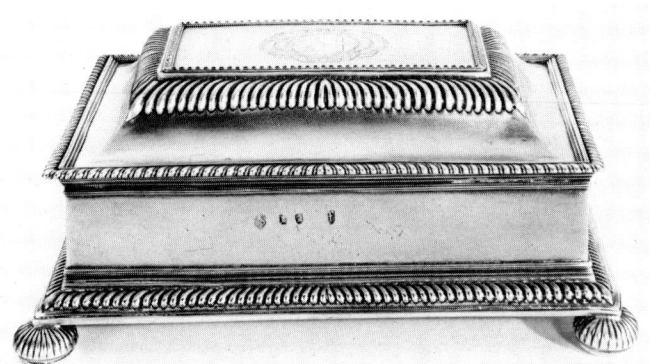

569 BODINGTON

570 CANNER

571 CANNER

567 Cup and cover
London, 1699
8 in (20.3 cm) high
35 oz 11 dwt (1,105 gr)
London, 17 V 1973, 107
£6,500 ($16,250)

568 Sugar bowl and cover
London, 1705
4¾ in (12 cm) diameter
6 oz 14 dwt (208 gr)
London, 20 IV 1972, 9
£600 ($1,500)

569 Casket
silver-gilt
London, 1701
9½ in (24.2 cm) wide
51 oz 1 dwt (1,587 gr)
Arms: Master impaling Legh for Sir Streynsham Master, Kt (died 1724), and his second wife Elizabeth, daughter of Richard Legh of Lyme, co. Chester, whom he married in 1690.
See catalogue, Christie's, 24 November 1971, lot 48 for a pair of bowls by Bodington bearing the same armorials, also no. 556
London, 20 VI 1974, 86
£3,400 ($8,160)

Christopher Canner
London; free 1688, died 1708. Specialist caster maker
Mark Grimwade, 258; Jackson, p.151

570 Casters, three
London, 1689
7½ in and 5½ in (19 cm and 14 cm) high
16 oz 3 dwt (502 gr)
London, 3 XII 1953, 335
£370 ($1,039)

571 Casters, three
London, 1704
7¼ in and 8¾ in (18.4 cm and 22.2 cm) high
26 oz 17 dwt
London, 20 II 1975, 194
£2,700 ($6,210)

572 WARD

577 BIRD

578 BIRD

573 WARD

576 GIBSON

579 BIRD

580 COOPER

574 WARD

Joseph Ward
London; free 1689
Mark Grimwade, 2989, 3856

572 Sugar bowl and cover
London, 1700
4½ in (11.4 cm) diameter
8 oz (248 gr)
Inscribed: This Sugar Dish was presented in July 1703 to Mrs Roberta Jones by Mrs Elizabeth Dodsworth. And it was frankly given back again in Sept 1742 by the said Mrs Jones to Miss Eliz. Dodsworth Grand-daughter of the Doner
London, 24 III 1960, 33
£950 ($2,669)

573 Chalice and paten
silver (loaded)
London, 1707
7 in (17.8 cm) high
London, 13 V 1976, 190
£352 ($633)

574 Beaker and cover
London, 1708
3¼ in (8.2 cm) high
4 oz 15 dwt (147 gr)
London, 8 VI 1972, 67
£1,100 ($2,750)

575 Covered jug
London, 1714
10 in (25.4 cm) high
30 oz 6 dwt (942 gr)
London, 14 XII 1972, 203
£4,500 ($11,250)

William Gibson
London; apprenticed to George Garthorne, free 1690
Mark Grimwade, 824

576 Coffee Pot
London, 1701
10½ in (26.4 cm) high
24 oz 16 dwt (833 gr)
See Hayward, *Huguenot Silver*, pl.49A, for a similar pot by George Garthorne.
New York, 17 VI 1981, 45
$46,200 (£22,320)

Joseph Bird
London; first mark 1697, died 1735. Specialist candlestick maker
Mark Grimwade, 177–9, 1120, 3614–5

577 Candlesticks, pair
London, 1701
6¾ in (16.5 cm) high
29 oz 19 dwt (931 gr)
London, 9 V 1974, 189
£3,800 ($9,120)

578 Candlesticks, pair
London, 1703
7¼ in (18.4 cm) high
30 oz 5 dwt (940 gr)
London, 19 VI 1969, 208
£2,000 ($4,800)

579 Candlesticks, pair
London, 1704
6 in (15.5 cm) high
25 oz 14 dwt (799 gr)
London, 19 VII 1979, 133
£3,080 ($1,502)

Robert Cooper

London; active c. 1675–1717.
Mark Jackson, p.146; Grimwade, 380

580 Candlesticks, pair
London, 1699
7 in (17.8 cm) high
34 oz 18 dwt (1,085 gr) including later nozzles, not illustrated
London, 8 XI 1973, 198
£2,700 ($6,480)

581 Covered jug
London, 1708
9¼ in (23.5 cm) high
29 oz 3 dwt (906 gr)
Arms: Sir Thomas Morgan of Kinnersley Castle, co. Hereford (died 1716)
See Burke and Savill, *Guide to Country Houses*, London, 1978–81, vol.II, p.40, for Kinnersley Castle.
London, 24 IV 1969, 259
£4,800 ($11,520)

582 Ewer
London, 1702
9¼ in (23.5 cm) high
24 oz (746 gr)
London, 30 V 1963, 46
£1,900 ($5,320)

583 Spoon tray
(London), c. 1720
Maker's mark only struck four times
6¼ in (16 cm) wide
4 oz 11 dwt (141 gr)
Arms: Thomas Frewen (born 1687) of Bonby Hall, co. Lincs, and his wife Martha, daughter of Henry Turner of Cold Overton Hall, co. Leics whom he married in 1713.
London, 20 IV 1972, 10
£260 ($650)

Seth Lofthouse

London; mark entered 1699, died by 1727
Mark Grimwade, 1945

584 Cup and cover
London, 1697
9½ in (24.2 cm) high
31 oz 17 dwt (990 gr)
London, 22 V 1969, 230
£2,600 ($6,240)

585 Ecuelle
London, 1697
11 in (28 cm) overall
15 oz 2 dwt (496 gr)
London, 22 X 1970, 214
£2,300 ($5,520)

575 WARD

581 COOPER

582 COOPER

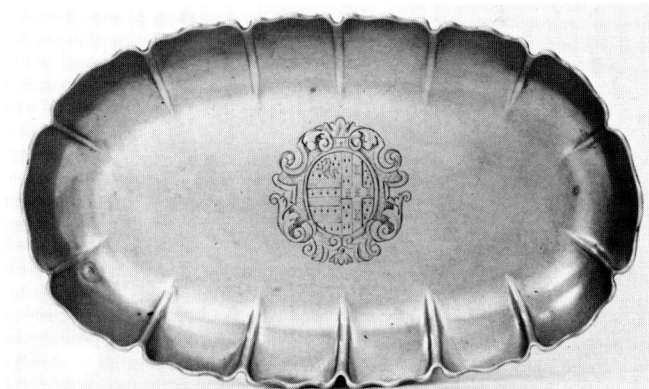

583 COOPER

584 LOFTHOUSE

585 LOFTHOUSE

586 YORSTOUN

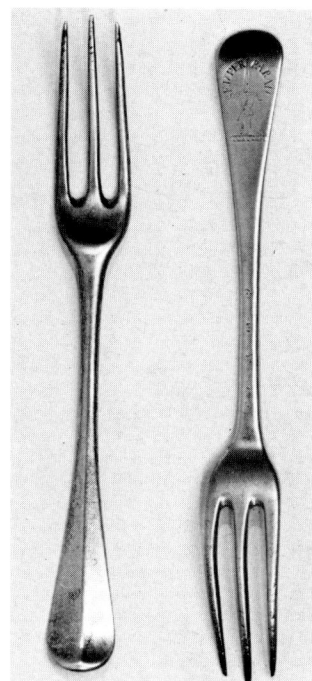

587 YORSTOUN

590 BOLTON

588 KER

591 BOLTON

589 KER

Mungo Yorstoun
Edinburgh; admitted to Incorporation 1702
Mark Jackson, p.500

586 Communion cups, pair
Edinburgh, 1719
Assay Master: Edward Penman
9 in (22.9 cm) high
35 oz 13 dwt (1,108 gr)
London, 31 X 1974, 145
£2,100 ($4,830)

587 Dessert forks, six
Edinburgh, 1719
Assay Master: Edward Penman
9 oz 17 dwt (306 gr)
London, 4 VII 1968, 156
£1,000 ($2,400)

592 BOLTON

593 BOLTON

594 BOLTON

595 BOLTON

596 BOLTON

597 BOLTON

Thomas Ker
Edinburgh; admitted to Incorporation 1694
Mark Jackson, p.501

588 Shaving dish and ewer
Edinburgh, 1702/3
Assay Master: James Penman
13½ in (34.2 cm) wide
46 oz 15 dwt (1,453 gr)
London, 19 X 1961, 156
£2,650 ($7,420)

589 Salvers, pair
Edinburgh, 1704
Assay Master: Edward Penman
11½ in (29.2 cm) diameter
57 oz 18 dwt (1,800 gr)
London, 16 III 1961, 113
£2,400 ($6,744)

Thomas Bolton
Dublin; free 1686, died 1736.
Became Lord Mayor of Dublin:
Bolton Street is named after him
Mark Bennett, p.340; Jackson, p.609

590 Cup and cover
Dublin, 1701
9¼ in (23.5 cm) high
30 oz 6 dwt (942 gr)
London, 18 VII 1968, 102
£2,900 ($6,960)

591 Wine jug
Dublin, 1702
12½ in (31.8 cm) high
49 oz (1,523 gr)
Arms: Royal, Queen Anne
See no.592.
London, 8 VI 1972, 73
£7,000 ($17,500)

592 Ewer
Dublin, 1702
9½ in (24.1 cm) high
47 oz 6 dwt (1,471 gr)
Arms: Royal, Queen Anne
Compare this piece with the wine jug (no.591): the engraving is probably by the same hand.
London, 19 VI 1969, 240
£7,000 ($16,800)

593 Bowl and cover
Dublin, 1696–9
5 in (12.7 cm) square
16 oz 16 dwt (522 gr)
Inscribed: The gift of Amelia Viscountess Powerscourt to her Goddaughter Lady Arabella Scott
London, 27 VI 1963, 93
£1,550 ($4,340)

594 Salvers-on-foot, pair
Dublin, 1704–6
9½ in (24.1 cm) diameter
39 oz 10 dwt (1,228 gr)
London, 16 X 1975, 186
£1,430 ($2,860)

595 Coffee pot
Dublin, 1706–8
10 in (25.4 cm) high
25 oz 8 dwt (790 gr)
London, 31 X 1974, 199
£2,600 ($5,980)

596 Beer jug
Dublin, 1717
8¼ in (21 cm) high
38 oz 1 dwt (1,183 gr)
London, 18 VI 1964, 129
£2,550 ($7,140)

597 Freedom box
22ct gold
Dublin, 1714
3¼ in (8.2 cm) diameter
5 oz 15 dwt (178 gr)
Arms: Robert, Earl of Kildare
London, 3 V 1984, 2
£26,400 ($36,696)

598 BOLTON

599 M. COOPER I

600 M. COOPER I

601 M. COOPER I

602 M. COOPER I

603 WALKER

598 Tankard
Dublin, 1718
8¾ in (22.2 cm) high
35 oz 18 dwt (1,116 gr)
London, 8 XI 1979, 181
£2,530 ($5,945)

Matthew Cooper I
London; apprenticed to Robert Cooper and Joseph Bird, first mark 1702, bankrupt 1731.
Mark Grimwade, 378, 2003

599 Candlesticks, pair
London, 1715
7¼ in (18.5 cm) high
21 oz 17 dwt (679 gr)
London, 19 XI 1953, 52
£185 ($519)

600 Snuffers stand and a pair of snuffers
London, 1704 and c. 1704
Snuffers bear maker's mark only struck four times
7 in (17.8 cm) high
8 oz 9 dwt (262 gr)
London, 20 IV 1972, 161
£600 ($1,500)

601 Tapersticks, pair
London, 1714
4¾ in (12 cm) high
5 oz 18 dwt (183 gr)
London, 15 X 1970, 40
£1,300 ($3,120)

602 Candlesticks, pair
London, 1718
7¼ in (18.5 cm) high
27 oz 9 dwt (853 gr)
London, 17 V 1973, 183
£1,500 ($3,750)

Joseph Walker
Dublin; active 1690–1722
Mark Bennett, 258–9

603 Salver
Dublin, 1715
17¾ in (45.2 cm) diameter
85 oz 14 dwt (2,665 gr)
London, 16 X 1975, 188
£5,720 ($11,440)

Charles Adam
London; born 1667, first mark 1703, died 1738. Specialist caster maker
Mark Grimwade, 25

604 Caster
London, 1703
7¾ in (19.7 cm) high
9 oz (280 gr)
London, 3 XII 1953, 333
£120 ($337)

605 Caster
London, 1705
7½ in (19 cm) high
8 oz 16 dwt (273 gr)
London, 17 X 1968, 143
£900 ($2,160)

606 Caster
London, 1713
7¾ in (19.7 cm) high
8 oz 9 dwt (261 gr)
London, 19 VII 1982, 87
£1,012 ($1,811)

607 Casters, pair
London, 1717
6¼ in (16 cm) high
12 oz 7 dwt (384 gr)
London, 8 VI 1972, 54
£880 ($2,200)

604 ADAM

605 ADAM

606 ADAM

607 ADAM

608 BAMFORD

609 TIMBRELL & BELL

610 TIMBRELL & BELL

Thomas Bamford I

London; apprenticed to Charles Adam, first mark 1720. Specialist caster maker
Mark Grimwade, 109–10, 2687, 2704

608 Caster
London, 1725
5¼ in (13.4 cm) high
4 oz 5 dwt (132 gr)
London, 8 VI 1972, 36
£380 ($950)

Robert Timbrell and Joseph Bell I

London; in partnership 1707, Bell having been previously apprenticed to Timbrell.
See nos 564, 565
Mark Grimwade, 2707

609 Coffee pot
London, 1714
10¾ in (27.3 cm) high
29 oz 18 dwt (929 gr)
London, 12 XII 1974, 126
£5,000 ($12,000)

610 Sugar bowl and cover
London, 1712
5¼ in (13.3 cm) high
16 oz 18 dwt (525 gr)
London, 18 VI 1964, 161
£5,000 ($14,000)

158 GREAT BRITAIN IRELAND

611 UNMARKED

613 UNMARKED 614 P. HARACHE I

612 UNMARKED

Unmarked

611 Dessert basket
English, c. 1710
13 in (33 cm) overall
22 oz 8 dwt (696 gr)
London, 4 V 1978, 97
£1,155 ($3,136)

615 P. HARACHE I

616 P. HARACHE I

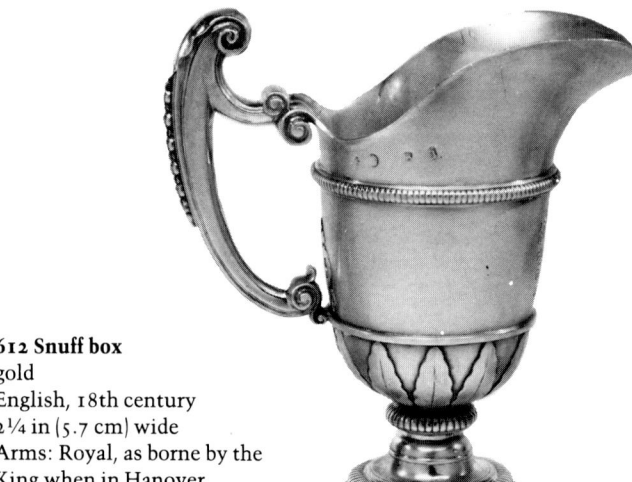

612 Snuff box
gold
English, 18th century
2¼ in (5.7 cm) wide
Arms: Royal, as borne by the King when in Hanover
London, 9 V 1974, 107
£1,450 ($3,480)

613 Rattle
gold and coral
English, c. 1725–30
Marks indecipherable
6½ in (16.5 cm) overall
London, 11 III 1982, 226
£4,070 ($7,285)

617 P. HARACHE I   618 P. HARACHE I   619 P. HARACHE I

620 P. HARACHE I

Peter (Pierre) Harache I and II

London; Huguenot father and son whose lives and work are still confused. 'After 1698 most recorded pieces are probably the work of Pierre II, although unfortunately few catalogues or authors distinguish between the marks and re-examination is needed to clarify the situation' (Grimwade, p.534). As this is not possible at present, 1698 has been taken as the date to separate their work.

621 P. HARACHE I

622 P. HARACHE II

Peter Harache I

London; born France, in England by 1682, died c. 1697
Mark Jackson, p.150; Grimwade, 936

614 Wine taster
London, 1684
5¼ in (13.3 cm) wide
4 oz 6 dwt (133 gr)
London, 23 I 1969, 201
£2,800 ($6,720)

615 Tray
London, 1686
22½ in (57.2 cm) wide
112 oz 2 dwt (3,486 gr)
Arms: Sir Henry Capel (later Lord Tewkesbury) and his wife Dorothy, daughter of Sir Richard Bennett
See no.623
London, 8 XII 1949, 153
£350 ($980)

616 Candlesticks, pair
London, 1692
6¼ in (15.9 cm) high
26 oz 17 dwt (835 gr)
London, 12 I 1961, 155
£600 ($1,686)

617 Ewer
London, 1693
Maker's mark rubbed
7¼ in (18.4 cm) high
33 oz 17 dwt (1,052 gr)
London, 18 VII 1968, 66
£1,000 ($2,400)

623 P. HARACHE II

618 Candlesticks, pair
London, 1692
8 in (20.3 cm) high
41 oz 11 dwt (1,292 gr)
London, 30 XI 1978, 137
£3,740 ($7,667)

619 Brush handle
silver-gilt
London, 1695
6 in (15.2 cm) high
Zurich, 18 XI 1977, 7
SFr.12,650 (£3,409 $6,306)

620 Salt cellars, pair
London, 1694
2¾ in (7 cm) diameter
7 oz 6 dwt (227 gr)
London, 4 XII 1969, 212
£370 ($888)

621 Cups, pair
silver-gilt
London, 1688
2 in (5.2 cm) high
7 oz 2 dwt (220 gr)
Exhibition: 25 Park Lane, 1929, no.495.
London, 10 II 1949, 144
£340 ($1,370)

Peter Harache II

See 'Peter Harache I and II', above.
London; born 1653, first mark 1698
Mark Grimwade, 937–9

622 Cup and cover
London, 1702
9¼ in (23.5 cm) high
57 oz (1,772 gr)
Arms: Sir William Strickland, 3rd Bt, succeeded 1684
London, 27 VI 1963, 36
£2,050 ($5,740)

624 P. HARACHE II

623 Casket
(London), c. 1700
Maker's mark only
5¾ in (14.6 cm) wide
22 oz (684 gr)
Arms: Dorothy, Lady Capel (died 1721)
See Oman, *English Engraved Silver*, p.63, where engraving, probably by the same hand, is attributed to 'Master of George Vertue', having previously been attributed to Gribelin (Christie's, 2nd December 1964, lot 21).
London, 28 II 1974, 122
£3,600 ($8,640)

624 Caster
London, 1703
6¾ in (17.1 cm) high
13 oz 16 dwt (429 gr)
London, 24 IV 1975, 171
£980 ($2,254)

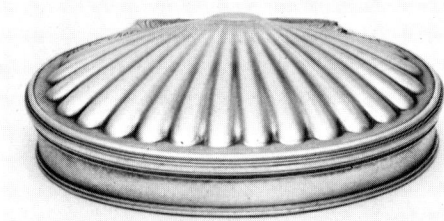

626 P. HARACHE II

629 D. WILLAUME I

625 P. HARACHE II

627 UNMARKED

625 Candlesticks, pair
London, 1704
6¼ in (15.9 cm) high
22 oz 15 dwt (707 gr)
London, 17 X 1963, 92
£820 ($2,296)

626 Snuff box
(London), c. 1715
Maker's mark and lion's head erased only
3¼ in (8.8 cm) overall
New York, 28–29 X 1977, 585
$450 (£243)

628 D. WILLAUME I

630 D. WILLAUME I

Unmarked

627 Snuff box
English, c. 1690
2½ in (6.4 cm) diameter
2 oz 7 dwt (73 gr)
London, 31 X 1974, 153
£250 ($575)

David Willaume I

London; born 1658, free 1693/4, married Lewis Mettayer's sister, retired 1728, died 1741.
His daughter married David Tanqueray; his sister-in-law was married to Simon Gribelin. Willaume ran one of the largest and most successful businesses of his day. See Honour, *Goldsmiths and Silversmiths*, pp.138–141.
Mark Grimwade, 512, 3192–4, 3859

628 Brazier
London, 1698
10 in (25.3 cm) wide
71 oz 10 dwt (2,223 gr)
London, 25 X 1973, 168
£4,000 ($9,600)

629 Candlesticks, four
London, 1700
6¾ in (17.2 cm) high
52 oz (1,617 gr)
London, 20 VI 1974, 109
£2,000 ($4,800)

630 Candlesticks, pair
London, 1706
7½ in (19.1 cm) high
37 oz 10 dwt (1,166 gr)
London, 3 III 1983, 60
£3,960 ($6,336)

631 Ewer and basin
silver-gilt (later)
London, 1702
Basin: 15¾ in (42 cm) wide
Ewer: 9½ in (24.2 cm) high
88 oz (2,736 gr)
Arms: Royal Arms of Queen Anne before the Union with Scotland
Provenance: Duke of Cumberland
Compare with no.670.
New York, 20–23 IV 1983, 336
$137,500 (£85,937)

631 D. WILLAUME I

632 D. WILLAUME I

632 Ewer
London, 1702
Scratch weight: 83 oz 6 dwt
14 in (35.5 cm) high
83 oz 3 dwt (2,585 gr)
Arms: Thomas Wentworth, Baron Raby, created Earl Strafford 1711; Ambassador to Berlin 1705–11 and to The Hague 1711–14. See no.672
London, 27 VI 1963, 52
£5,200 ($14,560)

633 Cream jug
gold
London, 1705
3½ in (8.9 cm) high
7 oz 18 dwt (245 gr)
Arms: John, Marquess of Monthermer, succeeded 1709 as 2nd Duke of Montagu, and his wife Mary, daughter of 1st Duke of Marlborough, whom he married 1705
London, 24 IV 1952, 161
£2,600 ($7,254)

633 D. WILLAUME I

634 D. WILLAUME I

634 Covered jug
London, 1708
6½ in (16.5 cm) high
12 oz 10 dwt (388 gr)
London, 24 X 1957, 118
£420 ($1,171)

635 Tea caddy
London, 1709
5¾ in (14.6 cm) high
16 oz 10 dwt (513 gr)
Arms: Wolryche impaling Weld, for Lady Elizabeth Wolryche of Dudmaston, died 1765
London, 12 XII 1974, 205
£1,600 ($3,680)

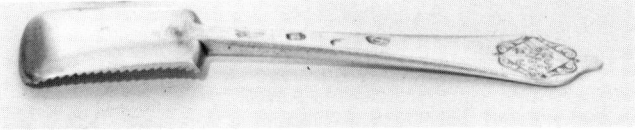

636 D. WILLAUME I

636 Butter spade
London, 1709
6 in (15.2 cm) overall
2 oz 4 dwt (68 gr)
Arms: as on no.635
London, 12 XII 1974, 207
£460 ($1,058)

635 D. WILLAUME I

637 D. WILLAUME I

638 D. WILLAUME I

637 Salvers-on-foot, pair
London, 1720
7 in (17.8 cm) diameter
34 oz 10 dwt (1,072 gr)
Arms: 4th Earl of Drogheda and his wife Charlotte, daughter of 1st Earl of Falmouth, whom he married 1720
London, 2 XII 1965, 178
£2,500 ($7,000)

638 Bowl
London, 1728
5¾ in (14.6 cm) diameter
29 oz 17 dwt (928 gr)
London, 27 VI 1963, 41
£950 ($2,660)

639 Candlesticks, pair
London, 1710
6 in (15.2 cm) high
21 oz 18 dwt (681 gr)
Maker's mark badly struck
Arms: Royal
London, 30 V 1963, 41
£1,350 ($3,780)

640 Sideboard dish
London, 1711
28½ in (72.4 cm) diameter
276 oz 15 dwt (8,606 gr)
Arms: added later within a contemporary cartouche: 2nd Viscount Clifden (1761–1836)
London, 19 VI 1969, 173
£4,200 ($10,080)

641 Cup and cover
London, 1712
16½ in (42 cm) high
170 oz 15 dwt (5,310 gr)
Arms: Watson impaling Proby for Hon. Thomas Watson Wentworth and his wife Alice, daughter of Sir Thomas Proby, Bt, whom he married in 1689
Exhibition: Seaford House, 1929, no.450
London, 16 VII 1970, 40
£5,500 ($13,200)

639 D. WILLAUME I

Louis Cuny
London; first mark 1697, died 1733
Mark Grimwade, 422–3, 3715

642 Sauceboats, pair
London, 1724
9½ in (24.1 cm) overall
41 oz 8 dwt (1,287 gr)
London, 9 IV 1959, 150
£1,700 ($4,777)

643 Tea caddy
London, 1718
5½ in (14 cm) high
12 oz 4 dwt (379 gr)
London, 20 VI 1974, 102
£950 ($2,280)

644 Cup
London, 1707
2½ in (6.3 cm) high
3 oz 1 dwt (94 gr)
London, 20 XII 1979, 83
£440 ($1,034)

640 D. WILLAUME I

641 D. WILLAUME I

642 CUNY

643 CUNY

644 CUNY

645 CHARTIER

646 CHARTIER

647 CHARTIER

John Chartier
London; first mark 1698
Mark Grimwade, 320–1, 1194

645 Cup and cover
London, 1699
9 in (22.8 cm) high
53 oz 16 dwt (1,673 gr)
Arms: Robert Packer (1670–1731) and his wife Mary, daughter of Sir Henry Winchcombe, Bt, whom he married in 1699.
See a similar cup bearing the arms of the 1st Duke of Newcastle in the Ashmolean Museum, Oxford (illus. Hayward, *Huguenot Silver*, pl.3)
London, 11 VI 1970, 232
£4,500 ($10,800)

646 Casters, three
London; two 1700, one 1702 or 1709
9 in and 6¾ in (22.7 cm and 17 cm) high
34 oz 18 dwt (1,085 gr)
Arms: Chetwynd, for Walter, Viscount Chetwynd (1678–1735/6), who married Mary, daughter of 4th Viscount Fitzhardinge.
London, 3 III 1983, 71
£5,390 ($8,624)

647 Sideboard dish
London, 1707
24½ in (62.2 cm) diameter
155 oz 10 dwt (4,836 gr)
Arms: Sir Edward Lawrence of St Ives, co. Hunts; Knight 1701, Baronet 1748
London, 15 X 1970, 9
£6,500 ($15,600)

648 CHARTIER

650 CHARTIER

649 CHARTIER

651 CHARTIER

652 PLATEL

648 Stirrup cup
London, 1714
2¼ in (5.7 cm) high
2 oz 19 dwt (91 gr)
London, 8 VI 1972, 59
£700 ($1,750)

649 Tea kettle on lamp stand
London, 1735
13½ in (34.2 cm) high
68 oz 3 dwt (2,119 gr)
London, 24 IV 1975, 16
£900 ($2,070)

650 Cruet frame, with casters and bottles
London, 1735
10½ in (26.8 cm) overall
49 oz 10 dwt (1,539 gr)
New York, 4 VI 1974, 64
$7,000 (£2,916)

651 Coffee pot
London, 1722
9¾ in (24.8 cm) high
23 oz 9 dwt (729 gr)
London, 28 I 1965, 120
£950 ($2,660)

Pierre Platel

London; mark entered 1699, died 1719
Mark Grimwade, 2200

652 Bowls and covers, pair
silver-gilt
(London), c. 1710
Maker's mark only
4½ in (11.4 cm) diameter
39 oz 7 dwt (1,223 gr)
New York, 6 VI 1980, 49
$33,000 (£12,765)

653 Powder flasks, pair
silver-gilt
London, 1711
7¼ in (18.4 cm) high
28 oz 10 dwt (886 gr)
London, 31 I 1946, 141
£200 ($806)

654 Salvers-on-foot, four
London, 1717
6¼ in (15.8 cm) diameter
39 oz 4 dwt (1,219 gr)
London, 8 VI 1972, 53
£3,000 ($7,500)

655 Candlesticks, pair
silver-gilt
London, 1711
6½ in (16.5 cm) high
27 oz (840 gr)
London, 14 XII 1972, 206
£2,000 ($5,000)

656 Candlesticks, pair
London, 1717
7 in (17.8 cm) high
31 oz 6 dwt (973 gr)
London, 4 III 1965, 161
£3,000 ($8,400)

653 PLATEL

654 PLATEL

655 PLATEL

656 PLATEL

657 PLATEL

658 PLATEL

657 Candlesticks, pair
(London), c. 1715
Maker's mark only
6 in (15.2 cm) high
22 oz 12 dwt (703 gr)
Arms: 6th Earl of Haddington (1680–1735), who married in 1696 Helen, sister of 1st Earl of Hopetoun
London, 13 VI 1983, 15
£3,520 ($5,632)

658 Mug
(London), c. 1715
Maker's mark only struck twice
3¾ in (9.5 cm) high
9 oz 7 dwt (290 gr)
New York, 4 VI 1974, 65
$900 (£375)

659 Salt cellars, twelve
London, 1717
2¾ in (7.2 cm) diameter
46 oz 10 dwt (1,446 gr)
Arms: crest, motto and cypher of George, Prince of Wales, later George II
Provenance: Duke of Cumberland
Exhibition: 25 Park Lane, 1929, no.435
London, 13 VI 1983, 11
£61,600 ($98,560)

659 PLATEL

660 PLATEL

661 W. LUKIN I

662 W. LUKIN I

663 W. LUKIN I

664 W. LUKIN I

665 W. LUKIN I

666 W. LUKIN I

William Lukin I

London; first mark 1699, bankrupt 1749. See Oman, *English Engraved Silver*, pp.88–9 on Lukin's connection with the engraver Joseph Sympson and their collaboration on Sir Robert Walpole's Exchequer salver.
Mark Grimwade, 1966, 3220

661 Inkstand
(London), c. 1700
Maker's mark only struck twice
9¾ in (25 cm) wide
58 oz (1,803 gr)
New York, 1 VI 1974, 1062
$10,000 (£4,166)

662 Chocolate pot
London, 1710
8¾ in (22.2 cm) high
27 oz (840 gr)
See Hayward, *Huguenot Silver*, pl.50B, for a pot, Thomas Corbet (1703), with an identical spout.
London, 26 I 1967, 160
£2,100 ($5,859)

663 Fountain and cistern
London, 1707
Fountain: 27¼ in (69.2 cm) high
Cistern: 27¼ in (69.2 cm) wide (not illustrated)
694 oz (21,583 gr)
Arms: Earls of Hopetoun
New York, 14–15 VI 1978, 819
$38,000 (£20,540)

664 Fountain
silver-gilt
(London), c. 1715
24¼ in (61.6 cm) high
262 oz (8,148 gr)
Arms: Royal
This piece is a 'duty dodger'.
New York, 16–17 XII 1976, 61
$13,000 (£7,647)

665 Tray
London, 1717
Engraving signed: Simpson Sculp
23¾ in (60.4 cm) wide
142 oz 12 dwt (4,434 gr)
See Oman, *English Engraved Silver* (cited above).
New York, 17 VI 1981, 72
$57,200 (£27,630)

660 Salvers-on-foot, pair
London, 1717
11 in (28 cm) diameter
64 oz 4 dwt (1,996 gr)
Arms: see no.659
London, 10 III 1960, 154
£2,200 ($6,182)

667 W. LUKIN I

669 P. ROLLOS I

668 P. ROLLOS I

670 P. ROLLOS I

666 Candlesticks, pair
London, 1719
6¼ in (15.8 cm) high
22 oz 10 dwt (700 gr)
London, 2 VI 1977, 37
£2,860 ($4,862)

667 Wine coolers, pair
London, 1716
8¼ in (21 cm) high
245 oz 2 dwt (7,622 gr)
Arms: Robert Walpole, 1st Earl of Orford
Exhibition: 25 Park Lane, 1929, no.760.
London, 2 XI 1950, 150
£2,500 ($7,000)

Philip Rollos I

London; free 1697 but possibly active from c. 1680. Subordinate Goldsmith to William III and Anne.
Mark Grimwade, 2383

668 Casters, three
silver-gilt
(London), c. 1705
Maker's mark only
10¼ in and 8¼ in (26 cm and 21 cm) high
73 oz 19 dwt (2,299 gr)
London, 13 VI 1983, 28
£96,800 ($154,880)

669 Salvers-on-foot, pair
silver-gilt
London, 1705
11½ in (29.2 cm) diameter
78 oz 13 dwt (2,446 gr)
Arms: Royal
These salvers formed part of the ambassadorial plate of Thomas Wentworth, created Earl of Strafford 1711, Ambassador to Berlin 1705–11 and to The Hague 1711–14. He died 1739.
See nos 632, 670, 671.
London, 27 VI 1963, 50
£3,100 ($8,680)

670 Ewer and basin
silver-gilt
London, 1705
24½ in (62.2 cm) diameter; 13½ in (34.2 cm) high
252 oz 4 dwt (7,843 gr)
Arms: Royal
Now in the Victoria and Albert Museum, London. See no.632 also. For other ambassadorial plate from the same property see nos 632, 669, 671.
London, 27 VI 1963, 49
£11,500 ($30,800)

671 P. ROLLOS I

672 P. ROLLOS I

673 P. ROLLOS II

674 P. ROLLOS II

671 Cup and cover
silver-gilt
London, 1712
13½ in (34.2 cm) high
108 oz 12 dwt (3,377 gr)
Arms: Thomas Wentworth, Earl of Strafford (see no.669)
See nos 690, 694.
London, 27 VI 1963, 53
£3,200 ($8,960)

672 Ewer and basin
silver-gilt
London, 1717
Ewer: 9 in (22.9 cm) high
Basin: 15¾ in (40 cm) wide
90 oz 10 dwt (2,845 gr)
Arms: Royal, of George I
See E.A. Jones, 'The Duke of Cumberland's English Plate', *Burlington Magazine*, January, 1924. See also no.631.
New York, 12–14 IV 1984, 374
$121,000 (£87,050)

Philip Rollos II
London; apprenticed to his father, Philip Rollos I, first mark 1705
Mark Grimwade, 2224, 2392

673 Tea set comprising tray, teapot, sugar bowl, milk jug and tea caddy
silver-gilt
London, 1721
164 oz 7 dwt (5,111 gr)
Arms: Royal
London, 8 IV 1954, 136
£12,500 ($35,125)

674 Tankard
London, 1721
7½ in (18.8 cm) high
31 oz 12 dwt (982 gr)
New York, 16 VI 1982, 18
$5,500 (£3,072)

675 Punch bowl
London, 1705
11¼ in (28.5 cm) diameter
57 oz 8 dwt (1,785 gr)
London, 1 VIII 1974, 333
£1,550 ($3,720)

675 P. ROLLOS II

676 METTAYER

677 METTAYER

678 S. PANTIN I

679 S. PANTIN I

680 S. PANTIN I

681 S. PANTIN I

Lewis Mettayer
London; apprenticed to David Willaume, who was married to Mettayer's sister; first mark 1700, died 1740. Mettayer was also closely connected with Peter Harache (see Grimwade, p.596)
Mark Grimwade, 1943, 2018, 3724

676 Andirons, pair
London, 1715
26 in (66 cm) high
Arms: 2nd Earl of Mountrath and his wife Isabella, daughter of 2nd Earl of Carnarvon
New York, 17 June 1981, 41
$176,000 (£85,024)

677 Sideboard dish and ewer
silver-gilt
London, 1720
Dish: 27¼ in (69.2 cm) diameter
Ewer: 13¼ in (33.7 cm) high
319 oz (9,920 gr)
Arms: Pocock
Inscribed: The Gift of Madam Pocock at the desire of her late Husband the Honble Brigr Gen Pocock. St. Martin's in the Fields 1732
London, 17 V 1973, 111
£26,000 ($65,000)

Simon Pantin I
London; apprenticed to Peter Harache, first mark 1701, died 1728
Mark Grimwade, 2124–5, 2606

678 Coffee pot
London, 1711
8¼ in (21 cm) high
18 oz 16 dwt (584 gr)
London, 18 XI 1965, 171
£2,000 ($5,600)

679 Incense Boat
London, 1702
4¾ in (12 cm) high
10 oz (311 gr)
London, 24 X 1946, 116
£75 ($302)

680 Hot milk jug
(London), c. 1705
Maker's mark only
4¾ in (12.1 cm) high
6 oz (186 gr)
London, 1 V 1969, 187
£900 ($2,160)

681 Candlesticks, pair
London, 1710
7½ in (19 cm) high
28 oz 11 dwt (887 gr)
London, 17 V 1973, 45
£2,500 ($6,250)

682 S. PANTIN I

684 S. PANTIN I

683 S. PANTIN I

685 S. PANTIN I

686 LIGER

682 Salvers, pair
silver-gilt
London, 1713
Scratch weights and numbered 1 and 2
15 in (38.2 cm) diameter
146 oz (4,540 gr)
Arms: Sir Henry Fetherstone, 2nd Bt
London, 30 XI 1978, 86
£30,800 ($63,140)

683 Bowls and covers, pair
silver-gilt
London, 1727
7¼ in (18.4 cm) wide
46 oz 18 dwt (1,458 gr)
Arms: Sir Nathaniel Curzon, 4th Bt (1675–1758), and his wife Mary, daughter of Sir Ralph Assheton, whom he married 1716
London, 17 V 1973, 177
£6,500 ($16,250)

684 Candlesticks, four
London, 1716/19
5¼ in (13.3 cm) high
38 oz 1 dwt (1,183 gr)
London, 9 V 1974, 230
£3,200 ($7,680)

685 Cup and cover
London, 1711
14 in (35.6 cm) high
95 oz 10 dwt (2,970 gr)
Arms: Sir Edward Bagot, 4th Bt, and his wife Frances, daughter of Sir Thomas Wagstaffe, whom he married 1697
London, 14 V 1959, 147
£1,250 ($3,512)

Isaac Liger

London; first mark 1704, died 1730. See Oman, *English Engraved Silver*, p.78, on his connections with Simon Gribelin and George Booth, 2nd Earl of Warrington.
Mark Grimwade, 1462, 1931

686 Bowls, two
London, 1717/26
11¼ in (28.5 cm) diameter
62 oz 10 dwt (1,943 gr)
Arms: George Booth, 2nd Earl of Warrington
Provenance: Sir John Foley Grey, 1921
London, 15 X 1970, 33
£4,200 ($10,080)

687 Teapot
London, 1729
4¾ in (12 cm) high
15 oz 1 dwt (466 gr)
London, 28 XI 1968, 224
£2,100 ($5,040)

687 LIGER

688 LIGER

689 LIGER

690 J. MARGAS

691 J. MARGAS

688 Snuffers and tray
The snuffers by Augustine Courtauld (see nos 759–761)
London, 1710
Tray: 7½ in (19 cm) wide
13 oz 16 dwt (429 gr)
Arms on tray: George Booth, 2nd Earl of Warrington; arms on snuffers: Grey quartering Booth impaling Bentinck, for 5th Earl of Stamford and his wife Henrietta, daughter of 2nd Duke of Portland, whom he married 1763
London, 18 XI 1965, 108
£1,150 ($3,120)

689 Toilet service (a selection illustrated)
silver-gilt
London, 1728
581 oz 14 dwt (18,090 gr)
Arms: Mary, Countess of Warrington or her daughter Lady Mary Booth, only child and heiress of 2nd Earl of Warrington, who married Henry, 4th Earl of Stamford 1736
The design of this service is influenced by a pattern book of engravings by C. de Moelder. See Hayward, 'A William & Mary Pattern Book for Silversmiths'.
London, 12 V 1966, 113
£14,500 ($40,600)

Jacob Margas
London; born 1684, apprenticed to Thomas Jenkins, first mark 1706, bankrupt 1725
Mark Grimwade, 1510, 1983, 3733–4

690 Cup and cover
With a salver *en suite*, Edmund Pearce
silver-gilt
London, 1725
13½ in (34.2 cm) high
165 oz 6 dwt (5,140 gr)
Arms: Royal
Probably a christening gift from George I to George Seymour (1725–45), son of 7th Duke of Somerset. See nos 671, 694
London, 3 V 1984, 54
£20,900 ($29,051)

691 Bowl
London, 1719
4 in (10.2 cm) diameter
4 oz 3 dwt (125 gr)
London, 16 VII 1970, 49
£1,400 ($3,360)

692 TANQUERAY

694 S. MARGAS

695 S. MARGAS

693 TANQUERAY

David Tanqueray
London; apprenticed to David Willaume, whose daughter he married; first mark 1713, died ?c. 1724
Mark Grimwade, 509, 2675

692 Dish
London, 1723
7 in (17.8 cm) diameter
10 oz 10 dwt (326 gr)
New York, 6 VI 1980, 45
$6,600 (£2,808)

693 Beer jug
London, 1723
9 in (22.9 cm) high
84 oz 3 dwt (2,617 gr)
Arms: Grenville quartering Temple with Nugent in pretence. George Grenville (1753–1813) was created Marquess of Buckingham 1784. He married Mary Elizabeth, daughter of 1st Earl Nugent, 1775.
The lot included another beer jug, Aldridge and Green (1785).
London, 22 V 1958, 103
£1,000 ($2,810)

Samuel Margas
London; born c. 1690, apprenticed to his brother Jacob (see above, nos 690, 691), first mark 1715, Subordinate Goldsmith to the King 1723–30 and 1732–3

694 Cup and cover
silver-gilt
London, 1721
13¼ in (33.6 cm) high
83 oz 2 dwt (2,584 gr)
Arms: Royal (George I); also of George Edgecumbe, son of 1st Baron Edgecumbe
See Hayward, *Huguenot Silver*, pl.10 for a cup of similar design, Philip Rollos, 1714, See also nos 671, 690.
London, 26 VI 1975, 63
£3,600 ($8,280)

695 Candlesticks, pair
London, 1717
6¼ in (15.9 cm) high
26 oz 8 dwt (821 gr)
London, 9 X 1969, 159
£1,950 ($4,680)

Thomas Folkingham
London; first mark 1707, died 1729
Mark Grimwade, 703, 2750

696 Candlesticks, four
silver-gilt, two Britannia Standard
London, 1725
Two: maker's mark only struck four times
5¾ in (14.6 cm) high
49 oz 12 dwt (1,542 gr)
London, 14 XII 1967, 116
£5,500 ($13,200)

696 FOLKINGHAM

697 FOLKINGHAM

698 FOLKINGHAM

699 DE LAMERIE

700 DE LAMERIE

701 DE LAMERIE

702 DE LAMERIE

703 DE LAMERIE

697 Casket
silver-gilt
London, 1725
10¼ in (26 cm) wide
109 oz 6 dwt (3,400 gr)
Arms: Charles Pepys, created 1st Earl of Cottenham 1850
See a similar pair of toilet vases, Christie's, 1 July 1970, lot 103.
Monaco, 30 XI 1975, 256
FFr.38,000 (£4,222 $8,445)

698 Candlesticks, pair
London, 1715
6¼ in (16 cm) high
23 oz 6 dwt (724 gr)
London, 2 VI 1977, 246
£2,860 ($4,862)

Paul de Lamerie

London; baptized 1688 at s'Hertogenbosch, Holland, apprenticed to Pierre Platel, first mark 1713, died 1751.
See Phillips, *Paul De Lamerie*; Honour, *Goldsmiths and Silversmiths*, pp.165–171. See also p.27.
Mark Grimwade, 1892, 2203-4

699 Candlesticks, pair
London, 1719
7 in (17.8 cm) high
42 oz 2 dwt (1,309 gr)
Arms: Morrell of Wallingford, co. Berks
London, 20 VI 1974, 107
£7,500 ($18,000)

700 Tea kettle on lamp stand
silver, Britannia Standard
London, 1725
12¼ in (31.1 cm) high
65 oz 7 dwt (2,032 gr)
London, 16 VII 1970, 84
£1,350 ($3,240)

701 Wall sconces, pair
silver-gilt, Britannia Standard (London), c. 1725
Maker's mark and leopard's head mark only
20½ in (52.1 cm) high
228 oz 12 dwt (7,109 gr)
Arms: 2nd Baron Foley, succeeded 1733, died 1766
London, 18 V 1967, 150
£23,000 ($64,400)

702 Waiter
London, 1730
6¾ in (17.2 cm) diameter
10 oz 1 dwt (311 gr)
London, 17 V 1973, 186
£3,600 ($9,000)

703 Caster
silver, Britannia Standard
London, 1730
6¾ in (17.2 cm) high
10 oz 9 dwt (324 gr)
London, 17 VI 1971, 173
£1,700 ($4,080)

704 DE LAMERIE

705 DE LAMERIE

706 DE LAMERIE

707 DE LAMERIE

708 DE LAMERIE

709 DE LAMERIE

704 Candlesticks, four
London, 1733/4
8 in (20.3 cm) high
83 oz 15 dwt (2,604 gr)
Arms: John, 3rd Earl Hyndford, showing the charge of the Eagle of Silesia granted by the King of Prussia after the Treaty of Breslau (1742)
London, 4 XII 1969, 246
£5,000 ($12,000)

710 DE LAMERIE

705 Coffee pot
London, 1734
8¼ in (21 cm) high
25 oz 15 dwt (800 gr)
Arms: Jerome, 2nd Count de Salis and his wife Mary, daughter of 1st Viscount Fane, whom he married 1735
London, 6 II 1958, 174
£1,350 ($3,793)

706 Candlesticks, four
London, 1734
7¾ in (19.2 cm) high
76 oz 15 dwt (2,386 gr)
London, 28 XI 1968, 263
£9,500 ($22,800)

707 Sauceboats, stands and ladles, pair
London, 1733/9
Sauceboats: 9¼ in (23.7 cm) wide
86 oz 10 dwt (2,690 gr)
Arms: Philip Yorke of Erddig, co. Denbigh, and his wife Diana Wynn, whom he married 1782
New York, 4 VI 1974, 84
$46,000 (£19,166)

708 Cake baskets, pair
London, 1734
9¼ in (23.5 cm) diameter
81 oz 10 dwt (2,534 gr)
Arms: Sir John Guise, 4th Bt, succeeded 1732
Compare with a basket, Thomas Folkingham, 1711, in the Victoria and Albert Museum, London, illus. Hayward, *Huguenot Silver*, pl.58B. See p.25.
London, 30 V 1963, 14
£15,500 ($43,400)

709 Strawberry dishes, three
London, 1734
9 in and 9½ in (22.9 cm and 24.2 cm) diameter
61 oz 2 dwt (1,900 gr)
Arms: *accolée* Royal Armorials for William IV, Prince of Orange, and Anne (Princess Royal), daughter of George II. They married 25 March 1734
London, 28 II 1974, 133
£17,000 ($40,800)

710 Sideboard dish
London, 1736
27¼ in (69.2 cm) diameter
272 oz 15 dwt (8,482 gr)
London, 16 VII 1970, 88
£27,000 ($64,800)

711 Ewer
(London), c. 1735
Maker's mark and lion passant only
15 in (38.2 cm) high
106 oz 10 dwt (3,312 gr)
Arms: Loftus, Earls of Ely
New York, 4 VI 1974, 80
$25,000 (£10,416)

711 DE LAMERIE   712 DE LAMERIE

713 DE LAMERIE

712 Ewer
silver-gilt
London, 1736
14 in (35.6 cm) high
78 oz 11 dwt (2,442 gr)
Exhibition: 25 Park Lane, 1929, no.46.
London, 17 XI 1960, 173
£4,200 ($11,802)

713 Set of three tea caddies, cream jug, two knives, twelve teaspoons, a mote skimmer and sugar tongs (case)
London, 1735
5½ in (14 cm) high
55 oz 16 dwt (1,735 gr)
Arms: Jean Daniel Boissier and his wife Suzanne Judith Berchère, whom he married 1735
Now in Leeds City Art Gallery; see catalogue of exhibition, 'Rococo', no.G1.
London, 21 I 1960, 158
£6,600 ($18,546)

176 GREAT BRITAIN IRELAND

714 DE LAMERIE

715 DE LAMERIE

716 DE LAMERIE   717 DE LAMERIE

718 DE LAMERIE

714 Tray
London, 1736
26¾ in (68 cm) wide
182 oz 13 dwt (5,680 gr)
Arms: Hasell impaling Williams, for Dorothy Williams, second wife of Sir Edward Hasell (1642–1707).
London, 25 X 1962, 177
£8,500 ($23,800)

715 Cup and cover
London, 1737
12¼ in (31.1 cm) high
56 oz 6 dwt (1,750 gr)
Arms: Richard Annesley, who succeeded as 6th Earl of Anglesey 1737, died 1761
London, 30 V 1968, 199
£1,800 ($4,320)

716 Soup ladle
London, 1738
14¾ in (37.5 cm) overall
13 oz 5 dwt (412 gr)
New York, 4 VI 1974, 72
$9,100 (£3,791)

717 Coffee pot
London, 1738
9 in (23.2 cm) high
25 oz 16 dwt (802 gr)
New York, 13 X 1981, 327
$42,900 (£23,966)

718 Tea kettle on lamp stand with tray
London, 1736/7
13 in (33 cm) high
106 oz 10 dwt (3,312 gr)
Arms: Sir John Lesquesne, knighted 1738
London, 27 VI 1929, 172
£1,550 ($7,517)

719 Tray
London, 1741
26 in (66 cm) wide
195 oz (6,095 gr)
Arms *accolée*: Child and Jodrell
New York, 6 VI 1980, 24
$192,500 (£81,915)

719 DE LAMERIE

720 DE LAMERIE

721 DE LAMERIE

722 DE LAMERIE

724 DE LAMERIE

723 DE LAMERIE

720 Tea caddies, three, with thirteen spoons and a pair of sugar nips, in contemporary case
London, 1741
5¼ in (13.3 cm) high
49 oz (1,523 gr)
London, 16 VII 1970, 97
£5,800 ($13,920)

721 Coffee pot
London, 1738
11 in (28 cm) high
34 oz (1,057 gr) including a cream jug
Arms: see no.718
See p.47; also Grimwade *Rococo Silver*, pl.60A, and catalogue of exhibition, 'Rococo', no.97.
London, 27 VI 1929, 171
£580 ($2,813)

722 Cream boat
silver-gilt
Unmarked, attributed to Paul de Lamerie
c. 1740
4½ in (11.2 cm) overall
10 oz (311 gr)
New York, 1–2 III 1978, 545
$7,000 (£3,783)

723 Cake basket
London, 1741
14½ in (36.8 cm) wide
55 oz 6 dwt (1,719 gr)
Arms: 2nd Baron Romney
London, 2 XII 1965, 181
£1,800 ($5,040)

724 Meat dishes, pair
London, 1741
17 in (43.2 cm) wide
80 oz 7 dwt (2,498 gr)
London, 24 III 1960, 6
£1,700 ($4,777)

725 DE LAMERIE

726 DE LAMERIE

727 DE LAMERIE

728 DE LAMERIE

729 DE LAMERIE

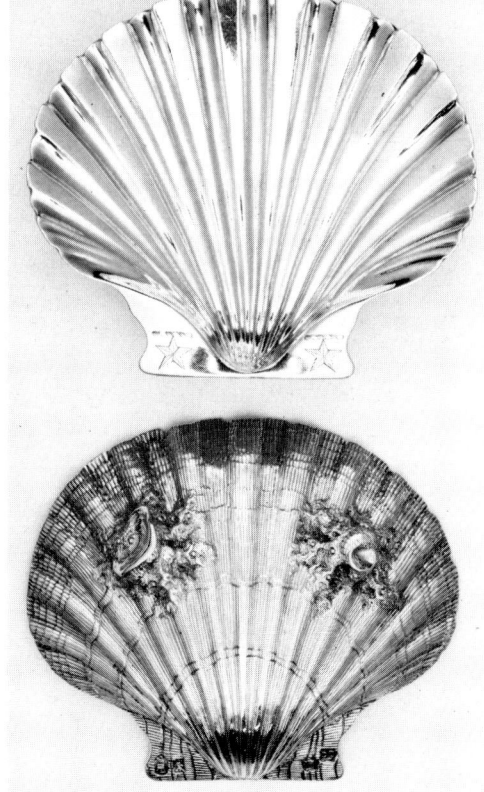

730 DE LAMERIE

725 Casters, three
London, 1738
Lamerie's mark overstruck by that of Phillips Garden (see nos 904–910)
7½ in and 9½ in (19 cm and 24.2 cm) high
42 oz 7 dwt (1,317 gr)
London, 26 XI 1953, 163
£105 ($295)

726 Waiters, pair
London, 1745
6 in (15.2 cm) diameter
26 oz 1 dwt (808 gr)
London, 17 XI 1960, 154
£850 ($2,388)

727 Cake basket
London, 1742
14 in (35.5 cm) wide
61 oz 10 dwt (1,912 gr)
See John D. Davis, *English Silver at Williamsburg*, Williamsburg 1979, no.119, for a similar basket.
New York, 17 VI 1981, 86
$93,500 (£45,170)

728 Meat dishes, pair, and a mazarine
London, 1744
20½ in (52 cm) wide
203 oz (6,313 gr)
London, 24 IV 1969, 242
£5,800 ($13,920)

729 Soup tureen and cover
London, 1741
17¾ in (45.1 cm) wide
139 oz (4,309 gr)
London, 11 XI 1982, 24
£74,800 ($119,680)

730 Butter shells, pair
London, 1742
5¼ in (13.3 cm) wide
15 oz 3 dwt (471 gr)
London, 17 VI 1971, 175
£3,200 ($7,680)

731 DE LAMERIE

732 DE LAMERIE

732 DE LAMERIE

733 DE LAMERIE

734 DE LAMERIE

735 DE LAMERIE

736 UNMARKED

731 Cup and cover
London, 1739
14 in (35.6 cm) high
98 oz 4 dwt (3,054 gr)
New York, 4 VI 1974, 75
$37,000 (£15,420)

732 Covered jug
London, 1747
10½ in (26.7 cm) high
21 oz 16 dwt (677 gr)
London, 13 VII 1967, 201
£1,250 ($3,500)

733 Cruet frames, pair
London, 1747
6½ in (16.5 cm) wide
43 oz 10 dwt (1,352 gr)
London, 16 VII 1970, 94
£5,000 ($12,000)

734 Inkstand
London, 1749
9½ in (24.2 cm) wide
22 oz 12 dwt (702 gr)
London, 24 III 1960, 5
£3,600 ($5,180)

735 Tea caddies, pair
London, 1751
6 in (15.2 cm) high
29 oz 12 dwt (920 gr)
London, 28 IV 1977, 184
£9,350 ($15,895)

Unmarked

736 Orange strainer
English, c. 1730
7 in (17.8 cm) overall
3 oz 7 dwt (104 gr)
London, 5 VI 1980, 80
£605 ($1,421)

737 FARREN

738 FARREN

739 FARREN

739 (DETAIL)

Thomas Farren
London; first mark 1707, died 1743; Subordinate Goldsmith to the King 1723–42
Mark Grimwade, 666, 2749, 2755, 3564

737 Cup and cover and salver-on-foot
silver-gilt
London, 1715
Cup: 11 in (28 cm) high; salver: 14¾ in (37.5 cm) diameter
141 oz (4,385 gr)
Arms: South Sea Company
Now in the Museum of London.
London, 20 IV 1972, 154
£7,800 ($19,500)

738 Cup and cover
silver-gilt
London, 1740
13 in (33 cm) high
99 oz 6 dwt (3,088 gr) including a plinth, Robert Garrard (1848)
Arms: Poulett
London, 18 XI 1981, 157
£9,350 ($16,736)

739 Cake basket
London, 1737
13 in (33 cm) wide
60 oz 15 dwt (1,889 gr)
Arms: John Shales Barrington
See no.868
London, 9 V 1974, 149
£5,500 ($13,200)

740 Coffee pot
London, 1733
9¼ in (23.5 cm) high
25 oz 4 dwt (783 gr)
London, 12 XII 1974, 116
£2,600 ($5,980)

Gabriel Sleath
London; born 1674, first mark 1707, died 1756. See Grimshaw, 'The Three Gabriels'.
Mark Grimwade, 890, 904, 907, 2568–9

741 Coffee pot
London, 1733
8¾ in (22.2 cm) high
22 oz 16 dwt (709 gr)
London, 5 XII 1968, 156
£3,200 ($7,680)

742 Tea kettle on lamp stand
London, 1715
12 in (30.5 cm) high
95 oz 4 dwt (2,960 gr)
New York, 17 VI 1981, 43
$27,500 (£13,285)

743 Porringer
London, 1713
4¼ in (10.8 cm) high
9 oz 6 dwt (289 gr)
London, 29 V 1975, 192
£350 ($805)

744 Sauceboats, pair
London, 1734
9 in (22.9 cm) overall
44 oz 12 dwt (1,387 gr)
London, 25 X 1973, 130
£7,000 ($16,800)

745 Tea kettle on lamp stand
London, 1745
13 in (33 cm) high
61 oz 5 dwt (1,904 gr)
London, 28 VIII 1969, 140
£400 ($960)

740 FARREN

741 SLEATH

745 SLEATH

742 SLEATH

746 SLEATH

743 SLEATH

744 SLEATH

747 SLEATH

746 Mugs, pair
London, 1730
3¾ in (9.5 cm) high
13 oz (404 gr)
London, 15 X 1970, 43
£380 ($912)

747 Beakers, pair
London, 1735
3¾ in (9.5 cm) high
15 oz (466 gr)
Arms: William Gouch (1681–1751), who was Governor of Virginia 1727
Johannesburg, 3 III 1975, 38
R.2,000 (£1,290 $2,967)

748 BAYLEY

749 BAYLEY

750 BAYLEY

751 BAYLEY

752 BAYLEY

753 BAYLEY

Richard Bayley
London; apprenticed to Charles Overing, first mark 1708
Mark Grimwade, 116, 2262, 2279, 3481, 3760–61

748 Hot milk jug
London, 1713
6¾ in (17.2 cm) high
12 oz (373 gr)
London, 16 VII 1970, 55
£3,600 ($8,640)

749 Coffee pot
London, 1715
9¾ in (24.8 cm) high
25 oz (777 gr)
London, 10 II 1949, 122
£420 ($1,692)

750 Coffee pot
London, 1715
9½ in (24 cm) high
24 oz 12 dwt (765 gr)
London, 17 X 1968, 199
£1,950 ($4,680)

751 Chocolate pot
London, 1729
9 in (23 cm) high
25 oz 7 dwt (788 gr)
London, 8 XI 1973, 36
£1,150 ($2,760)

752 Punch bowl
London, 1717
8¾ in (22.2 cm) diameter
29 oz (901 gr)
London, 8 VI 1972, 50
£1,600 ($4,000)

753 Tankard
London, 1737
8½ in (21.6 cm) high
33 oz 11 dwt (1,043 gr)
London, 20 VI 1974, 78
£850 ($2,040)

754 Teapot
London, 1713
5¾ in (14.6 cm) high
13 oz 4 dwt (410 gr)
Arms: Cowper, Earls of Cowper
London, 31 X 1974, 195
£900 ($2,070)

755 Teapot
London, 1737
5¼ in (13.3 cm) high
21 oz 2 dwt (656 gr)
Arms: Trapnell, co. Wilts
London, 24 IV 1969, 209
£3,200 ($7,680)

756 Tankard
London, 1743
17¼ in (43.8 cm) high
31 oz 9 dwt (978 gr)
London, 26 VII 1968, 325
£1,100 ($2,640)

754 BAYLEY

755 BAYLEY

756 BAYLEY

757 BAYLEY

758 BAYLEY

757 Sauceboats, pair
London, 1743
8¼ in (21 cm) overall
33 oz 18 dwt (1,054 gr)
London, 5 II 1948, 79
£220 ($886)

758 Beer jug
London, 1750
7½ in (19 cm) high
29 oz 1 dwt (903 gr)
London, 19 XI 1970, 174
£720 ($1,728)

Augustine Courtauld

London; born 1685–6, apprenticed to Simon Pantin, first mark 1708, died 1751
See Hayward, *The Courtauld Silver.*
Mark Grimwade, 18, 22, 385

759 Tea kettle on lamp stand with matching triangular stand
London, 1739/40
15¼ in (38.7 cm) high;
stand: 12 in (30.5 cm) wide
111 oz 14 dwt (3,473 gr)
London, 22 X 1970, 139
£800 ($1,920)

760 Caster
London, 1726
8¼ in (21 cm) high
16 oz 8 dwt (510 gr)
London, 24 III 1960, 13
£1,000 ($2,810)

759 A. COURTAULD

760 A. COURTAULD

761 Cup and cover
silver, Britannia Standard
London, 1725
11½ in (29.2 cm) high
73 oz (2,270 gr)
London, 13 XII 1973, 118
£2,400 ($5,760)

761 A. COURTAULD

762 VINCENT

763 (DETAIL)

Edward Vincent
London; free 1712
Mark Grimwade, 648–9, 2983, 3560, 3852

762 Salvers, two
London, 1728
One maker's mark: I.L., 1735
13½ in (34.3 cm) diameter
83 oz 10 dwt (2,596 gr)
Engraved with representations of the seals of office given to Sir Robert Eyre. The engraving attributed to Samuel Gribelin (son of Simon)
See Oman, *English Engraved Silver*, p.82.
New York, 6 VI 1980, 48
$198,000 (£84,255)

762 (DETAIL)

763 LE SAGE

John Hugh Le Sage
London; apprenticed to Louis Cuny, first mark 1718
Mark Grimwade, 1646, 1680–81, 2469, 3678A, 3683

763 Ewer
silver-gilt
London, 1725
15¾ in (40 cm) high
155 oz 15 dwt (4,843 gr)
This ewer has been separated from its dish (see *Connoisseur*, December 1936), which bears the arms of Sir Michael Newton, 4th Bt, created Knight of the Bath 1725
London, 23 VII 1970, 163
£3,400 ($8,160)

764 Cup and cover
London, 1734
13½ in (34.2 cm) high
100 oz 5 dwt (3,117 gr)
Arms: Henry, 2nd son of Sir William Courtney Bt of Powderham and his wife Catherine, daughter of 1st Earl Bathurst, whom he married 1737
London, 4 III 1965, 180
£2,800 ($7,840)

765 Salver
London, 1747
23½ in (59.7 cm) wide
155 oz 9 dwt (4,834 gr)
London, 27 VI 1963, 33
£2,100 ($5,880)

766 Flagons, pair
silver-gilt
London, 1746
Numbered 13 and 14
20½ in (52 cm) high
523 oz 10 dwt (16,280 gr)
Inscribed: The Gift of Mrs Eliz. Pocock to the Parish of St. Martin, Westmr 1746
Provenance: Church of St Martin in the Fields, London
London, 17 V 1973, 116
£14,000 ($35,000)

767 Candlesticks, pair
London, 1746
11½ in (29.2 cm) high
81 oz 12 dwt (2,537 gr)
London, 8 VI 1972, 14
£1,750 ($4,375)

René Hudell
London; mark entered 1718
Mark Grimwade, 1074

768 Sauceboats, pair
London, 1720
8½ in (21.6 cm) wide
28 oz 3 dwt (875 gr)
London, 15 VI 1961, 156
£2,900 ($8,149)

764 LE SAGE

766 LE SAGE

765 LE SAGE

767 LE SAGE

768 HUDELL

769 PILLEAU

770 PILLEAU

771 PILLEAU

772 PILLEAU

773 PILLEAU

774 PILLEAU

775 CRESPIN

Pezé Pilleau
London; baptized 1696, apprenticed to John Chartier, whose daughter he married; first mark c. 1720–24, died 1776
Mark Grimwade, 2195, 2212, 2217

769 Cruet frame, with three casters and two bottles
London, 1725
8 in (20.3 cm) wide
56 oz 5 dwt (1,749 gr)
Arms: 5th Baron Baltimore, who was Governor of Maryland 1732–3 and died 1751
London, 29 II 1968, 146
£1,950 ($4,680)

770 Covered jug
London, 1730
6½ in (16.5 cm) high
15 oz 7 dwt (477 gr)
London, 25 II 1954, 77
£620 ($1,742)

771 Tea kettle on lamp stand
London, 1731
13 in (33 cm) high
61 oz 6 dwt (1,906 gr)
Arms: Pollen impaling St John
London, 26 VI 1975, 203
£900 ($2,070)

772 Inkstand
London, 1735
8¾ in (22 cm) wide
15 oz 10 dwt (482 gr)
New York, 12–14 IV 1984, 356A
$2,750 (£1,978)

773 Bowl
London, 1737
5¾ in (14.6 cm) diameter
10 oz 3 dwt (315 gr)
London, 19 VI 1969, 150
£600 ($1,440)

774 Sauceboats, pair
London, 1752
8½ in (21.5 cm) overall
36 oz 5 dwt (1,127 gr)
New York, 16–17 XII 1976, 330
$2,500 (£1,470)

Paul Crespin

London; born 1694, first mark 1720, retired *c*. 1760, died 1770. One of the finest Huguenot craftsmen
Mark Grimwade, 406, 412, 2143a, 2146, 2149

775 Salvers, pair
London, 1727
7¾ in (19.7 cm) square
38 oz 4 dwt (1,188 gr)
Arms: 4th Earl of Chesterfield (see no.777)
London, 18 VI 1981, 106
£3,410 ($7,058)

776 Two tea caddies and a sugar bowl
The bowl possibly John Chapman
silver, Britannia Standard
London, 1724
Arms: Vernon
London, 11 IV 1934, 134
£170, ($850)

777 Candlesticks, four
London, 1727
8½ in (21.6 cm) high
105 oz (3,265 gr) including later nozzles
Arms: Royal
Formerly the property of Philip Dormer, 4th Earl of Chesterfield, author of the famous letters to his son. He was ambassador at The Hague 1728–32
London, 26 VII 1945, 72
£305 ($1,229)

776 CRESPIN

777 CRESPIN

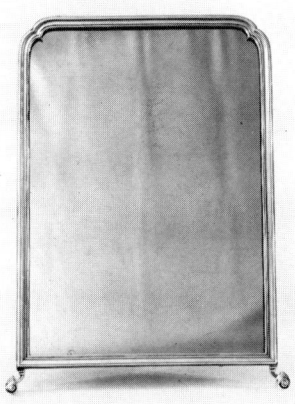
779 CRESPIN

778 Sideboard dish
silver-gilt
London, 1727
28 in (71 cm) diameter
405 oz (12,595 gr)
Arms: Richard Marquess of Buckingham, who married Lady Anna-Eliza Brydges 1796; he was later created Duke of Buckingham and Chandos
New York, 16–17 XII 1976, 60
$28,000 (£16,470)

779 Toilet mirror
silver, wood-backed
London, 1728
Scratch weight: 34 oz 6 dwt
19 in (48.2 cm) high
London, 4 III 1965, 144
£1,050 ($2,940)

778 CRESPIN

780 Salt cellars, pair
London, 1730
3¼ in (8.2 cm) diameter
12 oz 8 dwt (385 gr)
London, 4 III 1965, 151
£480 ($1,344)

781 Dishes, pair
London, 1733
6¼ in (15.9 cm) diameter
17 oz 18 dwt (556 gr)
London, 30 XI 1978, 120
£1,375 ($2,818)

782 Cream jug
(London), c. 1735
Maker's mark only struck four times
4¼ in (10.8 cm) high
8 oz 15 dwt (272 gr)
London, 1 II 1973, 88
£300 ($750)

783 Bowl
London, 1735
5¼ in (13.3 cm) diameter
11 oz 15 dwt (365 gr)
London, 15 VI 1978, 48
£990 ($1,831)

784 Cream boat
London, 1734
5¾ in (14.6 cm) overall
9 oz 16 dwt (304 gr)
London, 18 V 1967, 44
£750 ($2,100)

780 CRESPIN

781 CRESPIN

782 CRESPIN

783 CRESPIN

784 CRESPIN

785 CRESPIN

785 Soup tureens, two
One George Wickes (1738)
London, 1733
14¾ in (37.5 cm) wide
275 oz 5 dwt (8,560 gr)
See Barr, *George Wickes, Royal Goldsmith*, p.24.
London, 9 VII 1964, 102
£2,700 ($7,280)

786 Salt cellars, pair
London, 1735
3 in (7.6 cm) diameter
32 oz 14 dwt (1,016 gr)
London, 16 VII 1970, 65
£420 ($1,008)

786 CRESPIN

787 CRESPIN

788 CRESPIN

789 P. ARCHAMBO I

790 P. ARCHAMBO I

787 Epergne
London, 1742
8½ in (21.7 cm) high
195 oz 10 dwt (6,083 gr)
Arms: Thomas Watson Wentworth, later 1st Marquess of Rockingham
Johannesburg, 17–18 III 1978, 300
R.8,000 (£5,000 $9,250)

788 Chamber candlestick
London, 1744
7 in (17.8 cm) wide
11 oz 17 dwt (368 gr)
London, 24 IV 1980, 240A
£2,035 ($4,782)

Peter Archambo I

London; apprenticed to Jacob Margas, first mark 1721, died c. 1767
Mark Grimwade, 85, 2127–8

789 Dinner plates, twelve
silver-gilt
London, 1728
9¾ in (24.7 cm) diameter
257 oz 12 dwt (8,011 gr)
Arms: George Booth, 2nd Earl of Warrington
London, 13 VI 1983, 36
£41,800 ($66,880)

790 Salver
London, 1722
12¼ in (31.1 cm) diameter
41 oz 10 dwt (1,290 gr)
Arms: Baynard, Stukey, co. Norfolk
London, 18 XI 1965, 179
£3,000 ($8,400)

791 P. ARCHAMBO I

792 P. ARCHAMBO I

793 P. ARCHAMBO I

794 P. ARCHAMBO I

795 P. ARCHAMBO I

791 Salver
London, 1732
10¾ in (27.3 cm) diameter
42 oz 4 dwt (1,312 gr)
Monogram: George Booth, 2nd Earl of Warrington
London, 8 VI 1972, 29
£3,800 ($9,500)

792 Salvers, pair
London, 1738
15¾ in (40 cm) diameter
167 oz (5,193 gr)
Arms: George Booth, 2nd Earl of Warrington
London, 13 IV 1961, 150
£2,200 ($6,182)

793 Salt cellars, four
With spoons, maker's mark PR
London, 1735
2¾ in (7 cm) diameter
28 oz (870 gr)
London, 4 VII 1968, 86
£650 ($1,560)

794 Cake basket
London, 1735
12¾ in (32.5 cm) wide
58 oz 11 dwt (1,820 gr)
Arms: William Howard, Viscount Andover, who succeeded his cousin as 11th Earl of Suffolk 1745. In 1736 he married Mary, daughter of 2nd Earl of Aylesford
London, 18 XI 1965, 112
£1,300 ($3,640)

795 Cake basket
London, 1738
12¼ in (31 cm) wide
54 oz 3 dwt (1,684 gr)
London, 26 XI 1959, 153
£400 ($1,124)

796 Candlesticks, pair
London, 1744
10 in (25.4 cm) high
61 oz 15 dwt (1,920 gr)
London, 4 V 1978, 171
£1,925 ($3,561)

797 Sauceboats, pair
London, 1734
7½ in (19 cm) overall
34 oz 18 dwt (1,085 gr)
London, 10 VI 1965, 51
£1,150 ($3,220)

798 Candlesticks, pair
London, 1744
8¾ in (22.2 cm) high
51 oz 3 dwt (1,590 gr)
London, 26 I 1967, 157
£460 ($1,288)

799 Meat dishes, pair
London, 1738
16 in (40.7 cm) wide
133 oz 9 dwt (4,150 gr)
Arms: George Booth, 2nd Earl of Warrington
London, 16 III 1961, 59
£1,600 ($4,496)

796 P. ARCHAMBO I

797 P. ARCHAMBO I

798 P. ARCHAMBO I

799 P. ARCHAMBO I

800 P. ARCHAMBO I

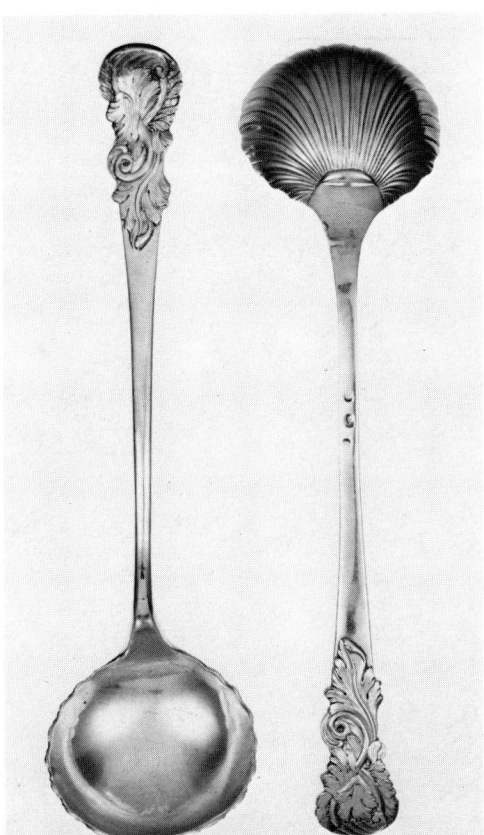

801 P. ARCHAMBO I

802 J. GOULD

803 J. GOULD

800 Tea caddies, pair
London, 1745
5 in (12.7 cm) high
34 oz 3 dwt (1,062 gr)
London, 20 VI 1974, 83
£850 ($2,040)

801 Soup ladles, pair
Maker's mark only struck thrice
(London), c. 1750
21 oz 10 dwt (668 gr)
London, 26 VI 1975, 183
£440 ($1,012)

James Gould

London; born c. 1700, first mark 1722, died 1750. See Fallon, 'The Goulds and Cafes, Candlestick makers', p.146
Mark Grimwade, 860, 1317–18, 1346–7, 3637

802 Candlesticks, pair
London, 1732
6¾ in (17.1 cm) high
25 oz 17 dwt (800 gr)
London, 18 VII 1968, 398
£2,000 ($4,800)

803 Candlesticks, pair
London, 1744
8¾ in (22.2 cm) high
38 oz 10 dwt (1,197 gr)
London, 20 II 1975, 153
£650 ($1,495)

William Gould

London; born c. 1710, first mark 1732, active until c. 1763. See Fallon, 'The Goulds and Cafes, Candlestick Makers', p.146
Mark Grimwade 868, 3134–5, 3149–50

804 Candlesticks, pair
London, 1736
6½ in (16.5 cm) high
25 oz 12 dwt (796 gr)
London, 21 VII 1977, 231
£1,078 ($1,832)

805 Candlesticks, four
London, 1745
9 in (22.9 cm) high
97 oz 12 dwt (3,035 gr)
London, 23 I 1969, 210
£3,600 ($8,640)

John Edwards II

London; first mark 1723
Mark Grimwade, 566, 573, 630, 1267–8, 1277

806 Toilet set
silver-gilt
London, 1725
344 oz 8 dwt (10,710 gr) excluding brushes
Arms: Joseph Gascoigne Nightingale and his wife Elizabeth, daughter of 2nd Earl Ferrers, whom he married 1725. She died 1731 (see their monument by Roubiliac in Westminster Abbey: *Official Guide*, 1965, p.85). Their daughter married the 1st Earl of Lisburne 1754
London, 27 VI 1963, 43
£9,700 ($27,160)

804 W. GOULD   805 W. GOULD

806 J. EDWARDS II

807 J. EDWARDS II   808 J. EDWARDS II

809 J. EDWARDS II

809 (DETAIL)

810 J. EDWARDS II

811 J. EDWARDS II

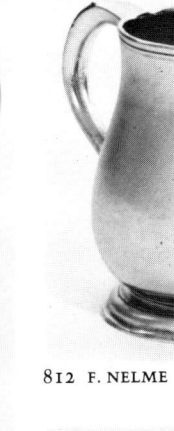

812 F. NELME

813 F. NELME

807 Beer jugs, pair
London, 1722
9¼ in (23.5 cm) high
63 oz 1 dwt (1,960 gr)
London, 30 V 1963, 27
£2,800 ($7,840)

808 Sauceboats, pair
London, 1729
8¼ in (21 cm) overall
29 oz 17 dwt (928 gr)
London, 20 II 1964, 90
£1,150 ($3,220)

809 Soup tureens, pair
London, 1739 and c. 1739
One maker's mark only struck thrice
15¾ in (40 cm) wide
312 oz 8 dwt (9,715 gr)
Arms: Sir Henry Featherstonhaugh of Uppark, co. Sussex, who succeeded his father (purchaser of Uppark in 1747) 1774 and died 1846.

Uppark is now a property of the National Trust
Provenance: see Sotheby's, 21 October 1965, lot 118
New York, 16–17 XII 1982, 576
$110,000 (£68,750)

810 Sideboard dish
London, 1729
19¾ in (50.2 cm) diameter
114 oz 4 dwt (3,551 gr)
Arms: Royal
Given to Sir William Strickland, 4th Bt, as a christening present for his son George, born 1729
London, 27 VI 1963, 35
£1,500 ($4,200)

811 Mug
London, 1728
4¾ in (12 cm) high
17 oz 2 dwt (531 gr)
London, 26 I 1967, 97
£620 ($1,736)

Francis Nelme

London; apprenticed to his father Anthony (see above, no. 544ff.), first mark 1723. His business was purchased by Thomas Whipham in 1739; by the early 19th century it had become Edward Barnard and Sons (see below, no. 1373ff.)
Mark Grimwade, 67, 702

812 Mugs, pair
London, 1729 and c. 1729
One maker's mark only struck four times
3½ in (9 cm) high
17 oz 10 dwt (544 gr)
London, 30 XI 1972, 111
£880 ($2,200)

813 Coffee pot
London, 1735
8¼ in (21 cm) high
23 oz 16 dwt (740 gr)
London, 24 IV 1975, 178
£1,600 ($3,680)

William Aytoun
Edinburgh; admitted to
Incorporation 1718
Mark Jackson, p.501

814 Coffee set
Edinburgh, 1718/20
Assay Master: Edward Penman
56 oz 18 dwt (1,769 gr)
London, 22 X 1970, 213
£9,800 ($23,520)

815 Tea urn
Edinburgh, 1736
Assay Master: Archibald Ure
13 in (33 cm) high
53 oz 10 dwt (1,663 gr)
New York, 28 X 1980, 553
$3,300 (£1,594)

816 Broth bowl
Edinburgh, 1733
Assay Master: Archibald Ure
6 in (15.2 cm) diameter
7 oz 17 dwt (244 gr)
London, 11 XI 1982, 16
£1,320 ($2,112)

817 Sugar bowl
Edinburgh, 1746
Assay Master: Archibald Ure
5 in (12.7 cm) diameter
7 oz 13 dwt (238 gr)
London, 26 II 1976, 139
£572 ($1,029)

James Ker
Edinburgh; admitted to
Incorporation 1723
Mark Jackson, p.502

818 Cream boat
Edinburgh, 1744
Assay Master: Hugh Gordon
6¾ in (17.2 cm) overall
7 oz 4 dwt (223 gr)
London, 14 III 1974, 195
£440 ($1,056)

819 Dish
Edinburgh, 1729
Assay Master: Archibald Ure
8½ in (21.5 cm) diameter
12 oz 18 dwt (401 gr)
London, 19 XI 1970, 226
£420 ($1,008)

820 Teapot
Edinburgh, 1742
Assay Master: Edward Lothian
5¾ in (14.6 cm) high
18 oz 13 dwt (580 gr)
Gleneagles Hotel, 28 VIII 1975, 64
£380 ($874)

814 AYTOUN

816 AYTOUN

815 AYTOUN

817 AYTOUN

818 KER

819 KER

820 KER

821 CALDERWOOD

822 CALDERWOOD

825 KANDLER

Charles Frederick Kandler

London; first mark 1727. Until the publication of Grimwade's *London Goldsmiths* in 1982 it was thought that Charles and Frederick were separate individuals
Mark Grimwade, 341, 689, 691–2, 1540, 1862–3, 3571

825 Caster
London, 1727
8¼ in (21.3 cm) high
19 oz (590 gr)
New York, 25–26 IV 1978, 745
$3,000 (£1,621)

823 CALDERWOOD

824 CALDERWOOD

Robert Calderwood

Dublin; free 1727, died 1766
Mark Bennett, p.341; Jackson, p.612

821 Beer jug
Dublin, 1747
11 in (28 cm) high
55 oz 13 dwt (1,730 gr)
London, 24 VII 1975, 205
£2,900 ($6,670)

822 Covered jug
Dublin, c. 1750
9¼ in (23.5 cm) high
29 oz 11 dwt (919 gr)
London 9 XI 1967, 181
£1,000 ($2,800)

823 Cups, pair
Dublin, c. 1740
4¾ in (12 cm) high
27 oz 6 dwt (849 gr)
London, 24 XI 1977, 108
£682 ($1,261)

824 Cream jug
Dublin, c. 1736
4 in (10.2 cm) high
3 oz 16 dwt (118 gr)
London, 23 IV 1981, 200
£352 ($728)

826 KANDLER

827 KANDLER

826 Soup tureen
London, 1728
14 in (35.6 cm) wide
130 oz 6 dwt (4,052 gr)
London, 4 V 1972, 174
£1,850 ($4,625)

827 Soup tureen and stand
silver, Britannia Standard
London, 1728
19¼ in (49 cm) wide
216 oz (6,717 gr)
London, 7 II 1957, 129
£1,850 ($5,161)

828 Candelabra, pair
London, 1751/2
14½ in (37 cm) high
116 oz (3,607 gr)
London, 19 I 1956, 106
£750 ($2,100)

829 Toilet mirror
London, 1777
27¼ in (69.2 cm) high
Arms: 3rd Earl of Bristol, died 1779
London, 16 VII 1970, 120
£780 ($1,872)

830 Candlesticks, pair
London, 1730
8¾ in (22.2 cm) high
61 oz 10 dwt (1,912 gr)
Compare with no.835
London, 14 X 1954, 149
£260 ($730)

831 Sauceboat
London, 1742
9¼ in (23.5 cm) overall
40 oz 10 dwt (1,259 gr)
London, 20 IV 1972, 147
£920 ($2,300)

828 KANDLER

830 KANDLER

829 KANDLER

831 KANDLER

832 KANDLER

834 KANDLER

835 HATFIELD

833 KANDLER

836 D. WILLAUME II

832 Cake basket
London, 1734
14 in (35.6 cm) wide
84 oz 4 dwt (2,618 gr)
Arms: Howard impaling Blount, for Edward, 9th Duke of Norfolk (1686–1777), and his wife Mary, daughter of Edward Blount of Blagdon, co. Devon. He inherited the title 1732. Their armorials also appear on a toilet box (Sotheby's, London, 9 October 1969, lot 153) and a caster (Christie's, 1 July 1970, lot 95), both Kandler (1727)
London, 8 VI 1972, 25
£4,400 ($11,000)

833 Coffee pot
London, 1728
9¾ in (24.7 cm) high
35 oz 6 dwt (1,097 gr)
London, 2 XII 1965, 171
£500 ($1,400)

834 Candlesticks, four
Silver (loaded)
London, 1765
14¾ in (37.5 cm) high
London, 24 X 1957, 68
£290 ($809)

Charles Hatfield
London; apprenticed to David Willaume, first mark 1727, died by 1740. Subordinate Goldsmith to the King 1723–39
Mark Grimwade, 324, 335, 944

835 Candlesticks, pair
London, 1728
8¾ in (22.2 cm) high
58 oz (1,803 gr) including later nozzles
See no.830 and p.24.
London, 26 VI 1952, 168
£200 ($558)

836 (ALTERNATIVE SETTING)

David Willaume II
London; born 1693, apprenticed to his father David I (see above, no.628ff.), first mark 1728, died 1761
Mark Grimwade, 514, 517, 3195

836 Centrepiece
David Willaume II and Anne Tanqueray
London, 1731
22 in (56 cm) overall
427 oz (13,279 gr)
London, 27 VI 1963, 47
£4,800 ($13,440)

837 D. WILLAUME II

837 Caster
London, 1730
7 in (17.8 cm) high
10 oz 14 dwt (332 gr)
London, 26 II 1976, 59
£660 ($1,188)

838 D. WILLAUME II

839 D. WILLAUME II

840 D. WILLAUME II

841 D. WILLAUME II

842 D. WILLAUME II

843 D. WILLAUME II

844 D. WILLAUME II

845 WICKES

846 WICKES

847 WICKES

838 Salt cellars, pair
London, 1732
3½ in (8.9 cm) diameter
11 oz 17 dwt (368 gr)
London, 3 II 1972, 134
£310 ($775)

839 Sauceboats, pair
London, 1737
8½ in (22.5 cm) overall
41 oz 3 dwt (1,279 gr)
London, 13 VI 1983, 48
£12,650 ($20,240)

840 Chargers, pair
silver-gilt
London, 1742
24 in (61 cm) diameter
398 oz (12,377 gr)
Arms: George Booth, 2nd Earl of Warrington
Provenance: Sir John Foley Grey, Bt, 1921
London, 8 VI 1972, 16
£7,200 ($18,000)

841 Salvers, pair
silver-gilt
London, 1743
Scratch weight 39.8 and 40.2
11 in (28 cm) diameter
79 oz 7 dwt (2,470 gr)
Cypher: George Booth, 2nd Earl of Warrington
London, 5 VI 1980, 44
£16,500 ($38,775)

842 Chamber pot
London, 1744
7 in (18 cm) diameter
33 oz 18 dwt (1,054 gr)
Arms: George Booth, 2nd Earl of Warrington
London, 14 VI 1984, 259
£10,450 ($14,525)

843 Casters, two
London, 1735
8½ in and 6¾ in (21.5 cm and 17.2 cm) high
30 oz 16 dwt (957 gr)
Arms: 2nd Duke of Grafton; succeeded 1690, died 1757
London, 13 V 1954, 81, 82
£380 ($1,067)

844 Candlesticks, pair
silver (loaded)
London, 1739
10¼ in (26 cm) high
With three-light branches, Robert Garrard (1859)
112 oz 14 dwt (3,504 gr)
London, 5 XI 1964, 147
£700 ($1,960)

George Wickes

London; baptized 1698, first mark 1722, died 1761. Because of the survival of many of Wickes' ledgers which document his business and that of his successors until the present-day firm of Garrards, we know a great deal about Wickes' clients and his associates within the trade. A full account is given by Barr, *George Wickes Royal Goldsmith 1698–1761*. See nos 854–864, 994–1000, 1002–1005, 1315
Mark Grimwade, 918, 921, 927, 3197

845 Mug
London, 1727
3¾ in (9.5 cm) high
9 oz 1 dwt (281 gr)
London, 27 I 1966, 73
£260 ($728)

848 WICKES

846 Casters, four
London, 1730
6½ in (16.5 cm) high
33 oz 13 dwt (1,046 gr)
See no.847
London, 4 V 1961, 75
£600 ($1,686)

847 Casters, pair
London, 1730
8½ in (21.6 cm) high
31 oz 4 dwt (970 gr)
New York, 11–12 XII 1973, 70
$3,500 (£1,458)

848 Dishes, pair
silver-gilt
London, 1739
10 in (25.4 cm) diameter
44 oz 2 dwt (1,371 gr)
Arms: Frederick Lewis, Prince of Wales (1707–51)
Made for the Earl of Scarborough. See Barr, op. cit., pl.95
London, 25 X 1973, 27
£2,800 ($6,720)

849 WICKES

850 WICKES

849 Candlesticks, pair
London, 1740
9½ in (24.2 cm) high
46 oz 1 dwt (1,432 gr)
London, 4 III 1971, 168
£550 ($1,320)

850 Ewer and basin
silver-gilt
London, 1735
Ewer: 14¼ in (36.2 cm) high
Maker's mark only struck four times
Basin: 21¾ in (55.2 cm) diameter
274 oz 5 dwt (8,530 gr)
scratch weights: ewer: 81 = 17, basin: 193 = 0
Arms and initials (later): William Stuart Stirling Crawfurd
Made for John Scrope (1662–1752) and presented to him by the Common Council of the Corporation of the City of Bristol. The cost was £149 15s 2d. See Barr, 'The Bristol Ewer and Basin'.
Exhibition: 'Rococo'.
London, 13 VI 1983, 45
£176,000 ($281,600)

851 Cake basket
London, 1740
13¼ in (33.6 cm) wide
61 oz 2 dwt (1,900 gr)
London, 14 X 1976, 198
£2,420 ($4,114)

852 Soup tureen and cover
London, 1742
17 in (43.2 cm) wide
110 oz 3 dwt (3,425 gr)
See Barr, op. cit., pl. 30a for a similar tureen (1739).
London, 7 III 1957, 137
£340 ($948)

853 Coffee pot
silver-gilt (later)
London, 1743
10½ in (26.5 cm) high
41 oz 15 dwt (1,298 gr)
London, 3 V 1984, 84
£5,280 ($7,339)

Edward Wakelin

London; apprenticed to John le Sage; first mark 1747, having joined George Wickes; died 1784. See nos 994–1000, 1002–1005. See also Barr, *George Wickes, Royal Goldsmith 1698–1761*, where a full account of Wakelin's association with Wickes is given, with details of the continuation of the business.
Mark Grimwade, 656

854 Tea caddies, three
London, 1751
4¼ in (10.5 cm) high
50 oz (1,555 gr)
Johannesburg, 3 III 1975, 140
R.4,500 (£2,905 $6,680)

855 Candlesticks, four
London, 1755
11 in (28 cm) high
186 oz 15 dwt (5,807 gr)
London, 18 VII 1968, 208
£4,000 ($9,600)

856 Condiment or spice boxes, pair
London, 1749
4½ in (11.6 cm) wide
31 oz 13 dwt (984 gr)
Arms: Sir William Irby, 2nd Bt, of Boston, co. Lincs.
London, 13 VI 1983, 46
£25,300 ($40,480)

857 Inkstand
London, 1755
11½ in (29.2 cm) wide
43 oz 2 dwt (1,340 gr)
London, 20 X 1966, 123
£950 ($2,660)

851 WICKES

852 WICKES

853 WICKES

854 WAKELIN

855 WAKELIN

856 WAKELIN

857 WAKELIN

858 WAKELIN

859 WAKELIN

860 WAKELIN

858 Jugs, pair
London, 1754
9½ in (24.2 cm) high
84 oz 18 dwt (2,640 gr)
London, 31 I 1963, 154
£2,100 ($5,880)

859 Wine cooler
London, 1754
8¾ in (22.2 cm) high
65 oz 5 dwt (2,029 gr)
Arms: 1st Viscount Folkestone
London, 10 II 1977, 163
£3,080 ($5,236)

860 Cream boat
London, c. 1750
4¾ in (12.1 cm) overall
12 oz 18 dwt (401 gr)
See Barr, op. cit., pl.34a.
London, 17 XI 1960, 151
£360 ($1,011)

861 WAKELIN

862 WAKELIN

861 Soup tureens, pair, with ladles
London, 1755
22½ in (57.2 cm) wide
513 oz 15 dwt (15,977 gr)
Arms: 9th Earl of Exeter (1725–93) and his wife Letitia, daughter of the Hon. Horatio Townshend
London, 16 VII 1970, 106
£7,500 ($18,000)

862 Soup tureen and cover
London, 1756; the stand, Parker and Wakelin, 1763
16¼ in (41.5 cm) wide
126 oz (3,918 gr)
Johannesburg, 3 III 1975, 51
R.4,000 (£2,580 $5,934)

863 Cruet stand
London, 1757
10 in (25.5 cm) wide
30 oz 16 dwt (958 gr)
Monaco, 30 XI – 1 XII 1975, 316
FFr.3,850 (£428 $856)

864 Tea kettle on stand, with draught excluder
London, 1757
16¾ in (42.5 cm) high
144 oz 10 dwt (4,493 gr)
New York, 14–15 XII 1977, 566
$2,800 (£1,513)

863 WAKELIN

864 WAKELIN

865 SWIFT

John Swift
London; first mark 1728
Mark Grimwade, 1651, 1689, 3686, 3708

865 Cup and cover
silver-gilt
London, 1765
16 in (40.7 cm) high
85 oz (2,643 gr)
After a design by William Kent; see Hayward, 'The Pelham Gold Cup', *Connoisseur*, July 1969
London, 3 XII 1970, 240
£900 ($2,160)

866 GILPIN

867 TUITE

Thomas Gilpin
London; first mark 1730
Mark Grimwade, 2758, 2768–9, 3825–6

866 Cup and cover
London, 1750
18 in (45.7 cm) high
211 oz 10 dwt (6,577 gr)
New York, 16–17 XII 1976, 84
$12,500 (£7,353)

John Tuite
London; first mark c. 1721–5. Specialist salver maker
Mark Grimwade, 1700, 1722

867 Salver
London, 1731
12 in (30.5 cm) square
33 oz 18 dwt (1,054 gr)
London, 24 III 1960, 9
£850 ($2,388)

868 ABERCROMBY

869 ABERCROMBY

Robert Abercromby

London; in partnership with George Hindmarsh May–October 1731, alone from 1731. Specialist salver maker
Mark Grimwade, 6a, 2254, 2258, 2260

868 Salver
London, 1733
20 in (50.8 cm) wide
95 oz 10 dwt (2,970 gr)
Arms: John Shales Barrington
See Oman, *English Engraved Silver*, ill.103, where engraving of very similar design on a salver by Thomas Farren (1733) is attributed to Joseph Sympson.
See also no.739.
London, 20 II 1964, 99
£2,050 ($5,740)

869 Salver
London, 1731
11¾ in (30 cm) diameter
27 oz 18 dwt (867 gr)
London, 11 IV 1968, 67
£1,450 ($3,480)

870 Salver
London, 1732
18¼ in (46.5 cm) diameter
101 oz (3,141 gr)
London, 14 XII 1961, 150
£1,400 ($3,920)

871 Salver
London, 1733
17½ in (44.5 cm) diameter
69 oz 11 dwt (2,163 gr)
London, 25 X 1973, 129
£2,000 ($4,800)

872 Salver
London, 1735
13½ in (34.2 cm) diameter
41 oz 19 dwt (1,304 gr)
London, 19 XI 1981, 145
£2,090 ($3,741)

870 ABERCROMBY

871 ABERCROMBY

872 ABERCROMBY

873 Salver
London, 1740
12 in (30.5 cm) diameter
34 oz 8 dwt (1,069 gr)
London, 12 XII 1974, 24
£380 ($874)

873 ABERCROMBY

Aymé Videau

London; apprenticed to David Willaume, free 1733/34
Mark Grimwade, 106–7

874 Coffee pot
London, 1738
9¼ in (23.5 cm) high
27 oz 1 dwt (841 gr)
London, 9 IV 1964, 136
£500 ($1,400)

875 Coffee pot
London, 1740
9¼ in (23.5 cm) high
28 oz 4 dwt (877 gr)
London, 18 VII 1974, 213
£720 ($1,728)

876 Cream pail
London, 1733
2¼ in (5.7 cm) high
3 oz 10 dwt (108 gr) including a ladle
London, 30 X 1975, 85
£154 ($308)

877 Cake basket
London, 1734
14¾ in (37.5 cm) wide
59 oz 18 dwt (1,856 gr)
London, 21 VII 1977, 252
£4,620 ($7,854)

878 Sauceboats, pair
London, 1735
8¼ in (21 cm) overall
34 oz 17 dwt (1,083 gr)
London, 27 VI 1963, 92
£360 ($1,008)

879 Milk jug
London, 1760
5½ in (14 cm) high
6 oz 15 dwt (209 gr)
London, 26 II 1976, 53
£297 ($534)

880 Tea kettle on lamp stand
London, 1741
14 in (35.6 cm) high
84 oz (2,612 gr)
London, 24 X 1957, 147
£200 ($558)

881 Sugar box and cover
London, 1743
5 in (12.7 cm) wide
15 oz 1 dwt (568 gr)
London, 17 XI 1960, 147
£240 ($674)

882 Cup and cover
London, 1747
14 in (35.6 cm) high
73 oz 4 dwt (2,276 gr)
London, 3 XII 1970, 133
£440 ($1,056)

883 Beakers, two pairs
London, 1743
1¾ in and 3¾ in (4.4 cm and 9.5 cm) high
14 oz 4 dwt (441 gr)
London, 28 I 1965, 163
£3,800 ($10,640)

884 Ewer, basin and a pair of scent bottles
silver-gilt
London, 1755
Ewer: 11 in (28 cm) high
106 oz 10 dwt (3,312 gr)
Arms: John Fleming, created baronet 1763
See no. 885
New York, 14–15 XII 1977, 597
$12,500 (£6,756)

885 Toilet mirror
silver-gilt
London, 1755
23¼ in (59 cm) high
63 oz 17 dwt (1,985 gr)
Probably from the same set as no. 884
New York, 27 IV 1976, 261
$2,200 (£1,222)

874 VIDEAU

875 VIDEAU

876 VIDEAU

877 VIDEAU

878 VIDEAU

879 VIDEAU

880 VIDEAU

881 VIDEAU

882 VIDEAU

883 VIDEAU

884 VIDEAU

885 VIDEAU

GREAT BRITAIN IRELAND

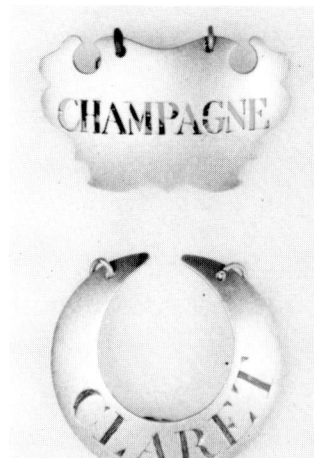

886 887 DRINKWATER

888 DRINKWATER

Sandylands Drinkwater
London; first mark 1735, died 1776. See Charles Reily and George Storer, no. 1346ff. Specialist wine label maker
Mark Grimwade, 2499, 3792

886 Wine label, for champagne, with another label
(London), c. 1739–55
London, 16 X 1975, 55
£88 ($176)

887 Wine label, for claret
(London), c. 1756–59
London, 16 X 1975, 57
£55 ($110)

888 Buttons, eight
Maker's mark and lion passant only; two S. Drinkwater, the remainder by others
(London), c. 1750–65
1 in (2.5 cm) diameter
London, 16 IX 1976, 187
£143 ($243)

Christian Hillan
London; first mark 1736
Mark Grimwade, 326, 333–4

889 Cream boat
London, 1738
4¾ in (12 cm) overall
5 oz 19 dwt (182 gr)
London, 26 II 1976, 56
£462 ($831)

890 Milk jug
silver-gilt
London, 1738
5 in (12.7 cm) high
8 oz 18 dwt (276 gr)
London, 3 XII 1953, 363
£115 ($323)

889 HILLAN

890 HILLAN

891 HILLAN

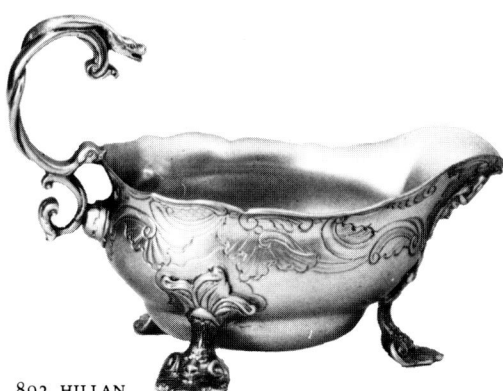

892 HILLAN

893 HILLAN

894 HILLAN

895 HILLAN

896 SHRUDER

897 SHRUDER

898 SHRUDER

899 SHRUDER

891 Sugar box and cover
(London), c. 1740
Maker's mark only
4 in (10.1 cm) high
9 oz 7 dwt (290 gr)
London, 9 V 1974, 62
£460 ($1,104)

892 Sauceboat
London, 1742
5½ in (13.8 cm) overall
5 oz 15 dwt (178 gr)
London, 10 II 1983, 92
£748 ($1,196)

893 Hot water jug
London, 1738
9½ in (24.2 cm) high
29 oz (901 gr)
New York, 6 VI 1980, 33
$15,400 (£6,553)

894 Sugar box and cover
London, 1739
4¼ in (10.8 cm) high
9 oz 4 dwt (286 gr)
See Grimwade, Rococo Silver, pl.68a.
New York, 16–17 XII 1980, 214
$7,150 (£3,455)

895 Cream bowl
silver-gilt
(London), c. 1740
Maker's mark and lion passant only
4 in (10.2 cm) diameter
9 oz 1 dwt (281 gr)
London, 13 III 1975, 75
£540 ($1,242)

James Shruder

London; first mark 1737. Trade card illustrated in Grimwade, *Rococo Silver*, pl.93a
Mark Grimwade, 1653, 1682–3

896 Covered jug
London, 1737
8¾ in (22.2 cm) high
24 oz (746 gr)
New York, 18 II 1982, 453
$3,300 (£1,845)

897 Casters, three
London, 1737
7¾ in and 6 in (19.7 cm and 15.2 cm) high
36 oz 5 dwt (1,127 gr)
London, 24 IV 1969, 203
£1,300 ($3,120)

898 Cake basket
London, 1738
13 in (33 cm) wide
51 oz 5 dwt (1,593 gr)
London, 14 X 1976, 150
£2,750 ($4,675)

899 Salver
London, 1739
6¼ in (15.9 cm) diameter
8 oz 18 dwt (276 gr)
London, 4 V 1978, 161
£308 ($569)

900 SHRUDER

901 SHRUDER

902 SHRUDER

904 GARDEN

903 SHRUDER

900 Cup and cover
London, 1739
13¼ in (34.7 cm) high
101 oz 18 dwt (3,169 gr)
London, 20 VI 1974, 179
£3,000 ($7,200)

901 Cake basket
London, 1742
12¾ in (32.5 cm) wide
55 oz 9 dwt (1,724 gr)
London, 15 VII 1976, 177
£2,200 ($3,960)

902 Candelabra, pair
London, 1742
The branches unmarked
14¾ in (37.5 cm) high
165 oz 19 dwt (5,161 gr)
London, 15 III 1962, 148
£900 ($2,520)

903 Tea caddies, pair
silver-gilt
(London), c. 1740
Maker's mark only
5 in (12.7 cm) high
32 oz 6 dwt (1,004 gr)
London, 31 X 1974, 191
£1,300 ($2,990)

Phillip(s) Garden

London; first mark 1738, bankrupt 1762. Garden purchased some of Lamerie's tools after his death in 1751 (see p.11)
Mark Grimwade, 2178–81, 2184–5

904 Salver
London, 1752
13¼ in (33.6 cm) diameter
43 oz 19 dwt (1,366 gr)
London, 19 VII 1979, 171
£737 ($1,510)

905 906 GARDEN

909 GARDEN

905 Cup and cover
London, 1751
14 in (35.6 cm) high
81 oz 18 dwt (2,547 gr)
Arms: as on no.906
London, 24 IV 1969, 190
£340 ($816)

906 Salvers, pair
London, 1752
7 in (17.8 cm) diameter
27 oz 18 dwt (867 gr)
Arms: Sir Henry Hicks of Beverstone Castle, co. Glos, died 1755
London, 24 IV 1969, 187
£750 ($1,800)

907 Covered beer jugs, pair
London, 1754
13½ in (34.2 cm) high
175 oz 12 dwt (5,461 gr)
Arms: Sir Henry Hicks
Exhibition: 'Rococo', no.G36
London, 24 IV 1969, 192
£17,000 ($40,800)

908 Cake basket
London, 1755
14½ in (36.9 cm) overall
61 oz 18 dwt (1,925 gr)
London, 8 II 1962, 130
£710 ($1,988)

909 Beaker
London, 1753
4½ in (11.6 cm) high
8 oz 6 dwt (260 gr)
Zurich, 22 XI 1978, 59
SFr.1,620 (£456 $934)

907 GARDEN

907 (DETAIL)

908 GARDEN

910 Candelabra, pair
London, 1756; the branches
1754 (not illustrated)
Sticks: 12½ in (31.7 cm) high
165 oz (5,131 gr)
London, 23 II 1967, 120
£1,500 ($4,200)

Ebenezer Coker

London; first mark 1738,
bankrupt 1781, died 1783
Mark Grimwade, 550, 556, 3538

911 Salvers, pair
London, 1772
15½ in (39.4 cm) diameter
99 oz 16 dwt (3,103 gr)
See Oman, *English Engraved
Silver*, pl.126 for a similarly
engraved salver, Coker, 1770.
London, 18 V 1967, 61
£1,300 ($3,640)

912 Tea tray
London, 1763
Engraved scratch weight: 138 oz
18 dwt
22 in (56 cm) wide
136 oz 12 dwt (4,248 gr)
London, 13 X 1960, 149
£1,000 ($2,810)

913 Salver
London, 1767
14 in (35.6 cm) wide
39 oz 12 dwt (1,231 gr)
Arms: Lewis Way of Denham
Place, co. Bucks and his wife
Sarah, daughter of Rev. Thomas
Payne of Holme Lacy, Hereford
whom he married 1755
London, 14 XII 1967, 217
£1,600 ($3,840)

914 Candlesticks, two pairs
London, 1761/8
10½ in (26.7 cm) high
93 oz 13 dwt (2,912 gr)
London, 3 IV 1969, 137
£2,500 ($6,000)

915 Candlesticks, eight
London, 1768
11 in (28 cm) high
183 oz 10 dwt (5,706 gr)
London, 23 I 1964, 58
£1,100 ($3,080)

John Cafe

London; born c. 1716,
apprenticed to James Gould, first
mark 1740, died 1757. Specialist
candlestick maker. See Fallon,
'The Goulds and Cafes,
Candlestick makers'
Mark Grimwade, 1203, 1228

916 Candlesticks, pair
London, 1748
10¾ in (27.3 cm) high
51 oz 14 dwt (1,607 gr)
London, 31 X 1974, 89
£800 ($1,840)

917 Candlesticks, pair
London, 1746
8 in (20.3 cm) high
35 oz 19 dwt (1,118 gr)
London, 31 X 1974, 33
£580 ($1,334)

918 Candlesticks, pair
London, 1748
9¼ in (23.5 cm) high
36 oz 13 dwt (1,140 gr)
London, 3 IV 1969, 174
£1,250 ($3,000)

910 GARDEN

911 COKER

912 COKER

913 COKER

914 COKER

915 COKER

916 J. CAFE

917 J. CAFE

918 J. CAFE

919 J. CAFE

920 J. CAFE

921 W. CAFE

922 W. CAFE

919 Candlesticks, four
London, 1752
9¾ in (24.8 cm) high
96 oz 2 dwt (2,988 gr)
London, 18 III 1982, 139
£7,040 ($12,601)

920 Taperstick, 'harlequin'
London, 1755
5½ in (14 cm) high
5 oz 13 dwt (175 gr)
London, 31 X 1974, 150
£360 ($828)

William Cafe

London; born c. 1727, apprenticed to his brother John (see above), first mark 1757, died 1802. See Fallon, 'The Goulds and Cafes, Candlestick Makers'.
Mark Grimwade, 3077

921 Candlesticks, two
London, 1763/4
10¼ in (26 cm) high
43 oz 15 dwt (1,360 gr)
London, 23 I 1969, 195
£1,350 ($3,240)

922 Candlesticks, four
London, 1765
10½ in (26.7 cm) high
91 oz 12 dwt (2,848 gr)
London, 22 V 1969, 236
£2,500 ($6,000)

923 Candlesticks, four
London, 1757
8¾ in (22.2 cm) high
70 oz 11 dwt (2,194 gr)
London, 30 I 1969, 48
£3,600 ($8,640)

924 Candelabra, pair
London, 1756
16½ in (42 cm) high
129 oz 7 dwt (4,022 gr)
London, 19 VI 1958, 131
£800 ($2,248)

923 W. CAFE

924 W. CAFE

Peter Taylor
London; mark entered 1740
Mark Grimwade, 2239

925 Sugar vases, three
London, 1751
7¼ in (18.4 cm) and 6 in (15.2 cm) high
46 oz (1,430 gr) including a sugar sifter
Arms: 1st Baron Sondes, who married 1752 Frances Pelham, niece of the 1st Duke of Newcastle
London, 15 V 1947, 133
£110 ($443)

Francis Crump
London; apprenticed to Gabriel Sleath, first mark 1741
Mark Grimwade, 670–72, 674, 907

926 Salver
London, 1758
21½ in (54.6 cm) wide
On a tripod table base, possibly Ambrose Stevenson, c. 1715
24½ in (62.2 cm) high
364 oz 3 dwt (11,325 gr)
London, 4 VII 1968, 135
£5,500 ($13,200)

927 Coffee pot
London, 1761
11½ in (29.2 cm) high
38 oz 12 dwt (1,200 gr)
Illus. Grimwade, *Rococo Silver*, pl.63.
New York, 16 VI 1982, 53
$5,500 (£3,072)

Benjamin Godfrey
London; married Elizabeth, widow of Abraham Buteaux (Grimwade p.455); first mark 1732, died 1741. See Barr, *George Wickes, Royal Goldsmith 1698–1761*, pp.23–4
Mark Grimwade, 170, 173–4

928 Cup and cover
(London), c. 1735
Bearing transposed and cancelled hallmarks
12¾ in (32.5 cm) high
90 oz 15 dwt (2,822 gr)
Arms: William Folkes Esq and his wife Mary, daughter of Sir William Browne of King's Lynn, Norfolk, whom he married 1747
London, 29 IV 1976, 21
£880 ($1,584)

929 Cup and cover
London, 1739
14 in (35.5 cm) high
98 oz 3 dwt (3,052 gr)
London, 17 V 1973, 106
£2,200 ($5,500)

925 P. TAYLOR

926 CRUMP

927 CRUMP

928 B. GODFREY

Eliza Godfrey
London; widow of Benjamin Godfrey (see above), mark entered 1741
Mark Grimwade, 591

930 Milk jug
(London), c. 1745
Maker's mark only
4½ in (11.4 cm) high
5 oz 6 dwt (164 gr)
London, 17 X 1974, 167
£270 ($621)

931 Tea caddies, pair
London, 1747
4¼ in (10.8 cm) high
41 oz 8 dwt (1,287 gr)
Arms: Sir Robert Grosvenor, 6th Bt, died 1755, and his wife Jane, daughter of Thomas Warre, whom he married 1730
London, 2 VII 1959, 138
£460 ($1,292)

932 Sauceboats, four
London, 1747
6½ in (16.5 cm) overall
79 oz 6 dwt (2,466 gr)
London, 7 III 1957, 155
£480 ($1,339)

933 Inkstand
silver-gilt
London, 1741
13½ in (34.3 cm) wide
46 oz 10 dwt (1,446 gr)
Arms: Osborne impaling d'Arcy, for Francis Godolphin, Marquess of Carmarthen, and his wife Amelia, daughter of the 4th Earl of Holdernesse. They divorced 1779 and she married John Byron (by his second wife the father of Lord Byron) and died 1784; he became 5th Duke of Leeds 1789
London, 30 XI 1978, 79
£6,050 ($12,402)

934 Sauceboats, four
London, 1764
8¾ in (22.2 cm) overall
81 oz 10 dwt (2,534 gr)
London, 31 I 1963, 122
£520 ($1,456)

935 Candlesticks, four
London, 1743
10 in (25.4 cm) high
123 oz 14 dwt (3,847 gr)
London, 2 V 1963, 32
£1,050 ($2,940)

929 B. GODFREY

930 E. GODFREY

931 E. GODFREY

932 E. GODFREY

933 E. GODFREY

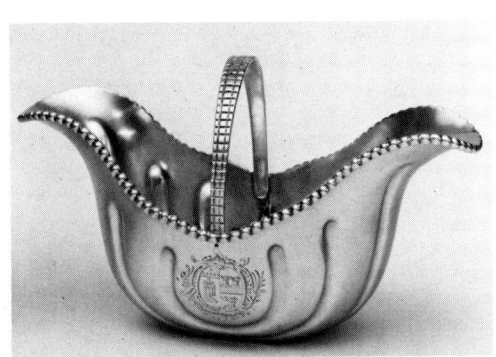
934 E. GODFREY

935 E. GODFREY

William Cripps

London; apprenticed to David Willaume II (see above, no. 836ff.), first mark 1743, died c. 1767
Mark Grimwade, 3056–8

936 Sauceboat
(London), c. 1750, marks rubbed
8½ in (21.6 cm) overall
23 oz 18 dwt (743 gr)
See a similar pair, Cripps (1749), illus. Grimwade, *Rococo Silver*, pl. 34C. Compare with no. 839.
London, 30 XI 1972, 41
£480 ($1,200)

937 Candelabrum
London, 1754
14¾ in (37.5 cm) high
59 oz 3 dwt (1,839 gr)
See Grimwade, *Rococo Silver*, pl. 78B.
London, 13 VI 1983, 55
£3,410 ($5,456)

938 Candlesticks, eight
London, 1744
8¾ in (22.2 cm) high
165 oz 10 dwt (5,147 gr)
London, 1 III 1956, 154
£740 ($2,072)

939 Soup tureen and cover
London, 1746
17¼ in (43.8 cm) wide
159 oz (4,944 gr)
London, 20 IV 1972, 158
£2,800 ($7,000)

940 Salver
London, 1754
27½ in (69.9 cm) diameter
226 oz 10 dwt (7,044 gr)
London, 20 XI 1969, 128
£850 ($2,040)

941 Soup tureen and cover
London, 1756
15½ in (39.4 cm) wide
144 oz (4,478 gr)
London, 20 II 1964, 95
£1,000 ($2,800)

Samuel Courtauld I

London; born 1720, son of Augustine Courtauld (see above, no. 759ff.), first mark 1746, died 1765
Mark Grimwade 2489–90

942 Tea kettle on lamp stand
London, 1748
15¾ in (40 cm) high
80 oz 10 dwt (2,503 gr)
London, 14 V 1970, 48
£680 ($1,632)

943 Mug
London, 1764
7 in (17.8 cm) high
39 oz 8 dwt (1,237 gr)
New York, 18–19 II 1981, 564
$1,870 (£903)

944 Coffee pot
London, 1757
10¾ in (27.3 cm) high
32 oz 16 dwt (1,020 gr)
London, 21 X 1971, 102
£600 ($1,440)

945 Coffee pot
London, 1748
10½ in (26.6 cm) high
32 oz 15 dwt (1,018 gr)
London, 9 V 1974, 222
£850 ($2,040)

946 Tea caddy and sweetmeat basket with twelve teaspoons, mote skimmer and sugar nips by others
London, 1759
23 oz 2 dwt (718 gr)
London, 28 II 1974, 88
£1,000 ($2,400)

936 CRIPPS

937 CRIPPS

938 CRIPPS

939 CRIPPS

940 CRIPPS

941 CRIPPS

944 S. COURTAULD I

945 S. COURTAULD I

942 S. COURTAULD I

946 S. COURTAULD I

943 S. COURTAULD I

947 S. TAYLOR

Samuel Taylor
London; first mark 1744.
Specialist maker of tea caddies
Mark Grimwade, 2645

947 Tea caddies, pair, and sugar bowl
London, 1763
5¼ in (13.3 cm) high
23 oz 1 dwt (716 gr)
London, 16 II 1978, 205
£1,375 ($2,543)

948 L. COURTAULD & G. COWLES

Louisa Courtauld and George Cowles

London; Louisa Courtauld widow of Samuel (see above). In partnership with Cowles *c.* 1768 and with her son 1777; died 1807
Mark Grimwade, 1907

948 Tea caddies, three
silver-gilt
London, 1770
6¼ in (15.9 cm) high
40 oz 6 dwt (1,253 gr)
London, 20 VI 1974, 122
£1,600 ($3,840)

George Michael Moser

London; born Schaffhausen 1706, died 1783; one of the founders of the Royal Academy, described in 1763 as 'chaser and painter in enamel colours'. See Snowman, *Eighteenth Century Gold Boxes*

949 Candlesticks, four
(London), *c.* 1740
Unmarked
After designs by Moser
14¾ in (37.5 cm) high
Now in the Victoria and Albert Museum, London. See catalogue of exhibition, 'Pattern and Design', no. 2.3.
London, 2 VI 1977, 254
£14,850 ($25,245)

950 Snuff box
four-colour gold
1774
Signed: GM Moser f 1774
2¾ in (6.8 cm) wide
London, 24 III 1980, 36
£29,700 ($69,795)

951 Nécessaire
gold and enamel
c. 1760
Signed: Moser F
4¾ in (12 cm) overall
Monaco, 29 XI 1975, 126
FFr.10,000 (£1,111 $2,222)

949 UNMARKED

951 MOSER

949 DESIGN BY MOSER

950 MOSER

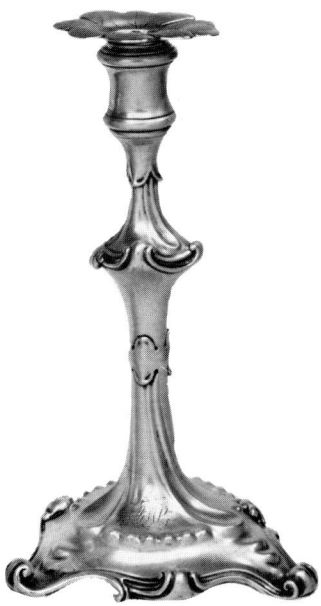

952 J. RÖMER

953 E. RÖMER

954 E. RÖMER

955 E. RÖMER

956 UNMARKED

John Römer

London; born c. 1715, possibly related to Emick Romer (see below); worked for Parker and Wakelin (see below, no.994ff.). See Barr, *George Wickes, Royal Goldsmith 1698–1761*, p.58
Mark Grimwade, 3677

952 Candlesticks, pair
London, 1763
10 in (25.4 cm) high
40 oz 15 dwt (1,267 gr)
London, 3 IV 1969, 158
£1,250 ($3,000)

Emick Römer

London; born Oslo 1724, active in London c. 1765–75, supplied silver to Parker and Wakelin (see below, no.994ff.); had returned to Norway by 1795
Mark Grimwade, 638

953 Tea caddies, pair
London, 1763
5½ in (14 cm) high
15 oz 13 dwt (485 gr)
London, 9 V 1974, 194
£780 ($1,872)

954 Epergne
London, 1770
17¼ in (43.8 cm) high
91 oz 19 dwt (2,859 gr)
London, 26 II 1976, 106
£770 ($1,386)

955 Cake basket
silver-gilt
London, 1767
15¼ in (38.7 cm) wide
39 oz (1,212 gr)
Lennoxlove, 24 VI 1980, 263
£990 ($2,326)

Unmarked

956 Salt cellars, pair
silver-mounted glass
English, c. 1760
3 in (7.6 cm) diameter
See Grimwade, *Rococo Silver*, pl.36D for a similar pair, Emick Römer.
London, 18 I 1979, 108
£286 ($586)

John Schuppe
London; possibly of Dutch origin, mark entered 1753
Mark Grimwade, 1686

957 Salt cellars, pair
London, 1754
4 in (10.1 cm) wide
5 oz 4 dwt (161 gr)
London, 20 II 1964, 63
£190 ($532)

958 A collection of cow creamers
London, 1757–68
London, 26 XI 1959, 96–107

959 Cow creamer
silver-gilt (later)
London, 1763
5¾ in (14.6 cm) overall
4 oz 4 dwt (130 gr)
London, 23 IX 1982, 91
£2,200 ($3,520)

960 Taperstick
London, 1765
5¾ in (14.6 cm) high
6 oz 8 dwt (199 gr)
London, 19 VII 1973, 55
£440 ($1,100)

Edward Aldridge I
London; first mark 1724, in partnership with John Stamper 1753–7, died c. 1766–7
Mark Grimwade, 526, 527, 3528–35

961 Stirrup cup frame with thirty-one glass tumbler cups
London, 1760
23 in (58.5 cm) high
70 oz 5 dwt (2,184 gr)
New York, 16–17 XII 1976, 331
$7,750 (£3,875)

Edward Aldridge I and John Stamper
See Edward Aldridge I, above
Mark Grimwade, 528

962 Cake basket
London, 1756
14½ in (37 cm) wide
44 oz 14 dwt (1,390 gr)
London, 2 VII 1970, 224
£620 ($1,488)

957 SCHUPPE

958 SCHUPPE

959 SCHUPPE

960 SCHUPPE

961 E. ALDRIDGE I

962 ALDRIDGE I & STAMPER

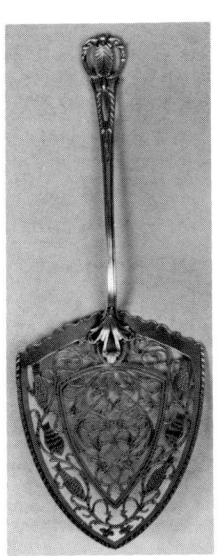

963 ALDRIDGE & GREEN

964 ALDRIDGE & GREEN

966 BUTTY & DUMÉE

965 HERNE & BUTTY

Charles Aldridge and Henry Green

London; Aldridge apprenticed to Edward Aldridge I, in partnership with Green 1772 (first mark 1775) until 1784
Mark Grimwade, 265

963 Fish slice
London, 1773
4 oz 11 dwt (141 gr)
London, 3 IV 1969, 51
£170 ($408)

964 Sweetmeat stand
London, 1782
10¼ in (26 cm) high
22 oz 10 dwt (700 gr)
London, 28 XI 1968, 301
£380 ($912)

Lewis Herne and Francis Butty

London; in partnership 1757. See Butty and Dumée below, nos 966–970
Mark Grimwade, 1930

965 Sauceboats, pair with two unmarked ladles
London, 1757
7 in (18 cm) overall
76 oz (2,365 gr)
See Grimwade, *Rococo Silver*, pl. 33B.
Zurich, 22 XI 1978, 60
SFr.38,880 (£10,952 $22,451)

Francis Butty and Nicholas Dumée

London; in partnership c. 1758–73. See Holmes and Dumée, below, nos 971–2
Mark Grimwade, 669

966 Coffee pot
London, 1765
11½ in (29 cm) high
36 oz (1,119 gr)
Johannesburg, 3 III 1975, 141
R.2,000 (£1,290 $2,967)

967 BUTTY & DUMÉE

968 BUTTY & DUMÉE

967 Salver
London, 1767
14¾ in (37.5 cm) diameter
55 oz 3 dwt (1,715 gr)
London, 18 VI 1981, 103
£1,210 ($2,504)

968 Epergne
London, 1767
14¾ in (37.5 cm) high
194 oz 3 dwt (6,038 gr)
London, 24 IV 1958, 68
£380 ($1,067)

969 Tea urn
London, 1768
20½ in (52 cm) high
99 oz 16 dwt (3,103 gr)
London, 30 XI 1978, 16
£1,375 ($2,818)

970 Soup tureen
London, 1769
16¾ in (42.6 cm) wide
107 oz 2 dwt (3,330 gr)
London, 6 XII 1979, 194
£6,380 ($14,993)

969 BUTTY & DUMÉE

970 BUTTY & DUMÉE

William Holmes and Nicholas Dumée

London; in partnership 1773–6.
See above
Mark Grimwade, 3176

971 Coffee jug
London, 1773
13½ in (34.3 cm) high
40 oz 18 dwt (1,271 gr)
London, 25 VII 1968, 147
£600 ($1,440)

972 Coffee jug
London, 1773
12½ in (31.8 cm) high
37 oz 4 dwt (1,156 gr)
London, 9 V 1974, 59
£850 ($2,040)

971 HOLMES & DUMÉE

972 HOLMES & DUMÉE

973 WEST

974 WEST

975 WEST

976 REW/RUGG

977 REW/RUGG

Matthew West

Dublin; free 1769, mentioned until 1804
Mark Bennett, p.348; Jackson, p.613

973 Dish ring
Dublin, 1773
8¼ in (21 cm) diameter
14 oz 2 dwt (438 gr)
London, 4 V 1978, 174
£1,320 ($2,442)

974 Dish ring
Dublin, c. 1780
8 in (20.3 cm) diameter
12 oz (373 gr)
London, 18 VI 1981, 159
£880 ($1,821)

975 Cups, pair
Dublin, 1771
5½ in (14 cm) high
28 oz (870 gr)
London, 20 VI 1974, 166
£300 ($720)

978 REW/RUGG

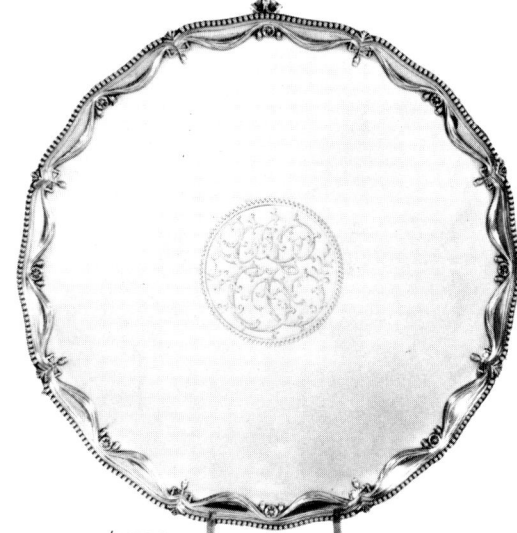

979 REW/RUGG

Robert Rew/Richard Rugg

Since the publication of Grimwade's *London Goldsmiths* (1982) it should be possible to distinguish between the marks of these makers, although not always. However, as the pieces illustrated below have not been re-examined, their work is grouped together. Robert Rew: mark entered 1754 (Grimwade, 2422); Richard Rugg: apprenticed to James Gould, first mark 1754, died *c.* 1795–1801 (Grimwade 2420–21)

976 Salver
London, 1770
14¼ in (36.2 cm) diameter
42 oz 10 dwt (1,321 gr)
London, 19 XI 1970, 156
£340 ($816)

977 Salver
London, 1757
23¼ in (59.1 cm) diameter
148 oz 15 dwt (4,623 gr)
London, 29 IV 1971, 183
£500 ($1,200)

978 Salver
London, 1781
19¼ in (48.9 cm) diameter
77 oz 9 dwt (2,408 gr)
London, 13 XII 1973, 144
£550 ($1,320)

979 Salver
London, 1776
13 in (33 cm) diameter
35 oz 16 dwt (1,113 gr)
London, 15 VII 1976, 180
£440 ($792)

Thomas Heming

London; first mark 1745, died between 1795 and 1801. Principal Goldsmith to the King 1760–82
Mark Grimwade, 2796–7, 3828

980 Cup and cover
London, 1750
15 in (38.1 cm) high
87 oz 13 dwt (2,725 gr)
London, 19 XI 1970, 159
£480 ($1,152)

981 Candelabra, pair
London, 1768
17¾ in (45.1 cm) high
148 oz 10 dwt (4,618 gr)
New York, 18–19 II 1981, 704
$33,000 (£15,950)

982 Casket
silver-gilt
London, 1758
10 in (25.3 cm) wide
63 oz 14 dwt (1,981 gr)
Provenance: Princess Elizabeth, third daughter of George III
London, 3 V 1984, 83
£7,920 ($11,008)

983 Cup, two-handled
London, 1765
7 in (17.8 cm) high
25 oz 6 dwt (786 gr)
London, 15 VI 1978, 150
£462 ($854)

984 Candlesticks, four
London, 1770
14¼ in (36.2 cm) high
188 oz 15 dwt (5,870 gr)
See Clayton, ed, *Collector's Dictionary of ... Silver and Gold*, ill. no.81 for a similar pair, Heming, 1770; also catalogue of exhibition, 'Rococo', no.G50.
London, 3 XII 1964, 157
£1,500 ($4,200)

985 Soup tureens, pair
London, 1771
14 in (35.5 cm) wide
204 oz 14 dwt (6,366 gr)
Arms: Royal, of George III; also of George Gordon, Marquess of Huntly (1770–1836), who succeeded as 5th Duke of Gordon 1827
London, 26 VI 1975, 50
£4,400 ($10,120)

986 Dishes, pair
London, 1780
9½ in (24.2 cm) wide
38 oz 4 dwt (1,188 gr)
Arms: Royal
London, 9 VI 1966, 155
£650 ($1,820)

980 HEMING

982 HEMING

983 HEMING

981 HEMING

984 HEMING

985 HEMING

986 987 HEMING

988 HEMING

989 HEMING

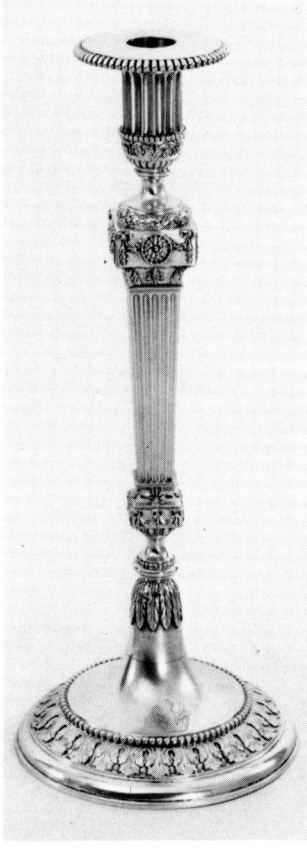

990 HEMING   991 HEMING

987 Dinner plates, twelve
London, 1780
9½ in (24.2 cm) diameter
211 oz 1 dwt (6,562 gr)
Arms: Royal
London, 9 VI 1966, 150
£1,350 ($3,780)

988 Sauce tureens, with stands and ladles, pair
London, 1769/70
9 in (22.9 cm) wide
152 oz 4 dwt (4,733 gr)
Arms: Nicholas Owen Smyth of Condover, co. Salop
London, 12 XII 1974, 147
£1,650 ($3,795)

989 Sauceboats, pair
London, 1770
8 in (20.4 cm) overall
43 oz 4 dwt (1,343 gr) (including a pair of ladles)
Arms: Royal
New York, 18–19 II 1981, 703
$15,400 (£7,440)

990 Punch bowl
silver-gilt
London, 1771
15¾ in (40 cm) diameter
194 oz 19 dwt (6,062 gr)
Arms: Sir Watkin Williams Wynn, 4th Bt, died 1789
Inscription: Chester Plates Won by Fop in the years 1769 and 1770
Now in the National Museum of Wales. See Rowe, *Adam Silver*, pp.37–8 on a drawing by Robert Adam for Sir Watkin Wynn
London, 18 V 1967, 102
£6,200 ($17,360)

991 Candlesticks, four
London, 1776
13¾ in (35 cm) high
115 oz 10 dwt (3,592 gr)
London, 1 II 1973, 161
£2,500 ($6,250)

992 S. & J. CRESPEL

995 PARKER & E. WAKELIN

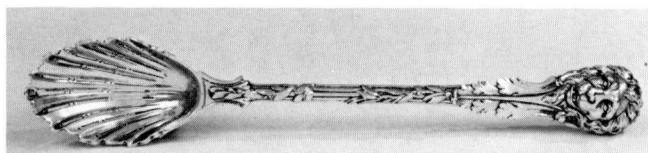

993 NO MAKER'S MARK

994 PARKER & E. WAKELIN

996 PARKER & E. WAKELIN

Sebastian Crespel I and James Crespel

London; active from c. 1760, closely associated with Wakelin and Taylor (see below, no. 1002ff.). Sebastian's daughter married Robert Garrard I; see no. 1005. See Barr, *George Wickes, Royal Goldsmith 1698–1761*
Mark Grimwade, 2497

992 Soup tureen
London, 1766
17 in (43.2 cm) wide
189 oz (5,877 gr)
Arms: 6th Baron Craven (died 1791) and his wife Elizabeth, daughter of 4th Earl of Bertie, whom he married 1767
London, 23 I 1964, 40
£1,650 ($4,620)

No maker's mark

993 Straining spoon
London, 1774
12½ in (32 cm) overall
9 oz 1 dwt (281 gr)
The marks, though visible, are pierced out except for the date letter.
London, 11 IV 1968, 117
£240 ($576)

John Parker and Edward Wakelin

London; in partnership 1760–76. Parker was apprenticed to George Wickes; see nos 854–864.
Mark Grimwade, 1602, 3757

994 Centrepiece
silver-gilt
London, 1771
23 in (58.4 cm) overall
199 oz 10 dwt (6,204 gr) including a later cover
Inscribed: This legacy was left to Assheton Curzon Esq. by his sister in law Mary Grosvenor who died Feb 1774 which Alas may serve as a token of remembrance of two kind sisters, Mrs. Dorothy Curzon surviving her only 14 days to lament her loss.
Assheton Curzon (born 1733) was created Viscount Curzon in 1802. He married Dorothy, sister of 1st Earl Grosvenor, 1766.
New York, 16–17 XII 1980, 235A
$17,050 (£8,236)

995 Sauceboats, four
London, 1761
8½ in (21.6 cm) wide
87 oz 10 dwt (2,721 gr)
Arms: William Douglas, Earl of March, who succeeded as 4th Duke of Queensbury 1778, died 1810
London, 15 X 1970, 46
£4,200 ($10,080)

996 Tray
London, 1761
20¾ in (52.7 cm) overall
88 oz 15 dwt (2,760 gr)
New York, 3–6 XII 1975, 56
$4,250 (£2,125)

997 Tea caddy
London, 1763
4½ in (11.4 cm) high
13 oz 15 dwt (427 gr)
See Barr, *George Wickes, Royal Goldsmith 1698–1761*, pl.77 for a similar caddy, Wakelin, 1752.
London, 18 V 1967, 41
£400 ($1,120)

998 Cake basket
London, 1773
12¼ in (31.1 cm) diameter
66 oz 18 dwt (2,080 gr)
London, 26 XI 1959, 134
£200 ($562)

999 Dessert dishes, four
London, 1772
12½ in (31.7 cm) wide
71 oz 1 dwt (2,208 gr)
See Barr, *George Wickes, Royal Goldsmith 1698–1761*, pl.91 for a supper set (1766)
London, 3 XII 1964, 159
£1,500 ($4,200)

1000 Sauceboats, pair
London, 1774
8¾ in (22.2 cm) overall
33 oz 9 dwt (1,040 gr)
London, 6 III 1969, 147
£1,400 ($3,360)

997 PARKER & E. WAKELIN

998 PARKER & E. WAKELIN

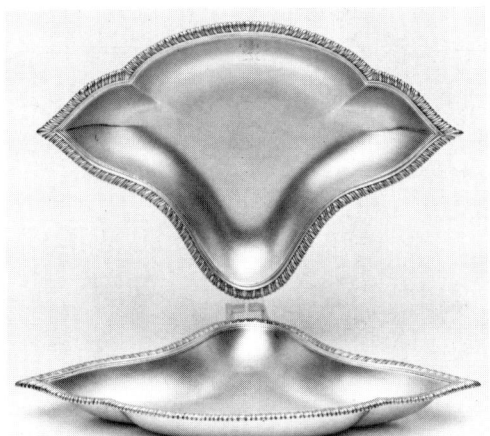

999 PARKER & E. WAKELIN

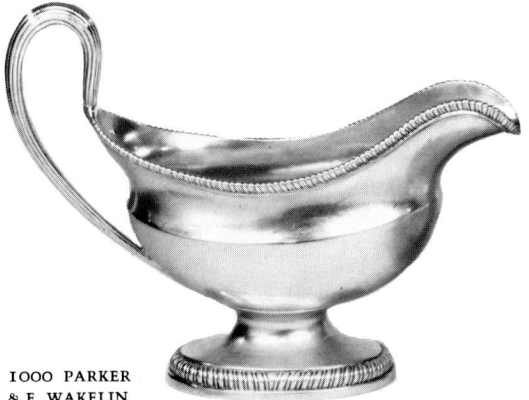

1000 PARKER & E. WAKELIN

1001 HEMING & CHAWNER

1002 J. WAKELIN & W. TAYLOR

1003 J. WAKELIN & W. TAYLOR

1004 J. WAKELIN & W. TAYLOR

George Heming and William Chawner I

London; Heming was the son of Thomas Heming (see above, no. 980), to whom he was apprenticed, as was Benjamin Laver; in partnership with Chawner 1774–c. 1781
Mark Grimwade, 821–2

1001 Candelabra, six
Two sticks and one branch, Benjamin Laver, 1783; four sticks, Heming and Chawner, 1780; three branches, Thomas Heming, 1780
London, 1780/81/83
15 in (38 cm) high
286 oz 3 dwt (8,900 gr) of weighable silver
London, 30 XI 1978, 104
£8,250 ($16,912)

John Wakelin and William Taylor

London; in partnership 1776–92. Wakelin was apprenticed to his father Edward (see above, no. 854ff.). See below, Wakelin and Garrard
Mark Grimwade, 1764

1002 Punch bowl
London, 1790
13½ in (34.5 cm) wide
50 oz 18 dwt (1,538 gr)
Monaco, 30 XI–1 XII 1975, 205
FFr. 14,300 (£1,590 $3,180)

1003 Dessert baskets and stands, pair
London, 1790
12 in (30.5 cm) wide
91 oz 16 dwt (2,854 gr)
London, 5 XII 1968, 310
£2,400 ($5,760)

1004 Tea urn
London, 1791
18 in (45.8 cm) high
123 oz (3,825 gr)
London, 20 IV 1972, 83
£380 ($950)

1006 (DESIGN)

1006 SMITH & SHARP

1005 J. WAKELIN & R. GARRARD I

1007 SMITH & SHARP

John Wakelin and Robert Garrard I

London; in partnership 1792–1802. See John Parker and Edward Wakelin, John Wakelin and William Taylor (above) and nos 1315ff.
Mark Grimwade 1760

1005 Wine coolers, pair
London, 1801
7 in (17.8 cm) high
99 oz 7 dwt (3,089 gr)
Arms: Arthur, 2nd Marquess of Devonshire, born 1753
London, 19 IV 1973, 199
£1,550 ($3,875)

Daniel Smith and Robert Sharp

London; in partnership c. 1763–1788. Smith may have retired 1788; Sharp died 1803. See Rowe, *Adam Silver*, pp. 35–7 etc. See also below, no. 1017 ff.
Mark Grimwade, 506–8, 3523

1006 Cup and cover, the Richmond Race Cup, 1764
London, 1764
18¾ in (47.5 cm) high
141 oz 18 dwt (4,413 gr)
Inscribed: Richmond Races 1764 Sir Marmyduke Wyvill Bart and Thomas Dundas Esq, Stewards
See Rowe, *Adam Silver*, pp.35–6, pls 7–9. This is one of the few pieces of silver known to be based on a drawing by Robert Adam.
London, 6 III 1969, 186
£5,200 ($12,480)

1007 Coffee jug
London, 1773
12¼ in (31.2 cm) high
31 oz 8 dwt (976 gr)
London, 11 IV 1968, 103
£500 ($1,200)

1008 Cup and cover
silver-gilt
London, 1768
17¼ in (43.8 cm) high
112 oz 17 dwt (3,510 gr)
Inscribed: Richmond 1768, Edwin Lascelles Esq, and Robert Shuttleworth Esq. Stewards
London, 6 III 1969, 180
£1,850 ($4,440)

1009 Sugar vases, three
London, 1771
7½ in (19.2 cm) and 8½ in (21.7 cm) high
39 oz (1,215 gr)
Arms: de Grey, Barons Walsingham
Monaco, 30 XI–1 XII 1975, 317
FFr.4,500 (£500 $1,000)

1010 Cup and cover
silver-gilt
London, 1772
Inscribed: Wm Pickett & Co., Fecit
17¾ in (45.2 cm) high
121 oz 2 dwt (3,766 gr)
London, 21 II 1980, 207
£4,180 ($9,823)

1008 SMITH & SHARP

1008 (DETAIL)

1009 SMITH & SHARP

1011 Cup and cover
silver-gilt
London, 1773
Inscribed: Pickett & Co Fecitt Ludgate Hill
17½ in (44.5 cm) high
109 oz 10 dwt (3,394 gr)
London, 19 VII 1982, 172
£2,420 ($4,331)

1012 Soup tureen
London, 1771
13¾ in (35 cm) overall
142 oz (4,416 gr)
Arms: 4th Earl Fitzwilliam (1748–1853), who married Charlotte, daughter of 2nd Earl of Bessborough, 1770
London, 28 IV 1977, 187
£4,840 ($8,228)

1013 Wine cistern
London, 1773
34 in (86.4 cm) wide
470 oz (14,617 gr) approximately
Arms: 3rd Earl of Rosebery (1729–1814)
See Penzer, 'The Great Wine Coolers'.
London, 10 III 1977, 205
£29,700 ($50,490)

1010 SMITH & SHARP

1011 SMITH & SHARP

1012 SMITH & SHARP

1013 SMITH & SHARP

1014 SMITH & SHARP

1014 Coffee pot
London, 1776
10¾ in (27.3 cm) high
23 oz 10 dwt (730 gr)
London, 9 V 1974, 153
£1,000 ($2,400)

1015 Toilet set
silver-gilt
London, 1783
Arms: Fane with Child in pretence for 10th Earl of Westmorland and Sarah Anne, daughter of Robert Child of Osterley Park, co. Middx, whom he married 1782
London, 14 XII 1961, 82
£9,600 ($26,880)

1016 Punch bowl
London, 1786
15 in (38 cm) wide
91 oz 10 dwt (2,845 gr)
Arms: John Fitzgibbon (1748–1802), created Viscount Fitzgibbon 1793 and Earl of Clare 1795. He married Anne, daughter of Richard Chapel Whaley, 1786
London, 28 II 1974, 144
£2,500 ($6,000)

Richard Carter, Daniel Smith and Robert Sharp

London; in partnership from 1778. Carter probably related to John Carter (see nos 1041–4); see above, nos 1006 ff.
Mark Grimwade, 2293

1017 Salver
London, 1779
16 in (40.7 cm) diameter
64 oz 8 dwt (2,002 gr)
London, 13 II 1969, 168
£1,200 ($2,880)

1015 (DETAIL)

1015 SMITH & SHARP

1016 SMITH & SHARP

1017 CARTER, SMITH & SHARP

1018 CARTER, SMITH & SHARP

1019 CARTER, SMITH & SHARP

1021 FOGELBERG

1020 CARTER, SMITH & SHARP

1022 FOGELBERG

1018 Entree dishes and covers, four
London, 1785
10½ in (26.7 cm) wide
164 oz 3 dwt (5,105 gr)
London, 11 III 1965, 162
£1,100 ($3,080)

1019 Sauce tureens, covers and stands, four
London, 1785
10 in (25.4 cm) wide
138 oz 4 dwt (4,298 gr) including four ladles
London, 11 III 1965, 163
£950 ($2,660)

1020 Vegetable dishes and covers, four
London, 1786
8¾ in (22.2 cm) diameter
168 oz 6 dwt (5,234 gr)
London, 4 VII 1968, 136
£2,400 ($5,760)

Andrew Fogelberg

London; born in Sweden c. 1732, active c. 1770–1793 when Paul Storr, his former apprentice, took over his premises; died 1815. See nos 1025–32. See also Rowe, *Adam Silver*
Mark Grimwade, 32

1021 Soup tureens and stands, pair
London, 1770
22¼ in (56.5 cm) overall
388 oz 15 dwt (12,090 gr)
London, 17 X 1963, 163
£2,900 ($8,120)

1022 Tea urn
London, 1771
21½ in (54.6 cm) high
145 oz 2 dwt (4,512 gr)
Arms: Sir Thomas Durrant, created Baronet 1784, and his wife Susanna Custance, whom he married 1773
London, 28 XI 1968, 212
£950 ($2,280)

230 GREAT BRITAIN IRELAND

1023 FOGELBERG

1023 Tankard
London, 1775
7¾ in (19.7 cm) high
26 oz 17 dwt (835 gr)
London, 27 XI 1975, 170
£650 ($1,300)

1024 Coffee set
London, 1775
48 oz 18 dwt (1,520 gr)
London, 27 XI 1975, 172
£1,100 ($2,200)

1024 FOGELBERG

Andrew Fogelberg and Stephen Gilbert

London; in partnership 1780–93. See Andrew Fogelberg (above). Gilbert apprenticed to Edward Wakelin (see above, no.854ff.), for whom he worked in partnership with James Ansill, before his association with Fogelberg. See Barr, *George Wickes, Royal Goldsmith 1698–1761*
Mark Grimwade, 36–7

1025 Cup and cover
silver-gilt
London, 1784
22¼ in (56.5 cm) high
132 oz 17 dwt (4,131 gr)
London, 27 VII 1967, 64
£350 ($980)

1026 Tea caddy and stand
London, 1785; the stand unmarked
6¾ in (17.2 cm) high
22 oz 17 dwt (710 gr)
Arms: Sir Henry Bridgeman, 5th Bt (1725–1800)
London, 1 II 1973, 153
£420 ($1,050)

1025 FOGELBERG & GILBERT

1026 FOGELBERG & GILBERT

1027 Pair of ewers and six goblets
silver-gilt
London, 1780
209 oz 10 dwt (6,515 gr)
Arms: The Hon. Thomas Fitzmaurice, second son of 1st Earl of Shelburne and brother of 1st Marquess of Lansdowne. The medallions are most probably based on designs by James Tassie.
London, 30 XI 1972, 165
£12,000 ($30,000)

FOGELBERG & GILBERT 231

1027 FOGELBERG & GILBERT

1028 FOGELBERG & GILBERT

1029 FOGELBERG & GILBERT

1028 Teapot
London, 1789
5¾ in (14.6 cm) high
24 oz (746 gr)
New York, 24 IV 1974, 224
$1,700 (£708)

1029 Bowl and stand
London, 1784
7½ in (19 cm) diameter
20 oz 11 dwt (639 gr)
London, 8 VI 1972, 6
£500 ($1,250)

232 GREAT BRITAIN IRELAND

1030 FOGELBERG & GILBERT   1031 FOGELBERG & GILBERT

1030 Pastille burner
London, 1785
7¾ in (19.7 cm) high
9 oz 17 dwt (306 gr)
London, 6 XII 1979, 184
£1,540 ($3,619)

1031 Punch bowl
silver-gilt
London, 1789
11 in (28 cm) diameter
69 oz 11 dwt (2,163 gr)
Now in the Victoria and Albert Museum, London. The medallions are taken from designs by Flaxman for Wedgwood and Bentley.
London, 29 IV 1976, 181
£3,520 ($6,336)

1032 Entrée dishes, four
London, 1789
9¾ in (24.8 cm) wide
92 oz 13 dwt (2,881 gr)
Arms: Edward, 4th son of George III, created Duke of Kent 1799, died 1820; father of Queen Victoria
London, 2 VI 1966, 132
£1,350 ($3,780)

1032 FOGELBERG & GILBERT   1033 DESVIGNES

1034 Candlesticks, pair
The branches, Andrew Fogelberg
London, 1775
Candlesticks: 11 in (28 cm) high
88 oz 3 dwt (2,741 gr)
London, 9 X 1969, 250
£1,200 ($2,880)

Peter Desvignes
London; mark entered 1771
Mark Grimwade, 2153

1033 Sugar vases, three
silver-gilt
London, 1778
7½ in (19 cm) and
8¼ in (21 cm) high
29 oz 10 dwt (917 gr)
London, 11 XI 1971, 147
£270 ($675)

Gabriel Wirgman
London; first mark 1772
Mark Grimwade, 922

1035 Cup and cover
gold
London, 1782
17 in (43.2 cm) high
100 oz 4 dwt (3,116 gr)
London, 24 I 1957, 134
£2,600 ($7,254)

1034 DESVIGNES

1035 WIRGMAN

1036 ROBINS

1037 ROBINS

1038 YOUNG & O. JACKSON

John Robins

London; first mark 1774, died 1831
Mark Grimwade, 1623, 3678

1036 Inkstand
London, 1792
10½ in (26.7 cm)
London, 24 IV 1975, 137
£920 ($2,116)

1037 Inkstand
London, 1800
6 in (15.2 cm) high
9 oz 10 dwt (295 gr)
London, 24 IV 1969, 170
£850 ($2,040)

James Young and Orlando Jackson

London; in partnership 1774
Mark Grimwade, 1767

1038 Tea set and tea urn
London, 1774
181 oz 9 dwt (5,643 gr)
Provenance: David Garrick
Now in the Victoria and Albert Museum, London.
London, 19 X 1961, 95
£1,000 ($2,800)

1039 YOUNG

1040 YOUNG

1041 J. CARTER II

1042 J. CARTER II

James Young
London; first mark 1760, active until *c*. 1790 (see above).
Mark Grimwade, 1765

1039 Centrepiece
London, 1786
25¾ in (65.5 cm) wide
800 oz (24,880 gr)
Arms: Fitzgibbon, probably for John Fitzgibbon (1748–1802), created Earl of Clare 1795
Compare this piece with the centrepiece, Paul Crespin (1741), in the Royal Collection (ill. E.A. Jones, *Gold and Silver of Windsor Castle*, Letchworth, 1911; catalogue of exhibition, 'Rococo', no.G17).
London, 22 X 1970, 157
£8,500 ($20,400)

1040 Bowl and stand
London, 1780
8 in (20.3 cm) high
67 oz 3 dwt (2,088 gr)
London, 2 V 1968, 197
£620 ($1,488)

1043 J. CARTER II

1047 SCOFIELD

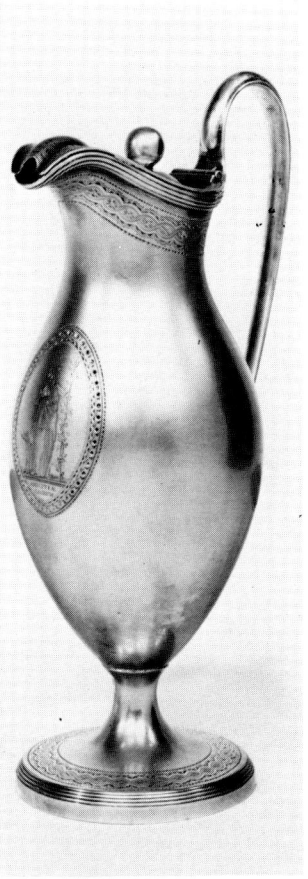

1048 SCOFIELD

John Carter II
London; first mark 1776 but active from c. 1769, retired 1777 when his workshop was taken over by R. Carter and R. Makepeace. Specialist salver and candlestick maker
Mark Grimwade, 1214–15

1041 Candlesticks, pair
silver (loaded)
London, 1771
12¼ in (31.2 cm) high
With a pair of three-light branches, Matthew Boulton, Birmingham, 1820, 108 oz 13 dwt (3,379 gr)
London, 19 I 1956, 157
£195 ($546)

1042 Candlesticks, four, with two branches to fit
London, 1771/3
10½ in (26.7 cm) high
134 oz 7 dwt (4,178 gr)
London, 19 VI 1969, 166
£3,800 ($9,120)

1043 Salver
silver, wood-backed
London, 1771
31¾ in (80.6 cm) overall
New York, 27 IV 1973, 16
$4,000 (£1,600)

1044 Candlesticks, four
London, 1774
10¾ in (27.3 cm) high
92 oz (2,861 gr)
London, 19 XI 1981, 49
£9,680 ($17,327)

John Scofield
London; first mark with Robert Jones 1776, alone 1778
Mark Grimwade, 1670, 3709, 3779

1045 Tea kettle on lamp stand
London, 1782
14¾ in (37.5 cm) high
63 oz 18 dwt (1,987 gr)
Arms: 2nd Baron Rodney (1753–1802)
London, 21 VI 1973, 66
£320 ($800)

1046 Wine cooler
London, 1792
8 in (20.3 cm) high
68 oz 2 dwt (2,117 gr)
London, 19 VII 1979, 159
£2,200 ($4,510)

1047 Coffee jug
London, 1786
11¾ in (29.8 cm) high
26 oz 9 dwt (822 gr)
London, 3 II 1972, 150
£380 ($950)

1048 Jug
London, 1787
10 in (25.4 cm) high
19 oz 15 dwt (614 gr)
London, 13 VII 1967, 81
£380 ($1,064)

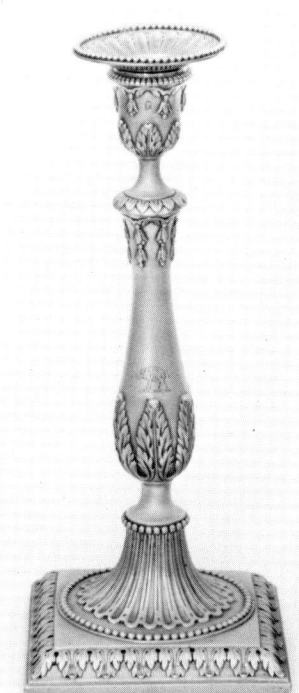

1044 J. CARTER II

1045 SCOFIELD

1046 SCOFIELD

1049 SCOFIELD

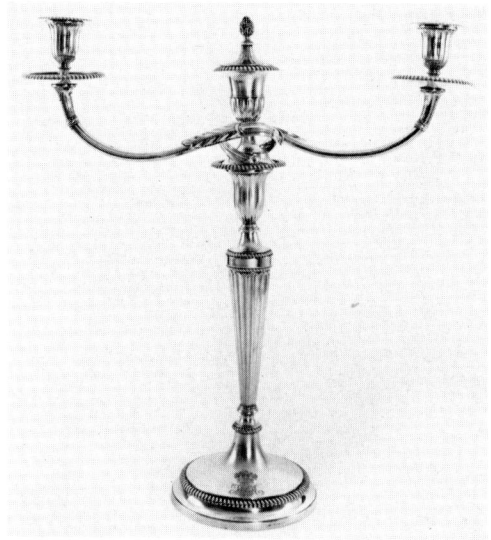
1050 SCOFIELD

1051 SCOFIELD

1052 T. PITTS I

1053 W. PITTS I & PREEDY

Thomas Pitts I

London; apprenticed to Charles Hatfield and David Willaume II, mark entered c. 1758. Specialist epergne maker; supplied Parker and Wakelin (see above, no. 994ff.)
Mark (formerly confused with that of Thomas Powell)
Grimwade, 2875

1052 Epergne
London, 1775
14½ in (36.8 cm) high
103 oz 9 dwt (3,217 gr)
London, 28 XI 1968, 88
£1,100 ($2,640)

William Pitts I and Joseph Preedy

London; in partnership 1791–9 (see below)
Mark Grimwade, 3272

1053 Sweetmeat stands
silver-gilt
London, 1792
4¾ in (12.1 cm) wide
31 oz 10 dwt (979 gr)
London, 17 IX 1981, 118
£1,012 ($1,811)

1054 Wall sconces, pair
London, 1796
17 in (43.2 cm) high
76 oz 5 dwt (2,371 gr)
London, 30 XI 1978, 133
£1,980 ($4,059)

1055 Candelabra, four
London, 1794
22 in (56 cm) high
184 oz 10 dwt (5,737 gr)
London, 23 I 1964, 96
£4,700 ($13,160)

1049 Candlesticks, two
One John Houle, 1814
silver-gilt
London, 1796
7½ in (19 cm) high
33 oz 2 dwt (1,026 gr)
Crest: William Beckford of Fonthill Abbey (1759–1844)
These candlesticks form part of a group made between the mid-1780s and 1817 (for others see Sotheby's, Lennoxlove, 24 July 1980, lots 258–261). See Snodin and Baker, 'William Beckford's Silver'; catalogues of exhibitions, 'Beckford and Hamilton Silver from Brodrick Castle', William Beckford Exhibition, 1976
London, 19 VII 1982, 198
£2,310 ($4,134)

1050 Candelabra, pair
London, 1794
22¼ in (56.5 cm) high
223 oz 17 dwt (6,961 gr)
Monogram: Harriet, Duchess of St Albans
London, 8 XI 1973, 179
£4,800 ($11,520)

1051 Candelabra, pair, and four candlesticks
silver-gilt
London, 1798
21¾ in (55.2 cm) and 9 in (22.9 cm) high
212 oz 12 dwt (6,611 gr)
London, 10 VI 1965, 162
£3,200 ($8,960)

1054 W. PITTS I & PREEDY

1055 W. PITTS I & PREEDY

1056 W. PITTS I

1057 W. PITTS I

1058 W. PITTS I

1059 W. PITTS I

1060 W. PITTS I

William Pitts I

London; apprenticed to his father Thomas (see above); first mark 1781, his son William apprenticed to him 1806. The connection, if any, between William Pitts I and the chaser and modeller William Pitts has not yet been clarified. The latter, who committed suicide in 1840, worked, for example, on the Wellington Shield for Green Ward and Green and on the Shield of Achilles for Rundells. See no.1175ff. see also Culme, *Nineteenth Century Silver Mark* Grimwade, 3263, 3272

1056 Candelabrum
London, 1800
17¼ in (43.8 cm) high
78 oz 16 dwt (2,442 gr)
London, 19 VII 1982, 202
£1,650 ($2,953)

1057 Epergne
London, 1790
12¼ in (31.1 cm) high
91 oz 8 dwt (2,842 gr)
London, 28 XI 1968, 146
£1,300 ($3,120)

1058 Centrepiece
silver-gilt
London, 1801
20¾ in (52.7 cm) high
195 oz 6 dwt (6,073 gr)
Crest: Brudenell, Earls of Cardigan
London, 26 VI 1969, 230
£680 ($1,632)

1059 Teapot
silver-gilt
London, 1783
6 in (15.2 cm) high
18 oz 19 dwt (589 gr)
London, 15 VI 1978, 15
£902 ($1,668)

1060 Dessert bowls, pair
London, 1802
11 in (28 cm) wide
72 oz 5 dwt (2,246 gr)
London, 28 XI 1968, 221
£1,600 ($3,840)

1061 Wine coolers, four
London, 1806
10½ in (26.7 cm) high
552 oz (17,167 gr)
London, 23 V 1963, 120
£1,000 ($2,800)

Peter Podio
London; in partnership with
Abraham Peterson 1783–90,
then mark entered alone
Mark Grimwade, 2215

1062 Milk jug
London, 1801
5½ in (14 cm) high
9 oz 15 dwt (303 gr)
The figures are based on
medallions of the Muses by
Josiah Wedgwood and Thomas
Bentley (see Mankowitz,
Wedgwood, pl. 100).
London, 26 II 1976, 51
£462 ($831)

Hester Bateman
London; baptized 1708, first
mark 1761, retired 1790, died
1794. See p.30; also Culme,
Nineteenth Century Silver, p.15
Mark Grimwade, 955, 958–61

1063 Wine labels, six
London, c. 1775
London, 20 II 1975, 146
£1,250 ($2,875)

1064 Tea caddy
London, 1782
5½ in (14 cm) high
11 oz (342 gr)
London, 30 I 1969, 171
£2,000 ($4,800)

1065 Tea caddy
London, 1784
5¾ in (14.6 cm) high
10 oz 18 dwt (340 gr)
London, 30 XI 1978, 15
£1,540 ($3,157)

1066 Sweetmeat basket
London, 1790
7 in (17.8 cm) wide
7 oz 10 dwt (233 gr)
London, 9 X 1969, 85
£400 ($960)

1067 Teapot
London, 1781
5½ in (14 cm) high
13 oz 4 dwt (410 gr)
London, 9 X 1969, 86
£380 ($912)

1068 Mustard pot
London, 1783
3 in (7.6 cm) high
3 oz 5 dwt (101 gr)
London, 9 X 1969, 83
£280 ($620)

1069 Teapot
London, 1783
5½ in (14 cm) high
13 oz (404 gr)
London, 9 X 1969, 84
£320 ($768)

1070 Argyle
London, 1781
4½ in (11.4 cm) high
9 oz 4 dwt (286 gr)
London, 29 V 1969, 228
£800 ($1,920)

1071 Tankard
London, 1783
7¼ in (18.4 cm) high
27 oz 19 dwt (70 gr)
London, 4 III 1965, 123
£620 ($1,736)

1061 W. PITTS I

1062 PODIO

1064 H. BATEMAN

1063 H. BATEMAN

1065 H. BATEMAN

1066 1067 1068 1069 H. BATEMAN

1070 H. BATEMAN

1071 H. BATEMAN

1072 H. BATEMAN

1073 H. BATEMAN

1072 Coffee pot
London, 1781
11¼ in (28.5 cm) high
27 oz 16 dwt (864 gr)
London, 28 II 1974, 93
£950 ($2,280)

1073 Milk jug
London, 1781
7 in (17.8 cm) high
5 oz 2 dwt (158 gr)
London, 10 XI 1977, 208
£396 ($732)

1074 Caster
London, 1786
5¾ in (14.6 cm) high
2 oz 7 dwt (73 gr)
London, 1 V 1969, 112
£200 ($480)

1075 Sauce tureen and cover
London, 1786
9½ in (24.2 cm) overall
13 oz 12 dwt (423 gr)
London, 28 II 1974, 89
£950 ($2,280)

1076 Cup and cover
silver-gilt
London, 1790
23¾ in (60.4 cm) high
151 oz 19 dwt (4,725 gr)
Arms: 1st Earl of Beauchamp
(1747–1816), who married
Catherine Denn
London, 12 VI 1980, 149
£8,250 ($19,387)

1077 Cake basket
London, 1789
14½ in (36.9 cm) wide
23 oz 6 dwt (724 gr)
London, 19 VI 1969, 133
£1,900 ($4,560)

1078 Mustard pot, with spoon
London, 1789
4 in (10.2 cm) high
4 oz 6 dwt (133 gr)
London, 19 IV 1973, 148
£360 ($900)

1079 Medallion
London, 1782
3 in (7.6 cm) overall
Inscribed: The Brotherly
Society; Love and Unity
London, 16 XI 1978, 79
£253 ($518)

Peter and Jonathan Bateman

London; sons of Hester Bateman
(see above); Jonathan born 1747,
in partnership with Peter
December 1790 until his death
(April 1791)
Mark Grimwade, 2142

1080 Milk jug
London, 1790
5¾ in (14.6 cm) high
2 oz 19 dwt (91 gr)
London, 18 VI 1981, 28
£935 ($1,935)

1081 Cucumber slicer
bone and silver
(London), c. 1790
8¾ in (22.2 cm) overall
London, 11 III 1982, 200
£550 ($984)

1074 H. BATEMAN

Peter and Ann Bateman

London; in partnership 1791–
1800. Peter was the son of
Hester Bateman (see above); Ann
was the widow of Jonathan (see
above)
Mark Grimwade, 2140

1082 Hot water jug
London, 1796
13½ in (34.3 cm) high
25 oz (777 gr)
New York, 17 VI 1981, 57
$3,300 (£1,594)

1083 Salver
London, 1799
10¾ in (27.3 cm) wide
19 oz 18 dwt (618 gr)
London, 14 XII 1972, 172
£500 ($1,250)

Peter, Ann and William Bateman I

London; in partnership 1800–
1805 (see Peter and Ann
Bateman, above). William (born
1774) was the son of Jonathan
and Ann Bateman. Ann retired
1805, died before 1813
Mark Grimwade, 2141

1084 Tea set
London, 1800
30 oz 12 dwt (951 gr)
London, 31 X 1974, 55
£750 ($1,725)

1075 H. BATEMAN

1076 H. BATEMAN

1077 H. BATEMAN

1078 H. BATEMAN

1079 H. BATEMAN

1082 P. & A. BATEMAN

1080 P. & J. BATEMAN

1081 P. & J. BATEMAN

1083 P. & A. BATEMAN

1084 P., A. & W. BATEMAN I

1085 P. & W. BATEMAN I

1086 CHAWNER

1087 CHAWNER

1088   1089 CHAWNER

Peter and William Bateman I

London; in partnership 1805–15 (see Peter, Ann and William Bateman, above). Peter died 1825, William died 1850
Mark Grimwade, 2143

1085 Beaker
London, 1811
4¼ in (10.8 cm) high
9 oz (280 gr)
London, 20 IV 1978, 192
£418 ($773)

Henry Chawner

London; born 1764, first mark 1786, in partnership with John Emes 1796, died 1851.
Mark Grimwade, 971–2, 977

1086 Teapot and stand
London, 1791
Teapot: 6¼ in (15.9 cm) high
19 oz 14 dwt (612 gr)
London, 10 II 1977, 49
£946 ($1,608)

1087 Sauce tureens and covers, pair
London, 1789
9¼ in (23.5 cm) overall
31 oz 5 dwt (971 gr)
London, 6 III 1969, 135
£1,250 ($3,000)

1088 Tea urn
En suite with no. 1089
London, 1790
14¼ in (36.2 cm) high
38 oz 7 dwt (1,192 gr)
London, 26 II 1976, 131
£700 ($1,260)

1089 Tea urn
London, 1790
22 in (55.9 cm) high
108 oz 2 dwt (3,361 gr)
Arms: Collings of Bury St Edmunds, co. Suffolk, with St Aubyn, co. Cornwall, in pretence
London, 26 II 1976, 130
£820 ($1,476)

John Crouch I and II and Thomas Hannam

London; Hannam in partnership with John I from c. 1770 and with the latter's son, John II, 1799–1808. Specialist salver makers
Mark Grimwade, 1233, 2805

1090 Salver
London, 1784
16 in (40.6 cm) diameter
58 oz 18 dwt (1,831 gr)
London, 16 II 1978, 172
£1,375 ($2,543)

1091 Dishes, pair
silver-gilt
London, 1802
18 in (45.7 cm) diameter
208 oz 8 dwt (6,481 gr)
Arms: Lygon, Baron Beauchamp
New York, 13 X 1981, 191
$11,000 (£6,145)

1092 Tray
London, 1806
29 in (73.7 cm) wide
162 oz 7 dwt (5,049 gr)
London, 13 VI 1974, 38
£1,300 ($3,120)

1093 Tray
London, 1799
37½ in (95.2 cm) wide
305 oz (9,485 gr)
London, 21 III 1963, 153
£800 ($2,240)

1090 CROUCH & HANNAM

1091 CROUCH & HANNAM

1092 CROUCH & HANNAM

1093 CROUCH & HANNAM

1094 PHIPPS & ROBINSON II

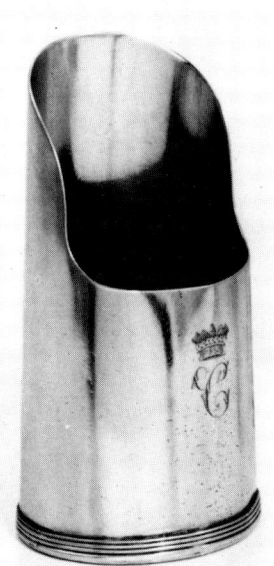

1095 PHIPPS & ROBINSON II

Thomas Phipps and Edward Robinson II

London; in partnership 1783–c. 1800. Robinson died 1816, Phipps died 1823 (see below)
Mark Grimwade, 2891

1094 Toothpick case
London, 1789
3½ in (8.9 cm) wide
See Delieb, *Silver Boxes*, p.58.
London, 26 VI 1975, 173
£250 ($575)

1095 Spice scoop
London, 1789
3½ in (8.9 cm) high
3 oz 6 dwt (102 gr)
London, 4 V 1978, 13
£308 ($570)

1096 PHIPPS & ROBINSON II

1098 T. & J. PHIPPS II

1099 R. HENNELL I

1097 PHIPPS & ROBINSON II

1100 R. HENNELL I

1101 R. HENNELL I

1096 Snuff box
London, 1791
3 in (7.6 cm) wide
London, 26 VI 1975, 174
£450 ($1,035)

1097 Bottle labels, ten
With cruet frame, R. and S. Hennell
London, 1804 and c. 1804
9¼ in (23.5 cm) high
14 oz 2 dwt (438 gr)
The labels are for Anchovy, Cavice, Soy, Ketchup, Cherokee, Lemon Pickle, Quin, Piquante, Kyan and Woods Fish Sauce.
London, 2 VII 1970, 177
£150 ($360)

Thomas Phipps and James Phipps II

London. In partnership 1816; Thomas and James previously in partnership with Edward Robinson II from c. 1811 (see above)
Mark Grimwade, 2893

1098 Coronation bell
silver-gilt
London, 1820
5 in (12.7 cm) high
6 oz 19 dwt (216 gr)
Inscribed: This bell was attached to the Canopy Borne by Charles Emmerson Esq. of Sandwich and other Barons of the Cinque Ports over HM George 4th at his Coronation AD 1821
London, 20 X 1977, 162
£2,860 ($5,291)

Hennell Family

London; business established by David Hennell I (1712–85) and continued as R. Hennell and Sons until 1899 in unbroken succession (see also nos 1427ff.). The firm is still in business. See Hennell, 'The Hennells'; also *Antique Collector*, June 1975/June 1979, which include a family tree 1712–1972

Robert Hennell I

Born 1741, first mark with his father David I 1763; alone 1772–95, died 1811.
Mark Grimwade, 2330–31

1099 Tea caddy
London, 1791
4¾ in (12 cm) high
6 oz 16 dwt (211 gr)
London, 6 VII 1972, 170
£280 ($700)

1102 R. HENNELL I & S. HENNELL

1106 T. HOLLAND II

1103 R. HENNELL II

1104 R. HENNELL II

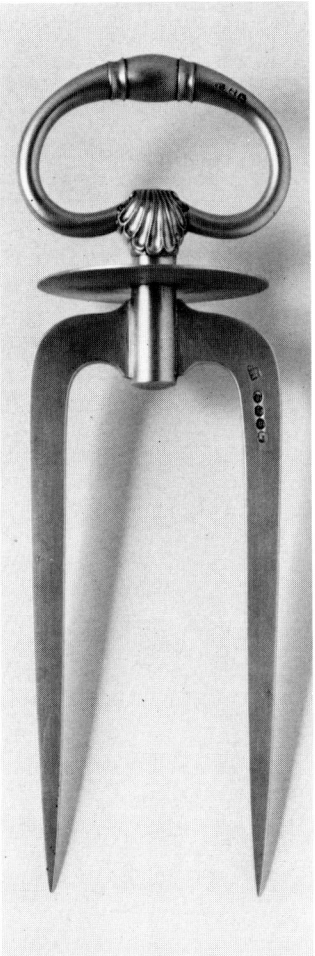

1105 ELEY, FEARN & CHAWNER

Robert Hennell II

London; born 1763, apprenticed to his uncle Robert I, mark alone 1809, retired 1833, died 1840
Mark Grimwade, 2332

1103 Toast racks, pair
London, 1824
6½ in (16.2 cm) wide
30 oz 18 dwt (960 gr)
London, 20 III 1980, 214
£1,320 ($3,102)

1104 Chamber candlestick
London, 1826
3½ in (9 cm) diameter
14 oz 8 dwt (447 gr)
London, 28 IV 1977, 110
£286 ($486)

William Eley I, William Fearn and William Chawner

London; in partnership 1808–14, previously and subsequently Eley and Fearn in partnership; the former, having been apprenticed to Fearn, died 1824. Specialist spoonmakers.
Mark Grimwade, 3114

1105 Roast fork
London, 1813
10¼ in (26 cm) overall
15 oz 16 dwt (491 gr)
New York, 13–15 X 1981, 181
$1,540 (£860)

Thomas Holland II

London; mark entered 1798
Mark Grimwade, 2789

1106 Teapot
London, 1806
5 in (12.7 cm) high
22 oz 16 dwt (709 gr)
New York, 16–17 XII 1980, 210
$1,320 (£637)

1100 Sweetmeat basket
London, 1792
5¼ in (13.3 cm) wide
5 oz 7 dwt (166 gr)
London, 20 XII 1979, 82
£506 ($1,189)

1101 Fish slice
London, 1776
11 in (30 cm) overall
New York, 26–27 X 1976, 269
$425 (£250)

Robert Hennell I and Samuel Hennell

London; Samuel (1778–1837) was son of Robert I; in partnership 1802–11
Mark Grimwade, 2338

1102 Tea caddy
London, 1803
5½ in (14 cm) high
17 oz 15 dwt (552 gr)
London, 4 XII 1969, 205
£240 ($576)

1107 T. HOLLAND II

1108 T. HOLLAND II

1107 Ewer
silver-gilt
London, 1807
13¾ in (34.9 cm) high
87 oz 3 dwt (2,710 gr)
Arms: Frederick, Duke of York
Provenance: Baroness Burdett Coutts, whose initials are on the body and foot
London, 22 VI 1967, 57
£800 ($2,240)

1108 Ewers, pair
silver-gilt
London, 1807
14¼ in (36.2 cm) high
168 oz (5,224 gr)
Arms: 5th Baron Aylmer (1775–1850)
London, 26 II 1976, 186
£3,300 ($5,940)

1109 T. HOLLAND II

1110 T. HOLLAND II

1111 STORR

1112 STORR

1113 B. SMITH II

1109 Ewer
London, 1807
13¾ in (34.9 cm) high
60 oz 2 dwt (1,869 gr)
London, 17 V 1973, 49
£1,200 ($3,000)

1110 Ewers, pair
London, 1807
14¼ in (36.2 cm) high
148 oz 10 dwt (4,618 gr)
Arms: 4th Baron Monson, born 1785, who married Sarah, daughter of 2nd Earl Mexborough, 1807
London, 15 X 1970, 57
£2,100 ($5,040)

Paul Storr

London; born 1771, apprenticed to Andrew Fogelberg, first mark in partnership with William Frisbee 1792, alone 1793, associated with Rundell, Bridge & Rundell 1807–19 (see separate entry, Paul Storr with Rundell, Bridge and Rundell, below, no.1113ff.), in partnership with John Mortimer 1822–38 (see Paul Storr and John Mortimer, no.1273ff., below), retired 1838, died 1844. See pp.32–4. See also Penzer, *Paul Storr*; Culme, *Nineteenth Century Silver*; bibliography for Rundell, Bridge and Rundell (below)
Mark Grimwade, 2233–5, 3133

1111 Candlesticks, pair
silver-gilt
London, 1800
7 in (17.8 cm) high
34 oz 13 dwt (1,080 gr)
Inscribed: Made for the Abbey at Fonthill by Vulliamy & Son 1800
See Snodin and Baker, 'William Beckford's Silver'.
London, 23 I 1964, 19
£1,200 ($3,360)

1112 Cake basket
silver-gilt
London, 1797
20½ in (52.1 cm) wide
272 oz (8,459 gr)
See Snodin, 'J. J. Boileau, a Forgotten Designer of Silver'.
London, 15 X 1970, 79
£7,000 ($16,800)

Benjamin Smith II

Born 1764, died 1823, worked alone 1807–8, 1812–16 and from 1818. In partnership with his brother James 1809 and with his son Benjamin 1816, having previously been with Digby Scott (see below). He worked for Rundell, Bridge and Rundell (see below), but not exclusively; he also worked, for example, for Green, Ward and Green (no.1113)
Mark Grimwade, 229–30

1113 Centrepiece
London, 1813
Stamped: Green Ward et Green Londini Fecerunt
22¼ in (56.5 cm) high
353 oz (10,978 gr)
London, 19 VII 1973, 88
£1,800 ($4,500)

1114 B. SMITH II

1114 Salts, pair
London, 1814
2¾ in (6.7 cm) high
19 oz 12 dwt (609 gr)
New York, 14–15 IV 1982, 251
$7,285 (£4,070)

Rundell, Bridge and Rundell

London; the leading retailers of silver and jewellery in the early 19th century. Philip Rundell (1743–1827) became a partner of William Pickett (see no. 1010) in 1772 and was joined by John Bridge (1755–1834) in 1777. They took over the firm in 1785, when it became Rundell and Bridge. In 1805 they took Rundell's nephew into partnership and the firm became Rundell, Bridge and Rundell. During this period the manufacture of their plate was chiefly divided between Digby Scott and Benjamin Smith II (see below) and Paul Storr (see Paul Storr with Rundell, Bridge and Rundell below). In 1807 Paul Storr became their managing partner in charge of the Dean Street workshops under the name Storr and Company. When this connection ended in 1819 Philip Rundell entered a mark which was used until his retirement in 1823, whereupon John Bridge entered a mark. On his death in 1834 the firm became known as Rundell, Bridge and Company; it ceased trading in 1843. In this latter period silversmiths who made pieces for Rundells included William Bateman, John Tapley and Edward Barnard and Sons. Those who designed for Rundells included John Flaxman, Thomas Stothard, William Theed (head of the design department until 1817) and Edward Hodges Baily (who worked for Rundells 1815–33). See Bury, 'The Lengthening Shadow of Rundells' and 'Flaxman as a Designer of Silverwork' in catalogue of the exhibition, 'John Flaxman, R.A.'; Oman, 'A Problem of Artistic Responsibility'; Culme, *Nineteenth Century Silver*

1115 SCOTT & B. SMITH II

1116 SCOTT & B. SMITH II

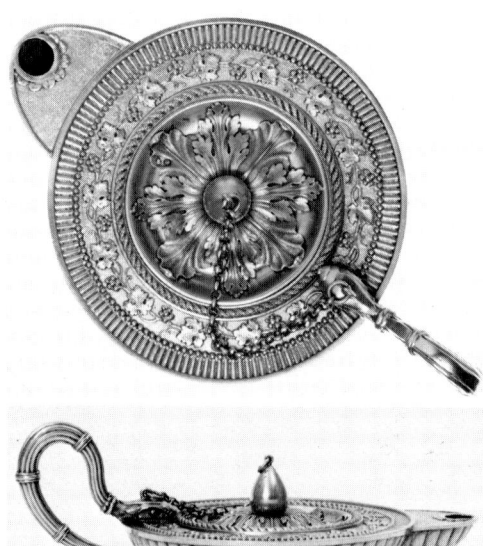

1117 SCOTT & B. SMITH II

Digby Scott and Benjamin Smith II

In partnership 1802–7
Mark Grimwade, 504–5

1115 Inkstand
silver-gilt
London, 1803
14 in (35.6 cm) wide
70 oz 5 dwt (2,184 gr)
Inscribed: Georgiana Stanhope Christened March 30 1802 God Father The King, God Mothers The Queen, and Her Royal Highness The Princess Augusta. The recipient was daughter of 5th Earl of Chesterfield and died aged 21.
London, 8 VI 1972, 3
£6,500 ($16,250)

1116 Salvers-on-foot, pair
silver-gilt
London, 1803
12 in (30.5 cm) diameter
94 oz (2,923 gr)
Arms: 6th Duke of Leeds (1775–1838)
London, 1 II 1973, 148
£2,200 ($5,500)

1117 Inkwell
silver-gilt
London, 1804
scratched: Rundell and Bridge
6 in (15.1 cm) diameter
10 oz 17 dwt (337 gr)
London, 11 XI 1982, 66
£1,540 ($2,464)

1118 Tea urn
silver-gilt
London, 1805
Stamped: Latin signature of Rundells
14¼ in (36.2 cm) high
219 oz (6,810 gr)
Arms: Charles, 4th Duke of Richmond and Lennox
See Sotheby Parke-Bernet, New York, 16–17 December 1982, lot 542, for a similar tea urn. See also Snodin, 'J.J. Boileau, a Forgotten Designer of Silver'.
London, 20 VI 1974, 48
£2,200 ($5,280)

1118 SCOTT & B. SMITH II

1119 SCOTT & B. SMITH II

1120 SCOTT & B. SMITH II

1119 Tea tray
silver-gilt
London, 1805
30¾ in (78.2 cm) wide
230 oz 10 dwt (7,168 gr)
London, 11 II 1971, 254
£1,800 ($4,320)

1120 Teapots, four
silver-gilt
London, 1806
3¼ in (8.2 cm) high
75 oz 16 dwt (2,357 gr)
Crest: Howard, Dukes of Norfolk
London, 4 V 1978, 93
£4,400 ($8,140)

1121 Sugar vase
silver-gilt
London, 1805
Stamped: Latin signature of Rundells
8¼ in (21 cm) high
31 oz 10 dwt (979 gr)
See nos 1122, 1150
London, 16 XII 1971, 40
£450 ($1,125)

1122 Sugar vases, four
silver-gilt
London, 1806
8 in (20.3 cm) high
131 oz (4,074 gr)
See nos 1121, 1150
London, 15 X 1970, 67
£1,900 ($4,560)

1121 SCOTT & B. SMITH II

1122 SCOTT & B. SMITH II

250 GREAT BRITAIN IRELAND

1123 SCOTT & B. SMITH II

1124 SCOTT & B. SMITH II

1127 SCOTT & B. SMITH II

1123 Candlesticks, pair
Fitted with branches, William Elliott, 1839
London, 1805
Stamped: Latin inscription of Rundells
19¼ in (49 cm) high
177 oz 16 dwt (5,529 gr)
London, 15 III 1973, 279
£700 ($1,750)

1124 Bowls, pair
silver-gilt
London, 1806
6¼ in (15.9 cm) high
45 oz 2 dwt (1,402 gr)
London, 26 II 1976, 166
£825 ($1,485)

1125 Soup tureens, pair
London, 1806
Stamped: Latin signature of Rundells
16¼ in (41.2 cm) wide
517 oz (16,078 gr)
See no.1759
London, 27 I 1966, 151
£3,300 ($9,240)

1126 Salvers-on-foot, pair
silver-gilt
London, 1807
Stamped: Latin signature of Rundells
12 in (30.5 cm) diameter
116 oz 18 dwt (3,635 gr)
Arms: Charles, 4th Duke of Richmond and Lennox
London, 20 VI 1974, 126
£3,600 ($8,640)

1127 Wine coasters, four
silver-gilt
London, 1807
Stamped: Latin signature of Rundells
5¼ in (13.4 cm) diameter
101 oz 9 dwt (3,155 gr)
London, 23 IV 1970, 194
£2,500 ($6,000)

1125 SCOTT & B. SMITH II

1128 SCOTT & B. SMITH II

1128 Wine labels, four
London, 1807
Others for Lisbon, Champagne, Vin-de-Grave
London, 24 IV 1969, 174
£480 ($1,152)

1126 SCOTT & B. SMITH II

1129 SCOTT & B. SMITH II

1131 STORR

1130 STORR

1132 STORR

Paul Storr

with Rundell, Bridge and Rundell; see p.248
Mark Grimwade, 2233-5

1130 Soup tureens, pair
London, 1806/7
Stamped: Latin signature of Rundells
17½ in (44.5 cm) high
1,039 oz (32,312 gr)
Initialled: EDC, for Ernest Duke of Cumberland; EA.F's (Ernst Augustus Fideikommis; the entailed estate of Ernest Augustus.
London, 15 X 1970, 89
£9,500 ($22,800)

1131 Tea set
silver-gilt
London, 1808/9
137 oz (4,260 gr)
London, 16 VII 1970, 136
£2,900 ($6,960)

1132 Tea tray
London, 1808
30½ in (77.5 cm) wide
214 oz 12 dwt (6,674 gr)
Arms: Duke of Cambridge, 7th son of George III
London, 26 VI 1975, 52
£4,200 ($9,660)

1129 Lloyd's Patriotic Fund Vase
London, 1808
Designer: John Flaxman
With a stand, B. and J. Smith (1809)
In a box with a label of Rundells
Vase: 15½ in (39.4 cm) high
362 oz 10 dwt (11,273 gr)
Inscribed: From the Patriotic Fund at Lloyds to Major General Sir John Stuart Commanding in Chief His Majesty's Troops at the Battle of Calabria on the 4th of July 1806...
One of some sixty-six vases presented to naval and military officers by Lloyd's Patriotic Fund, all of the same design. See S. Bury, 'Flaxman as a Designer of Silverwork', in catalogue of exhibition, 'John Flaxman, R.A.'.
London, 11 II 1971, 15
£1,700 ($4,080)

1133 STORR

1134 STORR

1138 STORR

1135   1136 STORR

1137 STORR

1139 STORR

1133 Dessert stands, pair
silver-gilt
London, 1808
8 in (20.2 cm) high
125 oz (3,887 gr)
See Charles Heathcote Tatham, *Etchings representing the best examples of Ancient Ornamental Architecture*, pl. 51, for the inspiration for this design, and compare with designs of Thomas Hope (*Anastasius The History of Architecture Household Furniture and Interior Decoration*, pl. 32).
See also nos 1165, 1166
London, 15 X 1970, 84
£1,550 ($3,720)

1134 Candlesticks, eight
silver-gilt
London, 1807/8
345 oz (10,729 gr)
London, 15 X 1970, 72, 73
£8,800 ($21,120)

1140 1141 STORR

1142 STORR

1143 STORR

1144 STORR

1135 Cruet
London, 1810
12½ in (31.8 cm) wide
London, 16 II 1978, 241
£1,050 ($1,942)

1136 Cruet
London, 1810
14¾ in (37.5 cm) wide
London, 16 II 1978, 242
£1,750 ($3,237)

1137 Centrepiece
silver-gilt
London, 1810
Stamped: Latin signature of Rundells
18½ in (47 cm) high
250 oz (7,775 gr)
Arms: De la Poer, Marquesses of Waterford
London, 22 VI 1972, 183
£1,900 ($4,750)

1138 Centrepiece
silver-gilt
London, 1809
Stamped: 345
17½ in (44.5 cm) high
231 oz 2 dwt (7,187 gr)
See Udy, 'Piranesi's Vasi, the English Silversmith and his Patrons'; Oman, 'A Problem of Artistic Responsibility'.
London, 9 XII 1976, 202
£16,500 ($28,050)

1139 Bowls and stands, two
silver-gilt
London, 1810
One unmarked, probably Cantonese work of Ch'ien Lung period made for export
15 in (38.1 cm) high
227 oz 8 dwt (7,072 gr)
Arms: 4th Baron Ducie and his wife Frances, daughter of 1st Earl of Caernarvon.
London, 23 I 1964, 63
£2,800 ($7,840)

1140 Sauce tureens, four
London, 1811
6½ in (16.5 cm) diameter
146 oz 13 dwt (4,563 gr)
London, 25 X 1962, 64
£1,050 ($2,940)

1141 Soup tureens, two
London, 1811/13
11¾ in (29.8 cm) diameter
310 oz 10 dwt (9,656 gr)
London, 25 X 1962, 65
£1,800 ($5,040)

1142 Dishes and covers, pair
silver-gilt
London, 1812
Stamped: Rundell Bridge et Rundell Aurifices Regis et Principis Walliae Regentis Britannias, 1764
9½ in (24 cm) diameter
69 oz 12 dwt (2,164 gr)
Arms: 3rd Duke of Northumberland
London, 3 V 1984, 112
£30,250 ($42,047)

1143 Theocritus Cup
silver-gilt
London, 1811/12
Designer: John Flaxman
Stamped: Latin signature of Rundells
14¼ in (36.2 cm) high
156 oz (4,851 gr)
The design is based on the description of the cup in the First Idyll of Theocritus. See Bury, 'Flaxman as a Designer of Silverwork' in catalogue of exhibition. 'John Flaxman, R.A.'; Penzer, *Paul Storr*, p.158.
London, 25 X 1973, 50
£9,000 ($21,600)

1144 Wine label
silver-gilt
London, 1812
London, 27 VI 1968, 156
£240 ($576)

1145 STORR

1147 STORR

1146 STORR

1148 STORR

1145 Salt cellars, four
silver-gilt
London, 1812
Probably designed by William Theed
Stamped: Latin signature of Rundells
4¼ in (10.8 cm) wide
105 oz 15 dwt (3,288 gr)
London, 16 VII 1970, 138
£3,600 ($8,640)

1146 Sideboard dishes, pair
silver-gilt
London, 1813
Designer: Thomas Stothard
One stamped: Rundell's Latin inscription
35 in (77.5 cm) diameter
724 oz 10 dwt (22,518 gr)
Arms: 3rd Duke of Northumberland
London, 3 V 1984, 105
£286,000 ($397,540)

1147 'Warwick Vase' wine cooler
London, 1812
Stamped: Latin signature of Rundells
20¼ in (51.5 cm) high
394 oz 10 dwt (12,268 gr)
Arms: 1st Viscount Exmouth (1757–1833)
The design is based on the marble vase purchased by the Earl of Warwick in 1774 and engraved by Piranesi. See Udy, 'Piranesi's Vasi, the English Silversmith and his Patrons'.
London, 13 XII 1973, 133
£3,000 ($7,200)

1148 Centrepiece
silver-gilt
London, 1813
23½ in (59.7 cm) high
394 oz 1 dwt (12,254 gr)
London, 24 IV 1969, 210
£5,200 ($12,480)

1149 Egg cruet
London, 1813
8½ in (21.6 cm) high
41 oz 17 dwt (1,301 gr)
London, 22 VI 1972, 170
£900 ($2,250)

1149 STORR

1151 STORR

1150 STORR

1152 STORR

1153 STORR

1150 Sugar vases, pair
silver-gilt
London, 1816
8¼ in (21 cm) high
61 oz 7 dwt (1,907 gr)
See Udy, 'Piranesi's Vasi, the English Silversmith and his Patrons'. See also nos 1121, 1122
London, 19 X 1978, 136
£4,400 ($9,020)

1151 Soup tureens and stands, pair
London, 1816
Stamped: Latin signature of Rundells
Probably designed by E.H. Baily
Stands: 23 in (58.4 cm) wide
754 oz (23,450 gr)
See no.1153
London, 16 VII 1970, 133
£9,000 ($21,600)

1152 Wine cups, pair
London, 1814
Stamped: Latin signature of Rundells
6¼ in (15.9 cm) high
28 oz 4 dwt (877 gr)
London, 22 VI 1972, 168
£1,250 ($3,125)

1153 Wine coolers, pair
London, 1817
Stamped: 93 and numbered
Probably designed by E.H. Baily
8¾ in (22.5 cm) high
285 oz 11 dwt (8,881 gr)
Arms: added 1844
See Oman, 'A Problem of Artistic Responsibility'.
London, 3 III 1983, 17
£39,600 ($63,360)

1154 RUNDELL

Philip Rundell

for Rundell, Bridge and Rundell;
see p.248

1154 Teapot
London, 1820
6 in (15.2 cm) high
30 oz (933 gr)
New York, 16–17 XII 1976, 327
$700 (£411)

1155 RUNDELL

1156 RUNDELL

1157 RUNDELL

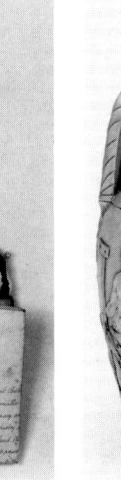

1158 RUNDELL

1159 RUNDELL

1160 RUNDELL

1155 Butter dish and stand
London, 1819
10¼ in (26 cm) diameter
64 oz 10 dwt (2,005 gr)
London, 20 VI 1974, 68
£1,300 ($3,120)

1156 Inkstand
silver-gilt
London, 1822
After a design by John Flaxman
Stamped: Rundell Bridge et Rundell Aurifices Regis Londini
16¾ in (42.9 cm) wide
184 oz 13 dwt (5,743 gr)
See Oman, 'A Problem of Artistic Responsibility', fig.6.
London, 3 V 1984, 131
£22,000 ($30,580)

1157 Seal box
London, 1822
7 in (17.7 cm) diameter
London, 19 VI 1969, 101
£1,300 ($3,120)

1158 Replica of the Portland Vase
silver-gilt
London, 1820
9¾ in (24.8 cm) high
89 oz 4 dwt (2,774 gr)
The Barberini Vase, purchased by Sir William Hamilton in 1780, was sold by him to the Duchess of Portland and became known as the Portland Vase. After her death it was borrowed and copied by Josiah Wedgwood. See Wolf Mankowitz, *The Portland Vase and the Wedgwood Copies*.
New York, 17 VI 1981, 78
$38,500 (£18,600)

1159 Stirrup cup
silver-gilt
London, 1821
4 in (10.4 cm) high
25 oz 3 dwt (782 gr)
London, 16 III 1978, 169
£3,520 ($6,512)

1160 Tankard
silver-gilt
London, 1820
Stamped: Latin signature of Rundells
11¾ in (29.8 cm) high
106 oz 10 dwt (3,312 gr)
New York, 16–17 XII 1982, 540
$26,400 (£16,500)

1161 The Shield of Achilles
silver-gilt
London, 1822
Inscribed: designed and Modelled by John Flaxman RA Executed & Published by Rundell Bridge & Rundell Goldsmiths & Jewellers to His Majesty London MDCCCXXII
36¼ in (92 cm) diameter
669 oz 10 dwt (20,821 gr)
Badge: 3rd Duke of Northumberland
See catalogue of Sotheby sale and Bury and Snodin, 'The Shield of Achilles by John Flaxman RA', *Art at Auction*, 1983/84.
London, 3 V 1984, 124
£484,000 ($672,760)

1162 RUNDELL

1163 BRIDGE

1162 Tea tray
silver-gilt
London, 1823
31¼ in (79.5 cm) overall
247 oz (7,681 gr)
Arms: 3rd Duke of
Northumberland (1795–1847)
The engraving is probably by
Walter Jackson (see Oman,
English Engraved Silver,
pp.123–6)
London, 3 V 1984, 113
£20,900 ($29,051)

John Bridge

for Rundell, Bridge and Rundell,
see p.248

1164 BRIDGE

1163 Inkstand
silver-gilt
London, 1825/34/35
The liner, mounts and base,
William Bateman
9 in (23.1 cm) diameter
31 oz 7 dwt (975 gr)
London, 3 III 1983, 12
£1,210 ($1,936)

1164 Inkwell
silver-gilt
London, 1823
3¼ in (8.3 cm) high
7 oz 7 dwt (228 gr)
*London (Belgravia), 21 II 1974,
134*
£600 ($1,440)

1161 RUNDELL

1165 BRIDGE

1167 BRIDGE

1166 BRIDGE

1166 BRIDGE

1168 STRACHAN

1169 STRACHAN

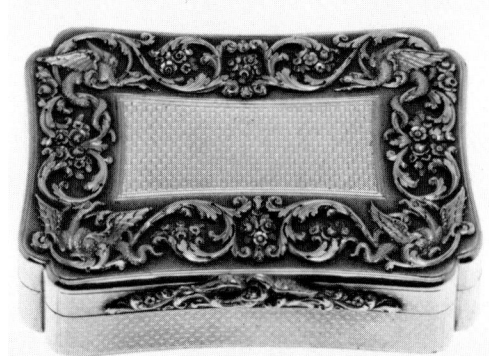

1170 STRACHAN

1171 STRACHAN

1165 Tea and coffee set
silver-gilt
London, 1828
120 oz 2 dwt (3,375 gr)
Arms: See no 1166
See nos 1133, 1257
London, 20 VI 1974, 114
£3,600 ($8,640)

1166 Vases, pair
silver-gilt
London, 1827
Designer: John Flaxman
6½ in (16.5 cm) high
66 oz (2,052 gr)
Arms: Hope impaling Beresford for Thomas Hope of Deepdene, Surrey, and his wife the Hon. Louisa Beresford. See nos 1133, 1165, 1257
New York, 10–11 VI 1975, 563
$9,250 (£4,021)

1167 Presentation cup
silver-gilt
London, 1830
Stamped: Rundell Bridge e Rundell Aurifices Regis Londini
13½ in (34.2 cm) high
53 oz 11 dwt (1,665 gr)
Inscribed: From his Imperial Majesty the Emperor of Russia to Edward Thomason Esqr 1831. Edward Thomason (1769–1849) was apprenticed to Matthew Boulton (see below, no.1194ff.) and later manufactured buttons, medals and silver and gold plate.
London, 12 XI 1970, 294
£600 ($1,440)

1172 STRACHAN

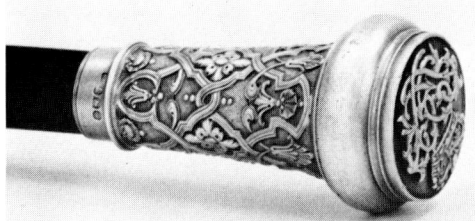

1173 STRACHAN

1174 UNMARKED

1175 W. PITTS

1176 W. PITTS

1177 W. PITTS

Alexander James Strachan

London; first mark 1799; the firm continued until c. 1842–50. Renowned for his gold boxes, which he supplied to Rundell, Bridge and Rundell (see above, p.248)
Mark Grimwade, 46

1168 Snuff box
silver-gilt
London, 1809
3¼ in (8.3 cm) wide
The spine engraved: 'Handel, Haydn, Mozart, Beethoven'
London, 19 VII 1979, 153
£2,970 ($6,088)

1169 Snuff box
two-colour gold
London, 1813
3 in (8 cm) wide
Geneva, 12 XI 1980, 35
SFr.10,450 (£2,435 $5,040)

1170 Snuff box
three-colour gold
London, 1825
3¼ in (8.5 cm) wide
London, 7 III 1983, 140
£2,200 ($3,520)

1171 Snuff box
gold inset with a Roman micro-mosaic panel
London, 1827
3¼ in (8.5 cm) wide
Geneva, 12 XI 1980, 34
SFr.20,900 (£4,871 $10,082)

1172 Toothpick case
two-colour gold
London, 1812
2¾ in (6.8 cm) wide
Geneva, 6 V 1981, 98
SFr.1,980 (£461 $954)

1173 Staff of office
London, 1820
Knop: 4 in (10.2 cm) long
See no.1221
London, 30 X 1975, 87
£374 ($748)

Unmarked

1174 Scent bottle
Attributed to A.J. Strachan
gold, enamel and glass
c. 1820
3¼ in (8.3 cm) high
London, 8 V 1978, 19
£3,300 ($6,105)

William Pitts

London; see p.237

1175 Sideboard dishes, pair
silver-gilt
London, 1809
15½ in (39.4 cm) diameter
London, 7 VI 1979, 71
£3,740 ($7,667)

1176 Charger
silver-gilt
London, 1814
Centred by an earlier plaque
22 in (56 cm) diameter
206 oz 6 dwt (6,415 gr)
Compare with two dishes, commissioned by Rundell, Bridge and Rundell from Pitts and sold to the Prince Regent, which are also inset with earlier medallions (one bearing Jacob Bodendick's mark): ill. Jones, *Windsor Castle Plate*, pl.XCVIII.
London, 11 VI 1970, 237
£850 ($2,040)

1177 Dish
silver-gilt
London, 1820
25½ in (65 cm) diameter
152 oz (4,727 gr)
New York, 12 XII 1973, 240
$2,800 (£1,166)

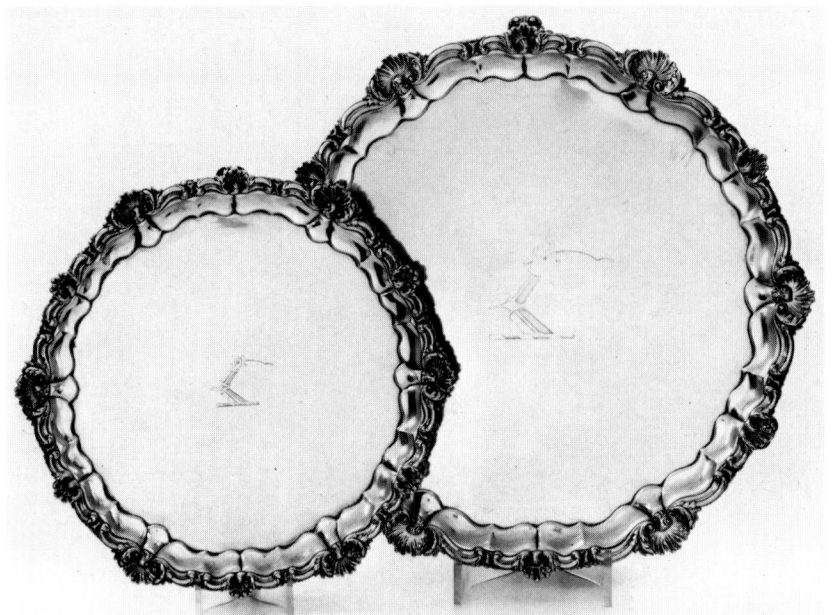

1178 W. BATEMAN II

1179 W. BATEMAN II

1180 W. BATEMAN II

1181 W. BATEMAN II

William Bateman II

London; apprenticed to his father William I (see nos 1084, 1085), first mark 1827, died 1874–7. Worked extensively but not exclusively for Rundell, Bridge and Company from c. 1834
Mark Grimwade, 3038

1178 Salvers, two
London, 1829
Stamped: 37/38
19 in (48.2 cm) and 14½ in (36.9 cm) diameter
110 oz 12 dwt (3,439 gr) and 59 oz 12 dwt (1,853 gr)
London, 24 VII 1975, 46, 47
£650 ($1,493) and £430 ($989)

1179 Salt cellars and spoons, pair
London, 1832/5
2½ in (6.4 cm) high
8 oz 17 dwt (275 gr)
London (Belgravia), 24 II 1972, 118
£90 ($225)

1182 W. BATEMAN II

1180 Tea and coffee set, five pieces
London, 1834/5
97 oz 5 dwt (3,024 gr)
Compare with no.1165
London (Belgravia), 7 VI 1973, 129
£580 ($1,450)

1181 Teapot
London, 1834
Engraved in freehand: 4811; probably for Rundell, Bridge and Company
4¾ in (12 cm) high
25 oz 5 dwt (784 gr)
London (Belgravia), 7 IV 1977, 495
£187 ($317)

1183 W. BATEMAN II

1182 Soup tureen
London, 1836
Stamped: Rundell Bridge & Co Aurifices Regis Londini
12¼ in (31.1 cm) high
174 oz 4 dwt (5,417 gr)
Arms: Royal
New York, 17 VI 1981, 59
$29,700 (£14,347)

1183 Cruet bottles, pair
glass, silver-mounted
London, 1836
8 in (20.4 cm) high
London (Belgravia), 1 V 1975, 111
£360 ($828)

1184 Sideboard dish
silver-gilt
London, 1834
For Rundell, Bridge and Company
Stamped: Rundell Bridge et Co. Aurifices Regis Londini
32 in (81.4 cm) wide
253 oz (7,868 gr)
Arms: HRH Adolphus Frederick, 1st Duke of Cambridge
Provenance: Collection of 2nd Duke of Cambridge, Christie's, 7 July 1904
The scene on this dish depicts the triumph of the Black Prince over the King of Bohemia at the Battle of Crécy (1346). The companion piece depicted the Battle of Agincourt and was made to the order of Thomas Hamlet as a birthday present to the duke from his wife in 1826.
London (Belgravia), 10 VII 1975, 168
£6,000 ($13,800)

1185 Tray
London, 1837
Stamped: Rundell Bridge & Co. Aurifices Reginae Londini
32¾ in (82.2 cm) wide
281 oz 9 dwt (8,753 gr)
Inscribed: The Gift of Queen Victoria to Lord Dundas as a token of Her Majesty's sense of the attentions shown by the late peer to her revered father His Royal Highness The Duke of Kent April 1838
London (Belgravia), 26 VII 1973, 204
£3,400 ($8,500)

1186 Posy holder
silver-gilt
London, 1835
For Rundell, Bridge and Company
6¼ in (15.7 cm) overall
London, 14 IV 1983, 337
£198 ($316)

1184 W. BATEMAN II

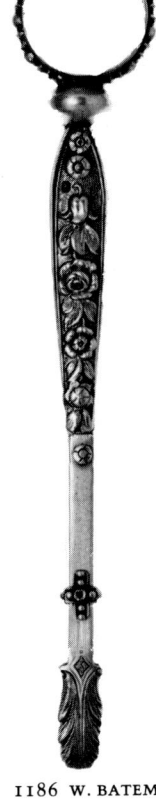

1185 W. BATEMAN II 1186 W. BATEMAN II

1187 W. BATEMAN II

1188 TAPLEY

1189 TAPLEY

1187 Coffee jug on lamp stand
London, 1838
Stamped: 9
12 in (30.5 cm) high
49 oz 19 dwt (1,553 gr)
London (Belgravia), 15 XI 1973, 166
£330 ($792)

John Tapley

London; first mark 1833.
Worked for Rundells and R.
Green and Company (formerly
Green, Ward and Green).
Mark Grimwade, 1720–21

1188 Tazza
silver-gilt
London, 1838
Scratched: 8810
For Rundell, Bridge and
Company
8¼ in (21.5 cm) diameter
26 oz 14 dwt (830 gr)
London, 26 V 1983, 112
£572 ($915)

1189 Sugar bowl
silver-gilt
London, 1842
6½ in (16.5 cm) diameter
13 oz 1 dwt (405 gr)
See Clayton, *Collector's Dictionary of ... Silver and Gold*, ill. no. 220, for a dessert service of this pattern
London (Belgravia), 13 IX 1973, 191
£320 ($768)

1190 Tea set
London, 1840
Scratched: 6285/6286/6287
48 oz 5 dwt (1,500 gr)
London (Belgravia), 11 IX 1975, 223
£407 ($814)

1190 TAPLEY

1191 TAPLEY

1191 Salt cellars, pair
London, 1848
Stamped: Green & Co.
3¾ in (9.4 cm) diameter
14 oz 6 dwt (443 gr)
London (Belgravia), 23 II 1978, 622
£198 ($366)

1192 TAPLEY

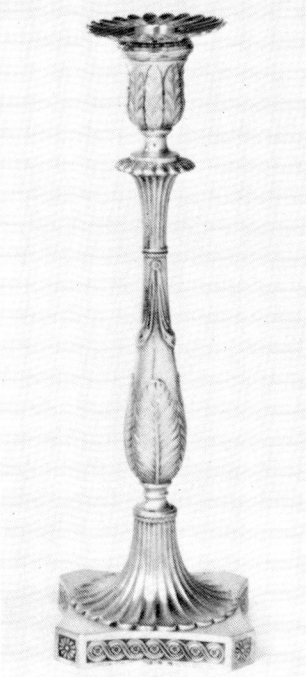

1193 TAPLEY

1194 BOULTON & FOTHERGILL

Matthew Boulton

Birmingham; born 1728, died 1809. In 1762 Boulton built a factory at Soho, north of Birmingham, and in 1773 was instrumental in the establishment of an assay office in the city. In partnership with John Fothergill 1762–81, and with James Watt 1775 to develop the steam engine. Also produced ormolu and Sheffield plate and worked with Josiah Wedgwood. After Boulton's death the firm continued as Matthew Boulton and Plate Company. See H.W. Dickinson, *Matthew Boulton*; Delieb and Roberts, *The Great Silver Manufactory*; catalogues of exhibitions, 'Matthew Boulton and the Toymakers', 'Birmingham Gold and Silver 1773–1973' (both with bibliographies).
Mark K.C. Jones, p.357

1195 BOULTON

1196 BOULTON

1192 Coffee pot
London, 1852
Stamped: Makepeace London
10½ in (27.4 cm) high
27 oz 6 dwt (848 gr)
London (Belgravia), 21 X 1976, 274
£407 ($692)

1193 Teapot
London, 1851
Stamped: Makepeace London
22 oz 6 dwt (696 gr)
London (Belgravia), 28 V 1981, 431
£198 ($409)

Boulton and Fothergill
See above

1194 Candlesticks, pair
silver (loaded)
Birmingham, 1773
11¾ in (29.9 cm) high
Compare with Rowe, *Adam Silver*, pls 50, 51A.
London, 28 III 1968, 155
£1,000 ($2,400)

Matthew Boulton
See above

1195 Candlesticks, four
silver (loaded)
Birmingham, 1805
13½ in (34.2 cm) high
London, 10 III 1977, 60
£1,760 ($2,992)

1196 Egg cruet, for six
Birmingham, 1808
10 in (25.4 cm) wide
53 oz 10 dwt (1,663 gr)
The spoons, Eley Fearn and Chawner (1811)
London, 21 VI 1973, 70
£900 ($2,250)

Matthew Boulton and Plate Company
See above

1197 Centrepiece
Birmingham, 1810
10¾ in (27.3 cm) high
95 oz 6 dwt (2,963 gr)
London, 17 X 1974, 57
£1,150 ($2,645)

1197 MATTHEW BOULTON & PLATE CO

1198 MATTHEW BOULTON & PLATE CO

1199 MATTHEW BOULTON & PLATE CO

1200 MATTHEW BOULTON & PLATE CO

1201 MATTHEW BOULTON & PLATE CO

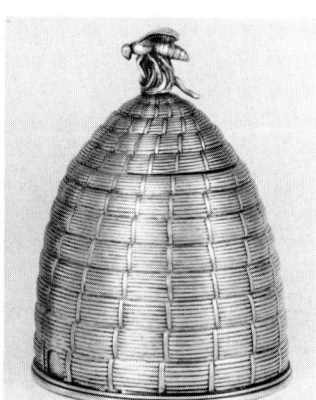

1202 J. EMES

1203 J. EMES

1204 J. EMES

1198 Epergne
Birmingham, 1823
12¾ in (32.5 cm) high
134 oz 2 dwt (4,108 gr)
London, 20 XI 1980, 69
£1,540 ($3,187)

1199 Wine coolers, pair
Birmingham, 1817
Stamped: Lewis Silversmith to HRH The Duke of York, St. James St London
11¼ in (28.5 cm) high
335 oz 5 dwt (10,426 gr)
London, 9 X 1969, 249
£1,800 ($4,320)

1200 Cup and cover
silver-gilt
Birmingham, 1810
15½ in (39.4 cm) high
150 oz 7 dwt (4,675 gr)
London, 3 IV 1969, 138
£520 ($1,248)

1201 Cup and cover
silver-gilt
Birmingham, 1826
Stamped: Hamlet Goldsmith to His Majesty HRH The Duke of Clarence & Royal Family
17 in (43.2 cm) high
124 oz (3,856 gr)
Inscribed: Burton Races 1827
London, 24 IV 1980, 327
£1,815 ($4,265)

John Emes

London; in partnership with Henry Chawner (see above, no. 1086ff.) 1796, first mark alone 1798, died by 1808. Continued business begun by Anthony Nelme in 1689 (see nos 544, 812, and below).
Mark Grimwade, 977, 1806–7

1202 Beehive honey pot
silver-gilt
London, 1800
5 in (12.7 cm) high
9 oz 13 dwt (300 gr)
London, 19 XI 1970, 139
£620 ($1,488)

1205 R. EMES & E. BARNARD

1206 CRADDOCK & REID

1203 Egg boiler and stand
London, 1802
13 in (33 cm) high
38 oz 14 dwt (1,203 gr)
London, 5 XII 1968, 134
£500 ($1,200)

1204 Brandy saucepan
London, 1804
3 in (7.6 cm) high
8 oz 4 dwt (255 gr)
London, 24 IV 1980, 139
£495 ($1,163)

Rebeccah Emes and Edward Barnard

London; Rebeccah, widow of John (see above), was in partnership with his former manager Edward Barnard 1808–29. The firm continued as Edward Barnard and Sons (see below, no.1373ff.).
Mark Grimwade, 2309–10

1205 Inkstand
London, 1823
18 in (45.7 cm) wide
130 oz (4,043 gr)
Arms: Joseph Kaye
London, 16 III 1978, 231
£1,925 ($3,561)

Joseph Craddock and William Ker Reid

London; in partnership 1812–25. Reid was married to a daughter of Edward Barnard, with whom he had business connections; died 1868
Mark Grimwade, 1236

1206 Entrée dishes and covers, four
with plated heater bases
London, 1819/20
12¼ in (31.2 cm) wide
293 oz 4 dwt (9,118 gr)
London, 21 VII 1977, 223
£2,860 ($4,862)

1207 CRADDOCK & REID

1208 WILLMORE

1209 WILLMORE

1210 WILLMORE

1207 Tray
London, 1823
27½ in (69.8 cm) overall
123 oz 11 dwt (3,842 gr)
Arms: George, 3rd Baron Walsingham (1774–1831), and his wife Matilda, daughter of Paul Cobb Methuen of Corsham, co. Wilts.
London, 4 V 1978, 86
£2,310 ($4,273)

Joseph Willmore

Birmingham; born 1790, first mark entered c. 1808, in partnership with Yapp and Woodward 1834 (their own mark entered 1845), died 1855. George Unite (who later took over Nathaniel Mills' premises) was apprenticed to him 1810. See Delieb, *Silver Boxes*
Mark K.C. Jones, p.354

1208 Apple corer
Birmingham, 1814
4 in (10.5 cm) overall
London, 19 XI 1981, 59
£260 ($465)

1209 Snuff box
gold
London, 1821
2½ in (6.5 cm) wide
Geneva, 16 XI 1983, 28
SFr.3,080 (£984 $1,367)

1210 Beaker
Birmingham, 1832
3 in (7.7 cm) high
7 oz 10 dwt (233 gr)
London (Belgravia), 30 V 1974, 219
£135 ($324)

1211 WILLMORE

1212 WILLMORE

1213 WILLMORE

1214 WALLIS & HAYNE 1215 UNMARKED

1216 UNMARKED

1217 LINNIT & ATKINSON

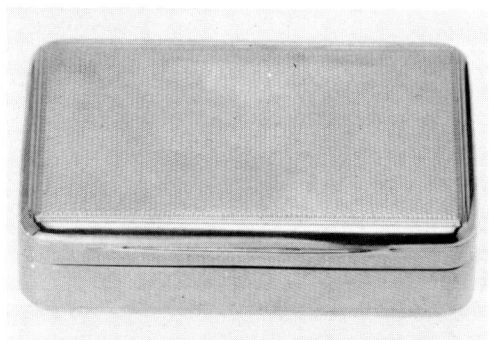
1218 LINNIT & ATKINSON

1211 Vinaigrette
parcel-gilt
Birmingham, 1813
1¾ in (4.5 cm) wide
London, 15 VII 1976, 128
£440 ($792)

1212 Inkstand
Birmingham, 1839
6¾ in (17.2 cm) overall
2 oz 14 dwt (84 gr)
London (Belgravia), 21 II 1974, 43
£130 ($312)

1213 Card case
Birmingham, 1835
3¾ in (9.5 cm) overall
London (Belgravia), 21 II 1974, 70
£155 ($372)

Thomas Wallis and Jonathan Hayne

London. In partnership 1810–21; then Wallis (who had founded the firm c. 1758) retired; he died 1836. Hayne died 1848. See no.1372
Mark Grimwade, 2978

1214 Snuff box
silver-gilt mounted tortoiseshell
London, 1820
3¼ in (8.5 cm) overall
London, 8 XII 1983, 40
£2,310 ($3,210)

Unmarked

1215 Group of tortoiseshell snuff boxes
Illustrated with no.1214.

1216 Wine label
English, first half of 19th century
4 in (10.4 cm) wide
London (Belgravia), 25 I 1973, 65
£400 ($1,000)

John Linnit and William Atkinson

London; in partnership 1809–15.
Mark Grimwade, p.367

1217 Snuff box
silver-gilt
London, 1811
3¼ in (8.2 cm) wide
London, 15 VI 1978, 122
£1,155 ($2,136)

1218 Snuff box
London, 1814
3 in (7.5 cm) wide
London, 6 VII 1981, 55
£1,430 ($2,960)

John Linnit

London; see above. Mark alone 1815
Mark Grimwade, 1833–4

1219 Snuff box
silver-gilt, inset with a Florentine pietra-dura panel
London, 1828
3 in (7.5 cm) diameter
London, 7 XII 1981, 40
£1,430 ($2,559)

1220 Beaker
silver-gilt
London, 1822
4 in (10.2 cm) high
8 oz 6 dwt (258 gr)
London (Belgravia), 31 VII 1975, 235
£260 ($598)

1221 Staff of office
London, 1831
40 in (101.7 cm) overall
Cypher: Royal, between crown and motto and with emblems of Scotland, England and Ireland
For a gold example bearing Linnit's mark see catalogue of exhibition, 'Touching Gold and Silver', no.148. See also no.1173
London, 19 VII 1979, 151
£1,265 ($2,593)

1222 Snuff box
London, 1837
4¼ in (10.7 cm) wide
9 oz 4 dwt (286 gr)
London (Belgravia), 19 II 1976, 293
£363 ($653)

1223 Snuff box
18 ct gold
London, 1849
3¾ in (8.3 cm) wide
5 oz 7 dwt (166 gr)
Arms: Chichester quartering Itchingham, Marquess of Donegal, probably for Earl of Belfast (1827–53), second son of 3rd Marquess of Donegal
London (Belgravia), 7 VI 1973, 152
£800 ($2,000)

1219 LINNIT

1220 LINNIT

1221 LINNIT

1222 LINNIT

1223 LINNIT

1224 LINNIT

1225 LINNIT

1226 LINNIT

1224 Standing cup
silver-gilt and oak
London, 1827
17 in (43.2 cm) high
Inscribed: This Cup was made from part of a Beam in Windsor Castle placed there when the castle was originally built by King Edward III.
New York, 20–23 IV 1983, 213
$14,300 (£8,937)

1225 'Pedlar' snuff box
silver-gilt
London, 1823
4 in (10.2 cm) overall
London, 18 VI 1981, 7
£2,145 ($4,440)

1226 'Pedlar' snuff box
London, 1825
4 in (10.2 cm) overall
London, 21 XII 1978, 193
£1,265 ($2,593)

1227 LINNIT

1228 MILLS

1229 MILLS

1230 MILLS

1231 MILLS

1232 MILLS

1233 MILLS

1227 Cup
18 ct gold
London, 1855
7½ in (19 cm) high
12 oz 18 dwt (401 gr)
London, 12 XI 1970, 275
£300 ($720)

Nathaniel Mills

Birmingham; born 1811, mark entered 1825, active until c. 1855, died 1873. Specialist 'toyman' or smallworker. See Delieb, *Silver Boxes*
Mark K.C. Jones, p.358

1228 Card case
silver-gilt
Birmingham, 1837
4 in (10 cm) overall
London (Belgravia), 13 IX 1973, 187
£200 ($480)

1229 Card case
Birmingham, 1837
3¾ in (9.5 cm) overall
London (Belgravia), 2 V 1974, 161
£115 ($276)

1230 Card case
Birmingham, 1844
4 in (10.1 cm) overall
Stamped and chased with a view of St Paul's Cathedral, London
London (Belgravia), 8 VI 1978, 209
£220 ($407)

1231 Cheroot case
Birmingham, 1839
4¾ in (12 cm) overall
Stamped with a view of Windsor Castle
London (Belgravia), 25 VI 1981, 214
£143 ($296)

1234 RAWLINGS

1235 RAWLINGS

1236 WYON

1237 FARRELL

1232 Vinaigrette
Birmingham, 1839
1¾ in (4.5 cm) overall
Cast with a view of Abbotsford
London (Belgravia), 1 V 1980, 361
£506 ($1,189)

1233 Vinaigrette
Birmingham, 1850
2 in (5.3 cm) overall
Engraved with a view of the Scott Memorial, Edinburgh
London (Belgravia), 5 VII 1979, 166
£82 ($169)

1238 FARRELL

Charles Rawlings

London; smallworker, first mark 1817, in partnership with William Summers from 1829, died 1863; the firm continued until 1896/7.
Mark Grimwade, 409–10, 414

1234 Snuff box
silver, inset with a Roman micro-mosaic panel
London, 1823
2¾ in (7 cm) wide
London, 15 VI 1978, 117
£715 ($1,322)

1235 Snuff box
London, 1825
3¼ in (8.2 cm) wide
London, 12 VI 1975, 179
£150 ($345)

Benjamin Wyon

London; born 1802, son of Thomas Wyon I and younger brother of Thomas Wyon II, each of whom held the post of chief engraver of seals at the Royal Mint, the position to which Benjamin was appointed in 1831; died 1858. See *Dictionary of National Biography*.

1236 Seal of William IV
London, 1831
4¾ in (12 cm) diameter
56 oz (1,741 gr)
New York, 4–5 XII 1974, 442
$3,500 (£1,521)

Edward Cornelius Farrell

London; born c. 1780, first mark 1813, died 1850. Closely connected with Kensington Lewis c. 1816–34, an important patron being the Duke of York. See Culme, *Nineteenth Century Silver*
Mark Grimwade, 584–5

1237 Sideboard dishes, pair
silver-gilt
London, 1816
Stamped: Lewis silversmith to HRH the Duke of York St. James's St. London
16½ in (42 cm) diameter
88 oz 13 dwt (2,757 gr)
The borders are after wood engravings by Thomas Bewick
London, 24 XI 1983, 203
£2,860 ($3,975)

1238 Mustard pot
London, 1821
3¼ in (8.5 cm) high
11 oz 12 dwt (360 gr)
New York, 16–17 XII 1980, 207
$2,200 (£1,062)

1239 FARRELL

1240 FARRELL

1241 FARRELL

1239 Tea and coffee set
silver-gilt, Britannia Standard
London, 1816/18
300 oz 12 dwt (9,348 gr)
New York, 16–17 XII 1980, 208
$17,600 (£8,502)

1240 Sideboard dish
silver-gilt
London, 1822
18 in (45.7 cm) diameter
55 oz 7 dwt (1,721 gr)
The central panel, depicting the Miracle of St Paul in Malta, is 17th-century; it is signed PG in monogram
London, 20 VI 1974, 59
£800 ($1,920)

1241 Sideboard dish
silver-gilt
London, 1823
27 in (68.6 cm) diameter
118 oz (3,670 gr)
London, 20 VI 1974, 57
£1,400 ($3,360)

1242 Snuff box
silver-gilt
London, 1824
3½ in (8.9 cm) wide
London, 4 V 1978, 78
£990 ($1,831)

1242 FARRELL

1243 FARRELL

1244 FARRELL

1243 Bowl
silver-gilt
London, 1820
Stamped: Lewis, silversmith to
HRH the Duke of York
St. James's St.
17 in (43.2 cm) wide
230 oz 4 dwt (7,159 gr)
Provenance: HRH Duke of
York sale, 19 March 1827, lot 71,
sold to Kensington Lewis for
£146 18s 10d
London, 15 VI 1978, 169
£3,520 ($6,512)

1244 Casket
silver-gilt, Britannia Standard,
inset with pietra-dura panels
London, 1835
6 in (15.2 cm) wide
London, 19 X 1978, 32
£2,420 ($4,961)

1245 Sauceboat
silver-gilt
London, 1824
9 in (22.8 cm) high
38 oz 8 dwt (1,194 gr)
New York, 16–17 XII 1980, 206
$8,800 (£4,251)

1245 FARRELL

1246 STORY & ELLIOTT

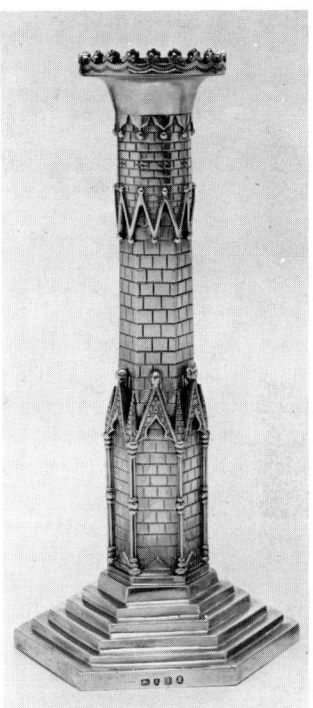

1248 ELLIOTT

Joseph William Story and William Elliott

London; in partnership 1809–13
Mark Grimwade, 1762

1246 Tapersticks, pair
London, 1811
4 in (10.2 cm) high
19 oz 14 dwt (612 gr)
London, 31 X 1974, 23
£480 ($1,104)

1247 Centrepiece
silver-gilt
London, 1811
13¼ in (33.6 cm) high
76 oz 4 dwt (2,369 gr)
London, 20 VI 1974, 113
£700 ($1,680)

1247 STORY & ELLIOTT

William Elliott

London; mark entered 1813
(previously in partnership with
J.W. Story, see above), died
1853–5. Elliott's mark is
frequently confused with that of
William Eaton, a spoon-maker.
For the latter's association with
Eley and Company, see Culme,
Nineteenth Century Silver,
pp.16, 17. Elliott occasionally
worked for Thomas Hamlet.
Mark Grimwade, 3107

1248 Candlesticks, four
London, 1814
11¼ in (28.5 cm) high
102 oz 16 dwt (3,197 gr)
London, 28 I 1965, 37
£600 ($1,680)

1249 ELLIOTT

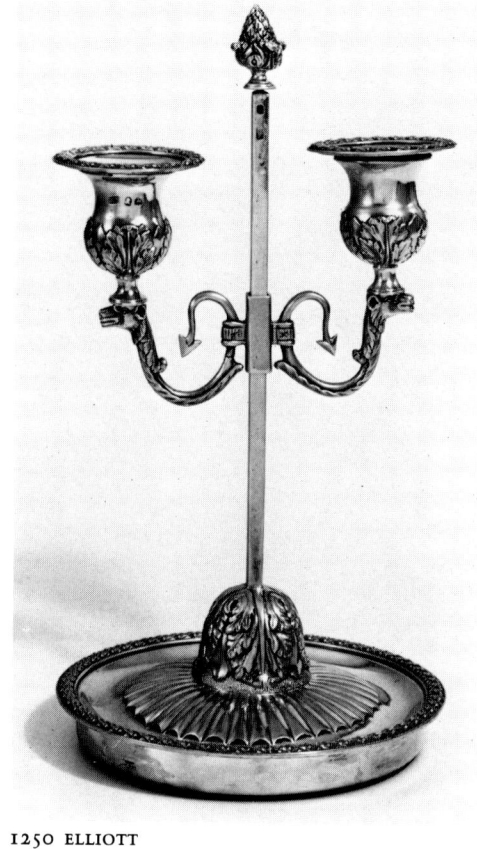

1250 ELLIOTT

1251 ELLIOTT

1252 ELLIOTT

1253 ELLIOTT

1254 ELLIOTT

1255 ELLIOTT

1256 ELLIOTT

1249 Candlesticks, pair
silver-gilt
London, 1818
7 in (17.7 cm) high
20 oz 7 dwt (632 gr)
London, 30 XI 1967, 121
£1,900 ($4,560)

1250 Library candlestick
silver (loaded)
London, 1820
10¼ in (26 cm) high
London, 15 VI 1978, 151
£2,090 ($1,129)

1251 Wine cups, pair
London, 1819
6 in (15.2 cm) high
26 oz 15 dwt (832 gr)
London, 1 II 1973, 127
£460 ($1,150)

1252 Casket
silver-gilt
London, 1820
11 in (28.2 cm) wide
96 oz 18 dwt (3,015 gr)
Inscribed: April 3rd 1821. This Box weighing 76 oz. 10 dwt. has been made to receive a chas'd medallion of Scripture History of unknown Assay weighing 18 oz. 5 dwt. which is to be added without solder.
Compare with a toilet set sold Christie's, 6 May 1959, as lot 48 (see no.1254).
Geneva, 10 XI 1981, 11
SFr.16,500 (£4,609 $8,250)

1253 Casket
silver-gilt
London, 1821
9¾ in (24.8 cm) square
68 oz 10 dwt (2,130 gr)
Arms: Ainsworth impaling Stirling
Inscribed: Nov 2d 1821. This Box weighing 72 oz. 2 dwt. has been Made to receive a Chas'd Medallion of unknown Assay weighing 5 oz. 18 dwt. which is to be added hereto without solder.
London, 20 VI 1974, 125
£1,350 ($3,240)

1254 Mirror
silver-gilt, wood-backed
London, 1825
24½ in (62.2 cm) high
See toilet set, Christie's, 6 May 1959, lot 48, and no.1252.
London, 14 XII 1972, 63
£1,300 ($2,990)

1255 Sugar vases, pair
silver-gilt
London, 1820
6 in (15.2 cm) high
19 oz 19 dwt (620 gr)
Arms: Royal
London, 20 VI 1974, 61
£780 ($1,872)

1257 ELLIOTT

1258 ELLIOTT

1259 ELLIOTT

1256 Tea caddy
silver-gilt
London, 1827
4¾ in (12 cm) high
8 oz 14 dwt (270 gr)
London, 24 IV 1969, 171
£420 ($1,008)

1257 Ewers, pair
silver-gilt
London, 1829
10¾ in (27.3 cm) high
72 oz 4 dwt (2,245 gr)
Compare with nos 1165, 1166
London, 20 IV 1972, 173
£1,600 ($4,000)

1260 ELLIOTT

1262 PRESTON

1258 Brandy saucepan
London, 1830
4 in (10.2 cm) high
9 oz 11 dwt (297 gr)
Motto and initials: Royal, of William IV
London (Belgravia), 25 V 1972, 173
£270 ($675)

1259 Claret jug
silver-mounted frosted glass
London, 1837
8¼ in (20.9 cm) high
For a similar jug by J.W. Figg see Sotheby's, Belgravia, 29 June 1972, lot 151.
London (Belgravia), 26 X 1972, 74
£180 ($450)

1260 Wine jug
silver (loaded)
London, 1847
11¾ in (29.8 cm) high
London (Belgravia), 24 I 1974, 201
£360 ($864)

1261 PRESTON

Benjamin Preston

London; apprenticed to Edward Barnard, mark entered 1825, retired c. 1865, died 1887. Associated with Kensington Lewis 1834–6.
Mark Grimwade, 206

1261 Salt cellars
London, 1831
4¼ in (10.8 cm) wide
55 oz (1,710 gr)
London, 16 II 1978, 71
£1,925 ($3,561)

1262 Dessert stand
silver-gilt
London, 1834
Stamped: K. Lewis St. James St.
6¼ in (15.7 cm) high
30 oz 9 dwt (946 gr)
London (Belgravia), 21 II 1974, 135
£360 ($864)

1263 B. SMITH III

1264 B. SMITH III

Benjamin Smith III

London; born 1793, apprenticed to his father Benjamin Smith II (see above, no.1113ff.), first mark alone 1818, died 1850, when the firm was continued by his son (see no.1439ff.).
Mark Grimwade, 231, 236

1263 Wine coolers, pair
London, 1824/5
10¾ in (27.3 cm) high
333 oz (10,356 gr)
London, 23 IV 1970, 193
£2,100 ($5,040)

1264 Mirror plateau
silver-gilt
London, 1828
23¾ in (60.4 cm) wide
London, 13 II 1969, 164
£3,600 ($8,640)

1265 Mug
London, 1847
3¾ in (9.5 cm) high
4 oz 6 dwt (136 gr)
London (Belgravia), 29 III 1979, 482
£143 ($293)

1265 B. SMITH III

1266 Centrepiece; the Macready Testimonial
silver, frosted and burnished
London, 1841
Designer: Charles Grant
30¾ in (77.5 cm) high
641 oz 13 dwt (19,913 gr)
William Charles Macready (born 1793), one of England's most celebrated actors, was presented with this testimonial in 1843 and made his farewell performance in 1851. Subscribers to the testimonial included Charles Dickens, Angela Burdett-Coutts and the Marquess of Lansdowne. It was shown at the Great Exhibition (1851) by Smith, Nicholson and Company, Benjamin Smith's successors. On loan to the Victoria and Albert Museum, London.
London (Belgravia), 22 IV 1976, 235
£9,900 ($17,820)

1266 B. SMITH III

1267 B. SMITH III

1268 B. SMITH III

1269 TERREY

1267 Goblet
silver-gilt
London, 1827
8 in (20.1 cm) high
18 oz 6 dwt (569 gr)
London, 9 II 1984, 99
£715

1268 Wine cooler
London, 1841
Stamped: B. Smith Duke St Linn Inn Fields
11½ in (29.3 cm) high
83 oz 8 dwt (2,593 gr)
London (Belgravia), 21 III 1974, 197
£800 ($1,920)

John Edward Terrey

London; initially in partnership with Samuel Hennell (see above, no.1102), worked alone from 1816, died or retired 1848.
Mark Grimwade, 1281

1269 Cup and cover
silver-gilt
London, 1817
16 in (40.6 cm) high
109 oz 19 dwt (3,419 gr)
London, 4 V 1972, 58
£460 ($1,150)

1270 Milk jug
silver-gilt
London, 1821
3¼ in (8.2 cm) high
10 oz 11 dwt (328 gr)
London, 22 X 1970, 94
£100 ($240)

1271 Bowl and stand
London, 1818
6½ in (16.5 cm) wide
45 oz 19 dwt (1,429 gr)
London, 6 III 1969, 146
£460 ($1,080)

1270 TERREY   1272 UNMARKED

1271 TERREY   1273 STORR & MORTIMER

Unmarked

1272 Teapot
silver-gilt
English, c. 1820
5½ in (14 cm) high
28 oz 8 dwt (883 gr)
See no.1273
London, 22 X 1970, 95
£260 ($624)

Paul Storr and John Mortimer

London; in partnership from 1822 until Storr's retirement in 1838 (using Storr's mark). See Paul Storr (no.1111ff.) and Mortimer and Hunt (below).
Mark Grimwade, 2233–5

1273 Teapot
silver-gilt
London, 1825
5¼ in (13.4 cm) high
25 oz 3 dwt (782 gr)
See no.1272 and p.48
London, 10 X 1983, 523
£7,150 ($9,938)

1274 STORR & MORTIMER

1275 STORR & MORTIMER

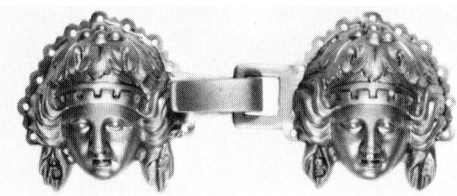

1276 STORR & MORTIMER

1274 Breakfast service
silver-gilt
London, 1829/32/36
Some stamped: Storr &
Mortimer
A few pieces by others
Tray: 31 in (78.8 cm) wide
513 oz (15,954 gr)
Arms: Robert Henry, 12th Earl
of Pembroke and 9th Earl of
Montgomery (1791–1862)
London, 10 III 1977, 201
£19,250 ($32,725)

1275 Wine cooler
silver-gilt
London, 1834
Stamped: Storr & Mortimer, 4
10¼ in (26 cm) high
194 oz 15 dwt (6,056 gr)
London, 16 II 1978, 248
£6,050 ($11,192)

1276 Cloak buckle
silver-gilt
London, 1830
3¼ in (8.3 cm) wide
1 oz 10 dwt (46 gr)
London (Belgravia), 11 IX 1975, 149a
£352 ($704)

1277 Stirrup cups, pair
silver-gilt
London, 1834
5½ in (14 cm) high
33 oz 2 dwt (1,029 gr)
London, 16 III 1978, 174
£8,250 ($15,262)

1277 STORR & MORTIMER

1278 Stirrup cup
London, 1834
5¾ in (14.6 cm) overall
19 oz 17 dwt (617 gr)
Inscribed: HRH Prince George of
Cambridge to Charles Davis
1835
London (Belgravia), 12 IX 1974, 241
£1,950 ($4,485)

1279 Candlesticks, pair
silver-gilt
London, 1823
9¼ in (23.5 cm) high
32 oz 9 dwt (1,009 gr)
London, 31 III 1966, 111
£900 ($2,520)

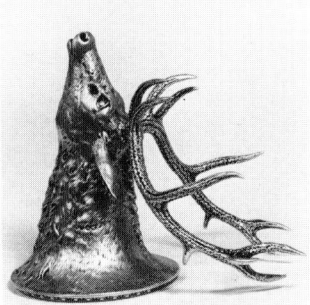

1278 STORR & MORTIMER

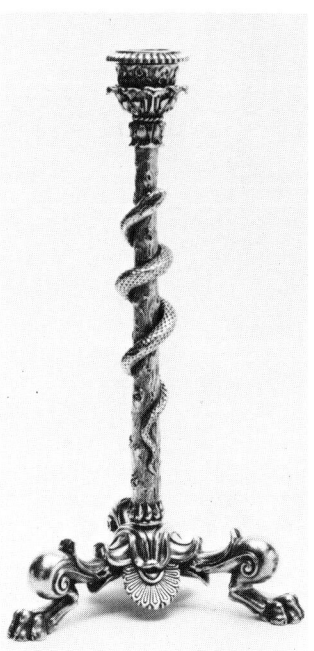

1279 STORR & MORTIMER

1280 STORR & MORTIMER

1281 STORR & MORTIMER

1282 STORR & MORTIMER

1283 MORTIMER & HUNT

1284 MORTIMER & HUNT

1285 HUNT & ROSKELL

1280 Figure of Hebe
After the original by Canova
London, 1829
Stamped: Storr and Mortimer
No. 8 . . .
35 in (89 cm) high
303 oz 18 dwt (9,451 gr)
Provenance: Duchess of St Albans
Four examples of this statue were made by Canova between 1796 and 1816. Storr's version is close to the original gesso maquette now in the Canova Museum, Possagno.
London, 5 II 1970, 92
£2,200 ($5,280)

1281 Cup and cover
silver-gilt
London, 1837
13½ in (34.2 cm) high
53 oz 15 dwt (1,671 gr)
Initials: probably Lady Victoria Ashley, daughter of 7th Earl of Shaftesbury, born 1837
London, 18 VII 1968, 115
£1,350 ($3,240)

1282 Salver
London, 1837
Engraved: no. 2
Scratch weight 121 oz 15 dwt
21 in (53.4 cm) diameter
120 oz 1 dwt (3,733 gr)
Arms: 4th Earl of Ashburnham
From the Ashburnham dinner service (Christie's, March 1914); see no. 1297.
London (Belgravia), 6 XII 1973, 166
£800 ($1,920)

Mortimer and Hunt
See Hunt and Roskell, below

Hunt and Roskell
London; after the retirement in 1838 of Paul Storr (see above, no. 1111ff and no. 1273ff.), John Mortimer and John S. Hunt went into partnership until the former's retirement in 1842. Robert Roskell then joined the firm and it was known as Hunt and Roskell 1842–97. John S. Hunt died in 1865; the firm was bought by J.W. Benson in 1889. The following marks were used:
1839   ISH crowned
1839–42   IM   ISH
1842–65   ISH crowned
1865–82   IH   RR
1882–89   RR   AR   IMH

1283 Caviar pail
silver-gilt
London, 1841
14¼ in (36.2 cm) high
187 oz 8 dwt (5,828 gr)
Arms: Prince Worontsov-Dashkov
London, 3 VII 1969, 249
£2,200 ($5,280)

1284 Vase
London, 1840
Stamped: Mortimer & Hunt 551
23¼ in (59 cm) high
178 oz 16 dwt (5,563 gr)
London (Belgravia), 13 XII 1979, 503
£2,860 ($6,721)

1285 Entrée dishes and covers, four
London, 1844
Stamped: Hunt & Roskell late Storr Mortimer & Hunt
12¾ in (32.4 cm) overall
244 oz 8 dwt (7,600 gr)
London (Belgravia), 9 I 1975, 279
£1,850 ($4,255)

278 GREAT BRITAIN IRELAND

1286 HUNT & ROSKELL

1287 HUNT & ROSKELL

1286 Dessert service, forty-seven pieces
silver-gilt
Twelve forks and twelve knives (agate handles), Francis Higgins
The remainder, G. Adams for Chawner and Company in a box of Hunt and Roskell
London, 1844–8
New York, 14–15 XII 1977, 387
$3,100 (£1,675)

1287 Centrepiece
London, 1847
30¼ in (77 cm) high
350 oz 10 dwt (10,900 gr)
Arms: Wilbraham Egerton of Tatton and his wife Elizabeth, daughter of Sir Christopher Sykes of Sledmere, whom he married 1806
London, 25 II 1971, 145
£880 ($2,112)

1288 Claret jugs on stands, pair
London, 1845
14 in (35.6 cm) high
Cypher: 2nd Earl of Zetland
London, 27 III 1969, 165
£920 ($2,208)

1289 Christening cup and cover
silver-gilt
London, 1841
Stamped: Mortimer & Hunt 759
16¼ in (41.3 cm) high
51 oz 10 dwt (1,601 gr)
Inscribed: To Victoria Alexandrina Leopoldine van de Weyer from her Godmother Victoria R 16 August 1842
London (Belgravia), 13 X 1973, 170
£680 ($1,632)

1288 HUNT & ROSKELL

1290 Cup
London, 1861
Stamped: Hunt & Roskell late Storr & Mortimer 1352
4¾ in (12 cm) high
5 oz (155 gr)
London (Belgravia), 12 X 1978, 244
£209 ($428)

1291 Dressing table mirror
silver-gilt
London, 1849
Stamped: Hunt & Roskell late Storr Mortimer & Hunt 3939
16½ in (42 cm) high
London (Belgravia), 22 I 1976, 261
£770 ($1,386)

1292 Salt cellar
London, 1844
6 in (15 cm) overall
23 oz 4 dwt (720 gr)
Bearing a contemporary Russian import mark
London (Belgravia), 7 IX 1978, 234
£396 ($811)

1293 Salt cellars, pair
silver-gilt
London, 1855
Stamped: Hunt & Roskell late Storr & Mortimer 7955
Possibly designed by William Theed
4½ in (11.4 cm) overall
36 oz 10 dwt (1,135 gr)
London, 11 XI 1982, 90
£2,200 ($3,520)

1289 MORTIMER & HUNT

1290 HUNT & ROSKELL

HUNT & ROSKELL 279

1291 HUNT & ROSKELL

1292 HUNT & ROSKELL

1293 HUNT & ROSKELL

1294 HUNT & ROSKELL

1295 HUNT & ROSKELL

1296 HUNT & ROSKELL

1294 Candelabrum
London, 1854
24½ in (62.5 cm) high
203 oz 10 dwt (6,332 gr)
London (Belgravia), 31 VII 1980, 527
£2,200 ($5,170)

1295 Christening bowl, cover and stand
silver-gilt
London, 1861
Stamped: Hunt & Roskell 1147/1042
Stand: 9¼ in (23.5 cm) diameter
43 oz (1,334 gr)
London (Belgravia), 22 IV 1976, 263
£715 ($1,287)

1296 Vase, Royal Hunt Cup, Ascot Races, 1860
London, 1859
Designer: A.J. Barrett
Stamped: Hunt & Roskell late Storr & Mortimer 295
24½ in (62 cm) high
131 oz 8 dwt (4,088 gr)
London (Belgravia), 6 III 1980, 320
£2,970 ($6,979)

280 GREAT BRITAIN IRELAND

1297 HUNT & ROSKELL

1298 HUNT & ROSKELL

1299 HUNT & ROSKELL

1300 HUNT & ROSKELL   1301 HUNT & ROSKELL

1297 Tea set, 'Ashburnham' pattern
London, 1871
Stamped: Hunt & Roskell late Storr & Mortimer 5667/5888/5798/6113
97 oz 2 dwt (3,022 gr)
See no.1282
London (Belgravia), 6 III 1980, 210
£1,650 ($3,877)

1298 Tea set, five pieces
London, 1874
Signed: Aristide Barré
111 oz 8 dwt (3,464 gr)
Aristide Barré (1840–1922) designed decorative silver and exhibited at the Paris Salon (1901)
London (Belgravia), 26 X 1971, 95
£500 ($1,250)

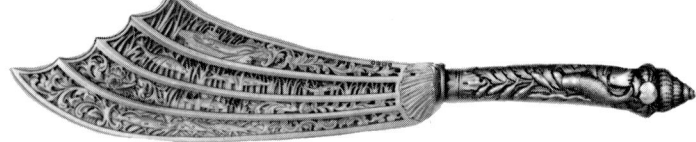
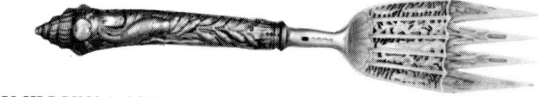

1302 FRANCIS HIGGINS & SON

1303 FRANCIS HIGGINS & SON

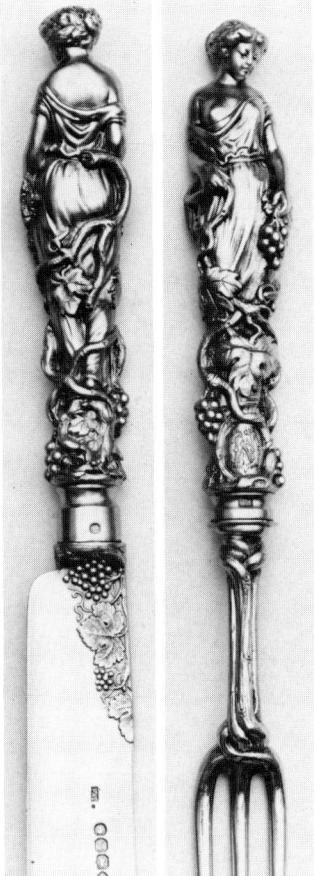

1305 FRANCIS HIGGINS & SON

1306 FRANCIS HIGGINS & SON

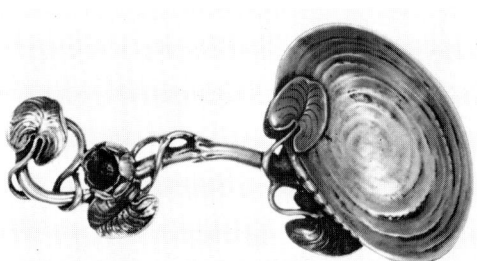

1304 FRANCIS HIGGINS & SON

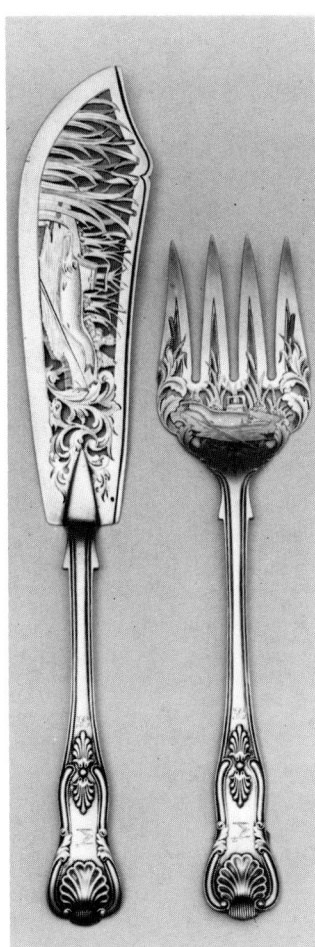

1307 CHAWNER & CO

1299 Dessert stands, pair
London, 1880
Stamped: Hunt & Roskell late Storr & Mortimer 8059
10½ in (26.8 cm) wide
52 oz 16 dwt (1,642 gr)
London (Belgravia), 2 V 1974, 180
£170 ($408)

1300 Christening set
silver-gilt
London, 1888
Knife, fork and spoon, Francis Higgins, 1854
Stamped: Hunt & Roskell late Storr & Mortimer 9492
See Sotheby's, Belgravia, 26 October 1971, lot 16, for an identical mug, Paul Storr, 1834.
London (Belgravia), 25 VII 1974, 320A
£220 ($528)

1301 Christening set
London, 1867
Knife, fork and spoon, Francis Higgins, 1866/7
Plate: 6¼ in (16.5 cm) diameter
15 oz 14 dwt (488 gr)
Inscribed: From Angela G. Burdett Coutts April 24th 1869
London (Belgravia), 11 IX 1975, 243
£198 ($396)

Francis Higgins and Son

London; first mark 1817; specialist spoon-maker, supplied cutlery to, among others, Hunt and Roskell (see above) and to R. and S. Garrard and Company (see below, no.1315ff.)
Mark Grimwade, 683–4

1302 Fish servers, pair
London, 1851
Slice: 14½ in (36.9 cm) overall
London, 12 XI 1970, 74
£45 ($108)

1303 Christening mug
silver-gilt
London, 1865
4½ in (11.4 cm) high
8 oz 5 dwt (256 gr)
London (Belgravia), 24 II 1972, 110
£130 ($325)

1304 Caddy spoon
parcel-gilt
London, 1854
3¼ in (8.5 cm) overall
This pattern was shown by Higgins at the Great Exhibition (1851)
London, 16 XII 1982, 284
£605 ($968)

1305 Dessert knife and fork
silver-gilt
London, 1861/2
10 in (25.4 cm) overall
London (Belgravia), 21 II 1974, 141
£90 ($216)

1306 Serving spoons, pair
silver-gilt
London, 1889
8¾ in (22.2 cm) overall
9 oz 17 dwt (275 gr)
London (Belgravia), 21 II 1974, 36
£90 ($216)

Chawner and Company

London; the firm's proprietor was George William Adams, whose mark is struck on the silver. Active from 1830s to 1880s, specialist spoon-maker, supplied cutlery to Hunt and Roskell (see above), R. and S. Garrard and Company (see below) and other firms
Mark Jackson, p.231

1307 Fish servers
London, 1853
10 oz 2 dwt (314 gr)
London (Belgravia), 30 V 1974, 305
£90 ($216)

1308 CHAWNER & CO

1309 CHAWNER & CO

1308 Dessert canteen, 108 pieces
silver-gilt
London, 1865/72
Maker's mark overstruck by
Robert Garrard
133 oz 19 dwt (4,165 gr)
*London (Belgravia), 6 XI 1975,
191*
£2,035 ($4,070)

1309 Ice cream spoons (six) and a pair of serving spoons
London, 1866/77
Maker's mark overstruck by
Robert Garrard
16 oz 10 dwt (513 gr)
*London (Belgravia), 9 X 1975,
247*
£121 ($242)

1310 Fish servers, pair
London, 1853/5
Slice: 14¾ in (37.5 cm) overall
London, 12 XI 1970, 76
£155 ($372)

1311 Fish servers
London, 1878
*London (Belgravia), 29 III 1979,
439*
£286 ($586)

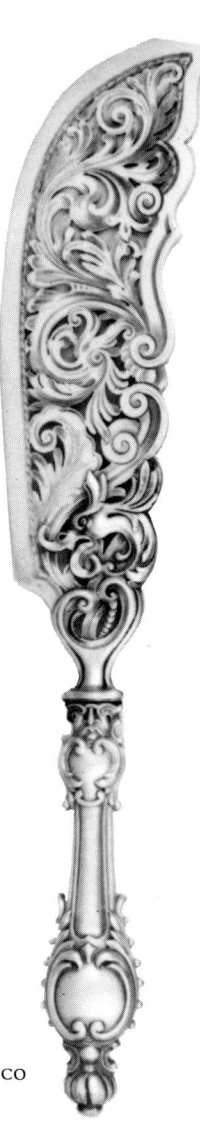

1310 CHAWNER & CO

1311 CHAWNER & CO

1312 Christening set
silver-gilt
London, 1868
4¾ in (12.1 cm) high
11 oz 19 dwt (371 gr)
London (Belgravia), 26 X 1971, 165
£150 ($375)

1313 Christening set
parcel-gilt
London, 1874
The knife, fork and spoon, Francis Higgins, 1868
4½ in (11.4 cm) high
8 oz 2 dwt (251 gr)
London, 18 VI 1970, 217
£70 ($168)

1314 Dessert canteen, forty-four pieces 'Canova' pattern
silver-gilt
London, 1871/2
74 oz 19 dwt (2,330 gr) excluding knives
London (Belgravia), 22 I 1976, 271
£1,540 ($2,772)

R. and S. Garrard and Company

London; Robert, James (retired c. 1835) and Sebastian Garrard (1798–1870) inherited the business of their father (see no. 1005) in continuation of the firm founded by George Wickes; first mark entered by Robert Garrard II (1793–1881) in 1818; appointed Goldsmiths and Jewellers to the King 1830. On Robert Garrard II's death his nephew James entered a mark on behalf of the firm (no. 1324). See nos 1529ff. for further entries. See also Honour, *Goldsmiths and Silversmiths*; Lever, *Goldsmiths and Silversmiths of England*
Mark Grimwade, 2322–3, 3769a

1315 Ewer
London, 1835
Stamped: Garrards Panton Street London
30 in (76.4 cm) high
446 oz 7 dwt (13,852 gr)
Probably the ewer shown by R. and S. Garrard and Company at the Great Exhibition (1851); see *Official Catalogue*, vol. II, class 23, no.98, item 30.
London (Belgravia), 13 I 1977, 166
£13,200 ($22,440)

1316 Entrée dish and heater base
London, 1836/42
12½ in (31.8 cm) wide
124 oz 15 dwt (3,879 gr)
Arms: Rothschild
London, 27 III 1969, 172
£680 ($1,632)

1312 CHAWNER & CO

1313 CHAWNER & CO

1314 CHAWNER & CO

1315 R. & S. GARRARD & CO

1316 R. & S. GARRARD & CO

284 GREAT BRITAIN IRELAND

1317 R. & S. GARRARD & CO

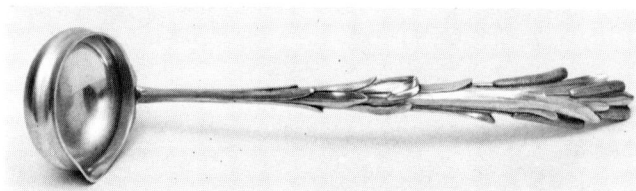

1319 R. & S. GARRARD & CO

1318 R. & S. GARRARD & CO

1320 R. & S. GARRARD & CO

1321 R. & S. GARRARD & CO

1317 Candelabra, pair
London, 1836
35 in (89 cm) high
844 oz (26,248 gr)
London, 20 XI 1980, 340
£14,795 ($30,625)

1318 Soup tureen and stand
London, 1839
14 in (35.6 cm) high
268 oz 10 dwt (8,350 gr)
Arms: James Brudenell, 7th Earl of Cardigan, commander of the cavalry in the charge of the Light Brigade at the Battle of Balaclava. He married Elizabeth Jane, sister of 1st Baron Tollemache, 1826
London, 18 VII 1968, 207
£2,400 ($5,760)

1319 Ladle
London, 1853
11¾ in (29.7 cm) overall
10 oz 15 dwt (334 gr)
London (Belgravia), 24 II 1972, 82
£200 ($500)

1320 Sweetmeat bowl
silver-gilt
London, 1839
9½ in (24.2 cm) high
64 oz 19 dwt (2,019 gr)
London, 27 III 1969, 159
£580 ($1,392)

1321 Figure salts, pair
London, 1856
7 in (17.8 cm) high
30 oz 16 dwt (957 gr)
London (Belgravia), 21 II 1974, 132
£1,000 ($2,400)

1322 R. & S. GARRARD & CO

1327 R. & S. GARRARD & CO

1322 Teapot and milk jug
London, 1851
Stamped: Garrards Panton Street London B/32
39 oz 12 dwt (1,229 gr) including five teaspoons
London (Belgravia), 20 V 1976, 186
£209 ($376)

1323 Centrepiece
The Queen's Cup, Ascot Races, 1852
London, 1852
Designer: Edmund Cotterill
Provenance: The Earl of Rosebery, Mentmore, 18–23 May 1977 (lot 1662)
The group is from Spenser's *The Faerie Queene*
London (Belgravia), 6 III 1980, 266
£7,150 ($16,802)

1325 R. & S. GARRARD & CO

1323 R. & S. GARRARD & CO

1324 Vase
London, 1885
28¼ in (71.7 cm) high
342 oz 8 dwt (10,648 gr)
London (Belgravia), 9 I 1975, 241
£1,400 ($3,220)

1325 Mustard pots, pair
London, 1854
4¼ in (10.8 cm) high
22 oz 13 dwt (707 gr)
London (Belgravia), 18 XI 1971, 148
£200 ($500)

1326 Candelabra, pair
London, 1856
22 in (81.3 cm) high
501 oz (15,581 gr)
New York, 4–5 XII 1974, 436
$14,000 (£6,086)

1327 Inkwell
silver-gilt
London, 1840
4¼ in (10.8 cm) high
London (Belgravia), 20 V 1976, 260
£264 ($475)

1324 R. & S. GARRARD & CO

1326 R. & S. GARRARD & CO

1328 R. & S. GARRARD & CO

1330 C. FOX II

1331 C. FOX II

1329 R. & S. GARRARD & CO

1332 C. FOX II

1333 C. FOX II

1328 Teapot and hot water jug
London, 1874
Teapot: 5½ in (14 cm) high
38 oz 10 dwt (1,197 gr)
London (Belgravia), 9 I 1975, 179
£200 ($460)

1329 Vase and cover
London, 1858
Stamped: R & S Garrard Panton St. London
21¾ in (55.3 cm) high
110 oz 10 dwt (3,436 gr)
Inscribed: The Gift of Her Majesty Queen Victoria to the Royal Yacht Squadron Cowes 1858
London, 11 XI 1982, 91
£2,310 ($3,696)

Charles Fox II

London; first mark 1822, active until 1840s
Mark Grimwade, 302–4

1330 Wine coolers, pair
London, 1834
10½ in (26.4 cm) high
304 oz 10 dwt (9,469 gr)
New York, 16–17 XII 1976, 16
$8,500 (£5,000)

1331 Christening mug
silver-gilt
London, 1837
5 in (12.7 cm) high
17 oz 19 dwt (558 gr)
London (Belgravia), 7 VI 1973, 147
£110 ($275)

1332 Vase and cover
London, 1841
7 in (18 cm) high
16 oz 12 dwt (517 gr)
London (Belgravia), 25 VI 1981,
396
£385 ($796)

1333 Tazza
parcel-gilt
London, 1829
16¼ in (41.3 cm) high
62 oz 2 dwt (1,931 gr)
Made to match a Flemish tazza
(c. 1660) sold as lot 41 for £1,050
($2,625)
London, 20 IV 1972, 40
£680 ($1,700)

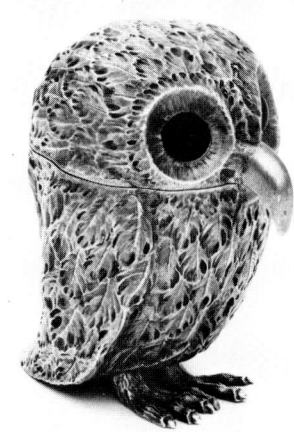

1334 C. T. & G. FOX

1335 C. T. & G. FOX

C.T. and G. Fox

London; Charles Thomas (born 1801) and George (born 1816), sons of Charles Fox II (see above), continued their father's business; closely associated with the retail firm of Lambert and Company. See Culme, *Nineteenth Century Silver*

1334 Owl inkstand
London, 1848
3¾ in (9.3 cm) high
6 oz 4 dwt (192 gr)
London (Belgravia), 12 X 1978,
277
£418 ($856)

1335 Inkwell
silver-gilt
London, 1863
8¼ in (21 cm) diameter
24 oz 13 dwt (766 gr)
London, 17 X 1968, 164
£480 ($1,152)

1336 Tankard
London, 1865
14½ in (37 cm) high
91 oz 10 dwt (2,846 gr)
London (Belgravia), 8 V 1980,
317
£1,540 ($3,619)

1337 Wine ewer
London, 1867
Stamped: Lambert, Coventry St.
London
9¼ in (23.5 cm) high
29 oz 9 dwt (915 gr)
This design was originally produced by Rundells.
London (Belgravia), 24 II 1972,
137
£240 ($600)

1336 C. T. & G. FOX

1337 C. T. & G. FOX

1338 Bell
London, 1871
Designer: Henry Fitz-Cook
4¼ in (11 cm) high
6 oz 19 dwt (216 gr)
London (Belgravia), 10 VII 1975,
225
£190 ($437)

1339 Cruet stand
London, 1878
5¼ in (13.3 cm) high
14 oz 2 dwt (441 gr)
London (Belgravia), 11 XII 1980,
239
£440 ($910)

1338 C. T. & G. FOX

1339 C. T. & G. FOX

1340 C. T. & G. FOX

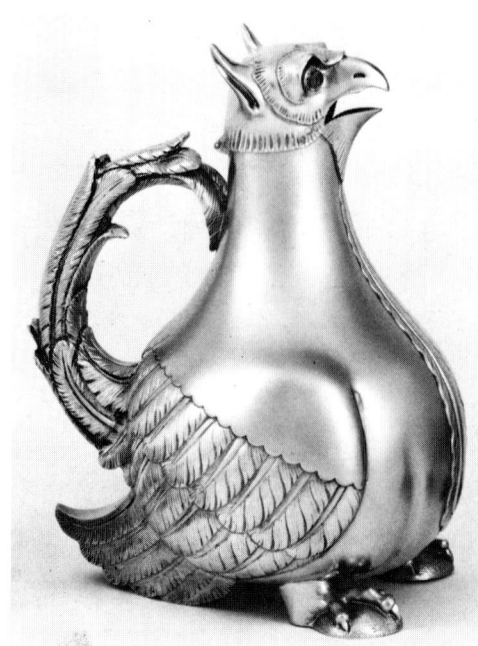

1341 C. T. & G. FOX

1342 C. T. & G. FOX

1340 Flagons, pair
silver-gilt
London, 1873
13½ in (33.6 cm) high
Initials: Baroness Burdett-Coutts
New York, 6–7 II 1980, 806
$6,600 (£2,808)

1341 Claret jug
parcel-gilt
London, 1879
8½ in (21.6 cm) high
25 oz 19 dwt (807 gr)
This wyvern jug is an almost exact copy of a porcelain chocolate pot made in Vienna 1744–9, the design adapted from a Mosan Romanesque aquamanile of *c.* 1160.
London, 25 II 1971, 89
£300 ($720)

1342 Ewer, Cellini pattern
London, 1872
11¼ in (28.8 cm) high
27 oz 18 dwt (869 gr)
Ewers of similar design were made by a number of firms, including Elkington and Stephen Smith.
London (Belgravia), 19 VI 1980, 534
£550 ($1,292)

1343 (DETAIL)

1343 EDINGTON

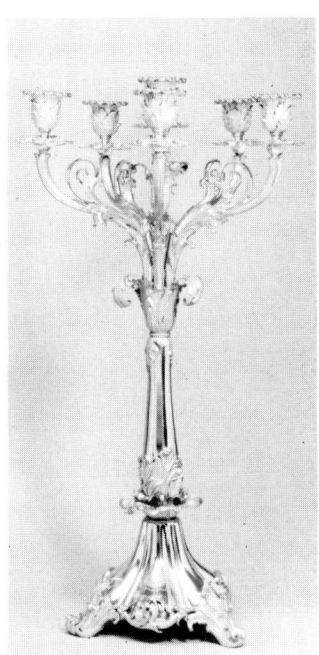

1344 EDINGTON

1345 EDINGTON

James Charles Edington
London; apprenticed to William Ker Reid, first mark 1828, closely associated with Green, Ward and Green
Mark Grimwade, 1794

1343 Candelabra, pair
London, 1837/8
Engraved: Green and Ward
42 in (106.5 cm) high
1,015 oz (31,566 gr)
Arms: Marquess of Sligo (born 1788)
London, 13 VI 1983, 102
£28,600 ($31,460)

1344 Candelabra, pair
silver-gilt
London, 1839/45
29¾ in (75.6 cm) high
415 oz 7 dwt (12,917 gr)
London, 13 VI 1983, 104
£9,900 ($15,840)

1346 REILY & STORER

1345 Ewer
silver-gilt
London, 1849
13 in (33 cm) high
39 oz 1 dwt (1,214 gr)
London, 3 VII 1969, 239
£460 ($1,104)

Charles Reily and George Storer
London; Reily born 1803, in partnership from 1829. The firm descended from Sandylands Drinkwater (see above, nos 886ff.).
Mark Grimwade, 413

1346 Vase
silver-gilt
London, 1837
Engraved: Robert Tate Fecit 204 Regent Street London
19 in (48.2 cm) high
147 oz 10 dwt (4,587 gr)
London (Belgravia), 1 V 1975, 197
£850 ($1,955)

1347 Decanters and labels, pair
silver-gilt mounted glass
London, 1840
11 in (28 cm) high
London (Belgravia), 8 V 1980, 307
£1,100 ($2,585)

1347 REILY & STORER

1348 REILY & STORER

1349 REILY & STORER

1348 Claret jug
London, 1840
Stamped: 209
12¼ in (31.2 cm) high
27 oz (839 gr)
The design is probably based on illustrations of Sir William Hamilton's collection of antiquities published by d'Hancarville (see Rowe, *Adam Silver*, p.27). Now in the Victoria and Albert Museum, London.
London, 25 II 1971, 119
£270 ($648)

1349 Mustard pot
London, 1841
Stamped: 607
2¾ in (7 cm) high
5 oz 11 dwt (172 gr)
London (Belgravia), 9 I 1975, 283
£70 ($161)

1350 REILY & STORER

1351 HENRY WILKINSON & CO

1350 Mug
London, 1851
4 in (10.5 cm) high
5 oz 18 dwt (183 gr)
*London (Belgravia), 11 XII 1980,
149*
£220 ($455)

1355 Fruit dish
silver, Britannia Standard
Sheffield, 1845
8¾ in (22.2 cm) wide
11 oz 8 dwt (354 gr)
*London (Belgravia), 20 V 1976,
276*
£220 ($396)

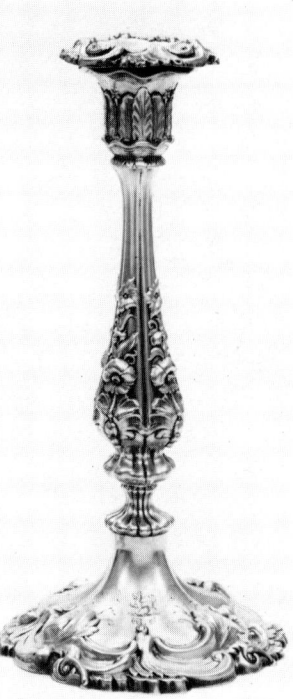

1354 HENRY WILKINSON & CO

Henry Wilkinson and Company
Sheffield; first mark 1831.
Mark Sheffield, pp.30, 58;
Jackson, pp.427

Joseph Angell II and John Angell
London; brothers, in partnership 1831–40. John Angell apprenticed to William Elliott (see above, no.1248ff.), died 1850. In 1840 Joseph went into partnership with his son (see below) and John with his son George, who later continued alone.
Mark Grimwade, 1772

1352 HENRY WILKINSON & CO

1355 HENRY WILKINSON & CO

1351 Mustard pots, pair
Sheffield, 1838/40
3 in (7.5 cm) high
7 oz 1 dwt (219 gr)
*London (Belgravia), 17 VI 1976,
307*
£165 ($297)

1352 Mug
Sheffield, 1858
Workman's mark: JR
4¼ in (10.4 cm) high
4 oz 5 dwt (132 gr)
*London (Belgravia), 3 III 1977,
235*
£352 ($598)

1353 Claret jug
London, 1867
Workman's mark: BS
14½ in (37 cm) high
26 oz 14 dwt (832 gr)
*London (Belgravia), 18 X 1979,
442*
£748 ($1,757)

1354 Candlesticks, pair
Sheffield, 1845
10½ in (26.5 cm) high
28 oz 18 dwt (900 gr)
*London (Belgravia), 6 III 1980,
286*
£950 ($2,232)

1356 Salt cellars, four
With four spoons by another
London, 1835
3½ in (8.8 cm) overall
21 oz 4 dwt (659 gr)
*London (Belgravia), 11 IX 1975,
303*
£544 ($1,088)

1357 Inkstand
London, 1838
10¾ in (27.4 cm) overall
43 oz 18 dwt (1,368 gr)
*London (Belgravia), 11 XII 1980,
166*
£440 ($910)

1358 Egg cruet
London, 1831/3
6¾ in (17.7 cm) high
14 oz 18 dwt (462 gr)
*London (Belgravia), 25 III 1976,
142*
£132 ($237)

1353 HENRY WILKINSON & CO

1356 J. ANGELL II & JOHN ANGELL

1357 J. ANGELL II & JOHN ANGELL

1358 J. ANGELL II & JOHN ANGELL

1359 (DETAIL)

1360 J. ANGELL II & III

1359 J. ANGELL II & III

1361 J. ANGELL II & III

Joseph Angell II and III

London; father and son. Mark entered 1840, in partnership until 1861

1359 Salver
silver-gilt
London, 1848
24 in (61 cm) diameter
167 oz (5,193 gr)
New York, 27 IV 1973, 28
$2,700 (£1,080)

1360 Tea set, three-piece
London, 1847
45 oz 12 dwt (1,418 gr)
London (Belgravia), 12 IX 1974, 85
£400 ($920)

1361 Ewer
London, 1845
10 in (25.5 cm) high
18 oz 12 dwt (579 gr)
London (Belgravia), 10 IV 1980, 541
£330 ($775)

1362 J. ANGELL III   1362

Joseph Angell III

London; born 1816, first mark alone 1849 after partnership with his father (see above). An exhibitor at the Great Exhibition (1851)

1362 Aesop's Fables: tea and coffee set
parcel-gilt
London, 1850
118 oz 19 dwt (3,699 gr)
Shown at the Great Exhibition (1851) and sold for £120. Now in the collection of the Goldsmiths' Company.
London (Belgravia), 29 III 1973, 162
£3,800 ($9,500)

1363 Wine ewer
London, 1851
Stamped: Angell 10 Strand
13½ in (34.3 cm) high
47 oz 13 dwt (1,485 gr)
Inscribed: Purchased by William Quilter at the Great Exhibition of 1851...
London (Belgravia), 13 IX 1973, 115
£1,300 ($3,120)

1364 Bowl
London, 1855
5 in (12.8 cm) diameter
8 oz 4 dwt (258 gr)
London (Belgravia), 22 XI 1979, 298
£198 ($465)

1363 J. ANGELL III

1365 JOHN HARDMAN & CO

1364 J. ANGELL III

1366 FIGG

John Hardman and Company

Birmingham; manufacturers of church furnishings, John Hardman (1811–67) in partnership with William Powell 1845, employed A.W.N. Pugin as designer until his death (1852).
Mark K.C. Jones, pp.344, 346, 351–2

1365 Chalice and paten
silver-gilt and gem set
Birmingham, 1869/77
9 in (22.7 cm) high
29 oz 1 dwt (903 gr)
London (Belgravia), 23 III 1978, 335
£935 ($1,730)

John Wilmin Figg

London; apprenticed to William Elliott (see above, no.1248ff.), first mark 1834; business merged with John Keith in 1880s.
Mark Grimwade, 1306

1366 Tea set, three-piece
London, 1836/7
49 oz 14 dwt (1,545 gr)
London (Belgravia), 27 II 1975, 171
£330 ($759)

1367 Casters, two
London, 1839/40
7¾ in (19.7 cm) and 6½ in (16.5 cm) high
19 oz (590 gr)
London (Belgravia), 9 I 1975, 253
£210 ($483)

1368 Jug
silver-mounted frosted glass
London, 1858
9¼ in (23.5 cm) high
London (Belgravia), 2 V 1974, 210
£100 ($240)

1369 Claret jugs, two
silver-gilt mounts
London, 1862/4
16¼ in (41.2 cm) high
London, 27 XI 1969, 168, 169
£200 ($480) and £240 ($576)

1370 Coffee pot
London, 1838
10¼ in (26 cm) high
28 oz 5 dwt (878 gr)
London (Belgravia), 11 X 1973, 179
£210 ($504)

1367 FIGG

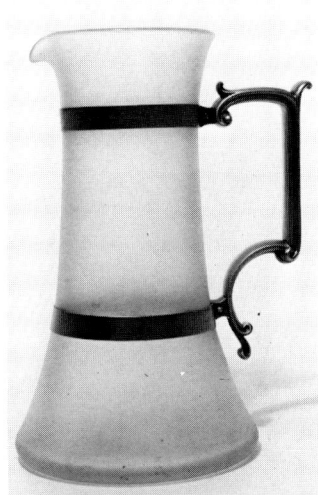

1368 FIGG

1371 Claret jug
silver-mounted glass
London, 1865
10½ in (26.7 cm) high
London (Belgravia), 27 IV 1972, 96
£390 ($975)

Samuel Hayne and Dudley Cater

London; in partnership from 1836. Hayne was the brother of Jonathan Hayne and apprenticed to Thomas Wallis (see no.1214). The firm, latterly known as S. Hayne and Company, continued until the mid-1860s.
Mark Grimwade, 2546

1372 Ewer
silver-gilt
London, 1855
17½ in (44.5 cm) high
93 oz 10 dwt (2,907 gr)
London, 3 VII 1969, 238
£560 ($1,344)

1369 FIGG

1370 FIGG

1371 FIGG

1372 HAYNE & CATER

294 GREAT BRITAIN IRELAND

Edward Barnard and Sons

London; first mark 1829: partnership of Edward (see no.1205), who retired 1846, and his sons Edward, John and William. The firm continues today. Customers included Rundell Bridge and Company, Thomas Hamlet, Green, Ward and Green, David Ellis and others. See Culme, *Nineteenth Century Silver*, pp.83–4; Bannister, 'The Barnard Ledgers'.
Mark Grimwade, 575

1373 Wine coaster wagons, pair
silver-gilt
London, 1829
Stamped: D. Ellis London Fecit
20¼ in (50.5 cm) overall
London, 3 V 1984, 143
£121,000 ($168,190)

1374 Tea set
London, 1831
55 oz 17 dwt (1,733 gr)
London (Belgravia), 1 XII 1976, 210
£770 ($1,309)

1375 Centrepiece
silver, with frosted glass dish
London, 1838
16½ in (41.8 cm) high
61 oz 8 dwt (1,905 gr)
London (Belgravia), 28 IX 1978, 210
£858 ($1,758)

1376 Teapot
London, 1838
Stamped: 697/U
6 in (15.5 cm) high
25 oz (779 gr)
London (Belgravia), 21 VI 1979, 349
£363 ($744)

1377 Tea and coffee set
London, 1839/41
860 oz 17 dwt (2,695 gr)
London (Belgravia), 22 IV 1976, 244
£1,265 ($2,277)

1378 Salver
London, 1842
13 in (33 cm) diameter
33 oz 2 dwt (1,031 gr)
London (Belgravia), 8 V 1980, 285
£385 ($904)

1379 Salver
London, 1851
Stamped: 189/D
16½ in (46.7 cm) diameter
85 oz 12 dwt (2,656 gr)
London (Belgravia), 29 IX 1977, 390
£605 ($1,119)

1373 EDWARD BARNARD & SONS

1374 EDWARD BARNARD & SONS

1375 EDWARD BARNARD & SONS

1376 EDWARD BARNARD & SONS

1380 Child's mug
London, 1851
Stamped: 121/G
3¾ in (9.2 cm) high
5 oz 9 dwt (169 gr)
Engraved with views of the Crystal Palace and Hyde Park.
London (Belgravia), 12 X 1978, 287
£176 ($360)

1381 Child's plate, with knife, fork and spoon
silver-gilt
London 1852/3
7 in (17.8 cm) diameter
7 oz 12 dwt (236 gr)
Engraved with a scene showing Queen Victoria, Prince Albert Edward (later Edward VII) and Prince Alfred (Duke of Edinburgh) in Windsor Great Park
London, 5 III 1970, 88
£180 ($432)

1377 EDWARD BARNARD & SONS

1378 EDWARD BARNARD & SONS

1379 EDWARD BARNARD & SONS

1380 EDWARD BARNARD & SONS

1381 EDWARD BARNARD & SONS

1382 EDWARD BARNARD & SONS

1383 EDWARD BARNARD & SONS

1382 Salver
London, 1860
Stamped: 34/E
17½ in (44.5 cm) diameter
56 oz 10 dwt (1,757 gr)
London (Belgravia), 30 V 1974, 310
£420 ($1,008)

1383 Centrepiece
silver-gilt
London, 1844
33½ in (85.2 cm) high
427 oz 15 dwt (13,303 gr)
Inscribed: The expression of a grateful sense entertained in the community of his liberal spirit and charitable disposition displayed Alike in Public and in Private and of his faithful unremitting and firm discharge of the duties of Chief Magistrate From a Numerous Circle of his Fellow Citizens to Sir James Campbell, Knight, Lord Provost of Glasgow from November 1840 to November 1843.
London, 27 III 1969, 106
£2,900 ($6,960)

1384 Taperstick
London, 1840
4 in (10.2 cm) high
6 oz 8 dwt (199 gr)
Now in the Victoria and Albert Museum, London.
London (Belgravia), 20 VII 1972, 190
£260 ($650)

1384 EDWARD BARNARD & SONS

1385 Presentation ewer
London, 1857
Engraved: A.B. Savory & Sons Fect.
19 in (48 cm) high
98 oz 15 dwt (3,071 gr)
With two goblets en suite maker's mark of William Smily of A.B. Savory and Sons, 1858
The illustration is a page from Savory's catalogue showing the ewer.
London (Belgravia), 12 X 1978, 389
£2,310 ($4,735)

1385 EDWARD BARNARD & SONS

1386 EDWARD BARNARD & SONS

1386 Claret jug
silver-mounted glass
London, 1874
12 in (30.5 cm) high
*London (Belgravia), 3 IV 1975,
187*
£220 ($506)

1387 Ewer on stand
London, 1858
21 in (53.3 cm) high
141 oz 5 dwt (4,392 gr)
Inscribed: Presented by The Earl of Eglinton, Lord Lieutenant of Ireland. Won by The Earl of Howth's Botheration Howth Races 1859
The design was executed by Fréret, a Frenchman who worked for C.F. Hancock during the mid-1850s. See no.1388
London, 12 XI 1970, 305
£500 ($1,200)

1388 Ewer on stand
London, 1859
21 in (53.3 cm) high
145 oz 4 dwt (4,515 gr)
See no.1387
London, 1 V 1969, 146
£550 ($1,320)

1389 Ewer
London, 1860
PODR: 29 November 1854
13 in (33 cm) high
28 oz 11 dwt (888 gr)
Engraved with designs after John Flaxman.
London, 12 XI 1970, 246
£210 ($504)

1390 Mug
London, 1865
4¾ in (12 cm) high
8 oz 14 dwt (273 gr)
London (Belgravia), 19 IV 1979, 399
£110 ($225)

1387 EDWARD BARNARD & SONS

1388 EDWARD BARNARD & SONS

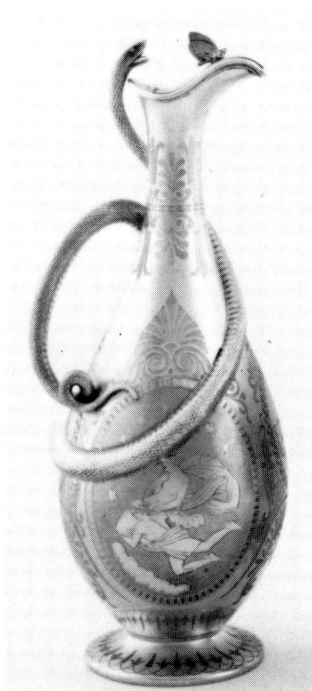

1389 EDWARD BARNARD & SONS

1391 EDWARD BARNARD & SONS

1391 Ewer
London, 1861
12 in (30.5 cm) high
25 oz 7 dwt (788 gr)
London (Belgravia), 26 X 1972, 117
£140 ($350)

1392 EDWARD BARNARD & SONS

1392 Ewer
London, 1863
Stamped: 198
PODR: 29 November 1854
13¼ in (33.5 cm) high
26 oz (806 gr)
London (Belgravia), 23 III 1978, 350
£462 ($854)

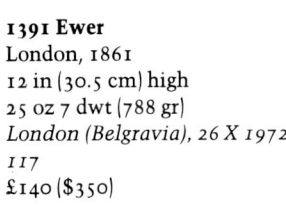

1390 EDWARD BARNARD & SONS

298 GREAT BRITAIN IRELAND

1393 EDWARD BARNARD & SONS

1394 EDWARD BARNARD & SONS

1395 EDWARD BARNARD & SONS

1393 Tray
London, 1879
PODR mark: 27 March 1880
Maker's mark overstruck by Frederick Elkington for Elkington and Company.
14 in (35.7 cm) overall
26 oz 16 dwt (834 gr)
London (Belgravia), 19 II 1981, 518
£396 ($819)

1394 Figure salts, pair
London, 1865
Stamped: 743/744
8¼ in (20.9 cm) high
33 oz 18 dwt (1,054 gr)
London (Belgravia), 21 III 1974, 236
£1,400 ($3,360)

1395 Mug
London, 1875
4½ in (11.4 cm) high
8 oz 6 dwt (260 gr)
London (Belgravia), 21 VI 1979, 288
£148 ($303)

1396 EDWARD BARNARD & SONS

1397 EDWARD BARNARD & SONS

1398 EDWARD BARNARD & SONS

1396 Tea and coffee set
London, 1878
Stamped: 993/K;234/K;922; 690/K
London (Belgravia), 11 XII 1980, 219
£1,375 ($2,846)

1397 Cup, based on a Greco-Roman original
silver-gilt
London, 1884
Stamped: 330/E
10 in (25.4 cm) high
66 oz 18 dwt (2,080 gr)
London (Belgravia), 1 III 1973, 6
£280 ($700)

ELKINGTON & CO   299

1399 EDWARD BARNARD & SONS

1398 Card case
parcel-gilt and pearl-finished
London, 1880
3¾ in (9.5 cm) overall
London (Belgravia), 2 V 1974, 148
£200 ($480)

1399 Tea set
parcel-gilt and pearl-finished
London, 1877
Teapot: 5½ in (14 cm) high
17 oz 7 dwt (539 gr)
London, 12 XI 1970, 149
£120 ($288)

Elkington and Company Ltd

Birmingham; founded by George Richards Elkington (1801–65) and associates. In 1840 Elkington patented the electroplating process upon which the firm's fortunes were based. In partnership with Josiah Mason as Elkington Mason and Company, the firm was then styled as Elkington and Company until it became a limited company. After G.R. Elkington's death the business was continued by members of the Elkington family, the silver being marked by Frederick Elkington. Merged with Mappin and Webb 1963 as British Silverware Ltd. Designers employed by the firm included Leonard Morel-Ladeuil, A.A. Willms (head of the design department until 1899).
Mark K.C. Jones, pp.333–4, 340–42; Bury, *Victorian Electroplate*, pp.62, 63

1400 ELKINGTON & CO

1401 ELKINGTON & CO

1402 ELKINGTON & CO

1400 Wall plaque
silver, Britannia Standard
Birmingham, 1844
21½ in (54.6 cm) diameter
79 oz (2,456 gr)
London, 5 III 1970, 186
£260 ($624)

1401 Inkstand
parcel-gilt
Birmingham, 1853
12½ in (31.7 cm) overall
45 oz 1 dwt (1,401 gr)
London (Belgravia), 11 X 1973, 183a
£700 ($1,680)

1402 Cup
silver, electrotype, Britannia Standard
Birmingham, 1844
From a model by Benjamin Schlick
4¼ in (10.8 cm) high
16 oz (500 gr)
See catalogue of exhibition, 'Birmingham Gold and Silver 1773–1973'.
London (Belgravia), 31 VII 1980, 529
£660 ($1,551)

1403 Tea and coffee set
Birmingham, 1854
85 oz 13 dwt (2,663 gr)
London, 13 VI 1983, 101
£5,720 ($9,152)

1404 Card case
parcel-gilt electrotype
Birmingham, 1864
Designer: George Stanton
3¾ in (9.5 cm) overall
3 oz 18 dwt (121 gr)
Card cases of this design were shown by Elkington at the International Exhibitions in Paris (1855) and London (1862).
London (Belgravia), 21 VII 1976, 641
£165 ($297)

1405 Tankard
parcel-gilt
Birmingham, 1859
Stamped: 1334
7¼ in (18.4 cm) high
16 oz 12 dwt (515 gr)
An electrotype copy of an Indian tankard.
London (Belgravia), 17 VI 1976, 334
£264 ($475)

1406 Ewer and basin
parcel-gilt
Birmingham, 1874
Designer: Morel Ladeuil
Ewer: 16 in (40.6 cm) high
Basin: 21 in (53.3 cm) diameter
131 oz 15 dwt (4,097 gr)
Identical with a ewer and basin shown at the International Exhibition, Paris (1878).
London, 5 XII 1968, 62
£450 ($1,080)

1407 Toast rack
Birmingham, 1859
8 in (20.1 cm) wide
23 oz 14 dwt (739 gr)
London (Belgravia), 6 III 1980, 310
£550 ($1,292)

1408 Figure, 'The Goddess of Sleep'
Birmingham, 1893
9¾ in (24.7 cm) high
15 oz 8 dwt (479 gr)
After an original by L. Morel Ladeuil for the table, 'Sleep', shown by Elkington at the International Exhibition (1862), which was bought by the City of Birmingham as a marriage gift to the Prince and Princess of Wales.
London (Belgravia), 1 III 1973, 151
£125 ($312)

1409 The Milton Shield (from *Paradise Lost*)
electroplated copper electrotype
Signed: Morel Ladeuil Fecit 1866
34 in (86.4 cm) high
The original in silver and damascened iron, made for the Paris Exhibition (1867), is now in the Victoria and Albert Museum, London.
London (Belgravia), 29 VI 1972, 35
£165 ($412)

1403 ELKINGTON & CO

1404 ELKINGTON & CO

1406 ELKINGTON & CO

1405 ELKINGTON & CO

1407 ELKINGTON & CO

1408 ELKINGTON & CO

1409 ELKINGTON & CO

1410 ELKINGTON & CO

1411 ELKINGTON & CO

1412 ELKINGTON & CO

1410 The Bunyan Shield (from *The Pilgrim's Progress*)
electroplated copper electrotype
Signed: Morel Ladeuil inv & fecit 1878
34¼ in (87 cm) high
London (Belgravia), 3 XI 1977, 120
£605 ($1,119)

1411 Dish 'Perseus and Andromeda'
electroplated copper electrotype
c. 1888
Designer: after an original by L. Morel Ladeuil
12¾ in (37.4 cm) diameter
London (Belgravia), 6 XI 1975, 114
£55 ($110)

1412 Shield, 'The Battle of the Amazons'
silver electrotype
Birmingham, 1871
From the original by Antoine Vechte
26¾ in (68 cm) diameter
108 oz 18 dwt (3,386 gr)
London (Belgravia), 13 I 1977, 216
£990 ($1,683)

1413 ELKINGTON & CO

1414 ELKINGTON & CO

1413 Jewel casket
parcel-gilt silver electrotype
Birmingham, 1865
Probably designed by
A.A. Willms
PODR: 7 December 1865
10¼ in (26 cm) wide
52 oz 16 dwt (1,642 gr)
See Culme, *Nineteenth Century Silver*, p.173.
London, 25 II 1971, 159
£380 ($912)

1414 Centrepiece, mirror plateau and two fruit dishes, 'Egyptian pattern'
Birmingham, 1870/73
15¼ in (39 cm) and 7 in (18 cm) high
129 oz 1 dwt (4,018 gr)
London (Belgravia), 25 IX 1980, 348
£1,210 ($2,504)

1415 ELKINGTON & CO

1416 ELKINGTON & CO

1415 Tea set and tray, with a pair of Kutani porcelain cups and saucers
parcel-gilt and pearl-finished
Birmingham, 1874
PODR: 10 July 1875; tray: 4 June 1874
Tray: 16½ in (42 cm) overall
52 oz (1,618 gr)
London (Belgravia), 11 XII 1980, 218
£1,540 ($3,187)

1416 Claret jug
silver-mounted mauve glass with electro-deposited silver decoration
Birmingham, 1897
14 in (35.5 cm) high
London (Belgravia), 13 I 1977, 247
£550 ($935)

1417 ELKINGTON & CO

1417 Salver
parcel-gilt
London, 1879
PODR: 27 March 1880
The mark of Elkington overstrikes another, probably E. Barnard and Sons
12 in (30.5 cm) wide
26 oz 5 dwt (816 gr)
London, 12 XI 1970, 192
£155 ($372)

1418 ELKINGTON & CO

1419 ELKINGTON & CO

1420 HANCOCK

1418 Centrepiece and mirror plateau, 'Pompeian pattern'
parcel-gilt
Birmingham, 1875
Designer: A.A. Willms
PODR: 3 May 1862
29¼ in (74.4 cm) high
418 oz 3 dwt (13,005 gr) of weighable silver
A Pompeian pattern dessert service was manufactured by Elkington for the International Exhibition (1862). See *Art Journal illustrated catalogue*, p.240
London, 11 XI 1982, 95
£6,600 ($10,560)

1419 The Brighton Cup, 1871
parcel-gilt, partially frosted on an ebonized wood plinth with chased electroplated frieze
Birmingham, 1870
Probably designed by A.A. Willms
Engraved: Elkington, Regent St. London
33 in (84.2 cm) high
321 oz 11 dwt (9,999 gr)
Provenance: Earl of Rosebery
Mentmore, 19 V 1977, 1667
£9,900 ($16,830)

Charles Frederick Hancock

London; born *c.* 1808, associated with Storr and Mortimer and Hunt and Roskell (see above, nos 1273ff. and 1283ff. respectively) before starting his own business 1848, retired 1870 when the firm was renamed Hancock and Company and continued by his sons, died 1891. Employed Raphael Monti and H.H. Armstead. See Culme, *Nineteenth Century Silver*; Gere, *European and American Jewellery 1830–1914*
Mark Jackson, p.233

1420 Centrepiece, the Doncaster Cup, 1857
London, 1857
Designer: H.H. Armstead
24¾ in (62.8 cm) high
487 oz 5 dwt (15,153 gr)
See Culme, *Nineteenth Century Silver*, p.165.
London (Belgravia), 26 VII 1973, 123
£1,750 ($4,375)

1421 HANCOCK

1422 HANCOCK

1421 Model of an owl
London, 1871
19¼ in (49 cm) high
136 oz 18 dwt (4,260 gr)
London (Belgravia), 8 V 1980, 292
£4,290 ($10,081)

1422 Scent bottle
gold-mounted glass
c. 1865
Stamped: Hancock & Co. 38 & 39 Bruton St
4 in (10 cm) high
London (Belgravia), 22 IV 1976, 45
£220 ($396)

1423 HANCOCK

1423 Punch bowl
parcel-gilt
London, 1858
21¾ in (55.2 cm) diameter
320 oz 10 dwt (9,967 gr)
New York, 12–14 IV 1984, 248
$24,200 (£17,410)

1424 Vase
silver-gilt
Probably designed by H.H. Armstead
25¾ in (65.4 cm) high
257 oz 9 dwt (8,006 gr)
The scene around the body depicts the crowning of Henry VII after the battle of Bosworth Field (1485).
London, 25 II 1971, 176
£480 ($1,152)

1425 Centrepiece, the Brighton Cup, 1869
frosted silver and bronze
London, 1869
Designer: Raphael Monti
23¾ in (59.7 cm) high
The group depicts British warriors on the rocks of Pevensey Bay, assembling to resist the landing of Caesar.
Mentmore, 19–23 V 1977, 1665
£14,300 ($24,310)

1424 HANCOCK

1425 HANCOCK

1426 HANCOCK

1427 R. HENNELL & SONS   1428 R. HENNELL & SONS

1429 R. HENNELL & SONS

1430 R. HENNELL & SONS

1426 Vase
London, 1885
22¼ in (56.5 cm) high
143 oz 10 dwt (4,462 gr)
*London (Belgravia), 30 V 1974,
261*
£620 ($1,488)

R. Hennell and Sons

London; see above, Hennell Family (no.1099ff.) for the earlier history of this firm. Robert Hennell II was succeeded by his son, Robert Hennell III: born 1794, first mark 1834, died 1868 (nos 1427–31); mark, Grimwade, 2333. Robert Hennell IV was born 1826, first mark 1869, died 1892 (nos 1432–6). James Barclay, brother of Robert Hennell IV, was born 1828, first mark 1877, died 1899 (nos 1437–8)
Mark Antique Collector, June 1979, also Jackson, pp.232, 233, 234. See p.38

1427 Wine cup
London, 1866
5½ in (14 cm) high
7 oz 1 dwt (219 gr)
London, 18 VI 1970, 159
£45 ($108)

1431 R. HENNELL & SONS

1428 Egg cruet, for six
London, 1851
9½ in (23.8 cm) wide
33 oz (1,026 gr)
London (Belgravia), 11 XII 1980, 186
£605 ($1,252)

1429 Covered jug
London, 1855
13½ in (34.3 cm) high
68 oz 15 dwt (2,138 gr)
London (Belgravia), 2 V 1974, 208
£900 ($2,160)

1430 Tea set
London, 1860
52 oz 12 dwt (1,630 gr)
London, 18 VI 1970, 167
£210 ($504)

1431 Tea and coffee set
London, 1856/7
Stamped: CF Hancock, 39 Bruton St. London
99 oz 18 dwt (3,106 gr)
London (Belgravia), 6 XI 1975, 217
£1,045 ($2,090)

1432 R. HENNELL & SONS

1433 R. HENNELL & SONS

1434 R. HENNELL & SONS   1435 R. HENNELL & SONS   1436 R. HENNELL & SONS

1437 R. HENNELL & SONS   1438 R. HENNELL & SONS

1439 SMITH, NICHOLSON & CO   1440 SMITH, NICHOLSON & CO

1432 Small tea and coffee set
London, 1868/70
23 oz 4 dwt (721 gr)
London (Belgravia), 10 X 1974, 98
£360 ($828)

1433 Vase
parcel-gilt
London, 1870
Stamped: Whistler fecit, 11 Strand London
18¼ in (46.4 cm) high
52 oz 18 dwt (1,648 gr)
London (Belgravia), 18 X 1979, 487
£990 ($2,326)

1434 Teapot
London, 1874
7½ in (19 cm) high
20 oz 7 dwt (632 gr)
London (Belgravia), 13 I 1977, 265
£154 ($261)

1435 'Mr Punch' mustard pot
London, 1873
PODR: 22 February 1868
3¾ in (9.3 cm) high
7 oz 18 dwt (245 gr)
London (Belgravia), 8 VI 1978, 116
£638 ($1,180)

1436 Salt cellars, four
London, 1869
4¼ in (10.7 cm) high
33 oz (1,026 gr) including four spoons
London (Belgravia), 24 II 1972, 175
£440 ($1,100)

1437 Ash tray
London, 1884
4¼ in (10.1 cm) diameter
2 oz 4 dwt (69 gr)
London (Belgravia), 17 XII 1981, 283
£253 ($452)

1438 Milk jug
London, 1877
3½ in (8.7 cm) high
8 oz 5 dwt (256 gr)
London (Belgravia), 25 VII 1974, 292
£120 ($288)

Smith, Nicholson and Company

London; Stephen Smith (son of Benjamin Smith III; see above, no.1263ff.) and William Nicholson, in partnership after Benjamin Smith's death in 1850.

1439 Dessert dish stand
London, 1861
10¾ in (27.3 cm) high
71 oz 14 dwt (2,225 gr)
London (Belgravia), 22 VI 1978, 361
£682 ($1,261)

1440 Tankard
London, 1863
10¼ in (26 cm) high
38 oz 8 dwt (1,196 gr)
London (Belgravia), 25 VI 1981, 372
£396 ($819)

Stephen Smith and Son

London; successors to Smith, Nicholson and Company (see above).

1441 Tea and coffee set
London, 1869/70
PODR: 6 January 1868
86 oz 2 dwt (2,680 gr)
London (Belgravia), 11 XII 1980, 197
£1,100 ($2,277)

1442 Coffee pot
London, 1871
PODR: 6 January 1868
10¼ in (26 cm) high
28 oz 6 dwt (880 gr)
London (Belgravia), 19 II 1976, 242
£231 ($415)

1443 Tea caddy
London, 1865
5 in (12.5 cm) high
18 oz (560 gr)
London (Belgravia), 18 X 1979, 559
£462 ($1,085)

1444 Wine ewer
silver-gilt, frosted
London, 1865
13 in (33 cm) high
20 oz 9 dwt (635 gr)
London (Belgravia), 21 III 1974, 134
£270 ($648)

1445 Two-handled cup
silver-gilt
London, 1877
24½ in (62.2 cm) high
161 oz 18 dwt (5,035 gr)
London, 18 VI 1970, 226A
£420 ($1,008)

George Ivory

London

1446 Mug
London, 1851
4 in (10 cm) high
7 oz 10 dwt (236 gr)
London (Belgravia), 25 VI 1981, 369
£198 ($410)

1441 STEPHEN SMITH & SON

1442 STEPHEN SMITH & SON

1443 STEPHEN SMITH & SON

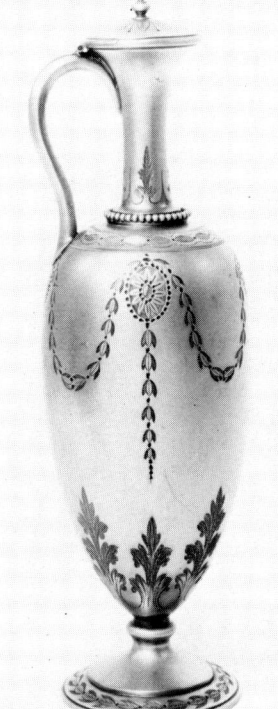

1444 STEPHEN SMITH & SON

1445 STEPHEN SMITH & SON

1446 IVORY

1447 IVORY

1448 MACRAE

1447 Ewer
London, 1856
Stamped: Turner's 58 & 59 New Bond St
18 in (46 cm) high
109 oz 6 dwt (3,402 gr)
London (Belgravia), 18 X 1979, 543
£2,420 ($5,687)

Alexander Macrae

London; specialized in centrepieces, dessert stands and candelabra

1448 Centrepiece
London, 1861
33½ in (85 cm) high
297 oz 13 dwt (9,237 gr)
London (Belgravia), 11 V 1978, 351
£3,850 ($7,122)

1449 (DETAIL)

1449 Candelabra, pair
silver-gilt
London, 1876
22 in (56 cm) high
154 oz (4,789 gr)
London (Belgravia), 19 II 1976, 303
£1,540 ($2,772)

1450 Centrepiece
parcel-gilt
London, 1857
Maker's mark overstruck by G.R. Elkington
29½ in (74.8 cm) high
168 oz 18 dwt (5,252 gr)
London (Belgravia), 27 VI 1974, 381
£680 ($1,632)

1449 MACRAE

Thomas William Dee and Son

London; founded c. 1830 by T.W. Dee in partnership with John Fargus; known as T.W. Dee and Son from 1853 until Thomas' death in 1869. The business was then continued by his sons Henry William and Louis as H.W. and L. Dee until the former's retirement c. 1879, when Louis continued until his death in 1884

1451 Box
ivory and wood with silver mounts
London, 1863
6 in (15 cm) wide
London (Belgravia), 17 VI 1976, 69
£220 ($396)

1450 MACRAE

1452 Vinaigrette/posy holder
silver-gilt, with a red hardstone cap
London, 1866
4¾ in (12 cm) overall
4 oz 18 dwt (155 gr) of silver
London (Belgravia), 6 III 1980, 470
£1,045 ($2,455)

1453 Posy holder
silver-gilt
London, 1866
4¼ in (10.5 cm) high
3 oz 14 dwt (114 gr)
London (Belgravia), 22 IV 1976, 220
£154 ($277)

1454 Vinaigrette
silver-gilt
London, 1867
PODR: 28 November 1867
Engraved: Jenner & Knewstub 33 St. James St. & 66 Jermyn St.
3½ in (9.5 cm) overall
London (Belgravia), 26 X 1972, 108
£230 ($575)

Henry William and Louis Dee
London; sons of Thomas William Dee (see above)

1455 Lady's companion
enamel and silver-gilt
London, 1870
Engraved: Payne & Son, 32 Lowndes St.
5 in (12.7 cm) overall
London (Belgravia), 27 VI 1974, 125
£260 ($624)

1456 Scent flask
enamel mounted in silver-gilt
London, 1872
Painting attributed to Lucien Besche after 'La Bascule' by Fragonard
6½ in (16.5 cm) high
London (Belgravia), 6 XI 1975, 52
£2,750 ($5,500)

1457 Fusee box, formed as an anchor
London, 1872
PODR: 20 July 1872
Engraved: Jenner & Knewstub, 33 St. James St. & 66 Jermyn St.
3½ in (8.9 cm) overall
London (Belgravia), 27 VI 1974, 134
£130 ($312)

1458 Spirit flask
London, 1879
6 in (15 cm) high
7 oz 16 dwt (243 gr)
London (Belgravia), 19 II 1981, 516
£165 ($341)

1451 THOMAS WILLIAM DEE & SON

1452 THOMAS WILLIAM DEE & SON

1453 THOMAS WILLIAM DEE & SON

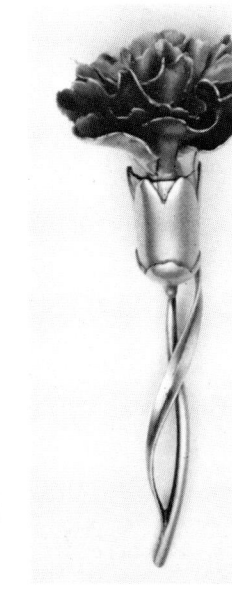

1454 THOMAS WILLIAM DEE & SON

1455 H. W. & L. DEE

1456 H. W. & L. DEE

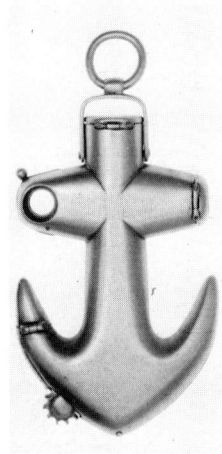

1457 H. W. & L. DEE

1458 H. W. & L. DEE

1459 L. DEE

1460 L. DEE

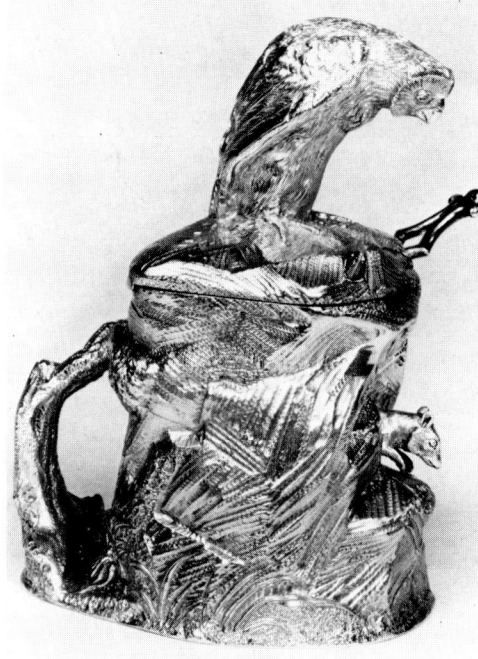

1461 L. DEE

1462 STOCKWELL

1463 STOCKWELL

1464 STOCKWELL

1465 STOCKWELL

Louis Dee
London

1459 Chamber candlesticks, pair
London, 1880
Engraved: Henry Wilson 60 Pall Mall
5 in (12.7 cm) high
34 oz 6 dwt (1,066 gr)
The design is based on the crest of Cathcart.
London (Belgravia), 27 VI 1974, 333
£380 ($912)

1460 'Punch and Judy' decanters, two
silver-mounted clear glass
London, 1881
PODR: 7 June 1879
Engraved: P & F Schafer, 27 Piccadilly
9¼ in (23.5 cm) high
London (Belgravia), 15 XII 1977, 371, 372
£242 ($447) and £286 ($529)

1461 Mustard pot
London, 1882
4½ in (11.4 cm) high
7 oz 8 dwt (230 gr)
London (Belgravia), 9 XII 1971, 95
£155 ($387)

Edward H. Stockwell
London; born 1840. Specialist smallworker.

1462 Snuff box
London, 1865
4½ in (11.6 cm) wide
London (Belgravia), 25 VI 1981, 359
£231 ($478)

1463 Claret jug
silver-mounted glass
London, 1880
7¼ in (18.4 cm) high
London (Belgravia), 11 IX 1975, 216
£220 ($440)

1464 Vinaigrette
London, 1880
3 in (7.5 cm) overall
1 oz 8 dwt (43 gr)
London (Belgravia), 7 XI 1974, 230
£500 ($1,150)

1465 Lady's companion
silver-mounted glass
London, 1871
6 in (15.3 cm) overall
London (Belgravia), 26 X 1972, 75
£100 ($250)

1466 STOCKWELL

1467 SAMPSON MORDAN & CO

1468 SAMPSON MORDAN & CO

1469 SAMPSON MORDAN & CO

1470 SAMPSON MORDAN & CO

1471 SAMPSON MORDAN & CO

1472 SAMPSON MORDAN & CO

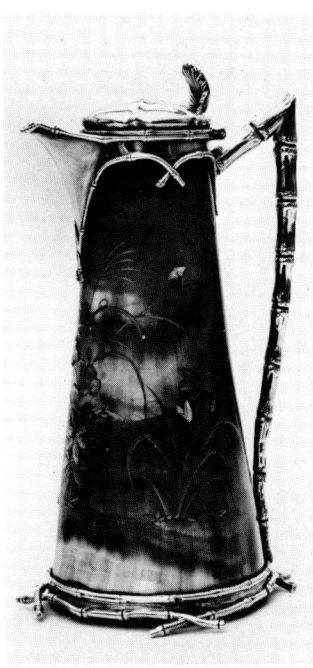

1473 SAMPSON MORDAN & CO

1466 Scent flask
London, 1877
PODR: 28 November 1877
2¾ in (7 cm) high
3 oz (93 gr)
London (Belgravia), 12 X 1978, 311
£264 ($541)

Sampson Mordan and Company

London; established as propelling pencil manufacturers c. 1813 but chief output in 1870s and 1880s was in silver smallwork

1467 Vinaigrette
silver-gilt
(London), c. 1860
1½ in (3.7 cm) overall
London (Belgravia), 6 IV 1972, 159
£300 ($750)

1468 Scent flask
parcel-gilt
London, 1873
3¼ in (8.4 cm) high
London (Belgravia), 1–2 XII 1976, 407
£104 ($177)

1469 Card case
parcel-gilt and frosted
London, 1878
4¼ in (10.4 cm) overall
London (Belgravia), 21 II 1974, 66
£140 ($336)

1470 Lady's companion
London, 1874
4¼ in (10.4 cm) high
London (Belgravia), 13 I 1977, 197
£385 ($654)

1471 'Mussel' vinaigrette
London, 1876
PODR: 29 February 1876
2 in (4.7 cm) overall
London (Belgravia), 13 I 1977, 183
£242 ($411)

1472 Claret jug
silver-mounted glass
London, 1881
11½ in (29.2 cm) high
London, 25 II 1971, 90
£320 ($768)

1473 Jug
silver-mounted lacquered horn
London, 1882
8½ in (22 cm) high
London (Belgravia), 6 IX 1979, 92
£495 ($1,163)

1474 SAMPSON MORDAN & CO

1475 MARTIN HALL & CO

1476 MARTIN HALL & CO

1477 MARTIN HALL & CO

1478 MARTIN HALL & CO

1474 Sewing case
London, 1876
1¾ in (4.4 cm) high
London (Belgravia), 7 IV 1977, 460
£198 ($336)

Martin, Hall and Company

Sheffield; founded 1854 by Ebenezer Hall and Robert Martin. See Vander, 'Some Sheffield Silversmiths'.
Mark Jackson, pp.428, 429; Sheffield, pp.36, 40

1475 Mustard pot
London, 1869
3½ in (9 cm) high
9 oz 11 dwt (296 gr)
London (Belgravia), 3 III 1977, 163
£187 ($318)

1476 Entrée dishes and covers, pair
Sheffield, 1859
PODR: 14 April 1857
13 in (33 cm) wide
102 oz 3 dwt (3,176 gr)
London (Belgravia), 21 II 1974, 146
£700 ($1,680)

1477 Lemonade jug and three mugs en suite
London, 1872
Jug: 7½ in (19 cm) high
57 oz 3 dwt (1,777 gr)
London (Belgravia), 20 VII 1972, 143
£280 ($700)

1478 Tray
silver, Britannia Standard
London, 1876
Stamped: 5153
30 in (76.3 cm) overall
134 oz 17 dwt (4,193 gr)
London (Belgravia, 27 VI 1974, 231
£700 ($1,680)

1479 Salver
silver, Britannia Standard
London, 1875
Stamped: 5153
21¼ in (54 cm) diameter
95 oz 2 dwt (2,957 gr)
London (Belgravia), 24 I 1974, 222
£480 ($1,152)

1479 MARTIN HALL & CO

1480 ROBERTS & BELK

1482 THOMAS BRADBURY & SONS

1481 ATKIN BROTHERS

1483 THOMAS BRADBURY & SONS

1484 THOMAS BRADBURY & SONS

Roberts and Belk

Sheffield; founded 1809, named Roberts and Belk from 1864, sold to C.J. Vander 1963. See Vander, 'Some Sheffield Silversmiths' *Mark* Sheffield, pp.40, 42, 49, 61; Jackson, p.430

1480 Tea and coffee set, with plated kettle
Sheffield, 1882
49 oz 12 dwt (1,544 gr)
London (Belgravia), 18 X 1979, 508
£748 ($1,757)

Atkin Brothers

Sheffield; mark entered 1853. On the death of Thomas Law in 1819 the business was continued by his son John with Henry Atkin and John Oxley. In 1958 flatware business sold to C.J. Vander, hollow-ware to Adie Brothers
Mark Sheffield, p.35 (H.A.)

1481 Tea set, four-piece, with six teaspoons and a pair of sugar tongs
Sheffield, 1890
PODR mark: 23277
39 oz 8 dwt (1,227 gr)
London (Belgravia), 27 XI 1980, 313
£407 ($842)

Thomas Bradbury and Sons

London and Sheffield; founded 1777, mark registered as Thomas Bradbury and Company 1832, T. Bradbury and Son 1858; bought by Atkin Brothers 1947. See Vander, 'Some Sheffield Silversmiths'; Bradbury, *A History of Old Sheffield Plate Mark* Jackson, pp.235, 431; Sheffield Assay, pp.30, 38

1482 Tea set, four-piece
London/Sheffield, 1918–20
60 oz (1,862 gr)
London (Belgravia), 25 III 1976, 126
£242 ($435)

1483 Ewer
London, 1873
10¼ in (26 cm) high
28 oz 7 dwt (881 gr)
London (Belgravia), 22 V 1975, 248
£280 ($644)

1484 Entrée dishes and covers, pair
London, 1899
Incuse workman's initials: EM
10¼ in (26 cm) wide
93 oz 4 dwt (2,898 gr)
London (Belgravia), 2 V 1974, 110
£360 ($864)

1485 Tea and coffee set
London, 1871/2
PODR mark: 24 July 1871
67 oz 2 dwt (1,927 gr)
London (Belgravia), 17 VI 1976, 304
£858 ($1,544)

Christopher Dresser
Born 1834, began to design silver early in 1860; most of his work is executed in electroplate. Designed for Elkington and Company 1875–88, Hukin and Heath from 1878 and James Dixon and Sons from 1879; died 1904. See Hughes, *Modern Silver*; *Phaidon Encyclopaedia of Decorative Arts*; catalogue of exhibition, 'Touching Gold and Silver', no.166 (ill. of Dresser's stamp)

J.W. Hukin and J.T. Heath
London and Birmingham; nos.1489, 1492 bear mark of J.T. Heath and J.H. Middleton for Hukin and Heath. Employed Christopher Dresser as designer from 1878 (see p.41).
Mark K.C. Jones, pp.345, 354

1486 Travelling tea set
London, 1880
3¼ in (8.5 cm) high
London (Belgravia), 25 IX 1981, 241
£528 ($945)

1487 Jug
glass with electroplated mounts
c. 1880–90
Design attributed to Christopher Dresser
8¾ in (22.5 cm) high
London, 13 IV 1984, 54
£82 ($113)

1488 Jug
glass with silver mounts
London, 1892
Design attributed to Christopher Dresser
16½ in (42 cm) high
London, 13 IV 1984, 55
£660 ($917)

1489 Jug
glass with silver mounts
London, 1881
Designer: Christopher Dresser
PODR: 9 May 1881
8½ in (22 cm) high
London, 13 IV 1984, 56
£1,045 ($1,452)

1490 Dish
London, 1881
After a design by Christopher Dresser
6½ in (16.2 cm) overall
London (Belgravia), 8 II 1980, 124
£82 ($152)

1485 THOMAS BRADBURY & SONS

1486 HUKIN & HEATH

1487   1488   1489 HUKIN & HEATH

1490 HUKIN & HEATH

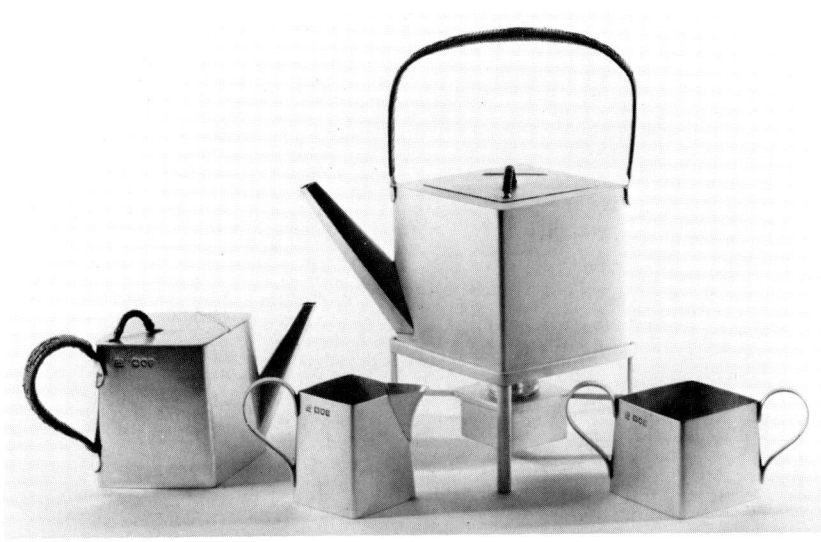

1492 HUKIN & HEATH

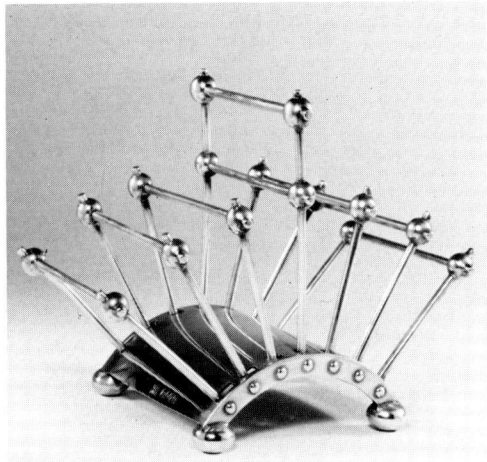

1491 HUKIN & HEATH

1493 JAMES DIXON & SONS

1494 WILLIAM HUTTON & SONS

1495 WILLIAM HUTTON & SONS

1496 WILLIAM HUTTON & SONS

1491 Toast rack
London, 1881
Designer: Christopher Dresser
5 in (12.5 cm) overall
London (Belgravia), 5 XII 1980, 86
£440 ($910)

1492 Tea set
London, 1894/Birmingham, 1901
Exhibition: 'Birmingham Gold and Silver 1773–1973', no.E 16.
London (Belgravia), 1 IV 1976, 134
£572 ($1,029)

James Dixon and Sons

Sheffield and London; founded 1806, manufacturing Britannia metal and plate; styled James Dixon and Sons prior to and following James Dixon's retirement in 1842. The firm is still in business. See Vander, 'Some Sheffield Silversmiths' *Mark* Jackson, p.429; Bury, *Victorian Electroplate*, p.34

1493 Teapot
London, 1880
Designer: Christopher Dresser
PODR: 25 November 1880
Engraved: Ch. Dresser
4 in (10.5 cm) high
London (Belgravia), 8 III 1972, 169
£750 ($1,875)

William Hutton and Sons

Birmingham and Sheffield; founded 1800 by William Hutton (1774–1842) and became leading electroplate manufacturers. Merged 1930 with James Dixon (see above).
Mark K.C. Jones, p.374

1494 Lemonade jug
silver-mounted glass
London, 1892
After a design by Christopher Dresser
8¾ in (22 cm) high
London (Belgravia), 28 II 1979, 164
£209 ($428)

1495 Tea and coffee set
London, 1900/1901
Designer: Kate Harris
Stamped: W.C. Connell, 33 Cheapside London (retailer)
London (Belgravia) 30–31 III 1977, 116
£2,200 ($3,740)

1496 Box
Birmingham, 1908
2½ in (6.5 cm) diameter
London (Belgravia), 11 VII 1979, 97
£132 ($270)

1497   1498
GUILD OF HANDICRAFT LTD

1499 GUILD OF HANDICRAFT LTD

1500 GUILD OF HANDICRAFT LTD

1501 GUILD OF HANDICRAFT LTD

Guild of Handicraft Ltd

London and Chipping Campden, Gloucestershire; founded by Charles Robert Ashbee (1863–1942) in 1888, first mark 1896, active until 1907/8
Mark Gere, p.148

1497 Butter knife
London, 1900
6½ in (16.2 cm) overall
London (Belgravia), 20 VII 1977, 73
£330 ($561)

1498 Spoon
London, 1905
Designer: C.R. Ashbee
7½ in (19.3 cm) overall
London (Belgravia), 4 VII 1980, 320
£352 ($827)

1502 GUILD OF HANDICRAFT LTD

1503 GUILD OF HANDICRAFT LTD

1504 GUILD OF HANDICRAFT LTD

GUILD OF HANDICRAFT LTD – LIBERTY & CO   317

1499 Decanter
silver-mounted green glass
London, 1901
8 in (20.5 cm) high
See Culme, *Nineteenth Century Silver*, p.111, illustrated in colour
London (Belgravia), 27 XI 1975, 129
£1,650 ($3,300)

1500 Hand mirror
London, 1902
10 in (25.6 cm) overall
London (Belgravia), 8 II 1978, 108
£176 ($325)

1501 Dish, with spoon and glass
London, 1903/4
Designer: C.R. Ashbee
7¼ in (18.5 cm) overall
London (Belgravia), 18 IV 1980, 47
£715 ($1,680)

1502 Cup and cover
London, 1903
Designer: C.R. Ashbee
11½ in (29.2 cm) high
London (Belgravia), 1 IV 1976, 143
£1,320 ($2,376)

1503 Tazza
London, 1904
11 in (27.7 cm) high
London, 13 IV 1984, 61
£2,200 ($3,058)

1504 Tazza
silver and enamel
London, 1905
6 in (15.2 cm) high
London (Belgravia), 13 X 1978, 101
£1,430 ($2,931)

Liberty and Company

London and Birmingham; founded 1875 by Arthur Lasenby Liberty, first mark entered 1894. Cymric range of silver and jewellery launched 1899 (until 1927). Most of the silver made by W.H. Haseler of Birmingham. Designers included Archibald Knox, Rex Silver and Oliver Baker. See Tilbrook, *The Designs of Archibald Knox for Liberty and Co*; Adburgham, *Liberty's*; catalogues of exhibitions, 'Liberty's, 1875–1975', 'Birmingham Gold and Silver 1773–1973'
Mark K.C. Jones, p.356

1505 Coffee spoons, six
Imported by Liberty 1893
Maker's mark: S.M. (Japanese)
London, 15 VII 1983, 107
£506 ($809)

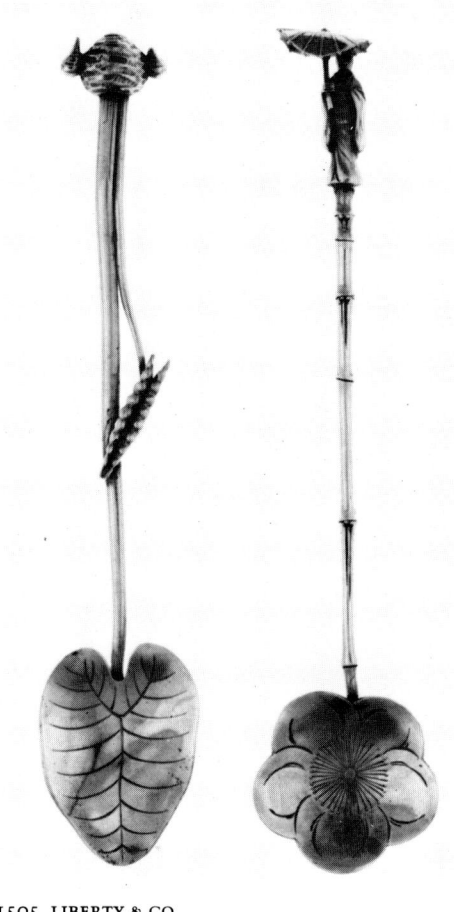

1505 LIBERTY & CO

1507 LIBERTY & CO

1508 LIBERTY & CO

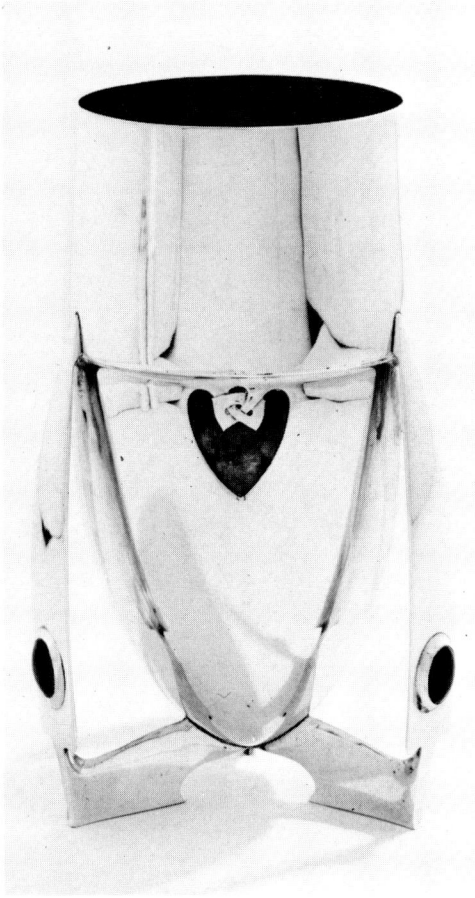

1506 LIBERTY & CO

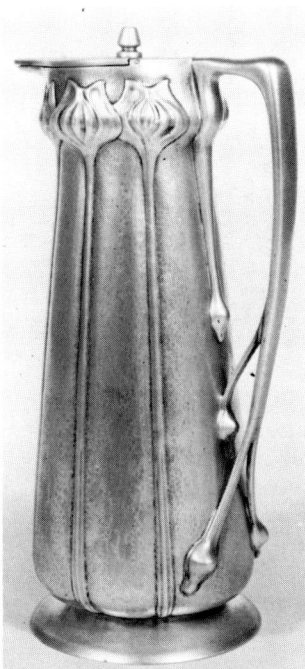

1509 LIBERTY & CO

1507 Bowl and stand
Birmingham, 1899
Design attributed to Oliver Baker
4¼ in (11 cm) high
London (Belgravia), 25 IV 1979, 73
£242 ($496)

1508 Candlesticks, pair
silver and enamel
Birmingham, 1901
6 in (15.2 cm) high
London (Belgravia), 25 IX 1981, 266
£495 ($886)

1509 Covered jug
Birmingham, 1901
9½ in (24.5 cm) high
London (Belgravia), 30–31 III 1977, 82
£374 ($635)

1506 Vase
silver and enamel
Birmingham, 1902
Design attributed to Archibald Knox
10 in (25.7 cm) high
London (Belgravia), 28 IV 1983, 67
£2,420 ($3,872)

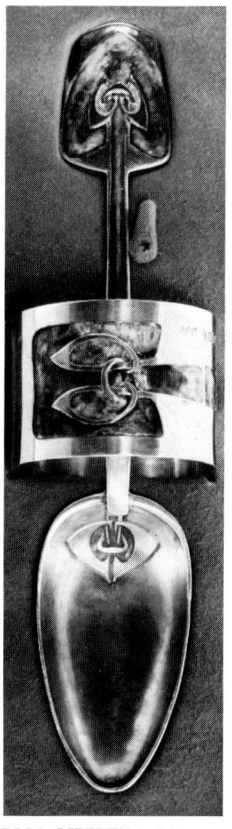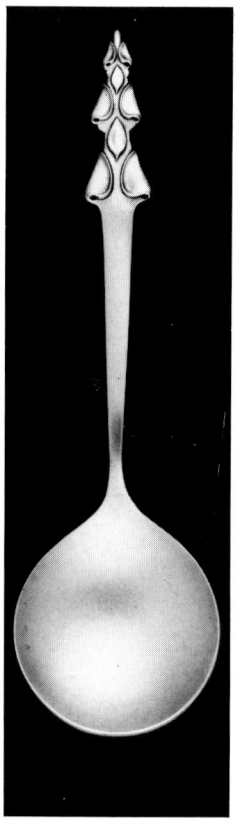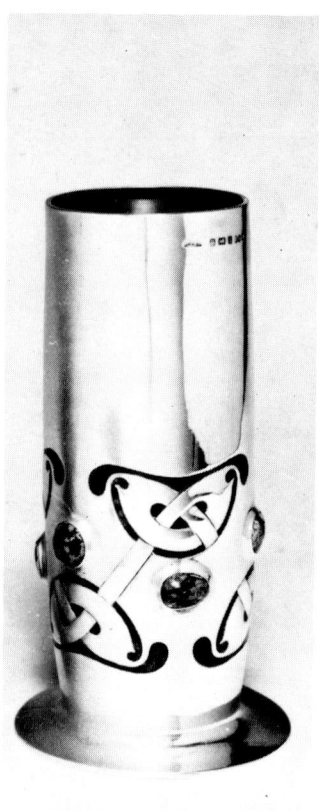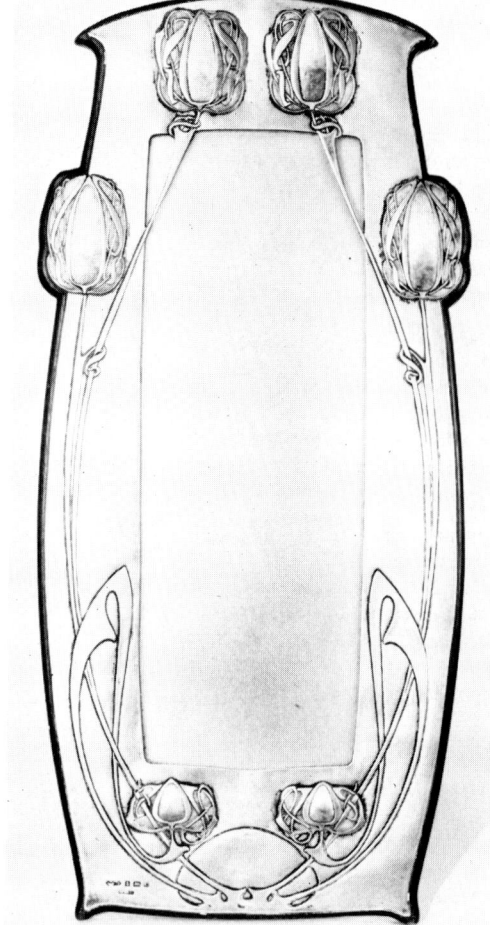

1510 LIBERTY & CO   1511 LIBERTY & CO   1512 LIBERTY & CO   1513 LIBERTY & CO

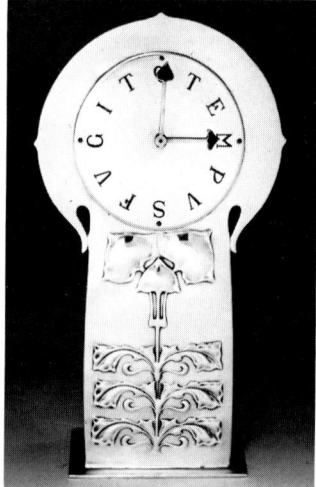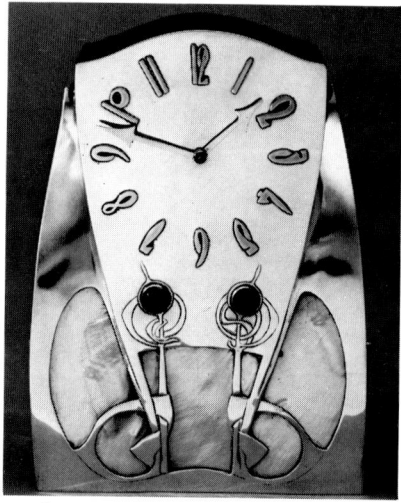

1514 LIBERTY & CO   1515 LIBERTY & CO   1516 LIBERTY & CO

1510 Napkin ring and spoon
silver and enamel
Birmingham, 1902
Designer: Archibald Knox
Stamped: Cymric
7½ in (19 cm) overall
London (Belgravia), 25 IV 1979, 69
£550 ($1,127)

1511 Serving spoons
London, 1899
8 in (20 cm) overall
London (Belgravia), 30 IV 1981, 54
£132 ($273)

1512 Vase
silver and enamel
Birmingham, 1904
Design attributed to Archibald Knox
Stamped: Cymric Rd.
No.369138 no.244
7½ in (19 cm) high
London (Belgravia), 5 XII 1980, 67
£4,180 ($8,652)

1513 Mirror Frame
Silver and enamel
Birmingham, 1902
Design attributed to Archibald Knox
18¾ in (47.5 cm) high
London (Belgravia), 13 III 1975, 35
£2,400 ($5,520)

1514 Clock
silver and enamel
Birmingham, 1903
Stamped: Cymric
10 in (25.7 cm) high
London (Belgravia), 22 IV 1982, 211
£2,640 ($4,275)

1515 Clock
Birmingham, 1903
Stamped: Cymric
Design attributed to Rex Silver
10 in (25.7 cm) high
See catalogue of exhibition,
'Liberty's 1875–1975',
cat. no. D99B
London (Belgravia), 1 IV 1976, 127
£935 ($1,870)

1516 Clock
silver, mother-of-pearl and lapis lazuli
Birmingham, 1903
Stamped: Cymric 5191
London, 30 XI 1983, 53
£6,050 ($8,409)

1517 Spoons, six
silver and enamel
Birmingham, 1903
London (Belgravia), 20 XI 1974, 28
£250 ($575)

1518 Vase
silver and enamel
Birmingham, 1903
Stamped: Cymric
8¼ in (20.6 cm) high
London (Belgravia), 12 VII 1978, 158
£374 ($692)

Gilbert Marks
London, born 1861, active from late 1880s for Johnson, Walker and Tolhurst, entered mark 1897, died 1905

1519 Goblet
London, 1896
Signed: Gilbert Marks –97–
13 in (33 cm) high
32 oz 16 dwt (1,020 gr)
London (Belgravia), 6 XI 1975, 189
£275 ($550)

1520 Rose bowl
London, 1897
Engraved: Gilbert Marks 97
13 in (33.3 cm) diameter
67 oz 18 dwt (2,017 gr)
London (Belgravia), 15 XII 1977, 224
£935 ($1,730)

1521 Rose bowl
silver-gilt
London, 1897
Signed: Gilbert Marks 97
12½ in (31.7 cm) overall
45 oz 9 dwt (1,413 gr)
London (Belgravia), 10 X 1974, 152
£380 ($874)

1522 Flower vase
silver, Britannia Standard
London, 1898
Engraved: Gilbert Marks 1898
10½ in (26.7 cm) high
46 oz 6 dwt (1,437 gr)
London (Belgravia), 29 IX 1977, 274
£990 ($1,831)

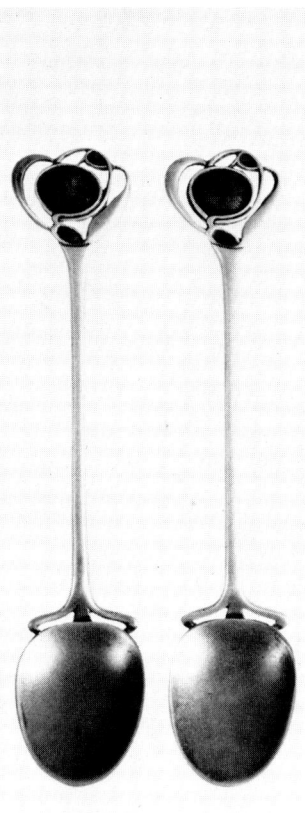

1517 LIBERTY & CO

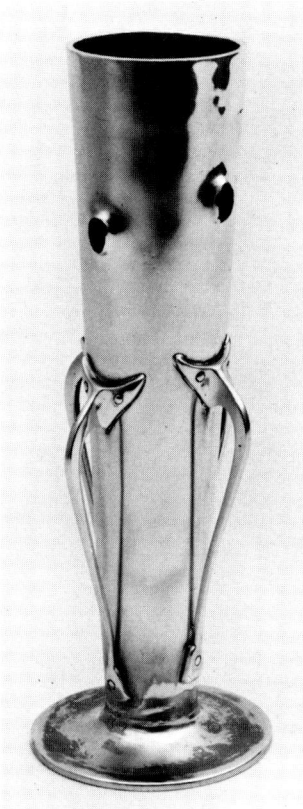

1518 LIBERTY & CO

1519 MARKS

1520 MARKS

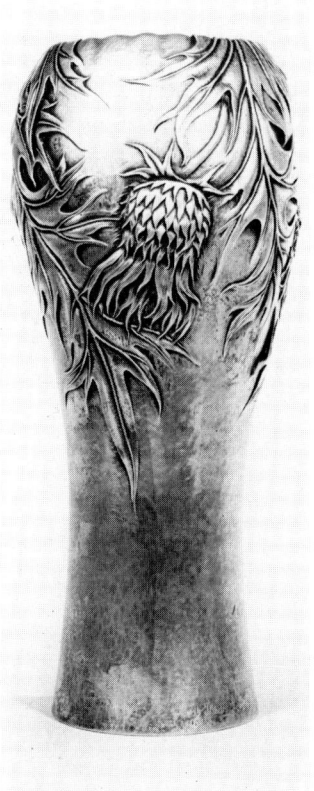

1522 MARKS

1521 MARKS

320 GREAT BRITAIN IRELAND

1523 MARKS

1524 MOVIO

1523 Vases, four
London, 1897
Stamped: Gilbert Marks 97
8¼ in (20.8 cm) high
35 oz 6 dwt (1,097 gr)
London (Belgravia), 19 VI 1975, 242
£440 ($1,012)

Latino Movio
London; specialist chaser, closely connected with Holland, Aldwinckle and Slater, whose retail clients included Johnson, Walker and Tolhurst; active c. 1894–1915, believed to have been associated with Gilbert Marks

1524 Rose bowl
London, 1904
Mark of W. Walker and B. Tolhurst
Engraved: Johnson Walker & Tolhurst Ltd 172 New Bond St. W
Signed: L. Movio 1904
10 in (25.5 cm) high
75 oz 19 dwt (2,357 gr)
London (Belgravia), 28 IX 1978, 76
£935 ($1,916)

1525 Sideboard dish
silver, Britannia Standard
London, 1907
Mark of Holland, Aldwinckle and Slater
Signed: L. Movio
22½ in (57.1 cm) diameter
136 oz 17 dwt (4,256 gr)
London (Belgravia), 12 IX 1974, 204
£780 ($1,794)

Goldsmiths and Silversmiths Company Ltd
London; established 1890, became a public company 1898, bought by Garrards 1952. See Hughes, *Modern Silver*

1526 Jug
London, 1901
20½ in (51.5 cm) high
London (Belgravia), 3 XI 1971, 10
£180 ($450)

1527 Bacon dish and stand
London, 1918
10¼ in (26.1 cm) overall
76 oz 6 dwt (2,373 gr)
London (Belgravia), 10 I 1980, 278
£935 ($2,197)

William Comyns and Sons
London; founded 1848 by William Comyns and continued by his sons until 1953 when bought by Bernard Copping. See Hughes, *Modern Silver*
Mark Jackson, p.235

1528 Coffee pot and hot milk jug
London, 1910/12
9¾ in (24.5 cm) high
45 oz 10 dwt (1,417 gr)
London (Belgravia), 18 X 1979, 188
£682 ($1,602)

1525 MOVIO

1526 GOLDSMITHS & SILVERSMITHS CO LTD

R. and S. Garrard and Company

London; mark entered by Sebastian Garrard (son of James, see no.1315ff.) 1900. Firm acquired by the Goldsmiths and Silversmiths Company 1952.
Mark Jackson, p.235

1529 Treasury inkstand
silver-gilt
London, 1912
Stamped Garrard & Co. Ltd./ Calcutta & London
9¾ in (25 cm) wide
57 oz 2 dwt (1,778 gr)
London (Belgravia), 19 IV 1979, 213
£594 ($1,217)

1530 Caster
London, c. 1925
7 in (18 cm) high
11 oz 14 dwt (366 gr)
London (Belgravia), 11 XII 1980, 112
£126 ($260)

Charles Rennie Mackintosh

Born 1868, architect and designer, a leading figure of the 'Glasgow School', died 1928

1531 Two spoons and a fish knife
electroplated
(1912)
Stamped: Miss Cranston's
Made for the Chinese Room in the Ingram Street Tea Rooms
London (Belgravia), 15 II 1980, 45
£264 ($620)

Birmingham Guild of Handicraft

Birmingham; founded 1890 by Arthur Dixon (1856–1929), active as guild until 1910
Mark K.C. Jones, p.325

1532 Teapot
Birmingham, 1899
6 in (15.1 cm) high
16 oz 6 dwt (507 gr)
London (Belgravia), 25 IV 1979, 116
£143 ($293)

1527 GOLDSMITHS & SILVERSMITHS CO LTD

1528 WILLIAM COMYNS & SONS

1529 R. & S. GARRARD & CO

1530 R. & S. GARRARD & CO

1531 MACKINTOSH

1532 BIRMINGHAM GUILD OF HANDICRAFT

1533 RAMSDEN & CARR

1534 RAMSDEN

1535 RAMSDEN

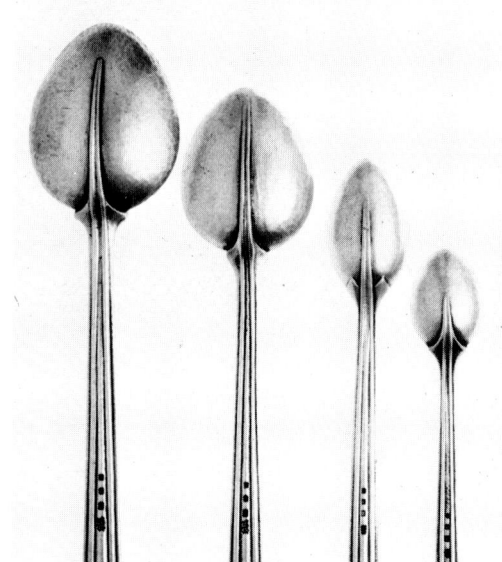

1536 RAMSDEN

Omar Ramsden and Alwyn Carr

See Omar Ramsden (below)

1533 Tea set
silver inset with cabochon chrysoprases
London, 1912–14
66 oz 18 dwt (2,080 gr) excluding tray
London, 18 XII 1975, 57
£1,550 ($3,100)

Omar Ramsden

London; born 1873, in partnership with Alwyn Carr (1872–1940) 1898–1919 (see above), then alone until his death 1939. Employed, among others, A.E. Ulyett as senior chaser and Henri de Konigh as enameller. See catalogue of exhibition, 'Omar Ramsden, 1873–1939'

1534 Claret jug
London, 1929
Engraved: Omar Ramsden me fecit
14¼ in (36.2 cm) high
London, 23 V 1974, 147
£800 ($1,920)

1535 Ladles, three
London, 1923
6¾ in (17 cm) and 8 in (20.5 cm) overall
London, 15 VII 1983, 116
£660 ($1,056)

1536 Table silver, forty-four pieces
London, 1926–38
54 oz 8 dwt (1,691 gr) excluding knives
London, 26 II 1976, 18
£748 ($1,346)

1537 Candelabra, pair
silver (loaded)
London, 1936
16 in (40.7 cm) high
London, 19 IV 1973, 98
£1,300 ($3,250)

1538 Table candlesticks, pair
London, 1937
5¼ in (13.3 cm) high
69 oz 4 dwt (2,152 gr)
London, 8 III 1973, 76
£700 ($1,750)

1539 Mazer
silver-mounted
London, 1939
Engraved: Omar Ramsden me fecit
11¾ in (29.8 cm) diameter
London (Belgravia), 25 IV 1979, 91
£682 ($1,391)

1537 RAMSDEN

1538 RAMSDEN

1539 RAMSDEN

1541 RAMSDEN

1540 RAMSDEN

1542 NAPPER & DAVENPORT

1540 Presentation casket
silver-gilt
London, 1926
Engraved: Omar Ramsden me fecit
9 in (23 cm) overall
London, 30 XI 1983, 47
£2,090 ($2,905)

1541 Hot milk jug
London, 1939
7¾ in (19.6 cm) high
London (Belgravia), 25 IV 1979, 83
£308 ($631)

Napper and Davenport

Birmingham; first mark entered 1908
Mark K.C. Jones, p.359

1542 Teapot
Birmingham, 1922
5¼ in (13.2 cm) high
Now in the Victoria and Albert Museum, London. This 'cube' design, more commonly seen in electroplate, was made by a number of manufacturers (see, for example, Sotheby's, 13 April 1984, lot 67).
London, 30 IX 1983, 79
£935 ($1,299)

Adie Brothers

Birmingham; founded 1879: Adie & Lovekin, registered 1907; Adie Brothers, later incorporated into British Silverware Ltd, closed 1968
Mark K.C. Jones, p.321

1543 Tea and coffee set
Birmingham, 1925
Designer: Harold Stabler
Stamped: Stabler
Reg. Applied For
46 oz 10 dwt (1,444 gr)
See Sotheby's, Belgravia, 24 February 1982, lot 280, for a set of the same design (London, 1938).
London (Belgravia), 30 IX 1976, 102
£341 ($580)

1544 Tazza
silver and ivory
Birmingham, 1930
5 in (12.5 cm) high
London (Belgravia), 12 VII 1978, 211
£286 ($529)

Viners Ltd

London and Sheffield; founded 1907, one of the largest manufacturers of plate and stainless steel. See Hughes, *Modern Silver*
Mark E.V. in a rectangle

1545 Tea and coffee set
London, 1934/Sheffield, 1939
London (Belgravia), 27 II 1981, 137
£154 ($318)

H.G. Murphy

London; born 1884, active from 1913, later Principal of Central School of Art and Crafts, died 1939.
Mark Catalogue of exhibition, 'Touching Gold and Silver', no.178

1546 Bowl and cover
London, 1935
7¾ in (19.5 cm) overall
21 oz 6 dwt (662 gr)
London (Belgravia), 11 IX 1975, 165
£115 ($230)

1543 ADIE BROTHERS

1545 VINERS LTD

1544 ADIE BROTHERS

1546 MURPHY

North America

1548 CONEY

John Coney
Boston; born 1655, active from 1676, died 1722
Mark Ensko, p.191

1547 Tablespoon
Boston, c. 1690
7½ in (18.7 cm) overall
New York, 12–13 IV 1977, 168
$3,200 (£1,882)

1548 Tankard
Boston, c. 1700
6¾ in (17 cm) high
23 oz (715 gr)
New York, 6–8 XI 1975, 607
$4,200 (£2,100)

John Edwards
Boston; born 1671 London, arrived Boston 1688, active from 1691, died 1746
Mark Ensko, p.192

1549 Porringer
Boston, c. 1690–1710
7½ in (19 cm) overall
7 oz 5 dwt (225 gr)
New York, 19–22 XI 1980, 194
$3,960 (£1,913)

1550 Spoon
Boston, c. 1713
7½ in (18.8 cm) overall
New York, 30 VI 1982, 228
$990 (£553)

1551 Tankard
Boston, c. 1730
8 in (20.5 cm) high
26 oz 10 dwt (824 gr)
New York, 19–22 XI 1980, 193
$4,675 (£2,258)

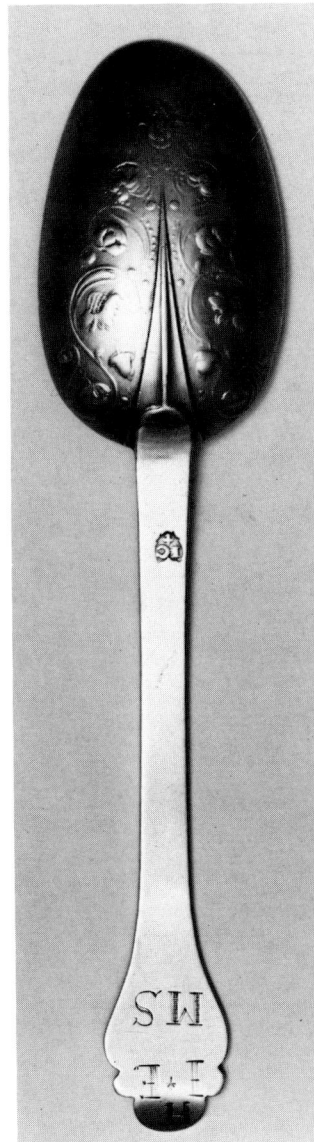
1547 CONEY

1549 J. EDWARDS

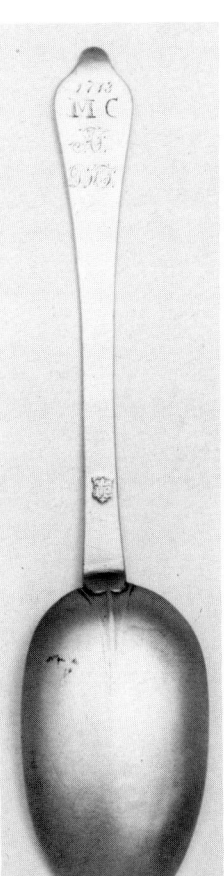
1550 J. EDWARDS

1551 J. EDWARDS

1552 J. BURT
1553 SOUMAINE
1554 SOUMAINE
1555 EYCK
1556 BOELEN
1557 BOELEN
1558 HURD
1559 HURD

John Burt
Boston; born 1691, active from 1712, died 1745
Mark Ensko, p.190

1552 Porringer
Boston, c. 1720
5 in (13 cm) diameter
8 oz (248 gr)
New York, 27 IV 1976, 122
$1,700 (£944)

Simeon Soumaine
New York; born 1685 in London, active from 1706, died 1750
Mark Ensko, p.235

1553 Kitchen pepper (dredger)
New York, c. 1730
3 in (7.6 cm) high
3 oz 10 dwt (108 gr)
New York, 27 IV 1976, 123
$1,500 (£833)

1554 Tankard
New York, c. 1720
7 in (17.8 cm) high
28 oz 18 dwt (898 gr)
London, 1 XI 1951, 119
£320 ($896)

Koenraet Ten Eyck
Albany, N.Y.; born 1678, apprenticed to Jacob Boelen, active from 1703, died 1753. He was a general merchant as well as a goldsmith
Mark Ensko, p.214

1555 Trencher salt
Albany, New York, c. 1710
3½ in (8.9 cm) diameter
2 oz 15 dwt (85 gr)
New York, 27–29 I 1983, 135
$28,600 (£17,875)

Henricus Boelen
New York; baptized 1697, son of Jacob Boelen (died 1729), whose business he continued; died 1755
Mark Ensko, p.184

1556 Bowl
New York, c. 1690
4¼ in (10.8 cm) diameter
2 oz 10 dwt (77 gr)
New York, 30 VI / 1 VII 1982, 236
$17,600 (£9,832)

1557 Tankard
New York, c. 1720
6½ in (16.5 cm) high
28 oz (870 gr)
New York, 21 III 1975, 80
$7,500 (£3,260)

1560 HURD

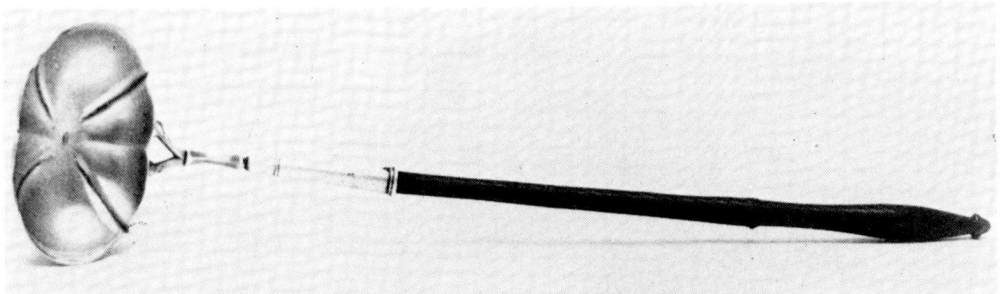

1561 HURD

Jacob Hurd
Boston; born 1702, active 1723–55, died 1758. See French, *Jacob Hurd and his Sons*
Mark Ensko, p.194

1558 Brazier
Boston, c. 1730
6 in (15.5 cm) diameter
17 oz (528 gr)
New York, 30 VI 1982, 231
$12,650 (£7,067)

1559 Tankard
Boston, c. 1730
7½ in (19 cm) high
25 oz (777 gr)
London, 26 II 1976, 75
£4,180 ($7,524)

1560 Dredger
Boston, c. 1730
3½ in (8.9 cm) high
2 oz 6 dwt (71 gr)
New York, 17 X 1972, 112
$1,950 (£780)

1561 Toddy ladle
Boston, c. 1740
16 in (40.6 cm) overall
New York, 6–8 XI 1975, 611
$2,600 (£1,300)

1562 Coffee pot
Boston, c. 1730–40
11 in (27.7 cm) high
39 oz 4 dwt (1,219 gr)
Inscribed: From a Friend to the Reverend Doctor Saml. Stillman
New York, 27–29 I 1983, 134
$44,000 (£27,500)

1563 Mug
Boston, c. 1750
5 in (13 cm) high
12 oz 5 dwt (380 gr)
New York, 1–4 II 1978, 667
$2,300 (£1,243)

1564 Pap boat
Boston, c. 1746
5¾ in (14.6 cm) overall
2 oz 5 dwt (70 gr)
New York, 28 III 1973, 140
$1,100 (£440)

1562 HURD

1563 HURD

1564 HURD

1565 J. RICHARDSON

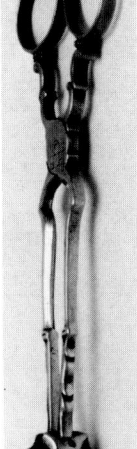

1566 J. RICHARDSON

Joseph Richardson
Philadelphia; born 1711, active from 1732, died 1784
Mark Ensko, p.197

1565 Sugar bowl and cover
Philadelphia, c. 1736
scratch weight 11:9
4½ in (11.4 cm) wide
11 oz 5 dwt (350 gr)
Initials: Oswald and Lydia Peel of Lancaster, Pa.
The order for this bowl is recorded in Richardson's account book for 1736, the cost being £5 3s for silver and £2 5s for making.
New York, 19–22 XI 1980, 189
$37,400 (£18,067)

1566 Sugar nips, pair
Philadelphia, c. 1750
1 oz (31 gr)
New York, 30 IV 1980, 171
$825 (£350)

1567 VAN DYCK

1570 MYERS

Peter van Dyck
New York; born 1684, apprenticed to Bartholomew Le Roux, whose daughter he married; died 1751
Mark Ensko, p.226

1567 Teapot
New York, c. 1720–40
7½ in (19 cm) high
22 oz (684 gr)
New York, 1–4 II 1978, 669
$47,000 (£25,405)

1568 VAN DYKE

Richard van Dyke
New York; born 1717, active from 1750, died 1770
Mark Ensko, p.227

1568 Bowl
New York, c. 1750
8¾ in (22.6 cm) diameter
26 oz 10 dwt (824 gr)
New York, 29 X 1977, 460
$16,000 (£8,648)

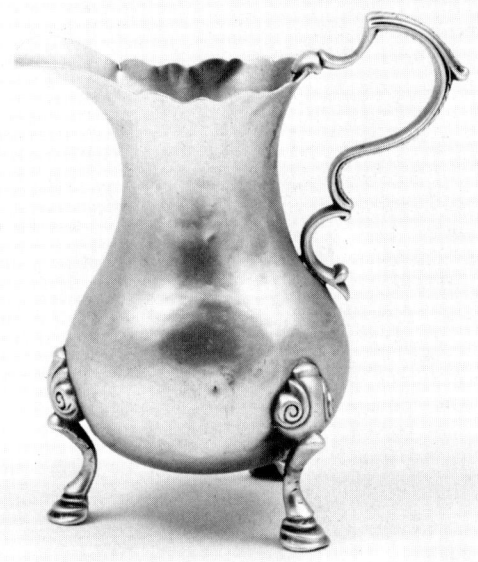
1571 MYERS

John Coburn
Boston; born 1725, active from 1750, died 1803
Mark Ensko, p.203

1569 Tankard
Boston, c. 1760
9 in (22.8 cm) high
31 oz 10 dwt (980 gr)
New York, 27–29 I 1983, 127
$9,350 (£5,843)

1569 COBURN

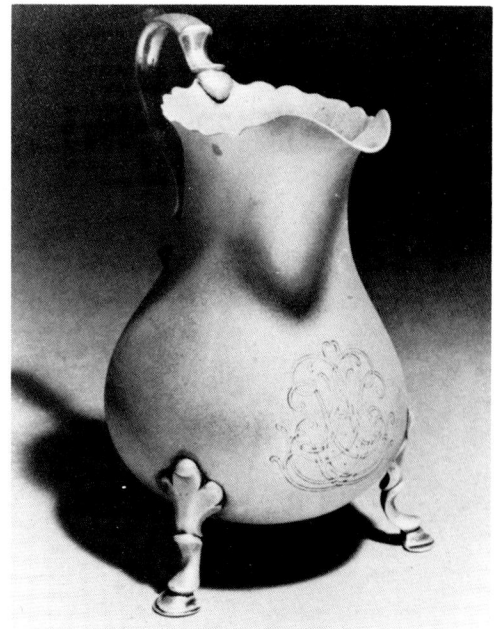
1572 MYERS

Myer Myers
New York; born 1723, active from 1745, died 1795
Mark Ensko, p.220

1570 Teapot
New York, c. 1750–60
7¼ in (18.4 cm) high
21 oz 10 dwt (668 gr)
New York, 27–30 I 1982, 197B
$63,250 (£35,335)

1571 Cream jug
New York, c. 1750–60
4½ in (11.4 cm) high
4 oz 10 dwt (140 gr)
New York, 27–29 I 1983, 131
$4,180 (£2,612)

1572 Milk jug
New York, c. 1760
Scratch weight: 7 oz
5¼ in (13.4 cm) high
6 oz 10 dwt (202 gr)
New York, 28 III 1973, 142
$3,800 (£1,520)

1573 Covered jug
New York, c. 1765
11¾ in (30 cm) high
52 oz 10 dwt (1,632 gr)
New York, 19–22 XI 1980, 179
$16,500 (£7,970)

1574 Sugar bowl
New York, c. 1770
4¼ in (10.8 cm) high
8 oz 10 dwt (264 gr)
New York, 31 I 1980, 531
$8,250 (£3,510)

1575 Teapot
New York, c. 1770
6 in (15.5 cm) high
19 oz (590 gr)
New York, 17–19 XI 1977, 414
$7,500 (£4,054)

1576 Buckle
gold
New York, c. 1765
2¼ in (5.9 cm) overall
New York, 14 VII 1981, 508
$11,000 (£5,314)

1577 Soup ladle
New York, c. 1780
14¼ in (36.2 cm) overall
New York, 30 VI 1982, 234
$4,950 (£2,765)

Philip Syng, Jr
Philadelphia; born 1703 in Cork, emigrated 1714, active from 1726, died 1789. See Honour, *Goldsmiths and Silversmiths*
Mark Ensko, p.226

1578 Mug
Philadelphia, c. 1760
4¾ in (12 cm) high
11 oz 10 dwt (357 gr)
New York, 30 IV 1980, 190
$990 (£421)

1573 MYERS

1574 MYERS

1575 MYERS

1576 MYERS

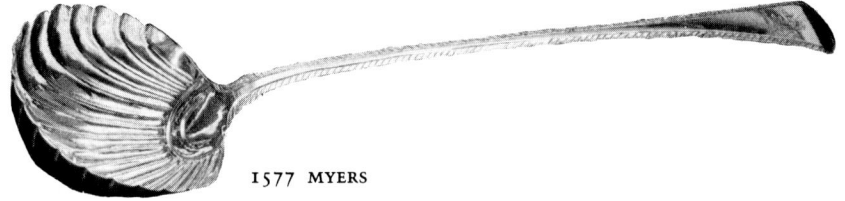

1577 MYERS

1578 P. SYNG, JR

1579 P. SYNG, JR

1579 Salt cellars, pair
Philadelphia, c. 1760
2½ in (6.7 cm) diameter
5 oz 10 dwt (171 gr)
New York, 18–19 VI 1974, 199
$1,900 (£791)

1580 Tankard
Philadelphia, c. 1770
7½ in (19 cm) high
33 oz 10 dwt (1,041 gr)
New York, 1–4 II 1978, 684
$13,500 (£7,297)

Benjamin Burt
Boston; born 1729, died 1805
Mark Ensko, p.160

1581 Tankard
Boston, c. 1780
7¾ in (19.6 cm) high
22 oz (684 gr)
New York, 1–4 II 1978, 666
$2,000 (£1,081)

1582 Porringer
Boston, c. 1750
5½ in (14 cm) diameter
8 oz 4 dwt (255 gr)
New York, 27–30 I 1982, 205
$2,640 (£1,475)

1583 Porringer
Boston, c. 1770
5½ in (14 cm) diameter
8 oz 5 dwt (256 gr)
New York, 25–26 IV 1975, 337
$1,900 (£826)

1584 Mug
Boston, c. 1780
6 in (15 cm) high
15 oz (466 gr)
New York, 15 XI 1974, 1024
$1,800 (£782)

Daniel Christian Fueter
New York; born Berne 1720, mark entered in London 1753, active New York 1754–79, died Berne 1785
Mark Ensko, p.167; Grimwade, 453

1585 Teapot
New York, c. 1755
7¼ in (18.2 cm) high
20 oz 10 dwt (637 gr)
New York, 19–22 XI 1980, 192
$27,500 (£13,285)

Daniel Henchman
Boston; born 1730, active from 1753, died 1775
Mark Ensko, p.168

1586 Teapot
Boston, c. 1760
6¼ in (15.9 cm) high
20 oz 4 dwt (628 gr)
New York, 27–30 I 1982, 207
$8,800 (£4,916)

1580 P. SYNG, JR

1581 B. BURT

1582 B. BURT

1583 B. BURT

1584 B. BURT

1585 FUETER

Thomas Hammersley
New York; born 1727, active from 1756
Mark Ensko, p.240

1587 Teapot
New York, c. 1760
16⅜ in (16.2 cm) high
18 oz 12 dwt (578 gr)
New York, 30 VI –1 VII 1982, 225
$9,350 (£5,223)

Paul Revere
Boston; born 1734, active from 1757, died 1818. Famous for his activities during the War of Independence and his 'ride' to New York and Philadelphia. See E. Forbes, *Paul Revere and the World he lived in*, 1942; Honour, *Goldsmiths and Silversmiths*
Mark Ensko, p.227

1588 Porringer
Boston, c. 1760–70
8 in (20.5 cm) overall
7 oz (217 gr)
New York, 30 IV 1980, 193
$9,625 (£4,095)

1586 HENCHMAN

1587 HAMMERSLEY

1588 REVERE

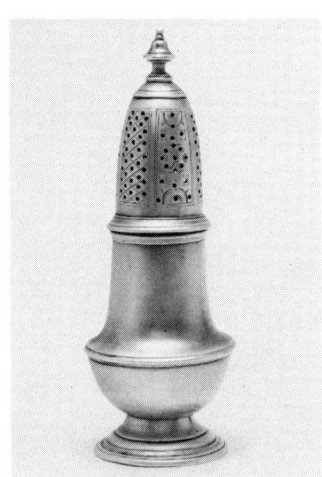

1589 REVERE

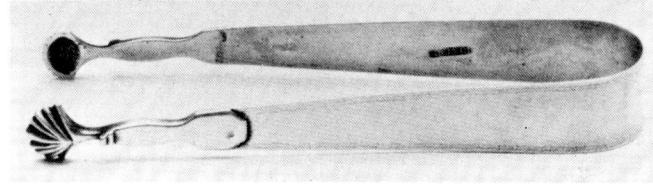

1591 REVERE

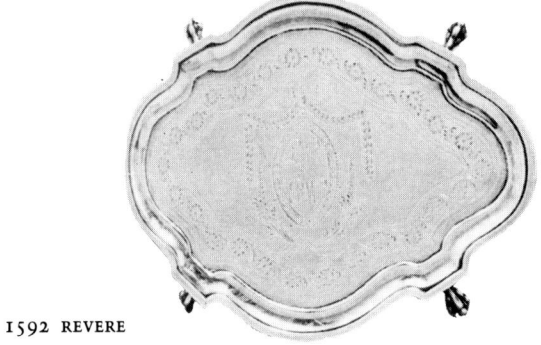

1592 REVERE

1590 REVERE

1589 Caster
Boston, c. 1770
5¼ in (13.7 cm) high
4 oz (124 gr)
New York, 17–19 XI 1977, 411
$5,000 (£2,702)

1590 Coffee pot
Boston, c. 1775
12¼ in (31.2 cm) high
42 oz 10 dwt (1,321 gr)
New York, 30 IV 1980, 184
$70,400 (£29,957)

1591 Sugar tongs
Boston, c. 1795
5¾ in (14.5 cm) overall
1 oz 15 dwt (54 gr)
New York, 1–4 II 1978, 685
$2,300 (£1,243)

1592 Teapot and stand
Boston, 1786
6 in (15 cm) high
New York, 18–20 XI 1976, 608
$37,000 (£21,764)

1593 REVERE   1594 REVERE

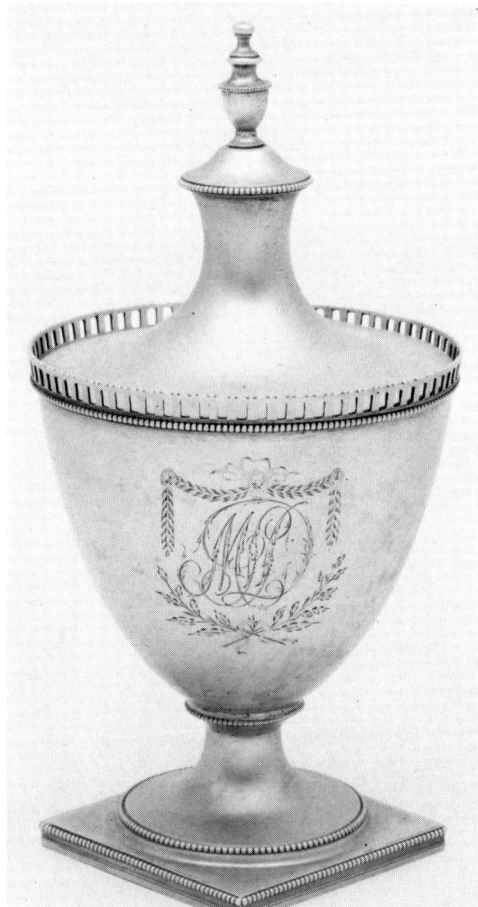

1595 DUBOIS   1596 J. RICHARDSON, JR

1593 Tankard
Boston, c. 1770
Scratch weight 29.16
8½ in (21.5 cm) high
29 oz 10 dwt (917 gr)
New York, 27 IV 1976, 127
$45,000 (£25,000)

1594 Coffee pot
Boston, c. 1795
Unmarked
13¼ in (33.7 cm) high
34 oz (1,057 gr)
Recorded in the daybook for 11
December 1795: cost £9 making,
£3 12s engraving, 6d wood
handle
New York, 28 III 1973, 160
$11,000 (£4,400)

Abraham Dubois
Philadelphia; active 1777–
c. 1807
Mark Ensko, p.151

1595 Sugar vase
Philadelphia, c. 1790
8¾ in (22.3 cm) high
14 oz (435 gr)
New York, 15 VII 1980, 338
$1,760 (£748)

Joseph Richardson, Jr
Philadelphia; born 1752, son of
Joseph Richardson (see above,
nos 1565, 1566); active 1773–
1810, continuing his father's
business; died 1831
Mark Ensko, p.197

1596 Sugar vase
Philadelphia, c. 1795
10 in (25.4 cm) high
16 oz 8 dwt (510 gr)
New York, 14 VII 1981, 505
$2,860 (£1,381)

1597 Milk jug
Philadelphia, c. 1800
4¾ in (12 cm) high
40 oz 10 dwt (1,259 gr)
New York, 14–15 VI 1978, 704
$800 (£432)

Joseph Lownes
Philadelphia; active from 1780
Mark Ensko, p.195

1598 Mug
Philadelphia, c. 1790
7 in (17.8 cm) high
33 oz 10 dwt (1,041 gr)
New York, 31 I 1980, 574
$7,700 (£3,276)

1599 Saucepan
Philadelphia, c. 1810
4¼ in (10.8 cm) diameter
6 oz 10 dwt (202 gr)
New York, 27–29 I 1983, 113
$2,750 (£1,718)

Joseph Anthony, Jr
Philadelphia; born 1762 in
Newport, R.I., active from 1783,
died 1814
Mark Ensko, p.189

1600 Coffee pot
Philadelphia, c. 1785
14 in (35.9 cm) high
50 oz (1,555 gr)
New York, 27–30 I 1982, 203
$20,900 (£11,675)

John Vernon
New York, active from 1787
Mark Ensko, p.199

1601 Mugs, pair
New York, c. 1790
5¼ in (13.2 cm) high
26 oz (808 gr)
New York, 17–19 XI 1977, 286
$3,250 (£1,756)

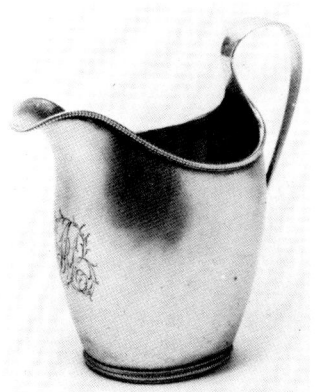
1597 J. RICHARDSON, JR

1598 J. LOWNES

1602 AIKEN

1599 J. LOWNES

1603 SAYRE

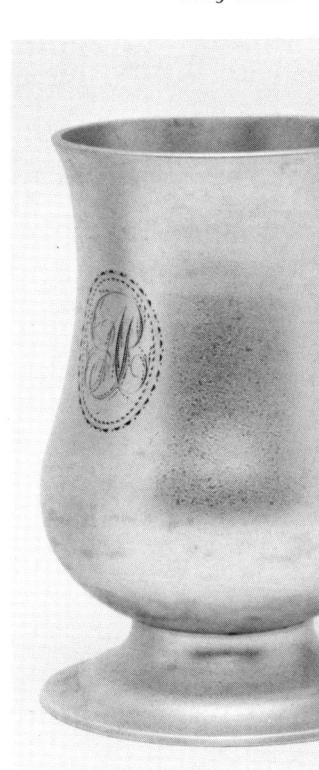
1600 ANTHONY

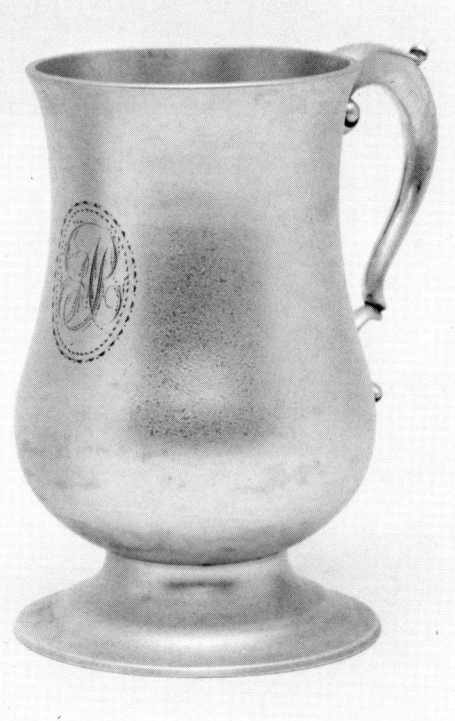
1601 VERNON

George Aiken
Baltimore; born 1765, active from 1787, died 1832
Mark Ensko, p.178

1602 Sugar bowl and cover
Baltimore, c. 1800
5½ in (13.9 cm) high
12 oz 15 dwt (396 gr)
New York, 27–29 XI 1979, 380
$1,045 (£444)

John Sayre
New York; born 1771, active c. 1792–1824, died 1852
Mark Ensko, p.198

1603 Tray
New York, c. 1795
30¾ in (78.2 cm) overall
130 oz (4,043 gr)
New York, 31 I 1980, 576
$22,000 (£9,361)

1604 SAYRE

1604 Tea set
New York, c. 1800
54 oz 10 dwt (1,694 gr)
New York, 19–22 XI 1980, 163
$4,950 (£2,391)

James Musgrave
Philadelphia; initially in partnership as Parry and Musgrave, active on own account from c. 1795
Mark Ensko, p.219

1605 Tea and coffee set, five pieces
Philadelphia, c. 1795
103 oz 10 dwt (3,218 gr)
New York, 30 VI–1 VII 1982, 214
$16,500 (£9,217)

John Targee
New York; active from c. 1797
Mark Ensko, p.199

1606 Cake baskets, pair
New York, c. 1810
13 in (33 cm) overall
52 oz 10 dwt (1,632 gr)
New York, 19–22 XI 1980, 160
$5,500 (£2,657)

John W. Forbes
New York; active from 1802

1607 Beakers, pair
New York, c. 1820
4¼ in (10.6 cm) high
8 oz 6 dwt (258 gr)
New York, 27–30 I 1982, 194A
$880 (£491)

1605 MUSGRAVE

Thomas Fletcher and Sidney Gardiner
Philadelphia; in partnership c. 1809–22
Mark Ensko, p.176

1608 Teapot and milk jug
Philadelphia, c. 1814
49 oz 8 dwt (1,536 gr)
New York, 30 VI 1982, 204
$660 (£368)

1609 Tea and coffee set
Philadelphia, c. 1820
168 oz (5,224 gr)
New York, 28 XI 1979, 373
$4,840 (£2,059)

1610 Cake basket
Philadelphia, c. 1820
16¼ in (41.2 cm) overall
44 oz 10 dwt (1,383 gr)
New York, 15 VII 1980, 323
$2,750 (£1,170)

1606 TARGEE

1607 J. W. FORBES

1608 FLETCHER & GARDINER

1609 FLETCHER & GARDINER

1610 FLETCHER & GARDINER

1611 FLETCHER

1612 THOMPSON

Thomas Fletcher

Philadelphia; active until 1850
(see above)
Mark Ensko, p.240

1611 Sauceboat and stand
Philadelphia, c. 1830
11 in (28 cm) overall
41 oz (1,275 gr)
New York, 18–20 XI 1976, 586
$2,500 (£1,470)

William Thompson

New York; active from c. 1810
Mark Ensko, p.251

1612 Milk jug
New York, c. 1825
7 in (17.9 cm) high
20 oz (622 gr)
New York, 28 XI 1979, 367
$550 (£234)

1613 ERWIN

1614 E. LOWNES

Henry Erwin
Philadelphia; active from 1817
Mark Ensko, p.184

1613 Cream jug and sugar bowl
Philadelphia, c. 1825
7½ in (18.1 cm) and 9 in (22.9 cm) high
34 oz (1,057 gr)
New York, 17–19 XI 1977, 367
$450 (£243)

Edward Lownes
Philadelphia; active from 1817, died 1834
Mark Ensko, p.174

1614 Milk jug and sugar bowl
Philadelphia, c. 1820
8¼ in (21 cm) and 11 in (28 cm) high
49 oz 15 dwt (1,547 gr)
New York, 17–19 XI 1977, 315
$425 (£230)

Ebenezer Cole
New York, active from 1818
Mark Ensko, p.172

1615 Tea set
New York, c. 1820
40 oz 10 dwt (1,259 gr)
New York, 26 I 1977, 319
$700 (£411)

1615 COLE

1616 KIRK   1617 KIRK

1618 KIRK

1619 EOFF & SHEPHERD

1620 BOYCE & JONES

1621 BOYCE & JONES

Samuel Kirk

Baltimore; born 1793, active from 1815, in partnership as Kirk and Smith until 1821, with his son from 1846 as S. Kirk and Sons, died 1872
Mark Ensko, p.214

1616 Hot water jug
Baltimore, c. 1850
8¼ in (21 cm) high
17 oz (528 gr)
New York, 17–19 XI 1977, 338
$600 (£324)

1617 Mug
Baltimore, 1828
4 in (10.2 cm) high
8 oz (248 gr)
New York, 17–19 XI 1977, 337
$550 (£297)

1618 Wine ewer
Baltimore, c. 1830
12½ in (32 cm) high
57 oz 4 dwt (1,778 gr)
New York, 14 VII 1981, 449
$4,400 (£2,125)

Eoff and Shepherd

New York; active from c. 1825
Mark Ensko, p.175

1619 Sweetmeat basket and milk jug
New York, mid-19th century
22 oz (684 gr)
New York, 1–4 II 1978, 613
$500 (£270)

Gerardus Boyce and William Jones

New York; in partnership from 1825
Mark Ensko, pp.158, 178

1620 Tea set
New York, c. 1830
70 oz (2,177 gr)
New York, 17–19 XI 1977, 350
$1,200 (£648)

1621 Tea set
New York, c. 1840
158 oz 5 dwt (4,921 gr)
New York, 17–19 XI 1977, 287
$1,900 (£1,027)

1622 W. GALE & SON

1623 GELSTON & TREADWELL

1624 BALL, TOMPKINS & BLACK

William Gale and Son

New York; in partnership from c. 1821 to 1823, firm became Gale and North in 1860s, later Dominick and Haff (purchased by Reed and Barton 1928)
Mark Ensko, p.246; Rainwater, pp.53–4

1622 Ewer
New York, 1862
13¾ in (34.9 cm) high
24 oz (746 gr)
New York, 28 XI 1979, 359
$550 (£234)

Gelston and Treadwell

New York; George S. Gelston active from c. 1835, later Gelston, Ladd and Company
Mark Ensko, p.179

1623 Inkstand
New York, c. 1835
15 in (38.2 cm) overall
120 oz 10 dwt (3,747 gr)
The central bottle is a replacement and one cover is missing.
New York, 31 I 1980, 552
$4,125 (£1,755)

1626 BALL, TOMPKINS & BLACK

1625 BALL, TOMPKINS & BLACK

Ball, Tompkins and Black

New York; successors to I. Marquand in 1839; partners were Henry Ball, Erastus O. Tompkins and William Black until 1851. See below.
Mark Rainwater, p.9

1624 Tea set
New York, c. 1840
69 oz (2,145 gr)
New York, 19–22 XI 1980, 133
$1,320 (£637)

1625 Pitcher (ewer)
New York, c. 1845
Mark of W. Forbes
For Ball, Tompkins and Black
11½ in (29.3 cm) high
34 oz (1,057 gr)
New York, 19–22 XI 1980, 125
$1,320 (£637)

1626 Cake basket
New York, c. 1840
Mark of J.C. Moore
Retailed by Ball, Tompkins and Black
12 in (30.5 cm) diameter
46 oz (1,430 gr)
New York, 28 XI 1979, 346
$1,430 (£608)

1627 Tea and coffee set, with plated tray
New York, c. 1850
167 oz (5,193 gr)
New York, 27–30 I 1982, 179
$6,160 (£3,441)

Ball, Black and Company

New York; Henry Ball and William Black, 1851–76
Mark Rainwater, p.9

1628 Pitcher (ewer)
New York, c. 1850
14½ in (37 cm) high
31 oz 15 dwt (987 gr)
New York, 17–18 XI 1978, 338
$600 (£292)

1629 Porringer
New York, c. 1855
Made by W. Forbes
With milk jug and pap boat by Eoff and Shepherd
For Ball, Black and Company
7½ in (19 cm) overall
20 oz 10 dwt (637 gr)
New York, 30 IV 1980, 110
$825 (£350)

Theodore B. Starr

New York

1630 Pitcher
New York, c. 1885
6½ in (16.4 cm) high
22 oz (684 gr)
New York, 12–14 VI 1980, 842
$1,870 (£795)

1627 BALL, TOMPKINS & BLACK

1629 BALL, BLACK & CO

1628 BALL, BLACK & CO

1630 STARR

1631 Tea and coffee set, six-piece
New York, early 20th century
129 oz (4,012 gr)
New York, 19–22 XI 1980, 14
$4,400 (£2,125)

Black, Starr and Frost
New York; successors to Ball, Black and Company (see above) from 1876 until 1929, when the firm merged with the retail store of the Gorham Corporation
Mark Rainwater, p.18

1632 Vase
New York, c. 1900
17¼ in (43.8 cm) high
64 oz (1,990 gr)
New York, 12–13 VI 1981, 190
$1,925 (£930)

Tiffany and Company
New York; founded by Charles Lewis Tiffany (1812–1902) in 1837 in partnership with John B. Young as a fancy goods store. Known as Tiffany and Company from 1853, began to manufacture silver 1868. On the death of the founder his son, Louis Comfort Tiffany (1848–1933), ran the firm and under his direction produced items in Art Nouveau taste including lamps and jewellery.
Mark Rainwater, p.181

1633 Wine jug
New York, c. 1866
Stamped: Tiffany & Co.
Mark of Gale & Willis (?)
13¼ in (33.6 cm) high
38 oz 6 dwt (1,191 gr)
London (Belgravia), 27 VI 1974, 312
£420 ($1,008)

1634 Vase
New York, 1880
8¼ in (21 cm) high
15 oz (466 gr)
New York, 12–13 VI 1981, 194
$1,210 ($584)

1635 Pitcher (ewer)
New York, c. 1885
7¾ in (19.5 cm) high
23 oz 16 dwt (738 gr)
London (Belgravia), 22 VII 1976, 262
£115 ($208)

1636 Pitcher (ewer)
New York, c. 1885
7 in (18.1 cm) high
25 oz 12 dwt (794 gr)
London (Belgravia), 23 II 1978, 372
£440 ($814)

1631 STARR

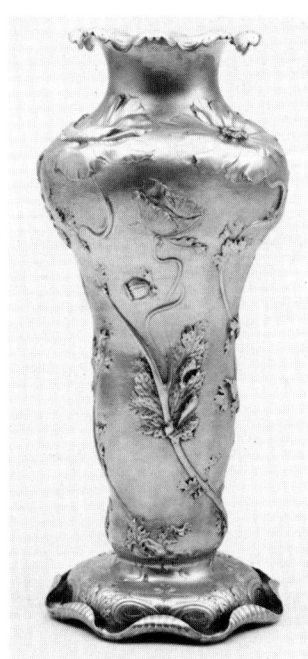
1632 BLACK, STARR & FROST

1633 TIFFANY & CO

1634 TIFFANY & CO

1635 TIFFANY & CO

1636 TIFFANY & CO

1637 TIFFANY & CO 1638 TIFFANY & CO

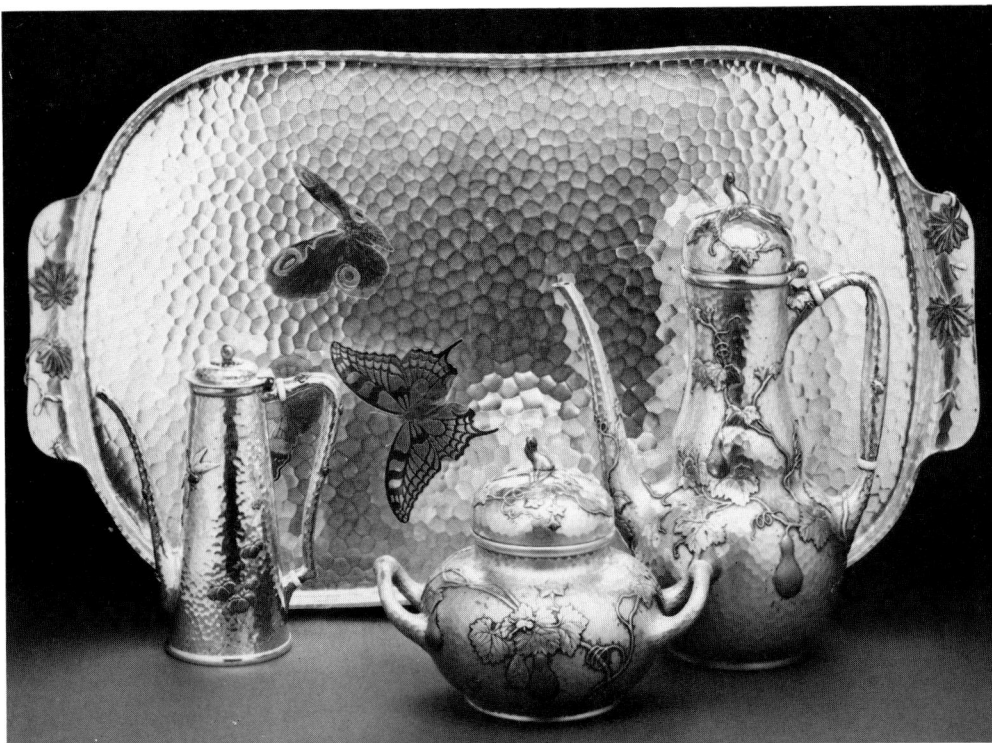

1639 1640 1641 1642 TIFFANY & CO

1643 TIFFANY & CO 1644 TIFFANY & CO

1637 Soup tureen
New York, c. 1880
13½ in (34.2 cm) overall
69 oz 5 dwt (2,153 gr)
New York, 28 XI 1979, 271
$2,530 (£1,076)

1638 Jardinière
New York, 1879–80
23¾ in (57.8 cm) overall
129 oz (4,012 gr)
New York, 27–29 I 1983, 63
$9,350 (£5,843)

1639 Coffee pot
New York, c. 1877
7 in (17.8 cm) high
11 oz (342 gr)
New York, 20–21 XI 1981, 327A
$1,870 (£1,044)

1640 Sugar bowl
New York, c. 1877
5½ in (14 cm) high
19 oz 4 dwt (597 gr)
New York, 20–21 XI 1981, 327
$2,860 (£1,597)

1641 Coffee pot
New York, c. 1877
11 in (28 cm) high
31 oz 8 dwt (976 gr)
New York, 20–21 XI 1981, 326
$4,840 (£2,704)

1642 Tray
New York, c. 1880
23 in (58.4 cm) wide
113 oz 16 dwt (3,539 gr)
New York, 20–21 XI 1981, 325
$7,700 (£4,301)

1643 Pitcher (ewer)
New York, c. 1875
8¾ in (22.5 cm) high
37 oz (1,150 gr)
New York 1–4 II 1978, 589
$850 (£459)

1644 Coffee pot
silver and enamel
New York, c. 1893
10 in (25.5 cm) high
19 oz 16 dwt (615 gr)
New York, 16–17 II 1983, 8
$4,235 (£2,646)

1645 TIFFANY & CO   1646 TIFFANY & CO

1647 TIFFANY & CO

1648 TIFFANY & CO

1649 TIFFANY & CO

1645 Punch bowl
New York, 1892
15 in (38.1 cm) diameter
261 oz 12 dwt (8,135 gr)
Exhibition: World's Columbian Exposition, Chicago, 1893.
New York, 21 V 1983, 13
$35,200 (£22,000)

1646 Tea kettle on lamp stand
New York, c. 1905
14 in (35.5 cm) high
69 oz (2,145 gr)
New York, 30 IV 1980, 13
$1,540 (£655)

1647 Centrepiece
New York, c. 1895
19 in (48.2 cm) diameter
121 oz 12 dwt (3,781 gr)
New York, 27–29 I 1983, 60
$6,600 (£4,125)

1648 Vase
New York, c. 1895
9½ in (24.1 cm) high
27 oz (839 gr)
London (Belgravia), 27 IV 1972, 66
£300 ($750)

1649 Vase
New York, c. 1900
8 in (20.3 cm) high
10 oz 12 dwt (329 gr)
London (Belgravia), 22 I 1976, 91
£137 ($247)

J.E. Caldwell and Company

Philadelphia; founded 1839
Mark Rainwater, p.26

1650 Tea and coffee set
Philadelphia, c. 1900
186 oz 16 dwt (5,809 gr)
New York, 20–21 XI 1981, 335
$6,600 (£3,687)

1651 Dessert dishes, four
Philadelphia, c. 1895
10 in (25.5 cm)
66 oz 12 dwt (2,071 gr)
New York, 27–29 I 1983, 39
$1,320 (£825)

1652 Vase
Philadelphia, c. 1890
17½ in (44.5 cm) high
36 oz 12 dwt (1,138 gr)
New York, 14 VII 1981, 402A
$935 (£451)

1650 J. E. CALDWELL & CO

1651 J. E. CALDWELL & CO

1652 J. E. CALDWELL & CO

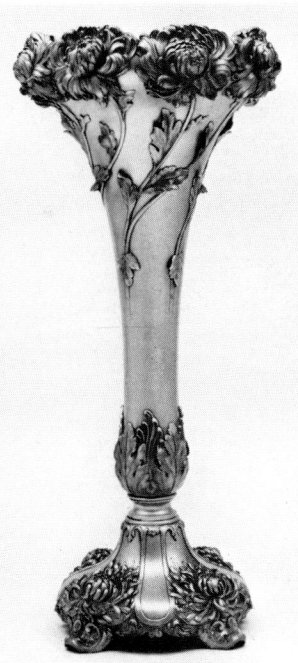

1653 WHITING MANUFACTURING CO

1654 WHITING MANUFACTURING CO

Whiting Manufacturing Company

New York; successor in 1866 to Tifft and Whiting, purchased by Gorham Corporation 1905
Mark Rainwater, p.199

1653 Vase
Providence, R.I., 1906
24½ in (62.2 cm) high
132 oz 12 dwt (4,123 gr)
New York, 21 V 1983, 32
$3,850 (£2,406)

1654 Bowl and a pair of servers
parcel-gilt and enamel
New York, c. 1890–1900
8 in (20.4 cm) diameter
23 oz 14 dwt (1,015 gr)
London (Belgravia), 15 XII 1977, 315
£352 ($651)

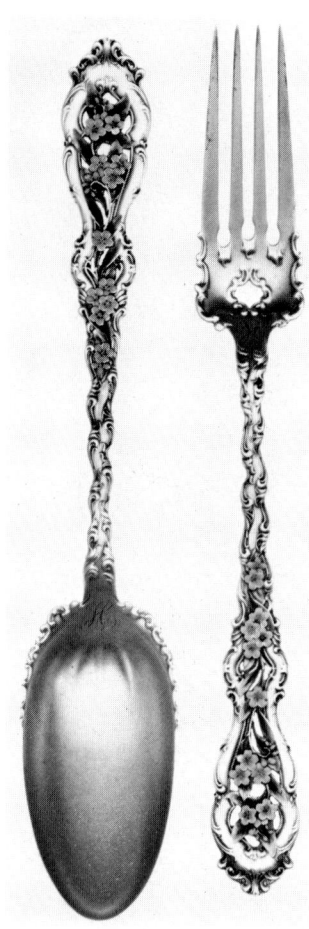

1655 WHITING MANUFACTURING CO

1655 Dessert servers, pair
silver-gilt and enamel
New York, c. 1895–1900
11 in (28 cm) overall
7 oz 6 dwt (226 gr)
London (Belgravia), 13 VII 1978, 164
£176 ($325)

1656 Pitcher
New York, c. 1880
7¼ in (18.4 cm) high
31 oz (964 gr)
New York, 20–21 XI 1981, 318
$5,280 (£2,950)

1657 Pitcher
silver and enamel
Newark, New Jersey, c. 1884
9½ in (24 cm) high
38 oz 15 dwt (1,205 gr)
New York, 21 III 1975, 98
$1,400 (£608)

1658 Desk set
New York, c. 1900
Inkstand: 18 in (45.7 cm) wide
205 oz 10 dwt (6,391 gr)
New York, 19 VI 1979, 107
$5,225 (£2,548)

1656 WHITING MANUFACTURING CO

1657 WHITING MANUFACTURING CO

1658 WHITING MANUFACTURING CO

1659 SIMPSON, HALL, MILLER & CO

1660 GORHAM MANUFACTURING CO

Simpson, Hall, Miller and Company

Wallingford, Conn.; founded by Samuel Simpson, manufacturing Britannia Metal, produced silver from 1895. Later joined the International Silver Company
Mark Rainwater, p.166

1659 Tea set
silver-gilt
Wallingford, Conn., c. 1900
52 oz 8 dwt (1,629 gr)
New York, 21 V 1983, 18
$2,200 (£1,375)

Gorham Manufacturing Company

Providence, R.I.; founded by Jabez Gorham (born 1792, retired 1847); known as Gorham and Company 1852–65, Gorham Manufacturing Company from 1865 until 1961, when it became Gorham Corporation. Their 'Art Nouveau' silver was sold under the name Martele.
Mark Rainwater, pp.59–61

1660 Claret jug
Providence, R.I., c. 1860
12½ in (31.7 cm) high
21 oz (653 gr)
New York, 30 IV 1980, 112
$1,100 (£468)

1661 Tea and coffee set, with tray
New York, c. 1865–71
Retailed by T. Kirkpatrick
435 oz 10 dwt (13,544 gr)
New York, 27–29 I 1983, 88
$12,100 (£7,562)

1661 GORHAM MANUFACTURING CO

1662 GORHAM MANUFACTURING CO

1662 Pitcher (ewer)
Providence, R.I., c. 1861
Retailed by Bigelow Brothers and Kennard
12½ in (31.7 cm) high
51 oz 5 dwt (1,593 gr)
New York, 28 XI 1979, 286
$1,540 (£655)

1663 GORHAM MANUFACTURING CO

1663 Coffee pot on lamp stand
Providence, R.I., 1869
15¾ in (40 cm) high
65 oz (2,021 gr)
New York, 19–22 XI 1980, 96
$2,420 (£1,169)

1664 Tea caddy
silver, gold and copper
Providence, R.I., c. 1878
3¾ in (9.5 cm) high
7 oz (217 gr)
New York, 4–5 II 1981, 188
$2,200 (£1,062)

1665 Cake basket
parcel-gilt
Providence, R.I., 1878
10¼ in (26 cm) wide
18 oz 10 dwt (575 gr)
New York, 30 IV 1980, 104
$550 (£234)

1666 Pitcher
Providence, R.I., 1905
9 in (23.2 cm) high
49 oz 5 dwt (1,531 gr)
New York, 31 X 1979, 19
$1,100 (£468)

1667 Hand mirror
Providence, R.I., c. 1900
Retailed by Bigelow, Kennard and Company
9½ in (24.1 cm) overall
New York, 16 VII 1982, 284
$1,320 (£737)

1668 Chafing dish
Providence, R.I., c. 1900
12 in (30.5 cm) high
154 oz (4,789 gr)
New York, 12–13 VI 1981, 188
$9,350 (£4,516)

1664 GORHAM MANUFACTURING CO

1665 GORHAM MANUFACTURING CO

1666 GORHAM MANUFACTURING CO

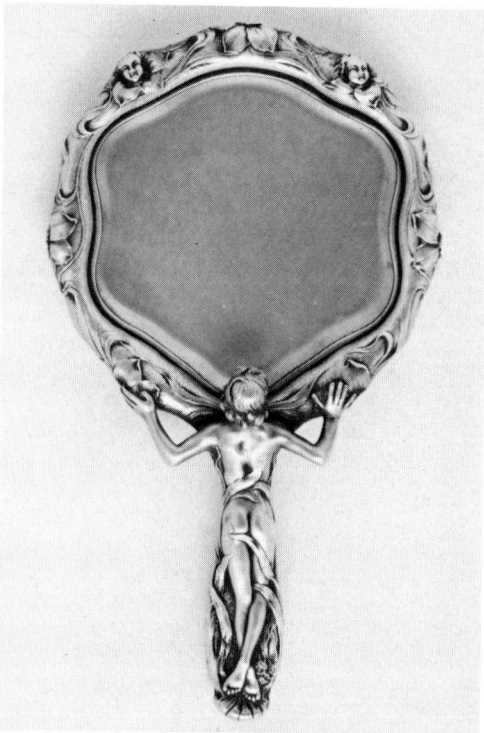

1667 GORHAM MANUFACTURING CO

1668 GORHAM MANUFACTURING CO

1669 GORHAM MANUFACTURING CO

1670 GORHAM MANUFACTURING CO

1671 GORHAM MANUFACTURING CO

1672 REED & BARTON

1669 Ewer and stand
Providence, R.I., c. 1900
15½ in (39.5 cm) high
98 oz 4 dwt (3,054 gr)
New York, 20–21 XI 1981, 336
$7,150 (£3,994)

1670 Sauceboat and stand
Providence, R.I., c. 1900
Stamped: Martele
Stand: 9½ in (24 cm) overall
29 oz 10 dwt (917 gr)
New York, 18–20 XI 1976, 561
$1,100 (£647)

1671 Wine cistern
Providence, R.I., c. 1900
24 in (61 cm) overall
400 oz (12,440 gr)
New York, 19–20 V 1982, 336
$30,800 (£17,206)

Reed and Barton

Taunton, Mass.; Henry Reed and Charles Barton continued the business of the Taunton Britannia Manufacturing Company (founded 1824); they were in partnership alone from 1840. The firm chiefly produced Britannia Metal and plated wares, silver from 1889. See Gibb, *The Whitesmiths of Taunton*, 1946
Mark Rainwater, p.138

1672 Tea set
Taunton, 1928
35 oz 12 dwt (1,107 gr)
New York, 21 V 1983, 76
$715 (£446)

France

Etienne Delaune
French engraver, born 1518/19, worked in Paris, Strasbourg and Augsburg, died 1583. See Hayward, *Virtuoso Goldsmiths*, p.180.

1673 Basin
silver-gilt
Unmarked
Last quarter of 16th century
20½ in (52 cm) diameter
123 oz 9 dwt (3,839 gr)
Most of the figures, embossed and chased in strapwork cartouches, are derived from engravings by Delaune. They show the Four Elements; seven planets and Hercules; Labours of the Months, and Signs of the Zodiac. See Hayward, *Virtuoso Goldsmiths*, pl.383.
London, 22 X 1970, 197
£18,500 ($44,400)

1674 Salt
silver-gilt
Maker's mark only, a squirrel
Dutch or German, early 17th century
4 in (10 cm) high
10 oz 12 dwt (329 gr)
The engraved figures of deities are after designs by Etienne Delaune. See Robert-Dumesnil, cat. nos 419 (Apollo), 418 (Diana), 417 (Minerva).
London, 11 II 1971, 194
£1,500 ($3,600)

1673 UNMARKED (AFTER DELAUNE)

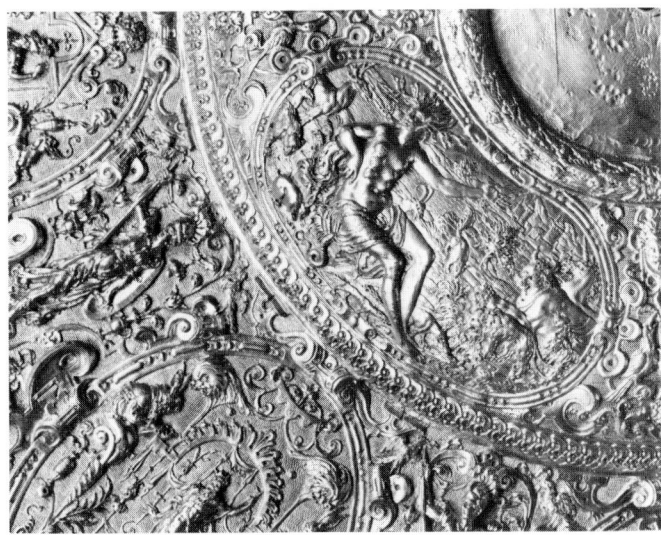

1673 (DETAIL)

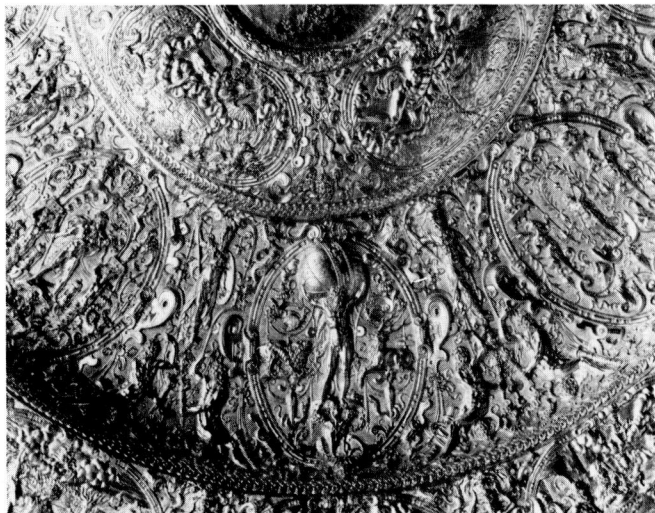

1673 (DETAIL)

1674 SQUIRREL (AFTER DELAUNE)

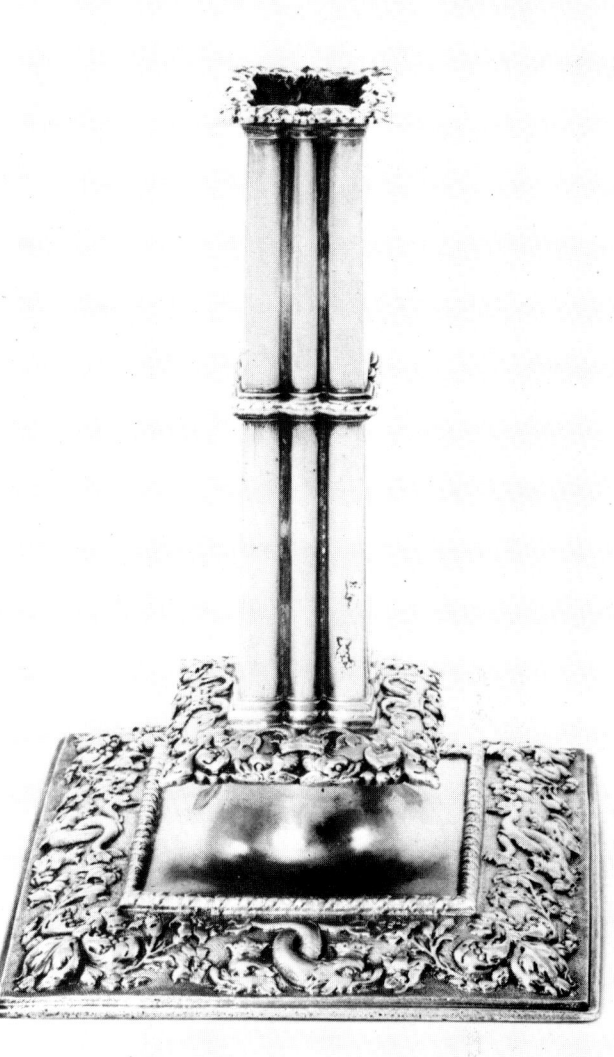

1675 MASSÉ

1674 (DETAIL)

Pierre Massé

Paris; master 1639, still recorded 1690
Mark Nocq, vol. III, p.211

1675 Candlesticks, pair
silver-gilt
Paris, 1664
6¾ in (17.4 cm) high
33 oz 13 dwt (1,046 gr)
Mentmore, 19 V 1977, 682
£33,000 ($56,100)

P.F.

1676 The Lennoxlove Toilet Service
silver-gilt
Paris, 1676
Monogram: Frances Teresa Stuart (1647–1702), wife of the 3rd Duke of Richmond and 6th Duke of Lennox, whom she married in 1667. She was granddaughter of the 1st Lord Blantyre.
Bought by the Royal Scottish Museum, Edinburgh. See in due course Godfrey Evans, catalogue of forthcoming exhibition, Edinburgh Festival, 1985.
London, 25 II 1954, 1
£17,000 ($47,770)

1676 P.F.

1676 P.F.

1676 P.F.

1676 P.F.

1676 P.F.

Claude Payen
Paris; master 1656
Mark Nocq, vol.III, p.306

1677 Bowl
silver-gilt
Paris, 1686
4¾ in (12 cm) diameter
9 oz 6 dwt (289 gr)
London, 16 X 1975, 133
£9,900 ($19,800)

Unknown maker

1678 Toilet mirror
parcel-gilt
Paris, discharge mark 1680–84
3¾ in (10 cm) wide
London, 20 III 1980, 133
£1,540 ($3,619)

1679 Snuff box
silver-gilt
Control mark only
French, c. 1685
3¾ in (9 cm) wide
London, 25 X 1973, 115
£750 ($1,800)

D fleur-de-lys above

1680 Candlesticks, pair
Lyons, probably 1697
5¾ in (14.5 cm) high
18 oz 4 dwt (566 gr)
London, 29 II 1968, 69
£1,800 ($4,320)

1677 PAYEN

1678 UNKNOWN MAKER

1679 UNKNOWN MAKER

1680 D FLEUR-DE-LYS ABOVE

1681 A. FILASSIER

1682 CORDIER

Antoine Filassier
Paris; master 1704
Mark Nocq, vol. II, p.172

1681 Candlesticks, pair
Paris, 1719
8½ in (21.6 cm) high
42 oz 9 dwt (1,320 gr)
Arms: Nantes de Pierredon of Provence
Mentmore, 19 V 1977, 668
£12,650 ($21,505)

Louis Cordier
Paris; master 1692, retired 1748
Mark Nocq, vol. I, p.296

1682 Candlesticks, pair
Paris, 1726
8¼ in (21.4 cm) high
26 oz (808 gr)
London, 4 III 1971, 87
£1,250 ($3,000)

1683 Ewer
Paris, 1729
10½ in (26.7 cm) high
39 oz 6 dwt (1,225 gr)
See Dennis, *Three Centuries of French Domestic Silver*, pl.CIII.
Zurich, 7 V 1980, 116
SFr.124,200 (£31,845 $74,835)

David André
Paris; master 1703, died c. 1743
Mark Nocq, vol. I, p.12

1684 Caster
Paris, 1705
8 in (20.5 cm) high
14 oz 8 dwt (447 gr)
London, 20 X 1966, 101
£1,450 ($4,060)

Jacques Joseph Giraud I
Marseilles; master 1705, retired 1751
Mark Helft, 59

1685 Ecuelle and Cover
Marseilles, 1724
11 in (28.2 cm) overall
23 oz 12 dwt (736 gr)
Monaco, 27 XI 1979, 726
FFr.49,950 (£5,150 $12,102)

Michel Filassier
Paris; master 1694, died before 1745
Mark Nocq, vol. II, p.171

1686 Candlesticks, four
Paris, 1715/16
8½ in (21.7 cm) high
76 oz 10 dwt (2,380 gr)
Geneva, 5 V 1981, 111
SFr.121,000 (£28,205 $58,384)

1683 CORDIER   1684 ANDRÉ

1685 GIRAUD

1686 M. FILASSIER

Nicolas Besnier

Paris; master 1714, died 1754. Father-in-law of Jacques Roettiers, grandfather of J-N. Roettiers.
Mark Nocq, vol.I, p.119

1687 Casket
Paris, 1714
11¼ in (28.5 cm) wide
106 oz 4 dwt (3,302 gr)
London, 13 IV 1961, 50
£2,900 ($8,149)

Guillaume Ledoux

Paris; master 1705, died 1751
Mark Nocq, vol. III, p.71

1688 Candlesticks, pair
Paris, 1731
9¾ in (24.7 cm) high
48 oz 4 dwt (1,500 gr)
Geneva, 6 V 1982, 61
SFr.37,400 (£10,447 $18,700)

Simon Gallien

Paris; master 1714, died 1757
Mark Nocq, vol. II, p.208

1689 Candlesticks, pair
Paris, 1740
9 in (23 cm) high
47 oz 2 dwt (1,464 gr)
London, 4 VII 1968, 129
£3,100 ($7,440)

Martin Berthe

Paris; master 1712
Mark Nocq, vol. I, p.114

1690 Spice boxes, pair
silver-gilt
One, Paris, 1723; the other Namur, 1720
5½ in (14 cm) overall
35 oz 10 dwt (1,105 gr)
Zurich, 18 XI 1977, 56
SFr.48,600 (£13,100 $24,235)

Charles-François Crose

Paris; master 1712
Mark Nocq, vol. I, p.320

1691 Beaker
Paris, 1749
4½ in (11.2 cm) high
7oz (219 gr)
Monaco, 27 XI 1979, 777
FFr.70,400 (£7,257 $17,053)

Jean-Louis Imlin II

Strasbourg; master 1720, died 1764
Mark Helft, 1077

1692 Beaker
silver-gilt
Strasbourg, 1736
3¾ in (9.4 cm) high
6 oz 10 dwt (205 gr)
Monaco, 27 XI 1979, 859
FFr.88,800 (£9,154 $21,512)

1687 N. BESNIER

1688 LEDOUX

1689 GALLIEN

1690 BERTHE

1691 CROSE

1694 ERHLEN

1693 Tumbler cups, pair
Strasbourg, 1758
2 in (5 cm) high
Arms: Falkenhayn of Alsace
Geneva, 12 V 1983, 40
SFr.14,300 (£4,268 $6,828)

Jean-Jacques Erhlen
Strasbourg; master 1728
Mark Helft, 1080

1694 Beaker
silver-gilt
Strasbourg, c. 1735
4 in (9.9 cm) high
5 oz 14 dwt (180 gr)
Geneva, 5 V 1981, 153
SFr.15,400 (£3,590 $7,431)

1695 Beaker
silver-gilt
Strasbourg, c. 1735
4 in (9.9 cm) high
6 oz 14 dwt (211 gr)
Monaco, 27 XI 1979, 778
FFr.60,500 (£6,237 $14,656)

1692 J.L. IMLIN II

1695 ERHLEN

Jean Baptiste Baube
Tours; master 1722
Mark Helft, 1179

1696 Wine taster
Tours, 1767
3 in (7.8 cm) diameter
4 oz 4 dwt (130 gr)
London, 31 X 1974, 75
£260 ($598)

S B

1697 Wine Taster
Lille, c. 1730
3¼ in (8.7 cm) diameter
3 oz 19 dwt (122 gr)
London, 20 IV 1972, 124
£350 ($875)

1693 J.L. IMLIN II

1696 BAUBE

1697 SB

1698 BERTRAND

1699 MOULINEAU

1700 MOULINEAU

1701 MARCQ

Jean-Louis Bertrand
Metz
Mark Helft, 535

1698 Ewer and basin
Ewer: maker's mark I, crowned
Metz, c. 1735–45
Basin: 15½ in (39.5 cm) wide
Ewer: 10¾ in (27.3 cm) high
73 oz (2,270 gr)
Geneva, 15 XI 1983, 114
SFr.209,000 (£66,773 $92,814)

Claude-Alexis Moulineau
Paris; master 1718, died c. 1748
Mark Nocq, vol. III, p.268

1699 Ewer
Paris, 1731
9¼ in (23.5 cm) high
22 oz 16 dwt (709 gr)
London, 17 VI 1971, 110
£1,350 ($3,240)

1700 Ewer
Paris, 1734
10½ in (26.5 cm) high
31 oz (965 gr)
Zurich, 16 V 1979, 89
SFr.18,360 (£5,170 $10,600)

1702 SOULAINE

Etienne-Jacques Marcq
Paris; master 1732, died 1781
Mark Nocq, vol. III, p.198

1701 Ewer
Paris, 1754
8¾ in (22.3 cm) high
29 oz 8 dwt (915 gr)
Geneva, 5 V 1981, 131
SFr.19,250 (£4,487 $9,288)

Paul Soulaine
Paris; master 1720, died 1759
Mark Nocq, vol. IV, p.32

1702 Spice box, double compartment
Paris, 1725
4¾ in (12 cm) wide
12 oz 10 dwt (390 gr)
Geneva, 15 XI 1983, 144
SFr.24,200 (£7,731 $10,746)

Jacques Besnier
Paris; born 1688, master 1720, died 1761
Mark Nocq, vol. I, p.121

1703 Candlesticks, pair
Paris, 1748
10 in (25.5 cm) high
42 oz 14 dwt (1,327 gr)
London, 2 V 1968, 113
£750 ($1,800)

PFB

1704 Candlesticks, pair
Paris, 1735
10¼ in (26 cm) high
64 oz 12 dwt (2,009 gr)
London, 24 V 1956, 72
£1,100 ($3,080)

Unknown maker

1705 Caster
Paris, 1737
No maker's mark
9½ in (24.2 cm) high
26 oz (808 gr)
See lot 71 for a matching pair, Lewis Pantin, London (1740).
New York, 11 XI 1975, 70
$17,000 (£8,500)

1703 J. BESNIER

1704 PFB

1705 UNKNOWN MAKER

1706 PLOT

Antoine Plot
Paris; born 1701, master 1729, died 1772
Mark Nocq, vol. III, p.345

1706 Dressing table candlesticks, pair
Paris, 1756
4¾ in (12.3 cm) high
18 oz 13 dwt (580 gr)
London, 30 XI 1967, 132
£2,400 ($5,760)

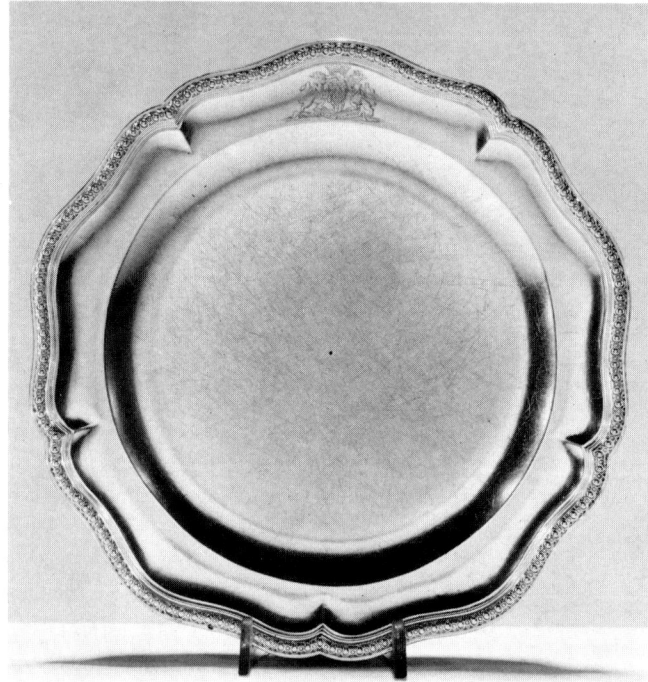

1707 J. ROETTIERS

1707 J. ROETTIERS

Jacques Roettiers
Paris; born 1707, master 1733, married in 1734 Anne-Marie, daughter of Nicolas Besnier, whose workshop he took over; retired 1772, died 1784.
Roettiers was 'a designer and workshop manager rather than a craftsman' (Honour). See Honour, *Goldsmiths and Silversmiths*, pp.192–7
Mark Nocq, vol. III, p.412

1707 Berkeley Castle service
Paris, 1735–8
Arms: Berkeley
The original order for this service most probably came from James, 3rd Earl of Berkeley, who married in 1710 Louise, daughter of 1st Duke of Richmond, for their son Augustus, born 1716.
London, 16 VI 1960
£207,000 ($581,670)

1707 J. ROETTIERS

1707 J. ROETTIERS

1708 Second course dishes, pair
Paris, 1738
11¼ in (28.5 cm) diameter
57 oz 5 dwt (1,780 gr)
Arms: St Clair Erskine impaling
Wemyss, for 3rd Earl of Rosslyn
London, 12 XII 1974, 156
£1,400 ($3,220)

Alexis Loir
Paris; master 1733, died 1775
Mark Nocq, vol. III, p.157

1709 Meat dishes, pair
Paris, 1744
14½ in (36.7 cm) wide
93 oz 4 dwt (2,900 gr)
Zurich, 16 V 1979, 92
SFr.75,600 (£21,295 $43,654)

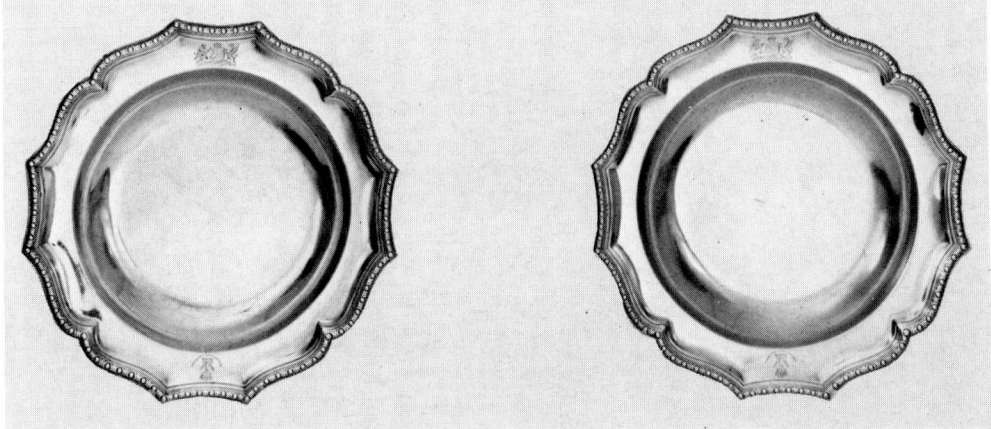

1708 J. ROETTIERS

1709 LOIR

1710 LOIR

1711 LOIR

1712 LOIR

1713 LOIR

1714 E-P. BALZAC

1715 E-P. BALZAC

1716 E-P. BALZAC

1710 Candlesticks, pair
Paris, 1740
10½ in (26.7 cm) high
58 oz 11 dwt (1,820 gr)
London, 22 V 1969, 200
£2,800 ($6,720)

1711 Candlesticks, four
Paris, 1749
11 in (28 cm) high
135 oz (4,200 gr)
Geneva, 10 XI 1981, 107
SFr.126,500 (£35,335 $63,250)

1712 Candlesticks, pair
Paris, 1752
9¾ in (25 cm) high
52 oz 8 dwt (1,630 gr)
Monaco, 6 XII 1983, 1165
FFr.99,900 (£8,597 $11,950)

1713 Candlesticks, pair
Paris, 1753
10¾ in (27.3 cm) high
51 oz 4 dwt (1,592 gr)
London, 17 VI 1971, 111
£2,000 ($4,800)

Edmé-Pierre Balzac

Paris; brother of Jean-François Balzac (see below, no.1731ff.), master 1739, recorded until c. 1780.
Mark Nocq, vol. I, p.60

1714 Ecuelle and cover
Paris, 1769
12¼ in (31 cm) overall
33 oz 18 dwt (1,055 gr)
Geneva, 12 V 1983, 20
SFr.15,400 (£4,597 $7,355)

1715 Ecuelle and cover
Paris, 1752
7¼ in (18.7 cm) diameter
22 oz 18 dwt (715 gr)
Arms: Marquis de Faletans
Geneva, 6 V 1982, 90
SFr.13,750 (£3,840 $6,873)

1716 Wine coolers, pair
Paris, 1757/8 and 1759/60
9½ in (24.5 cm) high
Arms: Louis-Philippe d'Orleans, before 1830.
These coolers formed part of a service which also included the work of Thomas Germain and Antoine Durand, bearing the same armorials.
Monaco, 24 VI 1976, 51
FFr.770,000 (£91,666 $165,000)

1717 Candlesticks, pair
Paris, 1767/8
10¾ in (27.3 cm) high
57 oz 10 dwt (1,788 gr)
London, 18 VI 1959, 61
£460 ($1,292)

1717 E-P. BALZAC

1719 BELLEVILLE

1722 LENHENDRICK

1723 LENHENDRICK

Pierre Belleville
Montpellier; master 1736, died 1765
Mark Helft, 564

1719 Candlesticks, pair
Montpellier, 1741–2
10½ in (26.7 cm) high
46 oz 18 dwt (1,460 gr)
Geneva, 12 V 1983, 38
SFr.11,000 (£3,283 $5,252)

1720 Chocolate pot
Montpellier, 1742
9½ in (24 cm) high
31 oz (964 gr)
New York, 3–4 X 1974, 156
$1,900 (£826)

1720 BELLEVILLE

Louis-Joseph Lenhendrick
Paris; apprenticed to Thomas Germain, master 1747, died 1783
Mark Nocq, vol. III, p.104

1721 Dishes, pair
Paris, 1775
9½ in (24 cm) square
45 oz 4 dwt (1,408 gr)
Arms: Nogaret de Trellans of Geraudan
Zurich, 18 XI 1977, 57
SFr.13,500 (£3,638 $6,730)

1722 Candlesticks, four
Paris, 1753–4
10¾ in (27.5 cm) high
105 oz (3,265 gr)
London, 17 X 1963, 134
£3,200 ($8,960)

1721 LENHENDRICK

1723 Candlesticks, two
Paris, 1753/4
11½ in (29 cm) and 10½ in (26.6 cm) high
59 oz 10 dwt (1,850 gr)
New York, 5–6 X 1977, 424
$550 (£297)

1718 E-P. BALZAC

1718 Dessert service,
comprising 17 spoons, 18 forks, 15 knives, with a further 21 pieces by others
silver-gilt
Paris, 1769
104 oz 14 dwt (3,258 gr)
excluding knives
Arms: Arenberg, probably for Charles-Leopold (1721–78), Duke and Prince of Arenberg, who married Louise-Marguerite Countess de la Marck 1748.
Geneva, 30 XI 1982, 78
SFr.23,100 (£6,895 $11,032)

362 FRANCE

1724 CLÉRIN

1725 PONTUS

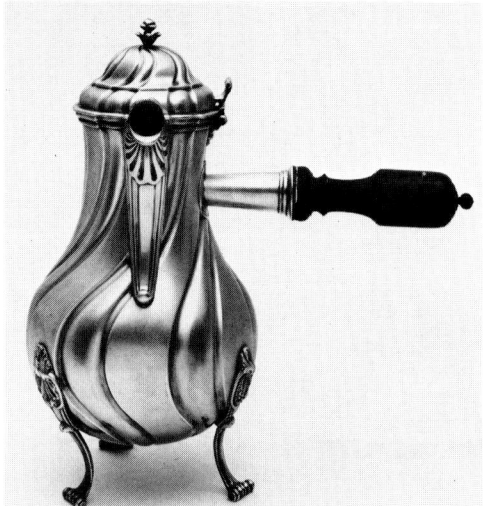

1726 IG CROWNED

1728 F-T. GERMAIN

1727 BAILLY

Lazare-Antoine Clérin
Paris; master 1741, died 1782
Mark Nocq, vol. I, p.275

1724 Teapot
Paris, 1764
6½ in (16.5 cm) high
28 oz 4 dwt (880 gr)
Geneva, 15 XI 1983, 121
SFr.66,000 (£21,086 $29,309)

Pierre-Joseph Pontus
Lille; born 1723, master 1746, died 1784
Mark Helft, 403

1725 Candlesticks, pair
Lille, 1768
9¼ in (23.7 cm) high
33 oz 14 dwt (1,050 gr)
Geneva, 30 XI 1982, 72
SFr.9,350 (£2,791 $4,465)

IG crowned

1726 Coffee pot
Lille, 1764
11¾ in (30 cm) high
45 oz (1,402 gr)
Monaco, 27 XI 1979, 739
FFr.33,300 (£3,432 $8,065)

Antoine Bailly
Paris; master 1748, died 1765
Mark Nocq, vol. I, p.45

1727 Beaker
Paris, 1759
4½ in (11.5 cm) high
7 oz 4 dwt (224 gr)
London, 2 VII 1970, 118
£620 ($1,488)

Francois-Thomas Germain
Paris; born 1726, son of Thomas Germain, master 1748, when he took over his father's workshop, bankrupt 1765, died 1791.
Mark Nocq, vol. II, p.243

1728 Toilet box
Paris, 1750
3½ in (9 cm) diameter
8 oz 16 dwt (275 gr)
Geneva, 15 V 1984, 207
SFr.25,300 (£8,083 $11,235)

1729 Dressing table candlesticks, pair
Paris, 1754
6½ in (16.2 cm) high
25 oz 14 dwt (802 gr)
Monaco, 27 XI 1979, 723
FFr. 85,470 (£8,811 $20,705)

1730 Toilet service
Paris, 1755
Dish: 10 in (25.5 cm) wide
87 oz 10 dwt (2,724 gr)
Monaco, 27 XI 1979, 731
FFr.666,000 (£68,660 $161,351)

Jean-François Balzac
Paris; brother of Edmé-Pierre Balzac (see above, no.1714ff.), born 1711, master 1749, died c. 1766
Mark Nocq, vol. I, p.61

1731 Mustard pot
Paris, 1755
5 in (12.6 cm) high
10 oz 1 dwt (312 gr)
London, 20 IV 1972, 66
£1,250 ($3,125)

1732 Candlesticks, pair
Paris, 1752
9½ in (24.2 cm) high
30 oz (933 gr)
New York, 13–14 VI 1977, 520
$2,700 (£1,588)

1733 Candlesticks, pair
Paris, 1757
9½ in (24.2 cm) high
32 oz 13 dwt (1,015 gr)
London, 5 II 1970, 48
£550 ($1,320)

Joseph-Pierre-Jacques Duguay
Paris; born 1724, master 1756
Mark Nocq, vol. II, p.118

1734 Cruet frame
Paris, 1771
12½ in (32 cm) wide
37 oz (1,150 gr)
New York, 21–24 II 1979, 62
$1,980 (£965)

1729 F-T. GERMAIN

1731 J-F. BALZAC

1730 F-T. GERMAIN

1732 J-F. BALZAC

1733 J-F. BALZAC

1734 DUGUAY

364 FRANCE

1735 DUGUAY

1736 WATTIAUX

1737 UNKNOWN MAKER

1739 CHERET

1740 CHERET

1738 DAPCHER

1735 Ewer and basin
silver-gilt
Paris, 1765
Ewer: 9¼ in (23.7 cm) high
52 oz 4 dwt (1,625 gr)
Geneva, 15 V 1984, 222
SFr.99,000 (£31,629 $43,964)

Pierre Joseph Wattiaux
Paris; master 1756
Mark Nocq, vol. IV, p.123

1736 Ewer
Paris, 1766
10½ in (26.2 cm) high
29 oz 9 dwt (915 gr)
London, 11 II 1971, 96
£1,350 ($3,240)

Unknown maker

1737 Ewer and basin
silver-gilt
Strasbourg, 1769
Maker's mark defaced
Ewer: 9½ in (24.1 cm) high
71 oz 14 dwt (2,230 gr)
Zurich, 7 V 1980, 143
SFr.66,960 (£17,170 $40,350)

Jean-François Dapcher
Paris; apprenticed to Thomas Germain, master 1751
Mark Nocq, vol. II, p.9

1738 Soup tureen and stand
Paris, 1772/3
10¾ in (27 cm) diameter
387 oz (12,035 gr)
Provenance: Count Alexander Sergeivich Strogonoff
London, 14 XI 1963, 171
£10,000 ($28,000)

Jean-Baptiste-François Chèret
Paris; born 1728, master 1759
Mark Nocq, vol. I, p.259

1739 Salts, four
Paris, 1762
3¾ in (9.5 cm) high
43 oz 8 dwt (1,350 gr)
Zurich, 16 V 1979, 202
SFr.41,040 (£11,560 $23,698)

1741 CHERET

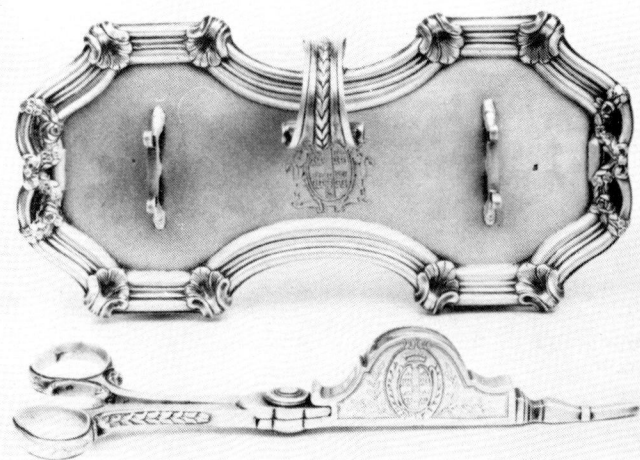

1743 LEMOINE

1744 ALBERTI

1742 LANGLOIS

1740 Toilex boxes, pair
Paris, 1784
6¼ in (16 cm) diameter
71 oz (2,208 gr)
Arms: Alexandre-Louis Auguste de Rohan-Chabot, Duc de Rohan, Prince de Léon and his wife Elizabeth, daughter of the Duc de Montmorency, whom he married 1785
Zurich, 18 XI 1977, 59
SFr.48,600 (£13,100 $24,235)

1741 Easel mirror
Paris, 1784
Signed: J.B. Cheret A Paris en 1785
Mark of Jean-Charles Roquillet-Desnoyers
34½ in (87.7 cm) high
210 oz (6,531 gr) approximately
Desnoyers was apprenticed to Pierre-Henri Cheret and made master 1772.
Arms: see no.1740
London, 20 IV 1972, 140
£3,600 ($9,000)

Nicolas-Martin Langlois
Paris; master 1757
Mark Nocq, vol. III, p.30

1742 Dessert Service, 50 pieces
silver-gilt
Paris, 1776–7
109 oz 6 dwt (3,400 gr)
Zurich, 16 V 1979, 86
SFr.17,600 (£4,957 $10,161)

Alexandre-Nicolas Lemoine
Paris; baptized 1736, master 1763
Mark Nocq, vol. III, p.98

1743 Snuffers stand and a pair of snuffers
Paris, 1771
8 in (20.7 cm) wide
13 oz 16 dwt (430 gr)
Arms: Boeuf of Lyon
Zurich, 7 V 1980, 92
SFr.29,160 (£7,476 $17,568)

Jacques-Henri Alberti
Strasbourg; master 1764, died 1795
Mark Helft, 1099

1744 Chocolate pot
Strasbourg, 1778
8¼ in (20.7 cm) high
18 oz 12 dwt (580 gr)
Geneva, 12 V 1983, 36
SFr.17,600 (£5,253 $8,404)

Jacques-Nicolas Roettiers

Paris; born 1736, son of Jacques Roettiers (see above, nos 1707, 1708), whose business he continued; master 1765, retired 1777
Mark Nocq, vol. III, p.413

1745 Dinner plates, twelve
silver-gilt
Paris, 1770
9¾ in (25 cm) diameter
231 oz 10 dwt (7,200 gr)
From the service of Prince Orloff; see no.1747.
Monaco, 24 VI 1976, 52
FFr.330,000 (£39,285 $70,713)

1746 Dinner plate
Paris, 1770
9¾ in (25 cm) diameter
23 oz 6 dwt (725 gr)
Arms: probably those of Chorot de Boisrerd of Dauphiné
Geneva, 30 XI 1982, 57
SFr.3,850 (£1,150 $1,840)

1747 Candlesticks, four
Paris, 1771
12¾ in (32.2 cm) high
240 oz (7,465 gr)
Part of the service of approximately three thousand pieces ordered by Catherine the Great in 1770 and given to Prince Gregory Orloff. The commission was received by J-N. Roettiers and completed with the aid of his father, Edmé-Pierre Balzac, Louis-Joseph Lenhendrick and others. Prince Orloff died in 1783, when the service was reacquired by Catherine.
Zurich, 7 V 1980, 87
SFr.528,000 (£135,385 $318,155)

Pierre François Goguelye (Gogly)

Paris; master 1768, still living 1793
Mark Nocq, vol. II, p.264

1748 Candelabra, pair
Paris, 1784
17¼ in (43.7 cm) high
133 oz (4,136 gr)
New York, 28 X 1980, 102
$29,700 (£14,347)

1745 J-N. ROETTIERS

1746 J-N. ROETTIERS

1747 J-N. ROETTIERS

1748 GOGUELYE

1749 OUTREBON

1750 OUTREBON

1751 BOULLIER

1752 F-D. IMLIN

1753 FERRIÉR

1754 R-J. AUGUSTE

1755 R-J. AUGUSTE

Antoine Boullier
Paris; master 1775, still active 1806
Mark Nocq, vol. I, p.168

1751 Candelabra, pair
Paris, 1781–2
25½ in (64.5 cm) high
259 oz 19 dwt (8,086 gr)
London, 9 VI 1966, 92
£2,900 ($5,320)

François-Daniel Imlin
Strasbourg; master 1780, died 1827
Mark Helft, 1109

1752 Beaker
silver-gilt
Strasbourg, c. 1795
3¾ in (9.5 cm) high
6 oz 4 dwt (195 gr)
Geneva, 12 XI 1980, 151
SFr.17,600 (£4,102 $8,491)

René Pierre Ferriér
Paris; master 1775
Mark Nocq, vol. II, p.168

1753 Sugar bowls and covers, pair
Paris, 1781
6¾ in (17.2 cm) overall
17 oz 10 dwt (544 gr)
New York, 31 V 1979, 104
$1,760 (£858)

Robert-Joseph Auguste
Paris; born c. 1730, master 1757, retired 1785, died 1805. See Honour, *Goldsmiths and Silversmiths*, pp.222–5
Mark Nocq, vol. I, p.31

1754 Sauceboat
Paris, 1776
8½ in (21.9 cm) overall
24 oz 15 dwt (770 gr)
London, 17 VI 1971, 70
£1,700 ($4,080)

1755 Wine coolers, pair
Paris, 1777
8¾ in (22.5 cm) high
on a pair of stands, Johann Jacob Gottlieb Matthias, Hanover, c. 1815
260 oz (8,095 gr)
Monogram: George III, King of England and Elector of Hanover (see nos 1757–8)
Monaco, 27 XI 1979, 840
FFr.555,000 (£57,216 $134,457)

Jean-Louis-Dieudonne Outrebon
Paris; master 1772
Mark Nocq, vol. III, p.292

1749 Ewer
Paris, 1788
11 in (28 cm) high
33 oz 10 dwt (1,041 gr)
New York, 12–13 XII 1978, 62
$6,600 (£3,219)

1750 Candlesticks, pair
Paris, 1778
10½ in (27.1 cm) high
38 oz 12 dwt (1,200 gr)
London, 11 VI 1970, 185
£750 ($1,800)

368 FRANCE

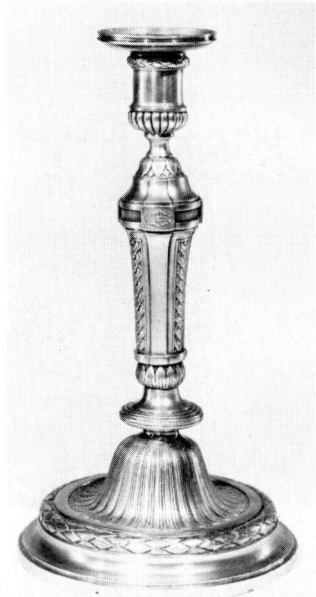

1756 R-J. AUGUSTE

1756 Candlesticks, eight
Paris, 1778/79/82
One St Petersburg, 1849
10¾ in (27.3 cm) high
259 oz 10 dwt (8,070 gr)
London, 23 X 1958, 117
£950 ($2,669)

1757 Soup tureens and stands, pair
Paris, 1778–80
19¾ in (50 cm) overall
595 oz (18,485 gr)
Monogram: as on nos 1755, 1758
Monaco, 27 XI 1979, 831
FFr.1,054,500 (£108,710 $255,468)

1758 Dinner plates, twelve
Paris, 1783
9¾ in (25 cm) diameter
285 oz 10 dwt (8,880 gr)
Monogram: George III, King of England and Elector of Hanover (see nos 1755, 1757)
Monaco, 27 XI 1979, 833
FFr.132,000 (£13,608 $31,978)

1757 R-J. AUGUSTE

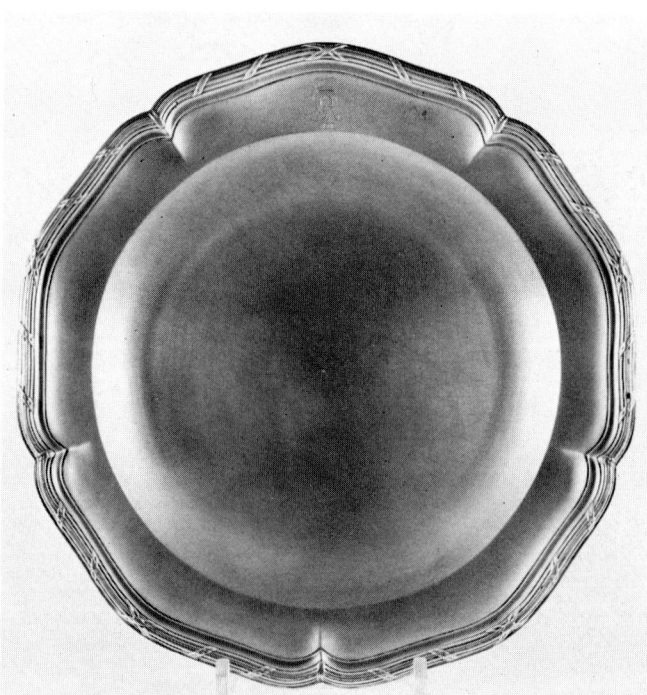

1758 R-J. AUGUSTE

Henry Auguste

Paris; son of Robert-Joseph (see above), born 1759, succeeded to his father's official appointment 1785, bankrupt 1809, died 1816 in Haiti.
Mark Nocq, vol. I, p.33

1759 Soup tureen and stand
Paris, 1787
Stand: 21 in (53.3 cm) wide
335 oz 10 dwt (10,434 gr)
See Sotheby's, New York, 20 April 1983, lot 250 for a tureen of this design by William Pitts. See also no.1125; Snodin, 'J.J. Boileau, a Forgotten Designer of Silver'.
New York, 18 VI 1974, 94
$38,000 (£15,833)

1760 Bowls on stands, pair
Paris, 1787
11 in (28 cm) diameter
159 oz 15 dwt (4,968 gr)
Geneva, 10 XI 1981, 123
SFr.24,200 (£6,760 $12,100)

1761 Soup tureen and stand
Paris, c. 1805
Stamped: Hy Auguste
18½ in (46.5 cm) wide
309 oz 8 dwt (9,622 gr)
London, 28 I 1965, 109
£1,100 ($3,080)

1759 H. AUGUSTE

1762 H. AUGUSTE

1760 H. AUGUSTE

1763 H. AUGUSTE

1761 H. AUGUSTE

1762 Ewer
silver-gilt
Paris, c. 1808
Signed: IP Auguste Fi à Paris
1808
19 in (48 cm) high
105 oz 6 dwt (3,274 gr)
Mentmore, 9 V 1977, 675
£2,200 ($3,740)

1763 Casket
silver-gilt
Paris, c. 1800
11¼ in (28.6 cm) wide
231 oz (7,184 gr)
London, 15 VI 1961, 113
£1,100 ($3,091)

1764 H. AUGUSTE

1766 BIENNAIS

1765 H. AUGUSTE

1767 BIENNAIS

1764 Dessert plates, twelve
silver-gilt
Paris, 1788
Four 8 in (20.5 cm) diameter
Eight 8½ in (21.8 cm) diameter
158 oz 11 dwt (4,930 gr)
London, 18 XI 1976, 164
£3,740 ($6,358)

1765 Wine cooler
Engraved: H. Auguste à Paris
1804
11 in (28 cm) high
88 oz 3 dwt (2,741 gr)
London, 31 III 1966, 95
£450 ($1,260)

1768 BIENNAIS

1769 BIENNAIS

Martin-Guillaume Biennais

Paris; born 1764, established in business by 1789 selling nécessaires, official goldsmiths to Napoleon and the Imperial family, retired 1819 and sold his business to Charles Cahier, died 1843. See Honour, *Goldsmiths and Silversmiths*, pp.232–7
Mark Beuque and Frapsauce, p.281

1766 Dinner plates, twelve
silver-gilt
Paris, c. 1810
9½ in (24.5 cm) diameter
217 oz (6,748 gr)
Arms: Prince Camillo Borghese (born 1775) and his wife Pauline Bonaparte (1780–1825), sister of the Emperor Napoleon
See also twelve plates (229 oz 7 dwt 7,132 gr), Sotheby's, London, 17 June 1971, lot 106; £4,500 ($10,800)
New York, 23 X 1973, 115
$7,500 (£3,125)

1767 Coffee pot
silver-gilt
Paris, 1798–1809
7¾ in (19.7 cm) high
14 oz 10 dwt (450 gr)
London, 21 III 1963, 59
£800 ($2,240)

1768 Supper set
silver-gilt
Paris, c. 1810
186 oz (5,784 gr)
Provenance: Marquess of Hertford and Sir Richard Wallace
London, 24 IV 1958, 38
£2,500 ($7,025)

1769 Cruet stands, pair
silver-gilt
Paris, c. 1805
10½ in (26.5 cm) high
114 oz 19 dwt (3,575 gr)
London, 1 II 1968, 152
£2,000 ($4,800)

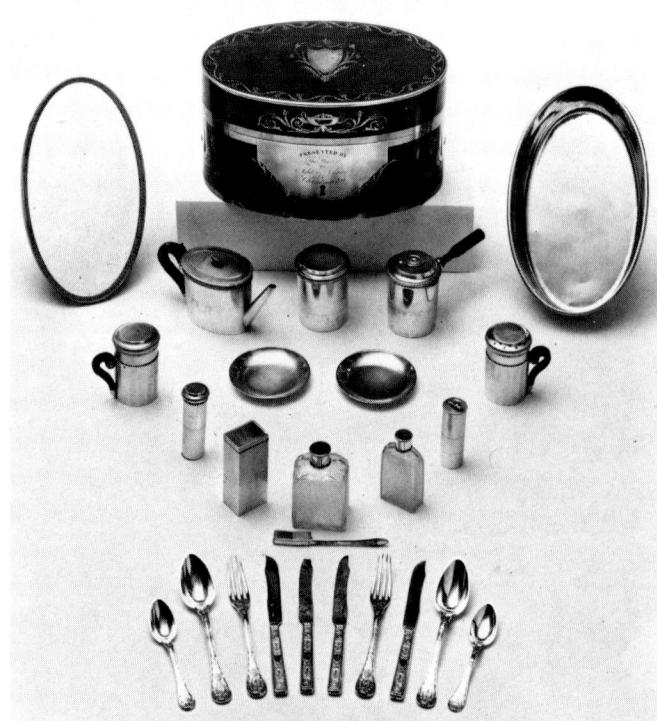

1770 BIENNAIS

1771 BIENNAIS

1772 BIENNAIS

1773 BIENNAIS

1774 HUGUET

1770 Nécessaire
silver and silver-gilt
Paris, c. 1810
Case: 13¼ in (33.7 cm) wide
116 oz 10 dwt (3,623 gr)
London, 17 VI 1971, 137
£950 ($2,280)

1771 Salver
silver-gilt
Paris, 1798–1809
Signed: Biennais orfevre de leurs Majestes
9¾ in (25 cm) wide
13 oz 15 dwt (427 gr)
London, 2 VI 1966, 57
£900 ($2,520)

1772 Bowl, cover and stand
silver-gilt
Paris, c. 1810
Stamped: Biennais
8¼ in (21.1 cm) diameter
27 oz 12 dwt (860 gr)
Geneva, 12 XI 1980, 322
SFr.17,600 (£4,102 $8,491)

1773 Soup tureen
The cover by another
Paris, c. 1810
14½ in (36.8 cm) overall
86 oz 1 dwt (2,676 gr)
Arms: apparently Jerome, King of Westphalia 1807–14 (died 1860), youngest brother of Napoleon
The service to which this tureen belonged was evidently enlarged by a German goldsmith and the cover is taken from one of the additional pieces.
London, 4 VII 1968, 42
£500 ($1,400)

Philippe-Jean-Baptiste Huguet

Paris; working by 1797
Mark Beuque and Frapsauce, p.330

1774 Bowl and cover
silver-gilt
Paris, *c.* 1810
8 in (20.5 cm) overall
20 oz 14 dwt (645 gr)
Geneva, 12 V 1983, 32
SFr.12,100 (£3,612 $5,779)

1775 Ewer
silver-gilt
Paris, *c.* 1800
15¼ in (38.7 cm) high
57 oz 16 dwt (1,800 gr)
Zurich, 22 XI 1978, 70
SFr.3,600 (£1,014 $2,078)

Jean-Charles Cahier

Paris; born 1772, bought business from Martin-Guillaume Biennais (see above) on the latter's retirement in 1819, retired 1849.
Mark Beuque and Frapsauce, p.309

1776 Coffee pot
silver-gilt
Paris, *c.* 1800
11½ in (29 cm) high
32 oz 14 dwt (1,019 gr)
Geneva, 6 V 1982, 96
SFr.6,820 (£1,905 $3,410)

1777 Centrepiece
Paris, *c.* 1816
Signed: Chles Cahier Orfvre du Roi et de Sale Monsieur. Paris 1816
23 in (58 cm) high
250 oz 10 dwt (7,790 gr)
Inscribed: to Major General Sir Hudson Lowe The City of Marseilles Grateful for Ever. Lowe was Governor General of St Helena during Napoleon's exile there 1816–21. This centrepiece was presented in gratitude for saving Marseilles from pillage after the battle of Waterloo.
London, 12 V 1966, 86
£850 ($2,380)

1775 HUGUET

1776 CAHIER

1777 CAHIER

1778 CAHIER

1779 CAHIER

1778 Wine coolers, pair
silver-gilt
Paris, *c.* 1820
Stamped: C. Cahier
8¾ in (22.3 cm) high
140 oz 10 dwt (4,370 gr)
Monogram: Grand Duke Mikhail Pavlovitch of Russia (1798–1849), 4th son of Emperor Paul I.
These wine coolers formed part of a service made by Cahier and Biennais.
Zurich, 18 XI 1977, 162
SFr.22,000 (£5,930 $10,970)

1779 Coffee pot
Paris, *c.* 1810
8¾ in (22.4 cm) high
22 oz (684 gr)
London, 3 VII 1980, 135
£1,375 ($3,231)

1780 CAHIER

1781 CAHIER

1782 LEBRUN

1783 LEBRUN

1780 Sauceboats, pair
Paris, 1819–38
Numbered 27 and 32
9¼ in (23.5 cm) overall
45 oz (1,399 gr)
Arms: Royal, of France
New York, 3–4 X 1974, 155
$1,600 (£695)

1781 Vegetable dishes and stands, pair
Paris, c. 1820
10½ in (27 cm) diameter
127 oz 10 dwt (3,965 gr)
Arms: Royal
Apparently ordered for the Tuileries Palace
New York, 31 V 1979, 100
$4,950 (£2,415)

Marc-Augustin Lebrun
Paris; master 1808
Mark Dennis, vol. II, no.217

1782 Toothpick holder
Paris, c. 1820
5¼ in (13.2 cm) high
8 oz 12 dwt (270 gr)
London, 7 III 1983, 230
£396 ($633)

1783 Cake basket
Paris, c. 1825
15¾ in (40.4 cm) wide
81 oz 10 dwt (2,535 gr)
Arms: Mecklenburg
Monaco, 27 XI 1979, 862
FFr.25,530 (£2,631 $6,182)

1784 LEBRUN

1785 LEBRUN

1786 J-B-C. ODIOT

1784 Teapot, coffee pot and milk jug
silver-gilt
Paris, c. 1810
38 oz 7 dwt (1,205 gr)
Zurich, 22 XI 1978, 76
SFr.5,400 (£1,521 $3,118)

1785 Bowl and cover
silver-gilt
Paris, c. 1825
7¼ in (18.5 cm) overall
18 oz 2 dwt (565 gr)
Geneva, 12 XI 1980, 321
SFr.11,000 (£2,564 $5,307)

Jean-Baptiste-Claude Odiot

Paris; born 1763, master 1785, died 1850. On his retirement the business was continued by his son Charles Nicholas (see below no.1798ff)
Mark Beuque and Frapsauce, p.282

1786 Vegetable dishes and covers, pair
Paris, c. 1800
8 in (20.5 cm) diameter
73 oz 18 dwt (2,300 gr)
Geneva, 30 XI 1982, 73
SFr.9,900 (£2,955 $4,728)

1787 Coffee pot
silver-gilt
Paris, c. 1800
12 in (30.5 cm) high
43 oz 19 dwt (1,365 gr)
London, 25 X 1973, 87
£1,900 ($4,560)

1788 Coffee pot
Paris, c. 1800
11 in (28.2 cm) high
26 oz 6 dwt (820 gr)
Geneva, 30 XI 1982, 60
SFr.6,820 (£2,035 $3,256)

1789 Bowl
silver-gilt
Paris, c. 1800
9¼ in (24 cm) diameter
51 oz 11 dwt (1,603 gr)
London, 11 VI 1970, 49
£480 ($1,152)

1790 Ewer
silver-gilt
Paris, 1809–19
9½ in (24.4 cm) high
22 oz (684 gr)
New York, 28 X 1980, 81
$9,900 (£4,782)

1791 Ewer
silver-gilt
Paris, c. 1810
10¼ in (26 cm) high
24 oz 10 dwt (765 gr)
Zurich, 18 XI 1977, 161
SFr.7,020 (£1,892 $3,500)

1792 Toilet vases, pair
silver-gilt
Paris, c. 1806
3¼ in (8.3 cm) high
16 oz 13 dwt (520 gr)
London, 9 V 1968, 60
£1,200 ($2,880)

1793 Mug
silver-gilt
Paris, 1809–19
4¾ in (12.4 cm) high
8 oz 15 dwt (272 gr)
New York, 14–15 VI 1978, 631
$475 (£256)

1787 J-B-C. ODIOT

1788 J-B-C. ODIOT

1789 J-B-C. ODIOT

1790 J-B-C. ODIOT

1791 J-B-C. ODIOT

1792 J-B-C. ODIOT

1793 J-B-C. ODIOT

1794 J-B-C. ODIOT

1794 (DETAIL)

1794 Soup tureen and cover
silver-gilt
Paris, 1819
Stamped: J. Bte.Cde.Odiot
19½ in (49.6 cm) high
277 oz 6 dwt (8,625 gr)
Arms: Branicki
Count François Zavier Branicki married in 1781 Alexandra Vassilievna Engelhardt (1754–1838), historically accepted as the daughter of Catherine the Great and Potemkin. This soup tureen was part of a service delivered to Countess Branicki in 1819. It is one of a pair (the other is now in the Rijksmuseum, Amsterdam) which cost approximately 17,200 francs. The design is attributed to Louis-Marie Cavelier (1785–1867)
Geneva, 30 XI 1982, 59
SFr.577,500 (£172,388 $275,820)

1795   1796 J-B-C. ODIOT

1795 Bowl and cover on stand
Paris, c. 1800
8 in (20.2 cm) high
39 oz 1 dwt (1,214 gr)
Arms (applied): Louis Philippe, Duke of Orleans
London, 25 X 1973, 86
£2,000 ($4,800)

1796 Ramekin dishes, eight
Paris, c. 1820
3 in (7.6 cm) diameter
28 oz 17 dwt (897 gr)
Arms (applied): Louis Philippe, Duke of Orleans
London, 25 X 1973, 85
£1,250 ($3,000)

1797 Double salt cellars, pair
silver-gilt
Paris, 1809–19
8½ in (22 cm) high
84 oz (2,612 gr)
New York, 12–13 IV 1977, 59
$4,400 (£2,588)

1797 J-B-C. ODIOT

1798 ODIOT

1799 ODIOT

1801 ODIOT

1800 ODIOT

Charles-Nicholas Odiot
Maison Odiot

Paris; born 1789, the son of J.B.C. Odiot (see above). After his father's retirement the firm was continued by Charles-Nicholas and subsequently became known as Maison Odiot. Charles-Nicholas Odiot died in 1869

1798 Ecuelle and stand
Paris, c. 1850
10 in (25 cm) diameter
43 oz 13 dwt (1,360 gr)
London, 6 XII 1979, 148
£682 ($1,602)

1799 Bowl and cover
silver, on plated stand
Paris, c. 1860
Stamped: Odiot à Paris
13¼ in (33.5 cm) wide
114 oz 2 dwt (3,550 gr)
Geneva, 30 XI 1982, 67
SFr.17,600 (£5,253 $8,404)

1800 Soup tureen and stand
Paris, c. 1880
Stamped: Odiot à Paris
21¼ in (54 cm) wide
273 oz 6 dwt (8,500 gr)
Geneva, 10 XI 1981, 138
SFr.36,300 (£10,140 $18,150)

1801 Entree dishes on lamp stands, four
Paris, mid-19th century
13½ in (34 cm) diameter
545 oz (16,949 gr)
New York, 11–12 XII 1973, 183
$6,250 (£2,604)

1802 ODIOT

1803 ODIOT

1802 Surtout-de-table
silver-gilt
Paris, 1828
98 in (248 cm) long
402 oz (12,500 gr) the figures
Geneva, 15 V 1984, 172
SFr.170,500 (£54,472 $75,716)
Arms: Emperor of Brazil, Dom
Pedro I (1798–1834)
Designer: after designs by
Cavelier inspired by Prud'hon

1803 Tea set
Paris, c. 1825
Stamped: Odiot a Paris
71 oz 4 dwt (2,214 gr)
London, 12 II 1981, 133
£935 ($1,935)

1804 Candelabra, pair
Paris, c. 1870
Stamped: Odiot a Paris
25¼ in (64.2 cm) high
364 oz 12 dwt (11,339 gr)
New York, 15–16 XII 1981, 55
$14,300 (£7,988)

1805 Candelabra, pair
Paris, c. 1875
Stamped: Odiot a Paris
16½ in (41.7 cm) high
94 oz 10 dwt (2,940 gr)
Monaco, 30 XI 1975, 65
FFr.20,900 (£2,322 $4,644)

1806 Table garniture
(Paris) c. 1860
Stamped: Odiot a Paris
Jardinière: 20½ in (52 cm) high
964 oz (30,000 gr) approximately
Geneva, 15 XI 1983, 140
SFr. 55,000 (£17,571 $24,423)

1807 Salt cellars, four
Paris, c. 1880
Stamped: Mon Odiot
4¼ in (10.9 cm) high
50 oz (1,560 gr)
Geneva, 12 V 1983, 47
SFr.8,800 (£2,626 $4,201)

François Durand
Paris; active 1828–74
Mark Beuque and Frapsauce,
p.293, no.2609

1808 Tea and coffee set
Paris, c. 1830
119 oz (3,700 gr)
New York, 4–5 X 1979, 73
$3,850 (£1,638)

Jean-Valentin Morel
Paris; born 1794, first mark
1827, in partnership with
Duponchel 1842, worked in
London 1848–52, died 1860

1809 Candlesticks, pair
silver-gilt and blue enamel
Paris, c. 1845
Stamped: Morel & Cie
9¼ in (23.5 cm) high
33 oz 18 dwt (1,054 gr)
Mentmore, 19 V 1977, 672
£1,100 ($1,870)

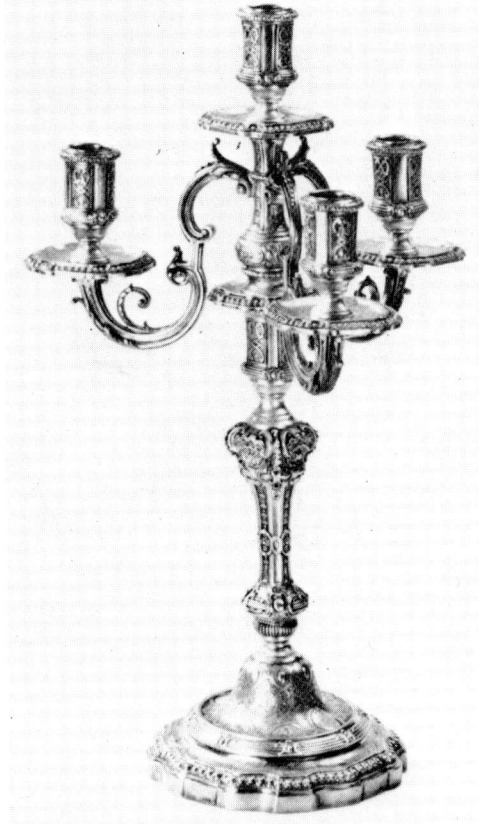

1804 ODIOT 1805 ODIOT 1809 MOREL

1806 ODIOT 1807 ODIOT 1810 UNMARKED

Unmarked

1810 Memorandum pad
silver mounts
Probably French, c. 1855
3¾ in (9.5 cm) overall
*London (Belgravia), 27 VI 1974,
130*
£70 ($168)

1808 F. DURAND

1811 UNMARKED

1812 BALAINE

1813 A. AUCOC

1811 Cup
Attributed to J.V.Morel
gold, rock crystal and enamel
c. 1850
8½ in (21.5 cm) high
London, 21 VI 1982, 90
£14,300 ($25,597)

Charles Balaine

Paris; active from 1829
Mark Beuque and Frapsauce,
p.284, no.2521

1812 Teapot
silver-gilt
Paris, c. 1845
Stamped: C. Balaine
8 in (20.5 cm) high
57 oz 18 dwt (1,802 gr)
London (Belgravia), 5 VII 1979, 386
£440 ($902)

1814 A. AUCOC

André Aucoc

Paris; founded 1821 by Casimir
Aucoc, succeeded by his son
Louis 1854 and then by André
Aucoc

1813 Ewer and basin
Paris, late 19th century
Ewer: 11 in (28 cm) high
109 oz (3,395 gr)
Monaco, 16 II 1983, 1632
FFr.21,090 (£1,745 $2,792)

1814 Candelabra, pair
Paris, c. 1890
19¼ in (48.5 cm) high
202 oz (6,285 gr)
Monaco, 27 XI 1979, 707
FFr.42,180 (£4,348 $10,217)

1815 Vegetable dish
Late 19th–early 20th century
Stamped: Aucoc Aine
13¾ in (34.8 cm) wide
135 oz 9 dwt (4,212 gr)
London (Belgravia), 9 I 1975, 67
£520 ($1,196)

1816 Vase
gold
c. 1900–1905
Designer: Edmond Becker
Inscribed: A.Aucoc orf.,
E.Becker sc.
7¼ in (18.5 cm) high
Geneva, 16 XI 1983, 164
SFr.30,800

Christofle et Cie

Paris; founded by Charles
Christofle (1805–63), continuing
the business of Joseph-Albert
Bouilhet (died 1837). In 1842
Christofle bought a licence from
Elkington and Company to
manufacture electroplate. The
firm is still in business. See
Bouilhet, *Christofle*

1817 Tea kettle on stand
Early 20th century
15¾ in (40 cm) high
101 oz 10 dwt (3,159 gr)
London (Belgravia), 29 III 1979, 301
£495 ($1,014)

1818 Dishes, pair
Paris, c. 1900
21½ in (54.5 cm) overall
139 oz (4,323 gr)
New York, 11–12 XI 1975, 63
$1,300 (£650)

1815 A. AUCOC

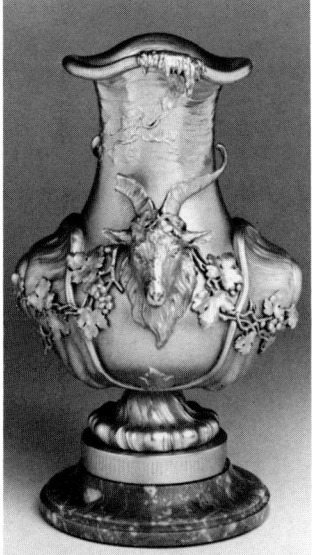
1816 A. AUCOC

1817 CHRISTOFLE ET CIE

1818 CHRISTOFLE ET CIE

1819 FROMENT MEURICE

1820 LALIQUE

1821 LALIQUE

1822 LALIQUE

Froment Meurice

Paris; firm founded by François-Desire Froment-Meurice (1802–55) and continued by his son Emile (1837–1913)

1819 Tea caddy
Paris, c. 1880
4¾ in (12 cm) high
15 oz (466 gr)
New York, 16–17 XII 1982, 444
$605 (£378)

René Lalique

Paris; born 1860, apprenticed to Louis Aucoc 1876; active principally as a jeweller until 1909, when he acquired his own glass factory; died 1945. See Lalique, *Lalique par Lalique*

1820 Vinaigrette
silver-mounted shell
c. 1900
Stamped: Lalique
2¼ in (6 cm) overall
London (Belgravia), 5 VII 1974, 161
£300 ($720)

1821 Chalice
Silver and glass
c. 1900
Stamped: Lalique 2
7½ in (19 cm) high
Monaco, 18 XI 1978, 285
FFr.33,300 (£3,660 $7,503)

1822 Dish
silver, enamel and bronze
c. 1900
Stamped: Lalique
8 in (20.5 cm) overall
Monaco, 7 XII 1981, 351
FFr.144,300 (£13,166 $23,567)

1823 CARDEILHAC

1824 CARDEILHAC

Cardeilhac

Paris; founded 1802 by Vital Antoine Cardeilhac and continued after 1860 by Ernest Cardeilhac (died 1904). The firm amalgamated with Christofle (see above) 1951

1823 Sugar basin and spoon
silver and ivory
c. 1895
7¾ in (20 cm) high
18 oz 4 dwt (566 gr)
New York, 12–13 XI 1982, 11
$3,300 (£2,062)

1824 Tea and coffee set
c. 1905
Stamped: Cardeilhac Paris
93 oz 4 dwt (2,901 gr)
London (Belgravia), 14 XII 1978, 147
£825 ($1,691)

1825 Bowl
c. 1905–10
2¾ in (7 cm) high
London (Belgravia), 18 IV 1980, 77
£99 ($232)

M.L.

1826 Wine coolers, pair
French c. 1910
12½ in (31.5 cm) high
922 oz 19 dwt (28,706 gr)
London, 10 XI 1983, 75
£35,200 ($48,928)

1825 CARDEILHAC

Jean Puiforcat

Paris; 1897–1945, son of Emile Puiforcat whose business he took over and whose mark (E.P. in a lozenge) he continued to use

1827 Coffee pots, two
20th century
9¼ in (23.5 cm) high
85 oz (2,643 gr)
New York, 6–7 II 1980, 544
$4,400 (£1,872)

1828 Coffee pot
20th century
9 in (22.8 cm) high
37 oz (1,150 gr)
New York, 6–7 II 1980, 543
$2,310 (£982)

1829 Tea set
c. 1920
Stamped: Jean E Puiforcat
London (Belgravia), 19 IX 1980, 352
£2,970 ($6,148)

1830 Tea set
c. 1925–35
London (Belgravia), 30–31 III 1977, 128
£935 ($1,589)

1826 M.L.

1831 Tea set
c. 1925–30
Stamped: Jean E Puiforcat Paris
Tray: 21¼ in (54 cm) wide
179 oz (5,565 gr)
Monaco, 19 IV 1982, 233
FFr.42,180 (£3,848 $6,887)

1832 Bowl
silver and lapis lazuli
c. 1925
Engraved: Jean E Puiforcat
9 in (23 cm) diameter
35 oz 6 dwt (1,099 gr)
Monaco, 25 VI 1981, 304
FFr.17,760 (£1,543 $3,194)

1833 Beaker
c. 1920
3 in (7.7 cm) high
London (Belgravia), 24 II 1982, 288
£121 ($216)

1834 Dish and cover
silver and ivory
c. 1925
Stamped: Jean E Puiforcat
13 oz 18 dwt (433 gr)
Monaco, 25 VI 1981, 303
FFr.4,218 (£366 $757)

1827 1828 PUIFORCAT

1829 PUIFORCAT

1830 PUIFORCAT

1831 PUIFORCAT

1832 PUIFORCAT

1833 PUIFORCAT

1834 PUIFORCAT

1835 PUIFORCAT

1835 Vase
c. 1930
Stamped: Jean E Puiforcat
France Saks Fifth Avenue
5 in (12.7 cm) high
*London (Belgravia), 20 VII 1977,
76A*
£308 ($523)

1836 PUIFORCAT

1839 GOULDEN

1837 PUIFORCAT

1838 PUIFORCAT

1840 CARTIER

1841 CARTIER

1836 Table silver, 196 pieces
c. 1930
247 oz 4 dwt (7,687 gr)
New York, 16–17 II 1983, 29
$12,375 (£7,734)

1837 Vase
c. 1930
Stamped: Jean Puiforcat Paris
Monaco, 25 V 1980, 155
FFr.7,770 (£800 $1,882)

1838 Vase
silver and wood
c. 1930
Stamped: Jean E.Puiforcat
9¼ in (23.5 cm) high
Monaco, 24–25 X 1982, 467
FFr.18,315 (£1,513 $2,420)

Jean Goulden

Paris and Reims; born 1878, died 1947; worked principally as an enameller

1839 Bowl
silver and enamel
Dated: '29'
Signed: Jean Goulden
7½ in (19 cm) high
Monaco, 25 VI 1981, 302
FFr.86,580 (£7,522 $15,570)

Cartier

Paris; founded 1859 by Louis François Cartier, succeeded by his son Alfred 1874; opened in London 1902 and New York 1912
Mark Gere, p.162

1840 Cigarette box
c. 1930
Stamped: Cartier, London JC
4½ in (11.2 cm) wide
Monaco, 25 V 1980, 154
FFr.9,990 (£1,030 $2,420)

1841 Cigarette box
black enamel and gold-coloured metal
c. 1935
Maker's mark: R in a lozenge
Engraved: Cartier Paris Londres New York
Stamped: 02237
5¾ in (14.5 cm) wide
London (Belgravia), 29 III 1979, 186
£1,760 ($3,608)

Italy

1843 (DETAIL)

1843 S.B.

1842 NO MAKER'S MARK

No maker's mark

1842 Ewer
Parcel-gilt
Messina, c. 1575
11 in (38 cm) high
35 oz (1088 gr)
New York, 24 VI 1983, 82
$18,700 (£11,687)

S.B.

1843 Dish
silver-gilt
Genoa, 1621
23½ in (60 cm) diameter
148 oz 16 dwt (4,630 gr)
Monaco, 6 XII 1983, 1139
FFr.999,000 (£83,250 $133,200)

388 ITALY

Gaspare Mola
Medallist and die-cutter, born 1567 in Coldre, active from c. 1592, died 1640. See Hayward, *Virtuoso Goldsmiths*, p.157; Honour, *Goldsmiths and Silversmiths*, pp.92–3.

1844 Charger
parcel-gilt
Probably made in Rome, 1630s
After designs by Giovanni Sadeleri
Signed by Mola and Sadeleri
21 in (53.3 cm) diameter
The charger commemorates the reform of the calendar by Pope Gregory XIII. It is the only surviving work by Mola in precious metals. See Hayward and Honour, cited in the biography above.
London, 25 VII 1935, 113
£650 ($3,204)

Unknown maker

1845 Ewer
Naples, late 17th century
Assay Master: A.A.C.
9 in (23.8 cm) high
24 oz 10 dwt (760 gr)
London, 6 XII 1979, 115
£2,200 ($5,170)

1844 MOLA

1845 UNKNOWN MAKER

1846 SIMOLI

Giuseppe Simoli
Naples
Mark Catello, p.151

1846 Ewer
silver-gilt
Naples, 1702
11½ in (29.2 cm) high
28 oz 15 dwt (894 gr)
London, 24 X 1968, 86
£2,500 ($6,000)

Unmarked

1847 Ewer
silver-gilt
Italian, early 18th century
13 in (33 cm) high
43 oz 16 dwt (1,365 gr)
Monaco, 24 VI 1976, 245
FFr.52,800 (£6,285 $11,313)

1847 UNMARKED

1848 PALMENTIERO

1849 SPINAZZI

1851 UNKNOWN MAKER

1852 1853 UNKNOWN MAKERS

Giuseppe Palmentiero
Naples
Mark Catello, p.145

1848 Ewer
Naples, c. 1720
9¼ in (23.5 cm) high
25 oz 10 dwt (793 gr)
London, 7 XII 1981, 68
£3,850 ($6,891)

Angelo Spinazzi
Rome; born Piacenza, active 1721–67
Mark Bulgari, p.433, no.989

1849 Ecuelle and cover
Rome, c. 1721
11¼ in (28.5 cm) wide
23 oz 8 dwt (727 gr)
Arms *accolée*: England and Poland, for Queen Maria Clementina, wife of James Stuart (the 'Old Pretender'), probably given to her on the birth of their son (later known as the Young Pretender) in Rome, 1720.
See no.1865
London, 12 V 1966, 101
£1,150 ($3,208)

1850 G. BARTOLOTTI

Giuseppe Bartolotti
Rome; born 1709, active 1731–75
Mark Bulgari, p.112, no.234

1850 Inkstand
Rome, c. 1740
11¼ in (28.6 cm) wide
39 oz 10 dwt (1,228 gr)
New York, 6–7 II 1980, 526
$7,425 (£3,160)

Unknown makers
1851 Dish
parcel-gilt
Possibly Pisa, c. 1700–50
19 in (48 cm) diam
54 oz 4 dwt (1,685 gr)

1852 Ewer
Genoa, c. 1720
9¾ in (24.8 cm) high
34 oz 10 dwt (1,072 gr)
London, 12 XII 1974, 185
£3,800 ($8,740)

1853 Dish
Genoa, 1733
13½ in (34.3 cm) wide
36 oz 4 dwt (1,125 gr)
London, 12 XII 1974, 186
£2,000 ($4,600)

1854 UNKNOWN MAKER

1854 Coffee pot
Venice, c. 1760
8¼ in (21.2 cm) high
14 oz 10 dwt (450 gr)
London, 20 IV 1972, 132
£420 ($1,050)

1855 UNKNOWN MAKER

1856 UNKNOWN MAKER

1857 UNKNOWN MAKER

1858 UNKNOWN MAKER   1859 UNKNOWN MAKER

1860 L. VALADIER

1855 Tray and two boxes
Como, c. 1730
Unmarked
Tray: 11¾ in (29.8 cm) wide;
boxes: 5½ in (14 cm) and 3¼ in (8.4 cm) wide
25 oz 11 dwt (794 gr)
See Sotheby's, London, 31 January 1974, lot 11 for an ewer and basin of identical design.
London, 26 VI 1975, 118
£1,900 ($4,370)

1856 Sugar box
Turin, c. 1760
4 in (10 cm) wide
5 oz 2 dwt (160 gr)
London, 12 III 1984, 214
£2,970 ($4,128)

1857 Sugar bowl
Genoa, 1762
5¾ in (14.5 cm) high
9 oz 19 dwt (305 gr)
Geneva, 30 XI 1982, 52
SFr.10,450 (£3,119 $4,990)

1858 Coffee pot
Genoa, 1768
No maker's mark
11¾ in (29.7 cm) high
46 oz 6 dwt (1,440 gr)
London, 12 III 1984, 226
£8,850 ($12,301)

1859 Coffee pot
Genoa, 1768
No maker's mark
12¼ in (31.3 cm) high
35 oz 12 dwt (1,110 gr)
Geneva, 5 V 1984, 150
SFr.20,900 (£6,677 $9,281)

Luigi Valadier

Rome; born 1726, trained in Paris, took over his father's workshop 1759, Court Silversmith to the Pope 1779, committed suicide 1785. See Honour, *Goldsmiths and Silversmiths*, pp.209–211
Mark Bulgari, p.496, nos 1055–7

1860 Salt cellar
silver-gilt
Rome, c. 1770
2 in (5 cm) diameter
4 oz 15 dwt (147 gr)
New York, 3–4 X 1974, 92
$1,900 (£826)

1861 L. VALADIER

1862 L. VALADIER

1863 L. VALADIER   1864 G. VALADIER

1865 UNMARKED; ATTRIBUTED TO VALADIER

1861 Serving dish
Rome, c. 1770
12 in (30.5 cm) wide
37 oz 10 dwt (1,166 gr) including two plates
New York, 27 IV 1973, 40
$7,500 (£3,000)

1862 Tray
silver-gilt
Rome, late 18th century
16¾ in (42.5 cm) overall
32 oz (995 gr)
From the same set as no.1860
New York, 11–12 XII 1973, 184
$8,250 (£3,437)

1863 Candlesticks, pair
Rome, c. 1770
6½ in (16.5 cm) high
17 oz 10 dwt (544 gr)
New York, 18 VI 1974, 100
$20,000 (£8,333)

Giuseppe Valadier

Rome; born 1762, the son of Luigi Valadier (see above), took over his father's workshop on his death in 1785 and used the same mark, died 1817. See Honour, *Goldsmiths and silversmiths*, pp.209–211
Mark Bulgari, p.495, nos 1055–7

1864 Oil lamp
silver (loaded)
Rome, c. 1800
20¾ in (52.5 cm) high
London, 6 VII 1981, 90
£935 ($1,935)

1865 Casket
silver-gilt
c. 1785
Unmarked, attributed to Luigi or Giuseppe Valadier
13 in (33 cm) overall
This casket forms part of a group of silver made for Cardinal York (1725–1807), younger brother of Charles Edward Stuart, the 'Young Pretender'. See no.1849
New York, 21 IV 1983, 187
$30,800 (£19,250)

1866 Table bell
Rome, c. 1790
5¾ in (14.8 cm) high
7 oz 6 dwt (230 gr)
London, 12 III 1984, 224
£1,760 ($2,446)

1866 G. VALADIER

1867 F.M.

1869 UNKNOWN MAKER

1870 UNKNOWN MAKER

1871 GRAZIOLI

1872 G. BELLI

F.M.
Rome
Mark Bulgari, 1185

1867 Coffee pot
Rome, c. 1795
11½ in (29.6 cm) high
24 oz 1 dwt (747 gr)
London, 6 VII 1981, 97
£3,520 ($7,286)

Unknown makers

1868 Sugar bowl
Turin, c. 1775
Assay Master: Bartolomeo Bernardi
5 in (12.8 cm) high
10 oz 18 dwt (340 gr)
Geneva, 30 XI 1982, 48
SFr.10,450 (£3,119 $4,990)

1868 UNKNOWN MAKER

1869 Coffee pot
Genoa, 1791
12 in (30.7 cm) high
33 oz 16 dwt (1,051 gr)
London, 5 V 1978, 144
£2,145 ($3,968)

1870 Coffee pot
Naples, c. 1815
13¾ in (35 cm) high
36 oz 4 dwt (1,125 gr)
London, 2 VI 1977, 108
£715 ($1,215)

Giuseppe Grazioli
Rome; born 1717, active from 1749, died 1792
Mark Bulgari, p.566, no.591

1871 Candlesticks, pair
Rome, c. 1790
9 in (22.8 cm) high
19 oz 17 dwt (617 gr)
London, 12 II 1981, 144
£1,430 ($2,960)

Giovacchino Belli
Rome; born 1756, active from 1787, died 1822
Mark Bulgari, p.124, no.241

1872 Ecuelle and cover on stand
silver-gilt
Rome, c. 1805
8¼ in (21 cm) high
53 oz 16 dwt (1,673 gr)
New York, 17 VI 1981, 1
$18,700 (£9,033)

Carlo Bartolotti
Rome; born 1749, active 1777–1824
Mark Bulgari, p.112

1873 Inkstand
Rome, c. 1790
14¼ in (36.5 cm) wide
25 oz 13 dwt (800 gr)
Mentmore, 19 V 1977, 622
£1,375 ($2,337)

Pietro Belli
Rome; born c. 1780, master 1825, died 1828
Mark Bulgari, p.125

1874 Soup tureen
Rome, c. 1825
11½ in (29 cm) wide
50 oz 8 dwt (1,570 gr)
London, 5 VII 1982, 37
£2,530 ($5,237)

1873 C. BARTOLOTTI

1874 P. BELLI

1875 GIANNOTTI

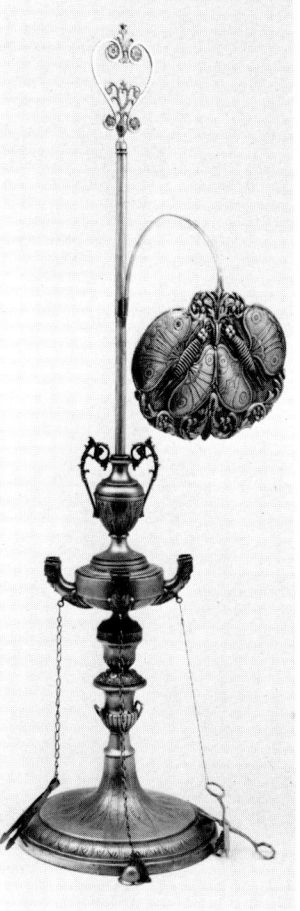
1876 GIANNOTTI

1877 CASOLLA

Angelo Giannotti
Rome; born 1798, master 1824, died 1865
Mark Bulgari, p.524

1875 Oil lamp
Rome, c. 1825
22¼ in (56.5 cm) high
36 oz 17 dwt (1,146 gr)
London, 9 V 1974, 81
£1,200 ($2,880)

1876 Oil lamp
silver (loaded)
Rome, c. 1830
39 in (99.1 cm) high
New York, 14–15 IV 1982, 170
$6,380 (£3,564)

Giovanni Casolla
Naples; born 1777
Mark Catello, p.129

1877 Ewer
Naples, c. 1830
13 in (33.5 cm) high
34 oz 18 dwt (1,085 gr)
London, 16 II 1978, 119
£572 ($1,058)

1878 CORTELAZZO

1879 BUGATTI

1880 BUGATTI

Antonio Cortelazzo

Born 1819 in Vicenza, exhibited at International Exhibitions in Florence (1861), London (1862) and Paris (1867)

1878 Tea set
silver and damascened steel
c. 1865–70
Signed: A Cortelazzo Di Vicenza Fece
Approx. 780 oz (24,258 gr)
See J. Culme, 'Antonio Cortelazzo and the Narishkine Tea Service', Art at Auction, London 1971–2, p.422.
London, 24 II 1972, 75
£3,500 ($8,750)

Carlo Bugatti

Italian designer, born 1855, died 1940, better known for his 'Moorish' furniture designs. See Philippe Dejean, Bugatti, 1982

1879 Tea set and tray
c. 1910
Designer: Carlo Bugatti
Engraved: A A Hebrard 8 Rue Royale Paris
Signed: Bugatti
Tray: 28¾ in (73 cm) overall
109 oz 4 dwt (3,398 gr)
London (Belgravia), 8 XII 1978, 141
£15,400 ($31,570)

1880 Teapot
c. 1910
Designer: Carlo Bugatti
Engraved: A A Hebrard 8 Rue Royale Paris
Signed: Bugatti
9½ in (24 cm) high
55 oz 6 dwt (1,722 gr)
London (Belgravia), 8 XII 1978, 140
£14,300 ($29,315)

Russia

1884 UNMARKED

1881 UNMARKED

1882 UNMARKED

1883 UNMARKED

Unmarked

1881 *Bratina*
parcel-gilt
Russian, early 17th century
4 in (10.5 cm) high
Zurich, 22 XI 1978, 16
SFr.11,880 (£3,346 $6,859)

1882 Beaker
silver-gilt and niello
Russian, late 17th century
4 in (10 cm) high
5 oz 14 dwt (180 gr)
Zurich, 22 XI 1978, 71
SFr.10,800 (£3,042 $6,236)

1883 Beakers, pair
silver-gilt and niello
Russian, late 17th century
4¼ in (11 cm) high
Zurich, 22 XI 1978, 77
SFr.30,240 (£8,518 $17,461)

1884 Beaker
parcel-gilt and niello
Russian, late 17th century
10 in (25.5 cm) high
Geneva, 6 V 1981, 315
SFr.38,500 (£8,974 $18,576)

1885 *Charka*
parcel-gilt
Russian, mid-17th century
5 in (12.5 cm) diameter
Zurich, 22 XI 1978, 30
SFr.8,640 (£2,433 $4,987)

1885 UNMARKED

1886 UNMARKED

1887 UNMARKED

1888 UNMARKED

1889 UNMARKED

1890 UNMARKED

1886 Kovsch
parcel-gilt
Russian, late 17th century
12¼ in (31 cm) overall
Zurich, 22 XI 1978, 54
SFr.30,240 (£8,518 $17,461)

1887 Kovsch
parcel-gilt
14½ in (37 cm) overall
Inscription: dated 1677 from
Tzar Theodore Alexeivich
(1676–82)
Geneva, 17 V 1984, 574
SFr.29,700 (£9,488 $13,188)

1888 Kovsch
parcel-gilt
Russian, c. 1683
Inscribed: 1683
14¼ in (36.5 cm) wide
24 oz 18 dwt (774 gr)
London, 20 IV 1972, 139
£2,600 ($6,500)

1889 Charka
silver-gilt
Russian, c. 1700
6 in (15.2 cm) diameter
6 oz 16 dwt (211 gr)
London, 18 VII 1974, 137
£450 ($1,080)

1890 Tankard
silver-gilt and niello
Russian, early 18th century
7¼ in (18.6 cm) high
Zurich, 22 XI 1978, 91
SFr.44,280 (£12,473 $25,570)

Peter Ivanov

Moscow; active 1686–1708
Mark Goldberg, p.189, nos 951–2

1891 Charka
parcel-gilt and niello
Moscow, c. 1700
1¼ in (3.2 cm) high
Zurich, 22 XI 1978, 73
SFr.4,320 (£1,216 $2,492)

G. Lakomkin

Moscow; active 1736–54
Mark Goldberg, p.182, nos 755–6

1892 Beaker and cover
silver-gilt
Moscow, c. 1745
6¼ in (15.9 cm) high
8 oz 10 dwt (265 gr)
Geneva, 6 V 1982, 7
SFr.3,960 (£1,106 $1,980)

1893 Beaker and cover
parcel-gilt
Moscow, 1759
11¼ in (28.5 cm) high
12 oz 16 dwt (400 gr)
Geneva, 12 XI 1980, 41
SFr.4,950 (£1,153 $2,386)

1891 IVANOV

1892 LAKOMKIN

1895 SEMYONOVITCH

1893 LAKOMKIN

1894 KOPPING

1896 UNMARKED

1897 UNMARKED

Johann Fredrik Kopping
St Petersburg; master 1748, died 1783, of Swedish origin
Mark Backsbacka, p.305, nos 661–2

1894 Hot water jug
St Petersburg, apparently 1768
8½ in (21.5 cm) high
26 oz 17 dwt (835 gr)
London, 18 VII 1974, 138
£700 ($1,680)

Y. Semyonovitch

1895 Plates, six
silver-gilt
Moscow, 1754
9 in (23 cm) diameter
80 oz (2,490 gr)
Zurich, 22 XI 1978, 105
SFr.13,200 (£3,718 $7,621)

Unmarked

1896 Sugar box and cover
silver-gilt
Russian, c. 1780
6¾ in (17 cm) wide
London, 21 VI 1982, 113
£2,640 ($4,725)

1897 *Kovsch*
parcel-gilt
Russian, c. 1751
11 in (28 cm) overall
13 oz 6 dwt (413 gr)
Inscribed (in Russian): Elizabeth the First ... Empress and Autocrat of All Russia ... gave this *kovsch* ... Saint Petersburg July 1751
London, 25 X 1973, 93
£3,200 ($7,680)

1898 UNKNOWN MAKER

1900 KUZOV

1899 UNKNOWN MAKER

1898 Teapot
Moscow, c. 1770
4¾ in (12 cm) high
London, 21 VI 1982, 115
£3,190 ($5,710)

1899 *Charka*
parcel-gilt and niello
Tobolsk, c. 1785
1¾ in (4.2 cm) high
Geneva, 16 XI 1983, 206
SFr.3,850 (£1,230 $1,709)

1901 S.I.

1902 JASCHINKOV

Semyon Petrovitch Kuzov

Moscow; active 1780–1800
Mark Goldberg, p.190, no.993

1900 Soup tureen
parcel-gilt and niello
Moscow, 1799
17¼ in (43.5 cm) overall
161 oz 16 dwt (5,035 gr)
Arms: Sheremetiev
Zurich, 22 XI 1978, 78
SFr.110,160 (£31,030 $63,611)

S.I.

1901 Coffee pot
silver-gilt and niello
Moscow, 1777
9¼ in (23.2 cm) high
London, 21 VI 1982, 127
£5,060 ($9,057)

1903 BEWERT

1904 POMO

1905 BUNTZELL

Alexander Jaschinkov
St Petersburg; active 1795–1825
Mark Goldberg, no.1197 (as assay master)

1902 Coffee pot
St Petersburg, c. 1820
7¾ in (19.5 cm) high
20 oz 8 dwt (634 gr)
London, 4 V 1978, 60
£385 ($712)

Johann Hermann Bewert
St Petersburg; master 1782, died 1822
Mark Goldberg, p.205, no.1375

1903 Dressing table candlesticks, pair
silver-gilt
St Petersburg, c. 1810
3¼ in (8.3 cm) high
18 oz 19 dwt (589 gr)
London, 15 VII 1976, 52
£770 ($1,386)

Georg Friedrick Pomo
St Petersburg; active 1797–1825
Mark Backsbacka, p.395

1904 Soup tureen
St Petersburg, 1811
16½ in (42 cm) high
412 oz (12,813 gr)
London, 13 VII 1967, 151
£880 ($2,464)

1906 NICHOLS & PLINCKE

Johann Theodor Buntzell
St Petersburg; born 1786, master c. 1810, died 1846
Mark Goldberg, p.214, no.1595

1905 Tea and coffee service
St Petersburg, 1837/8
282 oz (8,770 gr)
Zurich, 22 XI 1978, 37
SFr.19,440 (£5,476 $11,225)

1907 NICHOLS & PLINCKE

Nichols and Plincke
St Petersburg; retail business established 1815, continued until c. 1900
Mark Goldberg, p.216, nos 1651–4

1906 Dessert service, thirty-six pieces
silver-gilt
St Petersburg, 1856
London, 21 I 1980, 51
£3,960 ($9,306)

1907 Candelabra, pair
St Petersburg, late 19th century
Workmaster: P.K.
8 in (20.5 cm) high
Geneva, 17 V 1984, 571
SFr.4,180 (£1,335 $1,855)

1908 NICHOLS & PLINCKE

1909 NICHOLS & PLINCKE

1910 NICHOLS & PLINCKE

1908 Ewer
St Petersburg, c. 1890
10 in (25.4 cm) high
30 oz (933 gr)
New York, 4 XII 1980, 207
$1,700 (£821)

1909 Butter dish
silver and glass
St Petersburg, late 19th century
2¾ in (7 cm) diameter
London, 15 II 1984, 451
£209 ($290)

1910 Champagne jug
silver and frosted glass
St Petersburg, c. 1885
Workmaster: R.K.
15 in (39 cm) high
London, 15 II 1984, 431
£5,280 ($7,339)

1911 SAZIKOV

1912 SAZIKOV

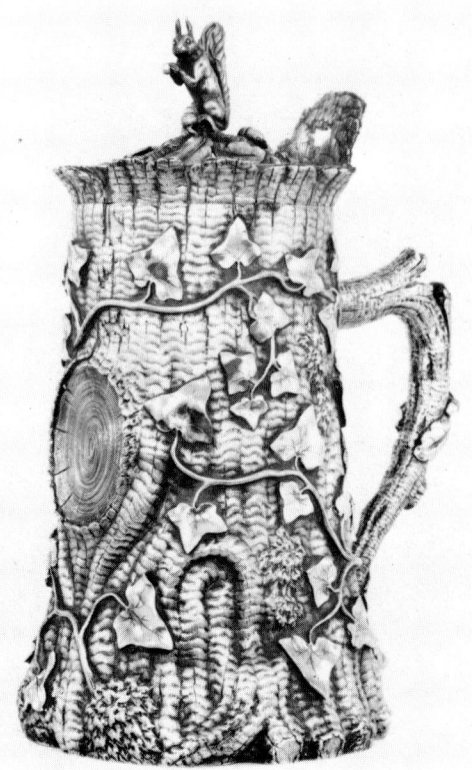

1913 SAZIKOV

1914 SAZIKOV

1915 SAZIKOV

1916 SAZIKOV

1917 SAZIKOV

House of Sazikov

St Petersburg and Moscow; held position of court supplier from 1846.
Mark Goldberg, p.190, nos 971–3, and p.202, nos 1297–8, 1301–2

1911 Beaker
silver-gilt and niello
Moscow, 1861
2¾ in (6.8 cm) high
Geneva, 6 V 1981, 312
SFr.825 (£192 $397)

1912 Tankard
silver and niello
Moscow, 1861
5½ in (14 cm) high
Geneva, 11 XI 1981, 389
SFr.4,180 (£1,167 $2,088)

1913 Tankard
silver-gilt
St Petersburg, 1855
10 in (5.4 cm) high
46 oz 18 dwt (1,458 gr)
London, 27 XI 1969, 75
£700 ($1,680)

1914 Candelabra, pair
St Petersburg, 1884
24¾ in (63 cm) high
643 oz (20,000 gr)
Geneva, 11 V 1983, 226
SFr.24,200 (£7,223 $11,556)

1915 Bratina
Moscow, 1883
4¾ in (12 cm) high
London, 4 X 1982, 364
£880 ($1,408)

1916 Tea and coffee set
Moscow, 1870
117 oz 16 dwt (3,663 gr)
New York, 17 XII 1982, 168
$4,125 (£2,578)

1917 Tea and coffee service
St Petersburg, 1882
Tray: 30½ in (77.5 cm) wide
344 oz (10,700 gr)
Geneva, 15 V 1984, 41
SFr.16,500 (£5,271 $7,326)

1918 SIMONSSON

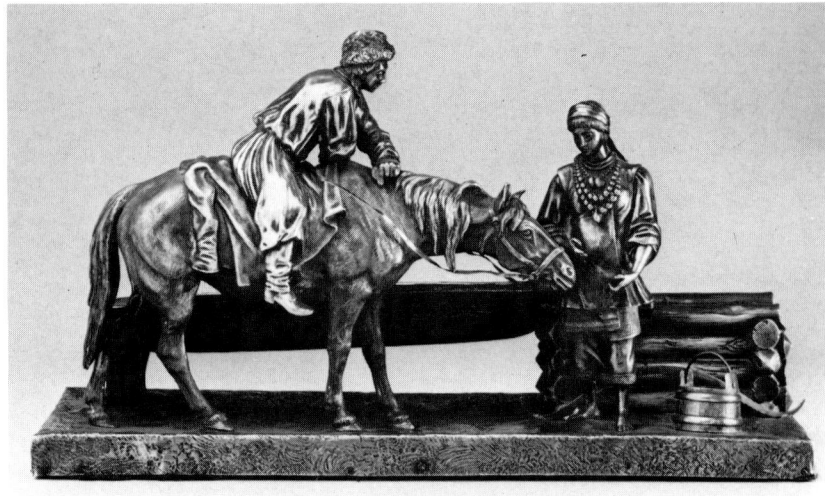

1920 OVCHINNIKOV

1919 SEMYONOV

1921 OVCHINNIKOV

Carl Gustav Simonsson
St Petersburg; born 1824 in Stockholm, master 1852
Mark Goldberg, p.211, nos 1516–17

1918 Teapot
parcel-gilt
St Petersburg, apparently 1857
7¼ in (8.4 cm) high
28 oz 5 dwt (878 gr)
London, 18 VI 1970, 128
£280 ($672)

Vasili Semyonov
Moscow; firm founded 1852
Mark Goldberg, p.182, nos 736–9

1919 Spoon
silver and niello
Moscow, 1869
7 in (18 cm) overall
Geneva, 6 V 1981, 321
SFr.880 (£205 $424)

Ovchinnikov
Moscow; firm founded 1853 by Pavel Ovchinnikov and continued by his four sons in St Petersburg also
Mark Goldberg, p.189, nos 958–9

1920 Group of two figures
Moscow, 1887
13¾ in (35 cm) wide
Geneva, 6 V 1981, 324
SFr.10,450 (£2,435 $5,040)

1921 Candelabra, pair
parcel-gilt
Moscow, 1883
22 in (56 cm) high
353 oz 8 dwt (10,990 gr)
New York, 5 III 1981, 248
$12,000 (£5,797)

1922 Samovar
Moscow, c. 1890
19 in (48 cm) high
London, 25 I 1982, 46
£2,200 ($3,938)

1922 OVCHINNIKOV

1923 OVCHINNIKOV

1924 OVCHINNIKOV

1923 Tankard
silver, niello and enamel
Moscow, 1874
6½ in (16.5 cm) high
Geneva, 11 XI 1981, 418
SFr.8,250 (£2,304 $4,124)

1924 Coffee pot
silver-gilt
Moscow, 1896
Mark of Michael Ovchinnikov
8¾ in (22 cm) high
Geneva, 17 V 1984, 533
SFr.9,000 (£2,875 $3,996)

1925 Kovsch, two
silver-gilt
Moscow, c. 1900
4½ in (11.2 cm) and 5 in (12.4 cm)
New York, 5 III 1981, 182
$1,500 (£724)

1925 OVCHINNIKOV

Michail and Semen Grachev

St Petersburg; firm founded 1866 by their father (who died 1873), active until 1917. Received the Imperial Warrant 1896
Mark Goldberg, p.200, nos 1241–3

1926 Hen and rooster boxes
St Petersburg, 1876
8 in (20.3 cm) wide
New York, 5 III 1981, 167
$3,600 (£1,739)

1926 M. & S. GRACHEV

1927 M. & S. GRACHEV

1927 Tankard
silver-gilt
St Petersburg, 1890
11½ in (29.5 cm) high
London, 14 IV 1983, 553
£1,650 ($2,640)

1928 Teapot
St Petersburg, 1893
4½ in (11.3 cm) high
Geneva, 6 V 1981, 339
SFr.£1,210 ($2,504)

1928 M. & S. GRACHEV

1929 KHLEBNIKOV

Ivan O. Khlebnikov

St Petersburg and Moscow; active in Moscow from 1870
Mark Goldberg, p.192, nos 1035–7

1929 Cigar box
parcel-gilt
Moscow, 1873
8 in (20.2 cm) wide
London, 26 VI 1975, 134
£2,300 ($5,290)

1930 FABERGÉ

1931 FABERGÉ

1932 FABERGÉ

1933 FABERGÉ

1934 FABERGÉ

1935 FABERGÉ

Peter Carl Fabergé

St Petersburg and Moscow; born 1846, in 1870 took control of the shop started by his father (who had retired 1860) in 1842 in St Petersburg. Received the Royal Warrant 1884 and opened in Moscow 1887. The firm closed 1918 and Fabergé died in Lausanne 1920. Famous for easter eggs, enamelled work and hardstones rather than silverware. Each workshop was headed by a workmaster. Julius Alexandrovitch Rappoport (1864–1916) became Fabergé's principal silversmith 1883 (mark I.P.). Michael Perchin (1860–1903) worked exclusively for Fabergé from 1886, making, for example, the Imperial easter eggs (mark M.II.). Johan Viktor Aarne (born 1863) joined Fabergé 1891 to make gold and enamel pieces (mark B.A. or J.V.A.). See Snowman, *The Art of Carl Fabergé* and *Carl Fabergé Mark* Goldberg, p.203, nos 1313–18, and p.186, no.870

1930 Kovsch
Moscow, c. 1875–1900
4 in (10 cm) wide
London, 20 VI 1977, 201
£700 ($1,190)

1931 Box
Moscow, 1892
6 in (15 cm) overall
Geneva, 11 V 1983, 301
SFr.8,000 (£2,388 $3,820)

1932 Tea caddy
Moscow, late 19th century
5 in (13 cm) wide
Geneva, 17 V 1984, 643
SFr.28,600 (£9,137 $12,700)

1933 Claret jugs
silver-gilt mounted glass
Moscow, 1908–17
13 in (33 cm) high
London, 19 VI 1978, 187
£3,300 ($6,105)

1934 Kovsch
silver-gilt and jewelled
Moscow, c. 1900
12¾ in (32.5 cm) high
New York, 10 VI 1981, 149
$16,000 (£7,729)

1935 Candelabra, pair
silver-gilt
c. 1900
15¾ in (40 cm) high
London, 26 VI 1972, 242
£1,900 ($4,750)

1936 Vodka cup
two-colour gold
St Petersburg, late 19th century
Workmaster: Michael Perchin
1¾ in (4.5 cm) high
London, 21 VI 1982, 100
£4,400 ($7,876)

1936 FABERGÉ

1937 FABERGÉ

1937 Tea set
St Petersburg, 1899–1908
Workmaster: JW
Geneva, 7 V 1982, 124
SFr.9,350 (£2,611 $4,673)

1938 Claret jug
silver-mounted cut glass
Moscow, 1899–1908
8 in (20.5 cm) high
Geneva, 6 V 1981, 469
SFr.8,800 (£2,051 $4,245)

1939 *Scherzbecher*
silver-gilt
Moscow, c. 1900
Workmaster: Julius Rappoport
9 in (23.2 cm) high
This is a copy of a 17th-century figure in the Armoury Museum, Moscow.
New York, 23 VI 1983, 582
$6,600 (£4,125)

1940 Crumb Tray
Moscow, 1899–1908
Workmaster: Julius Rappoport
9¾ in (25 cm) overall
Geneva, 12 XI 1980, 446
SFr.2,420 (£564 $1,167)

1941 Box
jewelled hardstone, gold-mounted
St Petersburg, late 19th century
Workmaster: Michael Perchin
2¼ in (5.8 cm) overall
London, 21 VI 1982, 93
£4,950 ($8,860)

1942 Frame
three-colour gold
St Petersburg, 1899–1908
Workmaster: Victor Aarne
3¼ in (8.4 cm) high
Geneva, 6 V 1981, 477
SFr.33,000 (£7,692 $15,922)

1943 Dessert dish
St Petersburg, c. 1900
Workmaster: Julius Rappoport
10 in (25.5 cm) wide
Zurich, 14 XI 1979, 514
SFr.9,288 (£2,380 $5,593)

1938 FABERGÉ

1939 FABERGÉ

1940 FABERGÉ

1941 FABERGÉ

1942 FABERGÉ

1943 FABERGÉ

Scandinavia

1945 ALBERTSZENN

1944 CLAUSSØN

1946 ALBERTSZENN

Mads (Matthis) Claussøn
Copenhagen; active c. 1606–35
Mark Bøje, p.83

1944 Tankard
Copenhagen, c. 1610
7¾ in (20 cm) high
28 oz 10 dwt (886 gr)
London, 15 VII 1976, 74
£4,950 ($8,910)

Jost Albertszenn
Bergen; active 1598–c. 1638
Mark Hansen and Kloster, p.355, no.26

1945 Tankard
Bergen, c. 1610
8 in (20.3 cm) high
19 oz 1 dwt (592 gr)
London, 15 VII 1976, 89
£6,050 ($10,890)

1946 Tankard
Bergen, c. 1625
9¾ in (24.8 cm) high
26 oz 4 dwt (814 gr)
London, 21 VI 1962, 22
£2,100 ($5,880)

Matts Eriksson
Stockholm; active c. 1595–1624
Mark Svenkst S., p.51

1947 Beaker
Possibly Matts Eriksson
Stockholm, c. 1620
3¼ in (8.5 cm) high
5 oz 4 dwt (161 gr)
London, 9 VII 1964, 49
£2,100 ($5,880)

Jan Reimers
Bergen; born 1610
Mark Hansen and Kloster, p.110

1948 Tankard
Bergen, c. 1660
4 in (10.4 cm) high
7 oz 12 dwt (236 gr)
London, 2 VI 1977, 166
£2,035 ($3,459)

1949 Spoon
Bergen, c. 1646
London, 5 XI 1964, 82
£48 ($134)

1947 ERIKSSON

1948 J. REIMERS

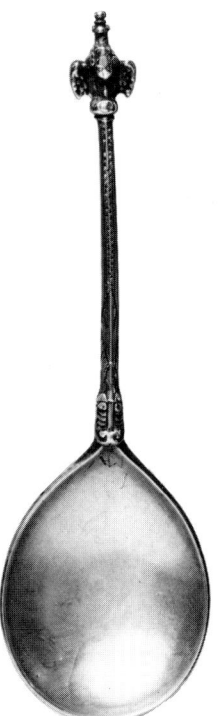
1949 J. REIMERS

1950 ENEVOLDSEN

1951 ENEVOLDSEN

1952 ENEVOLDSEN

Niels Enevoldsen
Copenhagen; active c. 1648–1700
Mark Bøje, p.90

1950 Tankard
parcel-gilt
(Copenhagen), c. 1650
Maker's mark only struck twice
5¾ in (14.6 cm) high
13 oz 4 dwt (410 gr)
London, 26 VI 1969, 175
£780 ($1,872)

1951 Tankard
Copenhagen, 1648
9 in (22.8 cm) high
43 oz 18 dwt (1,365 gr)
London, 26 VI 1947, 137
£350 ($1,410)

1952 Beaker
Copenhagen, 1663
4¼ in (11 cm) high
4 oz 16 dwt (150 gr)
Zurich, 13 XI 1979, 6
SFr.5,184 (£1,329 $3,123)

408 SCANDINAVIA

1953 OLOFSSON

1956 J. J. REIMERS THE ELDER

1954 P. J. REIMERS

1957 J. J. REIMERS THE ELDER

1955 J. J. REIMERS THE ELDER

1958 J. J. REIMERS THE ELDER

Bengt Olofsson
Stockholm; active c. 1631–66
Mark Svenskt S., p.59

1953 Tankard
parcel-gilt
Stockholm, c. 1650
6¾ in (17.2 cm) high
25 oz 4 dwt (783 gr)
London, 26 VI 1969, 171
£1,600 ($3,840)

Peder Johannessen Reimers
Bergen; born 1642
Mark Hansen and Kloster, p.133

1954 Tankard
Bergen, c. 1675
8¼ in (11 cm) high
32 oz 3 dwt (999 gr)
London, 9 VII 1964, 48
£820 ($2,296)

Johannes Johannessen Reimers the Elder
Bergen; active from c. 1660
Mark Hansen and Kloster, p.118

1955 Tankard
Bergen, c. 1674
7¼ in (18.5 cm) high
27 oz 4 dwt (845 gr)
London, 28 XI 1968, 136
£1,550 ($3,720)

1956 Tankard
(Bergen), c. 1685
Maker's mark only
7¼ in (18.6 cm) high
25 oz 7 dwt (788 gr)
London, 9 V 1974, 175
£2,000 ($4,800)

1957 Tankard
Bergen, 1703
7½ in (19.2 cm) high
24 oz 2 dwt (749 gr)
London, 17 VI 1971, 61
£1,850 ($4,440)

1958 Tankard
(Bergen), c. 1685
Maker's mark only
9 in (23.1 cm) high
33 oz 16 dwt (1,051 gr)
London, 22 VI 1972, 105
£1,750 ($4,375)

1959 Spoon
(Bergen), c. 1705
Maker's mark only
London, 15 VII 1976, 51
£308 ($554)

1960 Tankard
Bergen, c. 1710
9¾ in (24.7 cm) high
50 oz (1,555 gr)
New York, 14–15 IV 1982, 160
$7,150 (£3,994)

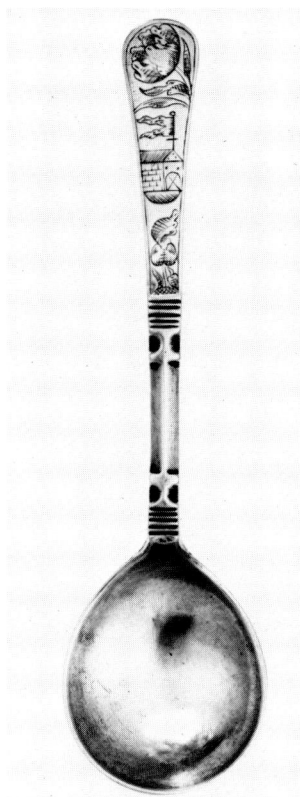

1959 J. J. REIMERS THE ELDER 1960 J. J. REIMERS THE ELDER

1963 DRAGMAN

Rudolf Wittkopf
Stockholm; active 1687–1723
Mark Svenskt S., p.83

1961 Tankard
parcel-gilt
Stockholm, 1701
7¾ in (19 cm) high
37 oz 11 dwt (1,167 gr)
London, 17 X 1963, 139
£1,100 ($3,080)

1962 Beaker and cover
filigree, silver-gilt
Stockholm, 1698
9½ in (24.2 cm) high
28 oz 3 dwt (875 gr)
London, 22 X 1970, 75
£1,600 ($3,840)

1961 R. WITTKOPF

1964 WALLMAN

Johann Dragman
Arboga; born *c.* 1670 in Uppsala,
master 1701, active until 1746
Mark Svenskt S., p.212

1963 Tankard
parcel-gilt
Arboga, *c.* 1710
7¾ in (19.8 cm) high
46 oz 19 dwt (1,553 gr)
London, 19 V 1960, 114
£800 ($2,248)

1965 H. A. REIMERS

Harmen Antoni Reimers
Bergen; born 1681, died 1721
Mark Hansen and Kloster, p.146

1965 Casket
silver, with an enamel boss
c. 1715
Maker's mark only
2¼ in (6 cm) wide
2 oz 4 dwt (68 gr)
London, 26 II 1976, 84
£1,045 ($1,881)

Johan Wallman
Gothenburg; master 1705, active
until 1739
Mark Svenskt S., p.584

1964 Tankard
Parcel-gilt
Gothenburg, 1727
7½ in (19 cm) high
43 oz (1,337 gr)
London, 18 V 1967, 133
£2,450 ($6,860)

1962 R. WITTKOPF

1966 J. F. STRAUB

1970 EBEN

1967 JOHNSEN

1968 JOHNSEN

1971 EBEN

Johann Friedrich Straub
Gothenburg; master 1722, active until 1731
Mark Svenskt S., p.279

1966 Tureen and cover
parcel-gilt
Gothenburg, c. 1725
15¾ in (40 cm) overall
70 oz 1 dwt (2,178 gr)
London, 12 V 1966, 109
£8,500 ($23,800)

Niels Johnsen
Copenhagen; born c. 1675
Mark Bøje, p.111

1967 Spice box, double-compartment
Copenhagen, 1743
Assay Master: Peter Nicolai v. Haren
4¼ in (11.1 cm) wide
9 oz (280 gr)
New York, 15–16 XII 1981, 28
$770 (£430)

1968 Coffee jug
Copenhagen, 1718
Assay Master: Conrad Ludolf
8¼ in (21 cm) high
22 oz 17 dwt (710 gr)
London, 4 VII 1968, 101A
£1,800 ($4,320)

1969 JOHNSEN

1972 BERG

1969 Coffee pot
Copenhagen, 1741
11 in (28 cm) high
28 oz 11 dwt (888 gr)
London, 5 II 1970, 66
£1,050 ($2,520)

Johann Georg Eben
Riga; master 1703, died 1710 of the plague
Mark Rosenberg, vol.IV, 7520

1970 Tankard
parcel-gilt
Riga, c. 1705
10¼ in (26.4 cm) high
55 oz 12 dwt (1,729 gr)
London, 12 XI 1974, 189
£2,800 ($6,440)

1971 Tankard
parcel-gilt
Riga, c. 1706
9¼ in (23.5 cm) high
43 oz 3 dwt (1,341 gr)
London, 26 VI 1969, 186
£1,300 ($3,120)

Johan Petterson Berg
Norrköping; master 1727, active until 1762
Mark Svenskt S., p.473

1972 Tankard
parcel-gilt
Norrköping, 1760
7½ in (19.4 cm) high
39 oz 10 dwt (1,228 gr)
London, 22 X 1970, 169
£1,550 ($3,720)

Henrik Wittkopf
Stockholm; born 1688, son of Rudolf Wittkopf (see above, nos 1961–2), master 1724, died 1756
Mark Svenskt S., p.103

1973 Coffee pot
Stockholm, 1748
11¼ in (28.6 cm) high
32 oz 2 dwt (998 gr)
London, 1 XII 1960, 98
£1,400 ($3,934)

Pehr Zethelius
Stockholm; born 1740, master 1766, died 1810
Mark Svenskt S., p.133

1974 Coffee pot
Stockholm, 1771
11½ in (29.2 cm) high
34 oz 17 dwt (1,083 gr)
London, 22 V 1969, 201
£5,000 ($12,000)

1973 H. WITTKOPF

1974 ZETHELIUS

Matthias Grahl
Gothenburg; born 1705, master 1740, active until 1776
Mark Svenskt S., p.280

1975 Sugar box
Gothenburg, 1759
6¼ in (15.8 cm) wide
10 oz 3 dwt (315 gr)
London, 18 V 1967, 135
£3,200 ($8,960)

Anders Castman
Eksjö; born 1743, master 1771, active until 1810
Mark Svenskt S., p.232

1976 Coffee pot
Eksjö, 1775
10¾ in (27.7 cm) high
28 oz 8 dwt (883 gr)
London, 11 VI 1970, 199
£3,800 ($9,120)

1975 GRAHL

1976 CASTMAN

1977 EKFELT

Zacharias Ekfelt
Arboga; active c. 1770–75
Mark Svenskt S., p.214

1977 Sauceboat
Arboga, 1771
7½ in (19.2 cm) overall
9 oz 9 dwt (293 gr)
London, 13 II 1969, 143
£1,400 ($3,360)

1978 WALLENIUS

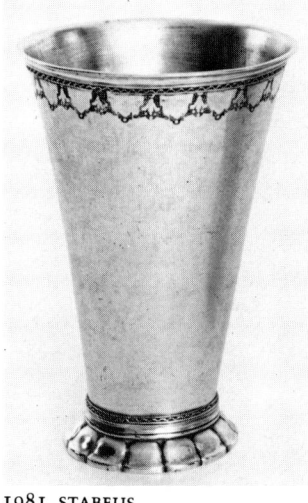
1981 STABEUS

1984 LEMON

1979 WENNERWALL

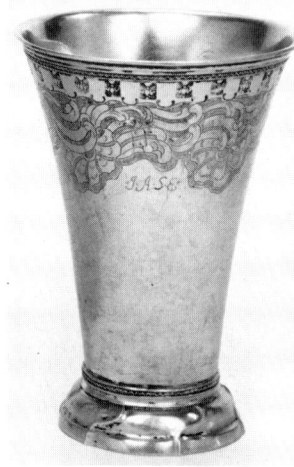
1982 STABEUS

1980 WENNERWALL

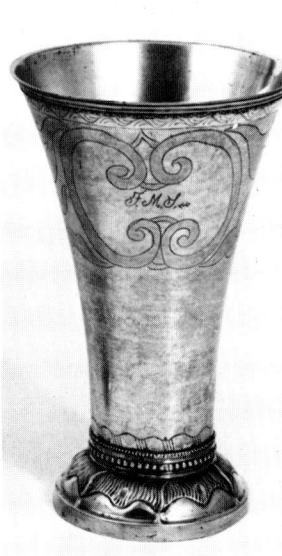
1983 LEMON

1982 Beaker
Stockholm, 1763
6¼ in (16 cm) high
9 oz 5 dwt (287 gr)
London, 9 X 1969, 170
£440 ($1,056)

Erik Lemon
Uppsala; born 1732, active 1761–1800
Mark Svenskt S., p.571

1983 Beaker
parcel-gilt
Uppsala, 1773
7¾ in (20 cm) high
8 oz 14 dwt (270 gr)
London, 20 VII 1978, 90
£495 ($915)

1984 Beaker
parcel-gilt
Uppsala, 1794
8¾ in (22 cm) high
12 oz 13 dwt (393 gr)
London, 4 VII 1968, 103
£520 ($1,248)

Petter Eneroth
Stockholm; born 1741 in Uppsala, master 1771, active until 1808
Mark Svenskt S., p.137

1985 Cruet frames, pair
Stockholm, 1787
13 in (33 cm) wide
78 oz 15 dwt (2,449 gr)
London, 5 II 1970, 57
£580 ($1,392)

Anton Michelson
Copenhagen; born 1809, started his own business 1841, Court Jeweller; after his death (1877) the firm was continued by his son Carl.
Mark Bøje, p.243

1986 Soup tureen and stand
Copenhagen, 1866
17 in (43.2 cm) high
449 oz 7 dwt (13,974 gr)
London (Belgravia), 24 II 1972, 43
£2,200 ($5,500)

Erik Wallenius
Stockholm; master 1731, died 1742
Mark Svenskt S., p.107

1978 Beaker
parcel-gilt
Stockholm, 1739
7¾ in (19.5 cm) high
17 oz 15 dwt (552 gr)
London, 20 X 1966, 83
£850 ($2,380)

Johann Wennerwall
Gothenburg; master 1737, died 1768
Mark Svenskt S., p.280

1979 Beaker
parcel-gilt
Gothenburg, apparently 1740
5¾ in (14.7 cm) high
8 oz 11 dwt (266 gr)
London, 9 X 1969, 169
£550 ($1,320)

1980 Beaker
Gothenburg, 1761
7¼ in (19 cm) high
12 oz 5 dwt (380 gr)
London, 4 VII 1968, 118
£700 ($1,680)

Lorens Stabeus
Stockholm; master 1745, died 1778
Mark Svenskt S., p.113

1981 Beaker
Stockholm, 1756
6¼ in (15.9 cm) high
10 oz 3 dwt (315 gr)
London, 20 IV 1972, 137
£380 ($950)

1985 ENEROTH

1986 MICHELSON

1987 MICHELSON

1988 MICHELSON

1987 Casket
silver and lapis lazuli
Copenhagen, 1852
4 in (10.2 cm) wide
13 oz (404 gr)
London (Belgravia), 27 VI 1974, 310
£110 ($264)

1988 Cup
c. 1860
Maker's mark only
9½ in (24 cm) high
18 oz 8 dwt (574 gr)
London (Belgravia), 11 XII 1980, 72
£385 ($796)

David Andersen

Oslo; established 1876, his business continued by his son, grandson and great-grandson.
See Hughes, *Modern Silver*

1989 Coffee service
silver-gilt and cloisonné enamel
Oslo, c. 1908
Tray: 19¾ in (50 cm) wide
London (Belgravia), 9 IX 1976, 71
£3,520 ($5,984)

1989 ANDERSEN

Georg Jensen

Copenhagen; born 1866, opened workshop 1904, assisted from 1906 by Johan Rohde as designer. The firm became a limited company 1916. After Jensen's death (1935) his son Søren Georg Jensen became chief designer. See Schwarz, *Georg Jensen*

1990 Dish
London, 1922
Designer: Johan Rohde
Stamped: 196
7¾ in (19.7 cm)
London (Belgravia), 8 XII 1978, 143
£880 ($1,804)

1991 Dish
Copenhagen, c. 1930
4¾ in (12.25 cm) high
London (Belgravia), 22 IV 1982, 227
£550 ($984)

1992 Pitcher
(Copenhagen), c. 1930
Designer: Johan Rohde
11½ in (29 cm) high
25 oz (777 gr)
New York, 12–14 VI 1980, 876A
$2,640 (£1,123)

1993 Water pitcher
Copenhagen, c. 1930
17 in (43.2 cm) high
58 oz 4 dwt (1,810 gr)
New York, 14 VII 1981, 45
$2,090 (£1,009)

1994 Tea and coffee set
Copenhagen, mid-20th century
45 oz 2 dwt (1,405 gr)
London (Belgravia), 18 X 1979, 231
£605 ($1,421)

1995 Cocktail shaker
Copenhagen, 1930s
Designer: Harald Nielsen
Stamped: Dessin HN Denmark
11 in (28 cm) high
London (Belgravia), 4 VII 1980, 156
£660 ($1,551)

1996 Tea set
Copenhagen, c. 1933–44
Tray: 20½ in (52.2 cm) wide
115 oz 8 dwt (3,589 gr)
New York, 18 XII 1980, 37
$4,400 (£2,125)

1997 Sugar caster
(Copenhagen), c. 1940
Designer: Harald Nielsen
4½ in (11.7 cm) high
London (Belgravia), 10 XII 1981, 97
£180 ($322)

1990 JENSEN

1991 JENSEN

1992 JENSEN

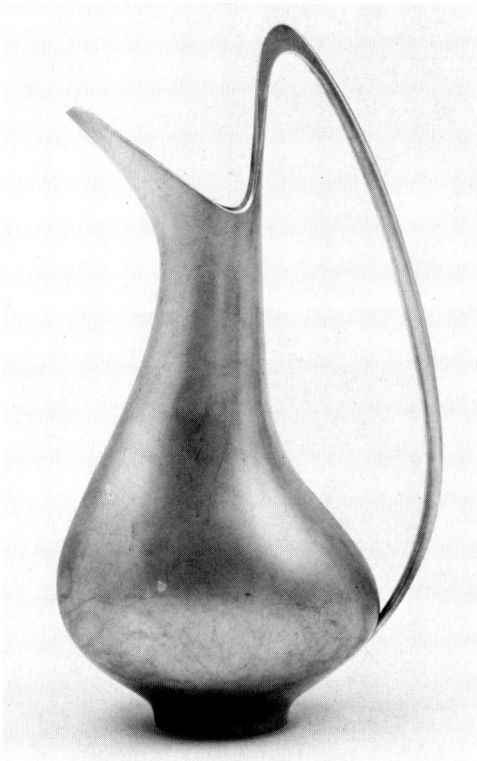
1993 JENSEN

1994 JENSEN

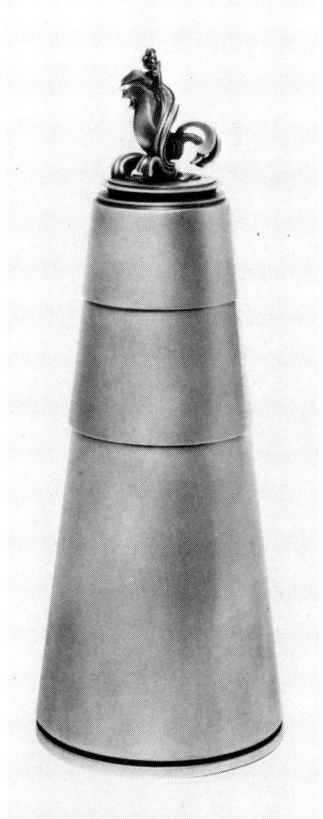

1995 JENSEN

1996 JENSEN

1997 JENSEN

1998 JENSEN

1999 JENSEN

1998 Sauceboat and ladle
Copenhagen, c. 1930
Stamped: 321
6 in (15.5 cm) high
Monaco, 19 IV 1982, 226
FFr.3,552 (£324 $580)

1999 Jug
London import mark 1927
9 in (22.7 cm) high
London (Belgravia), 10 XII 1981, 96
£605 ($1,082)

2000 Bowl
Copenhagen (1931 London import mark)
Designer: Harald Nielsen
15½ in (39.5 cm) wide
London, 30 XI 1983, 49
£1,430 ($1,987)

2000 JENSEN

Appendix 1
Family trees of Augsburg goldsmiths

The following genealogical tables have been compiled from information in Helmut Seling's *Die Kunst der Augsburger Goldschmiede 1529–1868* (Munich, 1980)

If a goldsmith's name is in italics, this indicates that he is represented in the catalogue of the present book; if his name is in a box, that he appears in one or more of the other tables (referred to by the letter T, followed by the number). The letter m before a year indicates the date the goldsmith became a master; d the year of his death; S his reference number in Seling.

Table 1

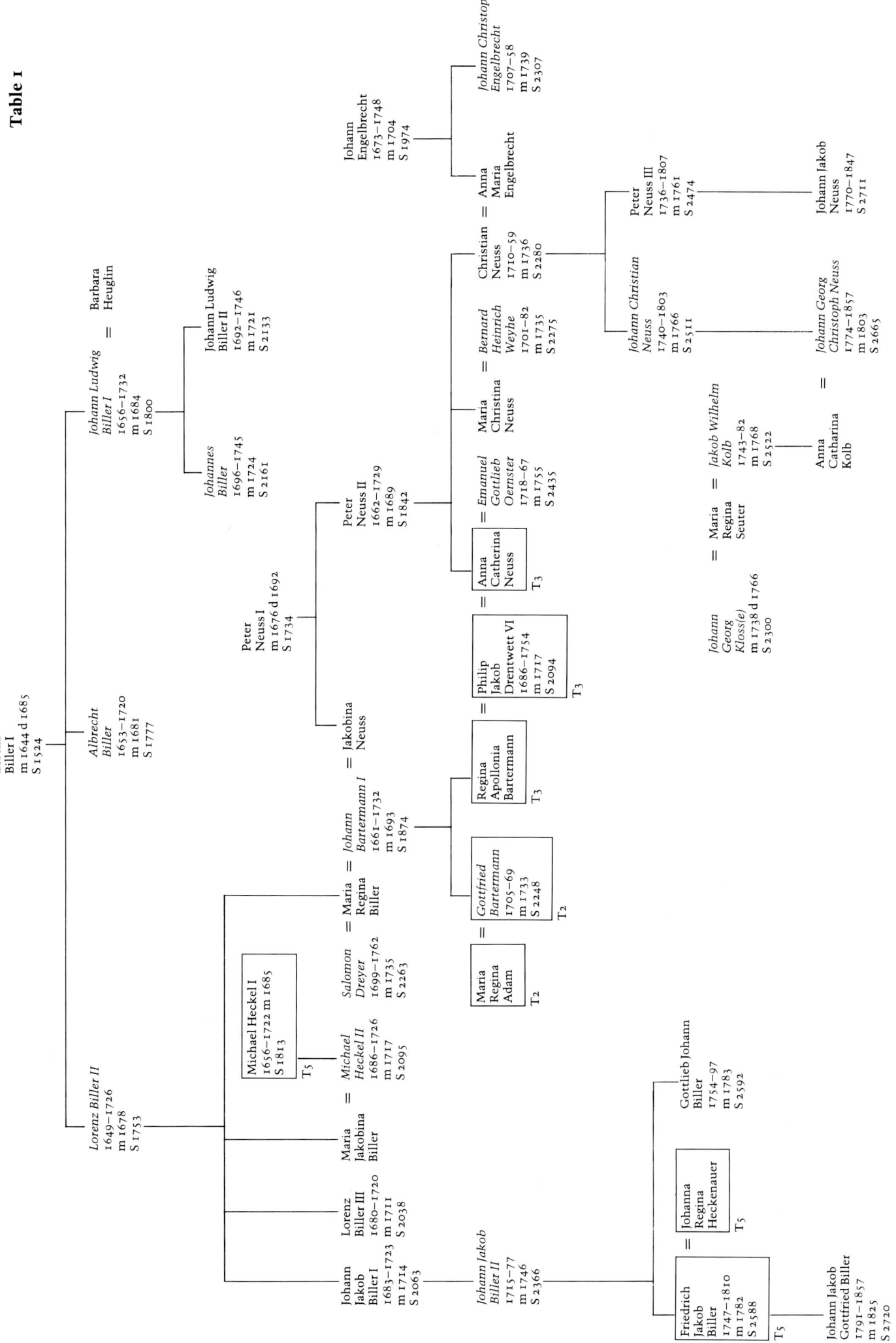

418 APPENDIX I

Table 2

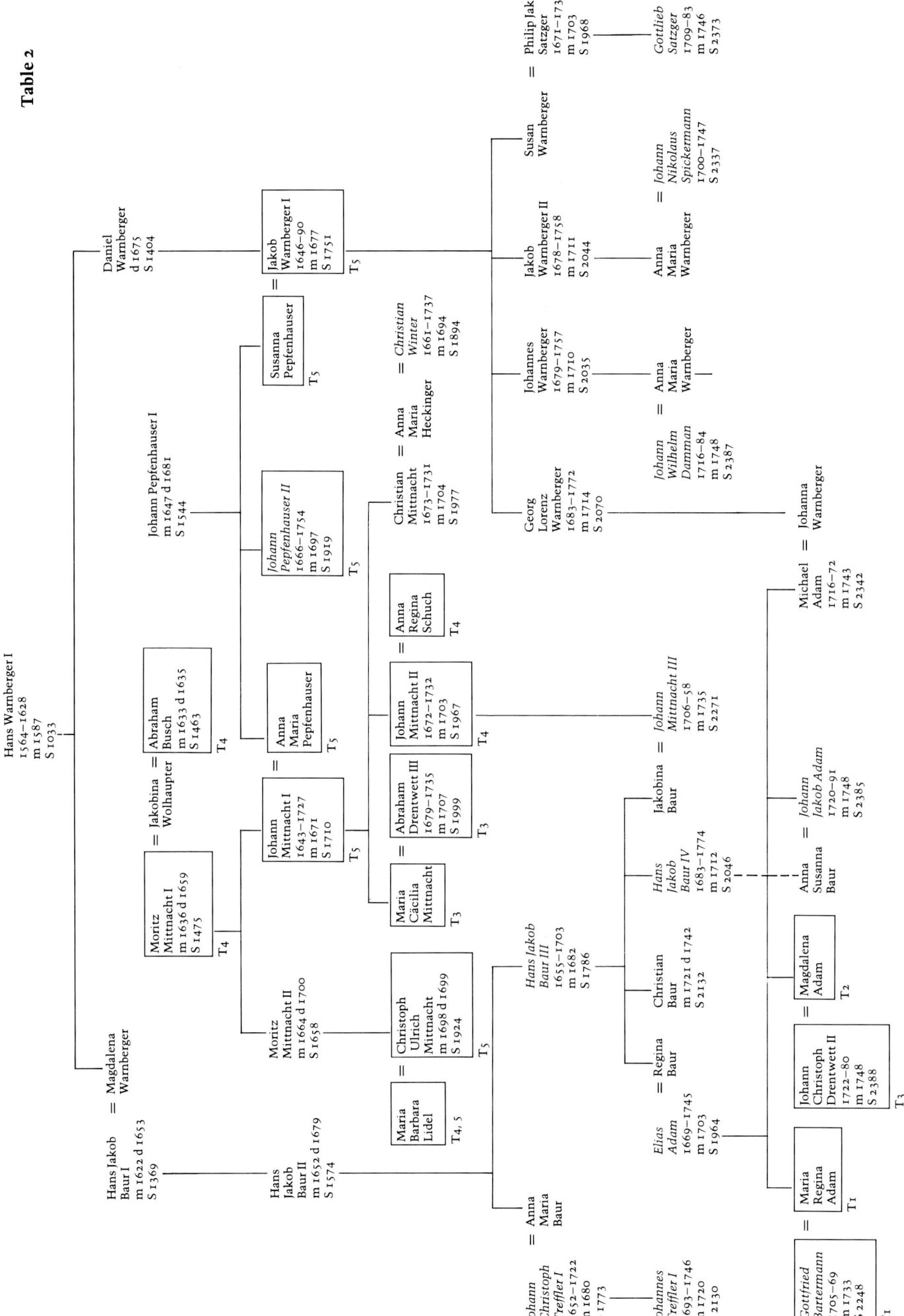

Table 3

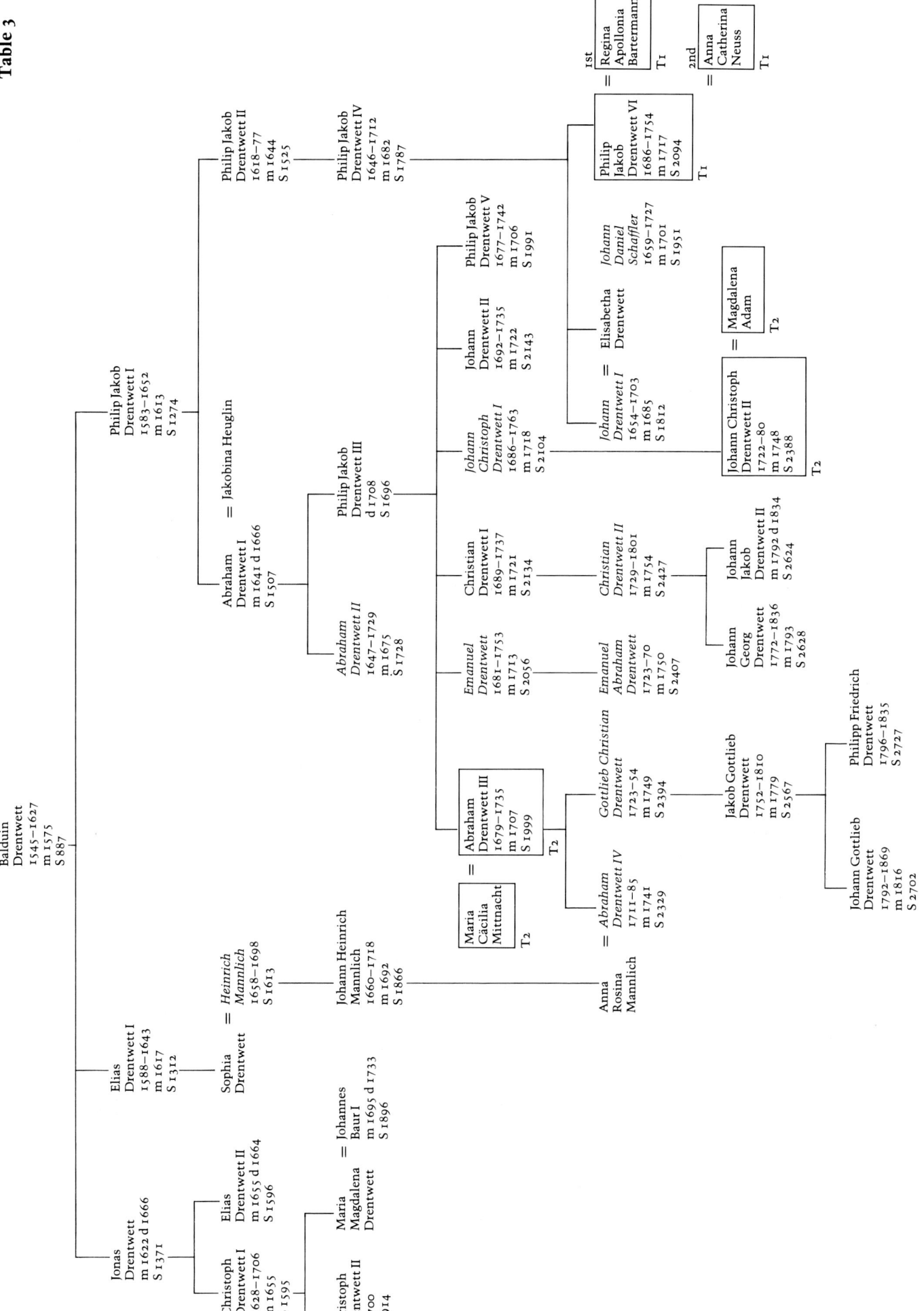

420 APPENDIX I

Table 4

```
                                                                                    Jeremias Busch
                                                                                    1644–1733
                                                                                    m 1672
                                                                                    S 1714
                              ┌─────────────────────────────────────────────────────┤
                              │                                                     │
                      Abraham Busch  =  Jakobina   =  Moritz                         │
                      m 1633 d 1635     Wolhaupter    Mittnacht I                    │
                      S 1463                          m 1636 d 1659                  │
                                                      S 1475                         │
                        T2                             T2                            │
                                                                                     │
                                                                    Hieronymus       │
                                                                    Schuch           │
                                                                    m 1644 d 1683    │
                                                                    S 1529           │
                                                         ┌──────────────┴─────────┐  │
                                                  Philippina  =  Matthäus    Johann Schuch I
                                                  Schuch        Baur II      1645–1715
                                                                1653–1728    m 1677
                                                                m 1681       S 1748
                                                                S 1776
                                                ┌──────────────────────┬───────────┐
                        Maria                   Johann Mittnacht II    Anna Regina   Catharina  =  Esaias Busch III
                        Barbara  =  Johann      1672–1732              Schuch        Barbara       1676–1759
                        Lidel       Ludwig      m 1703                               Schuch        m 1704
                        T2, 5       Baur        S 1967                 T2                          S 1973
                                    1665–1704
                                    m 1697      Matthäus Baur I
                                    S 1915      1616–79
                                    T5          m 1651
                                                S 1565
```

Esaias Busch I
m 1632 d 1679
S 1457

Johann Baptist
Busch I
m 1600 d 1629
S 1143

Esaias Busch II
1641–1705
m 1670
S 1701

Nikolaus   = Catharina Jakobina = Tobias Baur   = Johann Gottlieb
Ulrich   Busch   1660–1735   Baur
Heckel   m 1685   1686–1735
1658–1720   S 1809   m 1727
m 1704   S 2189
S 1976

Johann   = Anna
Christian   Maria
Girschner   Griessbeck
m 1738 d 1772
S 2298

Table 5

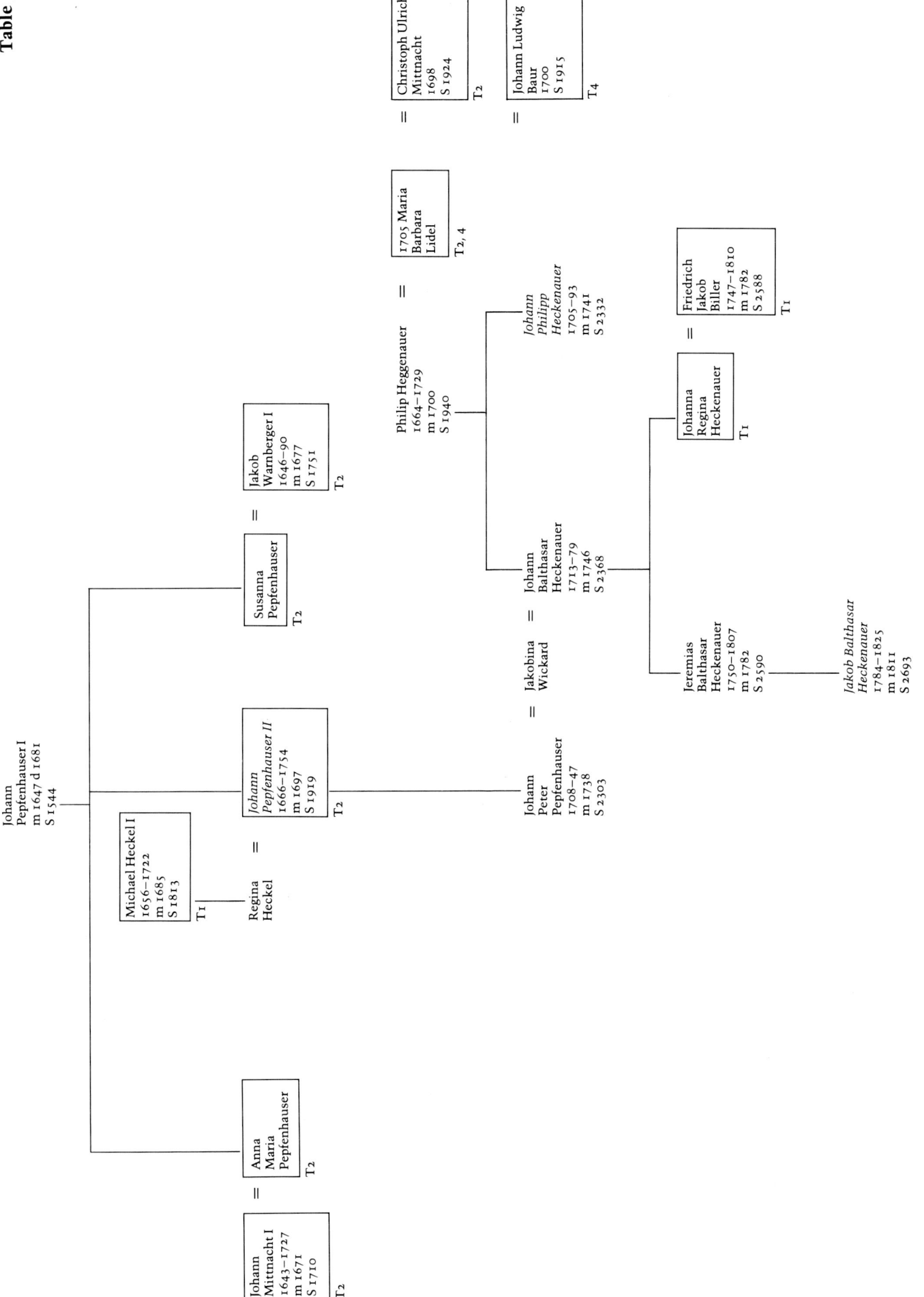

Appendix 2
Currency conversion and bullion price tables

Table 1
Currency conversions from sterling to U.S. dollars, 1925–71
From R.L. Bidwell, *Currency Conversion Tables: A Hundred Years of Change*, London, Rex Collings, 1970

1925 January	4.74	1949 January	4.03
1926 January	4.85	October	2.80
1927 January	4.85	1950 average	2.80
1928 January	4.87	1951 average	2.80
1929 January	4.85	1952 average	2.79
1930 January	4.87	1953 average	2.81
1931 January	4.87	1954 average	2.81
October	3.9	1955 average	2.79
1932 January	3.38	1956 average	2.80
1933 January	3.34	1957 average	2.79
June	4.05	1958 average	2.81
1933 October	4.5	1959 average	2.81
1934 January	5.0	1960 average	2.81
1935 January	4.93	1961 average	2.81
1936 January	4.93	1962 January	2.81
1937 January	4.91	May	2.81
1938 January	5.0	1963 average	2.80
1939 January	4.63	1964 average	2.79
1940 January	4.03	1965 average	2.80
1941 average	4.03	1966 average	2.79
1942 average	4.03	1967 January	2.79
1943 average	4.03	November	2.41
1944 average	4.03	1968 average	2.4
1945 average	4.03	1969 average	2.4
1946 average	4.03	1970 average	2.4
1947 average	4.03	1971 average	2.4
1948 average	4.03		

Table 2
Currency conversions from sterling, September 1971 to July 1984
From *Art at Auction*, London, Sotheby Publications

	US dollar	French franc	Swiss franc	Dutch guilder	South African rand
1971–2	2.5				
1972–3	2.5				
1973–4	2.4				
1974–5	2.3	9.3	5.8	5.55	1.55
Sept–Dec 1975	2	9	5.5	5.4	1.55
Jan–July 1976	1.8	8.4	4.5	4.9	1.55
1976–7	1.7	8.4	4.3	4.3	1.5
1977–8	1.85	8.75	3.71	4.25	1.6
1978–9	2.05	9.1	3.55	4.3	1.75
1979–80	2.35	9.7	3.9	4.55	1.8
1980–81	2.07	11.51	4.29	5.36	1.75
1981–2	1.79	10.96	3.58	4.65	1.9
1982–3	1.6	12.08	3.35	4.53	1.72
1983–4	1.39	11.62	3.13	4.27	1.77

Table 3
Annual average silver prices in London per troy ounce, 1925–84
London brokers' official yearly averages as published by Metal Bulletin

	d		d		p
1925	32 1/16	1948	45.00	1971	62.9p
1926	28 11/16	1949	49.24	1972	67.3p
1927	25 15/16	1950	64.80	1973	103.7p
1928	26 3/4	1951	77.86	1974	199.8p
1929	24 7/16	1952	74.39	1975	200.2p
1930	17 11/16	1953	73.94	1976	242.7p
1931	14 9/16	1954	73.48	1977	265.5p
1932	17 13/16	1955	77.54	1978	282.3p
1933	18 1/2	1956	79.13	1979	517.8p
1934	21 1/4	1957	78.93	1980	905.2p
1935	29	1958	76.22	1981	514.7p
1936	20	1959	78.83	1982	456.3p
1937	20 1/16	1960	79.38	1983	752.4p
1938	19 1/2	1961	80.22	1984	607.2p
1939	20 5/16	1962	91.51		
1940	23 7/16	1963	110.1		
1941	23 7/16	1964	111.9		
1942	23 1/2	1965	111.6		
1943	23 1/2	1966	111.8		
1944	23 1/2	1967	141.7		
1945	30.51	1968	219.4		
1946	48.70	1969	180.7		
1947	44.44	1970	176.8		

Bibliography
Books cited as references for marks

Most of the authorities listed here are cited in the text in the abbreviated forms given in the left-hand column

America

Ensko	Stephen G. Ensko, *American Silversmiths and their Marks*, New York 1948, reprinted New York, 1983
Rainwater	Dorothy T. Rainwater, *American Silver Manufacturers*, Hanover, Pa, 1966

Denmark

Bøje	Chr. A. Bøje, *Danske Guld og Sølv Smedemaerker*, vol. I, Copenhagen, 1979

England, Scotland and Ireland

Bennett	Douglas Bennett, *Irish Georgian Silver*, London, 1972
Gere	Charlotte Gere, *European and American Jewellery 1830–1914*, London, 1975
Grimwade	A.G. Grimwade, *London Goldsmiths 1697–1837, their marks and lives*, 2nd ed., London, 1982
How	G.E.P. and J.P. How, *English and Scottish Silver Spoons*, 3 vols, London, 1957
Jackson	Sir C.J. Jackson, *English Goldsmiths and their marks*, 2nd ed., New York, 1921
K.C. Jones	K.C. Jones, *The Silversmiths of Birmingham and their Marks*, London, 1981
Kent	T.A. Kent, *London Silver Spoonmakers 1500–1697*, London, 1981
Sheffield Assay	*The Sheffield Assay Office Register*, 1911

Readers are recommended to look out for John Culme's forthcoming work, *A Directory of Victorian and Edwardian Gold and Silversmiths 1838–1914*.

France

Beuque and Frapsauce	E. Beuque and M. Frapsauce, *Dictionnaire des Poinçons*, Paris, 1929
Dennis	Faith Dennis, *Three Centuries of French Domestic Silver*, New York, 1960
Helft	Jacques Helft, *Le Poinçon des provinces françaises*, Paris, 1968
Nocq	Henry Nocq, *Le Poinçon de Paris*, Paris, 1926 and 1931

Germany and Austria

Neuwirth	Waltraud Neuwirth, *Wiener Gold und Silberschmiede und ihre punzen 1867–1922*, 2 vols, Vienna, 1976
Scheffler, *Berlin*	Wolfgang Scheffler, *Berliner Goldschmiede*, Berlin, 1968
Scheffler, *Hesse*	Wolfgang Scheffler, *Goldschmiede Hessens*, Berlin, 1976
Scheffler, *Niedersachsens*	Wolfgang Scheffler, *Goldschmiede Niedersachsens*, Berlin, 1965
Scheffler, *Ostpreussens*	Wolfgang Scheffler, *Goldschmiede Ostpreussens*, Berlin, 1983
Scheffler, *Westfalens*	Wolfgang Scheffler, *Goldschmiede Rheinland Westfalens*, Berlin, 1973
Seling	Helmut Seling, *Die Kunst der Augsburger Goldschmiede 1529–1868*, Munich, 1980
Rosenberg	Marc Rosenberg, *Der Goldschmiede Merkzeichen*, 4 vols, Frankfurt am Main, 1922

Italy

Bulgari	Constantino G. Bulgari, *Argentierie Gemmari e orafi d'Italia*, Rome, 1958
Catello	Elio and Corrado Catello, *Argenti Napoletani*, 1973

Netherlands

Citroen (Amsterdam)	K.A. Citroen, *Amsterdam Silversmiths and their Marks*, Amsterdam, 1975
Frederiks	J.W. Frederiks, *Dutch Silver*, 4 vols, The Hague, 1961
Meestertekens	*Meestertekens van Nederlandse 1814–1963*, The Hague, 1963
Voet (Friesland)	Elias Voet, *Merken van Friese goud en zilversmeden*, The Hague, 1974
Voet (The Hague)	Elias Voet, *Merken van Haagsche*, The Hague, 1941
Zutphens zilver	W.J.S. van Alphen and M.M. Doornink-Hoogenraed, *Zutphens zilver*, Zutphen, n.d.
Exhibition catalogues	'Dordrechts goud en zilver', Dordrecht Museum, 1975 'Groninger Zilver', Groningen Museum, 1975 'Leids [Leiden] Zilver', Stedelijk Museum, Amsterdam, 1977 A.L. Blaauwen, ed., 'Dutch Silver 1580–1830', Rijksmuseum, Amsterdam, 1979

Norway

Hansen and Kloster	Thr. Krohn-Hansen and Robert Kloster, *Bergens Gullsmed Kunst fra Laugstiden*, Bergen, 1957

Russia

Backsbacka	L. Backsbacka, *St Petersburgs juvelerare guld-och silversmeder 1714–1870*, Helsinki, 1951
Goldberg	T. Goldberg, *l'Orfèvrerie et la bijouterie Russes XV–XX siècles*, Moscow, 1967

Sweden

Svenskt S.	E. Andren, B. Hellner, C. Hernmarck and K. Holmquist, *Svenskt Silversmide 1520–1850*, Stockholm, 1963

Switzerland

Gruber	Alain Gruber, *Weltliches Silber*, Zurich, 1977 'Schweizer Tafelsilber 1650–1850', exhibition catalogue, Schloss Jegenstorf, 1966

Books, articles and exhibition catalogues referred to in the text

Books

Alison Adburgham, *Liberty's, A Biography of a Shop*, London, 1975
Elaine Barr, *George Wickes, Royal Goldsmith 1698–1761*, London, 1980
Henri Bouilhet, *Christofle*, Paris, 1981
F. Bradbury, *A History of Old Sheffield Plate*, London, 1912
Herbert Brunner, *Old Table Silver*, London, 1967
Shirley Bury, *Victorian Electroplate*, London, 1971
C.H. and M.G. Carpenter, *Tiffany Silver*, London, 1979
Michael Clayton, ed., *Collector's Dictionary of the Silver and Gold of Great Britain and North America*, London, 1971
John Culme, *Nineteenth Century Silver*, London, 1977
John D. Davis, *English Silver at Williamsburg*, Colonial Williamsburg, 1979
Eric Delieb, *Silver Boxes*, London, 1968
J.W. Federiks, *Dutch Silver*, 4 vols, The Hague, 1952–61
Hollis French, *Jacob Hurd and his sons*, Cambridge, Mass., 1939
M.H. Gans and T.M. Duyvene de Wit-Klinkhamer, *Dutch Silver*, London, 1961
Philippe Garner, ed., *Phaidon Encyclopedia of Decorative Arts 1890–1940*, Oxford, 1978
Charlotte Gere, *European and American Jewellery 1830–1914*, London, 1975
George S. Gibb, *The Whitesmiths of Taunton*, Cambridge, Mass., 1946
A. Grimwade, *Rococo Silver*, London, 1974
Alain Gruber, *Silverware*, New York, 1982
J.F. Hayward, *Huguenot Silver in England*, London, 1959
J.F. Hayward, *The Courtauld Silver*, London, 1975
J.F. Hayward, *Virtuoso Goldsmiths*, London, 1976
Carl Hernmarck, *The Art of the European Silversmith*, London, 1977
Hugh Honour, *Goldsmiths and Silversmiths*, London, 1971
Graham Hughes, *Modern Silver*, London, 1967
Brand Inglis, *Silver*, London, 1980
M. and M.-C. Lalique, *Lalique par Lalique*, Lausanne, 1977
Christopher Lever, *Goldsmiths and Silversmiths of England*, London, 1975
Charles Oman, *Caroline Silver*, London, 1971
Charles Oman, *English Engraved Silver*, London, 1978
N.M. Penzer, *Paul Storr*, London, 1954, reprinted London, 1971
P.A.S. Phillips, *Paul de Lamerie, his Life and Works*, London, 1935
Robert Rowe, *Adam Silver*, London, 1965
W. Schwartz, *Georg Jensen*, Copenhagen, 1958
A.K. Snowman, *The Art of Carl Fabergé*, London, 1953
A.K. Snowman, *Carl Fabergé*, London, 1979
A.K. Snowman, *18th century Gold Boxes*, London, 1966
Peter Thornton, *17th Century Interior Decoration in England, France and Holland*, New Haven/London, 1978
A.J. Tilbrook, *The Designs of Archibald Knox for Liberty & Co.*, London, 1976

Articles

Judith Bannister, 'The Barnard Ledgers', *Proceedings of the Society of Silver Collectors*, vol. II, nos 9/10, 1974–6
Elaine Barr, 'The Bristol Ewer and Basin', *Art at Auction*, 1982/3
Shirley Bury, 'The Lengthening Shadow of Rundells', 3 pts, *Connoisseur*, February–April 1966
S. Bury, A. Wedgwood and M. Snodin, 'The Antiquarian Plate of George IV', *Burlington*, June 1979
John Culme, 'Kensington Lewis, a Nineteenth Century Businessman', *Connoisseur*, September 1975
C.C. Dautermann, 'Dream Pictures of Cathay, Chinoiserie on Restoration Silver', *Bulletin of the Metropolitan Museum, New York*, summer 1964
J.P. Fallon, 'The Goulds and Cafes, Candlestick Makers', *Proceedings of the Society of Silver Collectors*, vol. II, nos 9/10, 1974–6
M. Grimshaw, 'The Three Gabriels', *Proceedings of the Society of Silver Collectors*, vol. II, nos 7/8, 1972–4
J.F. Hayward, 'The Pelham Gold Cup', *Connoisseur*, July 1969
J.F. Hayward, 'A William and Mary Pattern Book for Silversmiths', *Proceedings of the Society of Silver Collectors*, vol. II, no. 1, 1966–7
Percy Hennell, 'The Hennells', *Connoisseur*, February 1973, and *Antique Collector*, June 1975, June 1979
T.A. Kent, 'Gabriel Felling, Goldsmith of Bruton', *Proceedings of the Society of Silver Collectors*, vol. II, nos 11/12, 1976–8
R.W. Lightbown, 'Christian van Vianen at the Court of Charles I', *Apollo*, June 1968
Charles Oman, 'A Problem of Artistic Responsibility', *Apollo*, March 1966
N.M. Penzer, 'The Great Wine Coolers', *Apollo*, September 1957
M. Snodin and M. Baker, 'William Beckford's Silver', *Burlington*, November 1980
Michael Snodin, 'J.J. Boileau, a Forgotten Designer of Silver', *Connoisseur*, June 1978
Hugh Tait, 'The Advent of the Two-handled Cup', *Proceedings of the Society of Silver Collectors*, vol. II, nos. 11/12, 1976–8
David Udy, 'Piranesi's Vasi, the English Silversmith and his Patrons', *Burlington*, December 1978
Richard Vander, 'Some Sheffield Silversmiths', *Proceedings of the Society of Silver Collectors*, vol. II, nos. 17/18, 1972–4

Exhibition catalogues

'Queen Charlotte's Loan Exhibition', Seaford House, London, 1929
'Loan exhibition of Old English Plate, 25 Park Lane, London, 1929
'Liberty's, 1875–1975', Victoria and Albert Museum, London, 1975
'Birmingham Gold and Silver 1773–1973', Birmingham City Museum and Art Gallery, 1973
'Omar Ramsden, 1873–1939', Birmingham City Museum and Art Gallery, 1973
'Johannes Schiötling', Rijksmuseum, Amsterdam, 1976
'Touching Gold and Silver', Goldsmiths Hall, London, 1978
'Vienna in the Age of Schubert, the Biedermeier Interior', Victoria and Albert Museum, London, 1979
'Dutch Silver 1580–1830', Rijksmuseum, Amsterdam, 1979
'John Flaxman, R.A.', Royal Academy, London, 1979
'Beckford and Hamilton Silver from Brodrick Castle', Spink and Son Ltd, London, 1980
'Matthew Boulton and the Toymakers', Goldsmiths Hall, London, 1982
'The Goldsmith and the Grape', Goldsmiths Hall, London, 1983
'Pattern and Design', Victoria and Albert Museum, London, 1983
'Rococo', Victoria and Albert Museum, London, 1984; see also 'Rococo ornament', published by the museum in connection with this exhibition and based on Peter Ward-Jackson, 'Some Main Streams and Tributaries in European Ornament from 1500 to 1750', Victoria and Albert Museum, London, 1967
'De Utrechtse Edelsmeden van Vianen', Centraal Museum, Utrecht, 1984–5

Index of objects

For the purposes of this index 'English' covers England, Scotland and Ireland; 'German' covers Austria, Germany, Hungary and Switzerland. References are to directory numbers.

andiron 461, 676
apple corer 1208
argyle 1070
ash tray 1437

badge 537; *see also* medallion
basin: *see* dish
basket: *see* cake basket; dessert basket, sweetmeat basket
beaker: 17th century (English) 430, 518, 520, 525, (German) 12, 14–16, 23, 26, 30, 43, 48, 51, 54, 69–71, 83, 85, 90, 92–96, 97, 107, (Low Countries) 283, 312, 313, 315, 316–321, (Russian) 1882–1884, (Scandinavian) 1947, 1952, 1962; 18th century (English) 574, 747, 883, 909, (French) 1691, 1692, 1694, 1695, 1725, 1752, (German) 108, 111, 126, 127, 129, 139, 150, 164, 177, 200, (Russian) 1892, 1893, (Scandinavian) 1978–1984; 19th century (American) 1607, (English) 1085, 1210, 1220, (Russian) 1911, 1941; 20th century (French) 1833; *see also* cup; travelling service
bell 369, 380, 1098, 1338, 1866; *see also* inkstand
bleeding bowl: *see* porringer
book cover 309
bottle: *see* label; toilet bottle; wine bottle; pilgrim bottle; scent bottle
bottle top 268, 269
bowl: 17th century (American) 1556, (English) 418, 438, 466, 503, 593, (French) 1677, (German) 27, 77, 84, 86, (Low Countries) 322; 18th century (American) 1568, (English) 550, 638, 652, 683, 686, 691, 773, 783, 816, 895, 1029, 1040, (French) 1760, (German) 141, 210, 216; 19th century (American) 1654, (English) 1124, 1139, 1243, 1271, 1295, 1364, 1507, 1520, 1521, (French) 1772, 1774, 1785, 1789, 1795, 1799; 20th century (English) 1524, 1546, (French) 1825, 1832, 1839, (German) 243, 270, (Scandinavian) 2000; *see also* dessert bowl, punch powl, sugar bowl
box 245, 257, 326, 1451, 1457, 1496, 1926, 1931, 1941; cigar/cigarette 1840, 1841, 1929 (*see also* cheroot case); freedom 597; seal 1157; snuff (17th century) 627, 1679, (18th century) 612, 626, 950, 1096, (19th century) 1168, 1169, 1170, 1171, 1209, 1214, 1215, 1217–1219, 1222, 1223, 1225, 1226, 1234, 1235, 1242, 1462; spice (17th century) 518, 520, 523, 524, (18th century) 856, 1690, 1702, 1967 (*see also* travelling service); sweetmeat 410, 504; tobacco (English) 517, (Low Countries) 325, 354, 365, 383, 384, 388; toilet (English) 459, 487, 506, 547, (Low Countries) 306, (French) 1728, 1740, (German) 116, 145, 193–195, 205, (Italian) 1855, (*see also* toilet set). *See also* canister; card case; casket; sugar box; toothpick case; vinaigrette
brandy bowl: *see* bowl: 17th century (Low Countries)
bratina 1881, 1915
brazier 628, 1558
breakfast service 1274
brush handle, 619: *see also* toilet set
buckle 1276, 1576
butter dish: *see* dish (butter)
butter knife/spade 265, 636, 1497
butter shell 730
button 888

caddy spoon: *see* spoon
cadinet 548
cake basket: 18th century (English) 708, 723, 727, 739, 794, 795, 832, 851, 877, 898, 901, 908, 955, 962, 998, 1077, 1112, (Low Countries) 361, 362, 370; 19th century (American) 1606, 1610, 1626, 1665, (French) 1783; 20th century (German) 279
candelabrum: 18th century (English) 828, 902, 910, 924, 937, 981, 1001, 1050, 1051, 1055, (French) 1748, 1751, (German) 197, 198; 19th century (English) 1056, 1294, 1317, 1326, 1343, 1344, 1449, (French) 1804, 1805, 1814, (German) 231, 232, 250, (Russian) 1907, 1914, 1921; 20th century (English) 1537, (Russian) 1935; *see also* centrepiece
candlestick: 17th century (English) 444, 446, 456, 552, 580, 616, 618, (French) 1675, 1680, (German) 52; 18th century (English) 531, 561, 577–579, 599, 602, 625, 629, 630, 639, 655, 656, 657, 666, 681, 684, 695, 696, 698, 699, 704, 706, 767, 776, 796, 798, 802–805, 830, 834, 835, 844, 849, 855, 914, 915, 916–923, 935, 938, 949, 952, 984, 991, 1034, 1041, 1042, 1044, 1049, 1194, 1354, (French) 1681, 1682, 1686, 1688, 1689, 1703, 1704, 1706, 1710, 1711–1713, 1717, 1719, 1722, 1723, 1725, 1729, 1732, 1733, 1747, 1750, 1756, (Low Countries) 331–334, 367, 371, 372–374, 377, 389–390, 393, 395, (German) 133–136, 143, 157, 171, 173, 174, 175, 180, 199, 202, 203, 213, 218, 221, (Italian) 1863, 1871; 19th century (English) 1111, 1123, 1134, 1195, 1248, 1249, 1250, 1279, (French) 1809, (German) 234, 237, 251, (Low Countries) 395, (Russian) 1903; 20th century (English) 1508, 1538; *see also* candelabra; chamber candlestick; taperstick; wall sconce; wax jack
canister 49, 53, 82; *see also* bottle; flask

card case 1213, 1228–1230, 1398, 1404, 1469
casket: 17th century (English) 488, (Low Countries) 308, 310; 18th century (English) 562, 569, 623, 697, 982, (French) 1687, (German) 151, (Italian) 1865, (Scandinavian) 1965; 19th century (English) 1244, 1252, 1253, 1413, (French) 1763, (Scandinavian) 1987; 20th century 1540; *see also* box; toilet box; toilet set
caster: 17th century (English) 570; 18th century (American) 1589, (English) 532, 557, 571, 604–608, 624, 646, 668, 703, 725, 760, 825, 837, 843, 846, 847, 897, 1074, (French) 1684, 1705, (German) 183, (Low Countries) 356, 358, 378; 19th century (English) 1367; 20th century (English) 1530, (Scandinavian) 1997; *see also* cruet; kitchen pepper
caudle cup 422, 428, 475: *see also* porringer
caviar pail 1283
censer 559
centrepiece: 18th century (English) 836, 994, 1039, (German) 182; 19th century (American) 1647, (English) 1058, 1113, 1137, 1138, 1148, 1197, 1247, 1266, 1287, 1323, 1375, 1383, 1414, 1418, 1420, 1425, 1448, 1450, (French) 1777; 20th century (German) 242, 263; *see also* candelabrum; cup; epergne
chafing dish: *see* dish
chalice 416, 573, 1365, 1821; *see also* communion cup
chamber candlestick 251, 512, 546, 788, 1104, 1459
chamber pot 842
charger: *see* dish (sideboard)
charka 1885, 1889, 1891, 1899
cheroot case 1231
chocolate pot: English 563, 662, 751; French 1720, 1744; German 186, 189, 190, 211, 212; *see also* coffee pot
christening set 1300, 1301, 1312, 1313, 1381; *see also* mug; table silver
church silver: *see* censer; chalice; communion cup; communion plate; crucifix; flagon; paten
clock 1514–1516
cocktail shaker 1995
coffee jug: English 971, 972, 1007, 1047, 1187; Scandinavian 1968
coffee pot: 18th century (American) 1562, 1590, 1594, 1600, (English) 576, 595, 609, 651, 678, 705, 717, 721, 740, 741, 749, 750, 813, 814, 833, 853, 874, 875, 927, 944, 945, 966, 1014, 1072, (French) 1726, (German) 142, 165, 167, 169, 187, 214, 220, 224, 226, (Italian) 1850, 1854, 1858, 1859, 1867, 1869, (Russian) 1901, (Scandinavian) 1969, 1973, 1974, 1976; 19th century (American) 1639, 1641, 1644, 1663, (English) 1192, 1370, 1442, (French) 1767, 1776, 1779, 1787, 1788, (German) 227, 229, 230, (Italian) 1870, (Russian) 1902, 1924; 20th century (English) 1528, (French) 1827, 1828; *see also* coffee jug; chocolate pot; tea and coffee set
coffee set 272, 814, 1024, 1989; *see also* tea and coffee set
coffee urn 148, 364; *see also* tea urn
communion plate 412, 555, 586; *see also* chalice; paten *etc*
cordial pot 521
cow creamer 958, 959
cream boat 722, 784, 818, 860, 889; *see also* jug (cream); sauceboat
cream jug: *see* jug (cream)
cream pail 876
crucifix 112
cruet frame/stand/bottle: 18th century (English) 650, 733, 769, 863, (French) 1734, (German) 222, (Low Countries) 381, (Scandinavian) 1985; 19th century (English) 1135, 1136, 1183, 1339, (French) 1769; *see also* caster; egg cruet; label; mustard pot
crumb tray 1940
cucumber slicer 1081
cup (including wine cup, standing cup, two-handled cup, communion cup etc): 17th century (English) 403–406, 423, 508, 526, 621, (German) 2, 4–7, 18, 28, 39, 47, 113, (Low Countries) 282, 311; 18th century (English) 644, 648, 823, 975, 983; 19th century (English) 1143, 1167, 1224, 1227, 1290, 1397, 1402, 1419, 1445, (French) 1811, (German) 249, 254, 256, 258, (Russian) 1936, (Scandinavian) 1988; *see also* cup and cover; caudle cup; chalice; centrepiece; goblet; porringer; stirrup cup; tumbler cup
cup and cover: 17th century (English) 445, 462, 529, 567, 584, 645, (German) 1, 3, 13, 21, 31–35, 46, 117; 18th century (English) 556, 590, 622, 641, 671, 685, 690, 694, 715, 731, 737, 738, 761, 764, 865, 866, 882, 900, 905, 928, 929, 980, 1006, 1008, 1010, 1011, 1025, 1035, 1076, (German) 138, 149, 166; 19th century (English) 1200, 1201, 1269, 1281, 1289, (German) 239, 248; 20th century (English) 1502
cutlery: *see* table silver

decanter 1347, 1460, 1499
desk set 271, 1658; *see also* inkstand
dessert basket/dish/stand/bowl: 17th century 407; 18th century 611, 999, 1003; 19th century 1060, 1133, 1262, 1299, 1439, 1651; 20th century 246, 1943; *see also* sweetmeat basket
dessert service: *see* table silver
dinner plate: *see* plate
dinner service 1707; *see also* plate; sauce tureen; soup tureen

dish: 16th century 1673; 17th century (English) 408, 426, 533, (German) 75, 78, 79, (Low Countries) 302, 314; 18th century (English) 692, 781, 819, 848, 986, (French) 1721, (German) 89, 99, 130, 155, 178, 191, 201, (Italian) 1853, 1861; 19th century (English) 1091, 1177, 1355, 1490, (French) 1796; 20th century (English) 1501, 1527, (French) 1818, 1822, 1834, (Scandinavian) 1990, 1991, (American) 1668; butter 1155, 1909; entree/vegetable (18th-century English) 1018, 1020, 1032, 1142, (19th-century English) 1206, 1285, 1316, 1476, 1484, (French) 1781, 1786, 1801, 1815; meat (18th-century English) 724, 728, 799, (French) 1708, 1709; shaving 588; sideboard (17th-century French) 1673, (Italian) 1843, 1844, (18th-century English) 640, 647, 710, 778, 810, 840, (19th-century English) 1146, 1175, 1176, 1184, 1237, 1240, 1241, 1411, (20th-century English) 1525; strawberry 709; see also dessert dish; ewer and basin; sweetmeat dish

dish ring 973, 974

dredger: see kitchen pepper

ecuelle: 17th century (English) 585; 18th century (French) 1685, 1714, 1715, (German) 140, 147, 154, 156, 161, (Italian) 1849; 19th century (French) 1798, (Italian) 1872; see also caudle cup; porringer

egg boiler/cruet 1149, 1196, 1203, 1358, 1428

entrée dish: see dish

epergne: 18th century 787, 836, 954, 968, 1052, 1057; 19th century 1198; see also centrepiece; sweetmeat basket/stand

ewer: 17th century (English) 476, 617, (German) 59, 60, 80, (Italian) 1842, 1845, (Low Countries) 324; 18th century (English) 582, 588, 592, 632, 711, 712, 763, 1027, (French) 1683, 1699–1701, 1736, 1749, (German) 159, (Italian) 1846–1848, 1852; 19th century (American) 1618, 1622, (English) 1107–1110, 1257, 1315, 1337, 1342, 1345, 1361, 1363, 1372, 1385, 1387–1389, 1391, 1392, 1444, 1447, 1483, (French) 1762, 1775, 1790, 1791, (Italian) 1877, (Low Countries) 396, (Russian) 1908; 20th century (American) 1669; see also ewer and basin/dish; flagon; jug

ewer and basin/dish: 17th century (English) 471, (Low Countries) 301, 303; 18th century (English) 631, 670, 672, 677, 850, 884, (French) 1698, 1735, 1737, (German) 179, 209; 19th century (English) 1406, (French) 1813, (German) 241; see also dish; ewer; toilet set; travelling service

feeding vessel 168

figure: see model

fish server/slice: 18th century 355, 368, 963, 1101; 19th century 1302, 1307, 1310, 1311

flagon 441, 494, 766, 1340; see also communion plate; ewer; jug

flask: see bottle; powder flask; scent flask; spirit flask

flatware: see table silver

fork 587, 1105; see also table silver

fountain (wine/water) 124, 663, 664

frame 1942

freedom box: see box (freedom)

gaming counter 413

garniture 468, 1806; see also mirror plateau; jardiniere; toilet set

ginger jar 453, 463, 468, 507, 551

goblet 1027, 1152, 1251, 1267, 1427, 1519; see also cup

honey pot 1202

incense boat 479

incense burner 465

inkstand/inkwell: 18th century (English) 543, 549, 661, 734, 772, 857, 933, 1036, 1037, (Italian) 1850, 1873; 19th century (American) 1623, (English) 1115, 1117, 1156, 1163, 1164, 1205, 1212, 1327, 1334, 1335, 1357, 1401, (German) 240; 20th century (English) 1529; see also desk set

jardiniere 1638

jug (including beer, claret, hot water, pitcher, wine): 17th century (English) 473; 18th century (American) 1573, (English) 575, 581, 591, 596, 634, 693, 732, 758, 770, 807, 821, 822, 858, 893, 896, 907, 1048, 1082, (Russian) 1894, (Low Countries) 385; 19th century (American) 1616, 1625, 1628, 1630, 1633, 1635, 1636, 1643, 1656, 1657, 1660, 1662, (English) 1259, 1260, 1288, 1328, 1341, 1348, 1353, 1368, 1369, 1371, 1386, 1416, 1429, 1463, 1472, 1473, 1477, 1487, 1488, 1489, 1494, (Russian) 1910; 20th century (American) 1666, (English) 1509, 1526, 1534, 1541, (German) 253, (Russian) 1933, 1938, (Scandinavian) 1992, 1993, 1999; see also coffee jug; decanter; jug (cream, hot milk, milk)

jug (cream, hot milk, milk): 18th century (American) 1571, 1572, 1597, (English) 539, 633, 680, 748, 782, 824, 879, 890, 930, 1073, 1080, (German) 172, 219, (Low Countries) 338; 19th century (American) 1608, 1612–1614, 1619, (English) 1062, 1270, 1322, 1438, (German) 227; 20th century 1541; see also cow creamer; cream boat; tea and coffee set

kettle: see tea kettle

kitchen pepper 1553, 1560

kovsch 1886–1888, 1897, 1925, 1930, 1934

label (bottle/wine), 886, 887, 1063, 1097, 1128, 1144, 1216, 1347

lady's companion 1455, 1465, 1470

ladle 716, 801, 1319, 1535, 1561, 1577; see also table silver

marriage casket: see casket: 17th century (Low Countries)

mazarine 728

mazer 1539

meat dish: see dish

medallion 284–290, 1079

memorandum pad 1810

milk jug: see jug (cream, hot milk, milk); tea and coffee set

miniature 342–352

mirror: 17th century 1678; 18th century 335, 779, 829, 885, 1741; 19th century 1254, 1291; 20th century 1500, 1513, 1667; see also toilet set

mirror plateau 1264, 1414, 1418

model: 17th century 24, 28, 42, 45, 87, 109, 113; 18th century 114; 19th century 261, 262, 1280, 1408, 1421, 1920

Monatsbecher: see beaker (German)

monteith: see punch bowl

mug: 17th century (English) 497, 498, 502, 515, 516, 530, 536; 18th century (American) 1563, 1578, 1584, 1598, 1601, (English) 658, 746, 811, 812, 845, 943; 19th century (American) 1617, (English) 1265, 1303, 1331, 1350, 1352, 1380, 1390, 1395, 1446, 1477, (French) 1793; see also christening set

mustard pot: 17th century (Low Countries) 323; 18th century (English) 1068, 1078, (French) 1731, (German) 183, (Low Countries) 378; 19th century (English) 1238, 1325, 1349, 1351, 1435, 1461, 1475; see also cruet

napkin ring 267, 1510

nécessaire: see travelling service

nef 17, 260

oil lamp 1864, 1875, 1876

pap boat 1564

pastille burner 1030

paten 508, 1365

pilgrim bottle 88; see also wine bottle

pitcher: see jug (including beer etc); ewer

plaque: 17th century 22, 61, 291, 292, 294–297, 1842; 18th century 121–123; 19th century 1400

plate (including dessert, dinner, soup): 17th century 511; 18th century 131, 542, 789, 987, 1708, 1745, 1746, 1758, 1764, 1766, 1895; 19th century 244; see also dish (meat); dinner service

porringer (including bleeding bowl; see Introduction, p.28): 17th century 409, 411, 420, 421, 424, 425, 427, 436, 455, 454, 482, 484, 485, 489, 491, 495, 500, 509, 510; 18th century 565, 743, 1549, 1552, 1582, 1583, 1588; 19th century 1629; see also caudle cup; ecuelle

posy holder 1186, 1452, 1453

powder flask 653; see also toilet set

punch bowl: 17th century (English) 528, 534, 564; 18th century (English) 675, 752, 990, 1002, 1016, 1031, (Low Countries) 359; 19th century (American) 1645, (English) 1423

rattle 613

Roemer: see beaker (German)

salt (including salt cellar, trencher salt, standing salt): 17th century (English) 620, (German) 8, 50, 1674, (Low Countries) 304, 1674; 18th century (American) 1555, 1579, (English) 538, 659, 780, 786, 793, 838, 956, 957, (French) 1739, (Italian) 1860, (Low Countries) 366; 19th century (English) 1114, 1145, 1179, 1191, 1261, 1292, 1293, 1321, 1356, 1394, 1436, (French) 1797, 1807

salver: 17th century (English) 477; 18th century (English) 589, 603, 682, 762, 765, 775, 790, 791, 792, 841, 867–873, 899, 904, 906, 911, 913, 926, 940, 967, 976–979, 1017, 1043, 1083, 1090, (German) 152, 172, (Low Countries) 336, 360, 363, 391; 19th century (English) 1178, 1282, 1359, 1378, 1379, 1382, 1417, 1479, (French) 1771; see also salver-on-foot; waiter

salver-on-foot: 17th century (English) 424, 425, 429, 433, 439, 440, 499, 508; 18th century (English) 513, 514, 594, 637, 654, 660, 669, 737, (German) 115, 153, 192; 19th century (English) 1116, 1126

samovar: see tea urn

saucepan 1204, 1258, 1599

sauceboat: 18th century (English) 642, 707, 744, 757, 768, 774, 797, 808, 831, 839, 878, 892, 932, 934, 936, 965, 989, 995, 1000, (French) 1754, (German) 196, 207, (Low Countries) 376, 379, (Scandinavian) 1977; 19th century (American) 1611, (English) 1245, (French) 1780; 20th century (American) 1670, (Scandinavian) 1996

sauce tureen 386, 988, 1019, 1075, 1087, 1140
scent bottle/flask 884, 1174, 1422, 1456, 1466, 1468
Scherzbecher 1939
scissors case 327
seal 1236; *see also* box: seal
Setzbecher: *see* beaker (German)
sewing case 1474
shield 29, 1161, 1409, 1410, 1412
snuff box: *see* box: snuff
snuffers stand and snuffers 340, 353, 600, 688, 1743
soup ladle: *see* ladle
soup plate: *see* plate
soup tureen: 18th century (English) 729, 785, 809, 826, 827, 852, 861, 862, 939, 941, 970, 985, 992, 1012, 1021, (French) 1738, 1757, 1759, (German) 181, 204, (Russian) 1900; 19th century (American) 1637, (English) 1125, 1130, 1141, 1151, 1182, 1318, (French) 1761, 1773, 1794, 1800, (German) 233, (Italian) 1874, (Russian) 1904, (Scandinavian) 1986
spice box: *see* box: spice; travelling set
spice scoop 1095
spice stand 10
spirit flask 1458
spoon: 17th century (American) 1547, (English) 398–402, 414, 415, (Scandinavian) 1949; 18th century (American) 1550, (English) 993, (Low Countries) 341, (Scandanavian) 1959; 19th century (English) 1304, 1306, 1309, 1505, 1511, 1517, (Russian) 1919; 20th century (English) 1498, 1531, (German) 268; *see also* table silver; travelling service
spoon tray 583
standing cup: *see* cup
stirrup cup 961, 1159, 1277, 1278
staff 1173, 1221
strainer 736; *see also* mazarine
sugar basin/bowl/box/vase: 18th century (American) 1565, 1574, 1595, 1596, (English) 568, 572, 610, 817, 881, 891, 894, 925, 1009, 1033, (French) 1753, (German) 223, (Italian) 1856, 1857, 1868, (Russian) 1896, (Scandinavian) 1975; 19th century (American) 1602, 1613, 1614, 1640, (English) 1121, 1122, 1150, 1189, 1255, (French) 1823; *see also* tea caddy; tea and coffee set
sugar nips/tongs 1566, 1591
sugar shaker: *see* caster
supper set 1768
surtout de table 1802
sweetmeat basket/dish/stand: 17th century (English) 417, 419, 452, (German) 25, 62–67, 118; 18th century (English) 946, 964, 1053, 1066, 1100; 19th century (American) 1619, (English) 1320
sweetmeat box: *see* box: sweetmeat

table silver: 18th century (French) 1718, 1742; 19th century (American) 1655, (English) 1286, 1305, 1308, 1314, (Russian) 1906; 20th century (English) 1531, 1536, (French) 1836, (German) 264; *see also* butter knife; christening set; fish slice; fork; ladle; spoon; travelling set
tankard: 17th century (English) 432, 434, 435, 437, 442, 443, 447–450, 470, 472, 478, 479, 480, 481, 483, 486, 490, 492, 493, 496, 501, 544, (German) 9, 11, 19, 36, 38, 40, 41, 55–58, 68, 72–74, 76, 81, 98, 100, 104, 105, 119, (Scandinavian) 1944–1946, 1948, 1950, 1951, 1953–1956, 1958; 18th century (American) 1548, 1551, 1554, 1557, 1559, 1569, 1580, 1581, 1593, (English) 554, 598, 674, 753, 756, 1023, 1071, (German) 101–103, 120, 128, 132, 137, 176, (Russian) 1890, (Scandanavian) 1957, 1960, 1961, 1963–1964, 1970–1972; 19th century (English) 1160, 1336, 1405, 1440, (Russian) 1912, 1913, 1923, 1927; 20th century (German) 252
taperstick 601, 920, 960, 1246, 1384
tazza: 17th century (German) 20, 37, 44, (Low Countries) 293, 299, 300, 305; 19th century (English) 1188, 1333; 20th century (English) 1503, 1504, 1544
tea caddy: 18th century (English) 635, 643, 713, 720, 735, 776, 800, 854, 903, 931, 946, 947, 948, 953, 997, 1026, 1064, 1065, 1099, (German) 215, (Low Countries) 357, 375, 392, 394; 19th century (American) 1664, (English) 1102, 1256, 1443, (French) 1819, (Low Countries) 394, (Russian) 1932
tea kettle: 18th century (English) 540, 560, 649, 700, 718, 742, 745, 759, 771, 864, 880, 942, 1045, (German) 162; 19th century (Low Countries) 397; 20th century (American) 1646, (French) 1817; *see also* tea and coffee set
teapot: 17th century (English) 505, (German) 91, (Low Countries) 330; 18th century (American) 1567, 1570, 1575, 1585–1587, 1592, (English) 535, 553, 687, 754, 755, 820, 1028, 1059, 1067, 1069, 1086, (French) 1724, (German) 146, 184, 185, 188, 208, 217, (Low Countries) 337, 339, 385, 387, (Russian) 1898; 19th century (American) 1608, (English) 1106, 1120, 1154, 1181, 1193, 1272, 1273, 1322, 1328, 1376, 1434, 1493, 1532, (French) 1812, (German) 236, (Russian) 1918, 1928; 20th century (English) 1542, (Italian) 1880; *see also* tea and coffee set
tea urn: 18th century (English) 815, 969, 1004, 1022, 1088, 1089; 19th century (English) 1118, (Russian) 1922; *see also* coffee urn; tea and coffee set
tea set/tea and coffee set: 18th century (American) 1605, (English) 673, 1038; 19th century (American) 1604, 1608, 1609, 1615, 1620, 1621, 1624, 1627, 1631, 1661, (English) 1084, 1131, 1165, 1180, 1190, 1239, 1297, 1298, 1360, 1362, 1366, 1374, 1377, 1396, 1399, 1403, 1415, 1430–1432, 1441, 1480–1482, 1485, 1486, 1492, (French) 1784, 1803, 1808, (German) 228, 235, 238, (Italian) 1878, (Russian) 1905, 1916, 1917, 1937; 20th century (American) 1650, 1659, 1672, (English) 1495, 1533, 1543, 1545, (French) 1824, 1829, 1830, 1831, (German) 272, 273, 276–278, (Italian) 1879, (Scandinavian) 1994, 1996; *see also* coffee set
tea tray: *see* tray
toast rack 1103, 1407, 1491
tobacco box, *see* box: tobacco
tobacco rasp 328
toddy ladle: *see* ladle
toilet bottle 457; *see also* toilet set
toilet set: 17th century (English) 431, 458, 464, 545, (French) 1676; 18th century (English) 541, 689, 806, 1015, (French) 1730, (German) 110, 116; *see also* entries for individual items: box (toilet); brush handle; ewer; mirror; powder flask; travelling service; vase
toothpick case 1094, 1172
toothpick holder 1782
travelling service/set: 17th century (English) 519, 522, (Low Countries) 280, 281; 18th century (English) 951, (German) 144, 158, 160, 206, (French) 1770; *see also* entries on individual items: bowl; ewer; ewer and basin etc

tray: 17th century (English) 460, 615; 18th century (American) 1603, (English) 665, 714, 719, 912, 996, 1093, 1764, (Italian) 1855, 1862, (Low Countries) 382; 19th century (American) 1642, (English) 1092, 1119, 1132, 1162, 1185, 1207, 1393, 1478; *see also* dish
tumbler cup 163, 961, 1693
tureen 1966; *see also* bowl; sauce tureen; soup tureen

vase: 17th century (English) 451, 468, (German) 125; 19th century (American) 1634, 1648, 1652, (English) 1129, 1158, 1166, 1284, 1296, 1324, 1329, 1332, 1346, 1424, 1426, 1433, 1522, 1523, (French) 1792, (German) 255, 259; 20th century (American) 1632, 1649, 1653, (English) 1506, 1512, 1518, (French) 1816, 1835, 1837, 1838, (German) 274, 275; *see also* centrepiece; cup; toilet set.
vegetable dish: *see* dish: entree/vegetable
vinaigrette 1211, 1232, 1233, 1452, 1454, 1464, 1467, 1471, 1820; *see also* lady's companion; posy holder

wager cup: *see* cup
waiter 702, 726; *see also* salver
waldhorn 106
wall sconce 298, 474, 701, 1054
wax jack 467
wedding heart 307
wine bottle 566; *see also* pilgrim bottle
wine bottle stand 558
wine cistern: 17th century (English) 469, 527, 663, (Low Countries) 329; 18th century (English) 1013; 20th century (American) 1671
wine coaster 1127, 1373
wine cooler: 18th century (English) 667, 859, 1005, 1046, (French) 1716, 1755, (German) 225; 19th century (English) 1061, 1147, 1153, 1199, 1263, 1268, 1275, 1330, (French) 1765, 1778, (German) 247; 20th century (French) 1826
wine cup: *see* cup; goblet
wine fountain: *see* fountain
wine label: *see* label
wine taster 614, 1696, 1697
wine wagon 1373

Index of goldsmiths
including assay masters, designers, retailers and engravers

The principal entries for goldsmiths listed in the directory appear in bold type, by directory number. Secondary entries and entries for assay masters, designers, engravers, retailers and goldsmiths who do not have a principal listing are in roman type. References in biographical details are listed under the immediately following directory number. References to the Introduction are in italics and indicate page numbers; only individuals who are not mentioned in the Directory Section are indexed.

Aarne, Johann Viktor 1930, 1942
AB conjoined 403–406
Abercromby, Robert 868–873
Ackermann, Johann Gottlieb 196
Adam, Charles 604–608
Adam, Elias 149
Adam, Joh. Jacob 206
Adam, Robert 990, 1006
Adams, G.W.: see Chawner and Company
Adie Brothers 1543, 1544
Aiken, George 1602
Alberti, Jacques-Henri 1744
Albertszenn, Jost 1945–1946
Aldridge, Charles 693, 963, 964
Aldridge, Edward, I 961–963
Andersen, David 1989
André, David 1684
Angell, John 1356–1358
Angell, Joseph, II 1356–1361
Angell, Joseph, III 1359–1364
Ansill, James 1025
Anthony, Joseph, Jr 1600
Archambo, Peter, I 789–801
Armstead, H.H. 1420, 1424
Ashbee, Charles Robert 1497–1504
Atkin Brothers 1481, 1485
Atkinson, William 1217, 1218
Aucoc, André 1813–1816
Aucoc, Louis 1813, 1820
Auguste, Henry 1759–1765
Auguste, Robert-Joseph 1754–1758, 1759
Aytoun, William 814–817

Bacher, A.B. 277
Bailly, Antoine 1727
Baily, Edward Hodges 1151, 1153
Bair (Bayr), Hans Jacob, I 20
Bair, Melchior 4–8
Bair, Paulus 32–35
Baker, Oliver 1505, 1507
Balaine, Charles 1812
Ball, Black and Company 1628, 1629, 1632
Ball, Tompkins and Black 1624–1627
Balzac, Edmé-Pierre 1714–1718, 1731, 1747
Balzac, Jean–François 1714, 1731–1733
Bamford, Thomas, I 608
Barde, Jean-Daniel 172
Barnard, Edward 1205, 1206, 1261, 1373–1399
Barnard, Edward, and Sons 812, 1205, 1373–1399, 1417
Barré, Aristide 1298
Barrett, A.J. 1296
Bartermann, Gottfried 178
Bartermann, Johann, I 124, 125
Bartolotti, Carlo 1873
Bartolotti, Giuseppe 1850

Bas, Hans 313
Bateman, Ann 1082–1084
Bateman, Hester 1063–1079
Bateman, Jonathan 1080, 1081
Bateman, Peter 1080–1085
Bateman, William, I 1084, 1085, 1178

Bateman, William, II 1163, 1178–1187
Baube, Jean Baptiste 1696
Baur, Hans Jakob, III 95
Baur, Hans Jakob, IV 173
Baur, Matthäus, II 90, 91
Baur, Tobias 116
Bayley, Richard 748–758
BB crescent below 504–506
Becker, Edmond 1816
Beham, Hans Sebald 283
Bell, Joseph, I 564, 609, 610
Bella, Stefano della 533
Belleville, Pierre 1719, 1720
Belli, Giovacchino 1872
Belli, Pietro 1874
Bentley, Thomas 1031, 1062
Bérain, Jean 21
Berg, Johan Petterson 1972
Bernardi, Bartolomeo 1868
Berthe, Martin 1690
Bertrand, Jean-Louis 1698
Besche, Lucien 1456
Besnier, Jacques 1703
Besnier, Nicolas 1687, 1707
Bettkober, Carl Samuel 210
Bewert, Johann Hermann 1903
Biennais, Martin-Guillaume 1766–1773, 1776, 1778
Bigelow Brothers and Kennard (Bigelow Kennard and Company) 1662, 1667
Biller family 163
Biller, Albrecht 110–113
Biller, Johann Baptist 62, 63
Biller, Johann Jakob, II 200–203
Biller, Johann Ludwig, I 114, 115
Biller, Johannes 166
Biller, Lorenz, II 112
Bird, Joseph 577–579, 599
Bird's Claw 293
Birmingham Guild of Handicraft 1532
Black, Starr and Frost 32
Blank (Plank), Matthäus 39
Blencke, Bernardus 340
Bodendick, Jacob 446–457, 1176
Bodington, John 566–569
Boelen, Henricus 1556, 1557
Boelen, Jacob 1555, 1556
Bogaert, Thomas: see Boogaert, Thomas
Böhm, Hermann 257–259
Boileau, J.J. 1112, 1118, 1759
Bolten, Arent van 291, 292
Bolton, Thomas 590–598
Bonnebakker, J.A. (Bonnebakker & Zn) 39
Boogaert, Thomas 304–306
Borthwick, John 496–499
Borthwick, Patrick 412
Bossard, Johann Karl 250, 251
Bosse, Abraham 56, 58, 315
Boullier, Antoine 1751
Boulton, Matthew (Matthew Boulton and Plate Company) 1041, 1194–1201
Bouman, Daniel 330
Boyce, Gerardus 1620, 1621
Bradbury, Thomas, and Sons 1482–1485
Brandt, Reynier 360–364
Bridge, John: see Rundell, Bridge and Rundell
Briot, François 18
Bry, Jan Theodor de 12, 16, 18
Bry, Theodor de 91, 280
Bugatti, Carlo 1879, 1880
Bunsen, Frantz Peter 221, 222
Buntzell, Johann Theodor 1905
Burt, Benjamin 1581–1584
Burt, John 1552
Busch, Esaias, I 48
Busch, Esaias, III 144–146
Buteaux, Abraham 928

Butty, Francis 965–970

Cafe, John 916–920, 921
Cafe, William 921–924
Cahier, Jean-Charles 1766, 1776–1781
Calderwood, Robert 821–824
Caldwell, J.E., and Company 1650–1652
Callot, Jacques 313, 315
Canner, Christopher 570, 571
Cardeilhac, Ernest 1823–1825
Carr, Alwyn 1533, 1534
Carter, John, II 1017, 1041–1044
Carter, Richard 1017–1020, 1041
Cartier 1840, 1841
Cary, Daniel 398, 399
Casolla, Giovanni 1877
Castman, Anders 1976
Cater, Dudley 1372
Cavalier, Louis-Marie 1794
CB in monogram 407, 408
Cellini, Benvenuto 36
Chartier, John 645–651, 769
Chawner, Henry 1086–1089, 1202
Chawner, William, I 1001
Chawner and Company 1286, 1307–1314
Cheret, Jean-Baptiste-François 1739–1741
Chevrier, Jacob/Jean 168
Christofle et Cie 1817, 1818, 1823
Claussøn, Mads 1944
Clérin, Lazare-Antoine 1724
Coburn, John 1569
Cockburne, James 496–499
C.O.D. 165
Coker, Ebenezer 911–915
Cole, Ebenezer 1615
Comyns, William, and Sons 1528
Coney, John 1547, 1548
Connell, W.C. 1495
Cook, Henry Fitz- 1338
Cooper, Matthew, I 599–602
Cooper, Robert 580–583, 599
Corbet, Thomas 662
Cordier, Louis 1682, 1683
Cortelazzo, Antonio 1878
Cotterill, Edmund 1323
Courtauld, Augustine 688, 759–761, 942
Courtauld, Louisa 948
Courtauld, Samuel, I 942–946, 948
Cowles, George 948
Craddock, Joseph 1206, 1207
Crespel, James and Sebastian 992
Crespin, Paul 775–788, 1039
Cripps, William 936–941
Crose, Charles-Francoise 1691
Crouch, John, I and II 1090–1093
Crump, Francis 926, 927
Cuny, Louis 642–644, 763

D fleur de lys 1680
D in script 507, 508
Damman, Johann Wilhelm 204
Dapcher, Jean-François 1738
Dautun, Pierre Henry 217–220
Dedeke, Lewin 140
Dee, Henry William 1451, 1455–1458
Dee, Louis 1451, 1455–1461
Dee, Thomas William 1451–1454
Delaune, Etienne 1673, 1674
Desnoyers, Jean-Charles Roquillet- 1741
Desvignes, Peter 1033, 1034
Dinglinger, Johann Melchior 48
Dixon, James, and Sons 1486, 1493, 1494
Dragman, Johann 1963
Drentwett, Abraham, II 87
Drentwett, Abraham, IV 191, 192
Drentwett, Christian, II 209, 210
Drentwett, Emanuel 179

Drentwett, Emanuel Abraham 207
Drentwett, Gottlieb Christian 205, 206
Drentwett, Johann, I 96
Dresser, Christopher 1486–1491, 1494
Dreyer, Salomon 174
Drinkwater, Sandylands 886–888, 1346
Dubois, Abraham 1595
Dufour, Jean et Frères 396, 397
Duguay, Joseph-Pierre-Jacques 1734, 1735
Duller, Hendrik 351
Dulliker, Johann Jakob 215, 216
Dumée, Nicholas 966–972
Durand, Antoine 1716
Durand, François 1808
Dyck, Peter van 1567
Dyke, Richard van 1568

Eaton, William 1248
Eben, Johann Georg 1970, 1971
Eckart, Johann Christoph 190
Eckloff, Paul 30
Edington, James Charles 1343–1345
Edwards, John (Boston) 1549–1551
Edwards, John, II (London) 806–811
Eelioet, Franssoys 282
EG between mullets 500–503
Ekfelt, Zacharias 1977
Eley, Fearn and Chawner 1105
Elkington and Company 1342, 1393, 1400–1419, 1450, 1486, 1817
Elliott, William 1123, 1246–1260, 1356, 1366
Ellis, David 1373
Emes, John 1086, 1202–1205
Emes, Rebeccah 1205
Emmerling, Nicolaus 16
Eneroth, Petter 1985
Enevoldsen, Niels 1950–1952
Engelbrecht, Johann Christoph 189, 206
Eoff and Shepherd 1619, 1629
Erhlen, Jean-Jacques 1694, 1695
Eriksson, Matts 1947
Erwin, Henry 1613
Everts, Warner 319, 320
Eyck, Koenraet ten 1555

Fabergé, Peter Carl 1930–1943
Farrell, Edward Cornelius 1237–1245
Farren, Thomas 737–740, 868
Felling, Gabriel 483–486
Ferriér, René Pierre 1753
Ferrn family: see SBF
Fesenmayr, Georg Wilhelm 50
Figg, John Wilmin 1259, 1366–1371
Filassier, Antoine 1681
Filassier, Michel 1686
Flaxman, John 1031, 1129, 1143, 1156, 1161, 1166, 1389
Fletcher, Thomas 1608–1611
F.M. 1867
Fogelberg, Andrew 1021–1032, 1111
Folkingham, Thomas 696–698, 708
Forbes, John W. 1607
Forbes, W. 1625, 1629
Fothergill, John 1194
Fournier, Johann Georg, II 227
Fox, Charles, II 1330–1333, 1334
Fox, C.T. and G. 1334–1342
Fréret 1387
Friedman, E. 278, 279
Froment-Meurice 1819
FS small s below 520–523
Fueter, Daniel Christian 1585
F.W. 441, 442

Gale, William, and Son 1622
Gallien, Simon 1689
Garden, Phillips 725, 904–910
Gardiner, Sidney 1608–1610
Garrard, Robert, I 992, 1005

INDEX OF GOLDSMITHS 429

Garrard, Robert, II, James and Sebastian: see Garrard and Company, R. and S.
Garrard, R. and S. and Company 738, 844, 845, 1302, 1307–1309, 1315–1329, 1526, 1529, 1530
Garthorne, Francis 509–514, 515
Garthorne, George 515–517, 576
GB in monogram 303
GC in monogram 461
Geffen, Arnoldus van 348, 349
Geffen, Johannes Adrianus van 350
Gelb, Johan 12
Gelb, Melchior, I 41
Gelston and Treadwell 1623
Germain, François-Thomas 1728–1730
Germain, Thomas 1716, 1722, 1728, 1738
Giannotti, Angelo 1875, 1876
Gibson, William 576
Gilbert, Stephen 1025–1032
Gilpin, Thomas 866
Giraud, Jacques Joseph, I 1685
Girod, Jacques 171
Girschner, Johann Christian 184, 185, 206
Godfrey, Benjamin 928, 929
Godfrey, Eliza 930–935
Goguelye (Gogly), Pierre François 1748
Goldsmiths and Silversmiths Company 1526, 1527, 1529
Goose in a dotted circle 489–495
Gordon, Hugh 818
Gorham Manufacturing Company 1632, 1653, 1660–1671
Gould, James 802, 803, 916, 976
Gould, William 804, 805
Goulden, Jean 1839
Grachev, Michail and Semen 1926–1928
Grahl, Matthias 1975
Grant, Charles 1266
Grazioli, Giuseppe 1871
Green, Henry 693, 963, 964
Green, Ward and Green/Green and Company 1113, 1188, 1191, 1343, 1373
Gribelin, Samuel 762
Gribelin, Simon 518, 520, 533, 623, 628, 686, 762
Guild of Handicraft 1497–1504

Haan, Cornelis de 369–372
Haan, Marcelus de 356–357, 369
Haan, Reynier de 358
Haas, Johann Wilhelm 106
Hamburgensis, Claus Sulsen 57
Hamlet, Thomas 1184, 1201, 1248, 1373
Hammersley, Thomas 1587
Hancock, Charles Frederick/Hancock and Company 1387, 1420–1426, 1431
Hannam, Thomas 1090–1093
Harache, Peter (Pierre), I 614–621, 676, 679
Harache, Peter (Pierre), II 614, 622–626, 676
Hardman, John, and Company 1365
Harris, Kate 1495
Haseler, W.H. 1505
Hatfield, Charles 835, 1052
Haydt, Balthasar 64–67
Hayne, Jonathan 1214, 1372
Hayne, Samuel 1372
Heath and Middleton: see Hukin and Heath
Hebrard, A.A. 1879, 1880
Heckel, Michael, II 150, 151
Heckenauer, Jakob Balthasar 234
Heckenauer, Johann Phillipp 197–199
Heming, George 1001

Heming, Thomas 980–991, 1001
Henchman, Daniel 1586
Hennell, Robert, I 1099–1102
Hennell, Robert, II 1103, 1104
Hennell, R., and Sons 1099, 1427–1438
Hennell, Samuel 1102, 1269
l'Herminotte, Joannes Andreas Gerardus 377–379
Herne, Lewis 965
Heuglin, Johann Erhard, II 152–158
Heuglin, Martin, II 81
Higgins, Francis and Son 1286, 1300, 1301, 1302–1306, 1313
Hillan, Christian 889–895
Hindmarsh, George 868
Hoffman, Josef 264–265, 267, 268, 269, 270, 272–276
Hogarth, William 12
Hohman, Eustachius 14
Holland, Thomas, II 1106–1110
Holland, Aldwinckle and Slater 1524, 1525
Holmes, William 971, 972
Hope, Thomas 1133
Hornung, Andreas 141
Hornung, Philip Christian 142
Houle, John 1049
Hound Sejant 409–411
Hudell, René 768
Huguet, Philippe-Jean-Baptiste 1774, 1775
Hukin and Heath 1486–1492
Hunt, John S. 1283, 1284, 1289: see also Hunt and Roskell
Hunt and Roskell 1283–1302, 1307, 1420
Hurd, Jacob 1558–1564
Hutton, William, and Sons 1494–1496

I.C. 138
IG crowned 1726
I.H. 444
I.I.B.: see Biller family
I.L. 762
I.M. (Muntinck) 318
Imlin, François-Daniel 1752
Imlin, Jean-Louis, II 1692, 1693
IN, bird below 420
Ingermann, Christian Heinrich 175
I.S. 136
Ivanov, Peter 1891
Ivory, George 1446, 1447

Jackson, Orlando 1038
Jackson, Walter 1162
Jamnitzer, Bartel 29
Jamnitzer, Wenzel 3
Jaschinkov, Alexander 1902
Jenkins, Thomas 468–475, 690
Jenner and Knewstub 1454, 1457
Jensen, Georg 1990–2000
Johnsen, Niels 1967–1969
Johnson, Walker and Tolhurst 1519, 1524
Jones, William 1620, 1621

Kandler, Charles Frederick 825–834
Keen, Pieter de 333
Keller (Kellner), Hans 15
Kent, William 865
Ker, James 818–820
Ker, Thomas 588, 589
Kessel, Th. van 301
Khlebnikov, Ivan O. 1929
Kirk, Samuel 1616–1618
Kirkpatrick, T. 1661
Klinge, J. 139
Klinkosch, J.C. 239, 242–246
Klinkosch and Mayerhofer 239–241
Klosse, Johann Georg 186–188, 211
Knox, Archibald 1505, 1506, 1510, 1512, 1513
Kolb(e), Hans (Johann) 49

Kolb, Jakob (Johann) Wilhelm 211, 212
Konigh, Henri de 1534
Kopping, Johann Fredrick 1894
Ködell, Johannes Adam 214
Kraer, Jacob 43
Kramer, Tobias 37, 38
Kuzov, Semyon Petrovitch 1900

Ladeuil, Leonard Morel- 1400, 1406, 1408–1411
Lakomkin, G. 1892, 1893
Lalique, René 1820–1822
Lamb, Adam 412
Lambert and Company 1334, 1337
Lambrecht family 56, 58, 59
Lambrecht, Hinrich 25
Lamerie, Paul de 699–735, 904
Langlois, Nicolas-Martin 1742
Laver, Benjamin 1001
Leake, Francis 479
Lebrun, Marc-Augustin 1782–1785
Ledoux, Guillaume 1688
Leeke, Ralph 526, 527
Lely, Tjeerd Jarigs van der 323
Lemoine, Alexandre-Nicolas 1743
Lemon, Erik 1983, 1984
Lenhendrick, Louis-Joseph 1721–1723, 1747
Lewis, Kensington 1199, 1237, 1243, 1261, 1262
Liberty and Company (Arthur Lasenby Liberty) 1505–1518
Liger, Isaac 686–689
Linnit, John 1217–1227
Lofthouse, Seth 584, 585
Logerat, Johannes 334
Loir, Alexis 1709–1713
Lossier, Pierre 169
Lothian, Edward 820
Lownes, Edward 1614
Lownes, Joseph 1598, 1599
Lukin, William, I 661–667
Lutma, Jan 306

Mackensen, Andrew 52
Mackintosh, Charles Rennie 1531
Macrae, Alexander 1448–1450
M.A.F. 303
Magnus, Antoni 315
Mair, Abraham 53
Mair, Melchior 19
Makepeace, Robert, I 1041
Makepeace 1192, 1193
Maler 235
Mannlich, Heinrich 78–80
Manwaring, Arthur 424–433
Marcq, Etienne-Jacques 1701
Margas, Jacob 690, 691, 694, 789
Margas, Samuel 694, 695
Marks, Gilbert 1519–1524
Marot, Daniel 21
Martin Hall and Company 1475–1479
Massé, Pierre 1675
Matthias, Johann Jacob Gottlieb 1755
Maundy, Thomas 417, 418
Maundy, William 419
Mayerhofer and Klinkosch 239–241
Meissonier, Juste Aurèle 14, 24, 25, 48
Metting, Jan 322
Mettayer, Lewis 628, 676, 677
Meurice, François-Désiré Froment- 1819
Michelson, Anton 1986–1988
Mills, Nathaniel 1208, 1228–1233
Mittnacht, Johann, III 176, 177
M.L. 1826
Moelder, C. de 689
Mola, Gaspare 1844
Monti, Raphael 1420, 1425
Moore, Andrew 424
Moore, J.C. 1626
Morel, Jean-Valentin 1809, 1811

Mortimer, John 1111, 1273–1284, 1289, 1420
Moser, George Michael 949–951
Moser, Koloman 264, 267
Moulineau, Claude-Alexis 1699, 1700
Movio, Latino 1524, 1525
Muller, B., and Son 260, 261
Muller, Michael 31
Muntinck family 318
Muntinck, Hindrick 317
Murphy, H.G. 1546
Musgrave, James 1605
Myers, Myer 1570–1577

Napper and Davenport 1542
Nelme, Anthony 544–560, 812, 1202
Nelme, Francis 812, 813
Neresheimer 260–262
Neuss, Johann Christian 224, 225
Neuss, Johann Georg Christoph 229–231
Neuss family 232, 233
Nichols and Plincke 1906–1910
Nicholson, William 1439, 1440
Nielsen, Harald 1995, 1997, 2000
Nieuwenhuys, Hendrik 386–388
Nieuwenhuzen, Gerardus Hendrikus 394
N.R. (Bavarian) 42
N.R. in script (Bamburg) 109

Odiot, Charles Nicholas/Maison Odiot 1786, 1798–1807
Odiot, Jean-Baptiste-Claude 1786–1797, 1798
Oernster, Emanuel Gottlieb 208
Olofsson, Bengt 1953
Orb and Cross 439, 440
Ostade, Adrian van 88
Outrebon, Jean-Louis-Dieudonne 1749, 1750
Ovchinnikov 1920–1925
Overing, Charles 748

Paap, Anton Hendrik 393
Palmentiero, Giuseppe 1848
Pantin, Lewis 1705
Pantin, Simon, I 678–685, 759
Papus, Elie 217–220
Parker, John 862, 952, 953, 994–1000, 1052
Passe, Simon de 284–290
Pastre, Jean Frédéric 213
Payen, Claude 1677
Payne and Son 1455
Pearce, Edmund 690
Peche, Dagobert 264, 273
Penman, Edward 586, 587, 589, 814
Penman, James 588
Pepfenhauser, Johann, II 133–135
Perchin, Michael 1930, 1936, 1941
Percier and Fontaine 32
Petzolt, Hans 13
P.F. 1676
P.F.B. 1704
Pfleger, Hans, IV 41
Phipps, James, II 1098
Phipps, Thomas 1094–1098
Pickett, William and Company 1010, 1011
Pilleau, Pezé 769–774
Pitts, Thomas, I 1052
Pitts, William, 1053–1061, 1175–1177, 1759
Plank, Matthäus: see Blank, Matthäus
Platel, Pierre 652–660, 699
Plot, Antoine 1706
Plummer, John 434–438
Podio, Peter 1062
Pomo, Georg Friedrich 1904
Pont, Jan Diederik 352–355
Pont, Willem 368
Pontus, Pierre-Joseph 1725

Pool, Matthys 325
Poppe, Cornelius 92, 93
Posen, Lazarus 252
Potthof, Herman 29
Powell, Thomas 1052
PR in cypher 467
Preedy, Joseph 1053–1055
Pressding, Nathaniel, I 76, 77
Pressding, Nathaniel, II 100
Preston, Benjamin 1261, 1262
Pribil, Anton 268
Prutscher, Otto 264, 272
Pugin, A.W.N. 1365
Puiforcat, Emile 1827
Puiforcat, Jean 1827–1838
Pyne, Benjamin 528–543

Quycke family 400–402

Ramsden, Omar 1533–1541
Rappoport, Julius Alexandrovitch 1930, 1939, 1943
Ratzersdorfer, Hermann 254–256
Rawlings, Charles 1234, 1235
Reed and Barton 1622, 1672
Rehfus, Georg Adam 236–238
Rehm, Johann Matthäus 132
Reid, William Ker 1206, 1207, 1343
Reily, Charles 886, 1346–1350
Reimers, Harmen Antoni 1965
Reimers, Jan 1948, 1949
Reimers, Johannes Johannessen, the elder 1955–1960
Reimers, Peder Johannessen 1954
Rennen, Peter/Salomon von der 60
Revere, Paul 1588–1594
Rew, Robert 976–979
RF mullet below 443
Richardson, Joseph 1565, 1566
Richardson, Joseph, Jr 1596, 1597
Richels, Jurgen 82
Riel, Reinhold 68–71
Ritter, Christof, I 1–2
Ritter, Christof, II 9
Ritter, Jeremias 23, 24
Ritter, Wolff Christof 40
Ritter family 61
Roberts and Belk 1480
Robins, John 1036, 1037
Robinson, Edward, II 1094–1097
Roettiers, Jacques 1687, 1707, 1708, 1745
Roettiers, Jacques-Nicolas 1687, 1745–1747
Rohde, Johan 1990, 1992
Rohde, Peter, II 72–74
Rohde, Peter, III 101
Rollos, Philip, I 473, 668–672, 673
Rollos, Philip, II 673–675, 694
Römer, Emick 952–956
Römer, John 952
Roskell, Robert: see Hunt and Roskell
Rossbach, Hertler and Kranert 228
Rugg, Richard 976–979
Rundell, Philip: see Rundell, Bridge and Rundell
Rundell, Bridge and Rundell/Rundell Bridge and Company 1112, 1113, 1115–1167, 1175, 1178, 1181–1186, 1188, 1337, 1373

Sadeler, Jan 293, 325
Sadeleri, Giovanni 1844
Sage, John Hugh le 763–767, 854
Sampson Mordan and Company 1467–1474
Satzger, Gottlieb 193–195
Savory, A.B., and Sons 1385
Sayre, John 1603, 1604
Sazikov, House of 1911–1917
S.B. (Genoa) 1843
S.B. (Lille) 1697
S.B.F. (Ferrn family) 83–85
Schafer, P. and F. 1460

Schaffler, Johann Daniel, I 147
Schaller, Matthäus 28
Schiotling, Johannes 380–385
Schlaubitz, Nathaniel 102–105
Schlick, Benjamin 1402
Schmidt, Niklaus 86
Schneider, Ludwig 159
Schultz, Christian Friedrich 223
Schuppe, John 957–960
Scofield, John 1045–1051
Scott, Digby 1113, 1115–1129
Semyonov, Vasili 1919
Semyonovitch, Y. 1895
S.H. 529
Sharp, Robert 1006–1020
Shepherd, Gilbert 421–423
Shruder, James 896–903
S.I. (Cologne) 136
S.I. (Russia) 1901
Silver, Rex 1505, 1515
Simoli, Giuseppe 1846
Simonsson, Carl Gustav 1918
Simpson, Hall, Miller and Company 1659
Sleath, Gabriel 741–747, 926
Smily, William: see Savory, A.B., and Sons
Smit, Jan 389, 390
Smith, Benjamin, II 1113–1129, 1263
Smith, Benjamin, III 1263–1268, 1439
Smith, Daniel 1006–1020
Smith, James 1129
Smith, Stephen 1342, 1439–1445
Smith, Nicholson and Company 1266, 1439, 1440
Smythier, Robert 444
Solanier, Paul 97–99
Sondagh, Rudolph 365–367
Soulaine, Paul 1702
Soumaine, Simeon 1553, 1554
Spickermann, Johann Nikolaus 161, 162
Spinazzi, Angelo 1849
Sprimont, Nicolas 27, 48
Stabeus, Lorens 1981, 1982
Stabler, Harold 1543
Stamper, John 962
Stanton, George 1404
Stapele, François van 338, 339, 373
Stapele, Martinus van 373–376
Starr, Theodore B. 1630, 1631
Stenglin, Philipp 126–128
Stevenson, Ambrose 926
Stockwell, Edward H. 1462–1466
Stoer, Thomas, the elder 18
Stoer, Thomas, the younger 44–47
Storer, George 886, 1346–1350
Storr, Paul 1021, 1111, 1112, 1130–1153, 1273–1282, 1420
Story, Joseph William 1246, 1247
Stothard, Thomas 1146
Strachan, Alexander James 1168–1174
Strant, Frederick van, II 342, 345–347
Strant, Willem van 342–344
Straub, Hans 3
Straub, Heinrich 26, 27
Straub, Johann Friedrich 1966
Straub family 27
Sudfeld, H., and Company 277
Sutton, John 480–482
Swift, John 865
Sy and Wagner 263
Sympson, Joseph 661, 665, 868
Syng, Philip, Jr 1578–1580
Syng, Richard 561–563

Tandler, Heinrich 277
Tanqueray, Anne 692, 836
Tanqueray, David 628, 692, 693
Tapley, John 1188–1193
Targee, John 1606
Tassie, James 1027
Tate, Robert 1346

Tatham, Charles Heathcote 1133
Taylor, Peter 925
Taylor, Samuel 947
Taylor, William 1002–1004
Terrey, John Edward 1269–1271
Terroux, Etienne 167–171
T.H., I.B. 94
Theed, William 1145, 1293
Thelott, Johann Andreas 117–123
Thompson, William 1612
Tiffany and Company (Charles Lewis Tiffany; Louis Comfort Tiffany) 1633–1649
Timbrell, Robert 564, 565, 609, 610
TK rosette below 476–478
Tobias, Willem 314
Toorn, Gregorius van der 359
Toorn, Johannes van der 391, 392
Townley, T.: see TT crowned
Treffler, Johann Christoph, I 88, 89
Treffler, Johannes, I 164
TT crowned 518, 519
Tucker, T.: see TT crowned
Tuillier, Jacques 335, 336
Tuite, John 867

Ulyett, A.E. 1534
Unicorn and Star 51
Unite, George 1208
Unknown makers 329, 993, 1678, 1679, 1705, 1737, 1842, 1852–1859, 1868–1870
Unmarked: English (17th century) 413, 416, 445, 460–466, 524, 525, 627, (18th century) 611–613, 736, 956, (19th century) 1174, 1215, 1216, 1272; French 1810, 1811; German etc 10–12, 22, 54–56, 75, 160, 226, 248, 249, 253; Italian 1847; Low Countries 281, 283, 307–313, 321, 324–328, 341; Russian 1881–1890, 1896–1899
Ure, Archibald 815, 816, 819

Valadier, Giuseppe 1864–1866
Valadier, Luigi 1860–1863, 1865
Vechte, Antoine 1413
Venables, Stephen 414, 415
Vernon, John 1601
Vertue, George, Master of 623
Vianen, Adam van 298–299
Vianen, Christian van 300–302
Vianen, Paul van 294–297, 303
Videau, Aymé 874–885
Vignon, Jan du 331
Vincent, Edward 762
Viners Ltd 1545
Vries, Jan de 337
Vulliamy & Son, 1111

Wagner, Johann 107, 108
Wakelin, Edward 854–864, 952, 953, 994–1000, 1002, 1005, 1025, 1052
Wakelin, John 992, 1002–1005
Walker, Joseph 603
Wallenius, Erik 1978
Wallis, Thomas 1214, 1372
Wallman, Johan 1964
Ward, Joseph 572–575
Warnberger, Abraham, IV 12
Wattiaux, Pierre Joseph 1736
Wedgwood, Josiah 1031, 1062, 1158, 1194
Weiss, Georg Daniel 148
Weiss, Johann Conrad 137
Weiss, Nicolaus 36
Wendel(s), Tilman 143
Wennerwall, Johann 1979, 1980
West, Matthew 973–975
Weyhe, Bernard Heinrich 180–183
WF conjoined 316
WF knot above 487, 488
Whipham, Thomas 812

Whistler 1433
Whiting Manufacturing Company 1653–1658
Wiber, Peter 21
Wickes, George 785, 845–853, 854–864, 994–1005, 1315
Wiener Werkstätte 264–276
Wilkinson, Henry, and Company 1351–1355
Willaume, David, I 628–641, 676, 692, 835–836, 874
Willaume, David, II 836–844, 936, 1052
Willmore, Joseph 1208–1213
Willms, A.A. 1400, 1413, 1418, 1419
Wilm, Hermann Julius 247
Winkler, Johann Abraham 206
Winter, Christian 129–131
Winterstein, Heinrich 17
Wirgman, Gabriel 1035
Wittkopf, Henrik 1973
Wittkopf, Rudolf 1961, 1962
Wolff, Bernt 332
Württembergische Metallwarenfabrik 42
Wyon, Benjamin 1236

Yorstoun, Mungo 586, 587
Young, James 1038–1040

Zethelius, Pehr 1974

Index of heraldry and inscriptions

References are to directory numbers

Abingdon, Earl of 555, 560
Aslefeldt and Blome, Denmark 336
Ainsworth 1253
Albemarle, Duke of 479
Andover, Viscount 794
Anglesey, Earl of 715
Anna, Princess of Holland 324
Anne, Queen of England 512, 513, 591, 592, 631; see also England, Royal arms of
Anne, Princess (dau. of George II) 709
Annesley (Anglesey) 715
Arenberg, Prince of 1718
Ashburnham, Earl of 1282
Ashburnham 477
Ashley (Shaftesbury) 1281
Assheton 683
Augustus I (the Strong), King of Poland 130, 131
Augustus III, King of Poland 175
Aylesford, Earl of 794
Aylmer, Baron 1108

Bagot, Bt 471, 476, 685
Baltimore, Baron 769
Banks 518
Barrington, Shales 739, 868
Baruth, Solus- 180
Bathurst, Earl 764
Baynard 790
Beauchamp, Earl of 1076
Beauchamp, Baron 1091
Beckford, William (of Fonthill) 1049, 1111
Belfast, Earl of 1223
Bennett 615
Bentinck (Portland) 688
Berchère 713
Beresford 1165, 1166
Berkeley 411
Berkeley, Earl of 1707
Bertie, Earl of 992
Bertie (Abingdon) 560
Bessborough, Earl of 1012
Blantyre, Lord 1676
Blount 832
Boeuf 1743
Boisrerd 1746
Boissier 713
Bonaparte 1766, 1773
Booth (Warrington) 686, 688, 689, 789, 791, 792, 799, 840–842
Borghese 1766, 1850
Branicki, Count 1794
Bridgeman, Bt 1026
Bristol, Earl of 829
Browne 928
Brudenell (Cardigan) 1058, 1318
Brydges (Chandos) 778
Buckingham, Marquess of 693, 778
Buckingham and Chandos, Duke of 778
Bulkeley, Viscount 560
Byron 933

Cambridge, Duke of 1132, 1184, 1278
Campbell 1383
Campden, Viscount 432
Capel (Tewkesbury) 615, 623
Cardigan, Earl of 1058, 1318
Carmarthen, Marquess of 933

Carnarvon, Earl of 676, 1139
Cathcart 1459
Catherine (the Great), Empress of Russia 1747, 1794
Charles I, King of England: as Prince of Wales 285
Charles II, King of England 461
Chester 429
Chesterfield, Earl of 775, 777, 1115
Chetwynd, Viscount 646

Chichester (Donegal) 1223
Child (of Osterley Pk) 719, 1015
Christian IV, King of Denmark 25
Cinque Ports 1098
Clare, Earl of 1016, 1039
Clifden, Viscount 640
Collings 1089
Cooks Company 494
Cottenham, Earl of 697
Courtenay, Bt 533, 555, 764
Coutts, Baroness Burdett 1107, 1266, 1301, 1340
Coventry, Earl of 556
Cowper, Earl of 754
Craven, Baron 992
Crawfurd 850
Cumberland, Duke of 233, 514, 631, 659, 660, 672, 1130
Curzon (Scarsdale) 527, 683
Curzon, Viscount 994
Custance 1022

d'Arcy (Holdernesse) 933
Dashkov, Prince Worontsov- 1283
De Grey (Walsingham) 1009
De la Poer (Waterford) 1137
Denmark, Royal arms of 25
Denn 1076
Dethick 518
Devonshire, Marquess of 1005
Dincklage 196
Dodsworth 572
Donegal, Marquess of 1223
Douglas (March/Queensbury) 995
Drogheda, Earl of 637
Ducie, Baron 1139
Dundas, 1006, 1185
Durrant, Bt 1022

E.A.F.s 514, 541, 1130
E.D.C. (Cumberland) 514, 1130
Edgecumbe, Baron 694
Egerton 1287
Eglinton, Earl of 1387
Elizabeth, Princess (dau. of George III) 982
Elizabeth I, Queen of England 290
Ely, Earl of 711
Engelhardt 1794
England, Royal arms of (the majority of references being for ambassadorial plate) 221, 222, 511, 612, 639, 664, 669, 670, 673, 690, 777, 810, 986, 987, 989, 1255; see also individual monarchs
Emmerson 1098
Ernst August, King of Hanover 191, 198
Erskine (Rosslyn) 1708
Exeter, Earl of 861
Exmouth, Viscount 1147
Eyre 762

Faletans, Marquis de 1715
Falkenhayn 1693
Falmouth, Earl of 637
Fane, Viscount 705
Fane (Westmorland) 1015
Featherstonhaugh 809
Ferrers, Earl 806
Fetherstone, Bt 682
Fitzgibbon (Clare) 1016, 1039
Fitzhardinge, Viscount 646
Fitzmaurice (Lansdowne) 1027
Fitzwilliam, Earl 1012
Fleming, Bt 884, 885
Foley, Baron 701
Folkes 928
Folkestone, Viscount 859
France, Royal arms of 1780, 1781
Frederick V, Emperor 289
Frederick Lewis, Prince of Wales 848
Frederick, Duke of York 1107, 1243
Frewen 583

Garrick, David 1038
George I, King of England, 514, 672, 694; see also England, Royal arms of
George II, King of England 659, 660, 709; see also England, Royal arms of
George III, King of England 221, 222, 982, 985, 1032, 1115, 1132, 1755, 1757, 1758; see also England, Royal arms of
George IV, King of England 1098; see also England, Royal arms of
Gordon, Duke of 985
Gouch 747
Grafton, Duke of 843
Grenville (Buckingham) 693
Grey (Stamford) 688
Grosvenor, Bt 931
Grosvenor, Earl 994
Guise, Bt 708

Haddington, Earl of 657
Hamilton, Sir William 1158, 1348
Hanover, King of 191, 198, 233, 612
Hanover, Elector of 221, 222, 1755, 1757, 1758
Hasell 714
Hertford, Marquess of 1768
Hicks 905–907
Hildesheim, Prince Bishop of 180
Hill, Emery 537
Hillebrandes 359
Holdernesse, Earl of 933
Holles (Newcastle) 566
Hope, Thomas 1165, 1166
Hopetoun, Earl of 657, 663
Howard (Norfolk) 832, 1120
Howard (Suffolk) 794
Howth, Earl of 1387
Hunhulton 449
Huntly, Marquess of 985
Hyndford, Earl 704

Imhof 13
Irby, Bt 856

James I, King of England 284, 286, 287
Jerome, King of Westphalia 1773
Jodrell 719
Jolliffe 474
Jones, Roberta 572

Kaye 1205
Kent, Duke of 1032
Kildare, Earl of 597
Kniphof 55

Lansdowne, Marquess of 1027, 1266
Lascelles 1008
Lawrence, Bt 647
Leeds, Duke of 933, 1116
Legh 569
Leiningen, Count 180
Lennoxlove 1676
Lequesne 718, 721
Leszczynski 52
Lintelo 315
Lisburne, Earl of 806
Lloyd's Patriotic Fund 1129
Loftus (Ely) 711
Lowe 1777
Lygon (Beauchamp) 1091

Macready, William Charles 1266
Mansell 536
March, Earl of 995
Marck, Countess de la 1718
Marlborough, Duke of 633
Master, Sir Streynsham 556, 569
Matthias, Emperor 288
Mecklenburg 1783
Methuen of Corsham 542, 1207
Mexborough, Earl 1110

Middleton, Baron 329
Mikhail Pavlovitch, Grand Duke of Russia 1778
Monck (Albemarle) 479
Monson, Baron 1110
Montague, Duke of 633
Montgomery, Earl of 1274
Monthermer, Marquess of 633
Montmorency, Duc de 1740
Mordaunt (Peterborough) 525
Morgan 581
Morrell 699
Mountrath, Earl of 676
Munster Goldsmiths 29

Newcastle, Duke of 566, 645, 925
Newton, Bt 763
Nightingale 806
Norfolk, Duke of 832, 1120
Northumberland, Duke of 1142, 1146, 1161, 1162
Nugent, Earl 693

Orford, Earl of 667
Orleans, Louis Philipe, Duke of 1716, 1795, 1796
Orloff, Prince 1745, 1747
Osborne (Leeds) 933

Packer 645
Paul I, Emperor of Russia 1778
Payne 913
Peel, Pa 1565
Pelham (Newcastle) 865, 925
Pembroke, Earl of 1274
Pepys (Cottenham) 697
Peterborough, Earl of 525
Philip V, King of Spain 115
Pierredon 1681
Pindar 409, 410
Pocock 677, 766
Poland, Royal arms of 130, 131, 175, 1849
Pollen 771
Portland, Duke/Duchess of 688, 1158
Potemkin 1794
Poulett 738
Powerscourt, Viscountess 593
Proby, Bt 641

Queensbury, Duke of 995
Quilter 1363

Richmond and Lennox, Duke of 1118, 1126, 1676, 1707
Rockingham, Marquess of 787
Rodney, Baron 1045
Rohan, Duc de 1740
Romney, Baron 723
Rosebery, Earl of 1013, 1323, 1419, 1425
Rosslyn, Earl of 1708
Rothschild, 1316
Russia, Czar of 25, 1167, 1887, 1897
Rutland, Earl of 432

St Albans, Duchess of 1050, 1280
St Aubyn 1089
St John 771
Salis, Count de 705
Salusbury, Charles 476
Savoy, Maria Louisa of 115
Saxony, Elector of 130, 131, 175
Scarborough, Earl of 848
Scarsdale, Baron 527; see also Curzon (Scarsdale)
Scott, Lady Arabella 593
Scrope 850
Seymour (Somerset) 690
Shaftesbury, Earl of 1281
Shelburne, Earl of 1027
Sheremetiev 1900
Shuttleworth 1008

Sligo, Marquess of 1343
Smyth 988
Somerset, Duke of 690
Sondes, Baron 925
South Sea Company 737
Spain, Royal arms of 115
Stamford, Earl of 688, 689; *see also* Warrington
Stanhope (Chesterfield) 775, 777, 1115
Stirling 1253
Strafford, Earl 632, 669, 671
Streatfeild 509
Strickland, Bt 622, 810
Stuart, Charles Edward (the Young Pretender) 1865
Stuart, James (the Old Pretender) 1849
Stuart 1129
Strogonoff, Count 1738
Suffolk, Earl of 794
Sussex, Duke of 301
Sykes 1287

Tewkesbury, Lord 615
Theodore Alexeivich, Tsar of Russia 1887
Tipping 519
Tongeren, von 301
Tollemache, Baron 1318
Townshend 861
Trapnell 755
Trellans 1721
Turner 583

Vernon 776
Victoria, Queen of England 1185, 1289, 1329

Wagstaffe 471, 685
Wales, Prince of 659, 660, 848
Walker 420
Wallace, Sir Richard 1768
Walpole (Orford) 667
Walsingham, Baron 1009, 1207
Warre 931
Warrington, Earl of 686, 688, 689, 789, 791, 792, 799, 840–842
Warwick, Earl of 1147
Waterford, Marquess of 1137
Watson 641, 787; *see also* Wentworth
Way 913
Weibel 128
Weld 409, 410, 635, 636
Wemyss 1708
Wentworth (Rockingham) 787
Wentworth (Strafford) 632, 669, 671
Westmorland, Earl of 1015
Weyer, van de 1289
Whaley 1016
William IV, King of England 1258
William IV, Prince of Orange 709
Williams 714
Winchcombe, Bt 645
Wolrych, Lady Elizabeth 635, 636
Wynn 86, 707, 990
Wyvill, Bt 1006

York, Cardinal 1865
York, Duke of 1107, 1243
Yorke, of Erdigg 707

Zetland, Earl of 1288

Frances Knight
from Bob
Christmas '90